Selected Readings on General Supervision

Selected Readings on General Supervision

Edited by

James E. Heald
Louis G. Romano
Nicholas P. Georgiady

The Macmillan Company
Collier-Macmillan Limited, London

First Printing

Library of Congress catalog card number: 75-112281

THE MACMILLAN COMPANY
866 THIRD AVENUE, NEW YORK, NEW YORK 10022

COLLIER-MACMILLAN CANADA, LTD., TORONTO, ONTARIO

PRINTED IN THE UNITED STATES OF AMERICA

Acknowledgments

Henry P. Knowles and Borje O. Saxburg, "Human Relations and the Nature of Man," *Harvard Business Review* (March-April 1967), 22-24.
© 1967 by the President and Fellows of Harvard College; all rights reserved.

Max. G. Abbott, "Intervening Variables in Organizational Behavior," *Educational Administration Quarterly* (Winter 1965), 1-14.
Reprinted by permission of Max. G. Abbott and the University Council for Educational Administration.

J. W. Getzels and E. G. Guba, "Social Behavior and Administrative Process," *The School Review* (Winter 1957), 423-441.
Reprinted by permission of J. W. Getzels and the University of Chicago Press, publisher. Copyright 1957 by the University of Chicago.

Herbert Sontoff, "What Is a Manager?" *Harvard Business Review* (November-December 1964), 24-26.
© 1964 by the President and Fellows of Harvard College; all rights reserved.

Amitai Etzioni, "Dual Leadership in Complex Organizations," *American Sociological Review* (October 1965), 688-698.
Reprinted by permission of Amitai Etzioni and the American Sociological Association.

Jack R. Gibb, "Dynamics of Leadership—Defensive and Emergent," *Vital Speeches of the Day* (April 1, 1967), 375-380.
By permission of *Vital Speeches of the Day*.

Edgar H. Schein and J. Steven Ott, "The Legitimacy of Organizational Influence," *American Journal of Sociology* (May 1962), 682-689.
By permission of Edgar H. Schein, J. Steven Ott, and the University of Chicago Press, publisher. Copyright 1961, 1962 by the University of Chicago.

Alan F. Brown, "Research in Organizational Dynamics: Implications for School Administrators," *Journal of Educational Administration* (May 1967), 36-49.
By permission of Alan F. Brown and *The Journal of Educational Administration.*

James G. Anderson, "The Authority Structure of the School: System of Social Exchange," *Educational Administration Quarterly* (Spring 1967), 130-148.
By permission of James G. Anderson and the University Council for Educational Administration.

Harlan A. Phillippi and Jack R. Childress, "The School Administrator and Organization Groupings," *The Clearing House* (September 1967), 54-56.
Reprinted by permission of *The Clearing House*.

Merlyn M. Gubser, "Anti-Democratic Attitudes of American Educators," *School and Community* (December 1967), 14-16.
Reprinted by permission of *School and Community.*

Donald J. McCarty, "Organizational Influences on Teacher Behavior," *American School Board Journal* (July 1961), 13-14.
Copyright assigned 1967 to the National School Boards Association. All rights reserved.

Don E. Hamachek, "Leadership Styles—Decision-Making and the Principal," *The National Elementary Principal* (April 1966), 26-31.
Copyright 1966, Department of Elementary School Principals, National Education Association. All rights reserved. Reprinted by permission of Don E. Hamachek and the Department of Elementary School Principals.

Andrew W. Halpin, "The Behavior of Leaders," *Educational Leadership* (December 1956), 172-176.
Reprinted with permission of the Association for Supervision and Curriculum Development and Dr. Andrew W. Halpin. Copyright © 1956 by the Association for Supervison and Curriculum Development.

Ralph B. Kimbrough, "The Behavioral Characteristics of Effective Educational Administrators," *Educational Administration and Supervision* (November 1959), 337-348.
Reprinted by permission of Ralph B. Kimbrough.

Neal Gross and Robert B. Herriott, "The EPL of Elementary Principals: A Study of Effective Professional Leadership," *The National Elementary Principal* (April 1966), 66-71.
Copyright 1966, Department of Elementary School Principals, National Education Association. All rights reserved. By permission of Neal Gross, Robert B. Herriott, and the Department of Elementary School Principals.

Harvey Goldman and James E. Heald, "Teacher Expectations of Administration Behavior," *Educational Administration Quarterly* (Autumn 1968), 29-40.
By permission of Harvey Goldman and the University Council for Educational Administration.

Donald C. Manlove and Robert Buser, "The Department Head: Myths or Reality," *NASSP Bulletin* (November 1966), 99-107.
Reprinted by permission of the National Association of Secondary School Principals and Donald C. Manlove.

Donald Thomas, "Which Organization—Department or Division—for Your School?" *NASSP Bulletin* (October 1965), 49-57.
Reprinted by permission of the National Association of Secondary School Principals and Donald Thomas.

Edwin M. Bridges, "Instructional Leadership: A Concept Re-Examined," *The Journal of Educational Administration* (October 1967), 136-147.
By permission of Edwin M. Bridges and *The Journal of Educational Administration.*

Bernard J. Lonsdale, "The 'Guese' of Supervision," *Educational Leadership* (November 1963), 69-74.
Reprinted with permission of the Association for Supervision and Curriculum Development and Bernard J. Lonsdale. Copyright © 1963 by the Association for Supervision and Curriculum Development.

Gertrude Moskowitz, "Toward Human Relations in Supervision," *NASSP Bulletin* (December 1966), 98-114.
Reprinted by permission of the National Association of Secondary School Principals and Gertrude Moskowitz.

Edmund J. Amidon, Kathleen M. Kies, and Anthony T. Palisi, "Group Supervision: A Technique for Improving Teaching Behavior," *The National Elementary Principal* (April 1966), 54-58.
Copyright 1966, Department of Elementary School Principals, National Education Association. All rights reserved. Reprinted by permission of Edmund J. Amidon, Kathleen M. Kies, and Anthony J. Palisi and the Department of Elementary School Principals.

Robert C. Day and Robert L. Hamblin, "Some Effects of Close and Punitive Supervision," *American Journal of Sociology* (March 1964), 499-510.
Reprinted by permission of Robert C. Day and the University of Chicago Press, publisher. Copyright 1964 by the University of Chicago.

Kurt R. Student, "Supervisory Influence and Work-Group Performance," *Journal of Applied Psychology* (Vol. 52, No. 3) 188-194.
Reprinted by permission of Kurt R. Student and the American Psychological Association.

Charles F. Malone, "A Design for Productive Classroom Evaluation," *The Clearing House* (February 1966), 348-354.
Reprinted by permission of *The Clearing House.*

Irving Flinker, "Reporting Teacher Observation," *The Clearing House* (September 1966), 9-12.
Reprinted by permission of *The Clearing House.*

George C. Kyte, "The Principal-Teacher Conference: A Case Study," *The National Elementary Principal* (April 1961), 25-32.

George C. Kyte, "Establishing Rapport in the Supervisory Conference," *The Educational Forum* (November 1963), 317-323.

N. A. Fattu, "Research on Teacher Evaluation," *The National Elementary Principal* (November 1963), 19-27.

"Evaluation of Teaching Competence," *NEA Research Bulletin* (October 1969), 67-75.

John H. M. Andrews and Alan F. Brown, *"Educational Administration and Supervison"* (July 1959), 234-242.

Jack R. Childress, "In-Service or Continuing Education for Teachers," *Journal of Education* (February 1965), 36-45.

Jack D. Roberts, "A Hard Look at Quality in In-Service Education," *The National Elementary Principal* (September 1964), 26-31.

Melvin M. Tower, "A Study of Orientation and In-Service Practices in the Indianapolis Public Schools," *Educational Administration and Supervision* (April 1956), 219-229.

John S. Morgan, "Keep Your Meeting on Target," *Supervisory Management* (May 1966), 4-8.

Thomas Sergiovanni, "Factors Which Affect Satisfaction and Dissatisfaction of Teachers," *The Journal of Education Administration* (May 1967), 66-82.

Henry A. Crooke, "The Supervisor and Staff Morale," *NASSP Bulletin* (October 1965), 86-96.

Table 1 from Mary Cronin in Henry A. Crooke, "The Supervisor and Staff Morale," *NASSP Bulletin,* Vol. 49 (October 1965), p. 92.

Frederick L. Redefer, "Factors That Affect Teacher Morale," *The Nation's Schools* (February 1959), 59-62.

Lawrence Borosage, "A Basis for Viewing Communication," *The National Elementary Principal* (May 1962), 6-12.

Douglas R. Bunker, "Communicating Person to Person," *The National Elementary Principal* (May 1962), 16-20.

Lloyd E. McCleary, "Communications in Large Secondary Schools—A Nationwide Study of Practices and Problems," *NASSP Bulletin* (February 1968), 48-61.

John A. Peoples, "The Relationship of Teacher Communication to Principal Behavior," *The Journal of Experimental Education* (Summer 1964), 407-411.
Reprinted by permission of John A. Peoples and the *Journal of Experimental Education.*

Egon G. Guba, "Diffusion of Innovations," *Educational Leadership* (January 1968), 292-295.
Reprinted with permission of the Association for Supervision and Curriculum Development and Egon G. Guba.

Ralph B. Kimbrough and Eugene A. Todd, "Bureaucratic Organization and Educational Change," *Educational Leadership* (December 1967), 220-224.
Reprinted with permission of the Association for Supervision and Curriculum Development and Ralph B. Kimbrough and Eugene A. Todd.

Ronald Urick and Jack R. Frymier, "Personalities, Teachers, and Curriculum Change," *Educational Leadership* (November 1963), 107-111.
Reprinted with permission of the Association for Supervision and Curriculum Development and Ronald Urick and Jack R. Frymier.

Bruce W. Tuckman and Wilmot F. Oliver, "Effectiveness of Feedback to Teachers as a Function of Source," *Journal of Educational Psychology* (Vol. 59, No. 4), 297-301.
Reprinted by permission of Bruce W. Tuckman and the American Psychological Association.

A. R. Crane, "Communication Within a Bureaucratic Organizational Framework: Implications for the Educational Administrator of Some Recent Investigations," *Journal of Educational Administration* (October 1967), 97-106.
Reprinted by permission.

Preface

To the practicing supervisor and the supervisory trainee, new and creative ideas concerning the art of supervision spring from many sources. From practitioners, theoreticians, and researchers come professional opinions based on experience, proposed models based on logic, and scientifically derived data based on research. Opinions, models, and research data are presented for consumption through textbooks, through books of readings, through courses of formal instruction, through professional contacts, through journals, and through numerous other ways.

This book of readings presents a variety of materials from a number of sources for the purpose of providing the student of educational supervision, experienced or inexperienced, a comprehensive contact with a multitude of ideas. Only in a book using many sources can the student gain maximum benefit from the many contributors. No single author can hope to provide his readers with expertise across such a broad front.

The editors have chosen the works with deliberation. When the best materials to generate new thoughts were outside education, they did not hesitate to seek contributions from other disciplines. The abundance of research reports reflects the editors' concerns for increasing the scientific base upon which supervision resides. The reliance on some older documents reflects the editors' recognition that newness is not always equal to quality.

The book was designed to stand alone as a text for courses or as a reference tool for the libraries of supervisors. In addition, the editors surveyed more than a score of texts in "supervision" to determine the areas in which supplemental readings would provide the highest complement to existing textual material.

Part One supplies materials that acquaint the reader with contemporary thought about the nature of *organizations* and the people who comprise them. Particular emphasis is placed upon the management and leadership aspects of organizational life.

From the views of organizational life in general, the reader is introduced to a re-examination of *educational organizations* in Part Two. Again, special attention is focused on the educational leader, manager, and administrator because it is he who, in education organizations, provides the bulk of the supervisory manpower.

Part Three takes an additional step from the general toward the specific as it contributes to an understanding of *supervision* as an organizational concept. From this point, it is possible to examine the roles and techniques of supervisors.

Evaluation techniques and practices, behavioral observations, follow-up conferences, in-service programs, and faculty meetings are among the *supervisory* techniques discussed in Part Four.

In conclusion, the editors realize that the best supervisors constantly encourage and accomplish both *individual and organizational improvements.* The concluding portion, Part Five, investigates the problems faced by the supervisor in building and maintaining staff morale and in building and improving processes of communication. The book closes with a reiteration of some of the many elements that must be considered by the supervisor as he plays the "agent of change" role within his organization.

Thus the book takes the reader through selections of general organizations, educational organizations, and the conceptualization of supervision to specific roles and techniques that can be employed by supervisors as they seek improvement in the quality of their organizations and in the performances of the personnel who comprise them.

J. E. H.
L. G. R.
N. P. G.

Contents

Part One

Organizations and Their Leadership

Human Relations and the Nature of Man	*Henry P. Knowles* *Borje O. Saxberg*	3
Intervening Variables in Organizational Behavior	*Max G. Abbott*	20
Social Behavior and the Administrative Process	*J. W. Getzels* *E. G. Guba*	31
What Is the Manager?	*Herbert Sonthoff*	44
Dual Leadership in Complex Organizations	*Amitai Etzioni*	54
Dynamics of Leadership–Defensive and Emergent	*Jack R. Gibb*	68
The Legitimacy of Organizational Influence	*Edgar H. Schein* *J. Steven Ott*	79

Part Two

Educational Organizations and Their Leadership

Research in Organizational Dynamics: Implications for School Administrators	*Alan F. Brown*	93
The Authority Structure of the School: System of Social Exchange	*James G. Anderson*	104
The School Administrator and Organization Groupings	*Harlan A. Philippi* *Jack R. Childress*	119
Anti-Democratic Attitudes of American Educators	*Merlyn M. Gubser*	122
Organizational Influences on Teacher Behavior	*Donald J. McCarty*	127
Leadership Styles–Decision-Making and the Principal	*Donald E. Hamachek*	131

The Behavior of Leaders — *Andrew W. Halpin* 138

The Behavioral Characteristics of Effective Educational Administrators — *Ralph B. Kimbrough* 144

The EPL of Elementary Principals: A Study of Executive Professional Leadership — *Neal Gross, Robert E. Herriott* 154

Teacher Expectations of Administrative Behavior — *Harvey Goldman, James E. Heald* 162

The Department Head: Myths and Reality — *Donald C. Manlove, Robert Buser* 173

Which Organization–Department or Division–for Your School? — *Donald Thomas* 179

Part Three

Supervision Within Organizations

Instructional Leadership: A Concept Re-Examined — *Edwin M. Bridges* 189

The "Guese" of Supervision — *Bernard J. Lonsdale* 199

Toward Human Relations in Supervision — *Gertrude Moskowitz* 206

Group Supervision: A Technique for Improving Teaching Behavior — *Edmund J. Amidon, Kathleen M. Kies, Anthony T. Palisi* 218

Some Effects of Close and Punitive Styles of Supervision — *Robert C. Day, Robert I. Hamblin* 224

Supervisory Influence and Work-Group Performance — *Kurt R. Student* 239

Part Four

Supervisory Roles and Techniques

A Design for Productive Classroom Evaluation — *Charles F. Malone* 251

Reporting Teacher Observation — *Irving Flinker* 258

The Principal-Teacher Conference: A Case Study — *George C. Kyte* 263

Establishing Rapport in the Supervisory Conference — *George C. Kyte* 273

Research On Teacher Evaluation	*N. A. Fattu*	279
Evaluation of Teaching Competence	*NEA Research Bulletin*	292
Can Principals Exclude Their Own Personality Characteristics When They Rate Their Teachers?	*John H. M. Andrews* *Alan F. Brown*	303
In-Service or Continuing Education for Teachers	*Jack R. Childress*	310
A Hard Look at Quality in In-Service Education	*Jack D. Roberts*	321
A Study of Orientation and In-Service Education Practices in the Indianapolis Public Schools	*Melvin M. Tower*	331
Keep Your Meeting on Target	*John S. Morgan*	342

Part Five

Encouraging Organizational and Personal Improvement

Factors Which Affect Satisfaction and Dissatisfaction of Teachers	*Thomas Sergiovanni*	347
The Supervisor and Staff Morale	*Henry A. Crooke*	361
Factors That Affect Teacher Morale	*Frederick L. Redefer*	369
A Basis for Viewing Communication	*Lawrence Borosage*	377
Communicating Person to Person	*Douglas R. Bunker*	388
Communications in Large Secondary Schools: A Nationwide Study of Practices and Problems	*Lloyd E. McCleary*	395
The Relationship of Teacher Communication to Principal Behavior	*John A. Peoples*	407
Diffusion of Innovations	*Egon G. Guba*	414
Bureaucratic Organization and Educational Change	*Ralph B. Kimbrough* *Eugene A. Todd*	418
Personalities, Teachers, and Curriculum Change	*Ronald Urick* *Jack R. Frymier*	423
Effectiveness of Feedback to Teachers as a Function of Source	*Bruce W. Tuckman* *Wilmot F. Oliver*	428
Communication Within a Bureaucratic Organizational Framework: Implications for the Educational Administrator of Some Recent Investigations	*A. R. Crane*	435

Part One

Organizations and Their Leadership

Human Relations and the Nature of Man

Henry P. Knowles and Borje O. Saxberg

> We all know how little boys love fighting. They get their heads punched. But they have the satisfaction of having punched the other fellow's head.[1]

> The principle of co-operation is the most dominant and biologically the most important.[2]

The point is constantly made that traditional organizations work on the assumption that people are essentially opposed to work and lack the capacity for self-direction and personal responsibility. Modern theories of organization take the opposite view; i.e., people do have the capacity to become psychologically involved in cooperative activity and, under certain conditions, to be virtually self-motivated and self-controlled.

Douglas McGregor, among others, has noted how these implicit assumptions about the nature of man influence organization and leadership in his now classic discussion of Theory X and Theory Y. The former assumes that man is innately lazy and unreliable, and leads to organization and control based on external or imposed authority. The latter assumes that man can be basically self-directed and creative at work if properly motivated; this assumption is said to lead toward an integrative organizational strategy.

However, neither McGregor nor other writers in this field have undertaken to reveal how deeply the roots of these assumptions about man penetrate our culture and thus how powerfully they influence human relations in our society. Not only are these assumptions important in theories of human organization, but they are also crucial in every system of thought involved with human and social control. Whether concerned with organizational strategy, the ancient social order of the Zuni, or the political theories of a Machiavelli or a Locke, one cannot escape the underlying relatedness and importance of what is assumed about man himself.

Managers need to know more about the nature, sources, and effects of one assumption or the other in order (1) to sort out and understand their own ideas

[1]Henri Bergson, *The Two Sources of Morality and Religion* (Garden City, New York, Doubleday & Company, Inc., Anchor Book edition, 1935), p. 284.

[2]Ashley Montagu, *Man in Process* (New York, New American Library, Mentor Edition, 1962), p. 50.

about the nature of humanity, and (2) to evaluate the fundamental influence of these ideas on managerial decisions. It may be asserted that no other variable weighs more heavily on the ultimate form and quality of organizational and interpersonal relations.

The question of the basic nature of man is, of course, as old as history and probably as old as society itself. The argument, in its many forms, stems from the ancient philosophical debate as to whether man is an end or a means. Reducing the argument to its simplest terms, and considering only the extremities of the spectrum, we treat a person as an *end* when we permit him to establish his own purposes and to choose and decide for himself. Contrariwise, we treat a person as a *means* when we limit his choices and utilize him primarily as an instrument for our own ends and purposes.

Implicit in these values are central assumptions concerning (a) whether man is "good" or "evil," (b) whether he has the ability to cooperate voluntarily or must be forced to cooperate, (c) whether he is a "pilot" capable of choosing or a "robot" imprisoned by circumstances and incapable of choice.[3] Values such as these lie at the very core of philosophies of religion, politics, education, organization, and human relations.

It is our intention in this article to describe how the choice of one or the other of these sets of values has influenced a number of systems of thought concerned with questions of human regulation and control. We do not intend to emphasize the growing body of empirical evidence which indicates that the quality of individual and group performance varies from one kind of assumption and system to the other. This area is adequately covered in the writings of such men as Chris Argyris, Rensis Likert, and, of course, McGregor. Rather, we shall explore some of the cultural roots and branches of optimistic-pessimistic assumptions about human nature in order to show that an underlying unity exists along this dimension in a variety of human-social control system.

Man: Pessimistic View

In their polar aspects, attitudes about human nature range from pessimism to optimism—from assumptions that evilness, predatory competition, and aggression on the one hand, to goodness, cooperation, and virtue on the other, constitute the central predispositions of men and, therefore, of the social order. Let us begin our discussion by examining how certain ideas about human-social control have been affected by the pessimistic or "means" view of man. This is the attitude that man is essentially evil and driven by aggressive and uncooperative motives and drives.

Fear Versus Love. As early giants in the history of Western idea makers, Niccolo Machiavelli and Thomas Hobbes—a pair of political scientists—provide us with a suitable starting point. It will be recalled that Machiavelli in *The Prince* (1515) urged that because of man's rebellious and uncooperative behavior, he must be

[3]The terms "pilot" and "robot" have been borrowed from Donald H. Ford and Hugh B. Urban, *Systems of Psychotherapy* (New York, John Wiley and Sons, Inc., 1965), pp. 595 ff.

strictly and ruthlessly controlled by anyone who aspires to gain or maintain a position of power. A ruler, in his view, must put aside any question of morality and must achieve control at any price and by whatever means he can find:

> It is much safer to be feared than loved . . . . For it may be said of men in general that they are ungrateful, voluble, dissemblers, anxious to avoid dangers, and covetous of gain.[4]

In all fairness, however, it must be made clear that he did not advocate his "end justifies the means" philosophy to benefit the prince or the ruler but to benefit the people. He assumed that only the ruler is competent to judge what the necessary ends are and must be. In furtherance of these ends, then, the ruler must resort to means which appear ruthless and deceitful.

Hobbes in the *Leviathan* (1651) outlined a theory of social relationships which makes him a direct intellectual descendant of Machiavellli. According to Hobbes, since men covet prestige, material goods, and power and expect to attain these at their discretion, they live in perpetual fear of their neighbors:

> And therefore if any two men desire the same thing, which nevertheless they cannot both enjoy, they become enemies.[5]

Law must therefore define what is honest and virtuous. But, in order for law to be applicable, a common authority must exist to enforce it. Man recognizes this need out of fear of loss of life and property. As a consequence, he enters into a social contract in which he gives up to a central authority whatever rights he has had in nature. In this way, he brings about the creation of a common wealth ruled by a sovereign. Each man is individually bound to this authority, or Leviathan and the latter's powers are irrevocable. The sovereign is a despot; whatever he wills becomes the people's will. As the Leviathan, he represents the supremacy of law, absolute authority and power, and the bureaucracy of the state.

Survival of the Fittest. Both Machiavelli and Hobbes viewed human nature primarily as a product of experience. They perceived in mankind a predominance of aggressive and selfish motives as a result of socialization rather than biological inheritance, and they designed political systems in order to constrain and control human behavior and thus create order in society.

Such orderliness in nature as a whole was also evident to Charles Darwin, who, through his research into the causes of variations in species and the contribution of these variations to the survival of species in nature, became convinced that survival was assured through a process of natural selection.

Darwin thought that survival was guaranteed only to those who were the best representatives of the species and best adapted to the conditions of the

[4]Niccolo Machiavelli, *The Prince and the Discourses* (New York, Random House, Modern Library edition, 1950), p. 61.

[5]Thomas Hobbes, *Leviathan* (Indianapolis, The Bobbs-Merrill Company, Inc., The Library of Liberal Arts edition, 1958), p. 105.

environment. The survivors were those who through physical prowess and mental agility were able to win in the competition for food and mate. The suggestion here is clear, that nature is a never-ending struggle—a competition—and that a permanent state of war exists among and between all species and the natural environment.

Darwin's interpreters suggested that as with animals so with man. Herbert Spencer, who was quick to find social implications in Darwin's biological theory, argued that among men the fittest survive; indeed, they are the only ones entitled to survive. In this, the process of natural selection in man's world favors the aggressive and the strong. Man, in this scheme, is a predatory creature. Spencer's interpretations of Darwinian theory underlie much of the creed of many nineteenth century U.S. industrialists and their philosophy of the "stewardship" of the rich and the "gospel of wealth."

(It is to be noted that Darwin himself was not willing to accept Spencer's theory that the law of natural selection applied to the human race. Actually, he turned the argument around. Man's weakness, Darwin thought, becomes his greatest strength; it forces man to establish cooperative relationships with others for protection and maintenance. In addition, Darwing attributed to man a moral feeling—one of sympathy and compassion—rather than indifference toward the weak and defective. Unhappily, it has been his fate to become associated with "survival of the fittest" as a scientific theory which is applied to man as well as other natural species.)

The Invisible Hand. Often associated with Darwin as a supporter of the idea of self-regulation in human society is Adam Smith. A century earlier, he placed his special emphasis on the automaticity of economic affairs. Under his doctrine of the invisible hand, there is a just allocation of a nation's scarce resources through the price mechanism which reflects supply and demand conditions of the market. By pursuing his self-interest, each individual can further not only his own fortune but also that of society as a whole.

It is this idea of self-interest as prime mover which has led many to assume that Smith considered man to possess a basically selfish, rather than a virtuous, nature. The economic doctrine of laissez-faire which Smith originated has meant "permission to do or make what you choose"; hence, noninterference with personal indulgence. This, when combined with self-interest as motivator, would seem, ergo, to support the notion that man is by nature self-seeking, predatory, and interested only in his own good at the expense of his weaker and less fortunate fellows. For example:

> It is not from the benevolence of the butcher, the brewer, or the baker that we expect our dinner, but from their regard of their own interest. We address ourselves not to their humanity, but to their self-love, and never talk to them of our own necessities, but of their advantage.[6]

Though there is ample evidence to indicate that Smith, like Darwin, recognized

[6]Adam Smith, *An Inquiry into the Nature and Causes of the Wealth of Nations* (New York, Ramdom House, Modern Library edition, 1937), p. 14.

that morality and government must and do govern the actions of men, he has nevertheless become, with Darwin, a symbol of individualism.

(Smith, at one time, occupied a professorial chair in moral philosophy and in *The Theory of Moral Sentiment* (1759) made it clear that he relied on natural law and, as a reflection of that, on a natural morality which prescribed three cardinal virtues: justice, prudence, and benevolence. Though he recognized some truth in the aphorism that private vices become public virtues, he clearly assumed that, as a reflection of a natural state of equality, men in pursuit of enlightened self-interest are characterized by adherence to justice—"a scrupulous refusal ever to hurt or injure anyone else, in the pursuit of one's own interest or advantage." Smith was not concerned with production and the accumulation of goods per se, but rather with the ends served thereby. In effect, the welfare of the ordinary man was on his mind to such an extent that he implicitly took the side of the underdog, which he perceived the ordinary laboring man to be.)

Sex and Aggression. Sigmund Freud, the father of psychoanalysis and the first to explore man's unconscious mind, took a clearer position on human nature than did Machiavelli, Hobbes, Darwin, or Smith. According to Freud, man is motivated by innate instincts and drives that he constantly struggles to pacify in ways which are antithetical to the norms of society. (These instincts and drives have been identified with sex and aggression but were really intended by Freud to refer to nature's and man's hankering to stay alive.) To the extent that society succeeds in curbing these animal forces, man becomes civilized and his energies can be turned toward socially acceptable goals. But, said Freud pessimistically:

> Psychoanalysis has concluded . . . that the primitive, savage, and evil impulses of mankind have not vanished in any individual, but continue their existence, although in repressed state . . . and . . . they wait for opportunities to display their activity.[7]

Freud further observed, in his *Civilization and Its Discontents* (1930), that society, itself, is perpetually threatened by the underlying hostilities which exist between human beings. Periodically, these feelings explode into open aggression which persists until the participants can once more be brought under control. However, society's attempts to neutralize destructive impulses through a "cultural superego," which defines for man what is "good" and what is "bad," create feeling of guilt. This, Freud said, is man's most urgent and important problem.[8] The anxieties generated by this constant clash between man's basic nature and the demands and needs of society increase human unhappiness and lead to mental illness. Thus, Freud seems to suggest, man is essentially doomed:

[7]Letter from Freud to Dr. van Eeden, quoted in Ernest Jones, *The Life and Work of Sigmund Freud,* Vol. II (New York, Basic Books, Inc., Publishers, 1957), p. 368.

[8]Sigmund Freud, *Civilization and Its Discontents,* translated by James Strachey (New York, W. W. Norton & Company, Inc. 1961), p. 81.

> From his [Freud's] point of view society, by its very nature, forces man to repress his inborn aggression more and more. The outlook for the future in that the more civilized he becomes, the more potentially destructive he becomes.[9]

Warrior and Weaponmaker. Recent evidence has been uncovered which seems to support the idea that man has been an aggressor and warrior since the beginning of his existence. Under the direction of L. S. B. Leakey, excavations conducted in South Africa—among what now appear to be the earliest remnants of man's ancestors—have uncovered man's earliest tools and have established that among them weapons occupied the most important place. The indications are that these were used not only for killing in the acquisition of food but also against man—for protection, in the defense of mate or of territory, and in the conduct of war. While the evidence is mixed, it has led some to theorize that a warlike, aggressive nature is part of every man's inheritance.

As a consequence, it can be argued that Darwin's law of nature, survival of the fittest, also applies to man. Such an emphasis on aggression over a span of hundreds of thousands of years, Robert Ardrey has argued, must have had a permanent effect on his hereditary structure:

> Man is a predator with an instinct to kill and a genetic cultural affinity for the weapon.[10]

In this view the urge to aggression, the desire to dominate others, is an instinct or drive transmitted from generation to generation through the genes.

The predisposition of men toward aggression has also been noted by one of the most renowned philosophers of our own time, Henri Bergson, who wrote:

> But no matter the thing taken, the motive adduced: the origin of war is ownership, individual or collective, and since humanity is predestined to ownership by its structure, war is natural. So strong, indeed, is the war instinct, that it is the first to appear when we scratch below the surface of civilization in search of nature. We all know how little boys love fighting. They get their heads punched. But they have the satisfaction of having punched the other fellow's head.[11]

Bergson clearly joins with those who take a pessimistic view of man. By assuming that innate, predatory, and selfish instincts are first causes, he cannot conceive of a human society—with its dependence on material possessions—as capable of avoiding conflict through the processes of reason and self-control.

Manager and Managed. The underlying ideas about human nature which have been previously outlined will also be found among some thinkers whose work

[9] Clara Thompson, *Psychoanalysis: Its Evolution and Development* (New York, Grove Press, Inc., first Evergreen edition, 1957), p. 151.

[10] Robert Ardrey, *African Genesis* (New York, Dell Publishing Co., Inc., 1961), p. 166.

[11] Henri Bergson, op. cit., p. 284.

focuses on the relationship between the manager and the managed in business and industry. These are the writers who are generally associated with the scientific management movement and who date from about 1900.

At this time, Frederick W. Taylor, who pioneered this movement in the United States, saw a need for management to exert close control over the indifferent behavior of workmen in order to ensure their adherence to the objectives and goals of business enterprise. In spite of all the human values which have been imputed to his writings, it seems clear that Taylor and his followers made these six basic assumptions about human nature:

1. The employee is a "constant" in the production equation. The implication here is that man has a fixed nature.
2. The employee is an inert adjunct of the machine, prone to inefficiency and waste unless properly programmed.
3. The employee is by nature lazy: only managers honor the "hard work" creed of the Protestant Ethic.
4. The employee's main concern is self-interest. At work, this is always expressed in economic values.
5. Given appropriate expression, these values will make man fiercely competitive among his peers as an accumulator of financial rewards.
6. Man (at least the working man) must therefore be tightly controlled and externally motivated in order to overcome his natural desire to avoid work unless the material gains available to him are worth his effort.

In accordance with these assumptions, Taylor thought that management must assume the responsibility for specifying in detail the method to be followed by the employee in order to gain an approximation of his full output potential. In addition, a piece-rate plan would have to be included as a financial incentive to ensure maximum performance.

At about the same time, a contemporary of Taylor was developing a similar pattern of thought in Europe regarding the relationship between manager and managed. While Taylor concerned himself mainly with the shop environment, Max Weber designed the features of his ideal bureaucracy viewing the organization from the top downward.

Again, in the elements of Weber's bureaucracy—specialization of personnel, impersonality, a hierarchy of authority relationships, entry and advancement by competitive examination, written policies, rules and procedures, and others—we find the Weberian image of man as a reluctant cog in an organizational machine. Thus the great majority of employees are confined to tightly controlled and dependent relationships with their superiors.

The pervasiveness of the Taylor-Weber approach to organization and management is evident throughout industrial organization today. Management scholars such as Urwick, Mooney, and Brown, as well as important business executives like Cordiner of General Electric, Greenwalt of DuPont, and Kapper of AT&T, have generally adhered to this model of managerial control and the underlying values which emphasize the need to minimize employee resistance to work—to support the Portestant Ethic—and a consequent need for autocratic rule and the traditional bureaucratic hierarchy.

Man: Optimistic View

Now let us turn from the foregoing cynical view of the nature of man to the view which emphasizes man's strength as a potentially creative, social being. As in dealing with the opposite view discussed earlier, we shall examine how an assumption that human beings have worth and goodness influences a wide-ranging sample of systems of social control. The examples used are not intended to be other than illustrative, straddling such divergent systems of human thought as political government, psychoanalysis, sociology, and business organization.

Social Instinct and Reason. Although separated in time by sixteen centuries, Marcus Tullius Cicero and John Locke shared remarkably similar ideas about the governing of men. Cicero in *On the Commonwealth* (51 B.C.) argued that men by nature believe in goodness and well-doing, and abhor savagery and baseness. On the assumption of mutual advantage,they come together in obedience to a social instinct and where enough individuals are involved form a democratic association or commonwealth for the benefit of all. Out of this emerges a leader who governs voluntary subjects through a moral claim to their allegiance rather than through regulation based on force.

Locke, in *The Second Treatise of Government,* contended that men of reason are inherently disposed toward mutual support and cooperation:

> The state of nature has a law of nature to govern it, which obliges everyone; and reason, which is that law, teaches all mankind who will but consult it that, being all equal and independent, no one ought to harm another in his life, health, liberty, or possessions.[12]

In other words, Locke argued that man's fundamental potential is reason and *reason itself* establishes cooperation as the basis for human relationships.

Under Locke's concept of the social contract, agreement is reached between free men to entrust to the community the authority to protect the common welfare. This custodianship is continued through tacit consent and is subject to the rule of majority. For Locke, man is naturally disposed toward doing good, and government is essentially a convenience. The sovereign is assumed to will what the people will. Locke believed that man's mind at birth is a *tabula rasa,* a blank sheet of paper and, therefore, that man becomes a person through sense impressions, mediated by reason, which he derives from social experience.

Thus the human mind and character are shaped by interaction with the world; whatever man becomes is a function of reason and social interaction. The function

[12] John Locke, *The Second Treatise of Government* (New York, The Liberal Arts Press, Inc., 1952), p. 5.

of government, therefore, is not to create its own laws as a controlling force but to discover what natural forces bring man to a state of reason *in which he can control himself.*

Cooperation and Survival. Two men of science, W. C. Allee, a biologist, and Ashley Montagu, a cultural anthropologist, have advanced ideas from their own fields about human nature which correspond in important respects with those of Cicero and Locke. They have argued that nature, from a biological standpoint, supports the concept of survival through cooperation rather than competition.

Allee reported in his *Cooperation Among Animals* the results of a wealth of research which provides evidence that cooperative, social relationships increase the probability of survival for any single individual as well as for a species as a whole. One of his simple experiments showed that it takes proportionately less toxic colloidal silver to kill a single goldfish in an aquarium than if the aquarium holds a number of goldfish. He suggested that the ability of a group of goldfish to neutralize a poison appears to increase faster than that of a single goldfish. He concluded his discussion of complex animal life in this way:

> The conclusion seems inescapable that the more closely knit societies arose from some sort of simple aggregation . . . such an evolution could come about most readily with the existence of an underlying pervasive element of unconscious proto-cooperation, or automatic tendency toward mutual aid among animals.[13]

As Allee explored further evidences of cooperation in higher animals, he came to this conclusion:

> All through the animal kingdom—from amoeba to insects, or to man—animals show automatic unconscious proto-cooperation or even true cooperation. There is much evidence that the drift toward natural cooperation is somewhat stronger than the opposing tendency toward disoperation [among crowded animals].[14]

However, in spite of his argument that a cooperative-social instinct is readily found in nature, Allee also recognized a counter-principle. This principle was that threat or force will be employed on the part of individuals, animal or man, to dominate others in a group in order to establish a hierarchy or pecking order. And he felt impelled to add that "much can be said for an established order of dominance and subordination."[15]

Allee pointed to evidences from the animal world which seem to reveal that any single individual thrives better where the pecking order is firmly established than where constant reorganization is in progress. He also saw evidence for this on the world scene. However, in all cases, Allee believed there will finally appear a subordinate to challenge the existing order. Thus he concluded that a pecking order

[13] W. C. Allee, *Cooperation Among Animals* (New York, Henry Schuman, 1951), p. 29.
[14] Ibid., p. 203.
[15] Ibid., p. 204.

brings peace and stability for the *short* run, but that an integrated unit characterized by natural cooperation promises stability for the *long* run.

Montagu agreed in all essential respects with Allee. He argued that from a biological point of view men prefer to survive through cooperation rather than competition:

> The principle of co-operation is the most dominant and biologically the most important.[16]

Montagu, of course, was particularly concerned with man rather than with the animal world. He believed that man from infancy on must rely on others for the satisfaction of his needs, and therefore affinity for interdependence is a fundamental reflection of the social state:

> All of man's natural inclinations are toward the development of goodness, toward the continuance of states of goodness and the discontinuance of unpleasant states.[17]

Thus warfare is considered by Montagu, as it was by Allee, as a human invention derived from economic or materialistic, rather than biological, considerations.

'Blank Page' Concept. On the basis of their more sanguine views of man's nature, these men, from Cicero through Montagu, have set forth behavioral concepts which support the idea of cooperation over aggression in human relationships and the need for strengthening these relationships through a constructive process of learning. Much of modern thought in psychoanalysis and psychotherapy, in sociology and social psychology, and in the field of organizational studies is also based on an optimistic view of man's nature. It resists Descartes' assumption that men are born with innate ideas and a more or less given nature.

Thus many modern behavioral scientists tend, like Locke, to think of man as entering life with a mind like a blank page on which experience is then impressed, and out of which the form and content of his personality are molded. To this way of thought, man's behavior is acquired in life and changes with experience. It is not solely predetermined by the genes, nor is it fixed and irrevocable. Out of these views have emerged new ways of perceiving man as an individual and as a member of a group.

Earlier, we outlined the pessimistic view of man on which Freud based his psychoanalytic theory. Freud's assumption about man's innate nature affected his theories in the same way as Hobbes's assumptions about man influenced his theories of government and society—man, left to his own devices, will prey on other men to satisfy his desires and must, in the interests of all, be restrained by forces in society.

The psychoanalysts who followed Freud have made distinctive contributions to

[16] Ashley Montagu, op. cit., p. 50.
[17] Ibid., p. 57.

modern views of the nature of man. From among them has emerged a group which broke with Freud on the issue of the basic nature of man, the so-called neo-Freudians, represented in this discussion by Harry Stack Sullivan, Erich Fromm, and Karen Horney. The neo-Freudians base their theories of human behavior on the assumption that the development of personality is influenced primarily by external societal forces and events rather than by biogenetically determined, innate instincts or drives.

Freud, of course, assumed that man and society are basically divided—on the one hand, a set of drives in man (sex and aggression) which are at the root of man's evil and, on the other, a set of rules in the human culture which inhibit and control the individual. The neo-Freudians argue that there is no dichotomy between man and society. According to Fromm:

> The most beautiful as well as the most ugly inclinations of man are not a part of a fixed and biologically given human nature but result from the social process.[18]

Necessarily then, if man is to be understood, major attention must be given to those forces in his environment which influence the molding of his personality.

J. A. C. Brown in *The Social Psychology of Industry* has described the difference between Freudian and neo-Freudian ideas about the nature of man as the difference between thinking of man as being "pushed from behind" or "drawn from in front." This, in a rough way, is the difference between psychological determinism or behaviorist psychology—with its focus on drives, instincts, or the conditioned reflex as a source of behavior—and subjectivist theories of psychology, which perceive psychic energy as being derived from personal goals and personal perceptions of reality. Sullivan's theory of personality development, like those of Fromm and Horney, belongs in this latter category.

According to Sullivan, the individual begins life with certain potentials and two basic goals: satisfaction and security. The extent to which he realizes his potential and achieves his goals depends on his experiences with other people. The pursuit of "satisfaction" has to do with satisfying physical needs like sleep, hunger, and sex.

However, the manner in which such needs are satisfied does not depend on the innate characteristics of an individual but reflects behavior patterns which are the product of interpersonal relations. It is in relation to other people that an individual seeks "security"—that is, in the avoidance of anxiety caused by feelings of disapproval or inadequacy in a social situation. Thus the matter of psychological security is culture-bound, and the form and content of the human personality is a product of specific cultural forces.

Sullivan defines the anxiety-free condition of "euphoria" as a tensionless state similar to that experienced by a new-born and sleeping child who has yet to discover that he has arrived in a threatening environment. Such an infant is at peace with the world or, in Rousseau's terms, in a state of oneness and harmony with

[18] Erich Fromm, *Escape from Freedom* (New York, Farrar and Rinehart, Inc., 1941), p. 12.

nature. Only exposure to the anxieties which arise out of human relationships can change this profound sense of well-being into a state of tension. This state of tension then promotes education and learning through which the self-system of an individual finally emerges.

The self-system, as Sullivan defines it, represents that portion of an individual's potential which is realized, while the "true self" contains the maximum potentialities which could have, under ideal conditions of experience, been developed. Since it is an unfortunate fact of life in our culture that interpersonal experience is far from ideal, Sullivan felt that most people are "inferior caricatures of what they might have been."[19]

Cultural Determination. Fromm does not accept the "blank page" concept of Locke but, nevertheless, strongly rejects the idea that instincts are the primary source of human behavior. Fromm concedes that man comes into existence with a set of drives and instincts. However, he argues that their particular patterns of development and their manifestation in the behavior of individuals are culturally determined:

> Any given social order does not *create* these fundamental strivings but it determines which of the limited number of potential passions are to become manifest or dominant.[20]

From this, it is clear that Fromm considers that human potentialities depend to a very large extent on the *will to productiveness which society succeeds in bringing to man.* The individual is shaped by society. The environment in which the individual exists, therefore, becomes a primary factor in the way he responds to life and work.

Fromm emphasizes in his theory that man is faced with a desire to be part of nature. Animals, through their instinctual equipment, seem able to accommodate themselves to the external environment through what appears to be an automatic process and, therefore, to achieve close ties with nature. Man, in contrast, through self-awareness and reason is alienated from nature.

In fact, in industrial society he is often alienated from himself, from meaningful human relationships, and from his work. In this process man is caught in a tug-of-war between self-reliance, power, control over nature, independence, and escape from isolation, competition, hostility, and insecurity. He must find his path by relating to things and to people. Ideally, he should succeed in establishing a productive relationship in which he is able to feel and act in accordance with his potential for contributing to constructive human life.

Pilot or Robot? As our final example of modern psychoanalytic thought, we consider Karen Horney. In her writings Horney agrees with Sullivan and Fromm in the view that Freud gave biological and genetic factors an excessive role in character formation. Taking the position that man's nature is not instinctive but learned, she was one of the first analysts to emphasize the importance of interpersonal relations

[19] J. A. C. Brown, *Freud and the Post-Freudians* (Baltimore, Penguin Books, Inc., 1961), p. 167.

[20] Erich Fromm, *The Sane Society* (New York, Holt, Rinehart & Winston, Inc., 1955), p. 14.

in behavior development. What an individual learns—that is, how he reacts to life with others—is influenced most by the way he is treated by others.

It was Horney's view that all individuals in their natural development seek sentiments of liking and approval from others. Where interpersonal relationships do not have such support, anxiety develops and begins to interfere with the growth of a healthy personality. In such cases people respond to others in three basic ways: (1) by "moving toward people"—feeling inadequate, they become attached and dependent; (2) by "moving against people"—rejected, they become rebellious and aggressive; or (3) by "moving away from people"—they seek comfort for rejection in symbolic substitutes and fantasy. Neurotic behavior occurs when there is conflict over which response pattern to adopt in a given situation. Various defense mechanisms help solve such conflicts but at the expense of genuineness in human relationships and of needed problem-solving behavior.

Because of her emphasis on the importance of situational factors in personality development, Horney tended to look to a person's present interpersonal involvements for the causes and solutions to neurotic problems. She did not deny that a connection exists between an individual's current responses and his early life—a connection which was so important a part of Freud's thinking—but she argued that one must look to the present situation for clues as to what triggered these responses.

Man is not, therefore, doomed by a set of prenatally determined instincts, nor are his patterns of behavior eternally established by early life experience. Horney's concept of man is cheerful and optimistic, not gloomy and pessimistic. Man is born neither a devil nor a saint; he simply reflects in his behavior the nature of relationships developed since the time of his birth with people who were important to him.

The insights into human nature which have been outlined above and which summarize the thinking of an important school of modern psychotherapy are based on the confident viewpoint that man is not doomed by a fixed and evil nature from which he cannot escape. Rather, they would seem to suggest just the opposite: man has within himself the potential to grow and develop significantly in cooperation with others. Man is a pilot not a robot. What is needed is not a method of controlling innately selfish or even predatory drives toward war with other men, but a means of tapping man's potential for joining in productive relationships with others.

Individual or Environment? One of the first social scientists to apply this concept of man to analysis of industrial organizations was Elton Mayo of Harvard University. Mayo's view of human nature was optimistic and anti-Freudian. To illustrate:

> The concealed assumption of the doctrine of original sin invalidates the psychoanalytic findings. The theory that life is a strenuous fight to subdue perversion, that the human mind is by nature "pathogenic" (i.e., predisposed to the pathological) is not a starting point for biological observation.[21]

[21] Elton Mayo, *The Human Problems of an Industrial Civilization* (New York, The Viking Press, 1960), p. 152.

In other words, the concept that life on earth is an atonement for original transgressions of God's laws, and that man is cursed with a set of evil instincts which must be curbed by society, is inadequate as a base for observing and understanding man's behavior in daily life.

Mayo argued that too much attention was being given in industrial settings to *individuals* as the source of noncooperative and unproductive relationships between the leadership of the organization and those who are employed to accomplish the work. He pointed out that developments in sociology and in social anthropology had already opened to serious question whether a merely psychological study of individuals in an organization is a logical approach to a comprehension of their behavior as workers.

On the contrary, Mayo said, such individuals constitute a group which develops responses to the total organizational environment. On the basis of this, the research interview program at the Hawthorne Works, originally consisting of isolated interviews, was restructured so that interviewers were assigned to study individuals over extended periods in relation to their jobs, the informal social organization in which they worked, and company policy.

The original isolated interviewing method was based on the premise that personal behavior or misbehavior was a result of personal rationality or irrationality; the second method assumed that the individual was only one of a number of interdependent variables relating to behavior. These other variables were part of the working environment and included such factors as leadership, working conditions, and working group membership. Science, inspired by the work of early sociologists and anthropologists, was at last begining to show, contrary to Hobbesian theory, that man was more victim than antagonist in his environment.

Behavioral Science Man. While the initial thrust toward change in managerial philosophy and practice can be traced back to the origin of the human relations movement in the 1930's, it has continued through the present time in two somewhat divergent directions: (1) toward the fusion of the scientific organizational behavior approach with a new, more humanistic management philosophy, and (2) toward organizational reeducation and change through sensitivity or laboratory training. In both cases the importance of the roles played by behavioral and other social scientists in defining the relationship between the manager and the managed is becoming more and more evident.

While Mayo's work resulted in increasing the emphasis on human relations mainly in normative terms, much of the subsequent direction of this work is based on the research and findings of the behavioral sciences of sociology, psychology, social psychology, and cultural anthropology. Research workers such as Argyris, McGregor, and Likert have identified themselves with A. H. Maslow's theory of the need hierarchy as an aspect of human nature. Given the assumption that a satisfied need does not motivate, man is seen as satisfying in ascending order the needs of hunger in an extended sense, safety, social affection, esteem, and finally self-actualization or self-fulfillment.

The challange for management today is seen by these authors as one of providing man at work with the opportunity to grow and mature continually into a human being who, because of a favorable working climate, is able to realize his own goals best by working for the success of the organization of which he is a member. Implicit in their assumptions is the idea that man has an essential nature which is defined by the broad spectrum of his needs, capacities, and tendencies. These needs, as expressed by Maslow, "are on their face good or neutral rather than evil."[22]

In a continuing reflection of the neo-Freudian view of man, we find McGregor stating, "If employees are lazy, indifferent, unwilling to take responsibility, intransigent, uncreative, uncooperative,"[23] this is due to the traditional bureaucratic assumptions and methods of organization and control. Argyris, in a similar vein suggests, "Mutual understanding trust, self-esteem, openness, internal commitment, fully functioning human beings who aspire to excellence . . . these values can not only be protected, but indeed increased, in an industrial setting."[24]

In the world of work, therefore, man is seen by the behavioral scientists as responding to the influences of his organizational environment. Given the opportunity, he will participate creatively in furthering the objectives of the organization. If frustrated, his behavior will characteristically revert to the basic need level of hunger; he will turn apathetic, slovenly, and totally alienated from an orientation toward work as a central life interest.

Such a basic underlying belief in man as a creative human being oriented toward constructive rather than destructive activities is even more clearly represented in the sensitivity training movement. Through this process of reeducation and skill development, Warren G. Bennis and his collaborators see the way to democratization of management—a condition which they view as essential in the face of accelerating technological change, the increasing proportion of professionals in the work force, and the consequent necessity of the organization to accept the values of science and scientific inquiry in order to survive in the future.

("Democracy" is here defined not as permissiveness or laissez-faire but as a system of values by which people in organizations are assumed to feel "internally compelled" to live. These include free communication, the consensus principle, influence based on competence rather than position, acceptance of emotion as fact, and a "basically human bias" in dealing with conflict.)[25]

In Bennis' terms, the "organization man" becomes a signpost on the road pointing the way to the kinds of flexibility and adaptability which are essential if the democratic environment in which science and scientists can flourish is to be realized. Whether one agrees or not, it is well known among men of science that

[22]A. H. Maslow, *Motivation and Personality* (New York, Harper & Brothers, 1954), p. 340.

[23]Douglas McGregor, *The Human Side of Enterprise* (New York, McGraw-Hill Book Company, Inc., 1960), p. 48.

[24]Chris Argyris, *Interpersonal Competence and Organizational Effectiveness* (Homewood, Illinois, Dorsey Press, Inc., and Richard D. Irwin, Inc., 1962), p. 5.

[25]See Philip E. Slater and Warren G. Bennis, "Democracy Is Inevitable," HBR March–April 1964, p. 51.

personalities are only of passing interest compared to the contribution they hope to make to the accumulation of new knowledge.

Where Do You Stand?

We have confined the discussion to the pessimistic-optimistic views for the sake of simplicity and clarity, although it is, of course, a matter of common observation that all of the possible social processes are located along a continuum whose polar extremities are mutual cooperation and predatory competition.

As opposite ends of a spectrum, cooperation and competition are closely related to love and hate, friendship and enmity, harmony and discord, collaboration and opposition. They may therefore be used to describe a person's *basic* or *characteristic* propensity toward his fellowman. In terms of his attitudes toward others, every man will find himself at some point on this spectrum depending on the particular situation in which he is involved.

However, each man is drawn by the force of his own history and experience toward some primary tendency, some central quality of being, which determines the general pattern of his social behavior. Peripheral changes occur in this pattern to accommodate the demands of the various roles he plays, but there would seem to be a core pattern which represents his basic beliefs concerning the nature of man. Man is evil or man is good, depending on man's experience with mankind.

The examples from the history of human thought that we have cited illustrate this concept of the *primary tendency* in the kind of view one man takes of another. They also clearly indicate that cooperation and competition, or goodness and evilness, as human characteristics are not discrete activities or qualities but rather exist in various mixtures in human nature.

Hobbes's *primary tendency,* for example, was to view man as evil. Nevertheless, his idea of the "social contract" contains the implicit assumption of *cooperative* activity among men by which they give up their rights to a ruling Leviathan to gain protection from one another. Bergson said that war in a materialistic society is natural, but he noted that collective ownership leads to cooperation within groups to protect members from outsiders. Even Freud, who comes closest to a concept of innately evil men straining against societal constraints to satisfy their needs, conceded that man may become "good" because of his dependency on others; he will, in short, *cooperate* when he finds helping behavior in other men.

Among those whose primary tendency is to view man as good we find similar ambivalences;

- Locke argued that reason evoked cooperation among men. However, he implied that the "social contract" exists between ruler and ruled to control man's acquired *competitive,* aggressive nature.
- The neo-Freudians believed that man's goodness or evilness was a product of experience—that is, competitive (hating) experiences lead to malfunctioning by societal standards, but cooperative (loving) experiences lead to satisfaction and to development.

The psychoanalytic assumptions and clinical findings of the neo-Freudians to the effect that man has basic worth and is capable of constructive psychic responses in an environment and understanding and encouragement have received scientific support among modern experimenters. Behavioral Science Man, whether the setting has been in the laboratory or in the field—in a business, education, or government organization—is a "good" man whose potential for productive growth and self-actualization has too often been stunted by his superiors' outmoded assumptions that he is "bad." Therefore, for their purposes, he must be manipulated like a puppet on a string.

Conclusion

The quality of human relations in any organization, from the political state to the business enterprise, reflects first of all its members', and particularly its leaders', views of the essential character of humanity itself. It makes a great deal of difference in systems of social control whether those involved tend to view man, in general, as good or evil. If we are to find a cause for behavioral failure, we are more apt to look outside the offender than inside and thus consider a whole new range of variables and contributory circumstances.

If, on the other hand, we assume that man himself is bad, a priori, then we are prone to assume that misbehavior is caused by something within him which we cannot alter directly. Accordingly, our attention will focus on limiting his feedom to choose and to act through external curbs or controls. In limiting the causes of behavior, we exclude ourselves from powerful internal sources of control.

Thus the underlying human value which predominates is readily perceived in (a) the way social relationships are structured, (b) the kinds of rewards and penalties that are used, (c) the character of the communication process which links people together, and (d) the other elements of social control that characterize a relationship or an organization.

Intervening Variables in Organizational Behavior[1]

Max G. Abbott

The current tendency in the study of organizational behavior is to identify the structural characteristics of the organization and the personal characteristics of the individual, and to analyze the relationships among structure, personality, and behavior.[2] This tendency has been highlighted by Merton, who has suggested that "studies of religious, educational, military, economic, and political bureaucracies dealing with the interdependence of social organization and personality formation should constitute an avenue for fruitful research."[3]

The following analysis conforms to this tradition. In addition to focusing on the structure and the individual, however, an attempt will be made to identify and to analyze some of the social forces, or *intervening variables*, which mediate the lack of a one-to-one correspondence between structure and personality, on the one hand, and goal-directed behavior on the other.[4]

Within the rubric of a structural and personal framework, a formal organization may be conceptualized as a social system consisting of two major dimensions. Getzels and Guba have described such a system as follows:

> We conceive of the social system as involving two major classes of phenomena, which are at once conceptually independent and phenomenally interactive. There are, first, the *institutions* with certain *roles* and *expectations* that will fulfil the goals of the system. Second, inhabiting the system there are the *individuals* with certain *personalities* and *need-dispositions*, whose interactions comprise what we generally call "social behavior . . . ."
>
> . . . to understand the behavior of specific role incumbents in an institution, we must know both the role expectations and the need-dispositions. Indeed, needs and expectations may both be thought of as *motives* for behavior, the one

[1] Although this analysis draws from the work of a number of people who have written in the area of organization theory, it will be apparent throughout the paper that I am especially indebted to Professor Jacob W. Getzels and his colleagues at the University of Chicago for the initial social systems model that is described here and for many of the concepts which are used in the remainder of the paper.

[2] For examples of this type of analysis, see Chris Argyris, "The Individual and Organization: Some Problems of Mutual Adjustment," *Administrative Science Quarterly,* II (June, 1957), 1-24, and Robert V. Presthus, "Toward a Theory of Organizational Behavior," *Administrative Science Quarterly* III (June, 1958), 48-72.

[3] Robert K. Merton, *Social Theory and Social Structure* (Glencoe, Ill.: The Free Press, 1957), p. 206.

[4] This use of the term *intervening variable* corresponds to that employed by Sergio Talacchi in his paper, "Organization Size, Individual Attitudes and Behavior: An Empirical Study," *Administrative Science Quarterly* V (December, 1960), 400. Talacchi asserts that "an intervening variable' . . . serves to mediate the lack of a one-to-one correspondence between external stimuli and behavioral responses on the part of individuals."

deriving from personal propensities, the other from institutional requirements. What we call social behavior may be conceived as ultimately deriving from the interaction between the two sets of motives.

The general model we have been describing may be represented pictorially as indicated in Figure 1. The nomothetic axis is shown at the top of the diagram and consists of the institution, role, and role expectations, each term being the analytic unit for the term next preceding it. . . . Similarly, the idiographic axis, shown at the lower portion of the diagram, consists of individual, personality, and need-dispositions, each term again serving as the analytic unit for the term next preceding it. A given act is conceived as deriving simultaneously from both the nomothetic and the idiographic dimensions. That is to say, social behavior results as the individual attempts to cope with the environment composed of patterns of expectations for his behavior in ways consistent with his own independent patterns of needs.

NOMETHETIC DIMENSION

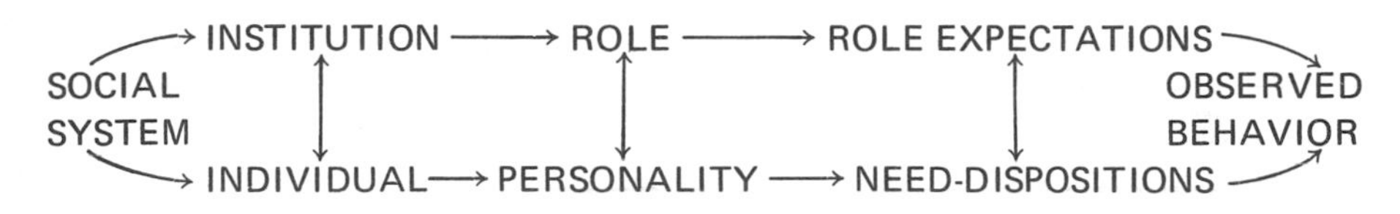

IDIOGRAPHIC DIMENSION

Figure 1. General model showing the nomethetic and the idiographic dimensions of social behavior. (Jacob W. Getzels and E. G. Guba, "Social Behavior and the Administrative Process," ***The School Review,*** **LXV (Winter, 1957), 423-41.)**

The heuristic value of this model of social behavior has been amply demonstrated by the research that it has generated in the field of educational administration during the past several years. The model is particularly useful in organizational theory, since it is sufficiently abstract to be applicable to any type of social system, large or small, formal or informal, impersonal or intimate. For specific purposes, however, the utility of the model may well be increased by some modification which enables us to specify additional variables which influence and control the behavior that occurs in an organizational context.

Although a formal organization may be conceptualized as a social system, analysis of such a system is enhanced when we recognize that it is a particular social system with a number of distinguishing characteristics:[5]

a) A formal organization is specifically goal-oriented,

b) The tasks of a formal organization are factored into subtasks and assigned to various positions as official duties,

c) The positions in a formal organization are arranged hierarchically and authority relationships are prescribed by the organization,

[5]These characteristics are essentially those which have been listed by Blau and Scott as the characteristics of a bureaucracy. *Cf.* Peter M. Blau and W. Richard Scott, *Formal Organizations* (San Francisco: Chandler Publishing Co., 1962), p. 32.

d) General and impersonal rules govern official actions and limit the scope of interpersonal interaction within such a system.

In a formal organization, as in other types of social systems, it is characteristic of roles that they do not represent a single set of behavioral expectations on which common agreement is easily reached. Rather, in any social system there is an array of roles which become associated with each office or position. This array of roles, or "complement of role relationships which persons have by virtue of occupying a particular social status," has been referred to by Merton as *role-set.*[6]

As Merton has pointed out, there is a distinction between role-set and the structural pattern which sociologists have termed *multiple roles.* Whereas the term multiple roles refers to the complex of roles associated with the various statuses in which individuals find themselves, the term role-set refers to the plurality of expectations which become associated with a single status.

Individuals within formal organizations are subject to conflicts and pressures deriving from the expectations associated with both multiple role and role-set affiliations. In reference to multiple role affiliations, for example, all members of formal organizations are also members of other groups, such as the family, civic clubs, and others. These groups may hold expectations for individual behavior which are in conflict with the expectations that are set by the formal organization.

In contrast, the role set is characterized by various expectations which are held for a single role or position within the organization. For example, the role of teacher in the educational institution may be subject to expectations which are held by such diverse groups as pupils, colleagues, administrators, the Board of Education, Parent-Teachers' Associations, and professional teachers' associations.

Conflicts and pressures arising from multiple role affiliations are largely outside the purview of the formal organization to which an individual belongs; thus, the individual must make his own accommodations to the incompatible expectations to which he is subjected because of these affiliations. On the other hand, conflicts and pressures arising from the role-set are both within the purview of, and significant for what occurs within, the organization. The frequently vague and contradictory expectations which constitute the role-set not only produce conflict and tension for a given role incumbent; they also tend to divert attention from the task performance which is required for efficient goal accomplishment.

Thus, both as a means of protecting members from undue pressures and as a means of assuring goal achievement, the formal organization is required to abstract from the array of vague and contradictory expectations which constitute the role-set a limited set of expectations which are reasonably consistent and which are related rationally to the organizations's goals. These expectations, which ideally are *functionally specific* and *universalistic*, are generally formalized and codified and adopted as the official rules of the organization.

In the same sense that some of the expectations which are held for institutional

[6] Merton, *op. cit.*, p. 369.s

roles may be irrelevant to organizational demands, so may some of an individual's need-dispositions be irrelevant to his performance within the organization. However, organizational analysis requires a focus on those facets of personality which structure the way in which the individual adapts to the position to which he is assigned. In other words, the concern of the organization is with those individual need-dispositions which determine an incumbent's role performance and his personal reactions to that performance.

In analyzing a formal organization, such as the school, it is necessary to take into account the limiting conditions which are characteristic of this type of social system. That is, it is necessary to focus on the limited set of expectations which are *officially* associated with a given role and on the limited set of need-dispositions which are most directly relevant to membership in the organization.

One of the important tasks confronting the controlling board of any organization is that of articulating conflicting demands and expectations which constitute the role-set for various positions within the organization. Such articulation occurs when a limited set of reasonably consistent expectations become formalized and codified. Although some expectations are so pervasive and so thoroughly understood by all members of the organization that they are never made explicit, many of these expectations are reduced to writing and are adopted as the official rules of the organization. These rules frequently take the form of policy manuals, staff handbooks, job descriptions, or some other such document. The officially sanctioned expectations, including those that are written and those that are generally understood, constitute for the formal organization a codified behavior system. This behavior system differs from generalized role expectations in that it has formal, official approval, and it has been made reasonably explicit.

The codified behavior system serves a useful purpose for the organization, both from the point of view of management and from the point of view of the employees. Since structural arrangements represent a response to demand for control from the hierarchy, any condition which enhances that control may be functional for the organization. The codified behavior system creates such a condition; it exerts an unusual influence upon individual behavior because it consists of an organized set of expectations which can be communicated with reasonable accuracy.

While the codified behavior system increases the organization's control over individual behavior it also performs a number of useful functions for organizational members. First, it mitigates the conflicts to which members might otherwise be exposed because of contradictions in the expectations associated with the role-set; second, it defines for members the minimum set of behaviors which are prescribed and proscribed, removing much of the ambiguity that would otherwise exist; and third, it protects the individual member from undue infringement upon his personal integrity by specifying the limits within which he may be subjected to authority.

The individual needs which are most relevant to organizational membership are those which are met largely in a social situation or which are accommodated through social interaction. One taxonomy of such needs has been provided by

Maslow[7] who has identified five general need areas, which have been arranged hierarchically as follows:

5. Self-actualization needs
4. Esteem needs
3. Belongingness needs
2. Safety needs
1. Survival needs.

There are two features of this formulation which are of particular significance in the present context. First, the needs as listed above are arranged in reverse of the order of their priority for the individual. Thus, survival needs are seen as primal or basic. Although needs related to all five areas may be present simultaneously for a given individual, the needs at any level become prominent when, and to the extent that, the needs at the lower levels have been met. Second, the needs are arranged in reverse of the order in which they require social interaction for their accommodation. Thus, the higher-order needs of self-actualization, esteem, and belongingness are satisfied primarily as individuals interact with other individuals in a social setting.

Since the needs related to belongingness, esteem, and self-actualization are accommodated largely in a social situation, these needs may be viewed as directly related to the motives an individual has for joining an organization, and to the personal goals he seeks to reach through organizational membership. Thus, an individual's own role concept may be conceived to be essentially an expression of his idiosyncratic pattern of belongingness, esteem, and self-actualization needs.

The development of this need pattern, *i.e.*, the acquisition of an individualized role definition, is largely a socialization process through which an individual learns from others the nature of institutional roles. Such learning includes two broadly defined processes which Sarbin has called *intentional instruction* and *incidental learning.*[8]

During the socialization period, each individual arrives at his own version of the idealized set of requirements which are attached to the positions or statuses found within a formal organization. Socialization involves essentially a transactional process in which there is a dynamic interaction of the individual need-dispositions and the institutional role definitions. Furthermore, socialization is a life-long process, beginning in early childhood and continuing throughout an individual's productive career.

The concept which is particularly useful in helping to understand the develop-

[7]A. H. Maslow, *Motivation and Personality* (New York: Harper & Row, Publishers, 1954).

[8]Theodore R. Sarbin, "Role Theory," *Handbook of Social Psychology,* ed. Gardner Lindzey (Reading, Mass.: Addison-Wesley Publishing Co., 1954), I, p. 226.

ment of an individual's role concept is that of selective perception.[9] In a sense, each individual may be said to be functioning in a world of his own making. His needs and values serve as a perceptual screen; he interprets his environment according to the way he perceives it; and he reacts to that environment in accordance with his interpretation.[10]

As a result of both incidental learning and intentional instruction, an individual who enters an organization in a given role will have some conception of the expectations which are held for that role. An example would be the teacher in her first assignment. No two such individuals would have the same role concept even though they had been subjected to highly similar experiences as judged by an observer. Each individual's own needs and values would determine to a great extent the particular expectations to be emphasized or de-emphasized from those available to him.

In recognition of this point, Riessman suggested that two factors are important in the use of the concept of "social role."

> First, the social role must always be seen in terms of a given situation. Secondly, allowance must be made for a range of individual role fulfillment based upon that person's experiences and values, if the *concept* of a social role is to be more adequately expressive of an *acting* individual. The alternative is rejected—that of structuring the social role exclusively in terms of the situation and ideal behavior patterns derived therefrom, with little or no concern for modifications due to individual definitions.[11]

As a member of a formal organization, then, each individual may be conceived to be functioning in two separate situations, the one imbedded in the other.[12] The first consists of the official definition of the position, the codified behavior system, and the second consists of the individual's own role concept, which represents essentially an expression of those facets of the personality which are relevant to organizational membership. The interaction of these two situations, a perceptual process, represents for each individual a *cognitive orientation to roles*.

The term cognitive orientation has been chosen deliberatly to emphasize

[9]For a discussion of the concept of selective interpersonal perception, see Jacob W. Getzels, "Administration as a Social Process," *Administrative Theory in Education,* ed. Andrew W. Halpin (Chicago: Midwest Administration Center, University of Chicago, 1958), p. 155.

[10]An example of the influence of selective perception is to be found in Bernard Berelson, Paul E. Lazarsfeld, and William N. McPhee, "Political Perception," *Readings in Social Psychology,* eds. Eleanor E. Maccoby, Theodore M. Newcomb, and Eugene L. Hartley (New York: Holt, Rinehart and Winston, Inc., 1958), pp. 72-85. See also, Max G. Abbott, "Values and Value-Perceptions of School Superintendents and Board Members," (Unpublished Ph.D. dissertation, University of Chicago, 1960).

[11]Leonard Riessman, "A Study of Role Conceptions in Bureaucracy," *Social Forces,* XXVII (March, 1949), p. 306.

[12]Getzels, *loc. cit.*

"dimensions of the individual's intellectual understanding; his concept of his job—what he thinks he is supposed to do and how he is to do it—and his concept of the organization and its objectives."[13] That is, an individual's cognitive orientation represents his perceptual response to the organization's codified behavior system.

Viewed in this way, the cognitive orientation to roles has to do with the rational aspects of an employee's understanding of (a) his own role, (b) the roles of others with whom he must interact, (c) the interrelationships of these roles, and (d) the relationships of the role definitions to the goals of the organization. Thus, an individual's cognitive orientation defines *for him* the position that he occupies, the way he is expected to relate to the incumbents of complementary positions, and the behaviors that are prescribed and proscribed by the organization. This orientation includes, but is not limited to, the conceptions of subordinate-superordinate relationships that employees have and that constitute the authority dimension of interaction.

Since, from the standpoint of the organization, the accuracy of an individual's cognitive orientation will determine the appropriateness of his behavior as he performs his role, most organizations make explicit provisions for bringing into congruence the organization's and the individual's role definitions. These provisions may consist of selective recruitment, close supervision during the early period of employment, pre- and in-service orientation sessions, or other similar arrangements. Regardless of the form that they take, these arrangements indicate a concern on the part of management regarding the importance of common understandings of role definitions.

An individual's cognitive orientation will not coincide exactly with either the institution's codified behavior system or the individual's idealized role concept, since the forming of a cognitive orientation is a perceptual process, and since perceptions are influenced by values and attitudes. However, this orientation will reflect elements of both the institution's and the individual's role definitions, and it will provide for a given individual the effective limits for his behavior.

At the same time that an individual is coming to a rational understanding of his position in an organization, he is also developing feelings and attitudes regarding that position. Thus, as he achieves a cognitive orientation to roles, he also acquires *affective responses to roles*. To the extent that an employee's cognitive orientation permits him to behave in ways that fit reasonably well with his idealized role definitions, the experience will be perceived as individually satisfying, his attitudes will be generally positive, he will be generally supportive of the organization, and his behavior will be expected to contribute most directly to the accomplishment of the organizations's goals.

On the other hand, to the extent that an employee is required to alter radically his own role definitions to conform to organizational demands, thus being required to behave in ways which deny the fulfillment of his own organizationally relevant needs, the experience will be perceived as individually dissatisfying, his attitudes

[13] Rensis Likert, *New Patterns of Management* (New York: McGraw-Hill Book Co., Inc., 1961), p. 198.

will be generally negative, he will be generally non-supportive of the organization, and his behavior will be expected to contribute less than maximally to the accomplishment of the organizations's goals.

Affective responses to roles, then, may be said to encompass that class of phenomena which is generally referred to as motivation. It is worth noting, however, that although the term motivation implies a proclivity to behave in some way, it does not necessarily imply behaving in ways that are productive for the organization. By using the two concepts of cognitive orientation to roles and affective responses to roles in place of the single concept of motivation, it should be possible to understand more thoroughly and to predict with greater accuracy the behavior that might be expected to occur under specified conditions. This is to say that knowing something about an individual's perceptions of the expectations attached to his role, and knowing something about his feelings regarding those perceptions, we should be able to predict with reasonable accuracy the behavior in which he will engage as he performs the role.

For example, it would be hypothesized that the individual who is satisfied with his cognitive orientation, whose behavior is individually satisfying while being organizationally productive, would conform to the production norms of the organization with a minimum of effort. On the other hand, it would be hypothesized that the individual who is dissatisfied with his cognitive orientation would encounter difficulty in conforming to production norms and would thus engage in a search for some alternative courses of action. Following March and Simon,[14] at least three such alternatives might be considered by an individual who found himself in this type of conflict situation:

a) For most employees, the alternative of leaving the organization would at least be considered,

b) Employees might conform to organizational demands even though to do so is viewed as personally dissatisfying,

c) Employees might decide to remain in the organization but seek opportunities for personal satisfaction without conforming to organizational demands.

The decision made by a given individual would depend upon a number of factors which would be considered simultaneously; regardless of that decision, his behavior at a given moment is conceived as deriving simultaneously from his cognitive orientation to roles and his affective responses to roles. This suggests that as long as an individual elects to remain in the organization, he will perform to some extent according to the way his position has been defined for him, or at least according to his concept of that position. His enthusiasm for his performance, however, will be affected by his attitudes and feelings, which are determined in turn by the personal satisfactions which he estimates will be forthcoming if he behaves in the required ways.

[14] James G. March and Herbert A. Simon, *Organizations* (New York: John Wiley & Sons, Inc., 1958).

Thus far, attention has been directed toward the officially sanctioned role definitions, the individual's idealized version of the role definitions, and the processes by which these two definitions converge. There has been no reference to other social forces which impinge upon the individual and which influence the behavior that occurs. Yet, such forces must be taken into account if one is to understand the complexity of organizational behavior.

It is meaningful to speak of an individual's cognitive orientation only at a given point of time. This orientation is subject to constant shifts and reformulations, and within any given organization there are forces which serve as feedback mechanisms and which determine in part the shifts which will occur. Two such mechanisms which appear to be particularly relevant to the topic of organizational behavior are the *reward systems* and *reference-group norms.*

Using the term "incentive system" in much the same way that the term reward system is being used here, Clark and Wilson have stated that "the incentive system may be regarded as the principal variable affecting organizational behavior."[15] This suggestion is derived from the largely common-sense assumption that all viable organizations must provide tangible or intangible incentives to individuals in exchange for contributions of individual activity to the organizations.

While the position of Clark and Wilson would appear to be sound, it seems reasonable to suggest that the reward system affects organizational behavior by altering an individual's cognitive orientation to roles. This is in keeping with the basic thesis of this paper, that each individual within an organization makes his own decisions regarding his behavior, but that those decisions are influenced by a number of forces which determine his perceptions of the situation. As Festinger has put it, "if a relation of dissonance exists [between cognition and behavior] there will arise forces to eliminate the dissonance and produce consonance. These pressures to reduce dissonance can act to change the behavior or to change some of the cognitive elements."[16]

It was suggested earlier that as long as an individual elects to remain in an organization, he will perform to some extent according to the way his position has been defined for him. In doing so, he anticipates a relationship between the expected performance and the rewards which the organization has to offer. Whether these rewards are in the form of promotion, increased pay, or some other type of recognition, they ary expected to be forthcoming when performance is in keeping with what the individual conceives his role to be.

If the anticipated rewards are not forthcoming following performance, or if the rewards are perceived by the employee to be negative rather than positive for him, a condition of dissonance may be said to exist. In seeking an explanation for the condition of dissonance, the individual will tend to question the accuracy of his

[15]Peter B. Clark and James Q. Wilson, "Incentive Systems: A Theory of Organizations," *Administrative Science Quarterly*, VI (Sept., 1961), 130.

[16]Leon Festinger, "The Relation Between Behavior and Cognition," *Contemporary Approaches to Cognition*, A Symposium Held at the University of Colorado (Cambridge, Mass: Harvard University Press, 1957), p. 131.

perceptions of the situation. Any shift in perceptions which occurs as a result of this questioning constitutes an altering of the cognitive orientation to accommodate the perceived disparities.

To illustrate, a teacher who conceives of her role as a faculty member as one which calls for ideas and suggestions may be expected to contribute ideas and to make suggestions as opportunities arise. To the extent that her ideas are accepted and recognized, the teacher's perceptions of the situation will be confirmed and her cognitive orientation will be reinforced. On the other hand, to the extent that her ideas are rejected or ignored, the teacher will be inclined to question the accuracy of her perceptions and she will restructure her cognitive orientation to fit her new perceptions of the situation. Any such alteration which occurs in the cognitive orientation to roles will be accompanied by a concomitant altering of the affective responses to roles. That is, as the cognitive orientation is altered, there will occur at least a temporary shift in attitudes and feelings regarding the role as it is thus perceived.

The influence of reference-group norms on individual behavior has been amply demonstrated in empirical research. Perhaps the classic studies in the area of group norms were those which were conducted at the Hawthorne plant of the Western Electric Company. In reporting on the behavior of the men in the bank wiring room, Homans has stated:

> They shared a common body of sentiments. A person should not turn out too much work. If he did, he was a "rate-buster." The theory was that if an excessive amount of work was turned out, the management would lower the piecework rate so that the employees would be in the position of doing more work for approximately the same pay. On the other hand, a person should not turn out too little work. If he did, he was a "chiseler"; that is, he was getting paid for work he did not do.[17]

Thus, Homans is describing the norms established by what Merton has called the "normative type" or inner reference group, which sets and maintains internal standards for individual performance.[18] In addition to this group, Merton has identified the "comparison type" or outer reference group, which provides a frame of comparison relative to which the individual evaluates himself and others.

Although an individual may be influenced simultaneously by the standards set by both types of reference groups, a thorough understanding of behavior within organizations requires attention to the primacy of these standards for different employees. Following the lead provided by Merton, for example, Gouldner has summarized the relevant research and has concluded that two latent organizational identities might be identified. They are:

1. COSMOPOLITANS: those low on loyalty to the employing organization, high on commitment to specialized role skills, and likely to use an outer reference group orientation.

[17]George C. Homans, "The Western Electric Researches," *Human Factors in Management*, ed. Schuyler D. Hoslett (New York: Harper & Brothers, 1951), p. 235.

[18]Merton, *op. cit.*, p. 283.

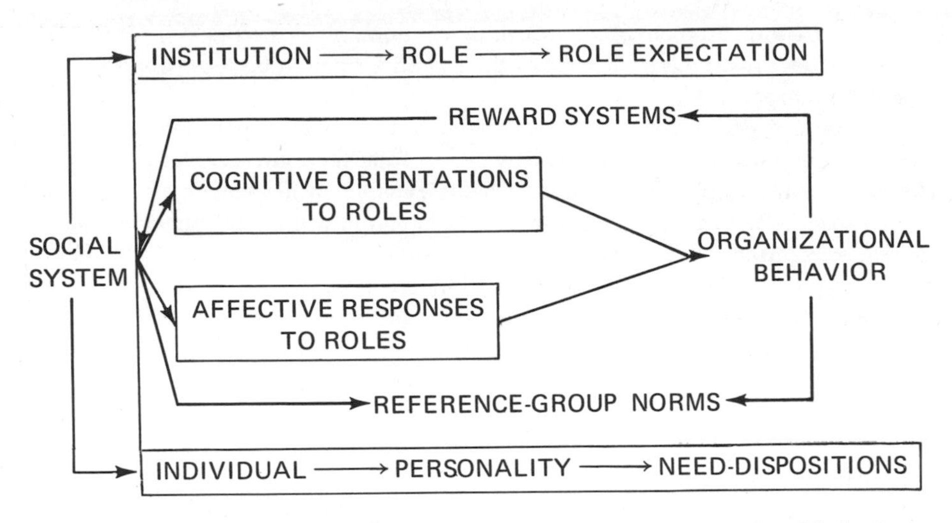

Figure 2. General model of the intervening variables in organizational behavior.

2. LOCALS: those high on loyalty to the employing organization, low on commitment to specialized role skills, and likely to use an inner reference group orientation.[19]

Those employees whose orientation is basically local may be expected to be readily amenable to influence by the standards of the normative or inner reference group. When the behavior of locals elicits negative sanctions from the inner reference group, such individuals will tend to question the accuracy of their cognitive orientations and will restructure these orientations to remove the dissonance which is perceived. They will tend to conform readily to organizational demands and will, eventually, adjust their own levels of aspiration so that personal satisfaction can be achieved within the limits or organizationally permissible behavior.

Those employees whose orientation is basically cosmopolitan may be expected to be less amenable to influence by the standards of the normative reference group. When the behavior of cosmopolitans elicits negative sanctions from the inner reference group, such individuals will tend to maintain their cognitive orientations but will increase their search for courses of action which are alternative to those proposed by the organization. For some of these individuals, increased search may eventuate in their leaving the organization, provided that opportunities for moving are available, and provided further that their *sunken costs* in the organization are not too great.

If leaving the organization proves not to be an acceptable alternative for the cosmopolitan, such a person will remain in the organization but will tend to seek opportunities for satisfaction without conforming to organizational demands. Such satisfaction may derive from recognition for research and/or publication in a professional field, from activity in professional or trade associations, or from other

[19] Alvin W. Gouldner, "Cosmopolitans and Locals," *Organizations: Structure and Behavior* (New York: John Wiley & Sons, Inc., 1963), p. 361.

similar activities. In any event, recognition from outside groups is sought and is substituted for the recognition not forthcoming from within the organization.

The model of organizational behavior which has been presented in this paper may be represented diagrammatically as shown in Figure 2.

In summary, a formal organization may be viewed as a specific social system in which role expectations become formalized and institutionalized. Such expectations constitute a codified behavior system, which is more or less explicit but which is generally understood by all employees. As specific individuals, with their own patterns of organizationally relevant needs, are socialized in respect to the organization's codified behavior system, they achieve a cognitive orientation to roles and they respond affectively to this orientation. Thus, behavior in a formal organization is conceived as deriving simultaneously from an individual's cognitive orientation to roles and his affective responses to roles.

Both the cognitive orientation to roles and affective responses to roles are modified over time, largely as a function of the operation of two feedback mechanisms within the organization: the reward system and the reference-group norms. Feedback, in this sense, is a perceptual process in which the cognitive orientation is monitored in terms of its congruence with the "real" situation.

Social Behavior and the Administrative Process

J. W. Getzels and E. G. Guba

Perhaps the most vigorous movement in administration in recent years has been directed toward the development of a comprehensive theory capable of generating both hypotheses for guiding research and principles for guiding practice. Despite many specific advances in special areas, such as hospital administration, public administration, business administration, and educational administration, there still is no general conceptual framework for systematizing and inter-relating our knowledge within and among these areas. It is still impossible to speak of administration in terms that would be acceptable to, or for that matter even readily understandable by, students and practitioners in the several special fields. This failure to conceptualize administration on a general theoretical level has been a major obstacle to the development of administration as a rigorous discipline, and the elaboration of theory is accordingly receiving increased attention both in "research" and "applied" administrative settings.

The purpose of the present paper is twofold: (*a*) to describe a socio-psychological theory of social behavior having broad application to the area of administration and (*b*) to illustrate the application of the theory to major issues in administration. The four major issues considered here are: the problem of institutional and individual conflict; the problem of staff effectiveness, efficiency, and satisfaction; the nature of various leadership-followership styles; and the problem of morale.

The process of administration deals essentially with the conduct of social behavior in a hierarchical setting (1). Structurally, we may conceive of administration as a series of superordinate-subordinate relationships within a social system. Functionally, this hierarchy of relationships is the locus for allocating and integrating roles, personnel, and facilities to achieve the goals of the system.

The term "social system" here is conceptual rather than descriptive; it must not be confused with "society" or "state" or as somehow applicable only to *large* aggregates of human interaction. Thus, within our framework, for one purpose a given community may be considered a social system, with the school a particular organization within the more general social system; for another purpose the school itself, or even a single class within the school, may be considered a social system in its own right. The theoretical model that we are proposing is applicable regardless of the level or the size of the unit under consideration.

We conceive of the social system as involving two major classes of phenomena, which are at once conceptually independent and phenomenally interactive. There are, first, the *institutions* with certain *roles* and *expectations* that will fullfil the goals of the system. Second, inhabiting the system there are the *individuals* with certain *personalities* and *need-dispositions*, whose interactions comprise what we generally call "social behavior." Social behavior may be apprehended as a function of the following major elements: institution, role, and expectation, which together constitute the *nomothetic*, or normative, dimension of activity in a social system; and individual, personality, and need-disposition, which together constitute the *idiographic*, or personal, dimension of activity in a social system.

To understand the nature of the observed behavior and to be able to predict and control it, we must understand the nature and relationships of those elements. The term "institution" has received a variety of definitions, but for our purposes it is sufficient to point out that all social systems have certain imperative functions that come in time to be carried out in certain routinized patterns. These functions—governing, educating, policing, for example—may be said to have become "institutionalized," and the agencies established to carry out these institutionalized functions for the social system as a whole may be termed "institutions." These institutions have certain noteworthy characteristics.

a) Institutions are *purposive*. They are established to carry out certain ends, and these ends serve as the criteria against which institutional practices are ultimately evaluated.

b) Institutions are *peopled*. If institutions are to carry out their prescribed goals, human agents are required. It should be noted, however, that here we are concerned with people, not in the personalistic sense, but in the actuarial sense. To avoid the possibility of confusion, we may adopt the term "actor" instead of "person" for this level of analysis.

c) Institutions are *structural*. To carry out a specific purpose requires an organization, and organization implies component parts and some rules about how these parts should be interrelated. If the goals and purposes of the institution are known, the tasks to achieve the goals may be specified, and these may be organized into *roles*. Each role is assigned certain responsibilities and concomitant resources, including authority and facilities for implementing the given tasks. A significant feature of such a blueprint or "table of organization" of roles is that it is most frequently set up *before* the selection of any real incumbents for the roles; it is set up in terms of *actors*, in the sense previously defined. And if we may anticipate ourselves a little here, the real person may or may not exactly fit the given roles. As we shall see, this question of fitness poses, in many ways, one of the critical dilemmas of administration.

d) Institutions are *normative*. The fact that tasks for achieving the institutional goals are organized into roles implies that the roles serve as "norms" for the behavior of the role incumbents or actors. The role expectations are obligatory upon the actor if he is to retain his legitimate place in the institution.

e) Institutions are *sanction-bearing*. The existence of norms is of no consequence unless there is adherence to them. Accordingly institutions must have at their disposal appropriate positive and negative sanctions for insuring compliance with the norms, at least within broad limits.

The most important subunit of the institution is the role. Roles are the structural elements defining the behavior of the role incumbents or actors. The following generalizations may be made about the nature of roles.

a) Roles represent *positions, offices, or statuses within the institution*. The role itself may be described, in the words of Linton, as the "dynamic aspect" (2:14) of such positions, offices, or statuses.

b) Roles are defined in terms of *role expectations*. A role has certain normative rights and duties, which may be termed "role expectations." When the role incumbent puts these rights and duties into effect, he is said to be performing his role. The expectations define for the actor, whoever he may be, what he should do under various circumstances as long as he is the incumbent of the particular role.

c) Roles are *institutional givens*. Since the role expectations may be formulated without reference to the particular individuals who will serve as the role incumbents, it is clear that the prescriptions do not depend on individual perception or even on typical behavior. Although the expectations may be misperceived or even serve as points of departure for the actual role incumbents, their crucial significance as blueprints for what *should* be done is not thereby nullified.

d) The behaviors associated with a role may be thought of as lying along a *continuum from "required" to "prohibited."* Certain expectations are held to be crucial to the role, and the appropriate behaviors are absolutely required of the incumbent. Other behaviors are absolutely forbidden. Between these extremes lie certain other behaviors, some of which would be recommended and others perhaps mildly disapproved, but all of which would be considered permissible, at least in the ordinary case. It is this flexible feature of roles that makes it possible for role incumbents with different personalities to fulfil the same role and give it the stamp of their individual styles of behavior.

e) Roles are *complementary*. Roles are interdependent in that each role derives its meaning from other related roles in the institution. In a sense, a role is not only a prescription for the role incumbent but also for incumbents of other roles within the organization, so that in a hierarchical setting the expectations for one role may, to some extent, form the sanctions for a second interlocking role. For example, the role of sergeant and the role of private in the army cannot really be defined or implemented except in relation to each other. This quality of complementariness fuses two or more roles into a coherent, interactive unit and makes it possible for us to conceive of an institution as having a characteristic structure.

So far in our analysis it has been sufficient to conceive of the role incumbents as only "actors," devoid of personal or other individualizing characteristics, as if all incumbents of the same role were exactly alike and implemented the given role in exactly the same way. But roles are filled by real, flesh-and-blood persons, and no two persons are exactly alike. An individual stamps the particular role he fills with the unique style of his own characteristic pattern of expresive behavior. Even in the case of the relatively inflexible roles of sergeant and of private, no two individual sergeants or privates fulfil the roles in exactly the same way. To understand the observed behavior of a specific sergeant and a specific private, it is not enough to know only the nature of the roles and of the expectations (although their behavior cannot be understood apart from these), but we must know the nature of the individuals inhabiting the roles and reacting to the expectations as well. That is, in addition to the nomothetic, or normative, aspects, we must also consider the *idiographic*, or individualizing, aspects of social behavior. Now, just as we were able to analyze the institutional dimension into the component elements of role and expectation, so we may analyze the individual dimension into the component elements of *personality* and *need-disposition*.

The term "personality," like that of "institution," has been given a variety of meanings. For our purposes, "personality" may be defined as the dynamic organization within the individual of those *need-dispositions* that govern his unique reactions to the environment. The central analytic elements of personality are the *need-dispositions*, which we may well define, with Parsons and Shils, as individual "tendencies to orient and act with respect to objects in certain manners and to expect certain consequences from these actions" (3:114). Or, as the same authors go on to say: "The conjoined word 'need-disposition' itself has a double connotation; on the one hand, it refers to a tendency to accomplish some end state; on the other, it refers to a disposition to do something with an object designed to accomplish the end state" (3:115).

Returning to the example of the sergeant and the private, we may now make an essential distinction between the behavior of two individuals with a need-disposition for "submission" in the roles of sergeant and private and the behavior of two individuals with a need-disposition for "ascendance" in the same roles. In short, to understand the behavior of specific role incumbents in an institution, we must know both the role expectations and the need-dispositions. Indeed, needs and expectations may both be though of as *motives* for behavior, the one deriving from personal propensities, the other from institutional requirements. What we call social behavior may be conceived as ultimately deriving from the interaction between the two sets of motives.

The general model we have been describing may be represented pictorially as indicated in Figure 1. The nomothetic axis is shown at the top of the diagram and consists of institution, role, and role expectations, each term being the analytic unit for the term next preceding it. Thus the social system is defined by its institutions; each institution, by its constituent roles; each role, by the expectations attaching to it. Similarly, the idiographic axis, shown at the lower portion of the diagram, consists of individual, personality, and need-dispositions, each term again serving as the analytic unit for the term next preceding it. A given act is conceived as deriving simultaneously from both the nomothetic and the idiographic dimensions. That is to say, social behavior results as the individual attempts to cope with an environment composed of patterns of expectations for his behavior in ways consistent with his own independent pattern of needs. Thus we may write the general equation: $B = f(R \times P)$, where B is observed behavior, R is a given institutional role defined by the expectations attaching to it, and P is the personality of the particular role incumbent defined by its need-dispositions.

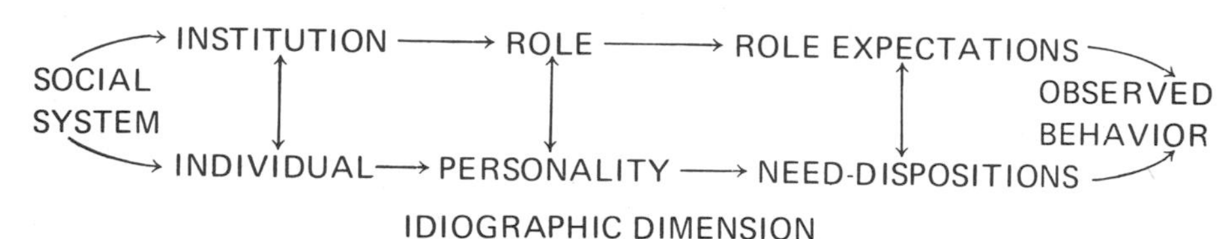

Figure 1. General model showing the nomothetic and the idiographic dimensions of social behavior.

The portions of role and personality factors determining behavior vary with the specific act, the specific role, and the specific personality involved. The nature of the interaction can be understood from another graphic representation shown as Figure 2. The factors entering into a given behavioral act may be conceived as occurring at a line cutting through the role and personality possibilities represented by the rectangle. At the left, the proportion of the act dictated by considerations of role expectations is relatively large, while the proportion of the act dictated by considerations of personality is relatively small. At the right, these proportions are reversed, and considerations of personality become greater than considerations of role expectations. In these terms, for example, the behavior of our army private may be said to conform almost entirely to role demands (Line *A*), while the behavior of a free-lance artist derives almost entirely from personality dispositions (Line *B*). In either case, behavior, insofar as it is "social," remains a function of both role and personality although in different degrees. When role is maximized, behavior still retains some personal aspects because no role is ever so closely defined as to eliminate all individual latitude. When personality is maximized, social

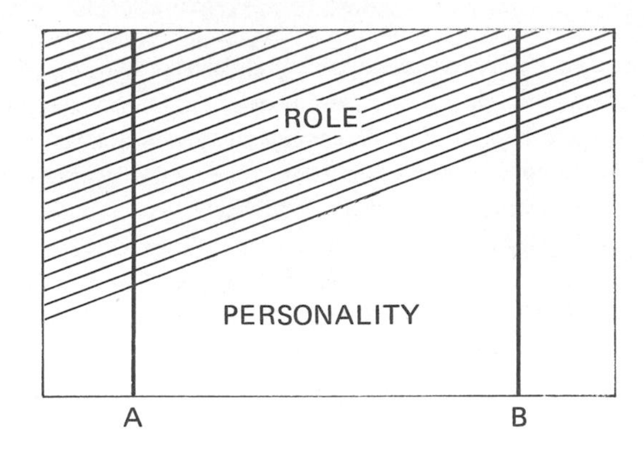

Figure 2. The interaction of role and personality in a behavioral act ($B = f[R \times P]$).

behavior still cannot be free from some role prescription. The individual who divorces himself entirely from such prescription ceases to communicate with his fellows and is said to be autistic.

The relevance of this general model for administrative theory and practice becomes apparent when it is seen that the administrative process inevitably deals with the fulfilment of both nomothetic role expectations and idiographic need-dispositions while the goals of a particular social system are being achieved. The unique task of administration, at least with respect to staff relations, is just this: to integrate the demands of the institution and the demands of the staff members in a way that is at once organizationally productive and individually fulfilling.

In the framework outlined here, we may proceed to a reformulation of certain recurring administrative problems and to a clarification of the issues involved.

1. Individual and Institutional Conflict

When an individual performs up to role expectations, we may say that he is *adjusted* to the role. Conversely, when an individual fulfils all his needs, we may speak of him as *integrated*. Ideally, the individual should be both adjusted and integrated, so that he may by one act fulfil both the nomothetic, or institutional, requirements and the idiographic, or personal, requirements. This would obviously be the case if institutional expectations and personal needs were absolutely congruent, for the individual would always will what was mandatory, and both his adjustment and his integration would be maximized. But absolute congruence of expectations and needs is seldom, if ever, found in practice, and as a consequence there is inevitably a greater or lesser amount of strain or conflict for the individual and the institution. In the present context this strain or conflict may be defined simply as the "mutual interference of adjustive and integrative reactions." The model points to three primary sources of conflict in the administrative setting (4).

a) Role-personality conflicts occur as a function of discrepancies between the pattern of expectations attaching to a given role and the pattern of need-dispositions characteristic of the incumbent of the role. Recall again our example of the individual with high need-dispositions for "ascendance" who is placed in the role of private. There is mutual interference between nomothetic expectations and idiographic dispositions, and the individual must choose whether he will fulfil individual needs or institutional requirements. If he chooses the latter, he is liable to unsatisfactory personal integration. If he chooses the former, he is liable to unsatisfactory role adjustment. In practice there is usually compromise, but, in any event, the nature of the forthcoming behavior is quite different when the expectations and the dispositions are discrepant than when they are congruent.

b) Role conflicts occur whenever a role incumbent is required to conform simultaneously to a number of expectations which are mutually exclusive, contradictory, or inconsistent, so that adjustment to one set of requirements makes adjustment to the other impossible or at least difficult. Role conflicts in this sense are situational givens and are independent of the personality of the role incumbent. They are evidence of disorganization in the nomothetic dimension and may arise in several ways:

(1) Disagreement within the referent group defining the role. For example, the principal of the school may be expected by some teachers to visit them regularly for constructive help and by others to trust them as professional personnel not in need of such supervision.

(2) Disagreement among several referent groups, each having a right to define expectations for the same role. For example, the university faculty member may be expected by his department head to emphasize teaching and service to students but by his academic dean to emphasize research and publication.

(3) Contradiction in the expectations of two or more roles which an individual is occupying at the same time. For example, a teacher may be attempting to be both a devoted mother and a successful career woman.

c) Personality conflicts occur as a function of opposing needs and dispositions within the personality of the role incumbent. The effect of such personal disequilibrium is to keep the individual at odds with the institution either because he cannot maintain a stable relation with a given role or because, in terms of his autistic reactions, he habitually misperceives the expectations placed upon him. In any case, just as role conflict is a situational given, personality conflict is an individual given and is independent of any particular institutional setting. No matter what the situation, the role is, in a sense, detached by the individual from its institutional context and function and is used by him to work out personal and private needs and dispositions, however inappropriate these may be to the goals of the social system as a whole.

In the terms of our model, these three types of conflict represent incongruence in the nomothetic and the idiographic dimensions, or in the interaction between the two dimensions of the social system under study. Such incongruence is symptomatic of administrative failure and leads to loss in individual and institutional productivity.

2. Effectiveness, Efficiency, and Satisfaction

A primary concern in any organization is the effectiveness, efficiency, and satisfaction of the staff (the role incumbents). The administrative problems concerned with effectiveness, efficiency, and satisfaction have been confused for want of an appropriate frame of reference. The terms have often been used interchangeably, and the significant issues and fruitful distinctions that the concepts imply are obscured altogether. The model we are using makes possible clear-cut and heuristic distinctions between the terms so that a given role incumbent may, for example, be seen as effective without being efficient, and efficient without being effective, and satisfied without being either effective or efficient.

We may recall our basic formulation of behavior in the administrative situation as a function of role expectations and personality dispositions. Effectiveness, efficiency, and satisfaction may be seen as relationships among these primary elements of the model. The relationships are shown in Figure 3.

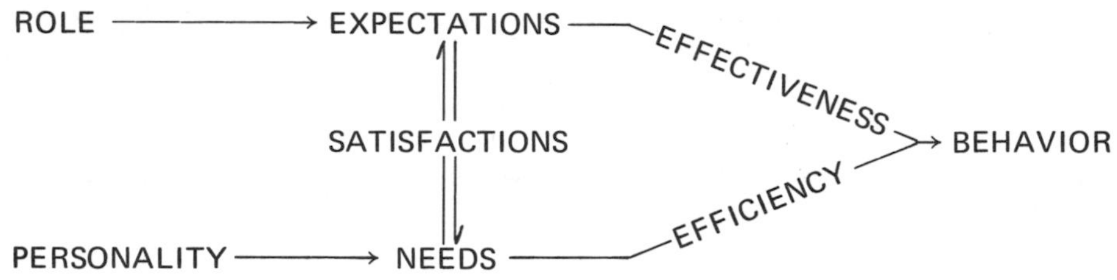

Figure 3. Relation of role expectations and personality needs to efficient, effective, and satisfying behavior.

a) The criterion for *effectiveness* is typically the observed behavior of the individual being rated. However, we maintain that the standard cannot be the behavior itself but the behavior *relative* to some expectation held by the rater for the behavior. Two crucial consequences follow from this. The first is that the same behavior may be labeled "effective" at one time and "ineffective" at another time by the same person, depending on the expectations he applies to the behavior. The second is that the same behavior may be labeled "effective" and "ineffective" simultaneously as a result of different expectations held by different referent groups. In either case, judgments of effectiveness and ineffectiveness are incapable of interpretation unless both the expectations being applied and the behavior being observed are known. In the terms of our model, effectiveness is a function of the congruence of behavior with expectations, and it must be assessed as such.

b) *Efficiency* is a relationship between needs and behavior. To the extent that needs and expectations are discrepant, behavior may conform to one or the other or, what is more likely, to some compromise between the two. When behavior conforms to the needs dimension, it appears "natural," even pleasurable, and is forthcoming with a minimum of strain or expenditure of psychic energy. In this sense, the behavior is efficient. When the behavior conforms to the expectations dimension and there is a gap between expectation and needs, behavior is "unnatural," even painful, and is forthcoming with a maximum of strain and expenditure of psychic energy. In this sense, the behavior is inefficient. In the terms of our model, we may say efficiency is a function of the congruence of behavior with need-dispositions.

c) When we consider *satisfaction* (5), we recognize that the administrator is faced with the dilemma of behaving in such a way as to produce maximal effectiveness or to produce maximal efficiency in the role incumbent. Usually he tries to maintain an appropriate balance between the alternatives. His dilemma would be resolved if the needs and the expectations could be made to coincide (selection and in-service training procedures are often directed toward just this goal). In that case, the behavior of the role incumbent would simultaneously meet situational expectations and personal needs. The relation of the individual to the organization would be ideal and presumably would produce maximum satisfaction for all concerned. In the terms of our model, satisfaction is a function of the congruence of institutional expectations with individual need-dispositions.

It should be apparent that, when expectations and needs are not congruent, satisfaction is reduced below the theoretical maximum. The individual may choose to maximize his effectiveness or to maximize his efficiency without necessarily being satisfied. We may summarize by suggesting that effectiveness is situational in origin and point of assessment, that efficiency is personal in origin and point of assessment, and that satisfaction is a function of the relationship between situation and person, the three concepts being entirely independent of one another in the present analysis.

3. Leadership-Followership Styles

The terms "leader" and "follower" in the administrative situation have been variously defined, and nothing will be gained by further elaboration here. For present purposes we may say that "to lead" is to engage in an act which *initiates* a structure in interaction with others, and that "to follow" is to engage in an act which *maintains* a structure initiated by another. The terms "leader" or "superordinate" and "follower" or "subordinate" in this usage are only relative; for the follower is not altogether passive in the relationship, and the leader is by no means always dominant. The nature of the relationship depends on the operating leadership-followership styles in the particular social system.

In the terms of our model, we have identified three distinct leadership followership styles: the nomethetic, the idiographic, and the transactional. These styles are represented pictorially in Figure 4. It should be noted that in this conception both the leader and the follower are goal-oriented, and their behavior is directed toward achieving a common institutional purpose. The three styles of leadership-followership are three *modes of achieving the same goal;* they are *not* different images of the goal. We may examine the variations in the three leadership-followership styles with respect to several major elements of our model: the proportion of role and personality factors in the behavior; the nature of the predominant conflicts recognized and handled; and the relative weight given to effectiveness, efficiency, and satisfaction.

a) *The nomothetic style* emphasizes the nomothetic dimension of behavior and accordingly places emphasis on the requirements of the institution, the role, and the expectation rather than on the requirements of the individual, the personality, and the need-disposition. In the equation $B = f(R \times P)$, P is minimized, R is maximized. It is assumed that, given the institutional purpose, appropriate procedures can be discovered, perhaps through time and motion studies and the

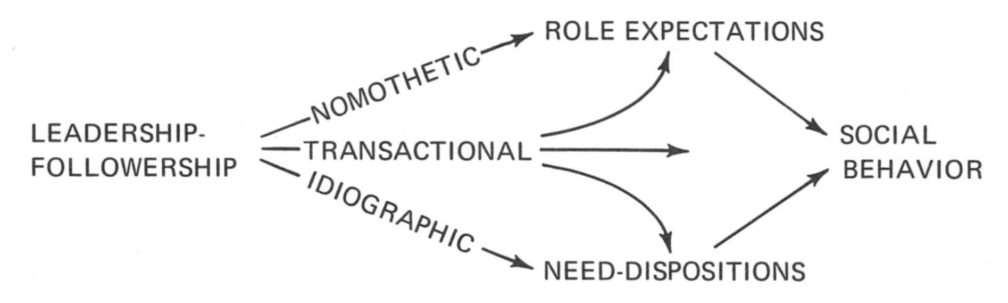

Figure 4. Three leadership-followership styles.

like. These procedures are then incorporated in the role expectations, and every role incumbent is required to adhere, in minute detail, to the expectations. It then follows that, if roles are clearly defined and everyone is held responsible for doing what he is supposed to do, the desired outcomes would naturally ensue regardless of who the particular role incumbents might be, provided only that they have the necessary technical competence.

In short, with the nomothetic style of leadership-followship, the most expeditious route to the goal is seen as residing in the nature of the institutional structure rather than in any particular persons. The obligation of the follower is to do things "by the book"; the obligation of the leader is to "write the book." The predominant conflict that is likely to be recognized is role conflict, since this is immediately related to the institution-role-expectation dimension of behavior. The standard of administrative excellence is institutional adjustment and effectiveness rather than individual integration and efficiency.

b) *The idiographic style* of leadership-followership emphasizes the idiographic dimension of behavior and accordingly places emphasis on the requirements of the individual, the personality, and the need-disposition rather than on the requirements of the institution, the role, and the expectation. In our equation $B = f(R \times P)$, R is minimized, P is maximized. This does not mean that the idiographic style is any less goal-oriented than is the nomothetic style; it means that the most expeditious route to the goal is seen as residing in the people involved rather than in the nature of the institutional structure. The basic assumption is that the greatest accomplishment will occur, not from enforcing adherence to rigorously defined roles, but from making it possible for each person to contribute what is most relevant and meaningful to him. This point of view is obviously related to the particular individuals who fill the roles at a particular time, and expectations must be kept vague and informal. In effect, change the individual role incumbent, and you change with him the definition of the role. Normative prescriptions of the sort included in typical role expectations are seen as unnecessarily restrictive and as a hindrance rather than a guide to productive behavior. The best government is the one that governs least, or, better, not at all. The predominant conflict that is likely to be recognized is personality conflict, since this is immeditely related to the individual-personality-needs dimension of behavior. The standard of administrative excellence is individual integration and efficiency rather than institutional adjustment and effectiveness.

c) *The transactional style* of leadership-followership, as might be expected, is intermediate between the other two and is, therefore, least amenable to "pure" or even clear-cut definition. Since the goals of the social system must be carried out, it is obviously necessary to make explicit the roles and expectations required to achieve the goals. And, since the roles and expectations will be implemented by flesh-and-blood people with needs to be met, the personalities and dispositions of these people must be taken into account. But the solution is not so simple as appears from just saying that one should hew to the middle course between expectations and needs, that is, between the nomothetic and the idiographic axes. Instead, the aim throughout is to acquire a thorough awareness of the limits and resources of both individual and institution within which administrative action may occur (that is, from the nomothetic to the idiographic extreme) and an intelligent application of the two as a particular problem may demand. In the equation $B - f(R \times P)$, P and R are maximized or minimized as the situation requires. Institutional roles are developed independently of the role incumbents, but they are adapted to the personalities of the individual incumbents. Expectations are defined as sharply as they can be but not so sharply as to prohibit appropriate behavior in terms of need-dispositions. Role conflicts, personality conflicts, and role-personality conflicts are recognized and handled. The standard of administrative excellence is individual integration and efficiency, satisfaction, and institutional adjustment and effectiveness.

4. Morale

Definitions of "morale," like those of "effectiveness," "efficiency," and "satisfaction," are necessarily more or less arbitrary. The model suggests one possible definition which takes into account the two elements most often identified with morale in the literature, namely, feelings of identification and belongingness, and suggests a third additional element, often overlooked, which is, however, as vital as the other two.

To understand the relevance of the model for morale, let us turn to Figure 5. We may again suppose that there exists a role incumbent subject to the expectations of his role and bringing to the role his individual pattern of needs. The goals to which the institution is directed may or may not represent the personal goals of the actor. Let us represent the terms, "expectations," "needs," and "goals," in a triangular relationship in the same way in which "expectations," "needs," and "behavior" were previously represented. Each of these three terms may overlap the other two to a greater or lesser extent. We may attach the designation "belongingness" to the needs-expectations congruence, "rationality" to the expectations-goals congruence, and "identification" to the needs-goals congruence.

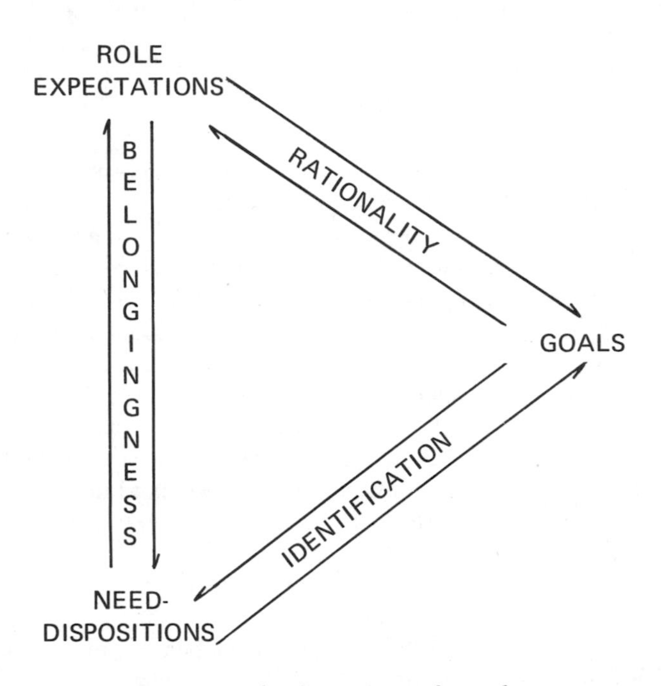

Figure 5. The dimensions of morale.

The variable *belongingness* represents the anticipation, on the part of the role incumbent, that he will be able to achieve satisfaction within the institutional framework, since it appears to him that meeting institutional expectations will also permit him to serve personal needs. Under such circumstances, as we have already observed, institutional activity is easy and natural to the subject, and he carries it out with a minimal cost in psychic energy. The energy so preserved is available for other purposes—a fact from which both the institution and the individual profit. If extra effort is required, the subject has available resources of energy upon which he can, and probably will, call.

The variable *rationality* represents the extent to which expectations placed upon a role are logically appropriate to the achievement of the proposed institutional goals. An individual may well have low morale if he sees little or no relation between what he is expected to do and what the institution as a whole is presumed to be doing. There seems to be little point in expending even normal effort on what appear to be tangential activities; putting forth extra effort would simply be useless.

The variable *identification* represents the degree to which the subject is able to integrate the goals and actions of the institution into his own structure of needs and values. Unless the subject is able to make this integration, it appears unlikely that he will be properly motivated to carry out the enterprise functions in an expeditious and thorough fashion. It is difficult to imagine how high morale, in the sense of a predisposition to put forth extra effort in the furtherance of group goals, might be maintained under such circumstances.

In terms of the model, then, morale may be understood as resulting from the interaction of three factors: belongingness, rationality, and identification. Morale cannot be high if even one of these factors is zero; morale can, however, reach acceptable levels if all three factors are maintained to some degree. In this sense, then, the task of the administrator seeking to develop high morale is the maintenance of reasonable levels of agreement among expectations, needs, and goals.

In conclusion, we wish to disown any implication that the improvement of administrative practice will automatically ensue from a knowledge or manipulation of concepts and variables of the sort proposed in this model. This would be like saying that the success of a medical practitioner depends solely on his knowledge of medical science—physiology, biochemistry, and such. On the other hand, there is little doubt that these are of no small value in successful medical practice. Similarly, the application of systematic concepts from social science to a real situation will help the administrator to sort out the problems confronting him, to examine them in appropriate contexts, and to understand something of their internal dynamics. Such formulations, though they may not provide generalized decisions for action, and at this time are perhaps of greater research value than applied value, may at least make it possible for the administrator to understand why certain decisions and practices work while others do not (6). There seems to us, in short, little doubt of the heuristic value of such models.

Notes

1. Our indebtedness to the work of Talcott Parsons will be self-evident throughout this and subsequent sections of the paper. See also J. W. Getzels, "A Psycho-sociological Framework for the Study of Educational Administration," *Harvard Educational Review,* XXII (Fall, 1952), 235-46.

2. Ralph Linto, *The Study of Man.* New York: D. Appleton-Century Co., 1936.

3. Talcott Parsons and Edward A. Shils, *Toward a General Theory of Action.* Cambridge, Massachusetts: Harvard University Press, 1951.

4. For some attempts at research in this area, see: (*a*) Samuel A. Stouffer and Jackson Toby, "Role Conflict and Personality," *American Journal of Sociology,* LVI (March, 1951), 395-406; (*b*) J. W. Getzels and E. G. Guba, "Role, Role Conflict, and Effectiveness: An Empirical Study," *American Sociological Review,*

XIX (April, 1954), 164-75; (*c*) J. W. Getzels and E. G. Guba, "The Structure of Roles and Role Conflict in the Teaching Situation," *Journal of Educational Sociology,* XXIX (September, 1955), 30-40.

5. The term "satisfaction," as it is used here, is more or less synonymous with "contentment" and should not be taken to include such additional concepts as fundamental agreement with institutional objectives or the feeling that the institutional environment lives up to the incumbent's standards of technical or professional adequacy. These concepts involve certain additional factors, as, for example, the level of aspiration of the incumbent, which are too complex to be handled here.

6. The relation of theory, research, and practice in administration generally has been discussed by J. D. Thompson, "On Building an Administrative Science," *Administrative Science Quarterly,* I (June, 1956), 102-11; and in educational administration specifically by A. P. Coladarci and J. W. Getzels, *The Use of Theory in Educational Administration.* Monograph No. 5. Stanford, California: School of Education, Stanford University, 1956.

What Is the Manager?

Herbert Sonthoff

The study of management has grown into the "management sciences." The use of this term points to our search for verifiable rules and "principles" as well as for descriptions of human "values," the full knowledge of which will presumably result in management techniques equally effective in all types of organizations. The question of the "scientific" nature of the study of management may trouble the businessman; not only does he seek practical operating information but, as a human being, he longs for a clear view of his place and role as a manager in a world seemingly governed by uncontrollably accelerated technological and scientific change. For the greater his own sense of responsibility, the more the manager today, as J. D. Batten puts it is *Tough-Minded Management,*[1] "is caught in a mainstream of self-examination and change."

We should keep this quest in mind whenever we turn to studies of managerial methods, processes, and objectives in order to gain some insight into what we are when we are managers, especially when the findings wear the imposing garb of "research." Such insight can in part be gained through the eyes of others, and we are about to consider a number of different views. Some of them are research findings, and others are straightforward observations and reflections. A search for managerial skills, leading to a consideration of the manager's role toward technical specialists and scientific executives, as well as of his specific responsibilities toward

[1] New York, American Management Association, 1963.

those for whom and with whom he works, may give us a new sense of the value of organizational relationships. But this is not enough. What the manager is asking us today is to help him develop an awareness of his particular kind of indispensability, an awareness of the form, to put it somewhat sententiously, of his particular existence as a manager. In this search, scientific inquiry, however defined, can be an aid, but only an aid.

Manager As Actor

Batten's is a no-nonsense approach to the question of how to be an effective manager. He attacks the increasingly popular assumption that—

> . . . imagination and dynamic things will happen when a major position is filled by a man who possesses, roughly, the following qualifications: at least one college degree (preferably two, sometimes three or more); considerable related experience; pleasant and personable mannerisms; and the ability to assuage feelings and pour oil on troubled waters. Many times a man with these flawless credentials is recruited and placed in charge of a department with high accompanying expectations.

Yet if the man moves into a "nonproductive climate" and simply remains a nice guy, he usually doesn't get the job done. "Individual talents," Batten argues, "must have specific targets within a climate of totally targeted activity. Individuals must have some real relationships between their own yearnings and the accomplishments of their department and company."

Too true to be denied. But just how does the manager develop a sense of this relationship? Batten does not embrace the many kinds of management development programs currently popular, whether they include role playing, buzz sessions, case studies, brainstorming, sensitivity training, problem solving, the in-basket technique, or managerial games. Devices and gimmicks all. Instead, he believes in post-appraisal counseling, which is, he says, "the best way currently known to bring about *development of the whole man*" [my italics]. In suggesting what this whole man looks like, Batten specifies 50 qualities of the "ideal tough-minded executive"; 20 additional qualities describe him as an individual, 10 more qualities spell out the prerequisities for his membership in society, and another 20 qualities set him apart as a manager.

While Batten does not tell us how we can acquire these admirable traits, the entire tenor of the book suggests his belief that modes of thinking and feeling can be developed much as strong muscles can be developed through constant exercise. If we decide to do so and possess the necessary innate qualities, he seems to imply, we can model ourselves in the image of the responsible, ethical, outgoing, action-minded, and results-oriented captain of industry—what, to Batten, the word "manager" stands for. The growing popularity of "how-to" books, lectures, and programs testifies to the attractiveness of this approach. It does have value as a primary step toward recognizing one's own ways of acting. But if adopted faithfully, it keeps the adopter on its particular level: he remains an *actor*.

Manager As Catalyst

"To get things done" will always remain the simple and accurate description of one basic managerial function. Nonetheless, in an industrial society increasingly ruled by the gray eminences of the laboratory, traditional views of managerial functions and organizational design become irrelevant. The good manager, say Ralph M. Hower and Charles D. Orth 3rd in *Managers and Scientists*,[2] now must become the kind of administrator "who will not drive scientists away, who will facilitate, not hamper the research effort," and who can be developed "without syphoning off into management any substantial portion of productive scientists."

This is a far cry from Batten's call for tough-mindedness. Hower and Orth, carefully documenting their analysis with detailed case studies, suggest certain policies which the manager of an industrial research organization should follow "in working out a pattern of administration which harmonizes professional needs with organizational needs." These policies, in the opinion of a participant in one of the cases, should encourage free exchange of scientific information within the laboratory, as well as close supporting relations with the operating divisions of the company. They should enable the scientist to do work which interests him as an individual by allowing him to choose the projects on which he would like to spend his time. They should help him achieve recognition in the scientific world through encouraging him to publish papers and attend professional meetings. They should give him financial security and also minimize administrative detail and red tape to maintain an atmosphere free from distraction.

There is nothing novel in these policy suggestions, but their implications may well be so because of what Hower and Orth call "the passive instrument assumption" of the classical he-man theory of organizational behavior. Their suggestions call for qualities and traits in the manager of an effective industrial research organization which are vastly different from those demanded by the classical theory. The classicists maintained that the more clearly structured the organization was and the more uncluttered the proverbial channels between its units were, the more effective the manager was. The human-relations rebellion against this view allows that the informal underside of an organization is far more potent than the side depicted by its hierarchical pattern. Under this newer view the manager is no longer an order-giver; he becomes a "motivator."

Hower and Orth now urge that the research firm cannot be described accurately in either conventional or progressive organizational terms—and neither, therefore, can the managerial function—because the R & D structure straddles two spheres which they perceive as the "management culture" and the "scientific culture."

Culture is a sonorous word. Whatever it describes, the distinction between the two spheres is quite significant for our purpose. It points toward a new sense of managerial identity. "The scientist," say the authors, "who favors the values and ideals of the scientific community has an orientation predominantly *external* to the company he works for. Getting ahead, for him, means impressing fellow

[2] Boston, Division of Research, Harvard Business School, 1963.

scientists–expecially the recognized authorities *outside* his company–by his technical achievements."

This seems rather a too business-like approach. Certainly, getting ahead is an important, powerful, and legitimate motive, governing scientists no less than anyone else. But surely the strongest motive of a scientist, the feeder root of his continuing competence, is curiosity–his desire for discovery, for growth of knowledge, for evidence, for certainty. Perhaps the very dilemma of our "scientific culture" is not that our existence is predestined by our scientists, but that the scientists seek the accolades of our "management culture" by putting recognition and worldly advancement before discovery.

Still, as part of an industrial firm the scientist must "identify with the management community" and so have "an *internal* orientation . . . . His carreer will be shaped largely by his ability to perform in relation to the value system prevailing in his own company." Hower and Orth devote considerable and necessary attention to the conflict between the scientific and the management cultures. Grossly oversimplified, this is a conflict between success in the marketplace and accomplishment in the laboratory. Of what significance is this conflict to the manager of an industrial R & D establishment?

The authors conclude that above all such a manager must have considerable skill in what is still called "human relations." He must have the capacity–

> . . . to communicate his feelings and ideas to others, to receive such communications from others, and to respond to their feelings and ideas in such a manner as to promote better mutual understanding in specific situations and to foster individual behavior which more effectively takes into account the many facets, complexities, and personal interests involved in those situations.

This idea of the major skill of an effective manager is hardly new, but its suggested uses are. It must be used in a situation characterized, in part, by the fact that the organization is staffed by professional men who have lost their traditional independence, and by resultant tensions which ' appear to be part of a cultural lag in which professional ideals and values inherited from the past persist with little modification in the face of radical changes in the scientist's role in society." To the closely reasoning scientific mind, many business activities are simply the result of sloppy thinking. To the business executive who must keep things moving, many concerns of the scientist are unrealistic and "impractical."

This conflict of attitudes is probably the main problem which the R & D manager must solve. He realizes that–

> . . . no one person is capable of seeing correctly a complex problem or of devising a good solution for it. Successful administration depends therefore upon obtaining the active assistance of technically competent people in defining problems, in devising solutions, and in following up the consequences.

The manager, then, is no longer the boss, the man of authority or the man in whose image the organization was and is molded. Nor is he merely an administrator relaying messages, applying policy, and regulating traffic between the in-baskets and the out-baskets. He becomes the Mr. Moderator of the daily R & D town meeting. He is a *catalyst.*

Manager As Guardian

The problem of "managing" the specialist and the expert *within* the organization has renewed a trend in the study of management which began when "scientific management" was supplanted by "people management" and when the "pure" problem of organization was distilled from the multiple problems of one particular form of organization, the competitive business firm. Today the systematic observer is deeply involved in the generic problem of organization management. We study and compare the functioning of a great variety of organizations in business, the professions, the public service, and in social and political life. Even the family is seen in organizational terms. And the student of management naturally asks: Are there views, methods, traits which the men who run these organizations have in common? Does their office require a uniqueness of disposition not found in other pursuits?

"The most important feature of the managerial mind is its commitment to the life and growth of the organization," says David W. Ewing in *The Managerial Mind.*[3] This "managerial emphasis" involves vastly more than what we must now call mere executive concerns with running an organization for results. The manager is *not* an executive, Ewing says, whose primary tasks are specific functions "where supervision is not the crucial element," and where coordination of activities is not essential.

The manager now is the organization man *par excellence,* and Ewing uses the term without critical implication or sociological overtones. The manager is the organization's anchor man. He ministers to its health, thus is an administrator in the true, literal sense of the word. The specifics of his functions and responsibilities derive their meaning from this commitment.

Ewing considers the strengths and weaknesses of the administrative point of view in great detail, attending in particular to the many aspects of supervision. Direction and control, to him, are more effective than manipulation. The attempt to manipulate people for the sake of organizational objectives, he says, is–

> . . . partly self-defeating–because the use of people as means to ends restricts their spirit and effectiveness, because power allows the manager to enforce and perpetuate his own errors, and because anxiety about these effects is a drain on his own capacity.

In some ways the manager, Ewing argues, has a professional mind. He values knowledge, disciplined thinking, analysis, objectivity, experience, standards, and selectivity. But in the more specific respects of his commitment, the manager must

[3] New York, The Free Press of Glencoe, 1964.

be more than a professional. He must cultivate individual differences, he must resist pressures toward conformity, value tension because tension is the soil of productivity, and he must support the harshness of creative relationships. He demands, disagrees, probes, caters, and nourishes.

What, then, is he? For Ewing, "the philosophy of expectation" not only gives the managerial mind internal consistency; it also sets it apart from other ways of thinking. Along with Hower and Orth, he holds, though he does not specifically say so, that in some ways an organization is an organism, with its own particular laws of internal motion, productivity, and existence. To the manager, his organization, whatever its specific tasks, is a vehicle not only of social progress but of survival. He is its *guardian.*

Manager As Friend

There is a certain air of self-conciousness about the field of management, if we may be permitted to pontificate. Practitioners as well as professional observers of the art seem to need continuously to demonstrate, if only by indirect reference, that management is a meaningful and useful pursuit, a valid field of knowledge, and a socially significant occupation. In many ways this is a sign of health which compares favorably with, for example, the present ossified state of the humanities: self-conciousness, even self-consciousness in a discipline, is a step toward self-awareness. It encourages the questioning of premises, it leads toward search for clarity, and it constantly impels those involved toward widening both their skills and their perception.

This self-conciousness understandably is most evident in the field of management development, partly because the very nature of this activity is the questioning of premises and–this being so–partly because different schools of thought vie for universal acceptance. Management development is no longer a movement, but by and large an established part of corporate life. This is not necessarily good. The problem of relating the contents of the innumerable programs and methods in management development and supervisory education to individual effectiveness will be with us until we have reached that stage of managerial commitment where the manager accepts the individual growth of his subordinates, within and beyond the context of their job functions, as his overriding responsibility.

To hold such a view, the manager must find in himself both the attitude and the intuition which will help him see the much-vaunted "whole man" in his subordinates. He must learn to understand what in their origin, make-up, and desires causes them to work and behave the way they do. If this sounds forbidding, it perhaps only shows how far we have strayed from our native sense of humanity. The order is large: perhaps only a whole man can see a whole man.

A recent study by David Moment and Abraham Zaleznik, *Role Development and Interpersonal Competence,*[4] points to one aspect of this problem. It focuses–to use its rather formidable phraseology–"on the ways in which the individual's total role

[4]Boston, Division of Research, Harvard Business School, 1963.

performance," which the study describes "with respect to its task, social, and interpersonal dimensions," maintains "historical continuity with his personal development over his life-time."

The authors conducted a series of experimental meetings in which business executives and specialists participated. Those taking part were grouped by the study into four major types, according to–

> . . . how each of them understood the particular subject of the meeting;
> . . . the way he "related to" the others;
> . . . the role which the group seemed to assign him and/or which the participant conceived himself;
> . . . the "degree and kind of social identity achieved by the participant."

The "role typology"–which presumably can be applied to most business meetings and management conferences–consisted of "stars," "technical specialists," "social specialists, and the "underchosen." Stars were congenial participants with good ideas; technical specialists were uncongenial participants with good ideas; social specialists were congenial group members without any particularly good ideas; the poor "underchosen" apparently were blessed with neither good ideas nor social grace.

Through an elaborate and impressive apparatus of questionnaires, interviews, and other research techniques, Moment and Zaleznik established that these roles express patterns of "combination of attitudes toward the world of work and people, behaviors consistent with the attitudes and behaviors and perceptions from others which reinforced the attitudes and behaviors." These patterns were correlated with each individual's life history, including especially his family relationships, and with his expectations, work experiences, and other aspects of his personal development.

The authors' assumptions about human nature implied in their method of inquiry and their terminology–largely those of social Freudianism–are beyond the ken of this discussion. For our purposes their study makes us realize that we must look beyond behavior if we want to help those with whom we work to improve what is called their "interpersonal competence." Management must give attention–

> . . . not only to selecting for participation those executives most prepared to use the help available in executive programs, but also to provide the initial help that enables an individual to use the experience to the utmost [and to explore] what range of alternatives are open to him for defining himself in the learning.

This means that the manager must be aware of "behavioral patterns within the context of *individual* development" [my italics] as well as "of the natural conditions under which significant change and learning can take place."

The more sophisticated the work and purposes of an organization, the more it depends for its success on individual creativeness and on the joy that comes from productive imagination. These are part of the capacity with which the person handles his life, and this capacity may become the first concern of the manager. In acting on this concern, is he a counselor, teacher, therapist, or personal trouble-shooter standing *in loco parentis?* He may have to be all these, but more than anything else, he must be—not just play the role of—that most unmanagerial of all beings: a *friend.*

Manager As Owner

A friend may listen and advise, but above all he comprehends. He comprehends the other person, in whatever straits and circumstances, ultimately in his awareness, with Kierkegaard, that "to be human is not a fact, but a task." As the manager's friend, what do we comprehend of him, what—to use a label in this age of labels—is our empathy toward him?

The arguments of the "managing-through-men" school were misunderstood almost as soon as they reached the light of day, and we rushed into "communication skills," "human relations" manipulation, indoctrination, and "scientific selection of personnel." The position of this school, however, centers on the manager's concerns not only *for* human beings, but on his concerns *as* a human being.

It is still largely an accepted truism that the manager's ultimate concern is for profit. Certainly there must be profit as sustenance and as a yardstick for the business firm to function effectively, but is it the principal guide of the manager's actions? Perhaps it takes a manager's friend to see the woods for the trees. As one of them, Abram T. Collier in *Management, Men, and Values,*[5] says straightforwardly:

> What impressed me throughout my recent experiences was that most of the successful men I talked with seemed to be guided by other objectives. I won't say they weren't concerned with making money, but it was almost a by-product from doing other things. They seemed to have a whole set of other values that guided them in making the decisions they had to make.

Collier is a manager's manager. As a lawyer and as a top executive of one of the largest American corporations, he is an observer—not merely an observer carefully keeping his distance, but one who is passionately and compassionately involved in the question of what makes a manager manage. He has written a series of realistic dialogues which are a search for "principles on which administrative decisions might be made." The lawyer in him is after principles of action which show that such decisions are more than simply matters of instinct and executive arbitrariness.

The dialogues are neither written for the stage nor do they follow the dull pattern of Plato's straight-man-versus-sage Socratic pronouncements. They set forth with great factual detail the different views and concerns, arising from a common sense of responsibility, which top management can have about major activities of the business organization. Collier inquires into such diverse matters as research,

[5]New York, Harper and Row, 1962.

management training, personnel assessment, selling, the business functions of professionals, retirement, and mergers.

In one well-known chapter, previously published as a prize-winning essay,[6] Collier says that the manager "conceives his function as a creative one. His role is to make the business grow—not just that it may survive, but in order that it may accomplish goals beyond survival." His dialogists express ideas which to our pragmatists will sound like the waving of tattered flags. One, for example, says:

> Every business I ever heard of was started as a response to a need of somebody outside of the business. I do not care whether a business is the transformation of somebody's vision, a complicated living organism, or the product of the economic and political environment in which it happens to find itself. What I do say is that it is nothing—nothing *except* the service it renders to others.
>
> To imagine a business existing without other organizations is just as impossible as to imagine a person living all alone in an empty world. An individual life has meaning only in relation to others. To describe a man in a meaningful way is always to show the relation.

And another of Collier's executives says:

> When we think of a man's power to choose, we begin to consider the possibility of moral values, to see that we have choices as to these values. Such values, many believe, are essential if we are to find the goals of a human organization. To work, they say, whether alone or in concert with others, has no significance, no human purpose, unless a man can look at the results of that work and can call them "good."

Well, what are those values? As a man of law, Collier knows the problem of the meaning of words and says perceptively that to answer this question "requires language that is several steps further removed from the realities it is supposed to represent." But he meets the question head-on. He is objective but not neutral, and does not imply, as our behaviorists seem to, that values are mere manifestations, much as and no more than manners, traditions, and habits are. As managers, he says, we are moved by "clusters of values" and by areas of conviction where we pass from one to the next as our awareness and sense of commitment increase. Self-teaching and volition, the sense of means, the desire for objectivity, the sense of impersonal compassion, and the "end value" of rising above and embracing all other values—these are the real values by which managers live. Not should live, but *do* live.

Collier cheerfully would plead *nolo* to the charge that he is searching for the idea of the manager as a moral person, but he would rightly deny any intent to codify moral rules. To me his intent is more aesthetic than ethical. He is looking for patterns, for the design of feelings and motivations which make up the personal qualities of the manager. These feelings seem similar to those we have toward personal property when we consider it not as an object of trade but as part of our existence. To Collier the manager is, in the widest sense of the word, an *owner.*

[6] "Debate at Wickersham Mills," HBR May–June 1960, p. 49.

Manager As Technician

Are all of the above reflections pointless? What is the use of inquiring into the manager's attitudes, motives, values, needs, and objectives? It is pointless, says Leonard R. Sayles in *Managerial Behavior,*[7] to try to spell out in textbook fashion, the "correct" managerial attitudes and human relations techniques, or to define the manager's position in terms of formal organizational relationships. Instead, we should look at his actual behavior within the particular system in which he works. "To distinguish alternative styles of administration, giving the manager the choice of being democratic or autocratic or something in between," the author says, is fashionable but unrealistic because "the manager does not have that choice open to him."

Not only will there always be a gap between doctrine and practice; the very dichotomy between the two is false. "There is only one organization process or system" for the manager. "For the most part," says Sayles, "management theory and management principles stress abstract categories and entities rather than *process* [my italics]. They are usually concerned with the nature of authority and its preservation. . . . As a result management principles fail to deal with the dynamic problems of human systems in action."

Some of the writings we have considered so far make it appear that Sayles is setting up somewhat of a straw man, an exercise not really necessary to support his arguments. Still, it *is* the traditional view that the manager's role is that of planning, decision making, and motivating. For Sayles, the manager is part of an "open system"; his behavior is a function of the organization; he is part of a network of relationships; he is effective only to the extent that he maintains or contributes to maintaining the continuity of this network; and his main objective is to seek and maintain predictable, reciprocating relationships. In Sayles's "process view" of management—

> . . . dynamic relationships, rather than compartmentalized jobs, are basic characteristics. Continuity of flow is the objective, tying together the independent parts of the total operation that have been fractionated by the need for specialists, departments, and organizational checks. There are not the neat beginnings and ends, the sharp demarcation lines between what is inside and what is outside, between what is past, what is present, and what is future that are associated with essentially legalistic, static models of human groups.

The entrepreneurial view of management is more transcendental than realistic, Sayles seems to think. "The essence of management is not of heroic proportions," he says. Rather—

> . . . most managerial behavior is mundane—and frustrating. . . . It involves meticulous assessment of the state of the organization system; and redirection of one's own and one's subordinates' activities in the light of the information derived from monitoring.

[7]New York, McGraw-Hill Book Company, Inc., 1964.

Balancing of controls, of competing sources of rewards and punishment, are no longer the central functions of the manager. Rather, he is a vital and viable part of a system of forever tense competition for the allocation of resources. The systems approach to business problems is here applied to management and enables Sayles to claim that the kind of managerial behavior which maintains and strengthens the system is learnable, much as is computer programming. In this view, the manager is a skilled craftsman, versed in keeping the organizational engine in tune and at peak efficiency. He is a *technician.*

Manager As Person

We have seen the manager, through the eyes of others and with intentional oversimplification, as *actor, catalyst, guardian, friend, owner,* and *technician.* Each represents a *sense* of managerial being, not a series, sequence, or choice of roles which can be adopted and abandoned at will. Each sense arises out of a particular kind of commitment to the felt needs of particular organizations. Each sense expresses a distinct form of human existence.

We tend to think of ourselves today, under the impact of our system of fractured learning, as a product–of emotions, traumas, heredity, circumstance, deprivation, needs. But we are more than the sum total of them all; we are individuals, each with our own particular make-up and configuration of traits and, therefore, with our own particular mode of self-fulfillment. It is this mode that prescribes our individual managerial sense. We cannot choose it at random. Our fulfillment, and hence our competence, depends on how clearly we recognize our own particular form of existence. This form is unique for each of us. In many ways we can be considered, treated, and reached "in terms of" our living–of our functions, of our social commitments, of our ideas, and of our fears. But beyond these, we each have our unique form of existence which shapes our work. Every manager has his own particular sense of commitment–because, above all, the manager is a *person* .

Dual Leadership in Complex Organizations

Amitai Etzioni

The theory of complex organizations, like the theory of other social systems, alternates between periods of emphasis on new imputs and periods of consolidation. In one of the earlier consolidations the quality of the theory was considerably improved by combining the formal structural tradition with the insights and findings of small group studies in the Kurt Lewin and Elton Mayo traditions.[1] The resulting product is symbolized by the pair concepts of formal and informal leadership). But the articulation of organizations with the groups in and around them is too vast a subject to have been exhausted by any one consolidation phase. The time may now be ripe for another effort to integrate small-group analysis with that of complex organizations.

One particularly promising approach seems to be a union of the Bales-Parsons structural-functional analysis of small groups with the main lines of analysis of complex organizations. Small group studies so far have obtained their data largely from groups created artificially in social science laboratories and from "natural"[2] groups in "natural" settings, mainly families in tribal and village communities.[3] Comparatively few data have been obtained, and few propositions formulated, for the structural-functional analysis of "natural" small groups within complex organizations, i.e., in artificial settings.[4] A theoretical articulation of this kind is the task of this article. To carry it out, I shall draw on one other recent development: the comparative study of organizations. I shall then attempt to show that if the theory so extended is valid, it has policy implications for major spheres of applied sociology, illustrating once more that theoretical effort is but one step removed from well-founded applied work.

From a theoretical point of view, articulation between small groups functioning within complex organizations and their organizational setting is two-fold: first, the organization affects the fulfillment of the functional needs of these groups, and second, the way these functions are served in turn affects the operation of the organization itself. It is essential to keep these two systems of reference apart: that the same act, role, or leader has both group and organizational functions by no means implies that these functions are identical.

Dual Leadership in Non-Organizational Settings

Drawing liberally on the right of interpretation I shall briefly summarize the Bales-Parsons analysis of small groups, which is based largely on experimental

[1] On this merger, see Rensis Likert, *New Patterns of Management*, New York: McGraw-Hill, 1962; and Amitai Etzioni, *Modern Organizations*, Englewood Cliffs, N.J.: Prentice-Hall, 1964, pp. 32-47.

[2] "Natural" groups are those whose culture and structure have evolved spontaneously. Since an element of artificiality (or self-consciousness and planning) characterizes most groups, "naturalness" is a matter of degree.

[3] For studies of differentiation in a "natural" group, see Oscar Grusky, "A Case for the Theory of Familial Role Differentiation in Small Groups," *Social Forces*, 35 (1957), pp. 209-217; and Francesca M. Cancian, "Interaction Patterns in Zinacanteco Families," *American Sociological Review*, 29 (1964), pp. 540-550.

[4] For one of the few relevant studies see Fred Strodtbeck and Richard D. Mann, "Sex Role Differentiation in Jury Deliberations," *Sociometry*, 19 (1956), pp. 3-11.

studies.[5] For my purposes here, by far the most important insight is that if small task-oriented groups are to operate efficiently, two kinds of leadership are required, and the two are to be mutually supportive.[6] Task-oriented groups tend to develop two kinds of leader: one, an expressive (or social-emotional) leader, who ranks higher than other actors in such interaction categories as "showing solidarity" and "asking for suggestions;" the other, an instrumental (or task-oriented) leader, who ranks higher than other actors in such categories as "giving suggestions" and "showing disagreement."

The distinction between expressive and instrumental orientations is not limited to a classification of leadership. All acts can be classified as expressive or instrumental. Roles can be classified according to the prevalence of one kind of act over the other. Moreover, the same analytical distinction can be applied to the functional needs of social systems. Here, *instrumental* refers to the need to acquire resources, or means, and to allocate them among the various role-clusters in the system, and *expressive,* to the need to maintain the integration of various parts of the system with each other as well as with its normative system.[7] Role clusters can then be classified as devoted primarily to the service of one or another functional need. Similarly, the same concepts are useful in classifying the elite roles of initiative and control, which direct the activities performed in various role-clusters by the respective followers.[8]

Finally, actors in general and leaders in particular have instrumental or expressive psychological propensities. Of course, this is in part a situational distinction. Whether an actor becomes an expressive or instrumental leader depends in part on the psychological predispositions of the *other* members of his group, and a person may acquire some of the "characteristics" of his kind of leadership (e.g., higher level of activity, ability to withstand hostility), once he has assumed the particular kind of leadership *position,* as he interacts with followers and with leaders of the complementary kind.[9] Still, one probably could predict, on the basis of a

[5] Robert F. Bales, "The Equilibrium Problem in Small Groups," in Talcott Parsons, Robert F. Bales, and Edward A. Shils (eds.), *Working Papers in the Theory of Action*, Glencoe, Ill.: The Free Press, 1953, pp. 111-161; and Robert F. Bales and Philip E. Slater, "Role Differentiation in Small Decision-Making Groups," in Talcott Parsons and Robert F. Bales, *Family, Socialization and Interaction Process*, Glencoe, Ill.: The Free Press, 1955, pp. 259-306.

[6] Effectiveness is studied more directly by Shaw than in the Bales studies. See Marvin E. Shaw, "Some Effects of Individual Prominent Behavior of Group Effectiveness and Member Satisfaction," *Journal of Abnormal and Social Psychology,* 59 (1959), pp. 382-386. See also Mauk Mulder, "Group-Structure and Group Performance," *Acta Psychologica,* 16 (1959), pp. 356-402.

[7] Here, my usage differs somewhat from that of the Parsonian tradition. Cf. Talcott Parsons, *The Social System*, Glencoe, Ill.: The Free Press, 1951, Ch. 4, esp. pp. 145-147; and Talcott Parsons, Robert F. Bales, and Edward A. Shils, "Phase Movement in Relation to Motivation Symbol Formation and Role Structure," in Parsons, *et al.*, *Working Papers in the Theory of Action*, *op. cit*., pp. 163-269.

[8] Amitai Etzioni, "The Functional Differentiation of Elites in the *Kibbutz*," *American Journal of Sociology*, 64 (1959), pp. 476-487.

[9] Philip E. Slater, "Role Differentiation in Small Groups," *American Sociological Review*, 20 (1955), pp. 300-310; and Godfrey Gardner, "Functional Leadership and Popularity in Small Groups," *Human Relations*, 9 (1956), pp. 491-504.

psychological test, the kind of leadership role a person is more likely to assume. Instrumental leadership seems to draw people who are more aggressive, more able to withstand hostility and more anxious to be respected, while expressive leadership attracts people who are more accommodative, less able to withstand hostility, and more anxious to be loved.

Drawing on these various levels of application of the twin concepts, expressive and instrumental, the dual leadership theory suggests—though here data are particularly lacking—that task-oriented groups will be more effective in terms of task-achievement and members' satisfaction, when the group commands both instrumental and expressive leaders.[10] It suggests further that while these two kinds of leadership might be provided by a single actor ("great man"), they tend not to be. Finally, when two actors carry out the two leadership roles, mutual support is required for effective leadership of the group.[11] This theory is contrasted with the approach prevalent in much of the psychological, administrative, and political science literature, which expects effective leadership to be provided by one man.[12]

Not all these statements are fully backed with empirical evidence, nor is the existing evidence immune to conflicting interpretation. Nevertheless, these statements may be used to develop additional propositions, which, of course, require validation in their own right.[13]

The dual leadership theory, briefly restated here, has been evolved largely in experimental, task-oriented groups and mainly applied to the study of "natural"

[10]For a review of the research on this question and for references to earlier works, see Robert F. Bales, "Roles in Problem-Solving Groups," in Eleanor E. Maccoby, Theodore W. Newcomb and Eugene L. Hartley (eds.), *Readings in Social Psychology* (3rd ed.), New York: Henry Holt, 1958, pp. 437-447.

[11]Robert F. Bales, "Equilibrium Problem in Small Groups," in Parsons, *et al.*, *Working Papers in the Theory of Action, op. cit.*, pp 148 ff.

[12]See Edgar F. Borgatta, Arthur Couch, and Robert F. Bales, "Some Findings Relevant to the Great Man Theory of Leadership," *American Sociological Review*, 19 (1954), pp. 755-759.

[13]Such validation should take into account that this is a functional theory. That is, it suggests that a group will be more effective *if* provided with both kinds of leadership, and *if* these kinds of leadership are mutually supportive. It also includes a nonfictional statement that differentiated leadership is more common than "great man" leadership, both because the psychological characteristics monoleadership requires are rare and because such leadership requires the same person to engage in opposing patterns of social behavior, e.g., to be assertive and accommodative simultaneously or at least in rapid succession.

On the other hand, the statement that the two kinds of leaders tend in fact to support each other is only an empirical finding (for the kinds of groups studied); it has neither a functional nor any other theoretical standing. Mutual support is a functional requirement of effective group action, but there is no reason, in theory, to state that most or even many small groups are effective. To refute this functional statement it would be necessary to show that when such support is lacking no dysfunction occurs, or that when provided, it does not increase effectiveness.

The functional model does not predict what pattern is common, but it does predict the *kinds* of pathologies that will occur if one of the two leadership roles is left vacant, or if mutual support is absent. Productivity will be low when the instrumental leader is missing, satisfaction when the expressive leader is missing; and both productivity and satisfaction will be reduced when the two leaders are in conflict rather than in coalition.

groups in the community.[14] But very little effort has been made so far to apply the dual-leadership theory to groups in complex organization. In studies of committees, the theory has been used as though the participants constituted another "natural" group, which is to disregard both the external organizational role-sets of the participants and the fact that they did not interact as individuals but as representatives of departments, services, agencies, or other organizations.[15]

Before attempting to join the dual-leadership and complex organization lines of analysis, I must make one more preparatory comment. To deal with the articulation of groups and organizations, I focus on the concept of leadership. Leadership is the ability, based on the personal qualities of the leader, to elicit the followers' voluntary compliance in a broad range of matters.[16] Leadership is distinguished from the concept of power in that it entails influence, i.e., change of preferences, while power implies only that subject's preferences are held in abeyance.

For small groups, leadership guides the activities by which their expressive and instrumental functional needs are served. The question here is: what contributions is the small group to expect from organizationally supplied leaders in its efforts to answer these needs? For the organization, the single most important bridge to participants' motivational and normative orientations is its ability to provide leadership to the small groups to which they belong. (Such a bridge is often not available, but it rarely exists without leadership.) If the participants accept the organizationally provided leader (i.e., one who is committed to the organization's goal, structure, and personnel), their non-calculative commitment to the organization can be obtained. If they reject the organizational leadership, the organization effectiveness is restricted to maintaining law and order and to carrying out the more routinized kinds of production, i.e., to tasks that require relatively little emotional commitment from the large majority of the participants.[17] The study of leadership—the consequences of its being supplied from various organizational ranks, its orientation toward the organization, and the scope of its influence—hence provides a rewarding approach to the study of small groups in complex organizations.

Dual Leadership in Organizations

Organizations differ from other collectivities in that within them power is, comparatively, more deliberately distributed and institutionalized. Power is focused

[14]Talcott Parsons, "Family Structure and the Socialization of the Child," and Morris Zelditch, Jr., "Role Differentiation in the Nuclear Family: A Comparative Study," in Parsons and Bales, *Family, Socialization, and Interaction Process, op. cit.*, pp. 35-131 and 307-351, respectively.

[15]Robert F. Bales, "In Conference," *Harvard Business Review*, 32 (1954), pp. 44-50.

[16]When only a narrow range is covered, referring to matters of little importance, influence rather than leadership is exercised.

[17]This point is elaborated in Amitai Etzioni, *A Comparative Analysis of Complex Organizations*, New York: The Free Press, 1961, Chs. 2, 3. This is not to say that the independent commitment of personnel to the organizational goals is not an analytically separate factor. Some types of organization (e.g., universities) do attract personnel with a high degree of such independent commitment.

in the formally recognized elite positions in which status symbols, the right to give and withhold economic rewards, and control of means of violence are concentrated. In experimental task-groups leadership rests solely on the followers' attitudes and reciprocations, so that few discrepancies arise between leadership and power positions, but such discrepancies are common in complex organizations. An actor may have only positional power, in which case he might be referred to as an "official;" only broad personal influence, in which case he might be called an "informal leader;" or both, in which case he is best labeled a "formal leader." If he commands neither, he is probably a follower. (See Figure 1.) These concepts are not new, but defined in this way, they become part of a systematic conception.

When the dual leadership proposition is applied to small groups in complex organizations, the critical issues are not only whether both kinds of leadership are provided for, and whether they are mutually supportive,

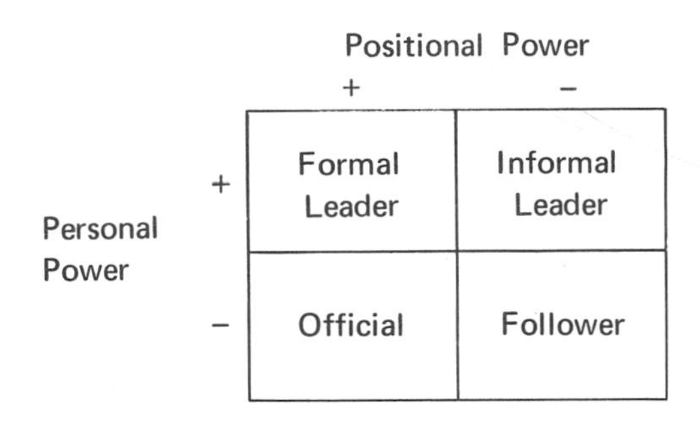

Figure 1

but also include the question of *how and to what extent the leadership is backed by organizational power.* A group in an organization where both types of leadership are exercised by informal leaders–persons without organizational positions–will be very different from a group where both types of leadership are exercised by formal leaders–persons in organizational positions–or a group where one type of leadership is provided by an occupant of an organizational power position while the other is not.

The organizational location of expressive and instrumental leadership affects (a) the degree of organizational control over the group; (b) the degree of collaboration between the two kinds of leaders; and (c) the power relations between the two kinds of leaders. Each of these points requires a brief elaboration.

Provision of leadership from organizational positions is a major source of organizational control over groups of participants. Holding an organizational position does not automatically assure the incumbent's loyalty to the organization's goal, its rules, or its higher-ranking leaders–nor does its lack necessarily imply alienation of the leader–but, all other things being equal, *informal leaders tend to be less loyal to the organization than formal ones.* Hence, by and large, an organization that provides both kinds of leadership (that is, its representatives are accepted by the small-group members as leaders), will have more control over the participants than one in which both kinds of activities are controlled by informal leaders.

The effectiveness of an organization that provides only one of the two kinds of leadership for the participants follows no definite pattern, for the effect of this configuration is contaminated by the nature of relations between the two leaders. This second variable, collaboration between instrumental and expressive leadership, is itself affected by the organizational positions of both leaders. All other things being equal, collaboration is more likely when both of the leaders hold organizational positions, or when neither does, than it is when only one of them does. (Exceptions are discussed below.) Where both leaders hold organizational positions, collaboration may be supported by various organizational mechanisms, such as rewards (e.g., more rapid promotions for leaders who "get along" with others) and rules and institutionalized points (e.g., the next higher in command) for resolving conflicts, and by shared training experience, organizational perspectives, and ideology. Of course, when this is not the case, as when one of the two leaders has been recently recruited from the outside, or is more anxious to please his subordinates than to be rewarded by the organization,[18] the likelihood of collaboration will decline; still, on the average such difference of background, perspective, and expectations should be less common between two formal leaders than between a formal and an informal leader.

Informal leaders are likely to be more similar to each other than to formal leaders because their income, prestige, interests, etc., are correlated with rank, and informal leaders of the same small group tend to be of similar rank. Being of similar rank, they may face a closed organizational level, into which they cannot be recruited (e.g., nurses facing the doctor's rank; enlisted men before the officer's rank); their organization may be slow to promote (e.g., young faculty at European universities); they may share the experience of having been left behind in an organization where rapid promotion is the rule, or of having refused on psychological or ideological grounds to accept a promotion into organizational leadership positions.

Finally, the relations between the expressive and instrumental leaders are much affected by their relative resources. These depend on their organizational positions, which in turn are influenced by the goals and compliance structure of the organization. In groups of four or five students meeting for four 45-minute discussion sessions, in a highly institutionalized situation, the only sources of power are personal; no member commands organizational power and hence it does not affect relations between the two leaders. But when the context is that of a complex organization, the question of their relative power is most important: which leader is superior in rank (or in other measures of organizational power)—the expressive or

[18]Graham M. Sykes, "The Corruption of Authority Rehabilitation," *Social Forces*, 34 (1956), pp. 257-262. See also Gresham M. Sykes, *Society of Captives*, Princeton, N.J., Princeton University Press, 1958.

the instrumental ones? Assuming all other things are equal, granting more organizational power to one kind of leader affects the goals to which the small group will be primarily devoted. That is, if the instrumental leader is superior, the group is more likely to be a task-oriented group, and if the expressive leader is superior, a socionormative group. One might expect the goals of the organization to determine whether a group operating within it is predominantly instrumental or expressive. But the organizational goals must gain support; they do not translate themselves into appropriate action automatically. By recruiting personnel whose leadership potential is high, through leadership-training and by deliberately allocating superior rank to one kind of leadership, the organization can bring groups into line with its goals. If the leadership hierarchy contradicts the organizational goals, however, a predominantly expressive group is quite likely to appear in a producing organization (workers "taking it easy," "chumming it up with the foreman," playing cards on the job, etc.) and the other way around.

The critical observation linking the small group and organizational lines of analysis is that to maximize it effectiveness the organization must not merely gain control of the group via its leaders, but also must *allocate power so as to establish the superiority of the desired kind of leadership over the other.* Mechanisms for this purpose include giving one leader a higher rank, symbols of higher prestige, greater backing by the next higher in command, etc. One might think that a complex organization should always support the instrumental leader, since it is basically an instrumentally-oriented unit. But the answer differs from one type of organization to another, and is to be sought in a cross-institutional comparative perspective (as distinct from a cross-cultural one).

Contrary to an assumption widely held and perpetuated in many textbooks on administration and industrial management, organizations differ strikingly in the degree to which effective operation requires them to gain control and loyalty of the small groups that function in them. In some organizations–for example, prisons–such control is hardly possible, rarely attempted, and not essential for effective operation. In other organizations–for example, religious or political movements–control is quite possible, often sought, and a prerequisite to effective operation. Organizational effects on relations between expressive and instrumental leaders should be examined against this comparative backdrop.

For our present purposes, it will suffice to classify organizations according to their goals and the corresponding needs to gain low, high, or medium commitment from the participants. Organizations whose goal is to segregate deviant members of the society–prisons, correctional institutions, and custodial mental hospitals–require relatively low commitment on the part of their inmates and most other personnel for satisfactory levels of operation. Their chances of gaining control of the small group within them by providing these groups with leadership are small in any case, since the participants, above all the inmates, are usually highly antagonistic to the organization and tend to reject any leadership it might attempt to provide, instrumental or expressive. Officials pursue their tasks by relying largely on power, not leadership.[19] Leadership in the small groups tends to be informal, and the expressive leader is likely to be superior, for alienated informal groups are primarily oriented not to tasks but to social and normative problems. These groups form the basis of social life in prison-type organizations and are the source of tension-management, aside from enforcing the special inmate code.[20] Instrumental leaders, such as the traders in various scarce (cigarettes) or forbidden (narcotics) goods tend to be lower in status and power than the "right guys," the expressive leaders of the inmates.[21] When the informal inmate groups are organized around escape efforts, and the instrumental leaders are in charge of the engineering and technical aspects of the escape, their status and power are higher, but they still tend to be subordinate to the expressive leaders. (This suggests that escape efforts are ritualistic and normative rather than rationally calculated operations.)

At the other extreme of the commitment continuum are organizations whose real goal is to socialize or re-socialize members of the society: schools, rehabilitation centers, therapeutic mental hospitals, and religious organizations.[22] Religious organizations belong in this category to the degree that one of their major goals is to strengthen their members commitment to a set of values, a commitment that tends to be eroded in secular life and, therefore, needs reinforcement. In this sense they are resocializing agencies.

Effective socialization requires a high level of commitment on the part of the participants, for without such commitment, without identification of the students, parents, parishioners with the organizational leadership and its goals, and rules, the organization cannot deeply affect their personalities.[23] Hence, these organizations must either provide the leadership of the small groups or gain the leaders' support. If such efforts are unsuccessful and loyalties are locked in the group and not extended to the organization, its failure is quite unavoidable. Conditions for achieving leadership of these groups are much better here than in the segregating

[19]The power of the inmate group is often sufficient to wring concessions from lower-echelon custodial officers in return for making their life bearable and not embarrassing them in the eyes of their superiors. In this sense the segregating type of organization can be said to work through the informal group to maintain its custodial control. See Seymour Rubenfeld and John W. Stafford, "An Adolescent Inmate Social System," *Psychiatry*, 26 (1963), pp. 241-256.

[20]Donald Clemmer, *The Prison Community*, New York: Holt, Rinehart, and Winston, 1958, pp. 111-134.

[21]Richard A. Cloward, "Social Control and Anomie: A Study of a Prison Community," unpublished doctoral dissertation, Columbia University, 1959.

[22]The following discussion assumes that schools are organizations for education and not just instruction; that successful therapy requires changes in a patient's personality, not just his following the therapist's advice, and that religious organizations are not just social clubs. This assumption is in part the consequence of implicit theoretical premises to the effect that the goals of these organizations cannot be served through instruction, advice, or "social" gatherings, but require deeper impact on the participants' personalities. Furthermore, organizations ought to be classified according to the business they are really in, however their licenses read. Thus, mental hospitals that do not cure but only keep inmates off the streets should be classified as segregating organizations, and so on.

[23]The theoretical reasons for this assumption cannot be spelled out here; they lie in the realm of psychology and their discussion would carry us far afield from the subject of this article.

type of organizations, however, for here participation is voluntary, and the means of control are largely symbolic and not coercive. Participants' attitudes are much more likely to be positive, and their groups more receptive to organizational leadership. The organization, in turn, makes a much larger investment in leadership training and symbolic control of the participants, and to the extent that it commands other kinds of power, it is much more reluctant to use it.

The subordinate leader of small groups in socializing organizations had best be the expressive one. The organization's prime aim is to affect the participants deeply; its agents for this purpose are the expressive leaders—teachers, therapists, ministers—who either interact directly with the participants or at least affect them indirectly by influencing the small group in which the participants are involved (e.g., classes or therapeutic groups). Each organization (and each small group) of course also has instrumental needs. Buildings need to be attended to, funds must be allocated, and so on. Still, these considerations pertain to the acquisition and allocation of resources whose nature differs from that of the organizational goals. Unlike the profit goal, socialization goals are such that merely combining resources better, or giving superior status to instrumental role-clusters and to instrumental leadership, reduces the effectiveness of the organization. (These statements, it should be stressed, refer not to the overall head of the various organizations under discussion, such as school principals, hospital directors, or other administrative heads, but to those in the ranks immediately above the members, i.e., teachers, psychiatric social workers, and parish clergy.)

Organizations whose goal is to produce goods, or services, or to exchange them—such as factories, shops, and banks—require more commitment from their participants, including the lower-ranking ones, than do segregating organizations, but they can function quite effectively with considerably lower levels of commitment than socializing organizations. As a rule, producing organizations operate more effectively if their leadership is accepted by the small groups within them. If organizational leadership is rejected, however, producing organizations still can operate more effectively than much of the current literature suggests. The participants can "trade" the organization a "fair day's work" for a "fair day's pay" without being committed to its goal (profit), to many of its rules, or to its management (treated as mere "officials"). This is especially the case when the work is routine, requiring little initiative or responsibility. The latter qualities are difficult to supervise or measure, and they require internal commitment and rewards other than remunerative ones. It is easier for an organization to build a pyramid without its participants' commitment than to conduct research leading to a lunar landing. Producing organizations, hence, tend to rely on a mixture of "official" power (especially remunerative) and leadership. What proportions are most effective depends on the kind of work carried out, according to the dimensions suggested above.

Apart from the amount of leadership an effective producing organization requires (and how much it actually commands), its maximum effectiveness is clearly served by making the instrumental superior to the expressive leadership. In this sense, producing organizations are in direct contrast to socializing organizations. Optimal combination of means is more directly relevant to the success of a producing organization than are its workers' moral and social lives. Production requires giving priority to calculations involving division of labor, assignment of personnel, and soon, and in fact, the interest of producing organizations in the expressive activities of participant groups is largely instrumental. Attention to expressive activities, including providing organizational leadership for them, is justified by the belief that it enhances organizational control of the *instrumental* activities. The need for expressive leaders is thus secondary. If expressive considerations were to prevail, production considerations would have to be significantly and regularly neglected to assure "good" social relations between the workers and the foreman. While foremen not infrequently give precedence to expressive considerations, this clearly is not the intent of the producing organization, and not what effective service of its goals requires.

Thus, each type of organization has a different need to control its participants, according to its goals and the degree of participant commitment these goals require.[24] This suggests an optimal relation between the instrumental and expressive leaders for each type of organization. Segregating organizations do not require much commitment of the lower participants for effective operation, and in any case can rarely affect relations between instrumental and expressive leaders, who both tend to be informal. Socializing organizations require deep commitment of the lower participants; the changed state of these participants is their main "product." This requires subordination of instrumental considerations to expressive ones, which in turn requires subordination of instrumental to expressive leaders. Producing organizations require a "medium" degree of commitment. Their handling of lower participants is subordinated to other, wider considerations of combining means of which the work of participants is only one, for their product is not a state of the participants but goods or services. The participants' morale (in the broadest sense of the term) is but one consideration among many, and the expressive leader in charge of this category of means is hence subordinated to the instrumental one, who is in charge of the broader combination of means and more "calculative" in his orientation to the workers. Thus a theoretical link exists between the kind of organization in question and the power relations between the two types of leaders.

Some Applications

The propositions I have advanced here are derived from two lines of analysis. Like all such theoretical derivations, they must stand the test of empirical research before they can be held valid. If validated, they would have significant implications for several seemingly unrelated areas of applied sociology; they would suggest revisions of the sociology of rehabilitation, therapy, labor relations, and education.

[24]Elsewhere I have proposed a typology of organizations: coercive, utilitarian, and normative. (See Etzioni, *op. cit.*) That typology provided a category for every complex organization. The present typology is not exclusive; it only provides for one or more examples of the most typical organizations in each of the three categories of the exhaustive typology. To note this difference, here the terms segregating, producing, and socializing are used.

Much of the literature in these fields stresses interpersonal relations, leadership styles, and group atmosphere, as if the structural contexts in which these are introduced were immaterial. A "sensitive" supervisor or "democratic" foreman can achieve leadership of participants' groups, thereby enhancing organizational effectiveness. But the preceding analysis suggests that structural and cultural factors strictly limit the degree to which an organizational "official," whatever his style, can gain the leadership of a group of participants, as well as the kind of leadership he can gain.

If the preceding analysis is valid, efforts to capture the expressive leadership of the inmate groups in segregating organizations by assigning a few professional workers (social workers, clinical psychologists, psychiatrists) must fail unless the basic nature of the organization (its security arrangements, restrictions of privileges, attitudes of guards or attendants, etc.) is changed. The inmates' groups in organizations tend to reject the organization's values (they feel the whole official conception of justice is distorted), its goals (they feel that their confinement is unjust), and its personnel (they feel that the guards or attendants are cruel and arbitrary). Anti-organization leaders and groups tend to prevail,[25] and though professional personnel in such a context may find isolated inmates who have not been assimilated and acculturated by the inmate community and who are amenable to their treatment, their efforts will largely be "washed out" by counterforces in the inmate community.[26]

The context changes when, instead of sending a few rehabilitation-oriented professionals into a segregating organization, their number and power in the organization is increased to a point where they can change some of its basic characteristics. But we are dealing then with a different type of organization, one that is, or is becoming, a socializing type. In segregating communities *per se*, isolated rehabilitation efforts, which require influencing inmates' expressive orientations and activities are liable to fail. A more effective approach would be to concentrate the available rehabilitation-oriented personnel in forces large enough to affect the basic structure of a few segregating organizations, and assign them to those most prone to change (as a result of favorable community interest, for example, or recent weakening of the coercive structure), rather than to distribute these scarce professionals among a large number of organizations on the assumption that they will convert other persons to their viewpoint, or in response to some sort of misplaced egalitarianism.

The preceding analysis implies that in producing organizations foremen trained in "Human Relations" workshops are likely to be least effective! The Human Relations tradition calls upon the foreman to be a "great man," which some might be and a few might become, but most are clearly not, nor are they capable of

[25] Norman S. Hayner and Ellis Ash, "The Prisoner Community as a Social Group," *American Sociological Review*, 4 (1939), pp. 362-369.

[26] Lloyd W. McCarkle and Richard R. Korn, "Resocialization Within Walls," *Annals of the American Academy of Political and Social Sciences*, 293 (1954), pp. 88-98. See also Stanton Wheeler, "Role Conflict in Correctional Communities," in Donald R. Cressey (ed.), *The Prison*, New York: Holt, Rinehart, and Winston, 1961.

becoming, great men. A foreman is expected to hold two roles simultaneously, to be both an instrumental and an expressive leader. Under pressure from management, he is expected to set specific work loads and assignments, to supervise production, and maintenance of machinery, to encourage adherence to rules, etc. He might accomplish this, if the workers consider their pay adequate and their working conditions satisfactory, if they are not politically antagonistic to the particular production system, and if he understands the work process. Suppose that he now enters Human Relations training; he attends seminars, workshops, meetings with representatives of the Labor Relations Department and so on. He is encouraged to become the workers' expressive leader as well, to be not only respected, but also liked, popular, loved; to be concerned with workers' personal problems, participate in their social life, be a "father" and a "friend."

To a limited degree an instrumental leader can exercise expressive leadership without commanding the rare talents of a "great man." A foreman can have a beer with his men or go bowling with them without corrupting his authority.[27] But sooner or later the relation between his expressive and instrumental commitments will come into question. When management increases its demands, the foreman must decide whether he will seek to circumvent the new demands, thus keeping his "popularity" with the workers, or impose them, which is likely to alienate the workers and undermines whatever expressive leadership he has attained.[28] Attempts to do both things simultaneously produces a high level of tension for the foreman. This role-strain[29] is heightened rather than reduced by Human Relations training.

Another important consideration here is that the foreman returning from Human Relations Workshop is likely to find the role of expressive leader filled, and the incumbent is likely to prevail in any conflict with the foreman over this position. The incumbent expressive leader may be an "old hand", a union steward, or merely an influential worker;[30] in any case, he has few, if any, instrumental demands to make of the workers and hence can be relatively "purely" expressive in his relation with them. Such leaders are, as a rule, selected by the workers themselves; they tend to be spontaneous rather than imposed leaders. But the foreman is not selected by the workers and, compared to the informal expressive leader, he is farther from them in terms of income and rank. Since he must, at least occasionally, transmit pressures from management in his instrumental capacity, a foreman is likely to lose in such a competition for expressive leadership. And not only does he fail to secure the expressive leadership role, he also jeopardizes a possible coalition with the incumbent expressive leader. Although the producing organization's goals would be advanced by such a coalition, the Human Relations

[27] Sykes, *op. cit.*, pp. 257-262.

[28] William F. Whyte and Burleigh B. Gardner, "The Man in the Middle: Positions and Problems of the Foreman," *Applied Anthropology*, 4 (1945), pp. 1-28.

[29] William J. Goode, "A Theory of Role Strain," *American Sociological Review*, 25 (1960), pp. 483-496.

[30] Leonard R. Sayles and George Strauss, *The Local Union*, New York: Harper, 1953.

approach in effect renders it improbable by teaching foremen to challenge the indigenous expressive leadership.

The preceding analysis is also relevant to the management of therapeutic mental hospitals. One controversy in this field focuses on the question: Should treatment be largely in the hands of psychiatrists or can other professionals fully participate? This is a complex issue with many ramifications, but one point is closely related to the matters at hand. Psychiatric treatment, like other socialization and re-socialization processes, involves a supportive element to provide emotional security, and a demanding one to encourage growth, experimentation, and learning.[31] In the primary family, as it existed among the middle classes in the 19th-century Germany and France, the mother (or nurse) was probably the primary source of support; the father, of growth. This is not to assert that one actor cannot fill both roles. In a successful psychiatric relationship the therapist probably provides both, varying the amount of support relative to pressure to grow from session to session, and in particular over various phases of the relationship. But a division of labor between the psychiatrist and another agent of re-socialization—a psychiatric nurse, social worker, clinical psychologist or the like—would make more treatment hours available for each patient, reduce costs per hour, and hasten the patient's advance, for the psychiatrist would be free to specialize more in pressure to grow if another staff-member provided support.

The theory advanced here, though, should not be viewed as simply supporting the participation of other professionals in the treatment process. Sharing the treatment would be effective only if the psychiatrist (as the instrumental leader) collaborates with other professionals (as expressive leaders). One of the best ways to assure such a coalition is to give a clear power (and status) advantage to one of the two kinds of leaders, and since no member of the treatment team has as much prestige, or power, as the psychiatrist, in Western medicine at least, the psychiatrist is the obvious person to coordinate the efforts of the treatment team. It follows that the psychiatrist can never act as a purely instrumental leader, for at least he is also charged with guiding the expressive aspects of the treatment and articulating them with his own work.

In therapeutic mental hospitals two or more staff members often participate actively in the treatment process. This does not necessarily reduce the effectiveness of treatment, as the Bales-Parsons dual-leadership theory might suggest, because the expressive and instrumental leadership roles may be distributed among more than two actors, as in an extended family. Such a division is attained when several professionals work simultaneously with the same patient.[32] Needless to say, the need to harmonize the treatment efforts, and hence to institutionalize psychiatric coordination, grows with the number of professionals participating.

[31] Parsons, *The Social System, op. cit.*, pp. 299-301. See also Talcott Parsons, "Illness and the Role of the Physician," *American Journal of Orthopsychiatry*, 21 (1951), pp. 452-460.

[32] This approach is often practiced by rehabilition officers. For an illustration, see Celia Benney, "Casework and the Sheltered Workshop in Rehabilitation of the Mentally Ill," *Social Casework*, 41 (1960), pp. 465-472, and Bertram J. Black, "Rehabilitation of Post-Psychotic Patients by Industrial Workshop," *Diseases of the Nervous System* (Monograph Supplement), 22 (1961), pp. 1-4.

Other applications of the preceding analysis can be mentioned only briefly here. Mostly Army infantry units have two institutionally-provided leaders, the officer and the NCO, whose division of labor seems to follow the instrumental-expressive line. Armies differ greatly, though, as to which kind of leadership is given the superior rank, for reasons that have yet to be explored. All religious organizations provide for expressive leadership, but they differ in the degree to which they provide instrumental leaders (as against leaving this role to the laity), and in the degree formal or informal[33] instrumental ones. Finally, for reasons that are far from clear, many American high schools provide no satisfactory formal expressive leadership. "Homeroom" teachers act as expressive leaders in some schools, but often they are "officials" who possess some specialized knowledge or are in charge of discipline so that a home-room teacher typically attempts little and succeeds even less in securing the expressive leadership of the student groups. Actually the rotating system of classes, which regularly redistributes the students from hour to hour, undermines the sociological importance of this organizational unit, and by default increases the importance of the non-organizational peer-group and its informal expressive leaders. This might well account for the limited effect of high-school teachers on the deeper normative orientations of their students.[34] Any organization that requires a positive commitment from its participants must provide the leadership of participant groups, instrumental and expressive, or gain the collaboration of the informal leaders, if it is to be effective, but not all such organizations do so.

Behind these and many other applied problems lies one analytical issue: the role of dual leadership in linking organizations and groups of participants. The leadership of groups in organizations is a major mechanism by which groups and organizations are articulated, one that in part reflects and in part affects the degree to which groups and organizations, and their expressive and instrumental considerations, work hand in hand or at cross purposes.

Dynamics of Leadership—Defensive and Emergent

Jack R. Gibb

People must be led. People perform best under leaders who are creative, imaginative, and aggressive—under leaders who lead. It is the responsibility of the leader to marshal the forces of the organization, to stimulate effort, to capture the imagination, to inspire people, to coordinate efforts, and to serve as a model of sustained effort.

[33] Paul M. Harrison, *Authority and Power in the Free Church Tradition*, Princeton: Princeton University Press, 1959.

[34] James A. Coleman, *The Adolescent Society*, New York: The Free Press, 1961.

The leader should keep an appropriate social distance, show no favorites, control his emotions, command respect, and be objective and fair. He must know what he is doing and where he wants to go. He must set clear goals for himself and for the group or institution and then communicate these goals well to all members of the organization. He must listen for advice and counsel before making decisions. But it is *his* responsibility to make decisions and to set up mechanisms for seeing that the decisions are implemented. After weighing the facts and seeking expert counsel he must make policy and rules, set reasonable boundaries, and see that these are administered with justice and wisdom, even compassion.

The leader should reward good performance and learn effective ways of showing appreciation. He must be equally ready to give negative criticism where warranted, and to appraise performance frequently, fairly, and unequivocally. He must command strong discipline, not only because people respect a strong leader, but because strength and firmness communicates care and concern. Good leadership requires good fellowship. People tend to follow good leaders. Leaders are born. Methods of election and selection are thus very important. Finding the right chairman or president is the critical variable in the success of a program or an institution. The quality of an organization is often judged by the perceived quality of the leadership.

The above is an oversimplified statement of one view of leadership theory and practice. A similarly oversimplified statement of an alternative viewpoint follows below.

People grow, produce, and learn best when they set their own goals, choose activities that they see as related to these goals, and have a wide range of freedom of choice in all parts of their lives. Under most conditions persons are highly motivated, like to take responsibilities, can be trusted to put out a great deal of effort toward organizational goals, are creative and imaginative, and tend to want to cooperate with others.

Leadership is only one of several significant variables in the life of the group or the institution. Leaders *can* be helpful and often are. The most effective leader is one who acts as a catalyst, a consultant, and a resource to the group. His job is to help the group to grow, to emerge and to become more free. He serves the group best when he is a whole person, is direct, real, open, spontaneous, permissive, emotional, and highly personal. The leader at his best is an effective member. He acts in such a way as to facilitate group strength, individual responsibility, diversity, nonconformity, and aggressiveness. The leader is thus not necessary to the group and quickly becomes replaceable, dispensable, and independent. The good leader tends not to lead. He permits, feels, acts, relates, fights, talks–acts human as do other members of the group and the institution. The leader is "present," "available" and "with" the group *as a person*, not as a role.

We find many shades and variations of each of these two oversimplified statements of the theory and practice of leadership in our society. Several years of consulting and research in representative organizations make it very clear to me that attitudes toward leadership tend to cluster around these two poles. This bifurcation finds analogues in current educational theory, politics, religion, philosophy, and administration.

The first view, described variously as authoritarian, paternalistic, or conservative, I classify as "defensive" because, dynamically, the view defends the administrator against his own fears and distrusts and against perceived or anticipated attack from the outside.

This authoritarian or defensive view is particularly appropriate to some viable aspects of the culture we live in: to organizational forms inherited from the medieval church and military; to a life of vertical hierarchy, prescribed role responsibilities, and delegated authority; to a highly competitive economic and educational system; to the current dominant values of efficiency, excellence, productivity, task performance, and perfectionism; to the impersonality, alienation, loneliness, impotence, and indifference in our people; to a world of automation, programming, data processing, and engineering; to a forensic, persuasive, public relations and marketing mode of interpersonal commerce; to a world continually at war, threatened by war, or preparing for war; in short, to a world of machines. It is not accidental that all around the country when administrators administer the ultimate forensic weapon in arguing against participative forms of leadership they say: "but it would never work in the military or on the production line." Actually, research indicates that this point is probably not true–but, in any event, the image of the leaders of our educational and governmental institutions using as a reference point for administrative theory the demands of the military organization and the production line is at least disconcerting.

It seems to me equally clear that defensive leadership is highly inappropriate and perhaps even fundamentally dissonant with another viable side of the world we live in: such education for growth, intimacy, authenticity, humanness, and creativity; with the Judeo-Christian ethics of love, honesty, intimacy, faith, cheek-turning, and brotherhood; with a climate for research, inquiry, scholarship, contemplation, and learning; with cooperation, group planning, team building, and various successful forms of group effort; with the new emerging models of industrial organization and manufacturing productivity; with what might be thought of as the "behavioral science" approach to organizational productivity and organizational change; with the world of ambiguity, feeling, conflict, sorrow, creativity, and diversity; with many new and exciting developments in education, architecture, the creative arts, economics, management, and all phases of modern life; in short, with the world of human beings, with people.

I have deliberatly drawn sharp and oversimplified distinctions in a problem area which is very complex and legitimately polemic. It is essential today that those who are administratively responsible for the colleges and universities of American see clearly this conflict and its implications for all facets of American life. It is my observation that much of the dysfunctional disturbance that the papers report daily from the college campuses is created as unintended but inevitable effects of defensive leadership practices among administrators of American colleges.

Let us look at the dynamics of defensive leadership. The major dynamic of the defensive model is fear and distrust. Observations indicate that people who have mild or more serious fears tend to do several things; have distrust for the people being led; filter the data that are given to the followers and develop strategies for such filtering and programming of data dissemination; attempt to control and manipulate the motivations of the followers; and attempt to control their behavior. The incidence and degree of low trust, strategic, persuasional, and controlling behavior varies directly with the amount of fear. Most of us who are leaders or are placed in leadership roles have varying degrees of fear, about our own adequacy, how we are seen by others, the effectiveness of our leadership strategies, the effects of rebellion, the anxieties about insubordination and other unfollowerlike behavior. I guess that our major fear has to do with anxiety about being followed!

The behavior of leaders tends to camouflage, perhaps even to themselves, the underlying fears which support the strategic, manipulative, and controlling behavior. For images of fear on assuming leadership roles one has but to think of the new teacher in the schoolroom, the new mother bringing back her first baby from the hospital, the new lieutenant guiding a patrol into action, or the newly appointed administrative official handling a student riot. The fears that we all have are quelled and softened by various adaptive, self deceptive, and facade-building mechanisms for presenting our selves to ourselves and to others.

It is my observation that some educational leaders are today more fearful than ever. In reaction to student strikes, riots, demonstrations, and protests, as well as to the more "normal" vicissitudes of campus life, college and university leaders utilize defensive practices that generate unintended by-products of fear, distrust, hostility, and counter-defensive behavior. The classical models of leadership are time and again proved to be ineffective. Why does defensive leadership arise and persist among educational leaders?

A reciprocal or circular process seems to be operating. Normal fears of life are exacerbated by the ambiguity, high control, and threat of the group or organization. However *necessary* this ambiguity and control is thought to be, it serves to create fears and hostilities which in turn call forth still more restrictive ambiguity and controlling behavior. This reciprocal fear-distrust cycle sustains the defensive behavior of leadership. The fears accompany and reinforce feelings of inadequacy and self-rejection in leaders and other members of the group or organization.

But the fears, hostilities, and distrusts are so successfully camouflaged in the social defenses that the casual observer might well think the above description of educational life to be strangely out of touch with reality as he sees it. Certainly it is not the conscious intent of educational leaders to create such a state of affairs.

Why is it then that we get in the university so many unintended effects? These unintended effects seem to result from a kind of self-fulfilling prophecy: Low-trust, high-fear theories, when put into practice, actually generate distrust and fears that not only confirm the assumptions underlying the theories, but also provide emotional support and strong motivation to continue the low-trust, high-fear behavior. An interactive and self-preserving cycle is thus set in motion, supported in depth by latent fear-distrusts and by rationalized theories which appear to be confirmed. Leadership behavior, thus supported, is exceedingly difficult to change.

Behind the facade of paternalism, politeness, one-big-happy-family-living, heartiness, and the accompanying soft-sell influence and velvet-glove control, lie defensive relationships that pervade the colleges. Defensive leadership is characterized by low trust, data distortion, persuasion, and high control. These four aspects of defensive leadership are parallel to four basic dimensions of all group or social behavior: the feeling climate, the flow of data within the system, the formation of goals and the emergence of control.

The key to defensive leadership is a state of low trust. The defensive leader assumes that: the average person cannot be trusted, he is essentially lazy and irresponsible, action must be taken to inspire and motivate him, and he requires supervision and control. The defensive leader can counteract his feelings of inferiority by assuming that his subordinates are less than they actually are, and he can service his hostile feelings by keeping the subordinate in demeaning, dependent, and inferior roles in relation to himself and to leadership as a class.

The defensive leader or administrator rationalizes the service of his needs by developing formal or informal leader theories which both justify and camouflage his fears and hostilities. An essential step in theory and in practice is to manipulate the flow of information and communication within the organization. Information sent down from the top is often deliberately "corrected" to increase morale, to allay fears, to put the best administrative foot forward, and to justify administrative action. "Correction" is achieved by consciously or unconsciously filtering and distorting information to present a good image, to encourage "positive thinking" or to build loyalty.

"Strategies" are devised to improve the administrative image: a worker's name is remembered to make him feel good; a birthday file is kept to demonstrate that the administrator feels the subordinate is important enough to warrant a birthday card. The "good" administrator is especially careful to smile acceptingly at those members of the "family" team towards whom he has temporary or sustained feelings of animosity. Interpersonal cues are thus manipulated and distorted to present a facade of warmth, friendliness or cohesiveness.

The defensive leader is continually challenged to create new prods, rewards and gimmicks as the old ones become ineffective. Thus the responsibility for sustaining motivations is thrust upon the administrator or teacher rather than upon the student. The inherent impetus to derive self-satisfaction and self-respect through accomplishment for its own sake becomes atrophied and lost. Self-satisfaction becomes dysfunctional as an incentive system.

The person who is being "motivated" by others through extrinsic rewards tends either to resist being influenced, or to come under the control of the rewarder. He is motivated, not to achieve something, but to gain the approval of the teacher or administrator, to hunt for his satisfactions in status, grade and social approval, rather than to look for his satisfaction *within*, in terms of self-respect, self-approval and the achievement of personal goals.

Thus the roots of dependence and apathy lie in the reward system, for the person who learns to find his values from without is always at the mercy of other persuaders—teachers, companions, demagogues, groups, or other sources of approval and authority. He becomes dependent, passive and susceptible to all sorts of external controls.

The reward system may, in others, foster resistance and rebellion, resentment, cynicism and a variety of negative and competitive feelings. People who work under competition learn to be competitive and the extrinsic rewards do not satisfy the deep needs for self-satisfaction and self-respect which are gained by achieving our personal goals as unique individuals.

Both dependency and resistance require controls, and the defensive leader expends a considerable amount of energy devising a variety of controls both for the people and for the processes of the enterprise. The more fearful and anxious he is, the more he feels caught in recurring emergencies and the greater is his need to control. Regulations are put on car-parking, coffee-break duration, channels of reporting, library schedules, methods of work, habits of dress, use of safety devices, more and more complex filing systems, rigid report systems–until all aspects of living in the organization are controlled.

The conscious and official reasons given for the controls usually relate to organization and productive efficiency, but the *underlying* impulses often spring from, or are reinforced by, the leader's personal needs for rigid order, or needs to demonstrate his superiority and strength, express hostility, exercise power, justify his position (what else would I do if I didn't plan these controls?), reinforce hierarchy, force people to be orderly or conforming, and "keep them in line."

Control systems become functionally autonomous–traditional and conventional elements of the organizational system–and often outlive any practical utility. Indeed, people seem to sense that many regulations actually serve personal needs for punishment or power and bear little relation to the actual needs of the organization itself. In looking at organizations, we have often found that many controls are universally violated in the system by common consent. In fact, there is clear indication–and often conscious awareness–that some controls are so dysfunctional that if everyone obeyed them the system would come to a grinding halt.

These defensive techniques of leadership produce certain predictable results. Fear and distrust begets fear and distrust. People who are distrustful tend to see untrustworthy behavior in others. If the relationship between an administrator and his subordinate is basically one of distrust, almost any action on either's part is perceived by the other as untrustworthy. Thus a cycle is created which nurtures self-corroboration leadership hypotheses.

This cycle is well illustrated in connection with communications. Any restriction of the flow of information and any closed strategy arouses energy devoted to circumventing the strategy and fosters counter-strategies that are at least as imaginative and often more effective than the original inducing strategy. A familiar example is the strategy of countering the "top brass" by distorting the upward-flowing data: feelings of hostility are camouflaged by deferential politeness; reports are "fixed up"; records are doctored or "cooked" to fit adminstrative goals and directives. Such attempts are augmented by emergency and threat; the greater the fear and distrust, the greater the circumvention, counter-strategy and counter-distortion.

Defensive leaders use various forms of persuasion to motivate subordinates towards the organization's goals, but often the results are either apathy and passivity or frenetic conformity. Persuasion is a form of control and begets resistance, which may take many subtle forms. Open and aggressive cold war between teachers and administrators for instance, is an obvious form. More common—and less easy to deal with—is passive, often unconscious resistance such as apathy, apparent obtuseness, dependent demands for further and more minute instructions, bumbling, wheel-spinning and a whole variety of inefficiencies that reduce creative work.

As we have seen, tight control leads to some form of dependency and its accompanying hostility; it may vary from the yes-man's deference and conformity to the no-man's rebellion against even the most reasonable and normal requests and rules. Deference and rebellion are cut from the same cloth. When unnecessary and arbitrary controls are imposed, or when normal controls are *seen* as unnecessary or arbitrary, as in the case when there is fear and distrust, then almost all members of the hierarchy become concerned with their feelings about authority. Most of us are ambivalent towards authority figures, and these mixed feelings are augmented in periods of stress and fear. In tightly controlled, disciplining and disciplined organizations, members demand clarity in rules and in boundary demarcations. But rules can never be made completely clear in practical work situations; boundaries are always permeable and inadequately defined. Thus the demands for further clarification are endless, and controls lead to further controls.

We see how the cycle is set up: hostility and its inevitable counterpart, fear, are increased by the distrust, distortion, persuasion-reward and control systems of defensive leadership, and the continuing cycle is *reinforced* at all stages, for as fear breeds distrust, distrust is rationalized and structured into theories which sanction distrustful leadership practices. The practices reinforce distrust; now the theorist is justified, and latent motivation to continue the cycle is itself reinforced.

Defensive leadership theories and practices permeate our society. We find them in the home, in school, and in the church, as well as in business organizations. Let us see, for instance, how the child-rearing patterns of our culture fit the picture described above. There are so many frightening things in the world that can harm helpless children. The fearful person can, with little effort, find a variety of frightening aspects in the environment of the child—anything from matches and electric outlets to busy roads and unacceptable playmates. Anxiety makes it easy to exaggerate the number of people ready to kidnap and even rape one's child; the fears of the parent embellish natural dangers and provide nourishment and comforting rationalization for defensive practices.

Communications must be managed for the good of the child. Because he might be worried or upset, emotional and financial discord must be camouflaged and a facade of security and serenity maintained. Children are inexperienced and immature, therefore they cannot be trusted to do things on their own. Moreover, since the natural interests of the child are likely to be frivolous, demeaning, or harmful, he should be carefully guided and persuaded to do what is right—to select appropriate playmates, read good books and generally adopt goals set by the parental culture or aspirations. To protect the child from ubiquitous dangers and to set his feet on the proper path, parents readily learn to use bribes, praise, and deprivation as tools of coercion. And because children are initially dependent and helpless, it is easy for the fearful parent to prolong the period of dependency.

Schools reinforce these patterns. They receive children whose dependency has been created by defensive parental techniques; and they maintain the dependency by continuing these practices. Having been distrusted, children continue to be untrustworthy. The insecure teacher finds it necessary to maintain a protective facade; she rationalizes her behavior by making a number of low-trust, tight-control assumptions about the children under her tutelage. She builds a changing repertoire of tricks to keep them busy, orderly, neat, attentive, and–she hopes–motivated. Impressed by the awesome culture heritage she is charged to transmit, she feels it imperative that she instill in her pupils the goals, ideals and rules of the culture. As bodies of knowledge become increasingly standardized, pressures towards indoctrination increase. By codifying rules, regulations, and standards, the teacher builds internal control systems–in the classroom, and hopefully, in the children themselves. As part of the informal curriculum, children are taught facade-building; they are encouraged to "put the best foot forward," to be polite, to be decorous, and to adopt the essentially hypocritical social graces of the dominant middle class.

What is the alternative to defensive leadership? This is not as easy to specify. The key to emergent leadership centers in a high degree of trust and confidence in people. Leaders who trust their colleagues and subordinates and have confidence in them tend to be open and frank, to be permissive in goalsetting, and to be noncontrolling in personal style and leadership policy. People with a great deal of self-acceptance and personal security do trust others, do make "trust assumptions" about their motives and behavior. The self-adequate person tends to assume that others are also adequate and other things being equal, that they will be responsible, loyal, appropriately work-oriented when work is to be performed and adequate to carry out jobs that are commensurate with their levels of experience and growth.

Just as we saw that distrust arises from fear and hostility, so we can see that people with little fear and minimal needs to be hostile are ready to trust others. Of course, there is some risk in trusting others, in being open and freedom-giving.

People naturally tend to share their feelings and concerns with those whom they trust, and this is true at the simplest and most direct level of interpersonal relationships as well as at more complex levels of organizational communication. Thus a high-trust system may institute open planning meetings and evaluation meetings; public criteria for promotion; easily available information on salaries, cost figures and budgets, and easy access to material in the files. There is comparatively little concern with public relations, with the corporate or family "image," or with "communications" programs. Communication in such a system is a *process* rather than a program.

The participative leader is permissive in his relations with subordinates, for he assumes that as people grow they learn to assess their own aptitudes, discover their deep-lying interests and develop their basic potentials. Therefore he gives his subordinates every opportunity to maximize self-determination and self-assessment, to verbalize their goals, to try new jobs or enlarge the scope of the work they are doing, and he trusts them to make mature judgments about job assignments. Where he is dealing with a work-team or a group, he lets the group make decisions about job allotments and work assignments.

This process of allowing people to be responsible for their own destinies, for setting their own targets, assessing their own development needs, searching out resources to aid in job accomplishment, and participating in setting organizational objectives is basic to high-trust leadership. Instead of using conventional defensive-leadership techniques of skilled persuasion to induce acceptance of leadership goals, the high-trust administrator participates in cooperative determination of goals and in cooperative definition of production and staff problems. He knows that goal-formation is a significant skill that must be learned, and that to develop such skill students and adults must exercise a variety of opportunities to make decisions, explore goals and experiment with many kinds of activities.

The participative administrator joins in creating a climate in which he has no need to impose controls. He knows that in a healthy group, controls emerge from group processes as the need is perceived. Then controls are mediated by group or organization objectives and by such relevant data as deadlines and target dates. People or groups who have set their own objectives and have clearly stated their own goals build internal tension-systems which maintain goal orientation and create appropriate boundaries.

Formal and written rules about such things as workspace, library use, and stock-room neatness are less and less necessary when people are engaged in a common task with others whose feelings and perceptions they freely share; when there is trust and mutuality, people are inclined to respect the rights and concerns of fellow-members. This principle applies to large and small systems alike—in either, the participative administrator reduces as far as practicable all formal controls evidenced by rules, regulations, written memoranda, signs, formal job-specification sheets, rigid lines of responsibility and authority, and the like.

The effects of participative leading are diametrically contrary to those of defensive leading. Love begets love. Respect begets respect. Trust produces trust. People who are trusted tend to trust themselves and to trust those in positions of responsibility. Moreover, the feeling that one is trusted encourages exploration, diversity and innovation, for the person need spend little time and energy trying to prove himself. His time and energy are freed to define and solve problems, accomplish work, and create new dimensions of his job. A fearful person uses a great deal of energy in defending himself against present or anticipated threat or attack; a confident and self-assured person can direct his energy toward goals that are significant to him as a person.

Again, openness begets openness. In the long run, at least, one who freely shares data, whether of feelings or figures, reduces fear and distrust in himself and in others. Defensive administrators build massive communication-programs, not to disseminate objective information but to mold attitudes, create favorable and appropriate "images," and influence people. Such persuasional and distortive communication produces resistance. Direct and open flow of information, on the other hand, serves to create an atmosphere which encourages people to share information with those above as well as with those below.

In general, openness and information-giving improves the decision-making process, for experience in giving information and expressing feelings enhances consensus, and the more nearly a group can reach consensus on operational issues, the higher the quality of the decision and the greater the group's commitment to the program.

Moreover, participative goal-information optimizes self-determination and self-assessment. Intrinsic motivations become increasingly relevant and powerful. People explore their own capacities and interests, and try to find or create work for themselves that is satisfying and fulfilling. They enlarge their own jobs, asking for more responsibility and more creative and interesting work. Such work is fulfilling to the person, and extrinsic rewards are secondary to satisfaction in accomplishing the task. Administrators find that people like to work; they "own" their jobs and feel great loyalty and responsibility toward the common goals of the group. People feel little need to escape from the work situation, and the "thank goodness it's Friday" clubs becomes less enticing. Concerns over salary and merit increases are symptomatic of defensive-leading pressures.

Participative administration creates interdependence and diminishes the problem of authority. For instance, work is allocated by concensus–people assess their abilities and select or create appropriate tasks. Where there is interdependence, conflict and disagreement are openly expressed and can thus be resolved and integrated into productive work. Where people feel they are working together for a common goal, the organization of work can be flexible, diverse and informal, with role-requirements. Channels of communication are free, open and spontaneous.

The attainment of emergent leadership on the college campus is a developmental task of awesome proportion. If the above analysis of the leadership problem has some validity, then it is clear where some responsibilities lie.

These concepts particularly are a challenge to the university. The Ohio State studies, particularly, showed how far behind even the military and industry the university administration is in achieving some kind of more participative and less authoritarian administrative relationships. The headlines today are filled with conflicts. The university is in many ways more susceptible to the pressures which produce fear than is industry, government, or business. The university is at one and the same time vulnerable to attacks from public opinion and also historically inviolate. The products of the university are highly intangible and it is difficult to apply vigorous controls to the product and to tell if the university is successful in the same way that a business or even the military has hard criteria for productivity, profit, or victory. Thus highly vulnerable the university has preserved a historical isolation from social pressures and administrative behavior is often strangely medieval and out of touch with the vigorous demands of democratic growth. The university, strangely, is sometimes a citadel for autocratic administrative behavior.

One of the discussion groups this morning has to do with ethics of academia. I should say a word about the implications of this model for ethical behavior. In abstract, this model of leadership specifies a theory of ethics. That behavior is more ethical when it is most trusting, most open, most self determining, and most interdependent. Thus one would look in the university setting for unethical of moral behavior in the areas of distrust, strategic filtering of feelings and ideas (honesty), manipulative abridgement of self determination, and dependency-producing or rebellion-producing high control behavior.

One of the seminars this morning has to do with planning. It seems to me that joint, interdependent, and shared planning is the central concept of the kind of participative, consultative leadership that we are considering. Planning, to be moral, in this framework, to be efficient, and to be growth-producing, must be organic to the institution, involve to an optimal degree all of the parcipants, and must be done interdependently. One does not have to go far to find illustrations on the university campus of architecture that is unrelated to experiential learning theory, fund raising methods that are planned by a special group of people who are usually collecting funds in ways that would be anathema to other members of the college community, athletic programs that arise from financial need rather than from educational policy, personnel practices that are inherited unabashedly from business institutions that have aims that are incommensurate with university goals, and many other illustrations where planning is a fragmentary, emergency process engaged in by small groups of people who are often out of touch with the university as a community.

One of the discussion groups deals with innovation. Our assumption here is that the blocks to innovation and creativity are fear, poor communication, imposition of motivations, and the dependency-rebellion syndrome of forces. People *are* innovative and creative. The administration of innovation involves freeing the creativity that is always present. The administrative problem of innovation is to remove fear and increase trust, to remove strategic and distortional blocks to open communication, to remove coercive, persuasional, and manipulative efforts to "pump" motivation and to remove the tight controls on behavior that tend to channel creative efforts into circumvention, counter-strategy, and organizational survival rather than into innovative and creative problem solving.

One of the discussion groups is concerned with the communication process. Valid, direct, authentic and open communication among all segments of the organic institution is a central process of effective leadership in the model we are examining. Effective leadership grows with communication in depth. Effective leadership is hampered by all forces which inhibit or restrain communication in depth. If emergent or participative leadership were prevalent on the campuses, communication programs would become less and less necessary. Defensive administration breeds the conditions that require an increasing escalation of massive communication programs to hopefully alleviate the conditions produced by the defensive leadership.

We are attempting to *become* as a people as a culture, We are in the process of discovering and creating models of interdependent, high trust, self determining, and open behavior. We are trying to create an interdependent, achieving, free, becoming culture. This has never before been done in the world and the strains of transition are awesome and somewhat frightening. But, for those of us who are dedicated to the university as a way of life, the challenge to the college and university administrator and leader is clear. The challenge is there. The road is unclear. The goal is at one and the same time the preservation of certain concepts we hold dear and the achievement of a more free, a more open, a more self-determining and a more human environment for learning and growth.

The Legitimacy of Organizational Influence[1]

Edgar H. Schein and J. Steven Ott

Attitudes toward the legitimacy of influencing various kinds of behavior in an organizational context are examined. An attitude survey revealed that samples from business managers, local union leaders, and college students were highly consistent in their ranking of behavior areas; the more job-related the area, the more it was considered legitimate to influence. In contrast, the samples differed significantly in the number of areas considered to be legitimate to influence, and in their responses to given behavior areas, for example, "attitudes toward unions."

There has been much concern in recent years over the infringement by corporations into areas of employee behavior which are usually defined as "private" in our culture. Corporations allegedly have norms about and influence where their managers should live, the types of women they should marry, the kinds of clothing they should wear, the kind of car they should drive, and so on. William H. Whyte and others see such organizational pressures as being supported by a new social ethic, the result of which is excessive conformity, the "organization man," and the atrophy of creativity and innovation.[2]

The fact that organizations and groups develop norms and behavior standards, enforce them, and consider such enforcement legitimate has been repeatedly demonstrated. The issue, then, is not whether influence occurs and whether such influence is considered to be legitimate, but what the boundaries of the area of legitimacy are for different groups and organizations. The present study does not attempt to determine either what attempts to influence actually occur in organizations or what *covert* attitudes exist toward such attempts. Rather, it

[1]Supported by the Sloan Research Fund of the School of Industrial Management at the Massachusetts Institute of Technology. We would like to acknowledge the help of John Glass, Usha Nand Sellers, and Susan Green, all of whom worked on various phases of the study.

[2]William H. Whyte, Jr., *The Organization Man* New York: Simon & Schuster, 1956).

explores the overt attitudes which people hold concerning the legitimacy of a superior's influencing areas of subordinate behavior or attitudes, at the managerial level of an industrial organization.

By overt attitudes, we mean attitudes which respondents are willing to state on a questionnaire. Such attitudes may not be related to the actual behavior of their holder, but they are nevertheless important in that they define at one level the rules of the game by which people in organizations tend to operate with one another. Yet such rules of the game are likely not to be talked about or clarified because of the tendency of each person in the organization to assume that others hold attitudes similar to his own on basic rules of conduct.

If such attitudes are actually different in a superior-subordinate relationship, that is, if superior and subordinate define the boundaries of legitimate influence differently, the foundation is laid for communication failure and the build-up of emotional conflict between them. For example, if an employee is gently chided about the kind of clothing he wears around the office, his emotional response will depend to a considerable extent on whether he regards this as a legitimate area of influence. If he does not grant his boss the right to guide his clothing he is likely to develop resentment and the relationship is likely to deteriorate; if he does grant his boss the right to influence his clothing he may be grateful or, at worst, embarrassed to have to be reminded, but there is less likelihood of basic tension growing between the two parties. This same argument applies to different groups, such as management and labor, within an organization. To the extent that they disagree on the areas of legitimate influence, tension and conflict will develop over any attempt to influence in an area for which such agreement has not been reached.

The present study focuses on two aspects of this problem: (1) identification of behavior or attitude areas which tend to be placed at the two extremes of the legitimacy scale by a wide cross-section of respondents (which, in a sense, reflects wider cultural norms), and (2) identification of behavior and attitudes areas which produce different responses in different subsamples of respondents for example, samples of managers and of hourly employees (which, in a sense, reflect agreement within a subculture but disagreement between subcultures). Behavior and attitude areas about which there is little agreement within a subsample may be the areas most likely to cause trouble between individual superiors and subordinates.

The Influence Questionnaire

In order to obtain data on legitimate and non-legitimate areas of influence a questionnaire was constructed according to the following criteria: sufficient simplicity to be easily administered to large populations with a minimum of verbal instructions; enough face validity to elicit the voluntary co-operation of the respondent; and power sufficient to tap attitudes in areas where the most common response might well be "it all depends on the situation."

Fifty-five behavior and attitude areas ranging from highly job related to highly personal were used in the questionnaire (see Table 1). Each respondent was asked

Table 1. Average Item Index Values[a]

Item	*Total Group (N = 812)* (1)	*Labor Leaders (N = 77)* (2)	*Students[b] (N = 223)* (3)	*MIT Executives[c] (N = 21)* (4)	*Company Executives[d] (N = 391)* (5)
27. His working hours	84	50	85	90	88
7. How much alcohol, if any, he consumes during the working day	84	43	83	87	91
34. The kind of temperament he exhibits on the job (i.e., how excitable or phlegmatic or aggressive or passive, etc., he is)	82	64	72	90	90
44. The tidiness of his office	79	65	68	77	88
1. How much importance he attaches to getting along with other people	79	66	52	84	95
36. How critical he is of the company in public	76	21	66	89	89
25. The amount of additional education he obtains in job-related areas	74	48	75	74	79
10. The amount of time he spends talking to his wife and children on the telephone while at work	74	66	75	68	77
6. Whether he uses profane language at work	72	28	67	83	82
45. How he divides up his working day among his various duties	65	59	55	60	74
19. The amount of time he spends doing job-related reading while at work	64	55	61	53	70
26. The location of his next job (assuming the company rotates its people to different geographical areas of the country)	59	46	55	62	63
52. How many drinks, if any, he has at lunch time	58	9	41	59	77
37. How he supervises his own secretary	54	− 2	50	56	67
16. The type of clothing he wears at work	47	20	44	48	54
38. The form of address he uses in talking to his colleagues	46	34	27	38	62
13. How active he is in recruiting others to join the company	28	− 1	21	19	40
39. The degree of formality of his clothing	26	−26	27	27	35
5. His attitudes toward unions	24	−40	11	49	35
14. How much he completes with his peers for promotion	12	8	6	5	18
42. The amount of company work he takes home with him	6	9	5	−11	12
40. Whether he uses the company product himself (i.e., drives the kind of car the company makes or whatever the product is)	− 1	−33	−21	− 9	21

Table 1. (Continued)

Item	Total Group (N = 812) (1)	Labor Leaders (N = 77) (2)	Students[b] (N = 223) (3)	MIT Executives[c] (N = 21) (4)	Company Executives[d] (N = 391) (5)
53. His degree of participation in non-company public activities (i.e., working for local political parties, organizations, etc.)	−11	−72	−48	3	20
48. The amount of leisure time he spends at company social functions	−13	−19	−35	−40	9
11. His willingness to play politics to get ahead	−19	−66	−29	− 6	− 7
35. His attitudes toward sexual morality	−19	−55	−59	−32	15
55. Whether he participates on a company athletic team (assuming he has the talent and is needed)	−21	2	−24	−54	−12
32. His attitudes toward money	−37	−60	−63	−45	−14
4. Whether he wears a beard or a mustache	−39	−79	−35	−29	−37
24. How much leisure time he spends with his subordinates	−49	−60	−43	−60	−47
46. How faithful he is to his wife	−54	−74	−79	−54	−36
43. His attitudes toward saving money	−57	−68	−78	−73	−37
47. How much he drinks at home	−59	−85	−73	−66	−43
30. What clubs or organizations he belongs to his superiors	−59	−83	−64	−64	−50
3. How much leisure time he spends with his superiors	−63	−74	−56	−76	−62
20. How much he buys on credit	−65	−77	−69	−71	−59
28. How much leisure time he spends with his peers	−68	−66	−69	−76	−66
2. The amount of money he gives to charity (assuming contributions are made at work)	−68	−71	−91	−80	−51
18. Who his friends are	−70	−83	−79	−73	−61
51. Whether he has close friends in a rival company	−70	−62	−68	−68	−73
41. The amount of life insurance he carries	−72	−82	−82	−80	−62
12. Where he lives	−74	−55	−74	−83	−74
33. His attitudes toward smoking	−77	−61	−78	−73	−81
8. Whether he owns his own house or not	−81	−76	−92	−97	−87
49. How much he entertains	−83	−85	−77	−90	−84
23. The kind of house or apartment he lives in	−84	−79	−85	−88	−82
54. Whether his wife works or not	−87	−81	−84	−92	−88
17. The kind of woman he marries	−88	−94	−91	−87	−84
9. The kind of car he drives	−89	−83	−87	−83	−93
15. What political party he belongs to	−92	−90	−93	−86	−92
21. How many children he has	−92	−69	−94	−98	−93
31. Where he sends his children to school	−94	−89	−94	−97	−95

Table 1. (Continued)

Item	*Total Group (N = 812)* *(1)*	*Labor Leaders (N = 77)* *(2)*	*Students*[b] *(N = 223)* *(3)*	*MIT Executives*[c] *(N = 21)* *(4)*	*Company Executives*[d] *(N = 391)* *(5)*
50. Where he maintains charge accounts for personal shopping	−94	−93	−93	−97	−94
22. Where he spends his vacations	−95	−84	−96	−97	−95
29. The church he attends	−96	−90	−98	−99	−95

[a]High positive indexes reflect a high percentage of "Yes" answers; values near zero reflect either a split between "Yes" and "No" answers or a high percentage of "No Answer"; high negative indexes reflect a high percentage of "No" answers. Items are ranked by col. 1 indexes.
[b] Includes University of Florida undergraduate and MIT graduate students.
[c] Combines executives enrolled in MIT's middle and senior management courses.
[d] Executives tested in their companies.

to indicate by stating "Yes" or "No" whether he felt it was legitimate or not legitimate for a manager to influence a subordinate in that area. If he felt unsure or thought it depended on the actual situation he was to leave the item blank and we scored in a "No Answer" (NA").[3]

The influence questionnaire was administered to a total of 812 respondents, who made up the following subsamples:

55 University of Florida undergraduates
168 graduate students in the School of Industrial Management at Massachusetts Institute of Technology (MIT)

[3]The exact instructions were as follows:

"In this questionnaire we are trying to find out in what areas you consider it to be legitimate for a manager (for example, the plant manager, superintendent, foreman, etc.) to attempt to influence his own subordinates. The 55 items listed below represent many possible areas of influence. Some of them will strike you as legitimate areas for a manager to be concerned about. On some of them you will feel that it depends entirely upon the specific situation whether attempts to influence in that area are legitimate or not. We are trying to locate those items about which you feel quite sure, regardless of the specific situation.

"Please put the letter *Y* for "Yes" next to those items where you feel sure that influence attempts are legitimate (i.e., where the manager has the right to attempt influence).

"Please put the letter *N* for "No" next to those items where you feel sure that influence attempts would not be legitimate, regardless of the situation or the specific job (i.e., where the manager does *not* have the right to attempt influence).

"Please leave blank those items where you are not sure or you feel that it depends on the particular situation or the particular kind of work.

"It is legitimate for a manager to attempt to influence his subordinates in terms of:

_____1. How much importance he attaches to getting along with other people.
_____2. The amount of money he gives to charity (assuming contributions are made at work)."

Here and throughout the discussion "He" in every case refers to the *subordinate*

83 Sloan Fellows attending MIT's middle management course
38 senior executives attending MIT's senior management course
391 managers from four different companies
77 local leaders of two international unions

There is considerable variation in the age, rank, and seniority of the managerial group but most of it could best be described as middle management. The labor leaders in the sample are regular employees of a number of companies and serve as presidents and secretary-treasures of their local unions.[4] These subsamples were chosen as being representative of different perspectives toward the organizational situation; the managers having the perspective of superiors, the labor leaders having the perspective of subordinates, and the students, most of whom will enter organizations after their schooling, representing the perspective of subordinates who are not yet part of the system.

To simplify the presentattion of the data, the total number of "YES," "NO," and "NA" responses to any given item for the total sample or any given subsample was reduced to a single index by subtracting from the total number of "Yes" responses the number of "No's" and 0.2 of the number of "NA's," dividing by the total number of respondents in the group and finally multiplying by 100 (i.e., $I = [\text{Yes} - \text{No} - 0.2(\text{NA})]/(N) \times 100$). The resulting index ranges from + 100 to −100 and expresses the degree of agreement within the subsample concerning a given item.[5]

Results

Over-all attitudes.—The results in terms of item indexes are shown in Table 1. The items of the original scale are rank ordered according to their index value for the total sample (col. 1) from those regarded as most legitimate to those regarded as least legitimate. The closer the index is to +100, the higher the percentage of the sample checked "Yes" to that item; the closer it is to −100, the higher the percentage of "No's" to that item.

The combining of graduate and undergraduate samples was based on the high rank-order correlation between the two sets of indexes (+.98) and their similarity in absolute level. The MIT management groups were also combined because of their similarity to each other.

The degree to which the subsamples resemble each other in their ranking of items is shown in Table 2 by rank-order correlations. Ranks for all items were based on

[4]The union group was given slightly modified instructions to insure that they would answer in terms of company managers and subordinates, not their own union officers.

[5]We gave some weight to "NA" responses because this answer implies that the respondent is considering at least some circumstances under which influence would not be legitimate. Thus if the respondents divided themselves equally between "Yes," "No," and "NA" on a given item, the index value would be slightly negative rather than zero. A zero index can be obtained if everyone answers either "Yes" or "No" and these are split evenly, or if there are enough "NA" responses in combination with "NO's" to offset the number of "Yes" responses. The weight of 0.2 was chosen arbitrarily after experimenting with different weights.

Table 2. Rank-Order Correlations Between Subsamples on Item Indexes

Subsamples	*Correlation*
Labor vs. students	+.91
Labor vs. MIT managers	+.88
Labor vs. managers in companies	+.89
Students vs. MIT managers	+.97
Students vs. managers in companies	+.95
MIT managers vs. managers in companies	+.98

their index values. The over-all agreement between groups varying widely in age, socioeconomic status, occupation, and rank suggests that there is considerable generality in attitudes concerning legitimate areas of influence in a superior-subordinate relationship. Only the labor group shows any degree of disagreement with the others.

High legitimacy items all concern behavior at the work place or attitudes toward work and the company. The low legitimacy items concern family relationships, matters of taste in non-job-related areas, place of residence, political and religious views, and the like.

It is interesting to note that even at the extremes opinion is not unanimous. Twelve respondents said "Yes" to item 22 (where he spends his vacations), and eight respondents said "Yes" to item 29 (the church he attends); twenty-seven respondents said "No" to item 7 (how much alcohol, if any, he consumes during the working day), and twenty-eight said "No" to item 27 (his working hours).

The high index score on item 34 (the kind of temperament he exhibits on the job) and item 1 (how much importance he attaches to getting along with people) poses an interesting problem because these are areas which are particularly difficult to influence.[6] If supervisors attempt to influence the temperament of subordinates, it is highly probable that they will encounter strong emotional resistance (even if a subordinate grants his boss the right to try to change him), leading to one of two outcomes: surface compliance and suppression of natural tendencies yielding undesirable emotional by-products such as displaced aggression, or to chronic conflict between them with neither being aware of the basic source of the difficulty.

If the attitude which is reflected in item 34 is combined with a company stereotype of the proper temperament for a given role, the groundwork is laid for strong organizational pressures on the individual to adopt the "correct" temperament. Since it is likely that he cannot voluntarily change his temperament, the probable outcome is suppression of all feeling and the adoption of a safe but sterile façade. The attachment to such façades, combined with the conviction that the

[6]We recognize, of course, that the word "temperament" may not mean the same thing to the manager as it does to the psychologist. In whatever sense he uses it, however, he is likely to be dealing with areas in which it will arouse resistance.

correct way to get along with people is never to let your real feelings show, is clearly revealed if one observes groups of managers in a human-relations sensitivity training group.[7] The rediscovery on the part of a participant that he has feelings and that others respond favorably to them is often a crucial event in a training group, leading to a reassessment of the belief that human relations must be conducted on a purely intellectual rational plane.

Items with index values near zero reflect conflict between respondents (equal numbers of "Yes" and "No" answers), inability on the part of respondents to decide (high number of "NA" responses), or both. Table 3 shows the items which elicited the highest conflict and highest "NA" frequencies for the total sample.

Table 3. High-Conflict and High "No Answer" Items[a]

Item	*Yes*	*No*	*NA*	*Index*
High "NA" and high-conflict items:				
39. The degree of formality of his clothing	52	21	28	+26
11. His willingness to play politics to get ahead	30	44	26	-19
35. His attitudes toward sexual morality	31	45	24	-19
14. How much he competes with his peers for promotion	48	30	22	+12
16. The type of clothing he wears at work	65	13	22	+47
4. Whether he wears a beard or a mustache	22	56	22	-39
40. Whether he uses the company product himself (i.e., drives the kind of car the company makes or whatever the product is)	41	38	21	- 1
30. What clubs or organizations he belongs to	12	67	21	-59
47. How much he drinks at home	11	68	20	-59
42. The amount of company work he takes home with him	45	35	20	+ 5
Other high-conflict items:				
48. The amount of leisure time he spends at company social functions	32	50	18	-13
5. His attitudes toward unions	53	32	16	+24
53. His degree of participation in non-company public activities (i.e., working for local parties, organizations, etc.)	39	46	15	-10
55. Whether he participates on a company athletic team (assuming he has the talent and is needed)	35	54	11	-21

[a] The numbers in the table are percentage of respondents who checked "Yes," "No," or "No Answer" ("NA") to a given item. The first group of items is ranked by the "NA" percentage.

[7]National Training Laboratory in Group Development, *Explorations in Human Relations Training: An Assessment of Experience, 1947-1953* (Washington, D.C.: National Education Association, 1953).

These items reflect three themes: behavior or attitudes which reflect on the subordinate's general moral fiber or character (items 11, 35, 14, 47); behavior which pertains to the subordinate's presentation of himself to others in his role as a member of the organization (items 39, 16, 4, 40, 30); and behavior or attitudes reflecting the subordinate's willingness to participate in company affairs beyond the strict demands of his job (items 42, 53, 48, 55). Item 5 (attitude toward unions) is a special area of potential conflict which will be discussed in greater detail later. On most of these high conflict items some 30 to 60 per cent of the respondents do consider it legitimate to influence subordinates.

Subsample differences.—The subsamples of labor, students, managers at MIT courses, and managers tested in their companies can be compared in several ways. We have already shown the high intercorrelation on item rankings. There remains the question of whether the degree of agreement on any given item is higher in some subsamples than others, and whether the over-all tendency to regard influence attempts as legitimate is higher in some subsamples than others.

To obtain such over-all data we computed an individual index for each respondent based on his number of "Yes," "No," and "NA" responses.[8] This index reflects the total number of areas a given respondent regards as legitimate. It varies from zero (all "No's") to +110 (all "Yes's"). In order to compare the subsamples we have presented the medians and the first and third quartiles of the distributions of such individual indexes (Table 4).

Table 4.· Median and First and Third Quartile Values of Individual Index Distributions and Average Number of "Yes," "No," and "NA" Responses in Subsamples

Subsample	*First Quartile*	*Median*	*Third Quartile*	*Yes*	*No*	*NA*
Labor leaders	44	35	29	17.7	34.9	2.4
Students	50	40	31	17.0	28.6	9.4
Managers at MIT courses	50	44	36	17.7	27.2	10.0
Managers in companies	58	47	41	22.7	26.8	5.6

To determine the significance of differences between the subsamples medians test were made for each one against each other one. The χ^2 significance levels are shown in Table 5.

There is a consistent and significant rise in the individual indexes with increasing proximity to the managerial role, reflecting an increasing willingness to regard more areas as legitimate areas of influence. Only the "student" and "managers at MIT"

[8]The individual index is similar to the item index and is obtained by subtracting from the total number of "Yes" responses the number of "No's" and 0.2 of the "NA's" then adding 55 (the number of items) to make all scores positive (ranging from 0 to +110); I = Yes − No − 0.2(NA) + 55.

Table 5. x^2 Significance Levels Comparing Subsamples on Median Individual Index Values

Subsample Level	*Significance Level*
Labor vs. students	.02
Labor vs. MIT managers	.001
Labor vs. managers in companies	.001
Students vs. MIT managers	.10[a]
Students vs. managers in companies	.001
MIT managers vs. managers in companies	.001

[a]Not significant.

subsamples fail to differ significantly from each other, but the difference is in the direction indicated above and just short of significance. An examination of the quartile scores shows that the shift is consistent for the whole distribution of indexes within a subsample. It can also be seen that there is considerable individual variation within a given subsample.[9]

Table 4 also shows the average number of "Yes," "No," and "NA" responses in each of the subsamples. It is interesting to note that the main difference between subsamples occurs in the frequency of "No" and "NA" responses, and that the two groups tested in an educational context have the highest frequency of "NA" responses. This suggests that one reason for the lack of resemblance between managers tested at MIT and those tested in their companies is the influence of the educational environment in which there is great pressure to question and re-examine corporate values.[10] The labor leaders, by contrast, have the lowest number of "NA" responses and by far the highest number of "No" responses, suggesting that they tend to have formed quite clear conceptions of the limits of legitimate influence.

A number of findings relating to subsample differences in the item areas emerge from an inspection of columns 2-5 in Table 1. On most items there is a consistent rise in index from labor to students to managerers, reflecting the greater tendency of the managerial group to sanction influence. The largest differences occur between the labor and management group (columns B and E), primarily in reference to behavior or attitude areas reflecting loyalty to the company (items 36, 13, 40), the subordinate's presentation of himself during the working day (items 7, 6, 52, 39, 4), degree of autonomy from the company (items 25, 53, 30), personal morality (items 11, 35, 32, 46, 43, 47), and some specific items like attitudes toward unions (item 5) and how a subordinate supervises his own secretary (item 37).

[9]In the present study we were not able to identify correlates of high or low individual influence scores, but the questionnaire is clearly capable of discriminating among individuals.

[10]We do not have sufficient information on the subsamples to rule out possible initial differences which could, of course, account just as well for the obtained results.

These differences strongly suggest that one source of tension between labor and management may be the value system underlying influence attempts, whether they are successful or not. If there is substantial agreement concerning legitimacy of influence in a given area, then both groups are playing within the "rules of the game"; but if influence is attempted in an area which one group considers legitimate while the other group does not, it is likely that the very attempt at influence will be strongly resented. For example, on item 53, 55 per cent of the managers tested in companies stated that it was legitimate to influence a subordinate's participation in non-company public activities, while only 10 per cent of the labor group agreed that it was legitimate. Under such circumstances it appears likely that even a routine compaign in a company newspaper to increase employee participation in community affairs might be strongly resented. Similarly 63 per cent of the managers consider it legitimate to attempt to influence a subordinate's attitudes toward unions, while only 29 per cent of the labor group consider this legitimate. These and other sharp differences in expressed attitudes strongly suggest the need to gather such data vertically within single companies to test whether tensions in fact do relate to such differences.

The student subsamples tend to differ from the managers on the same kinds of items as those cited above, but the differences are not as large. The fact that on most items the students fall between labor and management may be related to the fact that their socioeconomic status is potentially more similar to managers or that there is occurring in this group a certain amount of "anticipatory socialization" inasmuch as most of the students will enter business careers.

Summary and Conclusions

This paper describes the development of a questionnaire for assessing attitudes toward the legitimacy of organizational influence and on the first results obtained with it. Fifty-five items describing behavior or attitude areas ranging from highly job related to highly personal are to be answered "Yes," "No," or "No Answer" depending on whether the respondent feels it is legitimate for a superior to attempt to influence a subordinate in that particular area or not. Data from 812 respondents falling into subsamples of labor leaders, students, managers at MIT management courses, and managers tested in their companies were presented.

A high degree of agreement exists between subsamples on the relative ranking of the items implying that there are fairly well developed attitudes concerning legitimate and non-legitimate areas of influence in the population from which these subsamples were drawn. At the same time, with one exception, each sample differed significantly from all others in the mean amount of influence it considered legitimate, as measured by an index reflecting responses on all 55 items: Labor leaders were lowest on this index, followed in order by students, managers at MIT courses (who were not significantly different from students), and managers tested in their companies. This consistent rise in the number of areas considered as legitimate suggests that a social ethic of the kind which Whyte worries about is most likely to be found among managers who, of course, are in the best position to implement it.

Part Two

Educational Organizations and Their Leadership

Research in Organizational Dynamics: Implications for School Administrators

Alan F. Brown

Research into educational organizations is usually concerned with one of two distinct connotations–investigation into the patterns of deploying teachers and pupils, as in team teaching, or investigations into the nature of the organizations themselves. The latter approach has great promise for providing insights into administrative behaviour. The work of Katz and Kahn, Presthus and Carlson helps to provide such insights. Much attention is now being paid to the initiation of organizational change, especially as it affects the organizational climate. The results of a recent project in this area suggest that administrators who wish to change organizational climate may 1. "Thicken the mix" through freeing communication; 2. Sharpen perception through training in interpersonal awareness; 3. Improve output by not tinkering with the status of the organization.

Research into organizations today carries two distinct and usually unrelated connotations in educational studies. One has to do with patterns of deploying pupils or teachers, as in team teaching, for the sake of reaching some specified goals. An example of this is a paperback edited by Maurie Hillson, *Change and Innovation in Elementary School Organization.*[1] Relevant research is usually developmental in purpose and thus cannot safely be generalized. The second connotation has to do with the nature of organizations, as they are, and the variables that make them so. An example is the monumental *Handbook of Organizations*[2] recently published in the Rand McNally series. This is a new field. As James G. March, its editor, says of the book, "It could not have been written 15 years ago; certainly it will not survive another 15".[3] Research in this "semi-discipline" (the term is from March) is plentiful, sometimes insightful, and usually so diverse as to defy cross-communication among the various component social sciences. The study of organizations has, nonetheless, evolved as the focus for the conceptual groping-about which once characterized the era of "the interdisciplinary approach to administration."

[1] Hillson, Maurie (ed.) *Change and Innovation in Elementary School Organization.* New York. Holt, Rinehart and Winston. 1965.

[2] March, James G. (ed.) *Handbook of Organizations.* Chicago. Rand McNally. 1965.

[3] *Ibid.* p. xv.

The School qua Organization

School administrators have come to accept the notion that a school is an organization in the sense that it contains all the characteristic problems and potentialities possessed by organizations. It has both a formal and an informal structure, both necessary though possibly at variance. It pursues both manifest and latent purposes, loudly proclaiming the one but of necessity following dictates from the latter. It is characterized by internal-plus-external conflict; conflict that is as normal, as necessary, and as hazardous to social organizations as stress is to the person.[4] Katz and Kahn place the school as one of society's "maintenance organizations," as distinct from the productive and economic organizations, managerial and political organizations, or the adaptive and creative organizations.[5]

Disabling Conditions of Organizations

The anatomy of organizations contains several genetic disabilities, dislocations and nonarticulating passages. The print medium is often referred to as an example of a communications passage that the organization of the school has allowed to become clogged; interpersonal media represent passages that have yet to become fully developed. Some other disabilities will probably worsen before they get better.

Of the many divergent elements within a single school, one conflict that may be expected to intensify as teachers upgrade their qualifications lies between autonomy and bureaucracy, sometimes[6] called paternalism vs. professionalism. Trask, who recently confirmed the presence of this conflict, describes the dilemma:

> Professionals, we generally assume, are committed to individual autonomy . . . [which] appears to stand in direct contradiction to the bureaucratic requirements of hierarchical authority, characteristic of most large-scale organizations, especially as manifested in the supervision of subordinates' performance. Since the responsibility for supervising teachers within a school is usually delegated to the principal, he is the person confronted with trying to reconcile these divergent requirements.[7]

Three routes to harmony. By traditional methods this conflict would have had little chance to begin in the first place. Griffiths portrays the process in this way:

> Attempts are made to select individuals who have an inclination to accept the goals of the enterprise; they are submitted to an intensive program of

[4]E.g. Brown, Alan F. "Conflict and Stress in Administrative Relationships." *Administrator's Notebook*. 10, 7, March 1962. pp. 1-4.

[5]Katz, Daniel and Robert L. Kahn. *The Social Psychology of Organizations*. New York. Wiley. 1966. p. 112.

[6]Brown, Alan F. "Paternalism and Professionalism." *The English Teacher*. 3, 3, October 1963. pp. 31-37.

[7]Trask, Anne E. "Principals, Teachers and Supervision," *Administrator's Notebook*. 13, 4, December 1964. p. 1.

> indoctrination (commonly called orientation); they participate in continuing programs of indoctrination over long periods of time (commonly called in-service education) . . . .[8]

One may effect change in the personnel or in the changer himself. In Trask's research, principals clearly favour the latter approach. They seemed to suggest changing the notion of supervision to one of providing honest advice according to a mode not so much of the supervisor's choosing but to the supervisee's expectations for him.

There is another way out of this dilemma and that is by giving principals more latitude, by giving them a chance to exercise greater responsibility. Fettering their responsibilities provides a constant source of unproductive frustration that extends through the entire organization. With no budget and virtually no personnel authority, school principals learn less about how to use and be accountable for responsibility than young branch operators of relatively minor business enterprises. In the schools there is now a growing interest in what may be called "entrepreneurial administration." It is not the ideal phase, but "principal as entrepreneur" is the next phase through which the development of administration will move before it will be ready for the ideal. Unfortunately the biggest roadblock is the persistence of so many currently comfortable principals who, bewildered at the role of the entrepreneur, fail to exploit what opportunity they do have.

Unforseen Consequences

That identical stimuli will produce manifestly different responses in two individuals is the phenomenon called individual differences. Teachers know about this. Administrators exhort them to do something about it and, for the most part, they do a lot.

It appears strange, therefore, that administrators themselves behave so often as though there were such a thing as the "generalized teacher." Probably nine-tenths of the times that one experiences some other-than-anticipated happening to follow after an effort in instructional improvement, it is not a "fluke." Neither, if it is truly unexpected, can one honestly blame it on central office interference, departmental regulations, or the recalcitrant nature of the change-target. Instead it is generally one's limited knowledge (or failure to utilize one's full range of knowledge, which amounts to the same thing) of individual differences in organizational behavior. The frequency of unanticipated consequences is directly related to the administrator's state of knowledge at a given time.

Just how many actual unforseen happenings never so much as enter his awareness it is difficult to judge—for two reasons. First, subordinates have a way of concealing administratively undesirable consequences both as a protection to themselves and, paradoxically, to the administrator as well. Second, the very same handicaps that impair his ability to anticipate all the possible consequences blur his recognition of those that do occur. These handicaps refer partly to the administrator's heavy time

[8]Griffiths, Daniel E. *Administrative Theory*. New York. Appleton-Century-Crofts, 1959.

demands and the multiplicity of problems competing incessantly for his simultaneous attention, but also to his need to develop a variety of perceptual and analytic skills. Following are examples of unforseen consequences to organizational variables.

1. *Responses to supervision.* It has been experimentally indicated[9] that teachers sensing task-induced stress from their superiors will *appear* to randomize their behavior: some improve, many others decline while a few exhibit no measurable change in teaching effectiveness. Closer analysis, however, suggests these results *actually to have been predictable* from certain indentifiable personality characteristics, from traits which could have been assesed by a supervisor.

2. *Responses to subordination.* Argyris[10] finds subordination-frustration common to healthy individuals in a variety of organizations, and that these individuals–rather than reacting in a true subordinate fashion–develop defence mechanisms thereby avoiding both the frustration and, in a real sense, the organizations. Some leave the situation (teachers quit, change schools, or not uncommonly climb the organizational ladder to the principalship); some become defensive, apathetic; some from informal groups dedicated to non(not necessarily anti-) organizational goals; others chase the material rewards.

3. *Responses to the organizational press.* Individuals in an organization will accommodate to it in ways unintended by their leaders. Presthus[11] discovered three modes of accommodation: upward mobility, indifference, and ambivalence. They remind one of Will Cuppy's classic *How to Tell Your Friends From The Apes:*

(a) *The upward-mobile:* great energy, dominance, identifies with the organization and its goals, status conciousness, adaptive role-playing, power drive, two chief fears–fear of failure and fear of being sick, unflagging optimism, high morale, localism, impatient with opposition, respect for authority, strong need for control of his environment.

(b) *The indifferent:* refuses to compete, has low aspirations or else has aspired and lost, does what is required but major life interests are on the outside, keeps work and life apart.

(c) *The ambivalent:* wants the rewards of success but cannot achieve, may like individuals in authority but has no respect for authority, in conflict of interest will choose friends over organization.

The industrial findings of Presthus are corroborated for the educational organization. Griffiths[12] headed a New York University research team that, at board request, closely examined teacher mobility patterns in the city of New York.

[9] Brown, Alan F. "Conflict and Stress in Administrative Relationships." *op. cit.*

[10] Argyris, Chris. "The Individual and the Organization: An Empirical Test." *The Administrative Science Quarterly.* 4, September 1959. pp. 145-167.

[11] Presthus. Robert. *The Organizational Society.* New York. Knopf. 1962.

[12] Griffiths, Daniel E., Samuel Goldman and Wayne J. McFarland. "Teacher Mobility in New York City." *Educational Administration Quarterly.* 1, 1, Winter 1965. pp 15-31.

About one teacher in eight, particularly men, seemed to do just about anything to get out of the classroom. They were GASing (Getting the Attention of Superiors), and upwardly mobile by means of exploiting the visibility system. Two-thirds of the staff were "pupil-oriented" teachers, dedicated persons of low mobility attempting to provide the best education for the pupils assigned to them. A small group of five or six percent were classed "subject-oriented" teachers. Sometimes thought of as "intellectuals," their mobility was horizontal, in the direction of greater identification with their subject. In the fourth group of 15 percent, called "benefits-oriented," two subgroups appeared: those who genuinely were exploiting the benefits that accrue to the profession (security, vacation, hours, "moonlighting" or escape from boredom), being horizontally mobile towards the best "deal," and those others who appear to have once been GASers but to have become weary of the chase.

The Stance for Organizational Change

Carlson[13], working in the area of innovation in educational organization, has greatly influenced the direction of recent research. Many principals and superintendents, as educational innovators or change-agents, have taken heed. Carlson, charting the likelihood of successful innovation in school systems, finds change occurs more from bringing in the superintendent from outside the organization than from promoting him from within. There are several reasons, of course, why this should be so. The outsider, having moved, is more likely to be career-bound, the insider to be place-bound. The appointed outsider has a need to initiate change in order to legitimize his appointment; the promoted insider knows that seniority can pass for sufficient justification. Similarly the local organization, whether they like it or not, tends to expect change from the outsider whereas they knew the local man "back when;" the former enjoys a better change-readiness.

Considerable research corroborates Carlson's findings but Andrews and Greenfield[14] of the Ontario Institute for Studies in Education, are currently examining another aspect of the problem: has change wrought by the insider a "local" character to it? It is perhaps less flamboyant, or less obvious to an outside observer. But change it is. In Andrews and Greenfield's sense, locally-induced organizational change *occurs along* the organizational *theme* established locally, externally-induced organizational change *departs from* established organizational themes. It is this absence of a departure which is sometimes mistaken for an absence of change. A *theme* is a cluster of sub-culture value patterns which, though difficult for an observer to identify, dictates the dominant direction of the school.

[13] Carlson, Richard O. *Executive Succession and Organizational Change.* Chicago. Midwest Administration Center, University of Chicago. 1962.

[14] Andrews, John H. M. and T. Barr Greenfield. "Organizational Themes Relevant to Change in Schools." Paper read to 4th Canadian Conference on Educational Research, Toronto. June 1966.

Strategies for Organizational Change

Appropriate policy for the initiation of organizational change now may be suggested. The school administrator at various levels may utilize either a "clinical strategy" or a "growth strategy" depending largely upon whether change is to fulfil or depart from existing themes. A *clinical strategy* for change would be based upon a systems model of organizations and would use the medical analogue, proceeding through these steps.

(i) *Knowledge of the organism.* It begins with a thorough knowledge of the *organism,* without which we have administrative quackery. Ideally, this would require understanding not only of every part but also of the myriad interconnections between the parts, the sensitive spots and the environmental dependencies. Many of these knowledges are already available to the perceptive principal. More are acquired through experience and systematic study.

(ii) *Diagnosis.* The second stage is diagnosis. Here a skillful practitioner pinpoints the nature of the trouble and labels it something like "low morale," "non-involvement in educational goals," "no meaningful articulation between principal and new staff," or even "lack of acceptance of principal as person." Each of these four labels can be thought of either as a symptom, or as the malady itself.

(iii) *Prognosis*, as a third stage, represents an evaluation of the seriousness of the situation. This is an educated guess as to how it all will turn out, so that a favourable or a not-serious prognosis frees one's energies for other more urgent matters. This stage is badly confounded by the temperament of the administrator himself. Just as the pessimist runs himself wretched over his own bleak reports, the optimist lets things go until he stands in amazement when the organism dismantles itself about him.

(iv) *Prescription.* The indicated action, on the part of the administrator, may or may not be directly related to the diagnosis. Organizational prescriptions have a way of appearing somewhat devious so that we see "team teaching" suddenly developing into the new wonder drug that will cure low morale, lack of leadership, need for more layers in the hierarchy or simply to effect an "unfreezing" of tradition so that new traditions (the ones we favour) can be frozen in.

(v) *Follow-up*. In the final stage of the clinical process a follow-up is conducted to assess the extent to which treatment was successful, or even followed. There are many means; word from the grapevine, minutes of staff meetings, number and character of transfer applications, ratio of solicited to unsolicited suggestions from the principal, proportion of leadership acts initiating from staff, and so on. Organizational follow-ups, like prognoses, are so vulnerable to subjective confounding that, for the same reason, they demand objective support.

A *growth strategy* for change would be based upon a developmental model of organizations and, assisted by the biological analogue, would be governed by several postulates of natural organizational growth, the facilitation of which is seen as the administrator's chief responsibility. Relevant postulates would include the following:

(i) *Changing is a condition of organizations.* Just as learning is a fact of life to a

10 year old, change is a characteristic of organizations. Learning, defined simply as change in behaviour, is the raw process with which the teacher works. Organizational change, growth and development is the basic datum to the school administrator. Teachers seek to direct learning towards socially acceptable goals; this is called education. School principals seek to direct organizational growth towards educational goals; this is called administration.

(ii) *Change has directional quality.* Normally it is expected that growth is in some identifiable direction, and–in a living organism–is inevitable. It is very difficult to stunt a tree: the ming process takes much skill and patience. Human organizations, being man-made, are perhaps more vulnerable to stunting, decay, and death. Occasionally this is in line with overall direction of growth: committee-killing, once the committee has outlived its usefulness, permits other parts better growth.

(iii) *Normal change should imply progress.* Change which is in a direction away from an increase in value relative to goals is regarded as abnormal (c.f. "regression"). Whereas this is an essential part of the model it may not properly represent reality. This assumption causes the school administrator many an embarrassment when change does not bring progress. His attitude of disappointment generalizes to the staff, and the climate suffers, thereby adversely affecting future prospects of progress. Negative effects of some changes (e.g. population shifts, influx of inexperienced teachers) are normal and predictable.

(iv) *The basic energy is inherent potentiality.* Changers must assume a high degree of potentiality in the impetus towards development. A growth-centred attitude to organizational change will be one that, with Jeffrey, is

> . . . ready at all times to relax controls and to recognize that teachers generally are worthy of a greater measure of professional freedom and responsibility.[15]

Implications for Policy

By referring our two change strategies back to the studies on effecting change, it becomes possible to infer certain guidelines for administrative policy. When the desired change is judged to represent a *departure from* established organizational themes, a clinical strategy is indicated. When, however, the desired change is seen more as the *fulfilment of existing themes,* dictates of a growth strategy are more in order. Similar inferences may be drawn to bear upon executive selection and promotion policies in education. Appointment of the outsider, as distinct from promotion of the local, will more likely effect desired departure-change when the appointee utilizes clinical processes; fulfilment-change will be more effective when growth postulates guide the actions of the promotee.

Organizational Dynamics and the Cognitive Fallacy

By organizational dynamics one refers mostly to the inter-personal behaviours

[15] Jeffrey, G. B. (ed.) *External Examinations in Secondary Schools.* London. Harrap. 1958.

and small group processes that go on within a formal organization, like the school. Leadership, leader behaviours, climate and group mindedness are some examples. Research under each is plentiful, if somewhat less than helpful. Each term begs definition which, in turn, begs theory. Some research has aided definition at least, and from this may be drawn a practical inference or two. At present, however, a question far more pressing than "What is leadership or climate?" is "What *pay-off* will they bring?"

Looked at in educational terms, one typically seeks to answer the question with school marks, examination standings, standardized test results and the like. And one becomes trapped in what may be called "the cognitive fallacy" because there is absolutely no necessary logical reason for supposing good leader behaviour in and of itself to have a cognitive pay-off at the pupil level. The explanation lies in organizational, not educational terms. Good leadership, like other healthy organizational dynamics enhances the probability of, e.g. institutional policies being successfully implemented–*good* policies and *bad* policies alike. There is scarcely any organization that has no bad policies, no inept practices, no outmoded substantives. A school with top leadership, healthy climate, and open-minded teachers may be one in which the successful introduction of, let us say, a new method of teaching arithmetic, is facilitated. If the new method is good, leadership correlates with school marks; if the method is bad the leadership at that school is going to look negative when the statisticians are through with it.

The point is stressed because a large number of leadership, climate and openmindedness studies use a cognitive criterion. The administrator must be cautioned not to do likewise in practice. The cognitive outputs are the teachers' outputs; the organizational outputs are the administrator's. That the principal's effect on educational goals is only *mediated* through leadership and morale was clearly demonstrated in the National Principalship Study. In their report[16] of this nationwide project, the researchers first present a substantial-size correlation between leadership and pupil schoolwork, then demonstrate how the correlation shrinks step by step to zero as one organizational variable after another is partialled out (i.e. held constant). The principal does not try to take on the entire goal-structure of the organization but settles for these mediating processes as more proximate goals, those that are within both his grasp and his responsibility.

Organizational Climate

That every organization, once fully developed, has its own feeling-tone or atmosphere, or organizational climate, has been known for some time. Some interpersonally astute school inspectors could spot it the moment they entered the

[16]Gross, Neal and Robert E. Herriott. *Staff Leadership in Public Schools*. New York. Wiley. 1965. (Although the validity of the point referred to is established elsewhere, the study contains several weaknesses, as Donald A. Erickson points out in "Some Misgivings Concerning a Study of Leadership." *Educational Administration Quarterly*. 1, 3, Autumn 1965. pp. 52-60.)

staff room. Now that Halpin and Croft[17] have provided a way of measuring it, a whole new avenue of professional development has opened to school administrators. In Alberta, "Climate Clinics" sponsored by the administrator's association ran two years in a row, each time drawing over 165 principals interested in learning more about their schools' climates and what could be done about them. One overriding practical implication from such projects suggests that the main thing an officer of an organization can do about organizational climate is to study its climate. After that, specific practice suggests itself.

In his recent report on the state of the art, Halpin, following a review of the research, states "The blunt truth is that we do not yet know very much about how to change a climate."[18]

Stogdill, in his latest leadership research report entitled *Managers, Employees, Organizations*[19] clearly establishes morale and satisfaction as output (not input) variables along with productivity. This simply emphasizes the point that to organization theory the distinction between process and product is no longer useful. Further than that, however, one may enquire about the impact of various organizational dynamics upon the two output variables of morale and satisfaction. Just such an inquiry was made in the Alberta climate studies and reported by Andrews.[20] Not surprisingly, teachers in "open climate" schools, as distinct from schools with (reading down the scale) autonomous, controlled, familiar, paternal, or closed climates, expressed the greatest (a) teacher satisfaction, (b) confidence in their principal's effectiveness, and (c) confidence in the effectiveness of the school. The open climate is characterized by staff behaviours that are low on disengagement, low on hindrance, high on sprit, medium on intimacy; and by principal behaviours that are low on aloofness, low on production emphasis, high on thrust, and high on consideration.

Two Patterns of Leadership

A recent project involving the present author showed that administrative outputs are sensitive also to staff perceptions of a principal's leadership. Using the new edition of the Leader Behaviour Description Questionnaire Form 12[21] in the

[17]Halpin, Andrew W. and Don B. Croft. *The Organizational Climate of Schools*. Chicago. Midwest Administration Centre, University of Chicago. 1963.

[18]Halpin, Andrew W. "Change and Organizational Climate." *Ontario Journal of Educational Research*. 8, 3, Spring 1966. pp. 229-248. (See also *Journal of Educational Administration*. This issue.)

[19]Stogdill, Ralph M. *Managers, Employees, Organizations.* Columbus. Bureau of Business Research, Ohio State University. 1966. (A major study based partly upon the new LBDQ-12; see *Manual for Leader Behaviour Description Questionnaire Form* 12 by Stogdill, published 1963 by the Bureau.)

[20]Andrews, John H. M. "Some Validity Studies of the OCDQ." *Canadian Education and Research Digest*. 5, 4, December 1965. pp.317-34.

[21]*Ibid.*

largest reported study employing it in education to date[22], the project tested the staffs of 170 administrators, then brought the administrators together at a pair of seminars where personalized leadership analysis booklets were made available. In the research phase standardized school scores were obtained on each of the 12 dimensions of perceived leader behaviour covered by this instrument, namely Representation, Demand Reconciliation, Tolerance of Uncertainty, Persuasiveness, Initiation of Structure, Tolerance of Freedom, Role Assumption, Consideration, Production Emphasis, Predictive Accuracy, Integration, and Superior Orientation.

Inferences are difficult to draw from the LBDQ-12 if one fails to appreciate that a subscale score does not necessarily represent the principal himself but the average perception of him as held by his staff. Though this pooling of professional opinion may be accurate it does not extricate us from what Halpin[23] calls the "ubiquitous phenomenological box." (Halpin nicely illustrates the phenomenological dilemma with the anecdote of the indignant wife at the cocktail party chiding her husband, "Darling, don't you think you ought to stop drinking? Your face is already beginning to get blurred.") Users of LBDQ-12 assume that how a leader really behaves is less important than how the teachers *perceive* that he behaves; it is their perception of his behaviour–if anything–that influences their own actions and determines what we call leadership. And that is what one interprets from an LBDQ-12 subscale score.

To simplify matters, however, the twelve subscale distributions were submitted to factor analysis to discover the underlying dimensions of leadership. To our delight, two well-defined factors emerged, the first a set of leader behaviours that respond to the needs of the school *qua* system, the second a set of behaviours that respond to the needs of staff members *qua* person. They subsequently were named System and Person factors of leadership. From their intricate statistical combination, three distinct leadership styles may be identified. Leadership that is strongly System-oriented stresses Production Emphasis, Initiating Structure, Representation, Role Assumption and Persuasion, in that order. Person-oriented leadership stresses Tolerance of Freedom, Tolerance of Uncertainty, Consideration, and Demand Reconciliation. The Mixed pattern of leadership stresses Integration, Predictive Accuracy, and Superior Orientation.

Original subscale scores as well as derived factor scores were checked against administrative outputs in terms of teacher satisfaction, teacher confidence in principal, and teacher confidence in the school's effectiveness. These outputs were clearly found to be sensitive to teachers' perceptions of leadership. What is even more interesting, it turns out that a principal *can* make up for weakness on System-leadership with strength on Person-leadership, and *vice versa.* Strength on both, while certainly desirable and once thought to be the *sine qua non* of leadership, is simply an impossible goal for many mortals. School staffs accept this and express satisfaction and confidence in leadership situations strong on either.

[22]Brown, Alan F. "Reactions to Leadership." *Educational Administration Quarterly.* 3, 1, Winter 1967. pp. 62-73.

[23]Halpin. A. W. *op. cit.*

Weakness on both, or weakness on one without sufficient strength on the other, appears to be a sure prescription for unhealthy organizational dynamics.

To Effect Change in Organizational Dynamics

Admitting that three administrative outputs are sensitive to organizational dynamics, an administrator who wishes to work on them has several alternatives.

1. *Thicken the mix.* One way is to thicken the organizational "mix," to give dynamics more chance to operate, to create situations where climate and leadership can become visible, be scrutinized and flourish. This means heightening the free communication within one's own staff, and possibly across the other staffs through cooperative projects.

Although one does this partly through day to day interaction it requires some deliberate planning, some vehicles. Two such vehicles are the committee-structure of school organization, and team-teaching patterns of instructional organization.

Both allow for what an organization requires. The committee system in particular (and perhaps team teaching is just one example of the general case) reveals the health of the organization in no uncertain terms. As Chris Argyris[24] has pointed out, despite his previously cited research[25] showing some effects of existing organizations upon healthy individuals, a healthy organization is one in which the individual finds his own self-fulfilment.

Developing a committee structure facilitates internal communication by providing for the feedback processes vital to an awareness of the state of the system at any given time. Communication networks, loops, and meshes emerge naturally when the opportunity is established. An added value to the committee-system lies in its capacity to reveal certain symptoms of organizational pathologies. Some of these symptoms are revealed when committees shift their purpose or function. Some examples of committee-shift: an advisory committee becomes an administrative committee (perhaps to take over a weak administration); an advisory committee becomes a disseminative committee (internal public relations for a too-strong administration); a fact-finding or special problems committee becomes a policy or advisory committee; an *ad hoc* committee becomes a standing committee. These are particular instances of the more general case of goal-shift amid change.

2. *Sharpen your own perception.* It is difficult to do much about organizational dynamics wearing blinkers on one's own interpersonal perception. Using a semi-projective instrument developed earlier, it was possible to show[26] how even the most successful school principals will project their own style of leadership into their perceptions of individual staff members. The effective-rated teacher to the system-centred principal is quite different from the effective-rated teacher perceived by the individual-centred principal. Professional development activities

[24] Argyris, Chris. *Integrating the Individual and the Organization*. New York. Wiley. 1964.

[25] Argyris, Chris. "The Individual and the Organization: An Empirical Test." *op. cit.*

[26] Brown, Alan F. "A Perceptual Taxonomy of the Effective-Rated Teacher." *The Journal of Experimental Education.* 35, 1, Fall 1966, pp. 1-10.

for principals are beginning to take the refining of interpersonal perception as a promising conference activity.

3. *Don't bother with the statics.* It is well known that there are administrators who seem to need the support of some static condition affecting the organization, like school bus schedules, sparse population, old building, or dense population, to account for the leadership mess in their schools. They believe their problems to be not only unique, but to be unique because of the special combination of organizational statics under which they labour. In the leadership project cited above[27] data were secured on eight such props (size and type of school; social class of neighbourhood; staff age, sex, training, experience and longevity at that school) and none of them, together or in combination, bore weight. Combined elementary-secondary schools, as an exception, do suffer an organizational disadvantage—a finding confirmed by Andrews[28] with respect to climate. To improve organizational output by working on the dynamics, therefore, is not likely to be achieved by tinkering with the statics.

The Authority Structure of the School: System of Social Exchange

James G. Anderson

In this paper the bureaucratic authority structure of the school is viewed as consisting of an asymmetric system of role relationships with teachers' obligations and institutional expectations considered as an exchange system. It is suggested that the decision concerning how much authority to invest in teachers depends upon expectations of a return of the investment and an assessment of the risk involved. There appears to be a withdrawal of authority invested in teachers due to the perceived risk involved resulting in an abandonment of their professional orientation and a tendency to adopt a more rewarding bureaucratic orientation toward the schools. Since school administrators invest little authority in their instructional staff, teachers in turn have little authority to invest in students. Consequently, the school fails to draw upon the powerful societal norms of the adolescent subculture to reinforce achievement of the school's goals.

[27] Brown, Alan F. "Reactions to Leadership." *op. cit.*
[28] Andrews, John H. M. *op. cit.*

Organizational Authority as a System of Social Exchange

Formal organizations arise in order to coordinate the efforts of individuals in the pursuit of a common goal. Such coordination implies central direction of organizational activities. Power—the ability to influence the behavior of members of the organization in accordance with the wishes of a leader or administrative staff—makes such collective effort possible.[1]

Max Weber suggests that the legitimacy of such power must be recognized by the society in which the organization functions if officials of an organization are to perform their duties.[2] According to him, such legitimation of authority may be accomplished in one of three ways. First, it may be based upon a charismatic leader with extraordinary powers.[3] A body of disciples, assigned specific duties by him carries out his directives. Second, authority may be traditional, based on a body of customs handed down from generation to generation. The leader and his staff achieve a certain status in this instance by virtue of these traditions.[4] Third, it may be based on a body of general rules that delineate and circumscribe the behavior of members of the organization. Weber terms this final form of authority "legal-rational."[5]

Chester I. Barnard defines authority within formal organizations as that character of an order which causes it to be accepted by a member of the organization as a determinant of his behavior. The two essential features are the acceptance of the order by the subordinate and the character of the order making it acceptable to him. For Barnard, acceptance of the authority by the individual is essential and is dependent upon an exchange system. The organization offers certain inducements for an individual's contributions to the organization. It can maintain authority over members only so long as this balance is favorable for the individuals participating. Consequently, much of the administrative effort must be directed at maintaining a favorable balance of inducements for the individual so that he will accept the authority of the organization and provide the necessary contributions.

Additionally, Barnard equates the "system of communication" within the organization with the institution's "lines of authority." This system functions to provide information to positions of authority within the organization so that orders may be issued. Maintenance of an attitude conducive to acceptance of orders by

[1] Kenneth D. Benne, *A Conception of Authority* ("Contributions to Education," No. 895; New York: Teachers College, Columbia University, 1943), pp. 2, 39. Herbert Goldhammer and Edward A. Shils, "Types of Power and Status," *American Journal of Sociology*, XLV (September, 1939), 171-178.

[2] For an excellent discussion of Weber's concept of institutionalized authority see the introduction to A. M. Henderson and Talcott Parsons (eds.), *Max Weber: The Theory of Social and Economic Organization* (New York: Oxford University Press, 1947), pp. 56-77.

[3] *Ibid.*, pp. 358-373. Also see H. H. Gerth and Wright Mills (eds.), *From Max Weber: Essays in Sociology* (New York: Oxford University Press, 1958), pp. 245-252.

[4] A. M. Henderson and Talcott Parsons, *op. cit.*, pp. 341-358.

[5] *Ibid.*, pp. 329-341. Also H. H. Gerth and C. Wright Mills, *op. cit.*, pp. 196-244.

subordinates requires a careful structuring of the lines of communication from higher positions to lower ones.[6]

This notion of viewing a member's participation within an organization in terms of an exchange between the individual and the organization has been further developed by James S. Coleman.[7] He suggests that, in formal organizations, role expectations and role obligations constitute an exchange system based on a deferred payment plan. The structure is built around expectations and obligations for each individual occupying a position in the organization. Although such a set exists between each pair of role partners within the organization, direct reciprocity between the two is not necessary, and payment of obligations may occur over an extended period of time. Formal organizations consist of series of these asymmetric role relationships, which are then balanced by the organization itself. The institution guarantees that the role expectations of members will be met. It supplements those intrinsic rewards received by the individual from his interpersonal relations with the organizational members with whom he has role relations and with clients that the organization serves with extrinsic institutional rewards.

An example from the schools is the role relationship between a teacher and a student. From a student's (and his parent's) standpoint, expectations include qualified instruction, citizenship training, character formation, safety while under the auspices of the school, extracurricular opportunities, educational certificates, etc. His corresponding obligations are regular attendance, proper behavior, minimal effort, etc.

The teacher expects remuneration, status, security, and administrative support, in addition to enforcement of those obligations already specified for the student. His obligations include meeting to the best of his ability those expectations held by the student and his parents in addition to other purely institutional obligations and duties, such as continued professional development, discipline and control of students, compiling records and reports, sponsoring student activities, etc.

Both the teacher and the student look to the organization to balance this exchange and to enforce obligations. The school as an institution provides the teacher with remuneration and status, ensures attendance and acceptable behavior on the part of the student, and guarantees competence on the part of the teacher and an acceptable educational program. The organization also satisfies those expectations of the student and those of the teacher which are not intrinsic to their role relationship such as social intercourse and collegiality.

Not only does an exchange relation develop between members of the organization and its clients (in the case of the school, teachers and students) but several systems of exchange also develop within the institution. At first, as Barnard has suggested, an individual member submits to the authority of the organization in exchange for the rewards that organizational membership offers. But once he is established as a

[6]Chester I. Barnard, *The Functions of the Executive* (Cambridge, Mass.: Harvard University Press, 1954), pp. 161-184.

[7]James S. Coleman, "Systems of Social Exchange" (Johns Hopkins University, Baltimore, Md., February, 1963), pp. 20-21. (Mimeographed.)

member of the organization, the individual begins to submit to managerial authority because of emerging social norms that evoke social disapproval of opposition. In short, he exchanges compliance with institutional authority for the approval of his peers, as Blau points out.[8]

Such a pattern emerges because of the distinctive feature of institutionalized authority that causes it to be enforced not only by superiors but by individual members of the organization. For, although voluntary, social constraints make compliance imperative for the individual and preclude departure from accepted norms, rules, and directives. These social constraints arise as a result of a second form of exchange: that of the group to which the individual belongs which exchanges compliance with orders for a share of the rewards that the organization offers for such compliance and for group contributions. If these rewards exceed what is considered as a "fair exchange" for the cost of compliance and contributions, the collective approval of this exercise of control over the group's actions legitimates it.[9]

Thus, the collective obligations incurred for these rewards resulting from managerial actions and group approval of the exchange of compliance and services for them, creates group pressures that enforce compliance with institutional authority. To a large extent such social sanctions obviate the necessity for organizational sanctions.[10]

Moreover, coordination of group activities often involves social credit.[11] Employees are willing to comply with administrative demands in excess of their obligations with the expectation of a reward at some later date. If the administration is effective in securing greater rewards for them that would not have been obtained otherwise, this success buttresses superior claims to greater compliance in the future. In effect, it establishes credit which can be called upon at will.

Notwithstanding the exchange processes already described, Coleman has identified a third one that takes place within organizations: that of delegation of authority. It is this model that will be dealt with at some length.

Weber in characterizing a bureaucracy describes an incumbent of a particular office as limited to a sphere of competence with clearly defined jurisdiction. This requires a detailed specification of the responsibility for accomplishing some institutional subgoal for each position within the organization. However, concomitantly the organization must provide each incumbent with the requisite means to carry out this responsibility by providing him with the necessary authority and means of compulsion as well as with norms governing their use.

If we now look at this as an investment of authority by the organization in subordinates, we can analyze authority within an organization as investments in

[8]Peter M. Blau, *Exchange and Power in Social Life* (New York: John Wiley & Sons, Inc., 1964), p. 200.

[9]*Ibid.*, p. 207.

[10]*Ibid.*, pp. 208-209.

[11]*Ibid.*, p. 135; George C. Homans, *Social Behavior: Its Elementary Forms* (New York: Harcourt, Brace & World, 1961), pp. 297-299.

roles or offices as means for the accomplishment of the institutional goals. Responsibility or obligations then are the required return on the investment.[12] Since the incumbent may occupy the office for an extended period of time, a continued return on the investment is required. At the same time there is a continuing delegation or investment of authority in him.

The amount of authority invested, the expected return on the investment, and the time required for return on investment will vary within and between organizations. Consequently, it is possible to differentiate between organizations and between offices within an organization on this basis. One may ask on what basis does an organization invest authority in members at different levels of the hierarchy? Also how does it know how much authority to invest at each level? What is a sound investment? In all organizations these decisions are made and authority relations are prescribed for each office. In order to answer these questions we must focus attention on the investment decision itself.

The Investment Decision

Gain

In any organization authority may be centralized in key positions and little authority invested in subordinates at lower levels. This tendency to restrict investments appears to arise out of the organization's need to guarantee responsible action, to coordinate the performance of participants so that they will contribute to the accomplishement of the overall goals of the organization, and to utilize expert opinion in making decisions.

On the other hand, there is a countervailing tendency toward decentralization of authority and investment in subordinates. This seems to arise from the fact that much of the information relevant to decision making within the organization originates at the lower levels where the goal activities are carried on. Also, separation of decision making from these primary activities of an organization is time consuming, costly, and sometimes dysfunctional. Finally, there is utilization of the experience of participants, greater motivation and commitment, flexibility, and utilization of the experience of particpants, greater motivation and commitment, flexibility, and reinforcement of the organizational goals by the individuals involved.[13]

If an investment of authority is made, it may in turn by reinvested by the recipient. For example, if a broad investment of authority is made in a teacher, he can in turn invest it in his students. In this investment there is both the possibility of greater gain and of greater loss.

One of the examples that Coleman discusses is one in which the teacher reinvests authority in his students.[14] If the investment is made in such a way as to utilize the

[12]Coleman, *op. cit.*, pp. 22-23.
[13]Herbert A. Simon, *Administrative Behavior* (New York: Macmillan Co., 1947), p. 157.
[14]Coleman, *op. cit.*, pp. 24-26.

social organization of the classroom, the goals of the teacher will be reinforced and the teacher gains authority through the investment.

The same thing is true of the organization's investment of authority in the teacher. If a broad investment is made, the organization may gain from the reinforcement of the institution's goals by drawing upon the teacher's experience, knowledge, and initiative. Also the teacher may reinvest this authority in his students with the possibility of an additional gain for the school. Nevertheless, as in all investments, the possibility of loss is greater also. If the teacher is incompetent or if the students usurp the teacher's prerogatives, the school may lose through the investment.

The period of time between the investment of authority and the review of a subordinate's performance (this can be thought of as the requirement for an accounting or a return on the investment) is an indication of how much authority is invested or the level of his responsibility in the organization.[15] Lower participants are likely to have their performance evaluated quite often (a relatively short-term investment of authority) while a person occupying a more responsible position in the organizational hierarchy may only have his performance evaluated once a year (a much longer term investment).

In the schools this measures is quite valid in that new probationary teachers are subject to frequent observation and supervision by subject-matter specialists, department chairmen, and principals; but once a teacher has achieved tenure, he may be subject to supervision as little as once a year. The awarding of tenure and the autonomy accorded these teachers are indicative of a long-term investment of authority. Furthermore, reinvestment will occur from time to time. If the expected rate of return on the investment is met over a period of time, there is the likelihood that morc authority will be invested with the expectation of greater gain. Again this can be illustrated in those cases where a teacher is very successful and manages to attract the attention of his superiors. Over a period of time he may be permitted to teach brighter classes and may be given a great deal more latitude in subject-matter emphasis, text selection, and methods of instruction than the average teacher. However, those teachers who do not provide an adequate return on the investment may experience a withdrawal of authority over the same period of time as evidenced by closer supervision, a more rigid prescription of subject matter and teaching methods, etc.

In the case of the school these considerations appear to obtain. Since teaching is carried out by the lowest participants of the organization and is of an esoteric nature, a certain degree of authority must be delegated if the goals of the organization are to be met. The amount of authority delegated will depend upon expectations of gain for the organization resulting from the investment.

Let us examine the investment decision for a particular case, that of the secondary school teacher in the public schools. The administrator's decision concerning the scope of the investment in teachers is first a function of the

[15] Elliott Jaques, *Measurement of Responsibility* (London: Tavistock Publications, 1956), pp. 32-42.

anticipated gain from such an investment. In appraising potential gain, the first consideration is that of the competence of teachers in performing their tasks. Such an appraisal is complicated by the failure to date to devise generally acceptable measures of teaching effectiveness or to measure a particular teacher's influence on a group of students.[16] It is further compounded with vague esoteric goals such as character formation, problem solving ability, intellectual curiosity and a general lack of evaluative information concerning the efficacy of various teaching methods and curricula.

As a result, the administration limits its investment in teachers and instead relies on centralization of authority. Through rules it structures the action of teachers and relationships between them and other participants within the organization. Since the determining factor in accomplishment of the goals of the school is the contact between students and teachers in the institutional framework of the school, the main control that the organization has over the action of teachers in the accomplishment of the school's goals is the enforcement of rules concerning teacher behavior. Thus, the administrator can measure teacher compliance with these norms rather than teacher effectiveness since, unfortunately, for many administrators the two are synonymous.

In short, the decision in this case to limit the scope of the investment in teachers seems to be, to a great extent, a result of this inability to measure the gain that might be realized by making such an investment.

A second consideration in anticipating gain from an investment is an estimation of the commitment of the participants to the pursuit of the organization's goals. In this case we are dealing with the perception of motivation by the administration. This problem arises especially in large cities where teaching positions are not as desirable as in suburban areas or in private schools. Here the problem of producing some measurable change in the child's skill or knowledge, the problems of maintaining order and control, and the problem of morally accepting unaccustomed behavior of students make these positions undesirable. As a result, administrators perceive a lack of motivation on the part of teachers. This observation is reinforced by the large number of requests for transfers and the difficulty in recruiting qualified teachers to fill vacant positions.[17]

Since the administration is not assured that its interests will be preserved in delegating authority, the decision appears to be to restrict the investment in teachers. As before, authority is centralized with the development of a body of rules and procedures in order to prescribe behavior for teachers. One function of these rules is directional. They operate as guidelines for behavior so that an

[16] For two good summaries of attempts to measure teaching effectiveness see A. S. Barr *et al.*, *Wisconsin Studies of the Measurement and Prediction of Teacher Effectiveness* (Madison, Wis.: Dembar Publishing Co., 1961) and Dwight E. Beecher, *The Evaluation of Teaching: Backgrounds and Concepts* (Syracuse, N.Y.: Syracuse University Press, 1949).

[17] For a good discussion of the effect that these three problems have on teachers' career patterns see Howard S. Becker, "The Career of the Chicago Public School Teacher," *American Journal of Sociology*, LVII (March, 1952), 470-477.

individual can participate as a member of the organization.[18] In order to orient the contributions of members toward the fulfillment of organizational goals, obligations are specified and authority is delineated. Rules, then, communicate the expectations of the administration to those administered.

Rules may also be used to expand or contract the authority invested in teachers through several functions that they serve within organizations. First, they can legitimate the use of punishment by warning teachers of the probable consequence of improper behavior.[19] For example, the punishment for not submitting grades and attendance records at the close of the year may be the withholding of a teacher's pay check. Resorting to warnings of punishment to achieve proper behavior in a sense represents a withdrawal of investment in teachers. Instead the institution resorts to coercion, since one might say that no real alternative remains other than the prescribed one if punishment is to be averted.

However, an administrator may expand the investment in teachers by intentionally failing to enforce such rules prescribing punishment.[20] By refraining from exercising his legitimate power he creates an obligation on the part of the teacher, if you will, a social credit which can be called upon sometime in the future.[21] For example, a principal may choose not to enforce rules concerning signing in and out of school in return for acceptance of extracurricular assignments that require a great deal of time before and after school hours. This phenomenon may be considered as a periodic short-term investment by administrators in teachers. In this case the investment is limited and variable, the return is specific, and the period of investment is short.

Finally, in education there is one other factor that limits the realization of anticipated gain from an investment of authority in teachers, that is, the imbalance between authority and expected gain. There is usually an underinvestment of authority in the teacher at the same time that there is an overexpectation of gain. This occurs because the teacher's responsibility almost invariably exceeds his authority. Although he is responsible for demonstrating the progress of his students, he has little or no authority to control the environmental factors (social, political, and economic) that operate in and on the school and that have a decided bearing on the progress of students and affect the realization of the teacher's goals. Moreover, he has little choice of curricula or textbooks, has nothing to do with

[18] For an extended discussion of the role played by rules in formal organizations see James G. Anderson, "Bureaucratic Rules: Bearers of Organizational Authority," *Educational Administration Quarterly*, II (Winter, 1966), 7-34. Also for what he calls the "explicational" function of rules see Alvin W. Gouldner, *Patterns of Industrial Bureaucracy* (New York: Free Press, 1954), pp. 162-164.

[19] See Anderson, *op. cit.*, p. 22 and Gouldner, *op. cit.*, p. 170, for discussions of the "punishment legitimating" function of rules.

[20] This function of rules is termed the "bargaining function" by Anderson, *op. cit.*, pp. 22-23 and the "leeway function" by Gouldner, *op. cit.*, pp. 172-174.

[21] Blau, *op. cit.*, p. 206, notes that a superior may extend his control by refraining from exercising his formal power. Using this strategy, the superior exchanges some of his power for greater voluntary control over subordinates who are then obligated to him.

assignment to ability groups, can do little more than suggest that a child may need psychiatric counseling, and does not have the authority to curb severe behavioral problems by suspension or expulsion.

For example, a teacher assigned a basic class consisting of emotionally disturbed children, low-ability students, and discipline cases has no authority to control the innumerable variables that seriously affect the progress of these children, yet is responsible for each child's progress.

Risk

The decision concerning how much authority is to be invested also depends upon the risk involved for the institution. In evaluating risk for an investment one must assess the anticipated gain and weigh it against the possible loss. This estimation of risk then will affect the terms under which authority is invested, the amount invested, the anticipated return on the investment, and the period of investment. Homans has suggested that an individual, a group, or an organization will only act when the probability of realizing the anticipated gain from such an action exceeds that of the possible loss.[22] As a result, to a large extent, the investment decision will depend upon the range of consequences of actions taken by different members of the organization. Since actions of a particular participant in the institution may affect persons at higher and at lower levels of the hierarchy, when this range is wide, the higher levels of the organization must be assured that subordinates will behave in a manner so as to preserve their interests. This assurance may be occasioned by a coincidence of interests for the two levels. Or it may be assured by the technical competence and high commitment of those to whom authority is delegated. Nevertheless, in order to accomplish the goals of the organization, some authority must be delegated to the lower levels. If the possible loss to the organization is high, the institution may not choose to take the risk involved in a broad investment of authority in participants. In those areas where actions may have adverse affects for the institution, rules and procedural specification may be used to limit the scope of an individual's jurisdiction. If we again turn to the example of the school teachers, we may examine this factor in analyzing the investment of authority in teachers.

One of the reasons that an extensive investment of authority in teachers is considered to involve a high risk is the public belief in the critical nature of education. In our society the belief that students can be permanently influenced during the formative years of adolescence is prevalent. This is certainly evidenced by the repeated censorship of texts, criticism of social studies curricula, accusations of subversion among school teachers, etc. Due to this public concern and their idealistic expectations for the school, such as teaching citizenship, character formation, and group participation, there is the feeling among administrators that investing authority in teachers and allowing them to use their own judgment in educational matters involves a high risk, with a poor investment resulting in

[22] Homans, *op. cit.*

permanent damage to the student and in adverse criticism from society. Since students at this age are generally not considered mature enough to make individual value choices, an effort is made to insulate them from anything which is controversial or which requires an ethical choice. As a result, little authority is invested in teachers and many of their functions are specified, especially in social studies.

Moreover, the public may communicate its view of education through lay boards of education and state legislatures, thus directly affecting school program and policies. Notwithstanding these channels, parents whose child has been severely disciplined or injured or who strongly object to school policies may seek redress through the courts and may put pressure on school administrators through the newspaper, the PTA, as well as through organized interest groups.

Since the range of consequences of individual actions is great in this instance, affecting all levels of the public educational system, the necessity for restricting the authority of teachers appears evident, at least to most school administrators.

There may be another factor in the reluctance of school administrators to invest authority in teachers, due to the necessity for legitimating administrative authority. This reluctance may be motivated by the instability of the authority relationship between teachers and administrators. Instability is manifested in the functional supervision of teachers who are accountable both to subject-matter specialists and to the principal at the secondary level. Since the principal does not feel competent to judge the technical aspects of the teacher's performance, this job is relegated to specialists and curriculum coordinators.

Also, the formation of teacher organizations, such as unions, as countervailing forces to the administration and the reluctance of such organizations to admit school administrators suggests a further conflict between teachers and school administrators.[23]

Teachers identify school administrators with the bureaucratic structure of the schools, with its centralization of authority and tight prescription of behavior. Realizing their limited ability as individuals to affect changes in personnel policies, salary schedules, instructional procedures, etc., teachers are turning increasingly to group action. Through such action they attempt to modify the conditions under which they work as evidenced by the militancy of growing teacher unions.[24]

One might reasonably expect that this insecurity in the authority relationship between administrators and teachers (essentially a conflict between bureaucratic authority and professional autonomy) would result in a reluctance to invest authority in teachers.[25] Since there is some evidence that the interests of the higher

[23] For a good discussion of the emergence of informal groups in organizations see Philip Selznick, "An Approach to a Theory of Bureaucracy," *American Sociological Review*, VIII (February, 1943), 47-54.

[24] See Robert Dubin, "Decision Making by Management in Industrial Relations," *American Journal of Sociology*, LIV (January, 1949), 292-297.

[25] For a good brief discussion of this conflict in authority see Chandler Washburne, "The Teacher in the Authority System," *Journal of Educational Sociology*, XXX (May, 1957), 390-394.

levels of educational institutions are not coincident with those of teachers, especially in matters such as collective bargaining, there is a great deal of reluctance to invest authority. As a result, authority is centralized at the higher levels of the organization and teachers are viewed merely as employees of the school system, hired to carry out a prescribed job, and not as professionally responsible members of a profession.

Cosigners for the Investment

Another factor in the estimation of risk is the existence of cosigners who will offer collateral security for the investment. In the absence of permanent ties or a multiplicity of ties between the organization and the individual, collateral becomes the basis for security for investments. If we consider collateral in an intangible sense, educational institutions and professional associations through certification and licensing may be considered as cosigners for the investment of authority in an individual. When a bad investment is made, the cosigner may or may not be able to rectify the loss.

A profession traditionally renders a public service in return for which the public gives the profession a mandate to control admission and expulsion from the profession. This self-regulation presupposes that members acquire a certain expertise that can only be judged by their colleagues. It is then the profession's responsibility to prescribe and proscribe actions in accordance with a professional code of ethics. The profession rewards its members for the services they render to the public, which better enables clients to contribute to the community, which in turn awards the profession its mandate and status.[26]

To be admitted to a profession, an individual must heavily invest his resources in order to gain the necessary expertise and credentials (usually educational certificates and a professional license). Those individuals selected for admission, then, are strongly committed to the profession, in many cases irrevocably. Such a commitment impedes mobility and gives the professional association a great deal of power over its members due to their fear of sanctions or ultimate expulsion with the attendant loss of the resources that the individual has invested in gaining entry (money, time, effort, ego, etc.).[27]

Consequently, we may look at the reluctance of school systems to invest authority in teachers as a problem of professional autonomy. In general, professional autonomy pertains to a wide variety of decisions concerning conduct of members which are left to the discretion of the professional group. In delegating authority, the recipient of the authority is allowed to use his discretion since his training and experience allow him to make a more expert decision than the person delegating the authority. Therefore, professional autonomy means the latitude allowed the practitioner due to his expert skill and knowledge.

[26] For this observation see Blau, *op. cit.*, pp. 262-263.
[27] *Ibid.*, p. 161.

In most professions, the professional association and the educational institutions that offer the professional training act as cosigners for the investment of authority in an individual. Since they traditionally control entry into, and expulsion from, the profession, they provide some security for an investment of authority in an individual. This is due to the selective process and requirements for admission to the profession as well as the power of the association in sanctioning members who do not fulfill their obligations to a particular institution. Also, in the major professions the association controls the accreditation of schools which train practitioners for the profession. Consequently, they too provide security for an investment of authority in individuals by a particular organization.[28]

However, in education the lack of similar cosigners to provide security for investment in teachers is a decided limiting factor. Since there is widespread disagreement as to the role of the teacher, it is difficult to define what his expert professional functions comprise.

Furthermore, education, unlike other professions, generally does not control entry and expulsion through a board of practitioners of the profession. Rather state certification boards, usually state boards of education, are composed primarily of laymen in all but a few states and teachers possess a very limited representation on such boards. In this respect education even differs from other occupational groups such as barbers, beauticians, and architects where state licensing boards are composed entirely of practitioners.[29] Also unlike education, appointments to these boards are typically made by the professional association or from a list submitted by the association. This lack of professional representation on licensing boards for teachers is partially the result of laws in a number of states expressly prohibiting educators from serving on such boards.[30] Such policies have been defended repeatedly as necessary in order to preserve local control over the schools and to keep them responsive to the community.

A further limitation on the professional mandate accorded education by the public is the lay control over certification or licensing requirements, again a practice that differentiates education from the other professions. Teacher training institutions usually offer programs that satisfy minimal state certification requirements established both by the state legislature and by the state board of education. This arrangement attenuates local pressures and further weakens the professional associations' ability to guarantee expertise and competence.

After completing his study of teacher training programs in seventy-seven institutions in sixteen states, James Bryant Conant concluded that:

[28]For an excellent discussion of the problem of professional autonomy, certification, and accreditation see Myron Lieberman, *Education as a Profession* (Englewood Cliffs, N.J.: Prentice Hall, Inc., 1956), pp. 87-184.

[29]Lieberman (*Ibid.*, pp. 93-95) has reproduced several tables from *Occupational Licensing in the States* (Chicago: Council of State Governments 1952), pp. 84-87 to illustrate this point.

[30]Data contained in: U. S. Office of Education, Federal Security Agency, *State Boards of Education and Chief State School Officers* (Washington, D.C.: Government Printing Office, 1951), pp. 17-18, indicate that in 1951 ten states expressly prohibited professional educators from serving on state boards of education.

> The policy of certification based on the completion of state-specified course requirements is bankrupt; of this I am convinced. Unfortunately, the newer approved-program approach, which is intended to afford increased flexibility and freedom, involves the state department to such a degree that the dominant public school forces can use it to impose their own orthodoxy as easily as they used the older system. The specific course requirements and the approved-program approach as it is now developing have critical defects in common; they cannot be enforced in such a manner that the public can be assured of competent teachers, and they involve the states in acrimonious and continuous political struggles, which may not serve the public interest.[31]

Again, contrast this arrangement for licensing with that of other professions that license only after passage of a rigorous examination at the end of a lengthy formal education.[32]

Moreover, requirements for entry into the profession are appallingly low. Many states require in effect, less than a good baccalaureate program in the liberal arts (if the student majors in education at the undergraduate level) and little that the public considers as specialized professional training. To make matters worse, certification requirements are not rigidly enforced. On the pretense of filling shortages in instructional staffs, many local school districts easily circumvent state requirements by requesting "emergency" or "temporary" certificates.

Such diversity in the licensing requirements, minimal academic requirements, and the variety of certificates awarded in education drastically impede the mobility of teachers and give little assurance of the competency of teachers licensed in various states.

Finally, lack of professional control over the accreditation of professional training programs further reduces confidence in the educational profession in regards to certifying teacher competence.[33] Generally, there are three different means of accrediting professional schools: through a board of practitioners under the auspices of the professional association, through an agency created by the professional schools themselves, and through a council composed of representatives of both the association and the schools.[34] The stronger professions such as medicine, law, chemistry, and public health resort to the first means of guaranteeing quality in professional training.

Business administration, music and nursing employ the second means; while engineering, dentistry, and pharmacy utilize the third.

Along with state and regional accreditation, departments and schools of education and their programs are evaluated by a joint council known as the National Council for the Accreditation of Teacher Education (NCATE). However, the disproportionate representation on the council of members from the very

[31] James Bryant Conant, *The Education of American Teachers* (New York: McGraw Hill, 1964), pp. 54-55.

[32] See Lieberman, *op. cit.*, pp. 124-156 for a good discussion of the results of this practice.

[33] *Ibid.*, pp. 157-184.

[34] T. M. Stinnett, "Accreditation and the Professionalization of Teaching," *Journal of Teacher Education*, III (March, 1952), 30-39.

institutions being accredited (appointed by the American Association of Colleges for Teacher Education) and state school officials who are responsible for the establishment and operation of teacher education programs (appointed by the Council of Chief State School Officers, the National Association of State Directors of Teacher Education and Certification, and the National Commission on Teacher Education and Professional Standards), makes the adoption of rigorous criteria for accreditation inconceivable, since to do so would prevent many states from fulfilling their insatiable demand for additional teachers.

With little direct control over certification requirements and licensing, except through the lobbying of public school organizations, and with a professional accreditation agency primarily composed of persons who are directly involved in establishing or administering teacher education programs, the teaching profession has been unable to regulate the teacher education institutions upon which it relies for the professional training of practitioners. This has resulted in the admission to the profession of teachers with questionable training and competence.[35] Since the teaching profession cannot guarantee the competence of its members, there is, in effect, no reliable cosigner to substantiate the judgment of supervisors or administrators in evaluating the capabilities of teachers and differentially investing authority in them. Consequently, authority, due to the lack of security for an investment, is parcelled out sparingly and there is no general broad investment in practitioners as there is in other callings such as medicine and law that rely heavily on professional norms to curb abuses of professional autonomy and guarantee professional responsibility as the return on the investment.

Investment and Risk in the Schools: A Summary

From the preceding discussion it would appear that Coleman's investment model for authority in organizations focuses attention on the essential factor in institutional authority relations, the investment decision. An insight into the functioning of the organization is gained by asking such questions as: On what basis does an organization invest authority in members? How much authority does it invest at each level? What does the organization consider as the criteria for a sound investment? One can then differentiate between organizations and between different levels within an organization on the basis of the terms of the authority investment, such as its magnitude, the required return, and the time allowed for the return.

[35]The study entitled *Secondary School Science Characteristics and Service Loads* (Washington, D.C.: U. S. Government Printing Office, NSF 63-10, 1961) conducted by the National Association of State Directors of Teacher Education and Certification and the American Association for the Advancement of Science for the National Science Foundation estimates that almost half of the biology classes are taught by teachers who have completed less than thirty semester hours in their field. The percentages for mathematics in grades 9-12 and mathematics, general science and physics in grades 7-8 are much lower. Here it is estimated that twenty-three percent of the physics teachers and thirty-four percent of the math teachers have completed less than nine semester hours in their fields.

In examining the role of the school teacher in relation to this model, a number of factors militating against and limiting the investment of authority were identified. Limiting the expected gain from the investment are the inability to measure performance and results, the distrust of teachers' motivation, the use of coercive measures, variability of investment, and the imbalance between authority and expected return. Contributing to the possibility of loss are the public's view of the critical nature of education, the wide range of consequences of actions of teachers, the instability of the authority relationship between teachers and administrators, the formation of informal teachers' groups as countervailing forces within the organization, and the absence of reliable cosigners (professional associations) for the investment.

The result appears to be a withdrawal of authority invested in teachers due to the perceived risk involved. Increasingly teachers are part of a bureaucratic organization in which their conduct is circumscribed by rules. The result is two conflicting sources of authority—professional and bureaucratic.[36]

The knowledge, skills, and norms acquired through extensive professional training ideally permit the vesting of authority in individual practitioners rather than in a centralized authority communicated through a hierarchical structure. Self-determination and self-responsibility are the norms, with each practitioner exercising a great deal of autonomy in the performance of his professional speciality.[37]

However, in the schools these professional expectations of teachers receive little support. State boards of education and local school boards do not look to the teacher's professional association in licensing, recruiting, and promoting teachers. The teacher is rather an employee of the board of education whose welfare depends upon conformance to the bureaucratic authority exercised by the school administrators.

The overwhelming danger is that many teachers whose professional expectations are frustrated abandon them, accepting instead a more rewarding bureaucratic orientation characterized by apathy, a rigid legalistic adherence to rules and regulations, an impersonal attitude toward students, and an "upward-looking posture" that looks to school administrators for cues before decisions are made. These unprofessional attitudes, although decried by school administrators, school boards, and the public, are unanticipated results of bureaucratically structured school systems that inadvertently foster and reward such behavior.[38]

[36]Washburne, *op. cit.*, pp. 390-394.

[37]For two good discussions of how the typical bureaucratic structure of an organization is altered when authority is decentralized and professionalization of participants is relied upon see Arthur L. Stinchcombe, "Bureaucratic and Craft Administration of Production: A Comparative Study," *Administrative Science Quarterly*, IV (September, 1959), 168-187, and Amitai Etzioni, "Authority Structure and Organizational Effectiveness," *Administrative Science Quarterly*, IV (June, 1959), 43-67.

[38]See Anderson, *op. cit.*, for an exploration of the dysfunctional consequences of bureaucratically structuring educational systems. For an empirical examination of this problem see James G. Anderson, "Applicability of the Bureaucratic Model to the Organizational Structure of the School," U. S. Office of Education, Cooperative Research Project, S-043, 1964.

Another indirect consequence of the limited investment of authority in teachers is the teacher's inability to reinvest the limited authority he has in the students. Since little authority is invested, students assume little responsibility for their own education outside of attendance and a certain minimal compliance with regulations concerning their behavior in school. Rather than holding students responsible for independent effort, the responsibility for somehow getting them through resides with the teachers. In many schools department chairmen or principals regularly review grades and require teachers to account for marks that, in their estimation, are too low. Additionally, automatic promotion policies provide further evidence of the limited investment of authority in teachers and students.

Again the system has unanticipated consequences—the lack of motivation of students who create their own adolescent society with norms and values in many instances directly antithetical to those of the school.[39] This failure to invest authority results in a total inability of the schools to draw upon the powerful societal structure of the student subculture in the accomplishment of educational goals. In fact, it makes it more difficult and in some cases impossible to do so.

The School Administrator and Organization Groupings

Harlan A. Philippi and Jack R. Childress

Most secondary school administrators are at least vaguely aware of the informal groups that exist within their organizations and have some comprehension of the power of such groups over individual behavior. What is usually forgotten is that the kind of relationship established between these groups and the formal organization determines to a large degree how adequately and effectively the organization will function.

Any group can generally exercise more control over an individual than all the formal administrative directives in the world. Since most group norms are self-determined, group members are more likely to accept them. Unless secondary school administrators come to know and understand what motivates the groups in their organization, all attempts at teamwork and cooperation, whether at the classroom or the organizational level, will prove to be quite ineffective.

Several implications regarding organizational groupings can be drawn from the study we conducted of a large mid-western public school district.

First, administrators have no real control over how groups are formed in the organization. Consequently, the task of administrators is not to put people together

[39] See James S. Coleman, *The Adolescent Society* (New York: The Free Press, 1961).

into some workable combination, but rather to identify the workable combinations that have been formed by the people themselves. It was noted in this study that the factors that initially put people together such as organization prescription (being an English teacher, for example), spatial proximity, or character of the work performed, were not the factors that kept people together. In most respects it became meaningless to talk of a science or English department as if such departments were cohesive groups bound together by self-determined norms and capable of exerting control over individual members.

Within departments, sub-departmental groups existed which did not include all members of the department. In some instances the chairmen of departments had little to do with members of their department. Rather they confined their relationships to those matters dealing strictly with departmental routines. In one instance, a department chairman avoided all face-to-face contact with two members of his department. In another instance, two members of the same department who taught the same subject and at the same grade level were actively hostile towards each other and avoided any situation which could bring them together.

A second implication can be drawn from the first; the tangibles and intangibles that were inherent in an organization member's work, rather than the work itself, were the bases for group formation. A group cannot be imposed on an individual no matter how much his work is like another's and no matter how many reasons can be mustered why he should be an integral member of a group. Entrance into a group is still a choice of the individual. In this study, personal friendship determined that choice. So did an individual's appraisal of another's competence. So did the feeling that group association would have mutual advantages for those joining together.

Groups formed on these factors did not follow formal work patterns or formal prescriptions. Group membership cut across organizational lines, in a sense seeking its own level, and groups were formed almost as if the formal organization hierarchy did not exist. Thus groups included supervisors and supervisees, top-level administrators and non-administrators, professionally trained people and non-professionals, and a mixing of members of many departments.

A third implication relates to group control. As was previously stated, groups can generally exercise more control over an individual than can policies of an organization. Yet this control is not absolute. It is not absolute when individuals have alternatives to accepting this control. Administrative control is thus always precarious, since organization members have the alternative of informal groups being open to them. Also, members of one group may have the alternative of having other groups open to them. Groups are not static, either to size or duration.

Group control is also not absolute for the informal group leaders, the "high-influence" members as they were termed in this study. A "high-influence" individual may well risk doing something that would displease the group, since he may be able to lose safely some of this influence and still not jeopardize his position. The implication is that the "high-influence" group member becomes the one through whom administrators must work to gain support for the policies of the organizations. They also are the ones who are potentially the innovators of change in the organization. (Whether the low-influence group member is also potentially an innovator because of little to lose by displeasing the group is also a distinct possibility, as Homans has suggested.)[1]

An additional finding relates to what is termed "back group" formation. By definition, back groups are those that contradict or modify the decisions or directives of the formal organization, and which establish informal and personal communication networks that can circumvent the formal organization if the need arises.

Within the organization studied, organization members were generally aware of the formal channels through which they were supposed to work in meeting their organizational responsibilities. Some organization members, however, characteristically did not follow the formal channels, preferring to use unofficial channels and procedures. Unofficial channel users (back channel users as they were termed in this study) often formed together in groups. There were many "face" reasons why such back channels were formed and used: male-female differences, situations too personal to discuss with administrators, and administrators who were not well known by organization members. Most importantly however, back channels were formed and used because of administrative actions, particularly with reference to decision making. Back channels were characteristically used when decisions were made concerning areas important to organization members and when members were not involved in making such decisions.

In the organization as a whole, the feeling was prevalent that administrators and teachers represented two distinct groupings of people in varying degrees of conflict and disagreement (and cooperation), each group working towards goals for the organization (and for themselves) that were mutually conflicting. One group had the organizational authority to make rules and regulations concerning the functions of the other group. The receiving group, however, largely the teacher group, had the choice of complying or not complying with such decisions.

Secondary school administrators must come to realize that their ways of behaving may well be responsible for creating conditions that maximize the possibility of the formation of groups that are potentially destructive of organizational effectiveness. Back groups may be potentially destructive, but in many instances in the organization studied they were responsible for getting things done that might not have been accomplished otherwise. Yet, in so doing, much energy and talent was dissipated in the process—energy and talent which might have been more productive for the total organization if corrective measures could have been taken to broaden the decision-making process and to make the formal channels more effective. As it stood in the organization for many organizational imperatives, the formal channels stood empty and useless, and the incumbents of formal positions were left with little to do except engage in meaningless routines.

[1]George C. Homans, *Social Behavior: Its Elementary Forms.* New York: Harcourt, Brace and World, Inc., 1961.

Anti-Democratic Attitudes of American Educators

Merlyn M. Gubser

Educators should be the primary conservators of the democratic institutions, values and ideals supposedly held in high regard by our citizenry.

Within this decade, however, several questions have arisen relating to the ability of American teachers to manage this awesome responsibility. An increasing number of educators are currently questioning whether, during this era of concern for the rights of minorities and dissenters, American teachers may not be impeding rather than facilitating the learning of democratic values and the development of egalitarian behavior in our nation's schools.

The degree of the democratic or autocratic propensity of educators—both administrators and teachers—has only in recent years become the subject of scientific research and investigation. Harmon Zeigler, in a survey of 800 Oregon high school teachers, discovered that educators are not merely conservative in their political views, they possess a political apathy that may well be born of abject fear. In his study, the results of which were published by Prentice-Hall in March in "The Political Life of American Teachers," Zeigler finds that teachers have a decided fear of parents, administrators and school boards (14). The relationship between such fear and the political attitudes and behavior of educators was the subject of an earlier study.

In a survey of 86 elementary and secondary teachers conducted in 1959, Arthur Blumberg uncovered what he describes as a "fear syndrome" (3). The four basic components of the syndrome are fear of jeopardizing or losing job status, fear of change in work situation, fear of criticism, and fear of attracting disfavor of administrators and others teachers. The data implied that these fears lie behind teacher political and professional apathy and contribute to the low status of the teaching profession. As in any undemocratic group, Blumberg found that many teachers are afraid of asserting themselves as individuals.

Seventy-eight percent of his sample group believed that their colleagues were "too pliable and submissive" when confronted with an authority figure. Yet half of this 78 percent believed themselves to exhibit the same fearful responses (3). Blumberg observed that a common attitude of the teachers in his research group was that they feared ostracism from fellow teachers and administrative reprisals if they voiced views that differed from their school's established policy.

Weiser and Hayes (1966), employing the Purdue Opinion Poll—a survey of politico-social attitudes—to ascertain the political posture of 231 prospective and experienced teachers, recorded significant antidemocratic beliefs. Twenty-five percent of the teachers polled indicated that they would permit censorship of speech and press to a considerable extent (e.g., over 25 percent believed government should actively censor "some people" from making public speeches).

Over 50 percent of the 231 would allow police "or other groups" to ban or censor "certain books and movies in their cities." Approximately 40 percent said they would "allow the police or FBI to give a man the 'third degree' to make him talk.

Sixteen percent of the experienced secondary teachers included in the research group indicated that they would rescind the right of habeas corpus. One-third of the total group considered "a large mass of the people" to be incapable of determing what is and is not good for them," and one-fourth would prevent "criminal and moral misfits" from having children. Finally, over one-third of the teachers in this poll would require loyalty oaths of themselves. Another significant aspect of the Weiser and Hayes study was the relatively large number of teachers who indicated they were undecided as to how to respond to many of the above items (13). The researchers point out that the educators' responses to the Purdue Poll might not be unlike that of the average American.

This opinion is borne out by Theodore W. Parsons (1966) who has found evidence to indicate that teachers reflect—and follow—the standards of the community in which they live rather than being instruments of democratic innovation (11).

Additional studies of undemocratic attitudes of American educators further illuminate the dark corners of this problem. A. Montgomery Johnston (1959), applying the Bernreuter "Personality Inventory" to both democratic and autocratic teachers, concluded that the authoritarians were more emotionally unstable, more introverted, more easily dominated, and less self-sufficient than were the more democratic educators (10).

By subjecting these teachers to the "Hunter Test of Social Attitudes," Johnston determined that teachers about to retire and beginning teachers not on tenure tended to be more autocratic than their moderately-experienced peers. This would tend to support Blumberg's premise that insecurity and authoritarianism are positively correlated.

But what specific implications does the authoritarianism of the educator have for the training and instruction of his students? Blumberg's study indicates that teachers who are authoritarian may mold autocratic attitudes in their students:

> The results in the classroom would seem to be concerned with psychological phenomena of compensation and projection. For example, a compensatory reaction from one who is dominated by fear of authority is that he, in turn, will dominate others if he can. What better opportunity is there than the classroom with its built-in teacher-pupil authority relationships? . . . What seems to happen ultimately is that teachers succeed in projecting and transferring their own feelings about authority on to the student. The students soon learn that it is easier to get along by not differing from their teacher's ideas.

Thus conformity of thought and response is the hallmark of the autocratic teacher's classroom. As he is dominated, so shall he dominate.

The definitive work of H. H. Remmers in the area of student attitudes gives further insight into the relationship between the attitudes of the teacher and his students. When the results of the Weiser and Hayes study are compared with the data obtained by Remmers when he administered the Purdue Opinion Poll to students, the responses obtained are remarkably similar (12). But does this indicate that teachers' attitudes are being foisted off onto their students, or does it merely indicate that American educators have the same politico-social values as American adolescents and their parents?

Roy E. Horton (1963), in analyzing the results of a study in which the Purdue Opinion Poll was applied to 15,000 twelfth graders throughout the nation, found that those who had taken a civics or U. S. Government class showed no greater understanding of democratic principles than those who had taken no such course. In fact, Horton's research indicated that there is a tendency for students who have taken such courses to be more dogmatic and less in agreement with democratic principles than those who have not taken these courses. Horton concluded that this evidence should "give us pause," and indeed it should. Teachers of the social sciences, he further reasoned, should perhaps place ". . . greater emphasis upon the basic values of freedom upon which the existence of our democratic society depends (12).

If we can assume with minimal validity that teachers with antidemocratic leanings are not adequately inculcating democratic ideals and understandings in their students, can we not conclude that much of the responsibility for changing this situation lies with school administrators? For the administration hires and supervises the teachers and plays the most significant role as an authority figure in the teachers' professional environment.

Most textbooks on school administration point out the distinction between democratic and authoritarian leadership. The staunch autocratic administrator has been well defined by Bradford and Lippet (1945), who see him as a person primarily involved in "checking up on everyone to keep up production. He gives orders and expects them to be carried out." In dictatorial fashion the autocrat does not expect his teachers to think for themselves, but he establishes "policies" or makes "requests and suggestions" that have the weight of absolute law. Unfortunately, many administrators assume "democracy" to mean "benevolent despotism." The more benevolent of such authoritarians may ask their teachers to make decisions, but these "decisions" must conform to what the administrator has previously decided to do.

Harap (1959) has found that teachers and administrators often have a totally opposite view of their relationships to one another. The greater the discrepancy between their views, the lower the morale (8). Low morale contributes to the authoritarian syndrome. Teacher relationships in an autocratic situation break down rapidly. Groups of disgruntled and insecure teachers fragment from the faculty and form subgroups "which maintain themselves according to the satisfaction the members get from griping" (3). The autocratic administrator may or may not allow gossip and hearsay to influence his decisions, but in any event his teachers will become distrustful of one another and will suspect teachers outside of their own cliques of "apple polishing" and "selling out" to the administration. As autocracy thrives, teacher insecurity increases. And as teacher insecurity develops, classroom authoritarianism grows.

Research indicates (Cornell, 1954, and Davis et al., 1963) that more than any other factor, democratic administration can offset the effects of other elements that tend to produce teacher fear and insecurity. When teachers are actively involved in decision-making and their views are requested and respected, they "achieve great effectiveness . . . as teachers by stimulating adaptability and change necessary to improve instruction" (10). The direct effect would be a more tolerant atmosphere in which students would more efficiently learn the fundamentals and values of democracy.

> If the interpretations relative to security are valid, any administrative practices that foster teacher security might also tend to foster democratic practices. Some administrative practices which might foster security are higher salaries, salary schedules, tenure, better retirement programs, better merit rating programs, encouragement of experimentation, shared social activities of administration and staff, and a democratic administration (10).

To this list might be added administrative (1) support of teachers when controversial issues are discussed in the classroom, (2) respect for teacher time and privacy, (3) refusal to use the school intercom system as a "Big Brother" network for listening in on teacher conferences and class presentations, (4) support of teachers in parent-teacher confrontations, and (5) general respect for the teachers' professional competencies. Additionally, administrators should no longer exclusively hold on to such criteria as age and years of experience for teacher selection. Instead, teachers should also be chosen on the basis of their "confidence, self-sufficiency, and liberalism" (10). Though at the present time there are no tests of authoritarianism proven sufficiently reliable to perform such a sophisticated task, it may be justifiable, in light of the importance of the consequences, to consider personality inventories as an important inclusion in the teacher interview. But considering the unethical use to which such devices have sometimes been put in American commerce and industry, precaution must be taken to insure that personality tests are utilized to ward off authoritarianism—not to strengthen it.

Finally, reflections on anti-democratic attitudes of both teachers and administrators hold weighty implications for those concerned with teacher education. More stress must be placed on imparting democratic ideology to future teachers and administrators. We have learned that authoritarian attitudes of college students appear in the classroom when they become student teachers (DelPopalo, 1960). However, little thought has been given to eradicating these attitudes before turning autocrats loose on our public schools.

Who is to perform this surgery and what instruments they are to use constitute questions that only now can be answered philosophically. To actually solve these problems we must have more research and investigation of the influence of authoritarianism in education. The investigations noted herein are of the best available to date, despite several limitations and shortcomings. These studies need the sound validation and clarification that only supportive research can provide. We must improve our criteria for determining the differences between necessary organizational order and undue autocratic control in school leadership. More valid measuring devices of authoritarian group behavior must additionally be developed.

To scientifically examine the causes and effects of authoritarianism in American schools constitutes a highly complex endeavor with a myriad of concomitant political, social and psychological aspects. But when one considers the possible ramifications and the influences of the autocratic domain on education, this task becomes imperative.

Bibliography

1. Adorno, T. W.; Frenkel-Brunswik, Else; Levinson, Daniel J.; Sanford, R. Nevitt; *The Authoritarian Personality,* New York: Harper and Brothers, 1950.

2. Bernreuter, R. G., The Personality Inventory. Stanford: Stanford University Press, 1935.

3. Blumberg, Arthur, "Are Teachers Doormats?" *Educational Administration and Supervision,* 45: 215-219, July, 1959.

4. Cornell, F. G., "When Should Teachers Share in Making Administrative Decisions?" *Nation's Schools.* 53: 43-45, 1954.

5. Davis, Hazel; Ware, Martha; Shapiro, S.; Donald, Eleanor; and Stieber, Gertrude N., "Economic, Legal, and Social Status of Teachers," *Review of Educational Research,* 33: 398-414, October, 1963.

6. DelPopalo, Joseph A., "Authoritarian Trends in Personality as Related to Attitudinal and Behavioral Traits of Student Teachers," *Journal of Educational Research,* 53: 252-7, March, 1960.

7. Gage, N. L., *Handbook of Research on Teaching.* Chicago: Rand McNally and Company, 1963.

8. Harap, Henry, "Morale," *Nation's Schools,* 63: 55-57, June, 1959.

9. Hunter, E. C., *A Test of Social Attitudes.* New York: The Psychological Corporation, 1939.

10. Johnston, A. Montgomery, "Factors Influencing Democratic Practices," *Childhood Education,* 36: 122-25, November, 1959.

11. Parsons, Theodore W., "Discrimination Against Mexican-Americans, *Phi Delta Kappan,* 48: 86, October, 1966.

12. Remmers, H. H., *Anti-Democratic Attitudes in American Schools.* Evanston, Ill.: Northwestern University Press, 1963.

13. Weiser, John C., and James E. Hayes, "Democratic Attitudes of Teachers and Prospective Teachers," *Phi Delta Kappan,* 47: 476-81, May, 1966.

14. Zeigler, Harmon, *The Political Life of American Teachers.* Englewood Cliffs, N.J.: Prentice-Hall, Inc., 1967.

Organizational Influences on Teacher Behavior

Donald J. McCarty

The assertion that the profession of school administration is still in a depressed stage of development cannot be materially challenged. The modern school administrator is the unfortunate descendent of the teaching principal, an office historically restricted to second-rate clerical duties. Though the position has matured enough to include the management of substantial financial resources, no image of the public school administrator as a dynamic educational statesman has penetrated the public consciousness. Rather, typical job descriptions for administrative positions stress skills such as proper supervision of the money flows of the school system, keeping the enterprise solvent, and maximizing services by allocating the scarce resources among the different areas which have demand on them. Public relations chores are fastened on as unavoidable appendages; since the community rarely gives a clear policy mandate, the emphasis placed on external relationships tends to vary with passing, short term demands. Administrative meddling in the teaching-learning process itself, however, is not easily tolerated; "get good teachers and let them alone" is a shibboleth still held in high repute by the general public.

As a consequence, the subsequent administrative rejection of classroom supervision incites highly individualistic behavior on the part of staff members; the upshot of these independent tactics is person-oriented rather than goal-oriented conduct. For instance, within a system, one teacher may rule his domain with an "iron hand," another might be working on teacher-pupil planning, the next may have his class utterly out of control, while another might be subject-centered in approach.

In such a contingency, who provides the fundamental coordination, integration, and operational strategy? This is a key question. Since the public educational institution is a continuing enterprise and its survival is seldom at stake, isn't it entirely plausible that "keeping school" may become an end in itself? What we may commonly have is a financially well managed operation with little attention directed to the accomplishment of its genuine objectives. Almost by default the structural character of the enterprise itself is forced to act as a sort of psychological teacher and to mold individual teacher behavior in the dominant values of the school system.

The Board's Policy Making

One can argue that the board of education, through its all-absorbing policy making function, provides the energizing stimulus. This will be true to the extent that staff members really think of the overall goals of the organization, and common sense would dictate that this proviso is frequetly not met. Since school systems are essentially organized as bureaucracies, technical factors are apt to assume a pre-eminent position.

All educational enterprises are structured hierarchically with a system of roles graded by levels of authority which differentiate one person from another. Work is divided along specialized lines and personal discretion is limited through rules and regulations. Status symbols such as size and location of teaching stations dramatize and validate distinctions between roles. The operational consequence is a set of signals provided by the organization for its members which enable people to know where they belong. The total effect is to build rationality, certainty, and dispatch into the organization. Career advancement and psychic stability encourage the teacher to accept the prescriptions and the result is a fairly consistent behavior pattern on the part of individuals within the organization.

Such an organizational climate is likely to be a more salient influence on teacher behavior than the vague educational philosophy of the chief administrator, if known, or the theoretical mandates prescribed by the local teachers college, if understood. Working climates may vary from school to school, but each system structures its own situation so that behavioral expectations are quite clearly evident.

A School With Tradition

Consider a few examples. You have just been employed by Osopeachy High, an old venerated school with firmly built up traditions. Having prestige in educational circles, it caters almost exclusively to a college preparatory clientele. Located in a wealthy suburban area, the financial emoluments for teachers are superb. The impact of such an organization on you cannot help to be considerable; you must learn the behavior patterns which go along with your post. Both the formal and informal rules need to be mastered and these range from appropriate dress and deportment to the models established for pupil-teacher relationships. To violate these norms is to endanger your status in the organization.

You find that Brooks Brothers clothing or its reasonable facsimile is the preferred uniform, that you should try to handle your own discipline problems without referral to the administrative officers, and that your success in teaching will be evaluated by the results of your students on college board examinations. Smoking is permitted in the well appointed teacher lounges, and it is quite acceptable to enjoy a cocktail at the better restaurants in the vicinity. You are supposed to criticize education courses as superfluous and you should model your teaching techniques after the university professor. Competition among students for grades is good; social promotion is bad. And from these relatively gross expectations you are to keep a sharp lookout for the barely detectable cues which are constantly being given.

This example may seem slightly exaggerated, but is it? This school obviously has a clear advantage because its mind is made up before the teacher joins the group. In support of this point, research by Kurt Lewin and his associates revealed that an individual's behavior is sharply conditioned by the structure of his work group. Inasmuch as learning is a process of recognizing symbols or stimuli, learning is facilitated when the situation is understood.

Conflicting Groups

Contrast the previous case with the Sleepy Valley High School, a rural central school which services a culturally and economically deprived territory. The faculty is divided between two groups of approximately equal numbers. One group is made up primarily of middle-aged local women who are permanent fixtures in the community; in general, this group tends to be totally disinterested in changing the status quo, and is well satisfied with an inferior salary schedule.

The other group is less cohesive; it is younger, mostly transient, critical of the administration, salaries, facilities, and the like. However, teachers in this group escape with a jaded cynicism toward the organization and the community. Comments reflecting this attitudes such as "What the heck, it's their school," or "Oh, well, I'm leaving after this year anyway," are commonplace.

In this particular system you have to make a choice between two behavior patterns, and if you wish to remain, you would wisely select the more powerful group or assume a neutral position. To return to the point with which we started, the organization is a social microcosm, an ongoing society in itself, which acts as a socializing instrument. Successful teachers are those who can identify with the organization and accept as given the prevailing system; man is a remarkably adaptive animal and the most functional way of getting rid of anxiety in any situation is to conform to preferred models.

Given these facts, what is the dysfunctional result of the organization's pressure on the individual? One indictment can be made flatly: in developing and polishing men into similar molds, the tendency is to produce overconformity. If the position of teacher as defined by the organization does not adequately satisfy growth needs, the individual may ossify on the job or seek gratification outside school hours in such activities as building boats, raising flowers, and the like.

Since a school's overall success is irrevocably tied to a board of education's skill in forming, stimulating, and evaluating policy decisions, steps must be taken by the board to limit restrictive organizational influences.

Creativeness and Leadership

The first requirement is to sustain the truly creative teacher by permitting a certain amount of goal-oriented idiosyncratic behavior. For example, if the development of critical thinking powers in the student becomes a legitimate objective for a school, teachers should be permitted to experiment with techniques designed to achieve this end. A note of caution needs to be inserted here; eccentricity for its own sake and unrelated to the purposes of the school is pointless exhibitionism.

A second method of attack on organizational torpor is to increase the amount of participation by teachers in leadership acts. Job enlargement at all levels in the hierarchy is normally a more efficient way to structure an organization; if it doesn't seem to pay immediate returns in improved administrative services, the unexpected dividend may well be the boost given to a teacher's individual development. Douglas McGregor has argued that an individual's real potential is never discovered unless he is given an opportunity to self-actualize–that is, to participate in leadership activities as a valued colleague.

The most paramount function facing the board of education is the formulation of clear objectives for the school system. Since educational aims involve value choices selected from among a wide range of alternatives, it is mandatory that the public interest be operationalized in specific terms. Admittedly, to define the public interest is an exceedingly complex undertaking; however without a statement of principles the teacher has no standard against which to measure his performance. The exigencies of our times demand sound educational policies as guideposts for the professional conduct of our schools; improvisation on a day to day basis is hardly the desired alternative.

Since our final solution may appear on the surface as another impractical textbook remedy, let us examine the implications of the statement in a real situation. Suppose that a board of education were to state categorically that the principal aim of its schools shall be the development of the minds and the acquisition of knowledge by all children. All other aims, however important and desirable they may appear in themselves, shall be subordinated to this primary aim insofar as the functions of the schools are concerned.

Immediately, the administrative implications of this limited educational objective become apparent. With respect to children, this policy suggests ability grouping, heavy use of standardized achievement and ability tests, traditional type report cards, acceleration of gifted children and non-promotion of low achievers, and absolute standards for each grade level. Teacher in such a system will be encouraged to do graduate study in the arts and sciences excluding professional courses in education; teaching success will depend to a considerable extent on the performance of one's students on standardized tests; rigid conformist, authoritarian teacher types will be most successful.

Whether or not one agrees with the aforementioned policy statement, and only the board of education working within its own community context can make this determination, purposiveness is the essential ingredient needed to counteract the negative aspects of organizational inertia. And much more than mere intellectual understanding of educational aims is demanded. Teachers who affiliate with a school must believe in its cause and subscribe to its goals. Through this kind of firm commitment and personal identification with enterprise objectives, we are able to gain the healthy advantages of individual and self-directed effort without destroying organizational intent.

Leadership Styles—Decision-Making and the Principal

Don E. Hamachek

As I researched both ideas and people for this paper, I was quickly impressed with some rather consistent trends. Number one is that even among themselves, principals are in conflict about what their job is and what they ought to become if they are to survive. And number two, as near as I could tell from standard administration textbooks and professional journals, we have various theories to help us understand administration, but no theory or theories to help us understand administrators. I found that it is too easy to charge the principal with the responsibility for piloting the great ship U.S.S. School, while in reality the shifting crosscurrents of the job pressure him (if he allows himself to be pressured) to become not the ship's captain, but its mechanic.

The so-called "Traits Theory," for example, is useful for organizing a group of characteristic "leadership traits" such as forcefulness, intelligence, thoughtfulness, fairness, and the like, but it is useless for telling us how a man acquires these traits if he lacks them.

"Human Relations Theory" suggests that the leader is the person whom the group perceives as having the qualities and the power to help it achieve its goals. But what happens when a group is unable to define its own goals, or what happens when a man is delegated authority (like a principalship) and then doesn't know how to use it, or worse, misuses it?

Then there is something called "Organizational Theory," which asserts that within any informal organization, like a school, there develop informal organizations—such as those which form in coffee lounges, during lunch periods, and after school hours—which have as their main aim to decrease the basic causes of conflict, frustration, and failure. The theory states that both of these organizations—the formal and the informal—must be considered together as a total social system. The theory assumes, naturally enough, that the principal who uses this organizational framework to diagnose his problems not only will make wiser decisions but also will bring about better and more lasting changes.[1] But what about the principal who refuses to admit even the existence of informal groups (like those which form in teachers' lounges), much less consider them of any value in his decision-making processes?

What I am suggesting is that there seems to be a tendency to view the principal's role as change-agent and decision-maker from an organizational or power

[1] The reader will find a greater elaboration of these and related theories in "Educational Organization, Administration, and Finance. *Review of Educational Research* 31: 347-572; October 1961.

framework rather than from a person or personal framework. I have the feeling that the typical principal is so burdened with responsibilities–responsibilities for curriculum, teacher supervision and evaluation, staffing, pupil progress, records, guidance, discipline, transportation, public relations, budget, and assorted committee meetings–that he has little time to define himself to himself as a person, much less as a person within a professional role with a clear-cut educational view of his own. It is terribly unfortunate if one allows this to happen–particularly if it means that decisions are made and changes are brought about through purely mechanical, impersonal processes which follow formulas rather than convictions. Perhaps one of the reasons that principals seem to find so little time to examine their personal philosophy of education, their personal philosophy of "self," is that, much as prisoners do, they are inclined to fall in love with their chains.

The Crucial Concept

What we finally come to is a rather simple-minded but, I think, crucial concept. It is this: The kind of leader (or principal) one is depends on the kind of man or woman one is. If I say to a principal that he must have social sensitivity and action flexibility to be successful, this would matter not a whit unless he was a socially sensitive, flexible individual to *begin* with–unless he *valued* these, not simply as desirable *administrative* characteristics, but as desirable *personal* characteristics as well.

One's role as decision-maker and change-agent is more involved than, for example, a simple listing of desirable "leadership traits." It is more involved than the human relations theory idea that leadership grows from a group's consent to grant authority. It is more complicated than the simple recognition that informal power organizations meet to plot, scheme, and discuss at coffee breaks, lunch time, or after school. To tell you *what* you must do and *how* you must behave to be an effective change-agent and decision-maker is to dictate. Moreover, to explain decision-making or one's role as change-agent in terms of administration theory or theories serves only to unduly abstract and impersonalize the highly personal meanings and implications of any given leadership role–not the least of which is a principalship.

Rather than talking about the job and its demands or even the social setting and all of its relational systems, let us focus more specifically on the man. It is the man, if he is to amount to anything at all, who must ultimately determine his position, his status, indeed his decisions–*not* the job or the social setting although both do play a part in any role definition and decision-making process.

The man we want to look at is a leader. He's called a principal, but that is just the label we assign his role within a specific leadership context. Like a quarterback, he is sort of a field general, the responsible agent for the unfolding flow of events–someone people can either boo or cheer depending on how things go. For whatever else it is, leadership is a relation. It is a relation insofar as it involves interactions between two or more persons, one of whom makes decisions, the other of whom must abide by or follow these decisions. In order to understand the leadership process and one's related roles as change-agent and decision-maker it is first necessary to consider the personality of the *leader* in relation to the personality of the *followers* and then to relate these variables to the characteristics of the *situation.*

Leadership Models

Insofar as you are principals acting within a leadership context, each of you, either consciously or unconsciously, reflects a particular style of leadership and decision-making which best suits you as an individual. Each of you is a kind of "model" and, as such, is variously perceived by different persons on your staff either contemptuously, or with respect, or with envy, or with mixed feelings–or, perhaps, you are not thought of at all. Your reflection of principal "model" is less dependent on what you know about theories of personality or theories of administration as it is on the kind of person you are. (We keep returning to the crucial concept: The kind of leader one is depends on the kind of man one is.)

Let us speculate about three different leadership models. You may find that one seems to fit you best, or you may find bits and pieces of yourself in all three of them.

The Charismatic Leader

Consider first what we might call the "charismatic" leader. This is the person who is interested in keeping the attention focused primarily on himself. In many ways, he has a certain charisma, a certain bigger than life quality–he seems marked by his power, his energy, his commitment. By power, we have reference to sheer intellectual strength or uncommon perceptiveness and originality; by energy, we have reference to unusual force or vivacity of personality; and by commitment, we have reference to a deep absorption in the self and its work. Generally, we might expect to find all of these qualities present in the truly "charismatic" leader. We should remember, however, that energy without power is mere flamboyance and that power without energy or commitment is likely to reflect a detached, cold, impersonal individual.

Charismatic narcissism. Actually, this portrayal of the charismatic leader is only part of the story because there is still another dimension to his personality–namely, his narcissism, his self-love. This does not mean that this type of leader is necessarily vain or exhibitionistic; he may, in fact, be somewhat withdrawn, diffident, even humble. We assign him this narcissistic label only because he keeps the attention on himself. Being a "charismatic" leader has its dangers, however. Indeed, it is precisely the narcissistic overtones in this kind of leader which encourage either admiration or repulsion. Why is it that in one instance a person could be drawn with fierce loyality and admiration to one kind of charismatic leader, but be repelled by still another kind?

Perhaps we can understand it better if we examine a bit more closely the different forms of narcissism. On the one hand, there is a type of narcissism which makes a loud plea to all who care to listen. It cries, "Look at me! Look how wonderful I am! Admire me! Love me!" There is also a type of narcissism which is vindictive and vengeful; it says: "I love myself and who needs *you?*" We all know people with narcissistic traits of this sort. In either case, we frequently sense that the quality of their narcissism is somewhat stinted by strong personal needs, and for whatever "charisma" they may have, we generally find ourselves reluctant to become too involved or to be too influenced.

Autonomous narcissism. There is still another and rarer form of narcissism, and its impact on people is quite different. It is directed neither toward nor against other persons, but rather tends to be autonomous, internally fed, and capable of sustaining itself long after the applause has whispered away. It was just this form of narcissism which Freud was talking about when he wrote:

> . . . the charm of a child lies to a great extent in his narcissism, his self-sufficiency and inaccessibility, just as does the charm of certain animals which seem not to concern themselves about us, such as cats and the large beasts of prey. It is as if we envied them their power of retaining a blissful state of mind.[2]

This form of autonomous narcissism, when joined to other qualities, can make for a truly memorable leader. This kind of man invites us to identify with him, and we do so because it makes us feel stronger; he invites us to seek his protection and care, to share his psychological bounty. I think we can agree that John F. Kennedy had many of the qualities of this "autonomous narcissism." Indeed, it is precisely because so many identified with his strength in life that his death came as such a shattering, humbling experience, particularly to those who had forgotten about their own humanness–their own fallibility as individuals.

The Authoritarian Leader

Consider now a second kind of leadership style–the authoritarian model. Here we have the person who claims his power not through personal endowment, but through his office. He somehow is the agent of omnipotent authority. The charismatic leader, to some extent, is able to stand apart from his job and say: "I am valuable to myself and for what I am." The authoritarian leader, on the other hand, says in effect: "I am valuable for what I belong to. I am valuable because of my position and the power attached to it." The authoritarian leader starts with the simple assumption that he knows and others do not. His power, he feels, lies in what he knows and is able to accomplish rather than in his manner or personality.

Authoritarian characteristics. The authoritarian leader reflects interesting and consistent characteristics. For example, he is likely to be the sort of person who adheres to a tight schedule–not just at the office, but at home as well. Things may

[2]Freud, Sigmund. "On Narcissism." *Collected Papers.* (Edited by Ernest Jones.) London: Hogarth, 1934. Vol. 4.

have to be in certain places, events carefully planned ahead and anticipated. He tends to be somewhat intolerant of indecisiveness and ambiguity. Shades of gray bother him. Indeed, his academic interests usually lean toward the physical sciences rather than the social sciences, although not necessarily.

Advantages. We must admit that there are advantages to authoritarian leadership. This sort of leader is quick to offer his followers a definitive black and white picture which logs the route they are to follow. He presents not alternatives, but directives, and this always tranquilizes the insecure, anxious followers because they feel more comfortable and more secure knowing exactly what is expected. Not only does the authoritarian model demand dependency; he makes dependency easy.

Disadvantages. Let us also admit that there are disadvantages to authoritarian leadership. The follower of the authoritarian leader may purchase direction, force, security, and clarity, but he does so at a price. The price he pays is the sacrifice of some share of his own development. In many ways, he is no longer his own man; he no longer has his own unique identity because he is not free to pursue his own unique goals. His goals, like the goals of an oppressed person, are never his own, but someone else's. Most of all, the authoritarian "do-it-my-way" type leader is an inflexible despot who operates a one-way rather than a shared or two-way decision-making machine. The usual pillars of hierarchy, specialization, rules, and impersonality typically support his bureaucratic superstructure.

Make no mistake about it, authoritarian decision-making can be successful—alarmingly so. But it is successful at a price. It all depends on how much autonomy one is willing to give up to live under it.

The Therapeutic Leader

Shift now to still another brand of leadership model and look at what we can term "altruistic" guidelines. This is the kind of leader who frequently finds it difficult to make decisions for fear of hurting someone's feelings. Decision-making for him is transformed into a giant process of committees and sub-committees which research, discuss, and recommend—always in the name of democracy and fairness.

Therapeutic characteristics. Actually, our therapeutic leader comes closest of all to adhering to a democratic organizational framework. As contrasted to the typical bureaucratic operation of the authoritarian principal, we have here an operation more closely akin to an enterprise type organization, particularly in the sense of being personal, spontaneous, and adaptable to change.

The trouble with the therapeutic leader is that he is inclined to be *too* indecisive, *too* hesitant, *too* fearful of hurting feelings. He concentrates neither on himself, nor his role, nor on policy, but rather on the teacher or the student. He says, in effect: "I will help you become what you are." It is something like Michelangelo's approach to sculpture when he looked at a raw block of marble and tried to uncover the statue within it. The therapeutic leader operates in much the same way: he tries to uncover what is within each teacher, he works to help each individual teacher find out what is best and most essential within himself.

Danger signs. You may be thinking, "What a wonderful way to pilot a ship–what better course could there be?" But there are dangers in this kind of leadership, too. The leadership is selfless; it demands that the principal set aside his own desires and concerns and devote himself, totally, to the needs of another. Too often a therapeutic leader's altruism is born out of his own failure in self-esteem, his own lack of self-worth. There are some people who feel so worthless that they over-present themselves to others–they are *too* nice, *too* accommodating, *too* eager to please. What this suggests is that if the principal's altruism, his nice-guy attitude, is not genuine, then it is quickly seen as an expedient and shallow effort to get people to like and accept him. We have all had this kind of leadership from time to time, and we might remember the person as kind, or friendly, or very helpful, but we do it in a lukewarm way to conceal a polite disclaim.

There is a vast difference between the therapeutic principal who is sincerely interested in helping teachers emerge, develop, and become what they are capable of becoming and the therapeutic principal who is interested only in being liked and accepted. Democratic decision-making processes for the latter type of principal are used not to encourage individual autonomy and enterprise but rather to avoid taking the rap if the decisions happen to be the wrong ones.

Each of these three leadership styles has distinct implications for decision-making processes and the principal's role as a change-agent. It is not likely that any of us fits neatly any one of the three models. It is more likely that we find fragments of ourselves in each. The fact is, however, one particular leadership style fits us better than the other two. Furthermore, the kind of man one is on the job in his leadership role is not so different from the kind of man he is no matter where he happens to be. Each man brings to the job a "readiness" for being a particular kind of leader.

Followers' Personal Needs

There is still another dimension of leadership we must consider. It influences both decision-making processes and effectiveness as change-agent. This is the dimension of follower behavior and needs.

No matter what kind of leader you are, no matter how you arrive at your decisions, there will be those who accept you and those who reject you. Your rejection or acceptance will depend, for the most part, on how closely you meet the personal needs of those who work under you. Some people, we know, will strive mightily under the inspiration of a charismatic leader. Others want answers instead of inspiration and herald the authoritarian leader as their champion. Still others want neither inspiration nor answers but understanding, and flock to the therapeutic leader.

Suffice it to say that in *any* concrete leader situation, the follower's deep-lying attitudes and needs are background determiners of his reactions to the leader. Just as each of you brings to the job a certain "readiness" for a particular kind of leadership, so does each teacher bring a certain "readiness" to accept or reject certain leadership styles. If, for example, you have teachers on your faculty who lead ordered, scheduled, compulsive lives, who seem always uncertain about anything open-ended or unstructured, the chances are good that they will be uncomforable with you if you are inclined to be at all permissive, laissezfaire, or "therapeutic." If, on the other hand, you have bright, ambitious, creative teachers–the kind who are always wanting to try something different–the chances are equally as good that they will be more than a little distraught with you if you are inclined to be too authoritarian or too "schedule-conscious."

Situational Needs

We have just seen examples of "personal" needs and how they can influence reactions to the leader. In addition, "situational" needs must also be accounted for. We are referring here to needs which emerge not from the person but from the situation.

For example, in life-or-death situations, a man's need for warm approval is likely to be less important than his need to survive. He will be far less prone to accept the "nice guy" as a leader and much more likely to follow the man who appears able to help solve the immediate and pressing problem. To take a more concrete example, the buck private, under combat conditions, is more concerned about his sergeant's tactical ability than his "friendliness." Or the teacher asking you for advice on how to deal with an irate parent is more concerned about your ability to answer the question than about your willingness to be a friendly sympathizer. In situations where a specific goal is in sight, where a specific task must be done, where an immediate problem must be solved, there will be a preference for leaders who are "functionally competent," who, in short, are able to get the job done.[3]

Consider another kind of example. Assume that a new teacher comes to you because she is having trouble making friends, or adjusting to the town, or relating to her class. What kind of leadership "direction" is demanded here? This is a situation in which "functional" competence is probably less important than the ability to give psychological assistance, to be a friendly sympathizer, accepting and supporting.

These several examples indicate, of course, that the leader, whether he be a teacher, a principal, or a superintendent, must have built-in elasticity if he is to meet the multiple needs of his followers. Unfortunately, some leaders are chronic "nice guys" and cannot meet situational demands for strong directive authority. Others are chronic authoritarians who may desperately want to dominate others and who would be a severe handicap to a group with strong needs for individual initiative and freedom of expression.

[3]This is explained more fully by Sanford, F. H. "The Follower's Role in Leadership Phenomena," in *Readings in Social Psychology*, Swanson, Newcomb, and Hartley (editors). New York: Holt, 1952.

Defining Yourself to Yourself

There is one final dimension to consider. If a principal hopes to experience any success whatsoever in his role as decision-maker and change-agent, he not only has to know something about the social setting and something about the principles of intervention and diagnosis, but he has to know something about himself—what he stands for and what he doesn't. Robert Hutchins has written, "Education without a philosophy of education, that is, a coherent statement of the aims and possibilities of education, is impossible." In a similiar sense, "A *man* without a philosophy of *being*, that is, a strong belief about the aims and possibilities of *himself*, is impossible."

The principalship of a school is, it seems to me, a challenge second to none. You have responsibility both to your peers and to young people. You must define not only your educational and professional goals, but your personal goals. You must sort out who you are and what you believe in. In a word, you must define yourself to yourself or run the heavy risk of being tossed off course at the slightest change in the tides of public, staff, or student opinion. Somehow, every good principal must combine conviction with flexibility, and a sense of destiny with a sense of humility.

What is a good leader? Perhaps Walter Lippman has said it best: "The genius of a good leader is to leave behind him a situation with which common sense, without the grace of genius, can deal successfully."

The Behavior of Leaders

Andrew W. Halpin

We will greatly increase our understanding of leadership phenomena if we abandon the notion of "leadership" as a trait, and concentrate instead upon an analysis of the behavior of leaders. It is not easy to accomplish this shift in viewpoint, for our ways of thinking about "leadership" have been encumbered by many beliefs not in accord with behavioral facts. The problem is further exacerbated because "leadership" is a value-laden concept charged with much emotion. To be a leader is "good"; not to lead is "bad"—so each of us fancies himself a leader. We consequently have tended to use "leadership" primarily as a slogan, not as a strictly scientific concept. But even our gains from the use of this term as a rallying cry have been short-lived and spurious because we inevitably have been plagued by the fuzziness of our definitions. Hence, in the present context we first shall examine the definitional problem, noting the strategic advantage of studying *leader behavior* as distinguished from "leadership" *per se*; and shall then describe two leader behavior skills that clearly characterize "effective" leaders, and comment on their pertinence for teachers.

"Leadership" has been used in a variety of ways, most commonly in referring to the "leader" as an outstanding member of a class. Thus, radio and TV commercials proclaim that such-and-such is the leading brand of cigarettes, and that Marilyn Monroe is the leader of our current covey of actresses. Because of our American predilection for bigness, in no matter what sphere, the "leader" in this sense refers to the most popular product—or more specifically, to that item with the greatest sales-market potential. Similarly in education, we often confuse "leadership" with sheer bigness.

Problem in Definition

But this use of the term applies equally to either things or people, and fails to take into account the central psychological characteristic of leader behavior: that this is the behavior of a leader functioning vis-à-vis members of a group in an endeavor to facilitate the solution of group problems. The behavior of the leader and the behavior of group members are inextricably interwoven, and the behavior of both is determined to a great degree by formal requirements imposed by the institution of which the group is a part. For example, Mary Noel, fourth grade teacher, is the formally designated leader of the children in her class. How she behaves as a leader is influenced by the behavior of the children (which includes their expectations of how a teacher *should* behave as a leader) and is conditioned, moreover, by the policies and regulations, both written and unwritten, of the particular school system in which she is employed. As a result of the year which they spend with her, the children in Mary's class are expected to show certain minimum changes in behavior, especially in respect to scholastic achievement and skill in interpersonal relations. The accomplishment of these objectives is the salient group problem to the solution of which Mary must contribute, and it is presumed that her contribution will be greater than that of any other group member in her fourth grade class. This, of course, is why she was employed.

In accepting her assignment as teacher of the fourth grade, Mary assumes a role as leader of this group. This, however, tells us absolutely nothing about the "effectiveness" of her performance in this role, i.e., how effectively she contributes to the solution of group problems. What then, are we to mean by "leadership?" The assumption of a leader's role? The "effectiveness" with which this role is performed? Or the capacity of the individual to perform this role effectively? And here we are confronted by the further question: "effectiveness" in respect to what criteria? for research on leader behavior shows that "effectiveness" in respect to Criterion X is not necessarily correlated with "effectiveness" in regard to Criterion Y. For example, the behavior of a leader who is "effective" in maintaining high "morale" (a sticky term that requires a much clearer definition than has as yet been accorded it) and good human relations within the group is not necessarily "effective" in accomplishing high production and goal-achievement.

This definitional dilemma emerges from the fact that we have incorporated into the term "leadership" both descriptive and evaluative components, and have thus burdened this single word (and the concept it represents) with two connotations: one refers to a role and the behavior of a person in this role, and another is a straightforward evaluation of the individual's performance in the role. We have compounded this confusion even more by conceptualizing "leadership" as an essentially innate capacity of the individual manifested with equal facility regardless of the situation in which the leader finds himself. This belief, however, is unsupported by research evidence; for as Stogdill (14) and Gibb (3) have shown in their comprehensive surveys of the research literature on leadership, a large share of variance in leader behavior is associated with concomitant variance in specific situational factors. Stated baldly, this means that it is possible for Mary to function "effectively" as a leader in the fourth grade class of East Clambake Elementary School and yet operate quite "ineffectively" as a leader in the fourth grade class of West Clambake Elementary School. In brief, much depends on the situation.

How can we circumvent this semantic tangle? The first step is to focus our attention upon the *behavior* of leaders without imputing to the individual a fixed capacity for "leadership". Note that the phrasing of our questions dictates the form of our answers. Thus, if we ask the question, "What is leadership?"[1] we assume gratuitously that such a capacity exists. This assumption violates the warning of the semanticists who have stressed the point that words are to events as maps are to territories, and that a word is useful to only such extent as it corresponds to the territory of events it purports to describe.[2] On this score the term "leadership" is of dubious value and may be likened to a map for which no corresponding territory exists in the "real" world. Granted that the word possesses some hortatory appeal, there is little place for it in strictly scientific inquiry.

What, then, do we gain by shifting our emphasis from "leadership" to the analysis of the *behavior of leaders?* There are two major methodological advantages. In the first place, we can deal directly with observable phenomena, and need make no *a priori* assumptions about the identity or structure of whatever capacities may, or may not, undergird these phenomena. Secondly, this formulation keeps at the forefront of our thinking the importance of differentiating between the *description* of how leaders behave and the *evaluation* of the "effectiveness" of their behavior in respect to specified performance criteria.

Leader Behavior

This focus upon leadership behavior rather than upon "leadership," together with a careful differentiation between the *description* and the *evaluation* of the leader's

[1] A question phrased like this implies a materialistic theoretical model, rather than a mathematical one. For a discussion of the difference in these models in respect to the question, "What is electricity?" see the pertinent discussion by Young in his superb book, *Doubt and Certainty in Science* (16, p. 109ff.).

[2] This point was presented first by Korzybski (12), but a more readable discussion may be found in Johnson (11).

behavior, is an outstanding characteristic of the research approach used in The Ohio State Leadership Studies, a ten-year interdisciplinary program initiated in 1946 and undertaken to study the behavior of persons assumed to be in leadership positions in business, educational and governmental organizations. This program, under the aegis of the Personnel Research Board of the Ohio State University, is directed by Carroll L. Shartle, who has described some phases of this work in his recent book *Executive Performance and Leadership* (13). The separate studies have been reported in Air Force and Navy technical reports, and in the professional literature and a series of technical monographs[3] on this research has been published this year by the Bureau of Business Research of The Ohio State University. We shall note findings about leader behavior that are especially relevant for teachers.

A Leader Behavior Description Questionnaire (LBDQ) was devised to measure the behavior of leaders as perceived by members of their work-groups and by their immediate supervisors. The 150 items incorporated into the original form of the LDBQ were selected from a pile of 1,790 items. In the course of successive revisions, the number of items in this questionnaire has been reduced to 40, chosen on the basis of a factorial analysis by which we identified two major dimensions of leader behavior (8):

Initiating Structure-in-Interaction[4] refers to the leader's behavior in delineating the relationship between himself and the members of his group, and in endeavoring to establish well-defined patterns of organization, channels of communication, and ways of getting a job done. The leader establishes "Structure" in the way the group members interact with him and with each other so that whenever the group is confronted with a novel problem, the members can resort to these Structures-in-Interaction to facilitate the solution of group problems. Hence the group members are not dependent upon the leader for fresh and specific instructions on how to handle each new problem that arises.

Consideration refers to behavior that reflects friendship, mutual trust, respect and warmth in the relationship between the leader and group members. This represents the "human relations" aspect of leader behavior.

Originally, these two dimensions of leader behavior were identified in a study of aircraft commanders; but subsequent research has shown their applicability to factory foremen (2), school superintendents (6, 7), school principals (1), and chairmen of college departments (9). This LBDQ technique has not as yet been used in studies of classroom teachers, but there is strong presumptive evidence to suggest that these same two dimensions are of especial significance in the interaction between teachers and students.

Having developed a practical technique for describing how leaders behave, our next task was to determine the relationship between individuals' scores on these dimensions and their "effectiveness" as leaders. One of Halpin's (4) studies of aircraft commanders shows that the most "effective" commanders are those who

[3]The first of these, by Stogdill and Shartle (15), describes the plan of the series and lists the separate titles.

[4]This is a key concept in the theory of leadership developed by John K. Hemphill (10).

score high on *both* dimensions of leader behavior. Similarly, Hemphill's study of 22 departments in a liberal arts college shows that the departments with the best campus reputation for being well-administered were those whose chairmen scored above the average on both leader behavior dimensions. Studies on leadership ideology (5, 6) likewise indicate that "effective" leaders are characterized by high Initiation of Structure and high Consideration. These dimensions may be conceptualized according to the coordinate scheme presented in Figure 1, in which the four quadrants are designated by Roman numerals.

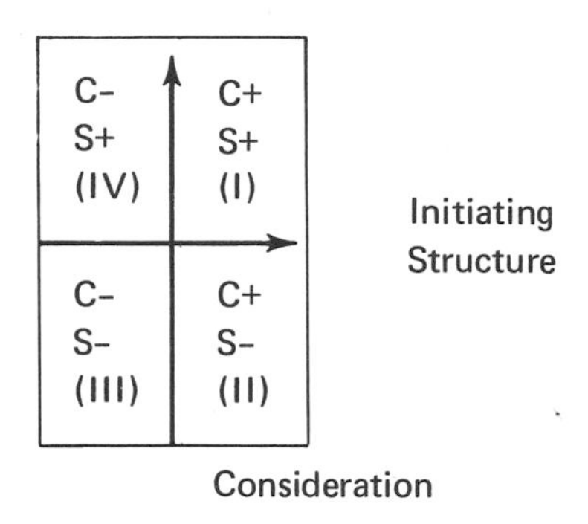

Figure 1. A coordinate scheme for conceptualizing the *initiating structure* and *consideration* dimensions of leader behavior.

The leaders described in Quadrant I are evaluated as highly "effective," whereas those in Quadrant III, whose behavior is ordinarily accompanied by group chaos, are characterized as most "ineffective." The leaders in Quadrant IV are the martinets and the "cold fish" so intent upon getting a job done that they forget that they are dealing with human beings, not cogs in a machine. The individuals described in Quadrant II are also "ineffective" leaders. They may ooze with the milk of human kindness, but this contributes little to "effective" performance unless their Consideration behavior is accompanied by a necessary minimum of Initiating Structure behavior.

The implications of these findings for teachers are obvious. The "effectiveness" of a teacher's behavior as a leader in his classroom will be augmented only to such extent as he increases *both* his Initiation of Structure and his Consideration. The current emphasis in education upon "human relations" and upon the group dynamics approach has developed, in part, as a protest against reactionary, and often even autocratic, leadership styles that have prevailed in many school situations. But in our enthusiasm for this new approach, have we perhaps swung the pendulum too far? In applying "human relations" principles, we must be sure that we do not overlook the responsibility imposed upon every leader by the institutional realities of the formal institution of which he is a part. The designated leader has a responsibility and, in fact, a contractual obligation to accomplish specified group objectives; and judgements in respect to these goals often are beyond the decision-making purview of the immediate work-group.

At this juncture, therefore, it is imperative to re-examine our ideas about establishing a desirable balance between "human relations" (i.e., Consideration) and Initiating Structure emphases in leader behavior. In education we have properly and quite successfully stressed the importance of maintaining a "democractic" relationship between the teacher and his students. This is good. But let us remember, too, that the primary responsibility of a leader is to lead, and that by doing so he in no way becomes less "democratic." The essence of leading is to Initiate Structure-in-Interaction, and to orient these structures continually toward the solution of group problems and the accomplishment of the goals prescribed for the group. Research indicates that this "structuring" can be engaged in with no sacrifice of Consideration.

In our opinion, leader behavior characterized by high Initiation of Structure *and* high Consideration represents the ideal of democratic leadership that we all seek. The advantage of the present approach is that by identifying the components of this leadership style in behavioral terms and by focusing our efforts, as we have, upon the *behavior* of leaders, we are placed in a better position to develop dependable techniques for training teachers as more "effective" leaders.

References

1. Benevento, Philip. "Administrative Communication: A Study of Its Relationship to Administrative Leadership." Unpublished Ph.D. Dissertation, Syracuse Univ., 1956.

2. Fleishman, Edwin A., and others. *Leadership and Supervision in Industry: An Evaluation of a Supervisory Training Program.* Columbus, Ohio: Bureau of Educational Research, The Ohio State University, 1955.

3. Gibb, Cecil A. "Leadership," in Lindzey, Gardner (Ed.) *Handbook of Social Psychology.* Vol. II. Cambridge, Mass.: Addison-Wesley Publishing Co., 1954, p. 877-920.

4. Halpin, Andrew W. *Studies in Aircrew Composition. III. The Combat Leader Behavior of B-29 Aircraft Commanders.* Bolling Air Force Base, Washington, D. C.: Human Factors Operations Research Laboratories, Sept. 1953, (HFORL Memorandum No. TN-54-7).

5. Halpin, Andrew W. "The Leadership Ideology of Aircraft Commanders," *Journal of Applied Psychology,* Vol. 39, No. 2, 1955, p. 82-84.

6. Halpin, Andrew W. "The Leader Behavior and Leadership Ideology of Educational Administrators and Aircraft Commanders." *Harvard Educational Review,* Vol. 25, No. 1, Winter 1955, p. 18-32.

7. Halpin, Andrew W. *The Leadership Behavior of School Superintendents.* Columbus, Ohio: University Press, The Ohio State University, 1956.

8. Halpin, Andrew W., and Winer, B. James, "A Factorial Study of Leader Behavior Descriptions," in R. M. Stogdill and A. E. Coons (Eds.), *Leader Behavior: Its Description and Measurement.* Columbus, Ohio: Bureau of Business Research, The Ohio State University, 1956

9. Hemphill, John K. "Patterns of Leadership Behavior Associated with the Administrative Reputation of the Department of a College." *Journal of Educational Psychology,* Vol. 46, No. 7, Nov. 1955, p. 385-401.

10. Hemphill, John K. "A Proposed Theory of Leadership in Small Groups." *Psychological Monographs,* in press.

11. Johnson, Wendell. *People in Quandaries.* New York: Marper Bros., 1946.

12. Korzybski, Alfred. *Science and Sanity.* Lancaster, Pa.: The Science Press, 1933.

13. Shartle, Carroll L. *Executive Performance and Leadership.* New York: Prentice-Hall, 1956.

14. Stogdill, Ralph M. "Personal Factors Associated with Leadership: A Survey of the Literature," *Journal of Psychology.* Vol. 25, 1948. p. 35-71.

15. Stogdill, Ralph M., and Shartle, Carroll L. *Methods in the Study of Administrative Leadership.* Columbus, Ohio: Bureau of Business Research, The Ohio State University, 1955.

16. Young, J. Z. *Doubt and Certainty in Science.* Oxford: Clarendon Press, 1951.

The Behavioral Characteristics of Effective Educational Administrations

Ralph B. Kimbrough

The problem of selecting school principals, supervisors and various administrative assistants has plagued school superintendents and boards of education for many years. School superintendents often find themselves in a state of indecision when forced to decide among numerous applicants for an administrative position. Many applicants may appear equally desirable "on paper" and seem to be a good bet in an interview situation. All too often the superintendent of schools may decide among "equally qualified" applicants on the basis of "experience" or subjective impression. Subsequently he may find that he has selected a person ill-fitted for the position.

Professors of school administration are or should be faced with the problem of selecting prospective good school administrators. Oftentimes the decision is made on standards of academic proficiency as measured by one or more objective tests. Rigid adherence to academic proficiency may turn up good prospects, but also among the lot are numerous "odd balls," misfits or persons who are for other reasons unsuccessful as administrators. Recognizing this problem many departments of school administration have added interviews, statements of references and other such devices in an attempt to get judgments of personality attributes. These attempts are often fraught with subjectivity because persons interviewing applicants possess no body of proven criteria regarding the characteristics necessary for effective school administration.

Fortunately, more and more research is being aimed at defining the kind of person who is likely to be effective as a school administrator. The staff of the Department of Educational Administration and Supervision at the University of Tennessee has conducted research for the past six years dealing with the question of what behavioral characteristics differentiate between effective and ineffective school administrators. The Tennessee project, supported jointly by the University of Tennessee and the W. K. Kellogg Foundation, has revealed some promising findings.

The Tennessee Staff began with the assumption that there are behavioral characteristics which can be described which differentiate between effective and ineffective school administrators. In approaching the task of defining effective and ineffective behavior, the Tennessee research staff attempted to define behavior which was most basic to the personality structure of the individual in terms of the job to be performed. The staff went far beyond earlier attempts to define personal effectiveness in terms of such things as dress, general poise with people, public speaking ability, intelligence, and other general qualitative descriptions.

The first step taken in the Tennessee project was to involve numerous educators and representatives from basic disciplines in an attempt to gain consensus regarding behavioral statements which might differentiate among effective and ineffective performance for school administrators. This involved a careful analysis of previous research dealing with the problem. The statements which emerged were subsequently incorporated in an instrument which became known as the Tennessee Rating Guide. The staff has invested much time and effort in determining the validity of this rating instrument.

Validity of the Rating Guide

The Tennessee Staff began early in the project to put the original rating instrument to the acid test in the field to determine its validity. The first guide consisted of seven divisions with more than 185 cumbersome statements representing varying levels of effectiveness. The present guide known as the Tennessee Rating Guide consists of six divisions and 125 discrete statements of varying degrees of effectiveness.

A study, typical of one approach to validate the Tennessee Rating Guide, involved asking three system-wide school administrators of a large school system to place school principals in their schools into three categories as follows: (1) The sixteen most effective principals in the system; (2) the sixteen least effective principals in the system; and (3) those who appear to be neither particularly effective nor ineffective. The sixteen effective and sixteen ineffective principals were rated in the field on the Tennessee Rating Guide by persons who were unaware of how the principals had been placed by the system-wide administrators. These data were carefully analyzed to determine which items on the rating guide clearly differentiated between the effective and ineffective principals in the study.

Another approach to validate the Tennessee Rating Guide was national in scope. Professors of school administration at various institutions of higher learning in the United States were asked to select three competent school administrators in their respective areas. Each of these "competent" school administrators was then asked to rate on the Tennessee Rating Guide one of the "most" effective and one of the "least" effective school administrators with whom he had worked.

Other studies to validate the Tennessee Rating Guide employed on-the-job descriptions of school administrative behavior in critical problem situations. Through using the results of the various validation studies the validity of the original rating instrument was greatly improved. In some instances items in the instrument failed to differentiate between groups of effective and ineffective school administrators. These items were deleted from the guide. All other items were carefully reviewed and revised in order to strengthen the instrument.

The validation studies, in addition to showing characteristics which did tend to differentiate, revealed certain areas of behavioral characteristics which failed to distinguish between the two extremes. In some instances this was due to inability to rate a person on the given series of statements. In others, even though reliable ratings were possible, the statements simply failed to show a differentiation between effective and ineffective school administrators. One such area was the condition of physical fitness or health. It now appears that many effective school administrators may be characterized as paying little attention to their health, some suffering conditions bordering on chronic health deficiencies. Of considerable surprise to the Tennessee research staff was the fact that certain categories of behavioral statements relative to emotional condition failed to show a distinction. For example, it has long been thought that recreational activity as a release from intellectual fatigue is necessary to effectiveness. The Tennessee study failed to support this notion.

Statements Descriptive of Effective and Ineffective School Administrators

Enough data have been collected through the development and use of the Tennessee Rating Guide to allow considerable description of the effective school administrator in behavioral terms. In order to conceptualize the effective school leader, it will be necessary to deal also with the characteristics of ineffectiveness in the following paragraphs. In the space below there are two columns of selected illustrative statements taken directly from the Tennessee Rating Guide. The first column is descriptive of the most effective administrators rated in the Tennessee study. The second column represents behavior of the least effective administrators studied.

Characteristics of Most Effective School Administrators	*Characteristics of Least Effective School Administrators*
1. Steadily warm and appealing in relationship with others.	1. Tends to be a lone wolf.
2. Consistently seeks and considers the opinions of others.	2. Generally ignores the viewpoints of others.
3. Moves surely and judiciously in effecting policies.	3. Tends to ignore or defer action on policies.
4. Urges the use of processes consistent with best democratic practices.	4. Uses any expedient method available to attain a predetermined end.
5. Recognizes and analyzes problems.	5. Tends not to recognize the existence of problems.
6. Is dependable and predictable in word and action.	6. Supports conflicting ideas; action characterized by inconsistency.
7. Tends to try out new ideas after careful study and follows through on basis of experimental evidence.	7. Tends to operate within traditional practices or on basis of hunches.
8. Recognizes his mistakes and seeks to avoid repeating them.	8. Frequently makes the same mistake but seldom admits it.
9. Appears to meet crises with a contagious calmness; others feel at ease in his presence.	9. Tends to be upset by everyday occurrences and keeps staff in continuous uproar.
10. Places principle above his own personal advantages.	10. Tends to weasel out of situations.
11. Chooses words which clearly convey thoughts; is able to express abstract ideas.	11. Expresses himself in a fuzzy, incomprehensible manner and tends to puzzle listeners concerning what he means.
12. Is attentive in trying to grasp ideas expressed by others.	12. Tends to listen only to himself.
13. Facilitates a stimulating and well-ordered climate conducive to reaching group decisions.	13. Is either at a loss or monopolizes discussion when appointed official leader of a group.
14. Involves general public, staff members in major policy formulation.	14. Formulates policies himself; rarely discusses them with others.
15. Continually strives for careful group problem analysis; helps group recognize points of agreement.	15. Contributes little to help group arrive at a working consensus.
16. Consistently seeks and employs new data.	16. Disregards new data that challenge the status quo.
17. Discusses intelligently major social, political and economic issues.	17. Does not seem to be informed about or interested in contemporary events.
18. Is aware of and actively concerned with desires and interests of community groups, agencies and organizations.	18. Considers the school an island that is competitive with non-educational groups

The above statements are thirty-six of a possible 125 statements of varying effectiveness incorporated in the Tennessee Rating Guide. A person need not and probably could not exhibit the most effective behavior in all areas. However, studies using the instrument indicate that even though a person may be rated low in some instances, he must rate generally high on the total guide in order to be effective.

Through extensive on-the-job visitations to rate school administrators it is possible to cite instances in which effective and ineffective characteristics were in evidence. In the following sections a narrative description of both extremes is attempted.

Example of an Ineffective Administrator

In the following paragraphs an account is given of a staff visit with a school principal who was judged ineffective by his superiors. A summary paragraph at the end of this section points to some behavioral statements in the Tennessee Rating Guide which partially characterize Principal A. The staff report of the visit with the ineffective principal follows:

> We arrived at School X at 10:00 A.M. to spend a prearranged period of observation of the principal, Mr. A. Upon our arrival at the office the school clerk conducted a scurrying search for Mr. A. After several minutes of search, Mr. A was found helping the custodian start the lawn mower. Mr. A greeted us rather casually explaining, "I am rather busy trying to get things organized today." We soon felt that, even though our visit had been arranged at his convenience, Mr. A. was slightly tense and uneasy at having to take time away from "his job." One of us started to explain that we could return later when the office phone rang.
>
> Mr. A answered the phone and engaged in a strange conversation and ended up by saying, "Well, if they call you, guess California. What is your phone number and I will call you back when we find the answer." Replacing the phone Mr. A turned to us and asked, "Do you know which state has the longest federal highway?" Before we could respond the phone rang again and he engaged in a similar conversation and ended it by taking another phone number with the promise he would personally see that they got an answer within the next ten minutes. Turning to us again Mr. A started to explain that a local radio quiz was underway. We were interrupted by a seventh grade teacher announcing the arrival of four new seventh grade children. Mr. A quickly instructed the teacher to get the three seventh grade teachers together and "thresh out where to put them." He explained that he was rather busy and had to talk to some visitors today.
>
> After a series of telephone calls involving the radio quiz program and the recording of a long list of telephone numbers, another teacher hurried into the inner office and asked, "Mr. A, may I use the movie projector next period?" After some discussion Mr. A answered, "No, I think Mrs. Smith is going to use it."
>
> Mr. A turned to speak to us again when the cafeteria manager interrupted.

"Mr. A, did you order the groceries for tomorrow?" Mr. A excused himself to use the phone in the outer office and engaged in discussion with the cafeteria manager. During this time the school clerk conversed with us about how hard Mr. A worked to keep the school going and the fact that ". . . many teachers simply don't appreciate how much he does to help them. They are always bothering him and then talk about him to his back. That man really does work hard."

Mr. A returned and was about to be seated at his desk when a teacher interrupted saying, "Mr. A, Mrs. Smith says she is not going to use the projector next period. Would it be all right if I use it?" Mr. A hesitantly answered, "Yes, go ahead and use it then." Whereupon the teacher indicated several of the children in her room needed to get into the store. Checking his watch quickly Mr. A said to us apologetically, "You folks find yourself at home here. I open the store at this break every day. It will be only a few minutes."

During his absence the school clerk who had been puttering around among files in the office "filled us in" on some more of her opinions about the operation of the school. "The way some of these teachers harp about meetings. Mr. A has explained and explained that we don't have time to fool around with petty problems. We wouldn't have any problems if everyone would follow Mr. A's instructions. He just cannot seem to get them to understand. He worked all summer setting up the teachers handbook and they just don't appreciate it. He has used every faculty meeting this year explaining the handbook. It's all down there in black and white just like Professor B told it to him in class. Still these old moss backs just harp and harp . . ."

Mr. A returned and joined the conversation. Among several things he stated, "Mrs. Bell (school clerk) is right. We really have no problems around here except poorly trained teachers. I have tried to tell those professors of yours up there that the University ought to lay off so much theory. Now I hired three teachers this year. They all looked well dressed, spoke nice and made good grades in college. But look what happened to two of them—complete flops. This happens to me over and over. Looks like you folks would learn some day."

At this point the teacher who had asked for the projector barged into the office and the following conversation took place:

"Mr. A the projector is broken."

"Well Mrs. Staley, what is wrong with it."

"The sprocket is broken."

"Which one—the front one or the back one?"

"I don't know."

"Well, you folks excuse me. I will be back in a little while."

Before Mr. A could return to the inner office where we waited for him a teacher hailed him and a very interesting conversation occurred.

"Mr. A, I have been trying to see you about my field trip to the water . . ."

"Now, Mr. Barnes, I told you we had a policy against field trips."

"Mr. A, It's not in the handbook."

"Handbook! Handbook! All I hear is handbook, handbook. Now I think it's about time, Mr. Barnes, that you and I decide who is going to run this school. My fifteen years experience compared to your measly one says I am principal of this school."

"But, Mr. A, I . . ."

"But! But! But! I get so fed up with everyone . . ."

"But, Mr. A, . . ."

"Confound it, shut up! I'm telling you that as long as I am principal, I am going to be principal. Now the policy is that there will be no field trips to the water works."

Mr. A had crescendoed into a shout by now and was figuratively "blowing his stack" at the young teacher.

Mr. A was hopping mad when Mrs. Poole, a parent, phoned complaining that her seventh grade youngster was placed in Mrs. Faire's room. "Now Mrs. Poole, we did the best we could. . . . Well, in that case, I will see what I can do about it."

Principal A was one of the judged ineffective principals in one of the studies to validate the Tennessee Rating Guide. Repeated visits corroborated the above brief account and pointed to the following kinds of statements of behavioral characteristics: (1) Formulates policies himself (in the above incident Mr. A wrote a handbook and imposed it on teachers. In other instances Mr. A was observed to make policies in the absence of coöperative help from others); (2) Runs the whole show himself (No delegation of responsibility in evidence in the above account of Principal A. Things appear to be in a state of disorganization); (3) Attempts to maintain outward calmness but explodes about trivial details (Interviews with teachers indicated the emotional outburst over the field trip in the above described episode was not uncommon); (4) Frequently makes the same mistake but seldom admits it (Mr. A censured colleges in general for his own repeated mistakes in hiring teachers.) These statements characterizing Mr. A are only a few which are incorporated in the Tennessee Rating Guide.

Statement Characterizing an Effective Administrator

Principal A in the above episode has opposites as revealed by many observed incidents of effective administrative performances. During the study of school administrators in the field, the Tennessee Research Staff made it a practice to talk with several persons in job association with the person being observed. A teacher gave the following narration of his principal:

Mr. X is the best principal with whom I have worked. I just put him at the top of the list. He is great.

I can give you one good example of why I think he is such a good principal. If we have a disagreement he takes it to staff meeting and we finally thrash it out. Just last spring we got all bothered about grades. Some teachers wanted to record letter grades and others wanted numerical marks. Mr. X came into faculty meeting and stated the problem. After talking about the problem briefly, he just leaned back in his seat and asked, "What do you want to do about it?"

You should hear one of these faculty meetings sometime—downright comical when you look back on them. Those old sisters get to going and shake their fists at each other. You have never heard such an argument. Mr. X just leans back and lets them go. But the surprising thing about it is we finally come out of these things happy about the whole matter. A decision is made. People seldom feel hurt after it is over. If you had told me a person could do this way before he came here, I would have said you were crazy. He has a hundred per cent backing of his faculty. Students like him too.

He always works to improve things. This school was run down at the heels when he came here. Parents were not interested. Students were unimpressed with school. Teachers were just going through the motions. Largely through his help we are now organized and at least think we know what we are doing. The gripe sessions are gone. Oh! of course, we complain about petty things, but I mean the chronic complaints.

For one thing the custodians were always fighting among each other and with teachers. The school building was filthy. You know what I mean. The toilets smelled to high Heaven. Mr. X talked to the custodians first. They began to work on a way to divide up the work. Mr. X was instrumental in getting someone from the state department to come in and of all things they had a custodian's school for the whole county. Then we had a joint meeting of the faculty and custodians. Even some students were invited. Mr. X presented a plan for keeping the building in order that he had worked out with the custodians. They had the neatest drawings of the school you have ever seen with indications of who would be responsible for what. Although it looked good to all of us, we thought it was just another straw in the wind—would soon blow over. It did not. We have the cleanest building in the county. He went to bat for us and got the building painted too. He is not afraid of going after anything for us if we believe in it. There is no more of this on again off again big I and little you.

From the descriptions of Mr. X by one teacher, one can begin to see several characteristics that differentiate Mr. X from Mr. A in the preceding section. It should be emphasized that such reports were only used to corroborate actual observations of behavior in one phase of the Tennessee study. Repeated observations pointed conclusively to characteristic behavior implied in the teacher's account. Some of these were: (1) Mr. X continually strives for careful group problem analysis; helps group recognize points of agreement; (2) Most people with whom he works have important responsibilities in which they are genuinely interested; (3) Attempts to involve staff members and students in major policy formulation; (4) Facilitates a stimulating and well-ordered climate conducive to reaching group decisions; (5) Moves surely and judiciously in effecting policies.

The Effective Educational Administrator

Having examined selected statements of behavioral characteristics and having seen them demonstrated in two accounts of administrative behavior, it is now possible to proceed with an abstract summary of the characteristics of the effective school administrator. This can be generally categorized under the paragraph headings which follow.

Interpersonal Relations. The effective school administrator instills close interpersonal relations with and among the group involved in the administrative endeavor. He promotes closeness as opposed to promoting distance between people. His constituents speak of him with a striking absence of defense. He helps groups organize in terms of purposes, interests and special abilities in order to fully release and achieve the coöperative utilization of the intelligence of the immediate group. The staff with whom he works reflects the stability and morale which accrue from judicious implementation of coöperatively developed school policies, plans, and procedures. The effective school administrator urges the use of processes consistent with democratic values.

Intelligent Operation. Effective educational administrators are critical in the identification and definition of educational problems in their situation. In fact, much of their discussion with people centers around problems about which they are seeking solutions. The effective school leader is consistent in terms of basic educational beliefs and has considerable ability to discuss why he took certain past actions as a person. He is especially cognizant of the special abilities and skills among the school staff. The effective school leader seldom repeats a mistake. In fact, he appears to have generally profited in increased understandings and skills as a result of recognizing personal mistakes. The effective educational administrator appears to have carefully reflected on his own status position and has assumed responsibilities commensurate with the truly important functions inherent in the status position.

Emotional Stability. The statement characterizing the most effective administrator on the Tennessee Rating Guide states, "Appears to meet crises with a contagious calmness; others feel at ease in his presence." Obviously this is not a characterization of the excitable person who shouts "fire" in a crowded gymnasium. However, it is just as important to see that this statement should not be interpreted as characterizing a moron who does not have enough insight to get excited. Anyone who has had experience with such a status leader will quickly recognize that he fails to promote a "contagious calmness" among a group. In fact, just the opposite is generally true in a crisis situation where no insightful leadership is present. The effective educational administrator helps create a calm, collected feeling which helps a group meet and confidently analyze a crisis.

Ethical and Moral Strength. The effective educational administrator tenaciously follows the truth as opposed to expediency as a means of action. He has definite, personally understood convictions and is willing to abide by them even though such action may not always be personally beneficial to him. This does not imply that he is a "pig headed" individual who insists that he has the truth yet refuses to have his truths examined experimentally. The effective educational administrator arrives at his truths through the coöperative use of experimentation. He may be observed publicly to admit he is "wrong" in the light of new evidence. No one doubts the effective educational leader's intentions in view of his high integrity. The staff members feel assured that he will not intentionally violate staff agreements reached through the coöperative use of intelligence.

Adequacy of Communication. The effective educational administrator promotes excellent communication in and among the group involved in an endeavor. One observes that he is effective in communicating abstract ideas to individuals and groups. In addition to his ability to clearly convey his position to others, he is good listener. Listening is one of the qualities of communication which many people overlook in prospective administrators. The Tennessee study indicates that the ability to listen, to grasp ideas expressed by others, is one of the characteristics necessary for success in school administration. The effective educational administrator interests people in and stimulates their considered analysis of new ideas in education. This is an element in his ability to communicate with people effectively. Finally, the effective educational administrator facilitates group communication and discussion through a climate conducive to reaching group decisions. He is highly skilled in helping discussion groups recognize and accept points of agreement through democratic processes.

Operation as a Citizen. Effective educational administrators are well informed about significant social, political, and economic trends and events which affect education. For example, they discuss intelligently the possible educational implications of such developments as automation in industry. They understand the importance of the school as an agency to improve living in the community and generally believe in the rights of all community groups to have a voice in the operation of the public schools. The effective school administrator has a working knowledge of the important community agencies and forces which affect education. In effect he is looked upon as one of the important leaders in the community.

Are Behavioral Characteristics the Only Determinants of Effectiveness?

The Tennessee staff does not contend that the quality of behavioral characteristics incorporated in the Tennessee Rating Guide are the only factors which determine effectiveness. For example, there is the matter of knowledge of the job to be performed. Certainly an effective school administrator needs a degree of sophistication in functional knowledge in the field of school administration. Since much of the experimentation at Tennessee has been toward selection of people at the pre-service level, it was not feasible to test for the degree of knowledge about the job. One would not expect pre-service students to possess a great body of knowledge about the field of school administration.

On the other hand, it is the considered opinion of the staff that a person with the effective behavioral characteristics described herein will tend to avail himself to the knowledge necessary to perform well on the job. An individual cannot define problems, experiment, interest others in ideas and profit from previous experience without assimilation of knowledge about any field of endeavor.

Looking at the problem from another standpoint, a person with ineffective behavioral characteristics may accumulate much abstract knowledge of the field of school administration and still fail to perform adequately the tasks of school administration. In fact, certain subjective evidence in the Tennessee study indicate this to be a strong hypothesis.

The Tennessee project has revealed that behavioral characteristics apparently make a difference in the degree of success a person enjoys in educational administration. Furthermore, the Tennessee Rating Guide appears to measure some areas of behavioral characteristics which are most critical. It appears that the findings in the Tennessee project have important implications for the preservice selection and training of school leaders. There is strong indication that the findings may in the future be of help to practicing school administrators in the matter of filling administrative positions within their organizations.

The EPL of Elementary Principals: A Study of Executive Professional Leadership

Neal Gross and Robert E. Herriott

Of all the administrative officials in the complex bureaucracy that manages public school systems in the United States, few have at their command greater potentialities for influencing *directly* the type and quality of education young pupils receive than has the elementary school principal. He is the school executive in closest contact with the central functions of the school: teaching and learning. His position of formal leadership provides him with the opportunity to motivate his staff and to improve their standards and performance in teaching. He can offer them valuable advice in their efforts to deal with classroom problems. He can make their meetings important and stimulating educational experiences. He can maximize the different skills of his teachers and help them develop their competencies. The elementary school principal, in short, enjoys substantial opportunities to provide a high order of staff leadership.

Although a conception of the elementary school administrator's role as the *professional leader* of his staff permeates the educational literature on the principalship, very little systematic evidence is available on either the determinants or the effects of such administrative behavior. One of the objectives of the National Principalship Study was to shed light on these questions through the identification of circumstances associated with the efforts of principals to conform to a leadership definition of their job.[1] The 175 elementary school principals participating in this phase of the Study were part of a national sample of all elementary and secondary

[1] This paper deals only with possible determinants of the professional leadership of elementary school principals. For findings about the effects on schools of this type of administrative performance as well as a more detailed consideration of the general findings presented here, see Neal Gross and Robert E. Herriott, *Staff Leadership in Public Schools.* New York: John Wiley & Sons, 1965. 247 pp.

school principals in American cities of a population of 50,000 or more during the 1960-1961 school year.

The central concept of this research, *Executive Professional Leadership* (EPL), refers to the behavior of a principal that can be viewed as his efforts to conform to a definition of his role which stresses his obligation to improve the quality of teacher performance. There are many ways in which conformity to this definition of the principal's role could be measured. Our approach was to ask a sample of teachers in each school to report how frequently (always, almost always, frequently, occasionally, almost never, never) their principal engaged in the following kinds of behavior:

1. Has constructive suggestions to offer teachers in dealing with their major problems
2. Displays a strong interest in improving the quality of the educational program
3. Gives teachers the feeling that they can make significant contributions to improving the classroom performance of their students
4. Helps teachers to understand the sources of important problems they are facing
5. Makes teachers' meetings a valuable educational activity
6. Considers "what is best for all the children" in his decisions affecting educational programs
7. Brings to the attention of teachers educational literature that is of value to them in their jobs
8. Maximizes the different skills found in his faculty
9. Treats teachers as professional workers
10. Gives teachers the feeling that their work is an "important" activity
11. Takes a strong interest in the professional development of teachers
12. Gets teachers to upgrade their performance standards in their classrooms.

The teachers' responses to these twelve questions were then summarized through the technique of Guttman scaling, and a single EPL Score was obtained for each of the 175 principals.[2] An inspection of these scores indicated that elementary school principals varied greatly in their conformity to a professional leadership definition of their role. What could account for this variation in performance?

Determinants of EPL: A Theoretical Formulation

The hypotheses we tested about determinants of EPL were based on certain theoretical ideas about the process of socialization or role learning to which administrators such as school principals are exposed. Prior to presenting the findings bearing on these hypotheses, it is relevant to consider the theoretical notions on which they were based.

[2]The technical details of the construction of the EPL Scale and a consideration of methodological problems pertaining to it are presented in Gross and Herriott, *op. cit.*, Chapter II and Appendix D.

A basic assumption of our inquiry was that school principals undergo a two-phased process of training. The first we designated as the *preparatory phase.* This is the period of formal training which must be undergone by principals in institutions of higher learning. There they are exposed to the skills, knowledge, values, and attitudes that professors of education judge to be prerequisites for entrance into the principalship. During this time, the neophytes encounter only a few of the hard realities that will confront them in the schools in which they will later work because training institutions typically have little *detailed* knowledge of the facts of life of the places where their students will eventually be assigned. In addition, the role definitions they teach are often idealized and general; they have, after all, only a limited period to impart knowledge, skill, and standards. Students who successfully complete the preparatory phase are then certified to carry out, with a minimum degree of competence, a specified administrative job in *some* organization. They have finished the initial and formal process of training, and we assume that they have internalized to some extent an ideal definition of their role. They are now ready to serve as principals.

The second phase of training begins when the individual, having successfully completed the preparatory phase, assumes his administrative position in a specific school. This may be described as the *phase of organizational reality,* the period when the administrator confronts the complex realities of organizational life. This is "the real thing." The neophyte no longer deals with the ideas of textbook authors or of his professors but with the values, attitudes, and convictions of individuals with and through whom he must work. He no longer writes examinations on hypothetical classroom problems but must resolve issues and make decisions directly bearing on his associates and the clients of the organization. In the words of many a new administrator, "Theory and practice are not the same!" In the preparatory phase, the neophyte occupied the position of learner, "played at" an administrative position, and received a general and idealized definition of his role for later use. In the organizational reality phase, however, he occupies a given position and must deal with the hard facts of life in a specific school system.

As just stated, we assumed that during the preparatory phase, the neophyte internalized to some degree an idealized conception of his role—a conception that provides him with standards for performing his role in the organizational reality phase. We further assumed that in the preparatory phase of training, the obligation to improve the performance of his professional staff is impressed upon him.

Subscribing to such standards is one thing; conforming to them is another. Of the many obstacles that might block an administrator's efforts to conform to this leadership definition of his role, we postulated that two are especially important.

The first obstacle is the claim of his subordinates to professional status. Teachers themselves have completed specialized training at institutions of higher learning and have been judged to possess at least the minimum competence required to carry out their organizational tasks in an essentially autonomous manner. Their employment by a school system indicates its provisional acceptance of their professional qualifications. If accorded "tenure," such personnel receive from the organization its full acknowledgement of their capabilities and their right to perform their tasks in an autonomous manner. Therefore, they may interpret any efforts of principals to influence their performance as invasions of their professional prerogatives. If, for example, administrators take the initiative in attempting to help their professional subordinates with problems, their efforts may be construed as betraying a lack of confidence and as being out of bounds. Or if principals urge their subordinates to try a new practice, it may be viewed as an encroachment on their rights as professionals. In short, the fact that subordinates have a claim to professional status could lead them to resist any efforts on the part of their administrators to serve as their leaders.

The second obstacle to a principal's EPL that we postulated is the heavy demand on his time made by routine administrative and clerical duties. The principal is responsible for and must devote time to the following kinds of activities: managing the office, dealing with correspondence, writing memoranda and bulletins, preparing reports for his administrative superiors, taking inventories of equipment and supplies, scheduling activities and keeping official records, handling disciplinary cases, ordering or distributing supplies, and handling organizational publicity. If we add to these tasks the responsibilities of being the organizational represenitive who deals with parents, community agencies, and officials in the higher administration, the principal could readily allocate nearly all his time and energy to these kinds of administrative functions. Thus, the many demands made on the administrator to accomplish routine managerial and clerical tasks could leave little time or energy for offering leadership to his professional staff.

Up to this point, we have made two major assumptions: the first is that a principal to some degree internalizes an EPL conception of his role during the preparatory phase of training; the second is that during the phase of organizational reality, certain obstacles will make it difficult to conform to this role definition. If these assumptions are tenable, it follows that an administrator's EPL will be a function, in part, of conditions that will lead to the maintenance, reduction, or surmounting of these obstacles. More precisely, the assumptions we made led us to expect that those conditions that perpetuate or accentuate the postulated blocks to professional leadership would serve to decrease EPL, while conditions that would reduce the obstacles or permit an administrator to overcome them would serve to increase it.

Such a formulation led us to reason about the kinds of conditions in the principal's work environment that would serve to maintain or reduce obstacles to his EPL or encourage him to surmount them. The hypotheses we tested about determinants of EPL involve circumstances of this kind. One set of hypotheses focused on the higher administrators of school systems and the ways their behavior could influence a principal's EPL. A second set of hypotheses dealt with characteristics of a principal's relations with his teachers that we reasoned would be associated with his leadership efforts. A third set of hypotheses concerned personal characteristics of principals which our theoretical formulation led us to anticipate would be related to his EPL.

Tests of Hypotheses: The Higher Administration and EPL

The theoretical formulation presented above to account for variation in EPL leads to an examination of those conditions present in the principal's work environment that serve to maintain or reduce obstacles to EPL or that encourage principals to surmount them. One possible source of such conditions may be located in an important characteristic of a public school as a social system: the school is a sub-unit of a larger organization. This means that although the principal is the chief administrative officer of his school, he is at the same time subordinate and accountable to other administrative officials. The circumstances to which he is exposed in this facet of his role network could have important effects on his EPL.

Just as teachers are exposed to principals who offer strong or weak professional leadership, so, in turn, principals may be given variable professional leadership by their superiors. Higher administrators who themselves conform to a professional leadership definition of their role can serve as models for the principal in his efforts to lead. In doing so, they show their principals that the obstacles can be overcome and demonstrate effective strategies and techniques to this end. Therefore, we assumed, other things being equal, that principals' own professional leadership will be directly affected by experiences of this kind with their superiors, and we developed the hypothesis that: the greater the EPL displayed by the principal's immediate administrative superior, the greater the EPL of the principal.

Our findings provided support for the hypothesis. Approximately one-quarter of the principals reported that their superiors infrequently helped them to understand the sources of their important problems or made principals' meetings a valuable educational activity. A similar portion described their superiors as not usually taking a strong interest in their professional development. And it was these principals who on the average had the lowest EPL scores.

We also found support for the hypothesis that the principals whose administrative superiors allowed them to participate in the evaluation of applicants for positions as teachers in their schools demonstrate a higher degree of professional leadership than those principals who are not permitted to participate. Nearly half of the elementary principals declared that they were not allowed to assess applicants. If principals must work with newly appointed teachers whose educational beliefs are contrary to their own or to those of others on the staff, or whose personal characteristics hamper cooperation, the result may be strain and tension between principals and teachers which may erode the principals' professional leadership. In addition, principals may readily interpret the failure of higher administrators to involve them in selecting teachers for their own schools as lack of confidence and respect for their judgment—a condition that may, in turn, undermine their confidence in their own abilities.

A third hypothesis that received empirical support was that principals whose administrative superiors strongly endorse their efforts to improve teaching methods exert greater EPL than those whose superiors do not. If, as we have maintained, the principals' attempts to give professional leadership to their staffs are often threatened with obstruction, they need to be strongly supported and rewarded by their superiors in their efforts to improve the performance of their staffs.

A fourth hypothesis we examined involved the social support given principals by their superiors. In conferences with their superiors, principals may or may not be made to feel that they can talk frankly about their difficulties with their staffs or about their other problems; they may or may not experience a catharsis and a sense of support and understanding. If we assume that a supportive climate will facilitate the efforts of principals to cope with obstacles to their EPL, then it follows that: the more social support a principal receives from his immediate administrative superior, the greater the EPL of the principal. The data also provided support for this hypothesis.

These findings strongly suggest that higher administrators would be well advised to examine carefully how their own performance may be influencing the EPL of their principals and to consider the possibility that any efforts to upgrade principals' EPL may call for changes in their own performance.

Principal-Teacher Relationships and EPL

We tested five hypotheses about dimensions of the principal's relationships with his teachers that our theoretical formulation led us to anticipate would be related to his EPL.

The first pertains to the influence on EPL of a principal's involvement of teachers in his decisions. We reasoned that a principal who permits his teachers to share in his decision making is thereby letting them know that he values their judgment and recognizes them as colleagues in a common educational endeavor. His teachers, in turn, would tend to view him as a superordinate who seeks to enlist their full cooperation in accomplishing school objectives. He would thereby be setting in motion forces that would reduce the barrier to EPL offered by the autonomy of his staff. On the basis of this reasoning, we hypothesized that the more a principal permits his teachers to share in his decisions, the greater his EPL. The data provided support for this hypothesis.

A second hypothesis that the findings supported was that the more egalitarian a principal's relationships with his teachers, the greater his EPL. We reasoned that a principal who minimizes distinctions of formal status would de-emphasize that he is the superior of his teachers and that, as a result, the teachers would not tend to view him primarily as a representative of the school bureaucracy. They would be less likely to perceive his interest or involvement in their teaching as interference with their professional prerogatives by an agent of the higher administration, and hence would be less likely to resist their principal's efforts to offer professional leadership.

The three other hypotheses we examined about EPL in regard to the principal's relationships with his teachers also received empirical support. They specified that: the more social support a principal offers his teachers, the greater his EPL; the greater the managerial support a principal offers his teachers, the greater his EPL;

and the greater the principal's support of his teachers in cases of conflict between teachers and pupils, the greater his EPL.

Personal Attributes of the Principal and EPL

On the basis of our theoretical formulation we also reasoned that certain personal attributes of the principal would be associated with his EPL. We found, as hypothesized, that the following characteristics of the principal were *positively* related to his EPL: self-evaluation of his ability to provide educational leadership to his staff, the time he devotes to his job, his academic record in college, and his interpersonal skills. Our data also revealed that principals who expressed a service motive for seeking the principalship, in comparison with those who did not, exhibited greater EPL.

Among the hypotheses we tested was one predicting a positive relationship between the degree to which principals internalize the professional leadership definition of their role and EPL and another predicting a negative relationship between the importance they attribute to their managerial tasks and EPL. As predicted, these general conceptions of role did indeed tend to be related to EPL—up to a point. However, the findings also revealed that in those principals who internalized the professional conception of their role to an extreme degree, EPL regressed, and that placing too little emphasis on their routine administrative tasks had a similar effect. Thus, the findings imply that principals must be on guard equally against overstressing the professional conception of their role and undervaluing their purely managerial obligations.

Other Findings About Determinants of EPL

In addition to testing hypotheses based on our theoretical formulation of determinants of EPL, we also examined the relationship to EPL of a number of other variables which are frequently assumed in educational literature or in practice to be associated with it.

Most school systems seek principals who will offer strong professional leadership to their staffs. How much weight should be given to the educational experience of candidates? What type and what amount of previous teaching experience in elementary schools should the candidates have who are being considered for the principalship? Should those who have had the most elementary teaching experience be given preference? Should teachers who have spent a longer time in the classroom, regardless of school level, be given priority? We found that neither type nor length of previous teaching experience discriminated among principals as to their EPL. Our findings suggest that school systems operating on the assumption that these characteristics should receive weight in the selection of principals need to reexamine their criteria of selection.

Is previous administrative experience related to EPL? Do principals who served as assistant or vice-principals tend to exhibit higher EPL than those who have not had this type of previous administrative experience? Our finding revealed that they do not: we found no relationship between previous administrative experience of this sort and EPL.

What about the formal education of principals? Is it related to EPL? We found that one of the three measures of educational preparation that we examined, graduate courses in educational administration, was negatively related to EPL and that the *trend* of the relationship between two other indices, undergraduate and graduate courses in education, and EPL was also negative.

Is the age of principals related to their EPL? The findings revealed that age was negatively related to Executive Professional Leadership: on the average, the older the principal, the lower his EPL score. Our data also showed that those appointed to their first principalship at the relatively late age of 45 years or older exhibited the weakest professional leadership, while those appointed between the ages of 36 and 40 exhibited the strongest. The mean EPL score of the last group, however, was only slightly higher than that of principals who had obtained their administrative positions when they were 30 or younger. Thus, appointing teachers who are beyond the age of 45 to elementary principalships may in general be a questionable practice, and to discriminate against young teachers who seek to become principals has little justification in the light of expectations for their EPL.

What about sex and marital status? Our findings revealed no simple relationships between sex or marital status and EPL. They also indicated that the principal's salary and the number of his administrative assistants were not related to EPL, and they provided no evidence in support of any patterning of EPL by size of city. We did discover, however, that in addition to the personal characteristics considered earlier, two others were positively associated with Executive Professional Leadership: the motive of service and the commitment of off-duty time to one's job.

Our findings suggest that if Executive Professional Leadership is to be the criterion, many school systems are selecting principals on grounds that appear to have little empirical justification: type or amount of teaching experience, experience as an assistant or vice principal, number of undergraduate and graduate courses in educational administration, sex, and marital status. They also suggest that characteristics that may require more consideration in appointing elementary principals are: a high level of academic performance in college, a high order of interpersonal skill, the motive of service, the willingness to commit off-duty time to their work, and relatively little seniority as teachers.

Our investigation, in summary, revealed that many widely held assumptions about correlates of EPL receive no empirical support. It also indicated the utility of a sociological perspective in the study of possible determinants of the professional leadership of principals. Such an approach led to the isolation of a number of variables involving the principal's relationships with the higher administration and his staff, in addition to his own personal attributes, that were associated with his professional leadership.

Teacher Expectations of Administrative Behavior

Harvey Goldman and James E. Heald

Contemporary concern about teacher-administrator relationships has been expressed in many ways. In this paper some factors related to teachers' affinity for their principals are explored, with particular emphasis on the impact of administrative behavior on the teacher-principal relationship. The analyses of the data are intended to serve as one means of bringing to the attention of those concerned with the administration of schools the expectations that teachers hold for principals and the conditions under which those expectations appear operative.

During 1966, a study was undertaken to determine which specific aspects of the administrator's total behavioral pattern have the greatest impact on teachers' attitudes toward that behavioral pattern.

In this study, the Executive Professional Leadership (EPL) Score represents a measure of a teacher's evaluation of the total behavioral pattern of his principal. The EPL Score, developed by Gross and Herriott, was designed as a measure of "the efforts of an executive of a professionally staffed organization to conform to a definition of his role that stresses his obligation to improve the quality of staff performance" (3, p. 22). Thus, the concept refers to the *behaviors* of formally designated executives (in this case principals) who operate within professionally staffed organizations. A basic assumption with regard to this concept is that any study of leadership behavior must take into account the situational context in which it is found (3, pp. 8-10).

The EPL Score was obtained by asking each participant to evaluate his principal's behavior, and a numerical value (ranging from 1 to 6) was assigned each answer. The individual scores were then averaged to obtain a composite score. The more positive the answer, the greater the numerical value assigned.

The 12 statements from which the Executive Professional Leadership Score was derived are as follows:

1. Gives teachers the feeling that their work is an "important" activity.
2. Gets teachers to upgrade their performance standards in their classrooms.
3. Gives teachers the feeling that they can make significant contributions to improving the classroom performance of their students.
4. Makes teachers' meetings a valuable educational activity.
5. Has constructive suggestions to offer teachers in dealing with their major problems.
6. Takes a strong interest in my professional development.
7. Treats teachers as professional workers.

8. Considers "what is best for all the children" in his decisions affecting educational programs.
9. Maximizes the different skills found in his faculty.
10. Brings to the attention of teachers educational literature that is of value to them in their jobs.
11. Helps teachers to understand the sources of important problems they are facing.
12. Displays a strong interest in improving the quality of the educational program.

A rapid inspection of the questions from which the EPL was derived clearly indicates each is quite general in nature. None seek to determine the specific techniques through which the leader's interest is expressed. Rather, each represents an attempt to obtain an evaluation of a leader's behavior in a "broad" area.

The five specific aspects of administrative behavior represent, on the other hand, attempts to measure specific behavioral patterns of principals which are related to the more generalized evaluation. When computing these scores the answers provided to the questions were assigned a numerical value which increased with the positive direction of the answer. The specific aspects measured (all of which were also derived from the Gross and Herriott study) are as follows:

1. Support of Teachers Authority–The extent to which the principal is seen as supportive of the teachers' authority.
2. Level of Egalitarian Relationships–The extent to which the teachers believe the principal promotes an atmosphere of equality between himself and his teachers.
3. Level of Staff Involvement–The degree to which teachers see themselves being involved in the decision-making processes of the school.
4. Level of Managerial Support–The extent to which they see their principal as providing and facilitating managerial services.
5. Social Support of Teachers–The degree to which the teachers perceive their principal as being an individual who understands and supports their positions.

The Social Support of Teachers' Authority Score was obtained from analysis of the answers given to the following statements:

1. Support a teacher's discipline decision that the principal believes is grossly unfair to the child.
2. Insist that students obey teachers' instructions first, and complain about them later.
3. Side with the teacher when a student complains about the teacher's behavior, even if the student's complaint is legitimate.
4. Back the teacher in any public controversy between teacher and student.

Answers to the following statements were the basis for determination of the Perceived Level of Egalitarian Relationships Score:

1. Encourage all teachers to call him by his first name when the students are not present.
2. Make it a practice to have lunch frequently with the teachers in his school.
3. Discourage teachers from treating him as "one of the gang" at informal gatherings of teachers.
4. Avoid first-name relationships with his teachers.
5. Insist, tactfully, that teachers show due respect for his position as principal.

Perceived Level of Staff Involvement was obtained from answers to the following statements:

1. Share with teachers the responsibility for determining the minimum level of satisfactory student performance in your school.
2. Share with teachers the responsibility for evaluating how good a job the school is doing.
3. Share with teachers the responsibility for determining how teachers should be supervised.
4. Share with teachers the responsibility for developing a policy for handling student discipline problems.

Perceived Level of Managerial Support was derived in the same manner as the others from reactions to the following statements:

1. Procrastinates in his decision-making.
2. Displays inconsistency in his decisions.
3. Has the relevant facts before making important decisions.
4. Requires teachers to engage in unnecessary paper work.
5. Makes a teacher's life difficult because of his administrative ineptitude.
6. Runs meetings and conferences in a disorganized fashion.

The last of the specific teacher-administrator scores to be considered here is the Perceived Level of Social Support. The statements from which the score was derived are:

1. Puts you at ease when you talk with him.
2. Rubs people the wrong way.
3. Develops a real interest in your welfare.
4. Makes those who work with him feel inferior to him.
5. Displays integrity in his behavior.

In review, the EPL Score represents a teacher's generalized evaluation of his principal's leadership qualities (within the limitations of the definition given previously) while the specific teacher-administrator scores refer to the teacher's evaluation of more specific behavioral patterns manifested by the principal (again, with each of the scores being limited by the definition assigned).

In order to gather the necessary data, a minimum of one personal visit was made to each of the 62 schools involved in the study. A meeting was held with the principal of each school, and the research study was also explained to and discussed with the teachers at building level staff meetings. It was clearly explained that participation was voluntary, and the materials were left with the teachers in stamped, addressed envelopes which could be placed in any United States mailbox after being completed.

The data from which the EPL and other specific behavioral scores were derived were taken from information provided by the participating teachers who completed the Teacher Section: The National Principalship Study, and all scores were calculated in the manner described by Gross and Herriott (3) in Chapter 7 of their book.

The Participants. Every teacher whose professional responsibilities included teaching in a classroom setting at least 50 per cent of the time was approached and asked to participate in the study. Four hundred and five elementary teachers (64.41 per cent) and 252 secondary teachers (52.73 per cent of the total) participated in the study. Forty-four elementary principals (84.61 per cent of the total) and 11 secondary principals (100 per cent of the total) also completed all the materials.

Comparative data regarding 44 respondents and a similar number of non-respondents were gathered for four characteristics–age, years of teaching, college degrees, and sex–in order to ascertain whether or not differences existed between those who did and those who did not participate. The differenbes between the two groups were insignificant except for one characteristic; in that case it was found that a larger proportion of the secondary non-respondents were males than was true for the participants.

With EPL as a dependent variable, a multiple correlation was calculated to determine the relationship of the five specific teacher-administrator relationship factors to the constant (EPL). The multiple correlation coefficient of +0.81 thus derived is indicative of a high degree of relationship between EPL and the five independent variables. It is clearly observable from Table 1 that two of the variables (Perceived Social Support of Teachers and Perceived Level of Staff Involvement) contributed more to the multiple correlation coefficient than did the other three factors (Perceived Support of Teacher Authority, Perceived Level of Egalitarian Relationships, and Perceived Managerial Support of Teachers).

This relationship is all the more apparent when the three independent variables which did not contribute materially to the multiple correlation coefficient were excluded and the correlation was calculated once again utilizing only the two more influential variables.

When only two of the variables were utilized, the multiple correlation coefficient was +0.80. Clearly, the two independent variables in Table 2 offered as good a measure of EPL as all five tested in the previous table. Utilizing only two variables the multiple correlation coefficient did not differ significantly from that obtained when all five were included.

Table 1. A multiple correlation with Executive Professional Leadership (the dependent variable) and the five teacher-administrator relationship factors (the independent variables)

Variable	*Multiple Correlation Coefficient*	*Partial Correlation Coefficient*
Executive Professional Leadership	+0.81	
Perceived Support of Teacher Authority		+0.08
Perceived Level of Egalitarian Relationships		+0.06
Perceived Managerial Support of Teachers		+0.18
Perceived Social Support of Teachers		+0.46
Perceived Level of Staff Involvement		+0.31

Table 2. A multiple correlation with Executive Professional Leadership the dependent variable and Perceived Social Support of Teachers and Perceived Level of Staff Involvement the independent variables

Variable	*Multiple Correlation Coefficient*	*Partial Correlation Coefficient*
Executive Professional Leadership	+0.80	
Perceived Social Support of Teachers		+0.64
Perceived Level of Staff Involvement		+0.35

In Table 3, a correlation matrix depicting the relationships between EPL and the five teacher-administrator relationship factors in terms of simple correlations is presented. Gross and Herriott found that all the independent variables correlated significantly with one another, and except for one such factor (Perceived Support of Teacher Authority) their findings were corroborated here. It is interesting to note that, in this case, Perceived Support of Teacher Authority did not correlate significantly with either the independent variables or the dependent variable; this is in marked contrast to the findings of Gross and Herriott who found that this factor correlated at the .001 level of significance with EPL. Nevertheless, all but one of the remaining intercorrelations was significant at the .01 level–the relationship between Perceived Level of Staff Involvement and Perceived Level of Egalitarian Relationships was significant at the .05 level.

Table 3. A correlation matrix depicting relationships between Executive Professional Leadership and five teacher-administrator relationship factors

	Perceived Support of Teacher Authority	*Perceived Level of Egalitarian Relationships*	*Executive Professional Leadership*	*Perceived Managerial Support of Teachers*	*Perceived Social Support of Teachers*	*Perceived Level of Staff Involvement*
Perceived Support of Teacher Authority	1.00					
Perceived Level of Egalitarian Relationships	0.03	1.00				
Executive Professional Leadership	0.17	0.31	1.00			
Perceived Managerial Support of Teachers	0.12	0.28	0.67	1.00		
Perceived Social Support of Teachers	0.15	0.35	0.77	0.73	1.00	
Perceived Level of Staff Involvement	0.12	0.21	0.64	0.54	0.59	1.00

It appears that Perceived Social Support of Teachers, alone, was the best single predictor of EPL. When correlated with EPL, that factor was nearly as good a predictor (r = +0.77) of EPL as the multiple correlation utilizing all five factors (+0.81).

When separated into sex categories there appeared to be little difference in extent or order of the importance attributed to the independent variables.

However, this high degree of intercorrelation should not serve to vitiate the significance of the results derived from the multiple correlations. This is particularly true since the two processes were not utilized for the same purpose, the simple correlations being computed to examine the degree of concomitance between and among the scores for each of the variables and the multiple correlations being computed for the purpose of determining which combinations of independent variables would serve as the best predictors of EPL. It would seem, therefore, that the high degree of intercorrelation between the independent variables does not pose a serious problem in this instance.

Table 4. A multiple correlation of female teacher responses with Executive Professional Leadership the dependent variable and the five teacher-administrator factors the independent variables

Variable	*Multiple Correlation Coefficient*	*Partial Correlation Coefficient*
Executive Professional Leadership	+0.81	
Perceived Support of Teacher Authority		+0.09
Perceived Level of Egalitarian Relationship		+0.07
Perceived Managerial Support of Teachers		+0.21
Perceived Social Support of Teachers		+0.41
Perceived Level of Staff Involvement		+0.34

It is obvious from Table 4 that the relationship which existed for the total group analysis also clearly represented the attitudes of female teachers, and this remained clear when the less influential variables were again factored out and another multiple correlation computed (Table 5).

Male teachers, too, appeared quite consistent in expressing their attitudes toward administrative behavior. It is clear from the data presented in Tables 6 and 7 that the men concurred with their female counterparts in emphasizing the importance for them of having the principals express support for and commitment to involvement of the teachers.

The results of a study by Dropkin and Taylor (1) led to the conclusion that perceptions of inner-city teachers differ from those of suburban teachers. This raised the possibility that teachers from inner-city "disadvantaged" schools might prefer different forms of administrative behavior than teachers from suburban-type "advantaged" schools. To facilitate making this distinction, those schools in this

Table 5. A multiple correlation of female teacher responses with Executive Professional Leadership the dependent variable and Perceived Social Support of Teachers and Perceived Level of Staff Involvement the independent variables

Variable	*Multiple Correlation Coefficient*	*Partial Correlation Coefficient*
Executive Professional Leadership	+0.80	
Perceived Social Support of Teachers		+0.63
Perceived Level of Staff Involvement		+0.36

Table 6. A multiple correlation of male teacher responses with Executive Professional Leadership the dependent variable and the five teacher-administrator factors the independent variables

Variable	*Multiple Correlation Coefficient*	*Partial Correlation Coefficient*
Executive Professional Leadership	+0.75	
Perceived Support of Teacher Authority		+0.11
Perceived Level of Egalitarian Relationships		-0.01
Perceived Managerial Support of Teachers		+0.06
Perceived Social Support of Teachers		+0.53
Perceived Level of Staff Involvement		+0.24

Table 7. A multiple correlation of male responses with Executive Professional Leadership the dependent variable and Perceived Social Support of Teachers and Perceived Level of Staff Involvement the independent variables

Variable	*Multiple Correlation Coefficient*	*Partial Correlation Coefficient*
Executive Professional Leadership	+0.75	
Perceived Social Support of Teachers		+0.60
Perceived Level of Staff Involvement		+0.29

study which qualified for federal grants based on concentrations of low income families were considered "disadvantaged" schools (18 schools). Those schools with similar characteristics, but which did not qualify or for which there were insufficient federal funds available, were not included (9 schools). The remaining schools were considered suburban-type (25 schools).

When the perceptions of teachers from the "advantaged" schools were examined to determine which behavioral qualities of principals were most desirable, the results were similar to those found when the responses of the total groups were analyzed (Table 8).

Table 8. A multiple correlation of advantaged teachers' responses with Executive Professional Leadership the dependent variable and the five teacher-administrator relationship factors the independent variables

Variable	*Multiple Correlation Coefficient*	*Partial Correlation Coefficient*
Executive Professional Leadership	+0.80	
Perceived Support of Teacher Authority		+0.11
Perceived Level of Egalitarian Relationships		+0.15
Perceived Managerial Support of Teachers		+0.16
Perceived Social Support of Teachers		+0.52
Perceived Level of Staff Involvement		+0.30

When the less influential elements were factored out (Table 9), the results were as follows:

Table 9. A multiple correlation of advantaged teachers' responses with Executive Professional Leadership the dependent variable and Perceived Social Support of Teachers and Perceived Level of Staff Involvement the independent variables

Variable	*Multiple Correlation Coefficient*	*Partial Correlation Coefficient*
Executive Professional Leadership	+0.79	
Perceived Social Support of Teachers		+0.66
Perceived Level of Staff Involvement		+0.33

The "advantaged" teachers clearly placed major emphasis on the need for social support on the parts of their principals.

A similar analysis of data supplied by teachers from "disadvantaged" schools provided the data for Tables 10 and 11.

The perceptions of teachers from "disadvantaged" schools were very much like those of the other teacher groups for whom data were available, except that they also placed considerably greater value on behavior related to managerial support of teachers than did the others.

Table 10. A multiple correlation of disadvantaged teachers' responses with Executive Professional Leadership the dependent variable and the five teacher-administrator relationship factors the independent variables

Variable	*Multiple Correlation Coefficient*	*Partial Correlation Coefficient*
Executive Professional Leadership	+0.86	
Perceived Support of Teacher Authority		+0.06
Perceived Level of Egalitarian Relationships		-0.01
Perceived Managerial Support of Teachers		+0.31
Perceived Social Support of Teachers		+0.44
Perceived Level of Staff Involvement		+0.35

Table 11. A multiple correlation of disadvantaged teachers' responses with Executive Professional Leadership the dependent variable and Perceived Social Support of Teachers and Perceived Level of Staff Involvement the independent variables

Variable	*Multiple Correlation Coefficient*	*Partial Correlation Coefficient*
Executive Professional Leadership	+0.84	
Perceived Social Support of Teachers		+0.72
Perceived Level of Staff Involvement		+0.36

It is interesting to note, contrary to public opinion, that none of the teacher groupings dealt with in this study expressed attitudes indicating that their general evaluation of administrative behavior was closely related to the degree of support of teacher authority which the principals provide. This was as true for teachers in "advantaged" schools as it was for those in "disadvantaged" schools. Perhaps the commonly accepted idea that teachers prefer principals who always "back them up" will require some modification. Future investigations might consider the conditions under which the need for support of teacher authority becomes operative and those in which the need diminishes.

The fact that, when multiple correlations were computed, none of the teacher groups participating in this study indicated that equality of relationships was a major factor in their evaluations of administrative behavior is of considerable importance. In light of the demands being made by teacher organizations directed toward greater involvement in the decision-making processes of the schools, this was an interesting development. It raises the possibility that teachers do not desire equality in their relationships with administrative personnel but instead would be content to accumulate power and influence within the organizational structure.

The extent of managerial support provided teachers by administrators did not appear to be a major factor with regard to their total evaluation of administrative behavior, but considerably more emphasis was placed upon the need for adequate managerial services by teachers from "disadvantaged" schools than by teachers from "advantaged" schools. One might anticipate the differential nature of the problems existing in both types of schools; furthermore, it is quite probable that the kinds of problems which face teachers and administrators in "disadvantaged" schools would have considerable impact on the quality of managerial services within those buildings.

The two specific behavioral qualities which consistently received the teachers' greatest emphasis in terms of relationship to their over-all evaluation of general administrative behavior were Perceived Level of Social Support and Perceived Level of Staff Involvement, but in every case it was quite clear that Perceived Level of Social Support bore the greater relationship to the teachers' general evaluation of administrative behavior.

Although, when correlated independently, Perceived Level of Staff Involvement was closely related to the general evaluation of administrative behavior, it was quite clear from the multiple correlation that it "ran a weak second" when compared to the teacher's emphasis on Perceived Level of Social Support. This appears closely related to the comments made earlier regarding the lack of emphasis placed on equality of relationships between teachers and principals. It would be logical to assume that extensive personal involvement would require a "team" approach in which all members were treated as equals. Thus, the teachers' tendency not to emphasize both types of behavior is related.

The heavy emphasis placed on Social Support of Teachers is understandable when viewed in a more comprehensive manner. The investigation of educators' needs from which this data emanated brought to light information indicating that teachers were generally an insecure group (2). This insecurity might well be the reason for their decision not to stress egalitarian relationships and staff involvement as major factors in evaluation of administrative behavior. Should this be true, it will be necessary for administrators to provide a highly supportive atmosphere prior to initiating any changes in administrative structure which would bring about greater teacher involvement in the decision-making processes of the schools. Changes in that direction, if expected to succeed, will apparently have to be curtailed until teachers are sufficiently secure to deal with the insecurity that change breeds.

Notes

1. Stanley Dropkin and Marvin Taylor. "Perceived Problems of Beginning Teachers and Related Factors," *Journal of Teacher Education,* 14, No. 4: 384-390, December, 1963.

2. Harvey Goldman. *A Study of the Teacher-Administrator Relationship and the Influence of Need Patterns,* Educational Research Series, Number 35, Educational

Publication Services, College of Education, Michigan State University, East Lansing, Michigan, July, 1966, 153+ pp. (financed by U. S. Office of Education Small Contract Research Grant, Project No. 6-8374).

3. Neal Gross and Robert E. Herriott. *Staff Leadership in Public Schools: A Sociological Inquiry,* (New York: John Wiley and Sons, Inc., 1965), 168+ pp.

The Department Head: Myths and Reality

Donald C. Manlove and Robert Buser

The position of the department head in the organization of the larger secondary school today is somewhat of an enigma. While many school administrators indicate some difficulty in operating with the position, most of them would not operate without it. Writers on supervision and administration typically devote little space to research on the department head, make few suggestions for enhancing the effectiveness of the position, and provide few–if, indeed, any–recommendations for alternative organizational patterns. All too often those writing and discussing the departmental organization are afforded the luxury of the second guesser so prevalent in today's society; that is, they criticize existing institutions but accept no responsibility to propose effective and realistic procedures for their improvement or replacement. In short, everybody seems to be talking about the position but no one appears to be doing much to improve it.

The practicing secondary school administrator may be confused by the assumptions made by several authorities in the field that: (1) there is a trend away from the use of the department headship; (2) there is a trend to replace the traditional heads of subject-area departments with division heads or coordinators; and (3) principals and teachers are generally dissatisfied with the position of the department head in the supervisory and administrative organization of secondary schools. Thus, the practicing school administrator discovers himself in a rather insecure position not unlike that of a traveler lost in a foreign country–he is not sure where he is, he is uncertain to whom he can turn for directions, and he may have difficulty interpreting directions once he receives them.

Objective Examination

The writers, who themselves were once high school principals, have a fellow-feeling for the conscientious secondary school administrator who hopes by the proper design and management of a departmental form of staff organization thereby to improve the supervision and administration of the instructional program in his school, for we recognize the many problems, shortcomings, and adverse criticisms that bedevil department heads and their conduct. It is not our intent in this paper to recommend either the establishment of departmental organizations where they do not exist or to argue for their elimination where they now are found. Rather, we have chosen to examine existing practices in regard to departmental organizational and from such an examination to propose some guidelines which, it is hoped, will lead to more positive and constructive use of department groups and department heads in those schools that now have them.

The guidelines recommended later in this article are based on the findings of three companion studies conducted at Indiana University in 1966 and the professional experiences of the writers. Buser[1] conducted a survey of the functions and characteristics of department heads as perceived by the principals of those public high schools that employed 40 or more teachers and which were members of the North Central Association of Colleges and Secondary Schools. The principals of 273 schools in 19 states responded to this study. Brenner[2] and Ciminillo[3] used the instrument developed by Buser in separate studies of the perceptions of teachers and department heads respectively of the department headship organization. They drew their sample from the schools responding to Buser's study. The following findings and conclusions were drawn from these studies.

Findings and Conclusions

First, *there was no trend away from the use of department heads.* Approximately 80 percent of the respondent schools employed heads of departments. The department head was most common in the large schools–those that employed 100 or more teachers–with 98 percent of the principals reporting their employment; 88 percent of the middle-sized schools–those with 70 but less than 100 teachers–utilized department heads; while 68 percent of the small schools–40 to 69 teachers–did so.

Second, *there was no trend to combine several subject areas into divisions for the purpose of assigning supervisory and administrative responsibility.* In fact, schools appeared to be establishing more specialized departments rather than consolidating existing ones into divisions.

[1]Robert L. Buser. *The Functions and Characteristics of Department Heads As Perceived by High School Principals.* Unpublished doctoral thesis. Bloomington: Indiana University, 1966. (Typewritten)

[2]Kenneth W. Brenner, *Functions and Characteristics of Department Heads As Perceived by Public High School Teachers.* Unpublished doctoral thesis. Bloomington: Indiana University, 1966. (Offset)

[3]Lewis M. Ciminillo, *The Department Head's Perception of the Functions and Characteristics of the Position.* Unpublished doctoral thesis. Bloomington: Indiana University, 1966. (Typewritten)

Third, *there was no widespread dissatisfaction with the departmental headship organization* evidenced by teachers, principals, or department heads. Ninety-seven percent of the principals of schools with department heads indicated that they would re-establish the departmental organization if they were reorganizing schools of the same type. Approximately 90 percent of the teachers and principals alike disagreed with the proposition that schools would be better off without department heads. Even though teachers were typically less satisfied with the position than both principals and department heads were, a large majority of teachers and principals felt that department heads generally have a broad outlook toward teaching and school problems. In short, teachers, principals, and department heads indicated that the department heads would generally provide effective supervision if they were given the time and authority to do so.

Fourth, *a close examination of the department-head position is necessary*, since more than one-third of the principals, teachers, and heads of departments surveyed agreed that it is the least understood position in the secondary school.

Fifth, teachers, principals, and department heads agreed that *leadership ability is the most important single characteristic of effective department heads*. The traits of superior teaching ability, knowledge and ability in curriculum development, willingness to work, administrative ability, and mastery of subject matter were also often listed as most important; most often listed as least important were seniority in the department, popularity among members of the department, and graduate study.

Sixth, *opinions varied on whether department-head positions were generally filled by the most qualified persons within the department.* Ninety percent of the principals answered affirmatively, but only 66 percent of the department heads and 48 percent of the teachers concurred.

Seventh, *there was no model organization used in lieu of departmentalization in the schools that did not have departmental organizations.* The functions commonly assigned to department heads usually became the responsibility of principals, assistant principals, curriculum directors, and systemwide supervisors.

Functions of the Position

Eighth, *the principals of schools that employed department heads saw the functions of department heads as both administrative and supervisory, although as somewhat more supervisory than administrative.* Over 90 percent of the principals marked the following as functions of department heads:

- provide leadership in the selection of textbooks and other instructional materials
- call attention to new ideas and developments within the field
- exercise leadership in the development of departmental course objectives, syllabi, and content, as well as in the development of the total school curriculum
- preside at departmental meetings
- orient new teachers into the system

- prepare written evaluations of the achievement and activities of the department
- conduct research and experimentation within their respective fields
- work with teachers in improving their procedures for student evaluation
- familiarize staff with community resources and facilities
- develop and implement in-service training programs for the members of the department
- order department supplies and equipment.

With the exception of developing and implementing in-service education, these functions were assigned department heads in 75 percent of the schools as reported by principals. However, a sizable number of principals indicated that the following functions were not, but should be, functions assigned department heads—and these are functions the present writer consider essential for effective supervision:

- conducting demonstration lessons for teachers of the department
- preparing written evaluations of the teachers of the department
- supervising the teachers of the department through classroom visits and observations
- developing and implementing in-service training programs for members of the department
- developing and maintaining a professional library
- recommending teachers of the department for promotion, continued employment, or dismissal

Even though teachers, department heads, and principals generally agreed as to the functions that should be assigned heads of departments, there were differences of opinion as to whether these functions were in fact assigned to the department heads in the schools of these studies. Apparently, teachers, principals, and department heads do not always have the same perceptions of policy and procedures in the process of supervision.

Finally, *teachers and department heads found the operational effectiveness of the departmental organization less effective than did the principals.* Principals perceived little conflict between functions that were and should not be, or were not and should be, assigned department heads, but both teachers and heads of departments perceived a significantly larger number of conflicts.

Myths Exploded

In summary, these studies seem to explode some myths about the department-head position as it exists in the larger public high schools. Some of these unfounded myths are: (1) that there is a trend away from the use of department heads in the larger secondary schools; (2) that the division organization is replacing the departmental organization; and (3) that there is widespread dissatisfaction with the position among department heads, teachers, or principals. It can be concluded from these studies that the departmental organization is typical rather than atypical in the larger high schools, and that teachers and principals alike view departmental organizations as offering considerable potential for effective supervision and administration.

The findings also point up some basic problems of the departmental organization as it currently operates in many schools

- A sizable number of teachers, principals, and heads perceive the position of the department head to be one of the least understood positions in the school system.
- There is disagreement as to the qualifications of department heads presently holding the positions.
- Both teachers and department heads perceive more conflicts between what are and should be the functions of department heads than do principals.
- There is some disagreement among teachers, principals, and heads of departments as to the characteristics most essential for the position.

The writers conclude, therefore, that if effective supervision and administration are to result from the departmental organization, several guidelines need to be considered. We have proceeded on the premise that departmentalization is only one form of organization for supervision and administration, even though by far the most common one. It is not our purpose to advocate or defend departmental organization, but rather to suggest means for more effective utilization of department heads in the schools that employ them.

Recommended Guidelines

We recommend the following guidelines for effective supervision and administration through the department headship.

I. Perhaps the most important ingredient for effective supervision and administration through the department headship is *a common understanding of the functions, responsibilities, selection procedures, and authority assigned department heads* by everyone involved in instruction—the superintendent, the principal, the assistant principals, the curriculum coordinator, the system-wide supervisors, the department heads, and the teachers. This requires that policy and job descriptions be established and effectively communicated to all personnel. Written job descriptions should be accompanied by policy statements of purpose and reinforced by on-the-job training for newly appointed department heads whenever feasible, to prevent development of such traits as autocratic behavior, resistance to change, dogmatism, empire building, and excessive competition among departments. These undesirable qualities commonly attributed to departmentalization often could be avoided through effective communication of roles and functions among all elements of the professional staff.

II. *A sound selection system* is needed, one which is compatible to and consistent with the functions assigned department heads. Criteria for selection should be established as a result of a study of the functions to be rendered by department heads. Certainly leadership ability, knowledge and ability in curriculum development, teaching ability, and willingness to work would be mandatory attributes. The principal should be the key person in the selection process. The practice of electing department heads by members of the department is a questionable one; one that is likely to reduce their status and effectiveness in the eyes of both teacher and administrators.

III. *The term of appointment* should be one year, with the understanding that the head would be reappointed providing he demonstrates capable leadership. Presumably, most department heads would serve several years. Frequent rotation of department heads or arbitrary limits to their term of office seem inconsistent with sound administrative practices since, typically, personnel changes produce discontinuity in policies and procedures.

IV. *Compensation* for the department head should be based on his professional qualifications, professional experience, and job performance. Released time from classroom teaching assignments should be a condition of appointment rather than compensation for the assignment. Financial compensation cannot substitute for released time since inadequate time, regardless of the reason, limits the opportunity to visit classes, confer with teachers, conduct demonstration lessons, and administer departmental affairs. The practice of releasing heads from student activity responsibilities may deprive students and teachers alike of a desirable professional model.

V. The *amount of time that department heads should be released from classroom teaching assignments* is directly proportional to the number of teachers in the department and the responsibilities assigned the department head. There is no substitute for time! It is difficult to understand the rationale of establishing heads of departments if they are not provided released time. It is equally difficult to understand the rationale of assigning time for supervision unless the time is used in classroom observations, teacher conferences, and other supervisory techniques.

VI. *Evaluation* is a key factor in the success or failure of departmentalization as an element in a design for supervision and administration. The effectiveness of department heads in implementing the philosophy of the school, as well as in carrying out their assigned functions, should be evaluated in some regular and systematic manner. The educational contributions of their departments must also be evaluated. Only if the evaluation is keyed to departmental contributions to the total school program can departments heads be encouraged not to measure their achievements in terms of additional staff members secured, budget achieved, addition of new courses, establishment of required or prerequisite courses, numbers of students enrolled in their respective departments, and other quantifiable but unreliable measures of a department's worth to its school. Without rigorous evaluation, the potential of the headship for professional growth and leadership will not be realized. Evaluation should be continuous, and it should be made by those to whom the heads are immediately responsible. Here, again, the principal plays the key role.

In conclusion, we re-emphasize that our purpose is to offer suggestions for improving the effectiveness of the department head in implementing improved instructional practices in secondary schools. In this paper we are not arguing either that departmentalization is or that it is not the most effective system for improving instruction. But we do believe that since it is such a widely used organization for administrative and supervisory purposes in secondary schools, it should be set up and operated with care. A new role and image of department heads must be developed in many schools where they are currently employed if more effective supervision and administration are to result.

Which Organization—Department or Division—for Your School?

Donald Thomas

The American high school is a unique educational institution. Having developed rapidly following World War I, it is today a significant American achievement. As the high school grew in size and complexity, it was soon evident that the principal was no longer able to carry out all of the original responsibilities of his position. The assistance needed by the principal and greater attention to subject matter areas soon produced the departmental organization with department heads as the dominant organizational structure for the secondary school.

Within recent years the department plan has come under increasingly more severe criticism. To replace it some have suggested a division organization combining several subject matter areas into instructional units. Each division is to be headed by a division chairman. This type of school structure has gained momentum in the Chicago suburban area, but has not yet given serious widespread challenge to the department concept.

It was the purpose of this study to determine the extent to which department and division secondary-school organizations met a pre-determined criterion composed of fifteen principles of secondary school organization. In the study, the secondary school was seen as a social unit and its organization was studied from the viewpoint of social science theories which define organization as consciously coordinated activies of people. It, therefore, analyzed the behaviors of teachers rather than presented a descriptive structure of the secondary school.

A criterion consisting of fifteen principles of secondary-school organization was first developed by a group of administrators in High School District 214, Arlington Heights, Illinois.[1] With the help of secondary school teachers, these principles were then broken down into specific acts of behavior. Questionnaire A was devised to

[1]See Table 1.

test the extent to which these behaviors were performed. Each principle was tested by five to eight statements of behavior acts. Questionnaire B was subsequently constructed which presented the principles being tested in addition to the statements of behavior acts.

The questionnaires were administered to teachers in eight high school districts in the Chicago suburban area—four organized on the department plan and four organized on the division concept. About two-thirds of the teachers completed Questionnaire A and about one-third completed Questionnaire B. The statistical design called for fifteen research hypotheses which stated that differences did exist between the responses of teachers in department and division schools on each of the fifteen principles. A two-tail t test for differences between means was used to verify or reject the null hypotheses. A .05 level of significance was chosen to indicate real differences. Both questionnaires were analyzed.

The two forms of the questionnaires verified each other. The results obtained did not differ when the organizational principles being tested were presented to the respondents. It was decided, therefore, to report only the data obtained by Questionnaire A. The data obtained by Questionnaire B were placed in the appendixes.

The data indicated that real differences do exist for eight principles examined (1, 2, 4, 5, 6, 9, 12, and 14), making it possible to reject the null hypotheses and accept the research hypotheses. Differences for seven principles (3, 7, 8, 10, 11, 13, and 15) were not significant at the .05 level.[2] The null hypotheses were, therefore, accepted for these seven principles.

An examination of the eight principles for which the research hypotheses were accepted indicated that seven of these principles (1, 2, 4, 5, 6, 9, and 12) appear to operate at a higher level in department schools and one (14) appears to operate at a higher level in division schools.

Conclusions

Differences do exist in the behaviors of teachers in department and division secondary schools when examined against a criterion of fifteen secondary school organizational principles. From these differences in behaviors it is inferred that the organization of the schools also differs when expressed in the form of organizational principles. It is assumed, therefore, that each type of organization (division and department) permits, allows, facilitates, and provides for cooperative actions at different levels or to a greater or lesser extent.

From this study it is possible to conclude that, except for one principle, these organizational principles operate as well or better in department organized schools than they do in division organized schools. The one that appears to operate better in division schools deals with continuous and cooperative evaluation and redirection of the organization. The ones that appear to operate better in department schools deal with supervision, communication, coordination, accountability, homogeneity

[2]See Table 2.

of responsibilities, essential programs, and the functions of specialists. The principles for which there appear to be no differences deal with maximum utilization of time and energy of members, responsibility and authority, democratic procedures, the principal as instructional leader, the teacher as the basic operative of the school, administrative leadership, and professional growth of members.

Assuming that what teachers say they do is an accurate reflection of what they actually do, and that the statements of behavior used are a valid test of the principles examined, it is then possible to formulate the following additional tentative conclusions:

1. Department organization permits each person to have only one superior to whom he is directly responsible to a greater degree than does division organization.
2. Department organization facilitates communication to a greater extent than does division organization.
3. Department organization allows members of the staff to function as coordinated parts to a greater degree than division organization.
4. Department organization provides for greater accountability for the proper discharge of responsibilities than does division organization.
5. Department organization utilizes more fully the talents and abilities of each member than does division organization.
6. Department organization provides for all essential programs, services, and activities more fully than does division organization.
7. Department organization utilizes supervisors, coordinators, or specialists as helpers and counselors to a greater degree than does division organization.
8. Division organization provides for continuous and cooperative evaluation and redirection of the organization to a greater extent than does department organization.

A final conclusion evolved which is not a basic part of the study. It is a conclusion which presents interesting possibilities for further research. It appears that some of the principles studied (1, 9, 12, 13, 14, 15) do not operate at a high level in either type of organization while others (2, 5, 6, 7, 10, 11) appear to operate at a high level in both organizations. Why?

Implications for Education

Although the department organization has been severely criticized, it does not yet appear that the division concept can correct the weaknesses attributed to the department plan. It does appear, however, that the division structure does facilitate democratic procedures as well as continuous and cooperative evaluation and redirection of the organization to a greater extent than does the departmental plan of organization. If secondary school organization is to be improved, it may be possible to develop a pattern of organization which combines the best features of both the division and department concepts. At the present time, neither is a panacea for the weaknesses of the other.

In deciding the organizational plan to adopt, school districts should first decide the organizational principles they wish to support. If the district values continuous and cooperative evaluation and redirection of the organization above all else, the division concept appears to be the organizational plan it should adopt. If, on the other hand, the district places greater value on supervision, communications, accountability, and homogeneity of responsibilities; then the department pattern appears to be the organizational plan it should establish. If a district values both continuous and cooperative evaluation and redirection of the organization *and* the principles which operate better in department schools, it may be possible to develop an organizational pattern which establishes large instructional divisions composed of smaller departments. That such an organization could facilitate the benefits of both the division and department concepts remains to be tested.

School districts presently organized on the department plan should be careful about suddenly deciding to adopt the division structure. Districts that have done so apparently have not solved the problems attributed to the department organization. It does not appear that communication, coordination, and supervision are improved by the division organization. The division concept appears to facilitate evaluation and redirection, but at the same time appears to weaken the effective operation of other principles.

Some may argue that the division structure has not been given a fair trial—that it has not been in operation for a long enough period of time when compared to the traditional department organization. Those who support the division concept also state that it is more effective to develop a division school originally than to change a department school into a division school. This position, however, is not yet supported by any objective studies. It is the author's opinion that the division concept may work better in one-high-school districts employing staff members who have not had extensive experience with the department organization than it does in multi-high-school districts having schools staffed with well-experienced teachers. On the other hand, the department organization appears to work as well or better than the division concept in either type of setting. These opinions are partially supported by the data obtained in this study, but they must be supported by further research in secondary school organization.

As with most studies the examination of these fifteen principles in division and department schools has raised a number of questions. Of particular interest is why certain principles, regardless of differences, operate at a low level in both department and division schools. If the division plan is not an effective replacement for the department concept, it is still necessary to improve the department organization or develop a new organizational pattern that will be an effective replacement. Principles which operate at a low level (1, 9, 12, 13, 14, 15) are vital to the operation of secondary schools and organizations must be devised that will facilitate their operation at a much higher level.

It is hoped that this study will now give impetus to a more objective appraisal of the department structure. At the same time it has been the purpose of the study to call attention to the division concept—to be further studied as an organizational pattern in its own right rather than as a replacement for the department plan. It is further hoped that those who favor one or the other organization will not be blind to the strengths of the plan they do not wish to adopt. As it has already been stated, it may be possible to combine the two concepts into a new organizational pattern which is more effective than either original structure. The author believes that is is unfortunate that some who have promoted the division plan have done so on a basis that the department pattern is obsolete and that it is not suited to the needs of a modern secondary school. On the other hand it is equally unfortunate that those who favor the department plan are not willing to acknowledge that the division plan does have some strength as well as weaknesses. It is hoped that this study may help to moderate the position of both groups.

Recommendations

Secondary school organizations have developed out of necessity and are based on subjective opinions of educators rather than sound objective data obtained from thorough research. At a time when the number of secondary schools being established is accelerating, it is imperative that greater attention be given to secondary school organization. Further research in this area is needed so that intelligent decisions can be made. With this in mind the author recommends further research to determine:

1. The extent to which the criterion used in this study differs when variables other than organization are examined:
    a. Union versus non-union secondary schools.
    b. Urban versus rural secondary schools.
    c. Multi-high-school districts versus one-high-school districts.
    d. Large high schools versus small high schools.
    e. High educational level of staff versus low educational level of staff.
    f. Long tenured staff versus short tenured staff.

If a sufficient number of such studies are made, it may be possible to develop a multi-factor index to guide the general development of the "ideal" secondary school. At some future point, for example, it may be possible to say that the fifteen principles examined operate best in a one-high-school district having a large high school organized on the department plan where the majority of teachers have the master's degree and where they do not belong to a union.

2. Why particular principles operate at different levels in different schools used in this study:
    a. Why does a particular principle operate at a high level in one school when it operates at the same low level in all other schools?
    b. Why does a particular principle operate at about the same level in all department schools while it has a wide range of levels in all division schools?
    c. Why does a particular principle have a wide range of operative levels?
    d. Why does a particular principle have a narrow range of operative levels?
3. Why some principles operate at a high level in all schools used in this study.
4. Why some principles operate at a low level in all schools used in this study.
5. The strengths and weaknesses of the department organization.
6. The strengths and weaknesses of the division organization.

7. The effects of changing from a department organization to a division organization.
8. Effective organizational principles for secondary schools.

The author further recommends that persons who are responsible for developing secondary schools be more careful in determining the type of organization to be established. Often this decision is based on size of staff, financial resources, or the recommendation of so-called organizational experts rather than desired outcomes or pre-determined values. It may be wiser to first determine the kinds of behavior the school district values and wishes to attain and then choose the organizational pattern which will facilitate them. Too often a change of organizational structure fails to attain desired ends because the organizational pattern selected was not chosen with ends and values in mind. The formulation of goals must always be the first step in considering organization. If the values of goals are determined first and are given primary consideration, the choice of organizational pattern becomes secondary. This is as it should be.

Table 1. Criterion, Secondary School Organizational Principles

1. The secondary school organization permits each person to have only one superior to whom he is directly responsible. Each staff member should, therefore, report to and be supervised by a single administrative officer.
2. The secondary school organization allows the channels of communication to be definitely known to all concerned. The structure of the organization should facilitate communication and promote cooperative understanding.
3. The secondary school organization should be such that it utilizes maximally the time and energy of every member.
4. The secondary school organization should facilitate maximum cooperation among the members of the organization. It should allow all members of the staff to function as coordinated parts rather than as individuals.
5. The secondary school organization provides that each unit and each administrative officer be held directly accountable for the proper discharge of his responsibilities. The functions, responsibilities, and working relationships of each staff member should be clearly defined and understood and should be recognized in actual practice. The area of responsibility assigned to each person should be reasonable in scope.
6. The secondary school organization allows the duties and responsibilities assigned to one person to be homogeneous. Such responsibilities and duties utilize fully the talents and abilities of each member.
7. The secondary school organization permits authority to act to be delegated to individuals who have been given responsibilities. Authority should be commensurate with the assignment of responsibility. Responsibilities and authority should be distributed among individuals in a manner consistent with the purposes of the school.
8. The secondary school organization facilitates democratic procedures. Operation should be based on the appropriate participation of the entire educational staff, the parents, and the students.

9. The secondary school organization provides for all essential programs, services, and activities. The organization must facilitate the attainment of the desired educational goals.
10. The secondary school organization recognizes the principal as the key person in the educational enterprise. It recognizes him as an instructional leader, staff officer, and head of his faculty.
11. The secondary school organization recognizes the teacher as the basic operative of the school system. While others deal with instruction, the teacher is primarily concerned with that function.
12. The secondary school organization makes possible the utilization of supervisors, coordinators, or specialists as helpers and counselors of teachers on special problems. In no case should they be charged with line or authoritative functions such as evaluating the competency of teachers or the direction of school programs.
13. The secondary school organization allows administrative personnel to lead, stimulate, coordinate, serve, and appraise instead of inspect and command. Line officers should be generalists with broad areas of responsibilities.
14. The secondary school organization provides for continuous and cooperative evaluation and redirection of the organization.
15. The secondary school organization provides for inservice training and for the professional growth of all members.

Table 2. Questionnaire A: Differences Between Means, Principles One Through Fifteen

Principle	*Department*	*Division*	$X_1 - X_2$	*F*	*t*
1	13.1205	14.5813	1.4608	1.65[a]	6.370[b]
2	12.0383	13.9612	1.9229	1.42[a]	7.529[b]
3	13.6630	14.0775	.4145	1.29	1.932
4	13.3726	14.0542	.6816	1.17	3.029[b]
5	10.1643	11.5813	1.4170	1.05	6.812[b]
6	10.7616	11.1279	.3663	1.05	1.990[c]
7	10.7068	10.9496	.2328	1.30	1.164
8	10.4438	10.3914	.0524	1.19	.291
9	14.2164	15.3333	1.1169	1.17	5.123[b]
10	11.6958	11.8837	.1879	1.45[a]	.8169
11	8.5452	8.5775	.0323	1.28	.1814
12	13.2794	13.9108	.6314	1.23	2.409[c]
13	14.0794	14.1317	.0523	1.04	.0528
14	16.5698	15.8798	.6900	1.37[a]	2.863[b]
15	16.8904	16.9069	.0165	1.00	.0168

[a]Significant at the .02 level.
[b]Significant at equal to or greater than the .01 level.
[c]Significant at equal to or greater than the .05 level.

Part Three

Supervision Within Organizations

Instructional Leadership: A Concept Re-Examined

Edwin M. Bridges

The concept of instructional leadership has been frequently discussed but rarely subjected to any rigorous analysis. In this paper four current views of instructional leadership–those of the principal as evaluator, helper, integrator and designer–are examined and the assumptions about human nature, skills, and knowledge underlying each of these views are identified. Following a critique of these assumptions, the author describes a "principal-as-experimenter" role which he maintains is a viable notion of instructional leadership given the present state of knowledge and the organizational necessity for informed decision-making.

Of the seven major task areas for which principals have responsibility[1] the area of curriculum and instruction has generated the most sound and fury. On the one hand, the principal has been exhorted to exert instructional leadership while on the other hand, he has been told flatly that such a role is beyond his or any other human being's capacity. The problem with these disputations is that the exponents of a given position have neither defined sharply what is signified by the concept of instructional leadership nor made their assumptions explicit. The aim of this paper is to bring each of these issues into sharper focus by developing four ideal types representing the major emphases of current notions about instructional leadership. Following a critique of these four types, the author will suggest a view of instructional leadership which is intended to overcome many of the deficiencies which are cited.

Four Views of Instructional Leadership

As implied in the introductory comments about instructional leadership, the literature dealing with this concept is checkered with diverse views. Since these overlap to some extent and differ mainly in the emphasis placed on tasks to be performed by the principal, these views will be re-constructed as ideal types to highlight the different instructional leadership roles educational theorists advocate for principals. No claim is made that these views exist in these pure forms in actual

[1]Campbell, Roald F., John E. Corbally, and John A. Ramseyer. *Introduction to Educational Administration.* Boston. Allyn and Bacon, Inc. 1962

practice; however, the author does contend that principals who do seek to exert instructional leadership manifest behaviors which, when taken in their totality, correspond closely to one of these four types. The four types are: the evaluator, the helper, the integrator, and the designer.

The first view, that of the principal as an *evaluator,* reflects a concern for the demands which the organization imposes on its members as a condition of employment. There is the recognition that individual teachers have a need for privacy which must be met if they are to be exempted from pressure to live up to the details of all organizational norms. However, it is felt that teachers who are fully insulated from observation by colleagues and superordinates may not live up to the minimum requirements of their role. Evaluation based on observation of role-performance is designed to meet the social requirement of accountability.[2] The teacher, according to this view, is an instrumental object who is charged with using certain kinds of materials and certain kinds of instructional techniques to achieve a prescribed set of ends or goals. The responsibility of the principal is to evaluate the instructional practices employed by individual staff members in order to: (1) make judgments about whether the goals of the organization are being achieved; (2) determine the extent to which the institutional policies and procedures are being followed; and (3) decide what teachers are to be retained, promoted, transferred, or discharged.

A second view of instructional leadership emphasizes a concern for people, the individuals who occupy teaching roles. This concern focuses on the importance of organizational members as people and seeks to minimize the restrictive influences of the organization. Operating from this perspective, the principal acts as a *helper* rather than as a judge of teachers. His role is to: (1) observe the teacher in action; (2) report his perceptions to the teacher; and (3) suggest a range of usable alternatives to the instructional task. Since evaluation is not considered to be in harmony with his consultant role, the principal is expected to avoid making formal value judgments about his teachers. His obligation is to provide the teacher with information about her instructional environment and to offer advice, suggestions, and assistance which the teacher hypothetically need not take into account in the enactment of her role.

The third view of instructional leadership reflects a dual concern. The system and its teachers are given equal emphasis. The principal is seen as one who should *integrate* the requirements of both the organization and the teacher. His work strategy, according to his viewpoint, involves establishing a cooperative relationship with his teachers on a one-to-one basis. In this way the principal works simultaneously for the good of the organization and the good of his staff. Performance targets are mutually agreed upon by the principal and each teacher and are consistent with the needs of the organization and the individual. The principal's leadership role is to: (1) communicate to each teacher what is expected of him; (2) provide the teacher with information about his performance; (3)

[2]Merton, Robert K. *Social Theory and Social Structure.* Glencoe, Illinois. The Free Press of Glencoe. 1957. pp. 375-76.

translate, in cooperation with the teacher, improvement needs into specific goals; (4) agree on what information will be used as evidence of growth; and (5) obtain assistance for the teacher when and as needed in order that the improvement needs may be achieved.[3]

In recent years a fourth view of instructional leadership has gained support.[4] This view is based on a number of trends including: the increasing specialization of school personnel, emerging conceptions of teaching and learning which demand more autonomy for faculty members, and the increasing bureaucratization of schools. These trends, according to the proponents of this view, demand a re-definition of the principal's leadership role in instruction. Evaluation of teachers will no longer be handled by the principal but by groups of teachers, "perhaps through mechanisms instituted by professional associations."[5] Improvement of instruction will occur through teachers turning to their fellow teachers for needed specialized assistance. The role of the principal is that of strategic coordination,[6] which involves the production of a unique "mix" of persons, facilities, materials, and activities that is most effective for that situation. In other words, his main function is to *design* an educational milieu which provides the combination of personalities, skills, materials, and programs needed in a particular school. The designer role calls for a principal who views the school as a system and who knows what its component parts are, what they do, and how they work together.[7] As a designer, the principal is expected to facilitate the basic processes and activities of the total system and to maintain a functional balance in the system. This requires him to view improvement or change in any component of the system in terms of its consequences for the entire system. "This orientation is based on the observation that, in organized systems, the behavior of any part ultimately has some effect on every other part."[8] To ignore this possibility may lead to a decision which is in the best interests of one component (e.g., Miss X's classroom) but does not serve best the system as a whole or a larger sub-system (e.g., the school building). Such a view further requires the principal to be aware of and sensitive to the dependence relationships between the system and its environment, i.e., all other factors (such as the community and forces at the state and national levels) which impinge upon the system.

[3]Kay, Emanuel. "A Modified System of Work Planning and Performance Review Within a General Electric Plant" in Zander, Alvin F. (ed). *Performance Appraisals.* Ann Arbor, Michigan. The Foundation for Research on Human Behavior. 1963. pp. 44-46.

[4]Erickson, Donald A. "Forces for Change in the Principalship," *Elementary School Journal* LXV, 2, November 1964. pp. 56-64.

[5]*Ibid.* p. 63.

[6]Erickson, Donald A. "Changes in the Principalship: Cause for Jubilation or Despair?" *The National Elementary Principal.* XLIV, 5, April 1965. pp. 16-20.

[7]Peach, Paul. "What is System Analysis?" Santa Monica, California. System Development Corporation. 1960.

[8]Ackoff, Russell L. "The Development and Nature of Operations Research and Its Relevance to Educational Media Research." A paper prepared for the Conference on "New Dimension for Research in Educational Media Implied by the 'Systems' Approach to Instruction," conducted by Center for Instructional Communications of Syracuse University, April 2-4, 1964. p. 8.

Assumptions Underlying Each View

These, then, represent the four major streams of thought regarding the concept of instructional leadership. Underlying each of these views are at least three sets of assumptions–(1) assumptions about human nature, (2) assumptions about skills, and (3) assumptions about knowledge. Each set of these assumptions will, in turn, be examined in relation to the various views of instructional leadership.

Underlying the concept of the evaluator is the notion that individuals prefer to be directed, wish to avoid responsibility, and must be urged to put forth adequate effort toward the achievement of organizational objectives.[9] The view of the principal as helper revolves around the idea that an individual will exercise self-direction and self-control in the service of objectives to which he is committed and will not only accept but seek responsibility under proper conditions. Everyone has the capacity to exercise a relatively high degree of imagination, ingenuity, and creativity in his movement toward attainment of the organization's goals.[10] With respect to the integrator view, it is assumed that individuals wish (1) to be told by their superiors where they stand and (2) to share in the planning of their work. Individuals, according to this view, will modify their behavior if conditions 1 and 2 prevail. The designer proceeds with the belief that teachers, like pupils, have individual competencies, needs and interests which may suit them for one situation or function and not another. Both teachers and students can perform their best when properly combined with facilities, materials, and program.

A second group of assumptions has to do with the skills required for each of these roles. For the evaluator to enact his role, he needs "coding" skills, i.e., adequate means and concepts for classifying and discriminating among the various instructional tactics and strategies which teachers use. The ability to discriminate among possible student reactions and to classify them reliably also constitute requisite "coding" skills. Implicit in this assumption about "coding" skills is the additional assumption, yet untested, that one can understand the process of instruction in a given classroom without having subject matter expertise since in this era of specialization no one can be expected to be knowledgeable in all subject matter fields. The evaluator further needs "weighting" skills, i.e., competence in arriving at value judgments which are consistent with the evaluative criteria and the information he has about the teacher. The helper, on the other hand, does not need "weighting" skills since he is not expected to reach value judgments about the teacher. Rather he needs "coding" skills and such inter-personal skills as the ability to listen, communicate, and provide non-evaluative feedback. As for the integrator, he requires "coding" skills, "weighting" skills, and such interpersonal skills as the ability to listen, communicate, provide evaluative feedback, and engage in collaborative decision-making. He must be able to "size up" each individual teacher and to determine what form of change strategy is likely to be most effective with

[9]McGregor, Douglas. *The Human Side of Enterprise.* New York. McGraw-Hill Book Company, Inc. 1960. p. 34.

[10]*Ibid.* pp. 47-48.

his teacher.[11] The designer must have skills in combining and coordinating the human and material components of a school and community to form an integrated educational system. In order to achieve this, he must be able to assess the differential influence of these components, individually and in interaction, on the output of the system.

The final set of assumptions has to do with the adequacy of present knowledge as a basis for rational, informed decision-making. Underlying the notion of the designer is the assumption that valid knowledge is available with respect to how the components of an educational system work in concert and with what consequences. With respect to the integrator, it is assumed that the behavioral sciences have developed to the point where there is knowledge which indicates what kinds of influence-strategies are likely to be effective with particular types of persons. All four concepts of instructional leadership presume that the current state of knowledge will enable one to specify the instructional tactics and strategies which are likely to produce a given outcome under certain kinds of conditions. These underlying assumptions of the four major views of instructional leadership, along with the required role behavior, are summarized in Table 1.

Critique of These Assumptions

Human nature and behavior are indeed complex, so complex that any one-sided analysis is inadequate. As Strauss has pointed out in his criticism of the self-actualization hypothesis, this view of human nature "overemphasizes individual's desire for freedom and under-emphasizes their desire for security."[12] Some people, as Eric Fromm suggests, are frustrated by freedom and want firm, secure leadership. There are those, because of early childhood experiences or their emotional make-up, who are dependent on others and are perfectly content to be directed by others. For some individuals their job is a primary source of satisfaction; consequently, they require little, if any, external motivation and direction. However, there are individuals who draw their principal satisfaction from work in the community, a hobby, or being a good parent. The presence of such individuals for whom work is not a central life interest has been documented by Dubin[13] in his study of industrial workers and by Presthus[14] in his examination of employees in all kinds of organizations including colleges and universities where the desire for self-actualization is presumed to be the greatest. These indifferents have much less of a desire for autonomy and freedom in their work than those whose lives revolve around their work, and consequently, require a much different type of treatment.

Of the four sets of assumptions concerning human nature, only the designer view

[11] Hunt, David E. "A Model for Analyzing the Training of Training Agents." Mimeographed. March, 1965.

[12] Strauss, George. "Some Notes on Power-Equalization" in Leavitt, Harold L. (ed.). *Social Science of Organizations.* Englewood Cliffs, New Jersey. Prentice-Hall, Inc. 1963. p. 50.

[13] Dubin, Robert. *The World of Work.* Englewood Cliffs, New Jersey. Prentice-Hall Inc. 1958.

[14] Presthus, Robert. *The Organizational Society.* New York, Random House, Inc. 1965.

Table 1. Summary Table

Role	*Underlying Assumptions*	*Role Behaviors Required*
Evaluator	1. Teachers wish to avoid responsibility: consequently, their work must be placed under surveillance to assure conformity to organizational policies and procedures. 2. The principal has adequate means and concepts for "coding" and "weighting" what occurs in the classroom. 3. The process of instruction can be reliably coded without a mastery of the subject matter being taught. 4. The current state of knowledge will enable one to specify the instructional tactics and strategies which are likely to produce a given outcome under certain kinds of conditions.	1. Observe what is going on in the classroom. 2. Record the "reality" of the classroom. 3. Compare the observed data with institutional requirements. 4. Make judgments about whether the goals of the institution are being achieved and procedures are being followed. 5. Make personnel decisions.
Helper	1. Teachers have the capacity to exercise a relatively high degree of imagination, ingenuity, and creativity in attaining the organization's goals and will exercise self-control under proper conditions. 2. The principal has the necessary means and concepts for "coding" what occurs in the classroom. 3. The process of instruction can be reliably coded without a mastery of the subject matter being taught. 4. The principal has such interpersonal skills as the ability to listen, communicate, and provide non-evaluative feedback. 5. The current state of knowledge will enable one to specify the tactics and strategies which are likely to produce a given outcome under certain kinds of conditions.	1. Observe what is going on in the classroom. 2. Record the "reality" of the classroom. 3. Report perceptions to the teacher. 4. Suggest a range of usable alternatives.

Table 1. Summary Table (Continued)

Role	*Underlying Assumptions*	*Role Behaviors Required*
Integrator	1. Teachers desire to know where they stand and will modify their performance to the betterment of the organization if given an opportunity to share in the planning of their work. 2. The principal has adequate means and concepts for "coding" and "weighting" what occurs in the classroom. 3. The process of instruction can be reliably coded without a mastery of the subject matter being taught. 4. The principal has such interpersonal skills as the ability to listen, communicate, provide evaluative feedback, and engage in collaborative decision-making. 5. The principal has a method for classifying people which suggests the means to employ in getting them to change their behavior. 6. The current state of knowledge will enable one to specify the tactics and strategies which are likely to produce a given outcome under certain kinds of conditions.	1. Communicate to each teacher what is expected of him. 2. Observe and record what is going on in the classroom. 3. Provide the teacher with feedback on how he is doing. 4. Work jointly with the teacher to translate improvement needs into specific goals. 5. Agree on what will be used as evidence of growth. 6. Provide assistance to the teacher as needed. 7. Determine with the teacher at some future specified point in time whether the goals have been achieved.
Designer	1. Teachers are unique individuals who are suited for some situations or functions and not others. 2. The principal has the skills required for "rationally and artfully" combining the human and material components of a school and community to form a functioning whole. 3. The principal has detailed knowledge of each component of the educational system and how these components work in concert and with what consequences.	1. Produce the "mix" of persons, facilities, materials, and program appropriate to a particular purpose for a particular situation. 2. Maintain a functional balance in the system. 3. Facilitate the basic processes and activities of the system.

would seem to be valid because it represents a broad view of human nature. It suffers, nevertheless, from a failure to specify the form that these individual differences may take. In over-emphasizing the uniqueness, rather than the universality, of human nature, the exponents of this view provide no directional focus for analysis and action with respect to human nature. This point should become clear to the reader as he examines the other three views. For example, if one assumes that an individual desires to become everything that one is capable of becoming (self-actualization) and will willingly work toward organizational objectives if he is achieving self-actualization, then the solution for the leader is to adopt policies which promote individual development and creativity. To say, however, that human nature is unique and to be no more specific than this obfuscates the situation and falls short of providing the administrator with the conceptual tools which he needs as he approaches the problem of instructional leadership.

What of the assumptions about the principal's skills? Are these assumptions valid, or are they subject to question as are those dealing with the assumptions about human nature? To answer this in part, the "coding" and "weighting" skills of principals will be examined since these skills are functional requisites to observing, analyzing, and evaluating teachers–activities for which the principal carries some responsibility. Barr has noted the subjective, impressionistic character of supervisory practices.[15] In this classic experiment, sixty supervisors observed the same teacher at the same time under the same conditions teaching two thirty-minute recitations and then were asked to rate and comment on the teacher's procedures. Barr found that the supervisors' comments were "guesses at fact" and contained no references to specific teacher and pupil activities. Of twenty-six ratings, fourteen were spread over the entire range of a ten point scale; eleven showed a nine point spread; only on one rating was there any substantial agreement. Work done much later by Hemphill, *et al.*[16] using films rather than "live" demonstrations revealed much the same kind of results. The present writer has encountered similar findings using tape recordings of classroom situations. Principals and other supervisors do not as a group possess the high level "coding" skills needed to perform the duties which they are expected to perform; in addition, principals do not seem to agree on the weights which they assign to what they observe in the classroom. Whether principals can acquire these coding skills will depend to a large extent on whether the process aspects of the classroom are subject matter specific. If indeed the instructional tactics and strategies which teachers use cannot be reliably coded unless one has a mastery of the subject matter being taught, then the evaluator, helper, and integrator views of instructional leadership are untenable.

As for the assumptions about the adequacy of present knowledge, these too

[15] Barr, A. S. *Characteristic Differences in the Teaching Performance of Good and Poor Teachers of the Social Studies.* Bloomington, Illinois. Public School Publishing Co. 1929.

[16] Hemphill, John K., Daniel E. Griffiths, and Norman Frederickson. *Administrative Performance and Personality.* New York. Bureau of Publications, Teachers College, Columbia University, 1962.

appear to be grounded on sand. For the designer to build an effective educational system, he needs detailed knowledge about how the various components of an educational system function and interact with one another. One has only to examine the conclusions drawn from hundreds of investigations reported in the *Handbook of Research on Teaching*[17] to learn how little is yet known about the ways in which the personal characteristics, tactics, and strategies of teachers influence what students learn. Knowledge of how the teacher and student components interact in an educational system would seem to await knowledge of their functioning; such knowledge is far from complete. The pioneer work of the Systems Development Corporation (SDC) in a case in point. SDC has simulated an actual educational system on a computer and attempted to predict certain outcomes from the utilization of a particular educational system that incorporates individual diagnosis and remedial treatment as components. These predictions were then compared with the actual outcomes of the system being simulated. Despite the fact that there was no great correspondence between the predicted and actual outcomes measured, more work of this nature is needed if designing an educational system is to be any more than a guessing game.

With respect to knowledge about influence-strategies, there is unavailable at present any typology which matches a constellation of factors for a given type of person with a corresponding set of treatment procedures.[18] What is needed is a method for classifying people which carries with it the treatment procedures, stages in the treatment, and criteria for determining whether the treatment has succeeded or failed.

A Revised Concept of Instructional Leadership

It appears from the preceding analysis that the popular notions of instructional leadership are indefensible because the assumptions underlying them are invalid. Each view of human nature in and of itself is inadequate in one or more respects. Furthermore, principals lack the coding skills required to fulfill the evaluator, helper, and integrator views of instructional leadership. Whether these skills can be developed has not yet been demonstrated. Finally, the current state of knowledge does not provide the designer with what he needs to know in order to construct an effective educational system, nor does it supply the integrator with what he needs to know about influencing people in order to change their behavior.

Nevertheless, the principal is confronted with the organizational necessity of making decisions and the problem of instructional leadership. In light of what is known and not known about instruction, change, human nature, and system design, is there a concept of instructional leadership for the principal which is legitimate, defensible, and congruent with his need to make decisions? The author believes that

[17] Gage, N. L. (ed.). *Handbook of Research on Teaching.* Chicago. Rand McNally and Company. 1963.

[18] Greenwood, Ernest, "The Practice of Science and the Science of Practice" in Bennis, Warren G. *et al.* (eds.). *The Planning of Change.* New York. Holt, Rinehart, and Winston. 1962. p. 79.

there is; this concept of instructional leadership is that of the *experimenter.* The experimenter view of instructional leadership calls upon the principal to establish an "experimental social system" in which he and other members of the social system continually try different approaches to their problems and examine the consequences of their actions for the functioning of the system. This means that the principal will need to take the initiative in working with his staff to specify what the system's functions and processes will be. The posture of the experimental social system will be one of continuous collection and evaluation of data relevant to goal setting, means selection, and system effectiveness. The principal will institutionalize feedback mechanisms regarding the functioning of system components and build in provisions for evaluation so that warranted conclusions and learnings can follow from an experimentally chosen action. In order to fulfill the experimenter role, the principal will need skills in collaborative decision-making and in establishing an inventory mechanism which will supply him with relevant, accurate, and objective information about the components of the system (e.g., teachers, students, and facilities) and their functioning. This means that the principal will require skills in data collection and analysis and the ability to conceptualize innovations in such a way as to generate the kinds of information needed to determine their impact on the functioning and output of the system. Finally, the principal will need knowledge of the various organizational arrangements for bringing students together with teachers–e.g., departmentalization, team teaching, the non-graded school, and the age-graded school–and the assumptions underlying each of these patterns.

This experimental approach to instructional leadership is based on two premises. The first is that the knowledge about educational systems and their components is inadequate. The second assumption is that the rate at which knowledge about educational systems will be developed is closely correlated with the rate at which new approaches to problems in this area are tried but tried in such a way as to yield valid generalizations. This concept of instructional leadership places the problem in its proper perspective. Definitive answers to significant educational problems are not yet available. If solutions are to be found it will require a climate of experimentation–a climate in which difficulties are continually identified by surveying instructional practices, records (e.g., achievement and aptitude), and perceptions; a climate in which a decision is reached to resolve these difficulties; a climate in which interpersonal support is given to those who implement the decision; and a climate in which the consequences, both anticipated and unanticipated, of the decision are studied and analyzed. This view prescribes an active role for the principal in matters relating to instruction. Whereas the behavior of the evaluator, helper, designer and integrator is mainly a reaction to events initiated by others, the behavior of the experimenter is largely self-initiated. While the former types are implementers, the latter is an inventor, one who seeks to create a state of events and in the process of creating, discovers solutions to important educational problems. This is the distinguishing mark of instructional leadership.

The "Guese" of Supervision

Bernard J. Lonsdale

One would think that, with the practice man has had in communicating through the ages he would have perfected his systems by now. There continue to be breakdowns that threaten relations between individuals, groups of people, and nations. A marginal note on a government report not intended for transmittal has been known to strain relations between nations that have been on friendly terms for years.

Hall in *The Silent Language* says:

> I am convinced that much of our difficulty with people in other countries stems from the fact that so little is known about cross-cultural communication.[1]

He continues:

> . . . . this formal training in the language, history, government and customs of another nation is only the first step in a comprehensive program. Of equal importance is the introduction to the non-verbal language which exists in every country of the world and among the various groups within each country. Most Americans are only dimly aware of this silent language even though they use it every day. They are not conscious of the elaborate patterning of behavior which prescribed our handling of time, our spatial relationships, our attitudes toward work, play and learning. In addition to what we say with our verbal language we are constantly communicating our feelings in our silent language—the language of behavior.[2]

From his background as a semanticist, Hayakawa pushes further the difficulties in communication both between and within groups:

> Today, the public is aware, perhaps to an unprecedented degree of the role of verbal communication in human affairs. This awareness arises partly, of course, out of the urgency of the tensions everywhere existing between nation and nation, class and class, individual and individual, in a world that is changing with fantastic rapidity. It arises, too, out of the knowledge on the part even of the most reflective elements of the population that enormous powers for good or evil lie in the media of mass communication. Thoughtful people in all walks of life feel, therefore, the need of systematic help in the huge task that confronts all of us today, namely, that of interpreting and evaluating the verbally received communications that pour in on us from all sides.[3]

[1] Edward T. Hall. *The Silent Language.* New York: Doubleday and Company, 1959, p. 10.
[2] *Ibid.*
[3] S. I. Hayakawa. *Language in Thought and Action.* New York: Harcourt, Brace and Company, 1949, p. iii-iv.

It appears as if man has put forth special efforts to keep language in certain slots—slots that belong to individuals, to groups, and to nations. Today we have the language of the banker, the jockey, the actor, the lumberjack, the surfer, and so on ad infinitum.

The banker uses such terms as amortization, bear market, callable, debenture, refinancing and many others.

The jockey talks about the totalizator, the mudder, odds, parimutuel, win, place and show.

The actor uses such terms as cues, loft, gels, wings, flats and sides.

The lumberjack talks about the whistle punk, sawyer, pond and edger.

The surfer[4] engages in such surfing expressions as over the falls, wipe out, goofy foot, hang ten, hot dogger and many others.

Language patterns, expressions and idioms peculiar to practically every trade and profession could be described. Language is coined and used in many instances to build an exclusion wall around a trade or profession. Such a wall is intended to give status and cohesiveness to the group, to make communication easier within the group and to create a brotherhood or in-group of the profession.

Speakers and writers frequently refer to the language peculiar to a trade or profession as the "guese"; for example, the language of educators is referred to as "pedaguese." If the butcher, the baker, the candlestick maker can afford the luxury of a "guese"—why cannot the educator have his pedaguese?

The blocks to communication and the threats to wholesome human relations in our society are not the "guese" but the failure of the in-group to interpret language to the out-group. One's social graces should dictate when a particular "guese" is proper and when it is improper. If a person has some money to invest with a banker or at the track he goes out of his way to learn the "guese" of the banker or of the racing expert. If individuals have an interest in education, they will go out of their way to find the meanings of the terms frequently used.

Many Voices—Many Languages

The writer has difficulty in recalling any glossary of educational terms prepared for public consumption which might improve communication between the school and the community. Those glossaries which have come out are directed to educators and most of them are attempts to lampoon terms used by fellow educators. It might pay dividends if every school district were to prepare a glossary which would be ready for each child to take home after his first day at school. The programs of parent organizations and other civic groups might be planned around the glossary, using a variety of techniques to enhance communication between the school and the community.

It is difficult to talk or write about the language of supervision apart from the many interrelated languages that affect educational programs—the language of the

[4] A teen-ager who read the manuscript said, "I could give you a lot of teen-age talk but if you used it your article would be dated because next year the talk will all be different."

child, the language of the mother and father to say nothing of the languages of the other members of the family, the language of the teacher, the principal, the superintendent, the school nurse, the psychologist, the school board–not to mention the languages of the power group and the various minority groups in the community.

True, democracy is made up of many voices and each voice has the right to be heard again and again. However, there are certain principles unique to the processes of democracy which make it possible to determine whether the voices ring true and whether the language expressed is in harmony with the principles of democratic living. Sometimes we hear the voices of the fakers riding on bandwagons who speak and write glibly about serving society and protecting the welfare of children. At other times we hear the dedicated educators who see the perpetuation and improvement of democracy as being realized through an education program custom-built for each individual so he will meet his needs and reach his highest potential.

Supervision in education has moved from the time when it meant demonstration and inspection. This function has become, in effect, a many-splendored thing set in a matrix of understandings, skills and values related to the growth of individuals as participating members of a democratic society. In earlier days supervision was a simple operation when it meant that someone from "downtown" or the "county seat" walked up and down the aisles of a classroom making notes in a little black book and then went back to the office to fill in a form, a copy of which was sent to the teacher, which answered, with *Yes* or *No,* such questions as:

Was the lesson socialized?
Did the children stand to recite?
Were the decorations in the room seasonal?

Franseth adds new dimensions to supervision in the statement:

> Today supervision is generally seen as leadership that encourages a continuous involvement of all school personnel in a cooperative attempt to achieve the most effective school program.[5]

In a summary statement Franseth suggests four ways in which supervision is most effective in realizing these new dimensions:

> (1) When it contributes significantly to the accomplishment of goals considered important by the teachers as well as by the supervisors; (2) When the teachers are meaningfully involved in making and carrying out plans that affect them, with a part in determining what the supervisory service should be; (3) When supervision provides an atmosphere of acceptance, support and understanding, and helps people experience feelings of worth; and (4) When supervision helps

[5]Jane Franseth. *Supervision as Leadership.* Evanston, Ill.: Row, Peterson Company, 1961. p. 19.

people make sound judgments and act on the basis of careful study of adequate and accurate information.[6]

The Supervisor's Language

As supervision moves to encompass new dimensions, the language of supervision talks about such things as:

The Goals of Education—The emphasis is on a statement of goals or a set of beliefs which is built school by school, district by district, with everyone affected by it participating in its preparation. The answers to the question of appropriate opportunities for children and youth will be found in a clearly defined statement in harmony with the principles of education in a democratic society. Such statements should provide the platform upon which to build programs suited to the needs of our times.

A publication of the California State Department of Education suggests the following questions as the basis for evaluating statements of goals:

1. Is the statement of the objectives available to all interested persons?
2. Is the statement in accord with the broad purposes of democracy?
3. Have legal requirements as established by the Legislature and the State Board of Education been met?
4. Is the statement based on the requirements of the course of study as established by the governing board of the school district or the office of the county superintendent of schools?
5. Is the statement in harmony with well-substantiated research in child growth and development?
6. Is the statement in harmony with well-substantiated research in mental health?
7. Are school practices consistent with the established goals?
8. Does the school have an organized plan to evaluate progress toward the fulfillment of the goals?
9. Do school personnel and members of the community refer to the goals when making decisions?
10. Are the goals reviewed and revised from time to time as the situation changes?[7]

Numerous statements of the purposes or goals of education in a democratic society have been prepared by committees of national repute. Accepting these statements for a particular school by a local committe or an administrator is one thing. Having them used for study purposes as a basis for working out statements that will fit their peculiar needs is quite another thing. The people whose nervous

[6] *Ibid., p. 29.*

[7] Bernard J. Lonsdale and Afton D. Nance. *Evaluating the Elementary School,* Revised. Bulletin of the California State Department of Education, Vol. XXX, No. 3, Sacramento: California State Department of Education, 1961. p. 29.

systems are most deeply affected by statements of goals or purposes are those who participated in their preparation.

Individual Differences in People—The stress is placed upon the differences—physical, social and intellectual—that characterize human beings. Each individual is recognized as a unique personality. Each has the right to develop to his fullest potential. Each is entitled to feel that he counts. Too often in our society some individuals feel that if everybody is somebody then nobody is anybody. The talk turns to "keeping certain people in their place." The question asked in supervision is, "How can the differences that characterize an individual be turned into assets for the good of the whole group?"

The Basic Human Needs That Individuals Must Satisfy—Unless an individual has opportunity to satisfy his basic needs which come out of the structure of his organism, the social context in which he develops, and his personal growth, he may be frustrated and spend his life in fruitless searching which often ends in despair and personality damage. Stress in the language of supervision is placed upon the need to sense the extent to which the basic needs of individuals are being met and as one meets his own needs to help others to meet theirs. The help to others may be shown in a warm smile, an invitation to coffee, a willingness to listen.

The Need to Know Children and Youth—Emphasis is placed upon a knowledge of the characteristics of growth and development of children and youth. These characteristics also apply to adult development. Each one goes through the same pattern but each goes through at a rate peculiar to himself. Each one comes through as a custom built job—some with more assets than others, some with more liabilities than others—but each with his own pocket full of stars. Stress in the language of supervision is placed upon the need for skill in the techniques of observing, studying and interpreting human behavior. Understanding that all behavior is caused and that the causes are many and interrelated is an important dimension in human relations. It may not be possible in many instances to know the cause, but to know that there is a cause contributes to better working relations.

Effective Teaching Methods—The language of supervision has stopped saying, through the use of directives, "This is the way to do it." Good supervisors realize that any change that might come from a directive can only be of the narrow routine type. The big changes, the really important ones, are those that come out of the teacher's changed behavior. Extensive research pertaining to effective methods of teaching has been done. Many of these research studies have set boundaries as to the most and the least effective ways of working. There is need for studies which will extend the boundaries set by this research. There is further need for research done by teachers who will be identified with the findings and who will put them into practice.

What evidence is there that certain methods of instruction are more effective than others? Could a particular method yield more learnings than another? Why does a child fail in one situation and succeed in another? How does one way of learning interrelate and support another? These questions are merely illustrative of the myriad questions teachers ask every day. The language of supervision suggests that teachers carry on research of significance to themselves. After they have defined a problem, they can state a hypothesis that will indicate the procedure to be followed and the outcomes to be expected. With this as a basis for starting, they have a laboratory in the classroom in which to collect data, evaluate it, and test the hypothesis. The emphasis in the language of supervision should be of the kind that will help teachers to create the design for the research, develop instruments needed for securing the necessary data, and interpret the records.

Use of Instructional Materials—Emphasis is placed upon the use of a variety of materials of instruction. As new insights are gained regarding the learning process, it becomes obvious that materials that have appeal to all the senses should be made available in classrooms. Each day, it seems, new materials come on the market which have learning value or which facilitate learning. Teachers are encouraged to experiment with these new materials and to use them in their research patterns. Too often new materials are condemned and passed over before they are even tried. Community resources are of immeasurable value as materials of instruction. People, places and things outside the classroom can contribute significantly to learning situations.

Creativity—A high premium is placed on the potential for creativity which is innate in each individual. The time has passed when creativity was thought to belong only to a chosen few. Kelley and Rasey say:

> Whenever an individual takes a set of known answers and contrives a new response, concept, or artifact he is creative. It is the process of taking the things we now have or now know and putting these together in such a way that something new emerges.[8]

This concept of creativity is furthered by Russell when he says:

> In one sense, all a child's learning is creative in that he arrives at what is, for him, new solutions. Some writers prefer to limit the more routine school and community learnings to the process of discovery and to describe by the term *creative thinking* only those processes which result in some product or solution of an original sort. Children's learnings may be described on a scale ranging from routine associative learnings through rather stereotyped problem-solving processes to highly original creative thinking resulting in new solutions for the individual and his subculture.[9]

The language of supervision urges an atmosphere in which teachers are encouraged to express themselves creatively. As teachers are motivated to develop their own creative abilities they in turn provide creative opportunities for children.

The creative personality does not develop under an autocratic regime. The language of supervision places a heavy stress upon the democratic processes because they hold most promise for freeing individuals to make their fullest contribution to the welfare of the individual and the group.

[8] E. C. Kelley and M. I. Rasey. *Education and the Nature of Man.* New York: Harper and Brothers, 1962, p. 116.

[9] David H. Russell. *Children's Thinking.* Boston: Ginn and Company, 1959, p. 326-27.

In part of the response to the question, "Is America Neglecting Her Creative Minority?" Toynbee[10] says:

> Potential creative ability can be stifled, stunted, and stultified by the prevalence in society of adverse attitudes of mind and habits of behavior. . . . When creative ability is thwarted, it will not be extinguished; it is more likely to be given an antisocial turn.

The challenge today in education is for everyone to think creatively. No one group of individuals in our society has an option on creative living. The satisfactions which are the by-products of creativity are available to all.

All of this supervision talk implies the need for continuous education, not only for teachers but for everyone responsible for planning educational programs. The language of supervision has a chance to be heard and understood by the types of in-service education programs developed cooperatively with the people who will profit from them.

The language of supervision will continue to talk about the goals of education, individual differences in people, the basic human needs that individuals must satisfy, the need to know children and youth, effective teaching methods, the use of instructional materials, and creativity.

It is evident that supervision means different things to different people. Many of the concepts held by the different individuals are inadequate as guides to the improvement of instruction. As a result, the language of supervision becomes a voice crying in the wilderness.

Supervision will never go back to inspection and demonstration. Through the thinking, action, and language, both spoken and silent, of dedicated educators its new role has emerged. Supervision will continue to improve instruction. The future greatness of our country will be built through the quality of education made available to every individual who is a part of this nation.

[10]Arnold Toynbee. "Is America Neglecting Her Creative Minority?" *Mills Quarterly* 44:5-6, May 1962.

Toward Human Relations in Supervision

Gertrude Moskowitz

"My cooperating teacher doesn't let me try out any of my own ideas."

"If only my cooperating teacher would leave the room when I'm teaching."

"In the middle of my lesson, my cooperating teacher thinks nothing of interrupting me to add a point or to correct what I'm saying."

"Yes, my student teacher seems to know his subject matter, but he doesn't know how to get the pupils interested and involved in the lesson."

"My student teacher has a number of good ideas, but she doesn't realize you have to lead pupils into new things slowly and not all at once."

"It's very difficult to give suggestions to my student teacher as he just can't take criticism."

Typical and timeless, such remarks are frequently heard by supervisors of student teachers, as well as by fellow student teachers and principals of cooperating schools. After several conferences, the college supervisor may conclude that his most prevalent problem is how to place the human element in the relationship between cooperating teachers and student teachers. Often supervisory conferences are spent accepting the feelings of dissatisfaction of cooperating teachers or student teachers,

"Yes, you probably would like to find out how you'll manage when your cooperating teacher leaves the room."

–and then trying to convey understanding or at least tolerance of one for the other.

"But perhaps your cooperating teacher feels that if she stays and watches you teach, she can be more helpful to you."

And so to help out the student teacher, at the next meeting with the cooperating teacher the supervisor exercises tact,

"And how does your student teacher seem to manage when you leave the room?"

–only to discover the justification of the cooperating teacher's staying, along with a complaint,

"Well, I haven't left as yet because my student teacher is having difficulty maintaining control. In fact I've told her to handle several situations, but she prefers to play it her own way."

—which leaves the supervisor facing round two in the role of appeaser.

Studies of Human Relations in Student Teaching

The literature on student teaching contains frequent mention of the importance of the cooperating teacher being highly skilled in human relations. Yet the few studies conducted in which student teachers revealed their feelings about their cooperating teachers indicated the student teachers felt that:

1. Cooperating teachers failed to encourage and inspire them.
2. Cooperating teachers did not relate to them with personal warmth.
3. Cooperating teachers criticized the student teachers, but failed to praise them sufficiently.

Other studies reveal that:

1. Cooperating teachers believed the conferences they had with student teachers were very nearly ideal. Yet observers of these conferences found a significant negative relationship between the ideal described by the cooperating teachers and the observed practices.
2. College courses dealing with the study of human relations do not give strong emphasis to many of the aspects of human relations that are relevant to the needs of student teachers.

Although the importance of a satisfying student teaching experience has been recognized, little has been done to better communication between cooperating teacher and student teacher so as to make this outcome more likely. Explanations, provocations, supplications do not seem to work. How, then, can a constructive and congenial supervisory relationship be developed?

A Study of Improving Supervisory Relations

A number of encouraging implications which relate to this problem are coming from an ongoing study under a Cooperative Research Project, hereafter referred to as Project POST.[1] Under Project POST the effects of training cooperating teachers in the Flanders system of interaction analysis are being investigated.

The Flanders system categorizes the verbal behaviors of teachers as they interact

[1]The Project on Student Teaching (POST) is being conducted for five semesters under a Cooperative Research grant and is directed by Professor Edmund Amidon of Temple University. This article reports findings from a correlative study, but one which was not funded by the grant. Without the help and encouragement of Professor Amidon, the research discussed here would not have been possible.

in their classrooms with their pupils. There are ten categories in the system—seven for teacher behavior, two for student behavior, and one for silence or confusion. The teacher behaviors are divided into two types of influence, *indirect* and *direct.* The indirect categories are those which expand the freedom of students to participate.

The categories of indirect teacher influence are: (1) accepts feelings of pupils, (2) praises or encourages, (3) accepts ideas of pupils, (4) asks questions. The categories of direct teacher influence limit the freedom of students to participate. The categories of direct influence are: (5) gives information, (6) gives directions, (7) criticizes or justifies authority. The two categories of student talk are: (8) teacher-initiated response, (9) student-initiated response.

To obtain a descriptive picture of what behaviors are used during a lesson, an observer tallies the classroom interaction every three seconds, as well as tallying every change of behavior by recording each time one of the ten categories. The tallies are entered into a 10-by-10 matrix, and the graphic picture of the lesson which results may then be studied and analyzed. From the matrix, a teacher may find out many specific things about his teaching. A few of these are:

1. What percentage of class time does the teacher talk?
2. What percentage of class time do the pupils talk?
3. Does the teacher use more indirect or more direct influence during a lesson?
4. Is the teacher more indirect or direct in the way he motivates and controls the class?
5. What kind of immediate feedback does the teacher give to pupils as they respond?
6. To what extent do pupils participate for extended periods of time?
7. What behaviors does the teacher use to elicit pupil response in the class?
8. To what extent are pupil responses which are called for by the teacher narrow, predictable ones and to what extent are pupils given the opportunity to bring in their own ideas?
9. What behaviors does the teacher use more extensively in communicating?

When the data are used as a feedback device, both in-service and preservice teachers have often developed new insights into their teaching and have subsequently made some changes in their patterns.

Focus of the Research

It was assumed in the present study that if cooperating teachers were trained to use interaction analysis, they would apply their knowledge to the interaction between their student teachers and themselves, thereby improving interpersonal relationships and insuring a more profitable experience for mature and inexperienced teachers. The focus of the research was the issue of whether the attitudes of cooperating teacher and student teacher toward one another would be influenced if either or both of them received training in interaction analysis, and if so, in what ways.

More specifically, the research sought answers to this multipart question:

> Does training in interaction analysis make a difference in the attitudes of cooperating teachers and student teachers toward each other when:
> - both the cooperating teachers and the student teachers receive the training?
> - only the student teachers receive the training?
> - only the cooperating teachers receive the training?
> - neither the cooperating teachers nor the student teachers receive the training?

Forty-four secondary education student teachers and their cooperating teachers were the subjects of this study in the spring semester of 1965. One-half of the cooperating teachers and one-half of the student teachers received training in the Flanders system. Each of the students and supervisors was assigned to one of the four possible combinations of training or no training in interaction analysis. In the present study, "no training" or "untrained" means that the subjects did not receive training in interaction analysis. The groups which evolved for the study are described in Table 1.

Table 1. Teacher-Student Groups Used in the Study

Group I Cooperating teachers with interaction analysis Student teachers with interaction analysis	*Group II* Cooperating teachers with no training Student teachers with interaction analysis
Group III Cooperating teachers with interaction analysis Student teachers with no training	*Group IV* Cooperating teachers with no training Student teachers with no training

The trained cooperating teachers received 25 hours of instruction in the use of interaction analysis as a supervisory tool in working with student teachers. They received two graduate credits, without cost, for taking this training. Applying the insights gathered from the study of interaction analysis to their own so-called regular teaching was not discussed in the cooperating teacher course since the focus, rather, was on how supervising teachers might help student teachers to gain the insights. The student teachers trained in interaction analysis focused on its application to their own teaching. These student teachers received a total of 60 hours of training in interaction analysis, consisting of a two-hour lecture and a two-hour laboratory period each week for one semester.

Procedures Used

Cooperating teachers who did not take the course in interaction analysis but who were supervising Temple University student teachers were asked to be participants in the study. These cooperating teachers and the student teachers not trained in interaction analysis formed the untrained groups. Both groups of cooperating teachers, trained and untrained, were volunteers.

Trained cooperating teachers who supervised trained student teachers tallied the interaction of a number of the lessons of their student teachers. The matrix of the lesson was then used as the basis for conferences. It was hypothesized that the common frame of reference of interaction analysis would open communication and understanding in the supervisory relationships. Since the student teachers understood the concepts of interaction analysis, the cooperating teachers did not have to resort to the classic procedure of telling the student teacher what the cooperating teacher *thought* happened during the lesson. And the student teacher, therefore, was not left feeling defensive. Saying to a student teacher, "You talked a great deal of the period," is different from the student teacher's seeing on a matrix that he spoke 85 percent of the time, during what was supposed to be a discussion lesson.

Going over a matrix together, the student teacher becomes his own vigorous critic, and the cooperating teacher then becomes a guide in the analysis by asking appropriate questions which can be answered by the student teacher. "What were the goals of your lesson?" and "Did your behavior match your intentions?" are leading questions in the conferences. The answers are found in the matrix and not in the student teacher's impressions of the lesson or the cooperating teacher's opinions of it.

If the goal of the lesson was to review material and to reinforce pupil responses, but the student teacher asked few questions, lectured a great deal, and gave little praise or acceptance of pupils' responses, then the lesson would not successfully have matched the intentions of the student teacher. What changes are desirable in order to fulfill these goals are then decided *by the student teacher.*

The trained cooperating teachers who supervised untrained student teachers were free to talk to their student teachers in broad terms about the concepts learned in the study of interaction analysis, *but without reference to a matrix* and without teaching the student teachers anything about the category system. It was hypothesized that, knowing interaction analysis, these cooperating teachers would be more sensitive about what to look for in the classroom teaching of their student teachers, and would be provided with a structure which would enable them to know more precisely what to communicate to their student teachers during their conferences together.

Two special instruments, the *Cooperating Teachers' Attitude Questionnaire* (CTAQ) and the *Student Teachers' Attitude Questionnaire* (STAQ), were devised by the author to assess the degree of satisfaction with and the attitudes toward one another of the cooperating teachers and their student teachers involved in this study. These were questionnaires generated from favorable and unfavorable comments made by student teachers and cooperating teachers about one another.

The two questionnaires consisted of parallel items in that the questions asked of cooperating teachers on the CTAQ were rephrased so as to apply to student teachers in the STAQ. Each questionnaire contained eleven items. Subjects were to check their reactions to each item along a nine-point scale. The highest possible score was 99. The higher the score, the more positive the attitude. The reliabilities of the questionnaires were: CTAQ, 0.92; STAQ, 0.87.

In the last week of the student teaching experience the appropriate attitude questionnaires were administered to the cooperating teachers and their student teachers to determine whether training in interaction analysis affected their attitudes toward one another.

Findings of the Study: Attitudes of Cooperating Teachers Toward Student Teachers

There appears to be no statistically significant difference in the attitudes of the trained and untrained cooperating teachers toward their student teachers, as is evident from the CTAQ mean scores given in Table 2. One can speculate that the reason for this lack of difference relates to the method of selecting all the cooperating teachers in the study—all teachers were volunteers, and all knew they were to have a part in a study which dealt with their role as cooperating teachers. It seems reasonable to suppose, therefore, that their attitudes were above average to start with.

Table 2. Mean Scores of Cooperating Teachers on the CTAQ

Trained Cooperating Teachers (Groups I & III)		*Untrained Cooperating Teachers (Groups II & IV)*			
Mean	*S.D.*	*Mean*	*S.D.*	*t*	*p*
82.14	9.94	76.91	16.37	1.25	not significant

In other words, these cooperating teachers might have had very satisfactory attitudes toward their student teachers, which had let them to volunteer for the study. Actually, this satisfaction may have applied even more to the untrained group, which was not taking the "free" two-credit graduate course dealing with interaction analysis, since those teachers received nothing tangible for participation in the study. In spite of these possibilities, it should be noted that such differences as were found did indicate somewhat more positive attitudes among the trained group than among the untrained teachers.

The reader will recall that four different teacher-student groups were used in the study (Table 1). A further refinement of the data regarding teacher attitudes toward their student teachers was obtained by determining the CTAQ scores for the teachers in each of these four groups. Mean scores for each of the groups are shown in Table 3. (This figure also contains some STAQ data which will be referred to later.)

Table 3. Mean Scores for All Four Cooperating Teacher and Student Teacher Groups on Attitude Questionnaires

	CTAQ	*STAQ*
Cooperating Teachers Trained Student Teachers Trained (Group I)	82.90	80.80
Cooperating Teachers Trained Student Teachers Untrained (Group III)	81.45	83.18
Cooperating Teachers Untrained Student Teachers Trained (Group II)	78.00	65.27
Cooperating Teachers Untrained Student Teachers Untrained (Group IV)	75.92	75.08

None of the differences between CTAQ mean scores was statistically significant. But differences did in fact occur and in a pattern that suggests that something more than pure chance is involved. It seems worth noting that

- The highest mean score was for cooperating teachers in Group I, in which *both* cooperating and student teachers were trained.
- Next in line was the mean score for cooperating teachers in Group III, in which *only cooperating teachers* were trained.
- Then came Group II, in which cooperating teachers were not trained but the *student teachers were.*
- The lowest mean score occurred in Group IV, where *neither* teacher group had had training in interaction analysis.

In other words, the attitudes of the cooperating teachers toward their student teachers were the most positive when both cooperating teachers and their student teachers were trained, and these attitudes decreased successively in positiveness as the degree of contact of the cooperating teachers with interaction analysis diminished.

Findings of the Study: Attitudes of Student Teachers Toward Cooperating Teachers

To turn now to the attitudes of student teachers, their attitudes toward their cooperating teachers were significantly more positive in the cases where the cooperating teacher had been trained than where they had not been trained (Table 4). And reference once more to Table 3 shows that in the four teacher-student categories the positive attitudes toward cooperating teachers ran highest in the two groups where the cooperating teachers had been trained in interaction analysis. Whether or not student teachers had had such *training* apparently was *not a factor* in determining their outlook on *trained* cooperating teachers.

Table 4. Mean STAQ Scores of Student Teachers Toward Trained and Untrained Cooperating Teachers

Student Teachers With					
Trained Cooperating Teachers (Groups I & III)		*Untrained Cooperating Teachers (Groups II & IV)*			
Mean	*S.D.*	*Mean*	*S.D.*	*t*	*p*
82.05	10.42	70.39	16.70	2.70	.01

Turning back to Figure 3 once more, it will be seen that the mean scores of the four groups of cooperating teachers on the CTAQ and the mean scores of the student teachers on the STAQ were surprisingly similar, pair by pair, with one exception, Group II. In this case, the cooperating teachers' attitudes were much more positive toward the student teachers than the student teachers' attitudes were toward these cooperating teachers. The student teachers in Group II, who themselves *had been trained* in interaction analysis but whose *teachers had not been* had the least positive attitudes toward their cooperating teachers.

It may be that this group of student teachers acquired certain awarenesses from their training which led to their having particular expectations of their cooperating teachers. Perhaps the cooperating teachers' lack of this training led to unfulfilled expectations in the student teachers, lessening rapport through an inability to communicate via a common frame of reference. The student teachers now knew something to which their cooperating teachers were not attuned. These student teachers may have wanted to try out new behaviors, only to find themselves working with someone less experimentally inclined.

On the other hand, the untrained cooperating teachers in Group II held more positive attitudes toward their trained student teachers than did the untrained cooperating teachers in Group IV toward their untrained student teachers. In other words, *untrained* cooperating teachers held more positive attitudes toward *trained* student teachers than did *untrained* cooperating teachers toward *untrained* student teachers. It appears as though training of the cooperating teachers in interaction analysis increased the rapport between these cooperating teachers and their student teachers. Training of *only* the *cooperating teacher accounted* for *very positive attitudes* in their student teachers, while training of *only* the *student teachers* seemed related to *very negative attitudes* toward the cooperating teachers.

Although the training in interaction analysis seems not to have affected significantly the attitudes of the cooperating teachers toward their student teachers, the training (or lack of it) on the part of teachers appears to have significantly affected the attitudes of the student teachers toward these cooperating teachers. If the attitudes of the cooperating teachers were quite positive to begin with, it may be that the effect of the training was not to improve their attitudes, but rather to increase their sensitivity in communicating with their student teachers.

How the Cooperating Teachers Were Perceived

What were some of the differences between the trained and the untrained cooperating teachers as perceived by their student teachers? An analysis of the individual items in the STAQ revealed the *greatest difference* to be that the student teachers found the trained cooperating teachers were much *more flexible and willing to make changes,* while the untrained cooperating teachers were seen as more set in their ways. Quite possibly, flexibility is the key element in developing positive human relations. The training in interaction analysis did, of course, focus on the concept of flexibility of behavior in classroom teaching. This, in turn, seems to have helped foster flexibility in the supervisory relationship.

When student responses on the STAQ were analyzed item by item, some differences between students' perceptions of trained and untrained cooperating teachers became apparent. Qualities more likely to be ascribed to the trained teachers than to untrained cooperating teachers are listed as follows, arranged in descending order of frequency of mention.

1. Had ideas about teaching which were more in agreement with those of their student teachers.
2. Made the student teachers feel like trying their cooperating teachers' suggestions and ideas more.
3. Praised their student teachers much more.
4. Made their student teachers feel more willing to discuss their lessons and problems in teaching.
5. Were more helpful in talks they had with their student teachers.
6. Offered criticism in a more acceptable way.
7. Were easier to work with.
8. Allowed their student teachers to use their own ideas in planning lessons more.
9. Understood and accepted somewhat more their student teachers' feelings concerning their teaching situations.
10. Gave the student teachers somewhat less negative criticism.

It is apparent that each of these differentiating behaviors tended to make for more favorable attitudes on the part of student teachers. Among other things in classroom teaching, this training focuses attention on the concepts of praise, criticism, and acceptance of pupils' feelings. Here, again, the insights from the training seem to have transferred into the one-to-one supervisory relationship, as indicated by items 3, 6, 9, and 10. As a result of their incorporating certain insights gained from their own study of interaction analysis, the trained cooperating teachers were seen by their student teachers as more helpful, easier to get along with, and more permissive.

Reciprocal Perceptions

Further comparative examination of the replies from teachers and students uncovered a number of other points worth consideration, especially as they reveal harmony or discord in the reciprocal feelings of the cooperating teachers and their student teachers.

1. Both groups of cooperating teachers responded that their student teachers frequently tried the suggestions or ideas offered to them. Yet the student teachers working with untrained cooperating teachers felt less willing to try them. Student teachers with untrained cooperating teachers apparently used the suggestions offered but did not particularly wish to do so.
2. The trained cooperating teachers felt they could allow their student teachers to use their own ideas in planning lessons more than did the untrained cooperating teachers. And the student teachers working with trained cooperating teachers felt they did have more freedom to use their own ideas.
3. Both groups of cooperating teachers saw their student teachers as flexible and willing to make the changes recommended to them, but the student teachers found the untrained cooperating teachers less willing to bend or mend their own ways.
4. Both groups of cooperating teachers felt that their student teachers generally accepted criticism. But the student teachers found the way the trained cooperating teachers criticized them was more readily acceptable. The trained cooperating teachers seemed to have developed skill in giving criticism graciously.
5. The untrained cooperating teachers felt they had to tell their student teachers what was wrong with their teaching somewhat more often. And these student teachers perceived that their cooperating teachers did indeed tell them what was wrong with their teaching more often. This type of communication may have led to some of the other dissatisfactions expressed by student teachers working with untrained cooperating teachers.
6. Although both groups of cooperating teachers responded that their student teachers did a number of things deserving of praise, the untrained cooperating teachers did not communicate their feelings to their student teachers.
7. The student teachers viewed the talks they had with trained cooperating teachers as even more helpful to them than their cooperating teachers had judged the talks to be. Student teachers of untrained cooperating teachers saw such talks as less helpful than their cooperating teachers had judged them to be. The perceived

differences in the ways the cooperating teachers used praise and criticism may have influenced their student teachers' judgments on the worth of these talks.

8. The trained cooperating teachers and their student teachers found each other very easy to work with. Student teachers seemed able to conceal some of their negative feelings from their untrained cooperating teachers, because student teachers rated untrained cooperating teachers as harder to work with than these cooperating teachers in turn rated the students.

9. There was little difference among the cooperating teachers in how willing they thought their student teachers were to discuss their lessons and problems in teaching with them. However, student teachers of trained cooperating teachers expressed even more willingness to discuss these issues than their cooperating teachers. Interestingly, student teachers of the untrained cooperating teachers found their ideas did not agree as much with their cooperating teachers' as their cooperating teachers supposed they did. The student teachers, even when they disagreed with the untrained cooperating teachers, seemed to go along, with the existence or extent of their disagreement undetected by their cooperating teachers.

In every case, the student teachers had more favorable reactions toward trained cooperating teachers than toward untrained ones. Of vital concern is the fact that, on most of the items, the untrained cooperating teachers were not aware that the attitudes of their student teachers were less favorable than the cooperating teachers believed them to be. This may be one more reason why there were no significant differences in the attitudes of the trained and untrained cooperating teachers toward their student teachers; the lack of sensitivity to the situation meant that the untrained cooperating teachers did not know that things were amiss in their supervision or that there was room for improvement.

Conclusions and Implications

The findings of this study seem to support these generalizations:

- Training cooperating teachers in interaction analysis appeared to affect in a positive direction the interpersonal relationships of the cooperating teachers and their student teachers.
- Training both cooperating teachers and student teachers in interaction analysis appeared related to more positive interpersonal relationships between the cooperating teachers and their student teachers.
- Training of only the student teachers appeared to affect the attitudes toward their cooperating teachers in a negative direction.

The findings of this study suggest that promoting more positive interpersonal relationships during the student teaching experience can best be accomplished by training cooperating teachers *and* their student teachers in interaction analysis. *If a choice had to be made* to train either cooperating teachers or student teachers, it appears that *cooperating teachers should be trained,* since their student teachers might thereby develop more positive attitudes toward their cooperating teachers, and consequently, have a more profitable student teaching experience. *Training only the student teachers does not seem desirable* inasmuch as the attitudes which developed in the student teachers toward their cooperating teachers tended, in this study, to be extremely negative.

Paradoxically, training in interaction analysis can be made more readily available to student teachers by means of course work required in professional education. Involving cooperating teachers may mean in-service training and workshops if similar training is not offered at the graduate level. It appears that more communication is needed between the principals of cooperating schools and the university so that training can be made available to in-service teachers and especially to cooperating teachers.

The in-service teacher needs to be up-to-date on what is current in the field. Placing student teachers who have certain newly-found insights and the desire to be experimental with cooperating teachers who are not aware of these learnings seems to establish a barrier between the two, since there is no common frame of reference. Representative of this barrier is the following statement by a trained student teacher working with two untrained cooperating teachers:

> According to my matrices, I moved from a neutral or middle-of-the-road position to one of a fairly indirect teacher. While this is good as far as I am concerned, I ran into a great deal of trouble with my cooperating teachers, who felt that my teaching was getting worse instead of better—based on the fact that I allowed my students to participate more, especially on something that I felt was important but my cooperating teachers didn't!

Student teachers who know how teaching can be analyzed through a category system seem to become critical of the teaching of others who do not share this knowledge. This appears to be a factor contributing to the negative attitudes of trained student teachers toward untrained cooperating teachers. By the same token, student teachers and in-service teachers who learn the Flanders system may tend to have less regard for principals not knowledgeable in this area now so productive of developments with many implications for the improvement of teaching.

Principals themselves, therefore, should have a working knowledge of the Flanders system. Quite possibly, the same results would follow the training of principals in the Flanders system as occurred with the training of the cooperating teachers: perhaps faculties would perceive their interpersonal relations with their principals more positively, with the principals becoming more sensitive about their own interaction with their teachers.

The student teaching experience is more than a practicum in teaching; it is a human relations experience as well. Differences in personality or varying viewpoints between cooperating teachers and student teachers have often led to anxieties and unprofitable experiences and may have even convinced some student teachers not to go into teaching at all. Tangible ways to improve the student teaching experience are needed.

Giving cooperating teachers and student teachers sensitivity training through a structure for objective feedback into their behavior is a concrete way to provide positive transfer into the student teaching experience. That training cooperating teachers in interaction analysis appeared to make a direct transfer into their interpersonal relations with student teachers is indeed an encouraging and exciting finding, one that deserves a more vigorous description than "incidental learning"!

Group Supervision: A Technique for Improving Teaching Behavior

Edmund J. Amidon, Kathleen M. Kies, and Anthony T. Palisi

The principal-teacher conference which usually follows observation of an instructional period is often conducted with the same air of confidentialness as the interview between doctor and patient or lawyer and client. This confidential approach to supervision, which has been widely promulgated and accepted, suggests that the discussion involves criticism of the teacher and that only he may profit from the interview. It suggests that the interview is concerned more with the teacher than with the act of teaching.

While this approach to supervision has value and is necessary at times, the authors propose that a different kind of supervision is at least equally appropriate. If supervision, defined as *the improvement of instruction,* can be carried out so that teachers perceive it as "challenge without threat," perhaps we can take another approach–an approach which directs attention to *the act of teaching,* rather than to the teacher.

In directing attention to the act of teaching, one might hypothesize that group supervision can be as effective as group counseling appears to be. One can also hypothesize that such a process is more economical of supervisory time and that the dynamics of small groups enhance both the effect of the process and interpersonal relationships among the faculty. Small group process almost invariably has these effects: 1) Communication is opened; 2) Cohesiveness is encouraged; 3) Group norms are clarified for general understanding; and 4) Group goals are clarified.

In attempting to explore the potential of group supervision, the authors felt it necessary to define the act of teaching. Combs and Snygg hold that the genius of good teaching lies in the ability to challenge students without threatening them and that the distinction between challenge and threat lies "not in what the teacher *thinks* he is doing, but in what the students perceive him to be doing."[1] Thus, the task is to study the act of teaching in terms of this ability to challenge without threatening, as perceived by students.

The communication between teachers and students is sometimes non-verbal; however, it is largely composed of verbal behavior, and by objectively observing this

[1] Combs, A., and Snygg, D. *Individual Behavior.* Evanston: Harper and Row, 1961.

talk, one can analyze the teachers' ability to challenge without threat. The authors' concern is to increase teachers' sensitivity to their own verbal behavior and their understanding of how this behavior affects classroom climate and individual pupils. The Flanders System of verbal interaction analysis provides the teacher with an instrument of objectivity through which he can compare his own performance with his intentions and study teacher-pupil dialogue.[2] This system was used as the basis for an in-service training program carried out by the authors.

The Flanders System

Flanders classifies classroom verbal interaction in ten categories, seven of which identify teacher talk. Categories 1, accepting and clarifying student feeling; 2, praising or encouraging student behavior; 3, accepting and clarifying student ideas; and 4, asking questions, are considered indirect teacher talk. Categories 5, lecturing, giving information or opinion; 6, giving directions; and 7, criticizing or justifying teacher authority, are considered direct teacher talk. Student categories 8, response to the teacher; and 9, student initiated talk, classify student talk. Category 10 is used to identify silence or confusion.

The observer, who may be present in the classroom or listen to a tape, records in sequence every three seconds the appropriate category numbers. When the lesson is over, the observer enters the numbers in the form of tallies in a 10-row by 10-column grid, called a matrix. The matrix reveals both quantification and patterns of verbal interaction.

Data which are related to quantification include the percentage of time consumed 1) by teacher talk, 2) by student talk, and 3) in silence or confusion. The percentages of time spent in each of the seven categories of teacher talk may be computed.

The matrix, while summarizing the data found by the observer, also maintains some of the sequence. The teacher can see the patterns of his reactions to student response, to silence, or to student initiation. He may find answers to such questions as, "Which of my verbal behaviors seem to elicit student response?" and "At what point in the interaction do I find it necessary to criticize?"

The Flanders System of interaction analysis does yield descriptive information about the teacher-pupil dialogue, but this information is *in no way* an evaluation of teaching. If any kind of value judgment about teaching is to be made, it is done by the teacher himself after studying his own interaction patterns.

This system was developed and refined by Flanders in the early 1950's. The first research related children's attitudes to patterns of teacher behavior. Results of the research indicated that pupils of teachers who were observed to be indirect had more positive attitudes toward the school, the teachers, and other pupils than did pupils of those teachers who were identified by observers as direct. This research supports the validity of interaction analysis as a tool for predicting general attitudes of children in a school classroom.

[2] Amidon, E. J., and Flanders, N. "The Effects of Direct and Indirect Teacher Influence on Dependent-Prone Students Learning Geometry." *Journal of Educational Psychology* 52: 286-91; 1961.

Several studies have been designed to relate pupil attitudes and pupil achievement to teacher behavior.[3] These studies, using interaction analysis, present supporting evidence for the following conclusion: above average achievement and positive student behavior appear to be related to certain kinds of teacher behavior such as acceptance and clarification of student ideas, use of direction and criticism, amount of time spent in talking, and the encouragement of student-initiated talk.

This research appears to have implications for teacher education, and studies have been conducted in which interaction analysis was taught as an observational tool to teachers or student teachers.[4] Findings of these studies indicate that interaction analysis does effect observable changes in teacher patterns of verbal behavior. After training, teachers were observed as: 1) more encouraging and accepting, 2) less critical, 3) more indirect, 4) more positive in their attitudes toward teaching, 5) more successful (by supervisors' rating) in student teaching, 6) talking less, 7) giving fewer directions, and 8) permitting more student-initiated talk. These are changes in the perception of teaching and attitudes toward teaching, as well as in actual teaching behavior. The researchers cited believe that the major cause of the changes was training in interaction analysis.

The In-Service Program

Unique in its simplicity, this system, nonetheless, does require study. To be able to interpret or to understand the interpretation of a matrix, teachers need about ten to twelve hours of training. A two-year in-service program was initiated in an elementary school so that the staff might learn to use this tool to aid in studying their own teaching. The school staff consisted of twenty-two teachers, the principal, and seven part-time specialists. Approximately twenty persons participated in the training program which consumed five two-hour meetings, held at weekly intervals. The primary objective of the first year of the program was to enable staff members to interpret matrices of their own lessons. Training included tape listening for practice in categorization and construction of matrices and some interpretative discussion of the matrix.

At the conclusion of the first year of the program, over half of the teachers

[3] *Idem.*

Amidon, E. J., and Giammatteo, M. *The Verbal Behavior of Superior Teachers.* Philadelphia: Group Dynamics Center, Temple University, 1964.

Flanders, N. A. *Teacher Influence–Pupil Attitudes and Achievement.* Final Report. U. S. Office of Education Cooperative Research Project No. 397. Minneapolis: University of Minnesota, 1960.

[4] Flanders, N. A. *Helping Teachers Change Their Behavior.* Ann Arbor: University of Michigan, 1962.

Hough, J., and Amidon, E. J. *An Experiment in Pre-Service Teacher Education.* Unpublished paper, Washington, D. C.: American Educational Research Association, NEA, February 1964.

Kirk, J. *The Effects of Teaching the Minnesota System of Interaction Analysis on the Behavior of Student Teachers.* Doctor's thesis. Unpublished. Philadelphia: Temple University, 1964.

Zahn, R. D. *The Effects of the Attitudes of Cooperating Teachers on the Attitudes of Student Teachers.* Unpublished paper. Glassboro, N. J.: Glassboro State College, 1964.

decided to analyze their teaching through the analysis of verbal interaction. In the traditional teacher-principal conference, these teachers were presented, without value judgment, matrices of their own teaching. Some of the teachers studied further and began to state objectives for particular lessons in terms of teaching patterns which they wished to develop.

At the end of the first year, the group discussion culminated with suggestions that students be given more time to frame answers to questions and that teachers give more attention to the phrasing of questions. This discussion clearly centered about the teacher-pupil dialogue and its application to supervision in a group setting. The teachers in the group were also concerned with problems which they perceived to be common to most group members. In this case, the teachers felt that recommendations ought to be given to the group as a whole rather than to any one individual. It is important to note, in this connection, that a distinction between "supervision in a group setting" and "group supervision" is made in this paper. The former is group emphasis on a problem seen as common to the group. The latter provides that "individuals explore and analyze their own problems" within a group. Focus on individual problems came during a second year, with the crystallization of the concept of group supervision and with a group analysis of tape recordings of their own teaching.

The ground rules accepted by the group established that feedback would be offered only in areas that were perceived as susceptible to change by the recipient if he so desired and that feedback would be in the form of observation rather than interpretation. At any time, any member of the group could request that the tape be stopped in order to raise questions or to offer feedback.

As each of the taped lessons was concluded, the interaction analysis data for the lesson were presented to the group for discussion. Coupling information about a teachers' interaction pattern with group feedback and his own objectives, the teacher was asked to analyze his teaching.

Some of the major concerns of the group were for: 1) communication among pupils, as well as communication between individual pupil and teacher; 2) the cueing behavior of teachers, as it affects pupil participation; 3) reflection of pupil ideas, as a powerful factor in influencing pupil participation, and 4) projection by teachers of their own reactions and feelings to children.

Some of the more important hypotheses developed by the teachers were those regarding the possible effect of interrupting a child, of anticipating student feelings, of questioning techniques, and of searching for *a* right answer in group discussions. They further designed in-class skill sessions for testing these hypotheses and experimented with behaviors which seemed to offer productivity.

Procedures and Ground Rules

As a result of the experience which the authors have had over a two-year period, several ideas have been developed which may be useful for those interested in doing this type of work with teachers.

The most important factor affecting climate of the group is the way in which members give feedback to one another about a tape recording which the group is auditing. A first step in setting up a successful group climate would seem to be the development of ground rules for giving feedback. The following rules were set up and used by the faculty group described in this article:

1. The person giving feedback describes, rather than evaluates, the pattern of teaching. He attempts to give as objective a description as possible of what he heard happening, and he avoids saying that it was good or bad.
2. Feedback is offered only in areas that are perceived as susceptible to change by the recipient. For example, there is really not much use in discussing a teacher's stuttering, since he may have no power to change this except through intensive therapy.
3. Feedback is given only upon request of the person whose teaching is being discussed. If a teacher is playing his tape and is interested in the group's reaction, observation, or perception, he will ask for feedback.
4. Feedback is concerned with those aspects of teacher behavior that are characteristic of the teacher at the time that discussion is taking place, rather than with aspects of behavior that are characteristic of an earlier time. This is to say that material open to discussion should be current, not that of a previous year.
5. Feedback does not require a teacher to defend his personal opinion or feelings about the way in which he is teaching. Feedback should help to clarify in the light of how others see a particular segment of teaching, rather than try to seek reasons for holding a particular philosophy or a particular attitude toward the teaching act.
6. Feedback is concerned with specific teaching acts, not with generalized interpretations. It can be concerned legitimately with the manner of questioning used, manner of responding to students, pace, or some other pattern of communication.

These ground rules were honored in the breach, generally, and were invoked only when feedback was perceived as being threatening to the recipient.

The writers also were concerned about what seemed to be the most appropriate composition and size of the group. The group has to be large enough to include all of the skills necessary for its successful functioning and yet small enough to give each teacher an opportunity to become involved and to discuss his own teaching. A reasonable size may be somewhere between five and twelve members. The size also seems to depend on the amount of time the faculty has available for the particular activity. Usually a staff using this process will want to adjust the size of the group to the amount of time available. Therefore, if a group has three hours a week, it might be appropriate to have from ten to fourteen in the group. On the other hand, if the group has only one hour a week, a smaller size would seem to be indicated.

Techniques

The first and most important activity is that of using *interaction analysis* to analyze one's own tape recording. Learning appears to be maximized if a teacher knows interaction analysis. Once he has learned it, he should be given the opportunity of classifying his own tape recording and also those of other teachers.

Role playing is perhaps one of the most widely used tools for improving teacher behavior. There are a number of ways of using role playing in combination with tape listening and interaction analysis. One type of role playing experience which the writers found useful was to ask a teacher to produce only certain kinds of behavior in a teaching situation. He might try to ask only very broad questions or only very narrow questions. He might try to produce only praise statements in response to a student, only statements accepting ideas in response to a student, only critical statements, or only direction-giving statements. The value of this technique is that it gives the teacher an opportunity to practice behaviors with which he may not be familiar and helps him to become more flexible in his behavioral repertoire. A secondary purpose is that it gives a teacher a chance to note the impact a particular kind of behavior is having on students. If a teacher becomes more critical than is his custom, he can see the impact of criticism on his students.

Role playing can be conducted in the group while a tape recording is playing; the tape can be stopped at a given point, and the principal can inquire, "How else could the teacher have asked that question?" and then teachers can role play different kinds of questions. Or, the tape recording can be stopped as the teacher responds to a student, and the principal can ask, "How else could the teacher have responded to the student?" Again, teachers will have an opportunity to role play various kinds of reactions. Role playing can also be done in the classroom after a teacher has been able to decide some of the things he would like to try. He can plan some teaching patterns he would like to try, go into his classroom and role play them, and tape the lesson in order to provide himself with feedback. When he listens to his tape, he will have some indication of the extent to which he has been successful in achieving the pattern he intended.

Tape recording, in general, is perhaps the most under-used teacher training technique. It is under-used in the sense that teachers seldom listen to their own performances. Yet the maching is simple to operate, it is usually available, and it provides immediate and live feedback for the teacher. Simple tape listening, with the group, has a major focus for the use of interaction analysis in this group supervision. Our procedure has been to play tapes of various teachers, with the option available to all group members of stopping the tape at any time to discuss a point. Sometimes, a more careful analysis of a given portion of the tape will be the outcome. Another use of tape listening is to play tapes other than those of the participants as examples of various teaching styles, so that the group may observe the differing results when the same lesson is taught in different ways. Obviously, it will be easily observed that there are many ways in which to teach the same lesson, and that there is no one "right" way.

For changing behavior, one of the essential requirements is the process of *developing hypotheses.* In the group, teachers have started out by listening to a tape and discussing it, analyzing a matrix, and then proceeded to the development of questions about certain aspects of the interaction pattern. These questions are concerned with the change that a teacher might decide to make in his interaction pattern.

One of the most exciting activities in which teachers can engage is simply *experimenting with teaching behavior.* Although similar in one way to the developing of hypotheses, this activity often leads to creative teaching, thus broadening the teachers' behavioral repertoire and helping them develop a truly experimental attitude.

Summary

It would appear that group supervision does provide some advantages that may be precluded in the traditional principal-teacher conference, particularly when confidentiality is not a requisite.

The authors believe that teachers did become sensitized to verbal interaction much as described in the cited research, and that the effect of group activity appeared to influence positively faculty interpersonal relationships, communications, goalsetting, and behavioral norms.

While group supervision may need to undergo the scrutiny of empirical research to provide data about the hypotheses advanced, the process appears to merit consideration.

Some Effects of Close and Punitive Styles of Supervision[1]

Robert C. Day and Robert L. Hamblin

An experiment based on a two-by-two factorial design was conducted to test hypotheses involving the relationship of four supervisory styles to aggressive feelings and actions of subordinates. The supervisory styles were arrayed on two continuums: the close versus general and the punitive versus non-punitive. Close as compared with general supervision produced significant increases in aggressive feelings toward the supervisor and in indirect aggression toward the supervisor through lowered productivity, an *in*significant increase in verbal agression toward the supervisor, and an increase of borderline significance in aggressive feelings toward co-workers. Punitive as compared with non-punitive supervision produced significant increases in indirect aggression through lowered productivity and in verbal aggression, but no significant increases in agression toward co-workers. The relationship between close supervision and aggressive feelings appears to be mediated by the self-esteem of the subordinate; an increase in

[1] This research was supported in part by a contract with the Office of Naval Research Nonr 816 (11), and the computer analysis was supported in part by a grant from the National Science Foundation, No. G-22296. The authors also wish to thank Professor Alvin W. Gouldner for his encouragement, suggestions, and criticisms.

aggressive feelings occurred only in subjects having low self-esteem. Finally the combined effect of the close and punitive supervision dimensions, for both aggressive feelings and indirect aggression, was not a simple function, but was less than would be predicted on the basis of additive assumptions.

Introduction

Close supervision was originally isolated and studied as a style or dimension of supervision by teams of researchers connected with the Survey Research Center at the University of Michigan and led by Daniel Katz.[2] In an early study of female workers in a large metropolitan insurance firm, Morse reported that workers subjected to a close supervision style were less satisfied with the supervisor's ability to handle people, less satisfied with the reasonableness of her expectations, and generally less satisfied with the rules she enforced.[3] These findings suggest a specific hypothesis that aggressive feelings are instigated by close supervision. Katz and Kahn reported finding this relationship between close supervision and aggressive feelings of workers in a tractor plant.[4] Furthermore, if lowered productivity is taken as a form of retaliatory aggression toward the supervisor, data reported earlier by Katz and his associates[5] are also consistent with this hypothesis. Gouldner produced evidence, from an illuminating study of a gypsum factory, that further supports the close supervision–aggression hypothesis.[6]

In the present study, close supervision is conceptualized as one end of a continuum that describes the degree to which a supervisor specifies the roles of the subordinates and checks up to see that they comply with the specifications. However, there are two other points of this continuum worth noting. The opposite extreme to close supervision might appropriately be termed "anomic supervision," as it would involve no specifications (that is, no expectations or norms) and no checkups. Somewhere in the middle area of this theoretical continuum, the general style of supervision can be postulated; it involves a moderate number of specifications and checkups, at least enough to let the workers know what they are supposed to do. Thus, in close supervision the attempt is to structure completely

[2]D. Katz and R. L. Kahn, "Some Recent Findings in Human-Relations Research in Industry," in G. E. Swanson, T. M. Newcomb, and E. L. Hartley (eds.), *Readings in Social Psychology* (2d ed.; New York: Henry Holt & Co., 1952), pp. 650-65; D. Katz and R. L. Kahn, "Leadership Practices in Relation to Productivity and Morale," in D. Cartwright and A. Zander (eds.), *Group Dynamics* (2d ed.; Evanston, Ill.: Row, Peterson Co., 1960), pp. 554-70; D. Katz, N. Maccoby, G. Gurin, and Lucretia G. Floor, *Productivity, Supervision and Morale among Railroad Workers* (Ann Arbor: Survey Research Center, University of Michigan, 1951); and D. Katz, N. Maccoby, and Nancy C. Morse, *Productivity, Supervision and Morale in an Office Situation,* Part 1 (Ann Arbor: Survey Research Center, University of Michigan, 1950).

[3]Nancy C. Morse, *Satisfactions in the White Collar Job* (Ann Arbor: Survey Research Center, University of Michigan, 1953).

[4]Katz and Kahn, "Leadership Practices . . . ," *op. cit.*

[5]Katz and Kahn, "Some Recent Findings . . . ," *op. cit.*

[6]A. W. Gouldner, *Patterns of Industrial Bureaucracy* (Glencoe, Ill.: Free Press, 1954).

the workers' behavior, and in general supervision, to structure it only to the point where the worker does not feel at a loss as to what to do; in anomic supervision no attempt is made at all to structure the behavior. Although it would have been interesting, anomic supervision was not included in the present investigation because of the limits of time.

To account for the relationship between close supervision and aggressive feelings or actual aggression, a softened version of the frustration-aggression hypothesis can be used,[7] since close supervision apparently is frustrating to the subordinate. To the extent that it is frustrating, then, the subordinate should be instigated to aggress against the supervisor as the agent of frustration and, in some cases, perhaps actually to translate his impulses into direct aggression, such as angry words, or indirect aggression, such as a conscious retalitory slowdown in productivity.

However, an important point to grasp here is that close supervision is not in itself aggression. For to be aggression, a manifest intention in applying it would necessarily be to hurt or injure the subordinate. But as Gouldner has suggested, the manifest intention involved in using the close style of supervision is probably to increase productivity.[8] The supervisor may not even be aware that his close supervision is frustrating, thus producing psychological pain or injury. In terms of intention or awareness, the close style of supervision may be contrasted with a second style, "punitive" supervision, which involves the intentional, conscious use of aggression to gain the compliance of subordinates.

To the extent that a supervisor enforces work specifications or rules by aggressing against those subordinates who depart from or violate the rules, he is using a punitive style of supervision. When the punitive supervisor uses aggression (most often in the form of angry, ego-lacerating reprimands), he is attempting to reinforce the avoidance of behavior that violates work rules. Thus, he is usually aware that his aggression is painful to the subordinate, and is in effect saying to him, "I know this hurts, but it is your own doing. If you want to avoid it in the future, follow my rules." Because it is so painful, he is probably aware that his aggression instigates subordinates to counteraggress, but because of his authority to hire, fire, promote, or demote, he evidently also assumes ultimate victory in any aggressive exchange. Furthermore, since the workers are aware of his superior power, he counts upon their not wanting to start an aggressive exchange of counteraggressing.

Yet, unresolved tensions have a way of being channeled into more subtle forms of indirect aggression that are not easily detected or eliminated, as, for example, when workers channel their aggressive impulses into conscious, retaliatory slowdowns in production. If artfully practiced, this form of aggression can hurt the supervisor badly while making it most difficult for him to fix blame or take active corrective measures. This evidently happened with railroad section gangs studied by Katz and his associates, who found that foremen of low-producing gangs tended to use a punitive style of supervision.[9]

[7] N. E. Miller, "I. The Frustration-Aggression Hypothesis," *Psychological Review,* XLVIII (1941), 337-42.

[8] *Op. cit.*

[9] Katz, Maccoby, Gurin, and Floor, *op. cit.*

Thus far, we have postulated that aggression is the over-all result of both the close and the punitive styles of supervision because both styles, whether intentionally or not, are painful to subordinates. Specifically, we have mentioned two forms of aggression: angry words and a conscious, retaliatory slowdown in production. But these may not be the only manifestations of aggression that result from the frustrations inherent in the close and punitive styles of supervision. Negative emotions often become displaced, and consequently could magnify out of proportion the aggression that sometimes accompanies routine conflicts among workers. Furthermore, these emotions might also be displaced to magnify any incipient dissatisfaction with the work situation itself. Thus, in hypothesizing that both the close and the punitive styles of supervision result in increased aggression, we are actually predicting that they both result in (1) an increase in the amount of verbal aggression toward the supervisor, (2) a decrease in productivity, (3) an increase in verbal aggression toward co-workers, and (4) an increase in dissatisfaction with the work situation. However, in making our predictions we should note that Pepitone and Reichling found that relationships based on displacement are usually weaker than the others.[10]

Although the close supervision-aggression hypothesis has been generally supported in a number of investigations, evidently the strength of the relationship is quite variable. Again, if lowered productivity is taken as an indication of indirect aggression, the data reported by Katz and his associates in 1950 show that a strong relationship exists where the close versus general styles are used by second-line supervisors in their relations with section heads, but only a moderate relationship in relations between section heads and their subordinates.[11] Data from a second study in 1951 by Katz and associates indicate no relationship at all between close versus general supervision and worker aggression.[12] These variations seem to indicate that a third variable mediates the relationship between close supervision and aggression. In this instance, the mediator is probably a characteristic of the subordinate that influences the amount of frustration he experiences when he is subjected to close and perhaps punitive supervision. The rationale for suggesting self-esteem as the mediating variable is best understood in the context of Goffman's dramaturgical theory of social behavior.[13]

Using the theoretical metaphor extensively, Goffman views the behavior of persons in social contexts as a sequence of carefully guided performances serving to create a "front" or an impression. In attempting to create and maintain a satisfactory self-image, the individual tries to define the situation in such a way that he is able to guide and control the impressions that others obtain of him in the situation. The individual's concern, then, is to put his act over successfully, to maintain by various techniques a favorable, creditable self-image. Thus, in a

[10] A. Pepitone and G. Reichling, "Group Cohesiveness and the Expression of Hostility," *Human Relations,* VIII (1955), 327-37.

[11] Katz, Maccoby, and Morse, *op. cit.*

[12] Katz, Maccoby, Gurin, and Floor, *op. cit.*

[13] We wish to express our appreciation to Alvin W. Gouldner for suggesting Goffman's theory as the conceptual context in which to discuss self-esteem as a mediating variable (E. Goffman, *The Presentation of Self in Everyday Life* [Garden City, N.Y.: Double day & Co., 1959]).

bureaucratic situation the workers may be viewed as striving to project a self-image to the supervisor and to co-workers, "and the characteristic issue, the crucial concern, is whether it [the self-image] will be credited or discredited."[14]

From the assumption that the workers are attempting to project a creditable self-image, it follows that the close and punitive styles of supervision would be frustrating for two reasons. First, the styles imply a lack of competence, a lack of skill on the part of the worker. Second, they imply a lack of motivation on his part to do the right thing or, in fact, a kind of malicious motivation to do the wrong thing. Thus, when a subordinate is subjected to either of these two styles of supervision, his self-image may be discredited severely. Furthermore, he may be able to do very little to change the situation so that he can create a more favorable impression.

However, and this is the critical assumption, not all subordinates may be equally concerned with maintaining the front, with presenting a creditable self-image. Specifically, our assumption is that some individuals have such strong, favorable self-images, such high *self-esteem*, that they are relatively *unconcerned* with impression management, whereas other individuals have such ambiguous, ambivalent self-images, such low *self-esteem*, that they are *highly concerned* with impression management, with maintaining a front and thus projecting a creditable self-image. If so, the amount of frustration an individual experiences when subjected to close or punitive supervision should vary inversely with his self-esteem. Furthermore, since the strength of the postulated relationship between either style of supervision and aggression should be a function of the amount of frustration experienced,[15] the strength of the relationship should also be a function of the self-esteem of subordinates. Perhaps a simpler statement is: The association between the two styles of supervision and the various aggression variables should be relatively weak among subordinates who have high self-esteem, but relatively strong among those with low self-esteem.

Method

The Experimental Groups

Twenty-four groups, each consisting of four women recruited from undergraduate classes and dormitories at Washington University, were used in the experiment. Controls were applied for age (17–19 years) and years of schooling (Freshmen and Sophomores).

The Experimental Situation

At an appointed time each group arrived at the laboratory and was ushered into an experimental room designed to stimulate reasonably well an industrial work station. Here the subjects were given a pre-experimental questionnaire and then task instructions. After these were completed, each group worked at the task for a

[14] *Ibid.*, p. 253.
[15] Miller, *op. cit.*

period of 40 minutes, and then completed a post-experimental questionnaire. The 40-minute experimental session included 10-minute periods with a supervisor (a trained member of the experimental staff) in the room and two intervening 5-minute periods during which the supervisor left the room for the expressed purpose of evaluating the workers' production. Her absence, however, was designed to give the subjects a chance to be alone and thereby some freedom to express any aggressive feelings toward the supervisor or the experiment. Her exits and entrances were timed precisely with a stopwatch that she held in her hand and that, in addition to accurate timing, provided a note of precision and authority. As in a factory setting, an impersonal buzzer was used to signal the beginning and end of the work period.

The task consisted of assembling models of molecules using pegs, springs, and various colored balls provided in Sargent Kits, which are often used in university chemistry classes. Drawings of elaborate, complicated molecular structures were provided as "blueprints" for molecule construction. These models seemed to be novel and complex enough to interest and involve the subjects for the required 40-minute work period. The fact that the task was complex and naturally suited for assembly-line procedures contributed to making this a natural situation where various styles of supervision could be used. (In any experiment it is important that the manipulation not be external to the situation and thus relatively obvious to the subjects, who usually are interested in guessing "what they're after." The general assumption is, of course, that subjects cannot systematically fake behavioral effects unless the goals of the experimenters are obvious.) In addition to providing a natural environment for the manipulations, the kits for molecule construction afforded a rather simple but reliable quantitative measure of productivity.[16]

To simulate an industrial setting, the member of the experimental staff who took the role of supervisor was introduced simply with, "This is Miss Bradshaw, your supervisor during the work period." To heighten the impersonality of the situation, subjects were not introduced to the supervisor, but were addressed by numbers conspicuously displayed at each of their work stations. In addition, words such as "supervisor," "worker," "blueprint," "material bin," "work efficiency," "production unit," "subassemblies," and "production line" were used to convey the atmosphere of an industrial situation. However, in order to promote interaction, the situation was designed to be different from the usual production line in one

[16]Several considerations went into the decision to set up a production line. First, it was desirable to standardize and keep constant the over-all sequence of operations for all groups. To this end, subjects were given definite subtasks to perform; that is, the groups did not determine their own division or non-division of labor. Second, it was undesirable either for the final combinations of operations to be so inefficient or slow that tension would be generated by the task itself, or for each worker to be allowed to proceed to construct whole models by herself in relative isolation, with no interdependence with the others. Although the latter procedure would have maximized productivity in the time allotted to the task, intersubject conflict would have been virtually absent even in high-tension situations. Consequently, although the sequence of operations chosen was efficient enough to keep frustrations at a minimum, it included enough interdependence among subjects to make some conflict inevitable.

important way: the subjects were stationed around an oval table that permitted each subject to view all co-subjects during the work period.

The Experimental Designs

Technically, the experiment involved a two-by-two factorial design with high-low manipulations of the two independent variables, that is, the close and punitive styles of supervision. Using a table of random numbers, six of the twenty-four groups were assigned to each of the four "cells," as shown in Figure 1.

	Close Supervision	General Supervision
High Punitive Style	6 Groups	6 Groups
Low Punitive Style	6 Groups	6 Groups

Figure 1

To operationalize the four styles of supervision, two lists of remarks were drawn up for use by the supervisor. To operationalize closeness of supervision, a set of clear, concise instructions (role definitions) was developed. In the general supervision situations, the eight most essential of these instructions were used by the supervisor to give a minimum definition of the situation. In the close supervision situations, forty instructions were used; also, certain amounts of obvious hovering and watching as well as repetitions of previous instructions were used as checkup techniques.

To operationalize the punitive style in both the close and general situations, a list of sarcastic, negative, status-deflating remarks was developed for the supervisor to use as punitive sanctions. In the high-punitive situation, she made forty such remarks; in the low-punitive situation, she made none at all.

Two members of the staff who observed verbal aggression by the subjects also counted the supervisor's punitive remarks. The experimenter kept a count of the instructions and checkups, and a system of lights informed the supervisor when she had given the required number of remarks for each situation.

Fourteen practice sessions were required to standardize and internalize the multiple facets of the supervisor's role.[17] All extraneous remarks had to be

[17]The supervisor's role demanded a person who could combine a certain ability to act with emotional stability, maturity, and general interpersonal insightfulness. The role was taken by a recent graduate in nursing who had a major in psychiatric nursing and whose past experience in therapeutic role-playing with mental patients and hospital-ward supervision constituted an excellent background for the job.

identified and inhibited, and important non-verbal gestures (facial and body) had to be standardized. She had to learn to recognize and "control" subjects who were skilled at becoming dependent on the supervisor through asking for support. To help the supervisor control and minimize support-giving, observers registered all supportive remarks by the supervisor during this training period. Finally, she had to practice giving instructions that were devoid of aggressive connotations.

Measurement

Self-esteem.—The measure of self-esteem used in this experiment was developed by de Charms and Rosenbaum[18] and was based in part on an earlier measure by Janis.[19] The subjects were instructed to choose an answer ranging from "strongly agree" through "strongly disagree" that best characterized their usual reactions. (In listing these and other items in this section, the numbering and order are appropriate to this presentation and consequently depart from the format used in the questionnaire.)

1. I feel capable of handling myself in most social situations.
2. I seldom fear my actions will cause others to have a low opinion of me.
3. It doesn't bother me to have to enter a room where other people have already gathered and are talking.
4. In group discussions I usually feel that my opinions are inferior.
5. I don't make a very favorable first impression on people.
6. When confronted by a group of strangers, my first reaction is always one of shyness and inferiority.
7. It is extremely uncomforable to accidentally go to a formal party in street clothes.
8. I don't spend much time worrying about what people think of me.
9. When in a group, I very rarely express an opinion for fear of being thought ridiculous.
10. I am never at a loss for words when I am introduced to someone.

Agreement with items 1, 2, 3, 8, and 10 and disagreement with items 4, 5, 6, 7, and 9 probably indicate high self-esteem or self-confidence and little concern with the presentation of self, that is, with the management of the image presented to others. On the other hand, opposite responses to these items indicate low self-esteem and low self-confidence and a great deal of concern and anxiety about the presentation of self in everyday situations.

Aggressive feelings.—To measure covert aggressive feelings toward the supervisor, that is, those aggressive feelings which did not erupt into overt behavior, the following items were used:

[18] R. de Charms and M. E. Rosenbaum, "Status Variables and Matching Behavior," *Journal of Personality,* XXVIII (1960), 492-502.

[19] I. L. Janis, "Personality Correlates of Susceptibility to Persuasion," *Journal of Personality,* XXII (1954), 504-18.

1. How often did you become annoyed with the supervisor?
2. How often did you become irritated with the supervisor?
3. If you were to participate in this group again, how would you feel about having the supervisor replaced?

On the first two items, the subjects were asked to make responses on a six-point scale ranging from "continually" to "never"; for the third item, a seven-point scale was used ranging from "extremely favorable" to "extremely unfavorable." The responses provided an estimate of the frequency with which each subject experienced aggressive feelings toward the supervisor during the work period.

Two sets of items similar to these were used to measure aggressive feelings toward co-workers and dissatisfaction with the task. The first set was identical with the above items except that the term "co-workers" was substituted for "supervisor." The response alternatives were the same except for the third item; here the subjects were asked to indicate the actual number of co-workers they would prefer to have replaced. In measuring dissatisfaction with the task, only the first two of the above items were used, but they were used twice, first with the term "molecules" and second with the phrase "job in general" substituted for the term "supervisor." Ranging from "continually" to never," the response alternatives were the same as before.

Overt aggression.—As may be recalled, we assumed that overt aggression might be expressed directly as verbal aggression or indirectly as a conscious slowdown in production. Two rather complex measures thus were required.

After two female observers had reached a level of competence where they could reliably code verbal aggression as it occurred during the experimental-work period, they independently entered marks on forms each time a subject (a) antagonistically criticized the supervisor or used indirect sarcasm with definite negative content in reference to the supervisor; (b) antagonistically criticized or used sarcasm about her co-worker; or (c) antagonistically criticized or joked about the task or the experimental situation. In general, the observers were asked to perceive and evaluate each remark simultaneously along two dimensions: objective content and effective content. All remarks that were negative in objective meaning were counted as verbal aggression regardless of effective content. Remarks that were not objectively negative but tended to carry negative effective connotations were more difficult to categorize reliably. However, 85 per cent agreement of two observers was obtained throughout the experiment on items, not just cell totals.

The production-line arrangement of work required to encourage interdependence in interaction among subjects virtually precluded the possibility of taking accurate or even meaningful measures of each subject's production rate. Consequently, a measure based on the group's total production was used. This was calculated as the sum of the model components (the colored balls, pegs, and springs) completed per 40-minute work period, minus errors and omissions.

Factor analysis.—Data from each of the scales administered in the pre- and post-experimental questionnaires were factor-analyzed using the principal axis method. The obtained factor weights were used, together with standardized scores for each of the subjects, to obtain indexes for each of the above-mentioned dimensions[20] (Table 1).

Table 1. Factor Analysis Weights[a] for Pre- and Post-Experimental Questionnaire Scales

	Item Number									
Scale	*1*	*2*	*3*	*4*	*5*	*6*	*7*	*8*	*9*	*10*
1. Self-esteem	0.77	0.42	0.74	−0.50	−0.42	−0.75	-0.35	0.38	−0.65	0.58
2. Aggressive feelings, supervisor	.94	.96	.78							
3. Aggressive feelings, co-workers	.97	.95	.64							
4. Dissatisfaction, task	0.90	0.89	0.88	0.92						

[a]These weights were extracted using the principal axis method. A separate analysis was done for each scale, and in each case the weights given are those obtained on the first factor.

Results

Analysis of the results began with group data and the testing of basic hypotheses for the stable effects. Then individual scores and a smaller number of independent variables selected on the basis of the initial analysis were used to test the more complex hypotheses involving the mediating variable, that is, the psychological dimension of self-esteem.

The Basic Hypotheses Tested with Group Data

Results relevant to the basic hypotheses are presented in Tables 2 and 3. For all the basic hypotheses, the analysis-of-variance results in Table 2 gives significance as well as explained variance. In Table 3 the means are given where significant relationships were found.

From Tables 2 and 3 it is apparent that close supervision produced a significant and large increment in aggressive feelings toward the supervisor. The data also indicate a moderate and near-significant increment in aggressive feelings toward co-workers. On the other hand, close supervision was not significantly related to dissatisfaction with the task, to verbal aggression against the supervisor or co-workers, or to verbal dissatisfaction with the task. Finally, the data indicate that close supervision results in a significant and rather substantial decrease in productivity.

Tables 2 and 3 also indicate that the punitive style of supervision resulted in a large, significant increment in aggressive feelings toward the supervisor. However, in this case the relationships between punitive supervision and aggressive feelings

[20]These procedures are outlined in detail in M. J. Hagood and D. O. Price, *Statistics for Sociologists* (New York: Henry Holt & Co., 1952), pp. 526-30.

Table 2. Summary of Two-Way Analysis of Variance Using Data Tabulated by Groups

	Close Supervision		Punitive Supervision		Interaction	
Dependent Variable	*F-Value*[a]	*Explained Variance*[b]	*F-Value*	*Explained Variance*	*F-Value*	*Explained Variance*
1. Aggressive feelings,[c] supervisor	10.3	.24	10.9	.25	3.0	.07
2. Aggressive feelings, co-workers	4.0	.16	0.0	.00	0.4	.02
3. Dissatisfaction, task	.6	.03	0.2	.01	0.1	.01
4. Verbal aggression, supervisor	1.8	.04	20.3	.48	0.9	.02
5. Verbal aggression, co-workers	2.8	.11	2.2	.09	0.1	.00
6. Verbal dissatisfaction, task	2.0	.09	1.4	.06	0.0	.00
7. Productivity	5.2	.17	4.2	.14	1.1	.04

[a]Results are significant at the 0.10 level if F is equal to or greater than 3.0; at the 0.5 level if F is equal to or greater than 4.4.

[b]The measure of explained variance is n.

[c]Using Bartlett's test, the variance of all dependent variables was tested for homogeneity. All variances were homogeneous except for this particular variable. To achieve homogeneity, the scale was transformed using the following formula: ¼(X – 100/50). We wish to thank Keith Miller for helping us find this and other transformations used later.

Table 3. Cell Means for Two-Way Analysis of Variance

	Means			
Dependent-Variable	*General Non-punitive Style*	*Close Non-punitive Style*	*General Punitive Style*	*Close Punitive Style*
1. Aggressive feelings, supervisor[a]	0.73	1.14	1.15	1.27
2. Aggressive feelings, co-workers[a]	1.84	2.07	1.70	1.84
3. Dissatisfaction, task[a]	1.90	2.06	1.64	2.01
4. Verbal aggression, supervisor[b]	0	4.5	10.8	11.7
5. Verbal aggression, co-workers[b]	5.2	14.0	15.2	19.2
6. Verbal dissatisfaction, task[b]	9.3	17.8	16.5	24.5
7. Productivity[c]	335	252	258	226

[a]These measures of aggressive feelings are based on standard scores which have little obvious meaning. However, the means are included here to give an idea of the relative magnitude of the effects of close and punitive supervision.

[b]All of these verbal measures are in terms of the number of aggressive or negative remarks.

[c]In terms of the number of correct connections of the pegs, springs, and balls completed during the work period.

toward co-workers or dissatisfaction with the task are both small and insignificant, as are the relationships between punitiveness and verbal aggression toward co-workers or verbal dissatisfaction with the task. Unlike close supervision, however, punitive supervision resulted in a large, significant increase in verbal aggression toward the supervisor. Finally, it is evident that punitive supervision also resulted in a relatively large decrease in productivity—a decrease which, because of a small *N*, is of borderline significance.

Thus far the data have not supported all of the basic hypotheses. The results with respect to direct verbal aggression and the displacement of aggressive feelings toward co-workers and the task were variable. Consequently, the more detailed analysis will be limited to two dependent variables: aggressive feelings toward the supervisor and productivity.

Table 4. Summary of Three-Way Analysis of Variance Involving Close Supervision, Punitive Supervision, and Self-Esteem, Using Data Tabulated in Terms of Individual Scores

	Aggressive Feelings, Supervisor[a]		*Productivity*	
Source of Variation	*F-Value*[b]	*Explained Variance*[c]	*F-Value*	*Explained Variance*
1. Close supervision	9.3	.08	23.7	.17
2. Punitive supervision	11.3	.10	18.0	.13
3. Self-esteem[d]	0.3	.00	0.1	.00
Close style X punitive style	2.7	.02	4.0	.03
Close style X self-esteem	5.0	.04	1.1	.01
Punitive style X self-esteem	1.0	.01	0.7	.00
1 X 2 X 3	0.0	.00	0.7	.01

[a]Using Bartlett's test, the variance of this dependent variable was tested for homogeneity with negative results. The unhomogeneous variance was corrected using a log χ transformation.

[b]Results are significant at the 0.10 level if *F* is equal to or greater than 2.79; at the 0.05 level if *F* is equal to or greater than 3.96.

[c]The measure used for explained variance is η.

[d]Because of unequal cells, the approximate method for analysis of variance was that presented in Helen M. Walker and Joseph Lev, *Statistical Inference* (New York: Henry Holt & & Co., 1953).

Hypotheses Involving Self-Esteem and Analysis in Terms of Individual Scores

The results relevant to the mediating hypotheses are found in Tables 4, 5, and 6. Table 4 gives the results of an analysis of variance, with significance levels and explained variance; Tables 5 and 6 show the means involved in the significant interactions. Before turning to these interactions, note that the relationships between punitive or close supervision, on the one hand, and aggressive feelings toward the supervisor or productivity, on the other, are much stronger in this than in the preceding analysis. This reflects the difference between group and individual data–largely the difference between an *N* of 24 (groups) and an *N* of 96 (individual subjects).

In Table 4 the findings indicate a significant interaction between closeness of supervision and self-esteem with respect to feelings of aggression toward the supervisor, but not with respect to productivity. In Table 5, the means indicate that

Table 5. Means Involved in Significant Interaction Between Close Supervision and Self-Esteem with Respect to Aggressive Feelings Toward Supervisor

Means	*Aggressive Feelings, Supervisor*
General style, low self-esteem	1.54
Close style, low self-esteem	1.74
General style, high self-esteem	1.64
Close style, high self-esteem	1.66

this significant interaction is precisely the one that was predicted. The relationship between close supervision and aggressive feelings toward the supervisor is much stronger among subjects with low than among subjects with high self-esteem. In fact, the difference between the means for subjects with high self-esteem is nil. In other words, the over-all relationship observed between closeness of supervision and aggressive feelings toward the supervisor is due primarily to the subjects with low self-esteem. Yet, at the level of indirect aggression apparently no difference existed, since the interaction between close supervision and self-esteem with respect to productivity involved very little variance and was insignificant as well. In the close supervision variations, the subjects with high self-esteem evidently engaged in indirect aggression through lowered productivity as readily as did those with low self-esteem. The difference apparently was in their emotional state; that is, whether or not aggressive feelings, perhaps anger, accompanied their decision to decrease productivity. However, it should be noted that this pattern could be an artifact of the group productivity scores.

In Table 4 it is apparent that the interactions between punitive supervision and self-esteem with respect to both aggressive feelings and productivity are insignificant. Apparently the experience of being aggressed against in the form of punitive supervision produces aggressive feelings as well as indirect aggression equally in subjects with high and low self-esteem. We can make this assumption with some confidence because the variance involved in the relevant interactions is very low and because we have seen that the measure of self-esteem is sensitive enough to detect rather precise effects.

Finally, are the effects of the two supervisory styles a simple additive function? If

Table 6. Means Involved in Significant Interactions Between Close and Punitive Supervision with Respect to Productivity

Means	Productivity: No. of Units	Productivity: Percentage Reduction
General style, non-punitive.	84	100
Close style, non-punitive	63	75
General style, punitive	65	77
Close style, punitive	56	67

they are, the interactions between close and punitive supervision with respect to any of the aggression variables will be insignificant. It is apparent in Table 4 that the interaction between the close and punitive styles of supervision with respect to aggressive feelings toward the supervisor only approaches significance at the 10 per cent level. However, the interaction with respect to productivity is significant, even though a modest amount of variance is involved. This result, of course, implies something more than a simple additive effect with respect to productivity. Apparently the effects of punitive and close supervision with respect to productivity are less than would be expected on the basis of the effects of close supervision alone and punitive supervision alone. As can be noted in Table 6, close supervision by itself reduces productivity by 25 per cent and punitive supervision reduces it by 23 per cent. Together they do not reduce it by 48 per cent as would be expected if the effects were a simple additive function, but only by 33 per cent. Since the decrease in productivity, indicating as it does an increase in aggression, is less than might be anticipated, we will refer to the phenomenon apparent in this interaction as the dampened-increment effect.

This dampened-increment effect might have occurred for one of two reasons. First, productivity in the experimental situation might have been very difficult to reduce below some minimal level regardless of aggressive feelings or impulses to reduce it still further. Second, the aggressive feelings themselves might not have been additive. In other words, double frustration may not lead to double aggressive feelings, but to something much less than double. As can be seen from the first line in Table 3, the data are consistent with this latter interpretation. The scores indicating aggressive feelings toward the supervisor are increased (from .73) 41 points by close supervision alone and 42 points by punitive supervision alone. Together, however, they increase the score only 54 points, as compared with an increment of 83 points that would be predicted if the effects were not dampened. These data, showing as they do a dampened-increment effect, are remarkably consistent with the data in the previous paragraph which showed a similar effect with respect to productivity.

Discussion

Over-all, the results present an interesting pattern that is laden with implications.

The lack of support for a number of the hypotheses matters very little, as these involved displacement which usually vitiates the strength of aggressive phenomena. But the interesting thing is that in the close supervision situations a certain amount of displacement evidently did occur. The subjects by and large expressed more than usual aggressive feelings against one another as co-workers. It is this tendency to displace, plus the absence of verbal aggression toward the supervisor, which distinguishes the close from the punitive supervision situations. In the latter, the tendency to displace aggressive feelings was conspicuously absent and verbal aggression toward the supervisor conspicuously present. Why should such a difference obtain?

A number of explanations are possible, but the one that suggests itself involves the generic distinction between close and punitive supervision made in the theoretical section, that of intention. Our argument there was that with close supervision the *intention* is simply to increase production; the resulting psychological pain is unanticipated, unintentional, and possibly even an unknown consequence. Therefore, close supervision was characterized as frustrating rather than aggressive. On the other hand, with punitive supervision, the pain-producing activities are used intentionally because the pain presumably reinforces the desired avoidance responses. Since activities used with the intention of producing pain or injury are by definition aggression, we pointed out that punitive supervision is a form of aggression. Thus, at a more generic level, the close supervision-aggression hypotheses tested here are simply variants of the basic frustration-aggression hypothesis, whereas the punitive supervision-aggression hypotheses are basically aggression-aggression hypotheses. Phrased this way, these hypotheses may appear to be circular, but they are not. What really is meant is: "To the extent that A frustrates B, B will be instigated to aggress against A," and "To the extent that A aggresses against B, B will be instigated to aggress against A." In other words, genuine causal relationships are involved in the hypotheses because the hypotheses involve an exchange between two individuals.

If this distinction is valid, then the difference in response patterns to close and punitive supervision may actually represent a more generic difference in response patterns to frustration and aggression. Evidently, when A either frustrates B or aggresses against B, the unvarying result is the instigation of aggressive feelings in B. Furthermore, if an indirect avenue of aggression is available, such as decreasing productivity, then in either case B will use this indirect aggression against A. However, a basic difference evidently arises at the level of direct verbal aggression. Although they recognized that the pain they felt was not intended, those subjects who were frustrated by the close supervision practices had a difficult time expressing their aggressive feelings directly at the verbal level, whereas those subjects who felt the aggression inherent in punitive supervision, perhaps because they recognized it as intentional, retaliated openly in kind. Apparently because the latter subjects were able to verbalize their aggressive feelings directly, they were not led into displacing the feelings as were the subjects who experienced the frustrations of close supervision.

Before concluding, we must pay tribute to the women who were subjects in this investigation. While their behavior was not predicted precisely, it was not entirely unpredictable, as we sometimes feared it would be. They probably reacted to the various styles of supervision in much the same way as men would have reacted; most differences probably would be a matter of degree. However, our empirical impression is that women suppress their tendencies to overt aggression, particularly verbal aggression, more than do men. Rather than express their negative feelings in words, they tend to express them more in nervous laughter, or alternatively to withdraw more than do men. In other words, if the experiment were duplicated using men, we think any change in results would be with respect to verbal aggression: verbal aggression would be much more frequent in the punitive situation, and a significant relationship might obtain between close supervision and verbal aggression.

Supervisory Influence and Work-Group Performance

Kurt R. Student

Incremental influence, a new concept for the study of organizational leadership, was empirically tested by relating 12 work-group performance measures with measures of supervisors' social power. Referent power and expert power were conceptualized as incremental influence and considered qualitatively different from reward power, coercive power, and legitimate power. Referent power and expert power are considered to be idiosyncratic in character and depend upon an individual's unique role behavior, while reward power, coercive power, and legitimate power are organizationally determined and designed to be equal for all supervisors on the same hierarchical level. As predicted, expert power was related to a low accident rate, referent power was somewhat related to measures of subordinate withdrawal, and both referent power and expert power were generally related to group measures of production performance. These results are regarded as supporting the concept of incremental influence.

A recent book by Katz and Kahn (1966) has súggested a new concept for the study of organizational leadership. The concept, incremental influence, is stated as follows:

> When we think of leadership in contrast to routine role performance, however, we become particularly interested in those kinds of individual behavior which go beyond required performance and realize more fully the potential of a given position for organizational influence. In other words, *we consider the essence of organizational leadership to be the influential increment over and above the mechanical compliance with routine directives of the organization* [p. 302].

The present research is an empirical investigation of the concept of incremental influence in an industrial organization. More specifically, this research will analyze some performance correlates of the first-line supervisors' incremental influence.

A five-fold typology of social power suggested by French and Raven (1959) was used as the framework for the author's analysis of supervisory influence. Although other bases of power could be cited, French and Raven specify these five as the primary by which an agent, O, can exert influence over a person. P: (1) *Reward power,* based on P's perception that O has the ability to mediate rewards for him. In order for O to use reward power to influence P, he must possess resources that P values, and P must believe that by conforming he will actually benefit by the resources in question. (2) *Coercive power,* based on P's perception that O has the ability to mediate punishments for him. Analogous to the situation for reward power, in order for O to use coercive power to influence P, P must want to prevent some act of O and believe that through conforming he will do so. (3) *Legitimate power,* based on internalized values in P that O has a right to influence P and that P has an obligation to accept this influence (4) *Referent power,* based on P's identification with O. French and Raven define identification as "a feeling of oneness of P with O, or a desire for such identity." If O is a person toward whom P is attracted, P will have a desire to be closely associated with O. This identification of P with O can be established or maintained if P behaves, believes, or perceives as O does. (5) *Expert power,* based on P's perception that O has some special knowledge or expertness in a given area. French and Raven hold that the strength of expert power varies with the extent of knowledge which P attributes to O and that the range of expert power is restricted to those cognitive areas in which O is believed to have superior knowledge. Experience, training, reputation, demonstrated ability, etc. are among the many reasons why P attributes expertness to O.

This five-fold typology of the bases of supervisory power makes possible an important conceptual distinction between the bases of power and leads to an operationalization of the concept of incremental influence. The areas in which reward power, coercive power, and legitimate power may be exercised are largely specified by the organization; on the other hand, areas in which the supervisor can exercise referent power and expert power are to a substantial degree uniquely determined by his own behavior and his interactions with his subordinates (expert power is personally determined, but the amount of information available may vary as a part of organizational structure). The extent and range of a supervisor's referent power and expert power cannot be specified by the organization. Expert power and referent power are idiosyncratic in character. On the other hand, reward power, coercive power, and legitimate power are nomothetic in character and result from the supervisor's occupancy of a position in the organization's role system. The formal organizational structure is designed to provide equal legitimate power to all supervisors on the same hierarchical level and to give them equal access to the use of organizational rewards and punishments. However, supervisors are not equal in their referent power or their expert power; the supervisor's referent power and his expert power constitute his particular utilization of his formal position. Thus the author concludes that referent power and expert power are conceptually and qualitatively different from reward power, coercive power, and legitimate power. Influential acts based on referent power and expert power constitute an increment in organizational influence ɞeyond the influence inherent in the routine functioning of the organization's rᴄˡᵅ system. Consequently, referent power and expert power are the basis of incremental influence, and incremental influence has been operationalized as the additive combination of referent power and expert power.

The present research relates incremental influence to work-group performance. Since recent research in a variety of organizational settings casts doubt on the validity of job performance as a unidimensional construct, a multiple-criteria approach to work-group performance was used. Supervisory influence will be related separately to 12 performance measures. These measures were conceptualized by a framework suggested by March and Simon (1958) who state that organizational members face two different decisions—the decision to participate and the decision to produce. Consequently, the performance measures are considered as measures of withdrawal, or as measures of production; accident rates are considered separately since this criteria does not fit into the withdrawal-production classification. An impressive body of research evidence (Kahn & Katz, 1960; Likert, 1961; Mann, 1965; Pfiffner, 1955) suggests that incremental influence (i.e., both referent power and expert power together) would relate to production measures. On the other hand, March and Simon (1958) hypothesized that withdrawal measures relate to satisfaction but not to performance, which in the author's terms would suggest that withdrawal measures relate mainly to referent power. Two studies support this view. Fleishman, Harris, and Burtt (1955) found a negative relationship between supervisory consideration and absenteeism; Fleishman and Harris (1962) found a negative relationship between supervisory consideration and turnover. Finally, in terms of the analytical model, the author considers that accidents are unintended consequences resulting from low supervisor "technical competence" (Mann, 1965, defines technical competence as the ability to use petinent knowledge, methods, techniques, and equipment necessary for the performance of specific tasks and activities) and the inability of the supervisor to impart his competence to his subordinates. Accordingly, one would expect that accidents relate mainly to supervisory expert power. Consequently, the operational hypotheses were that incremental influence (i.e., both referent power and expert power together) would relate to the production measures; referent power would relate to the withdrawal measures; expert power would relate to the accident rate.

Method

Research Site and Sample

This study employed data collected from a manufacturer of major home appliances. The data were collected for a larger study sponsored by the company and conducted by the Survey Research Center. The sample consisted of 486 hourly employees and 39 first-line supervisors representing 40 of the 52 work groups

Table 1. Relationships Between Measures of Supervisory Influence

Measure	*1*	*2*	*3*	*4*	*5*	*6*
1. Incremental influence						
2. Referent power	.83[c]					
3. Expert power	.89[c]	.49[b]				
4. Reward power	.44[b]	.32[a]	.43[b]			
5. Coercive power	.12	.12	.09	.45[b]		
6. Legitimate power	.35[a]	.38[a]	.24	.08	.41[b]	

Note.–Group means, $N = 40$.
[a] $p < .05$, two-tailed.
[b] $p < .01$, two-tailed.
[c] $p < .001$, two-tailed.

which comprised the company's two main plants, and the unit of analysis in this research was the work group. Measurements of attitudes, opinions, and perceptions of behavior were collected by paper-and-pencil questionnaires administered to nonsupervisory production employees during March 1964.

Questionnaire Measures of Supervisory Influence

The measures of supervisory influence were as follows:

Referent power. A single-item rating by subordinates of the extent to which they comply with their supervisor's directives because he is a "nice guy" and they don't want to hurt him.

Expert power. A single-item rating of the extent to which subordinates comply with their supervisor's directives because he can give special help and benefits to those who cooperate with him.

Coercive power. A single-item rating of the extent to which subordinates comply with their supervisor's directives because he can penalize or make things difficult for those who do not cooperate with him.

Legitimate power. A single-item rating of the extent to which subordinates comply with their supervisor's directives because he has a right, considering his position, to expect subordinates to do what he wants.

Incremental influence. As noted earlier, this concept was operationalized by summing the group mean for referent power and the group mean for expert power.

Table 1 presents the relationships between these measures of supervisory influence, while Table 2 presents the means and standard deviations of incremental influence and the bases of social power.

Measures from Company Records

For purposes of the larger study from which the present research data are taken, a roster of work-group performance measures was developed so that a number of

Table 2. Mean and Standard Deviation of Incremental Influence and Bases of Power

Measure	*M*	*SD*
Incremental influence	6.12	.92
Referent power	2.73	.47
Expert power	3.39	.59
Reward power	2.78	.40
Coercive power	2.32	.42
Legitimate power	3.43	.44

Note.–Group means, $N = 40$.

different measures of performance could be related to questionnaire data. Twelve of these work-group performance measures were used in the present research. These 12 measures were tabulated weekly by the company during a 17-week period from immediately preceding and following the questionnaire administration. Six of the measures were direct measures of frequency or amount, and these measures were converted to a per-employee basis for each work group; the other six measures were based on ratings of each work group by the department head. The ratings were on 4-point descriptive scales based on the firm's existing budgetary, allowance, or schedule standards. Actual group performance was compared against these abstract standards. Table 3 lists the 21 work-group performance measures taken from the company records and presents a description of each measure.

Note that a high score on any 1 of the 12 work-group performance measures may indicate either excellent or poor performance depending upon the specific measure in question.

Table 3. Listing and Description of Work Group Performance Measures

Rating measures of performance

Indirect costs (+)
  Performance rating based on actual versus budgeted amounts of inspection, stockhandling, general labor, make-up allowances, and rework labor (4-point scale).

Maintenance costs (+)
  Performance rating based on actual versus budgeted amounts for maintenance, considering both type and quality of maintenance orders (4-point scale).

Supply costs (+)
  Performance rating based on actual versus budgeted allowance for supplies (4-point scale).

Scrap costs (+)
  Performance rating based on actual versus budgeted amounts for scrap and rework (4-point scale).

Performance against schedule (+)
  Performance rating based on the extent to which the work group: stayed on or ahead of schedule (Rating = 4), required help to stay on schedule (Rating = 3),

Table 3. Listing and Description of Work Group Performance Measures (Continued)

Rating measures of performance
was behind schedule (Rating = 2), or was behind to the extent of causing down-time (Rating = 1).
Quality (+)
Performance rating based on actual versus anticipated numbers of rejects, taking into consideration the disposition, amount, and kind of reject (4-point scale).
Average earnings (+)
The average earnings per hour per man for each work group.
Excused absences (-)
The number of occurrences of excused absence, divided by the number of men in the work group.
Unexcused absences (-)
The number of occurences of unexcused absence, divided by the number of men in the work group.
Accidents (-)
The number of reported injuries divided by the number of men in the work group.
Turnover (-)
The number of quits, transfers, and formal bids for jobs in other work groups and not involving advancement, divided by the number of men in the work group.
Suggestions submitted (+)
The number of suggestions formally submitted, divided by the number of men in the work group.

Note.–In each case, direction of scale is indicated by a plus or minus sign. "+" means that a high numerical rating represents "good" performance.

Results

The first hypothesis predicted that expert power would be positively related to a low work-group accident rate. The results from an analysis of his prediction are presented in Table 4 indicating that the hypothesis is supported. Expert power is the only one of the five bases of supervisors' power to relate significantly to a low accident rate.

The second hypothesis predicted that measures of withdrawal–excused absences, unexcused absences, and turnover–would be related to referent power. Specifically, the author predicted that high referent power would be associated with low absences and low turnover. The results relating to this prediction are presented in Table 5.

Table 5 indicates that this prediction is only partially supported. As expected, referent power is associated with low excused absences. However, it was found that unexcused absences and turnover are not associated as expected with supervisory bases of power. Surprisingly, high referent power tends to be related to *high* turnover. This latter finding is contrary to most previous research which would suggest that supervisory behavior which is characterized by high referent power should result in employees' continuing in the system. In the present case, however, unexcused absences are not at all related either to referent power or to the other bases of supervisory power, while turnover is related in a direction opposite to that predicted.

The third hypothesis predicted high incremental influence (both referent power and expert power) would be related to good performance on those measures which were considered to represent measures of production. The results from an analysis of this prediction are presented in Table 6.

Table 4. Relationships Between Accidents and Supervisory Power

	Subordinate work-group's mean perception of their supervisor's					
	Incremental influence	*Referent power*	*Expert power*	*Reward power*	*Coercive power*	*Legitimate power*
Accidents	–.24	–.12	–.28*	–.03	–.16	–.20

Note.–Group means, $N = 40$.
*$p < .05$, one-tailed.

Table 5. Relationships Between Withdrawal Performance Measures and Supervisory Power

Withdrawal performance measure	*Subordinate work-group's mean perception of their supervisor's*					
	Incremental influence	*Referent power*	*Expert power*	*Reward power*	*Coercive power*	*Legitimate power*
Excused absences	–.36*	–.35*	–.28*	–.18	.16	–.12
Unexcused absences	.00	.02	.02	.18	.02	–.08
Turnover	.12	.23	.01	.14	.08	.01

Note.–Group means, $N = 40$.
*$p < .05$, one-tailed.

Table 6. Relationships Between Production Performance Measures and Supervisory Power

Production performance measure	*Subordinate work-group's mean perception of their supervisor's*					
	Incremental influence	*Referent power*	*Expert power*	*Reward power*	*Coercive power*	*Legitimate power*
Indirect cost performance	.27*	.40**	.10	.15	.22	.00
Maintenance cost performance	.12	.00	.18	–.20	–.30*	.10
Supply cost performance	.31*	.21	.32*	.31*	.08	.08

Table 6. Relationships Between Production Performance Measures and Supervisory Power (Continued)

Production performance measure	*Subordinate work-group's mean perception of their supervisor's*					
	Incremental influence	*Referent power*	*Expert power*	*Reward power*	*Coercive power*	*Legitimate power*
Scrap cost performance	.25	.33*	.13	.26	.12	.06
Performance vs. schedule	−.11	.05	−.21	−.06	.04	−.05
Quality	.36*	.32*	.31*	.13	−.08	.11
Average earnings	.01	.00	.01	−.40*	−.22	.05
Suggestions submitted	.28	.36*	.14	.09	.40**	.10

Note.—Group means, $N = 40$.

The predictions of this study are generally supported. For four production performance measures (indirect costs, supply costs, quality and suggestions submitted) the predicted zero-order relationships are significant. For two other production performance measures (scrap costs and maintenance costs) the predicted zero-order relationships; incremental influence is not related to good performance on average earnings or performance against schedule.

Discussion

Although legitimate power ranked first among the reasons for compliance with supervisory directives, legitimate power is not related to differences in the performance of these subordinate work groups. The data suggests, therefore, that when the supervisor has a choice in the bases of power he emphasizes, to achieve compliance with his directives the supervisor should attempt to create and to use referent power or expert power rather than rely too strongly on his legitimate power.

Reward power and coercive power, unlike legitimate power, do relate to a number of performance measures. However, the overall relationship between these two bases of power is two-sided. From the organization's point of view the correlates of reward power and coercive power are problematic and have unintended consequences for the organization. Organizationally speaking, reward power relates functionally to supply costs but dysfunctionally to average earnings; coercive power relates functionally to suggestions submitted but dysfunctionally to maintenance costs. Therefore the data suggest that the supervisor's use of reward power and coercive power should be tempered where possible by the creation of referent power and expert power. Since there appear to be no dysfunctional or organizationally unintended correlates of incremental influence, the latter should be created and used where possible.

As was noted above and as predicted, incremental influence has positive and organizationally functional correlates. However, it is important to note that only 7 of the 12 performance measures relate to incremental influence. Five measures, two withdrawal measures (unexcused absences and turnover) and three production measures (maintenance costs, performance against schedule, and average earnings), showed no relationship to incremental influence. The reason for the difference in relationship between incremental influence and performance is not altogether clear. Perhaps the five performance measures which do not relate to performance represent areas or factors over which the first-line supervisor has little or no control. Unexcused absences and turnover might be related to extraorganizational considerations or to organizational factors which are unrelated to compliance with the first-line supervisor. The three production measures which do not relate to incremental influence may be said to represent company-wide or system factors rather than to be related to factors at the first-line supervisory level of the company. Maintenance costs, performance against schedule, and average earnings may be related to company-wide policies regarding maintenance programs, production schedules, and pay rates, respectively.

Finally, it should be noted that the correlations for referent power and expert power are not generally additive, and referent power is a better predictor of performance that is expert power. Referent power is significantly related to five performance measures (excused absences, indirect costs, quality, suggestions submitted, and scrap costs), while expert power relates significantly to four measures (accident rate, excused absences, supply costs, and quality). Only in the case of quality is the correlation for incremental influence greater than the correlations for referent power and expert power, which suggests that in this case the bases of power are additive.

The present research has shown the concept of incremental influence to be a useful and viable one. The qualitative distinction between referent power and expert power on the one hand and reward power, coercive power, and legitimate power on the other was generally supported by the data. The performance correlates of referent power and expert power are surprisingly large in view of the fact that the research did not included only one level of management. Moreover, the first-line supervisor in the present research site is a supervisor who may be said to have a relatively small area of freedom; his role ranged is limited by industrial engineers, quality-control specialists, time and motion study men, and others, as well as by the standardized nature of high-volume, single-product production. In view of the limitations inherent in the role which was studies, the findings are encouraging and further research and validation of these findings are indicated.

References

Fleishman, E. A., & Harris, E. F. Patterns of leadership behavior related to employee grievances and turnover. *Personnel Psychology*, 1962, *15*, 43-56.

Fleishman, E. A., Harris, E. F., & Burtt, H. E. *Leadership and supervision in industry*. Columbus, Ohio: Bureau of Educational Research, Ohio State University, 1955.

French, J. R. P., Jr., & Raven, B. H. The bases of social power. In D. Cartwright, (Ed.), *Studies in social power.* Ann Arbor, Mich.: Institute for Social Research; 1959, Pp. 150-167.

Kahn, R. L., & Katz, D. Leadership practices in relation to productivity and morale. In D. Cartwright & A. Zander (Eds.), *Group dynamics.* (2nd ed.) Evanston, Ill.: Row, Peterson, 1960. Pp. 554-570.

Katz, D., & Kahn, R. L. *The social psychology of organizations,* New York: Wiley, 1966.

Likert, R. *New patterns of management.* New York: McGraw-Hill, 1961.

Mann, F. C. Toward an understanding of the leadership role in formal organization. In R. Dubin, G. C. Homans, F. C. Mann & D. C. Miller (Eds.), *Leadership and productivity*. San Francisco: Chandler, 1965. Pp. 68-103.

March, J. G., & Simon, H. A. *Organizations.* New York: Wiley, 1958.

Pfiffner, J. M. The effective supervisor: An organization research study *Personnel,* 1955, *31*, 530-540.

Part Four

Supervisory Roles and Techniques

A Design for Productive Classroom Evaluation

Charles F. Malone

Today's educational leader has been caught up in a ceaseless campaign of change; every facet of his existence, personal and professional, is constantly being made different. Unfortunately a good portion of present-day principals have been inadequately prepared for the jobs they now hold and their attempt to keep pace is very difficult; this statement rings true despite the fact that our administrators today are better prepared than any previous group. The changing demands of the job, however, have created a totally unique circumstance and a challenge which can be met only through aggressive, well-organized planning. Surely the principal-administrator who deteriorates in job efficiency by merely maintaining the status quo can expect his entire staff to follow suit. That this must be avoided is one of the chief objectives of this discussion.

Seawell and Holmes[1] have recommended procedures which may provide some help to administrators in the area of in-service training; their suggestions include employing assistants, time and money for educational experimentation, leaves of absence, opportunity for consultation and formal study, etc. The number of school districts presently developing administrative in-service programs is increasing, a trend which we must consider encouraging.

It is my purpose in this paper to offer ideas which will contribute to more competent principal leadership in the area acknowledged to be first and foremost in importance, namely, instructional supervision.

Specifically a five-step instrument (hereafter referred to as OEGT, Observable Evidences of Good Teaching) is presented which is designed to focus in on the generally accepted main aspects of classroom teaching. Ideally the instrument would be developed by an entire faculty in order that maximum agreement and understanding among all faculty and administrative members could be attained. Such an undertaking would require one or more years of allotted in-service growth time and so, therefore, I am presenting my own views in hopes that they may be used as a basis for study and try-out. At this point the reader should acquaint himself with the instrument; the discussion to follow will be more meaningful if this is done.

[1] W. H. Seawell and George W. Holmes, "Improving Administrative Leadership," *The American School Board Journal*, 148:9-10 (Feb. 1964).

Hints for Using the Instrument

The reader will note that the instrument calls for a completed copy to be handed to the teacher. In a few cases it might be desirable to send a copy to another person as well: the general supervisor, superintendent, etc. The latter practice would be exceptional, however, since the chief aim of this particular device is to improve communication between the principal and individual faculty members. It is this very communication which will lead to improved classroom teaching.

The cover sheet of OEGT infers and suggests a number of recommendations to be followed if maximum success is to be attained. The need for mutual teacher-principal agreement regarding effective teaching has been cited, so in some respects it matters little whether the principal completes the instrument alone or in conjunction with the teacher. A far more important step is to give attention to this filling-out-of-the-instrument and the follow-up conference within a two-day period. Ideally, the two step completion-conference cycle would be conducted on the day of visitation. In the large majority of cases careful planning will permit this.

Most principals who carry reasonably heavy administrative responsibilities will find it best to schedule one or possibly two visitations per day, excluding those days which we have all learned simply do not lend themselves well to classroom observation: party days, days on which holidays are scheduled to begin, etc. On these days the principal will find it best to demonstrate helpfulness in ways other than visitation.

The length of a visitation again will vary according to the classroom activity in progress. Teachers have expressed opinions about how many minutes a principal should observe and their feelings should be respected.[2] It is obvious to the trained visitor, however, that one may need to spend a longer time in observing an intermediate social studies lesson, for example, than the same class when it is concerned with spelling; the reason being that teachers generally allot more time to social studies, reading, mathematics, etc., than they do to spelling.

At this point a most significant recommendation needs to be made: namely, that *the length of visitation is not nearly so important as the absolute necessity to arrive prior to the initiation of instruction and to remain until that lesson is concluded.* This action constitutes the only fair treatment possible to a visit, for it insures the opportunity for the teacher to present both the goal-establishment and evaluation phases of instruction; similarly it allows the principal to make observations of these portions of the lesson which are the first and last cited in the instrument. To arrive even five minutes late may cause the observer to miss seeing the techniques a teacher employs to establish a goal or aim for the lesson at hand. The same can be said for the evaluation phase, though if one had to make a choice, it would be far better to leave a few minutes early in preference to arriving late.

Space is also provided for noting such information as the date of visitation,

[2]Charles F. Malone and Robert W. Ridgway, "Attitudes of Teachers Toward Supervisory Services," *University of Kansas Bulletin of Education*, Vol. 18 (Winter Issue, February, 1964), pp. 68-74.

subject observed, follow-up conference date, next planned visitation, etc. The principal will find it valuable to complete these various items, as the recorded information will prove beneficial as he plans future visits. For example, recording of the visitation date will be a guide, along with numerous other factors, as to when he will return to that same classroom; by indicating the subject or activity in progress during the visit the principal will be in a position to determine if he wishes to observe that same subject again or another; the follow-up conference date and next-planned-visitation date are equally important.

The skill of the principal in conducting the follow-up conference will be a main factor leading to better teaching. One can be a skilled observer, but if he fails to establish rapport easily or if he fails to open free and accessible channels of communication which can help lead the teacher to improved performance, his competence as an observer may be for naught. Therefore, the skills of successful conferencing need to be known and practiced.

Actually, the whole field of human relations is the framework of operation for the principal. His day-by-day professional behavior sets the tone of the school. How he reacts to all the demands made upon him by faculty is a main and contributing factor to the over-all school climate and atmosphere. Though he may be the officially designated leader, he must really earn the respect of his faculty each day, which is but another way of saying his "right to lead" must be proved daily. And it is teacher feeling about this behavior which will eventually contribute to or interfere with the success of the post visitation conference.

Allowing the teacher to express his own views and to state his own observations regarding the lesson is basically a sound practice. Teacher familiarity with the instrument is considered a requirement and will surely lead to more valid evaluation. It has been found that teachers are usually quite conservative in judging themselves, that far more often than not the principal observes many more evidences of good teaching than the teacher feels have occurred. This fact of itself is a rapport-establishing circumstance.

The many positive evidences observed probably should be reconstructed in the first minutes of the conference. We have learned the value of this practice in parent relations, as it paves the way for the sometimes constructive criticism which must follow. This need not be a "drummed-up or phony" environmental situation, for certainly the vast majority of our teachers are offering satisfactory leadership. We rightfully should have faith and confidence in classroom leadership and we should sincerely convey this feeling to our esteemed colleagues, the teachers, who make it possible.

The five major areas of leadership designated in OEGT should be discussed at each post-visitation conference. Evidences should be noted as observed by the principal and teacher, items of agreement recounted, notations of teaching which overlapped from one major area to another mentioned, etc. If proper rapport between the two parties exists, it seems logical to inject concerns and constructive criticisms in any major area as that area is discussed. Let it be understood now that concerns and constructive suggestion can be initiated by the teacher as well as the principal. *In fact this is far better, for it is evidence of the teacher's continuously-*

developing self-evaluation skill. This is certainly one of our major supervisory goals.

The Five Evidences

Briefly let us comment on the five areas which can bring thorough and complete teaching closer to reality.

(1) *Interpersonal Relations:* A case for classroom climate and environment hardly needs to be made. As students earlier and now as teachers we are very cognizant of the relationship between teaching success and the creation within a classroom of a challenging and motivating atmosphere. The observer should be keenly alert to the quality of human relations during visitation and should make note of evidences which contribute or interfere with the establishment of a maximum learning climate.

(2) *Physical Environment:* Assessment of the physical environment should take place immediately upon entering the classroom. Allot the first several minutes of your visit to a critical analysis of interest centers, bulletin boards, light, ventilation, etc. As the visitation continues, note if and/or how pupils are utilizing the learning centers, etc., to further their goals. If one considers student participation in the planning and creation of a stimulating physical environment important, and most authorities do, then evidence of this will be sought. One needs to learn to recognize the overall quality of room environment. We must discover how to make objective judgments in terms of learning value in the neat, everything-in-order classroom as well as the classroom which is characterized by pupil activity, problem-centered work habits, involvement of students, etc. The latter classroom will have that desirable "lived-in" look and climate.

(3) *Goal-Centered Instruction:* One can succeed in many ways in teaching, but one will almost surely fail if one is unable to establish meaningful goals to be pursued. Planning in this context has fallen woefully short of desired standards: too often our only aim is stated in some such vague description as "Complete page 67." We must recall that pages to be read and/or completed are but part of the techniques we should employ to accomplish what may be a briefly stated, but nevertheless clearly understood, lesson objective. *Every lesson, whether it is of 15 or 60 minutes duration, should include a planned attempt to establish a desired goal.* And this goal should be stated in pupil dialogue, for truly we cannot expect growth without understanding.

Unfortunately, too few teachers clearly understand what they want to accomplish. As the classroom teacher gains skill in stating his exact purpose and he is able to convey this more effectively to his pupils, learning will become a much more rewarding process. The observer is seeking, then, clear evidence of the teacher's effort to establish goal-centered teaching. Pessimistically, I feel that one will have to use all one's "detective instincts" to figure out a goal for many of the lessons observed. If so, is there not a real need for guidance?

(4) *Lesson Procedures:* To this point the observer has sought evidence of positive interpersonal relations, a stimulating physical environment, and goal-centered instruction. The procedures employed to accomplish the stated goal represent the

very core of the teaching process and therefore evidence of effective leadership will be sought. Items 1-12 should be used as the basis for evaluating the "procedures" phase of the observation period.

(5) Finally, evidence must be sought in the vital area of *evaluation.* Use of the OEGT instrument to date has revealed a rather alarming lack of evidence regarding both the quantity and quality of teacher effort toward appraisal/evaluation. It is recognized that a possible cause for this may be a poor selection of evidences one seeks in Area Five. But if a reasonable degree of evidence choice has been made, i.e., if the evidences are logical, then truly we have a significant task before us in our need to assist teachers in developing appropriate evaluative classroom experiences. To me a satisfactory solution must be found, for evaluation, properly planned and wisely conducted, is the stepping-stone to the next well-developed lesson plan. It has remedial and reteaching connotations which cannot be ignored.

The Instrument

Observable Evidences of Good Teaching (OEGT)

Note: The purpose of this instrument is to assist those responsible for the improvement of instruction to evaluate the teaching-learning situation. An attempt has been made to render this instrument as objective as possible; thus the heavy emphasis on *evidence* rather than opinion. What is presented is intended to be a guide only. You will find five important aspects of a lesson emphasized, one of which appears at the top of each page. The evidences on that page relate, then, to that main heading. I would encourage those working with the instrument to add or delete evidence in order to make the instrument more valuable to them. *Not all of the evidence will be observed in any one visit, of course.*

Classes observed____

Date of Visit____

Date of Follow-Up____

Next Planned Visitation____

Copy to: Principals________________Teacher________________Other________

Comments: (As this would be the cover sheet, much more space would be available here and on the back.)

Page 1

A. *Interpersonal Relationships Are of Such Nature Than an Overall Feeling of Rapport Exists– Thus Contributing to the Climate of Learning.* Evidences of Good Interpersonal Relations Are:

1. There is an attitude of mutual respect and confidence on both the part of

the teacher and her pupils, thus resulting in an atmosphere of friendliness and understanding between classroom participants.
(Space would be provided here and between each item on your own instrument.)

2. There are free and open channels of communication (Children to teacher, teacher to children, children to children).
3. Classroom activities and procedures suggest that teacher and pupils have planned together in establishing standards of behavior, committee work, independent activity, etc. Cooperativeness, a business-like attitude, enthusiasm, are readily apparent.
4. There is recognition and acceptance of sincere contributions and efforts of individual pupils. This is evidenced in the relations described in number 2.
5. Respect for the principles of child growth and development is evidenced by the manner in which physical, social, intellectual, and emotional needs are met.
6. Guidance techniques, both group and individual, are employed to promote the total development of class members. Problems of discipline are handled firmly, fairly, and with sympathetic understanding.
7. There is a balance between the freedom necessary to full development of individual personality and the controls necessary to productive group work.

Page 2

B. *There Is a Stimulating Physical Environment That Will Afford a Variety of Appropriate Learning Opportunities.*

1. There is evidence of learning through the arrangement of appropriate displays and materials on tackboards, tables, chalkboards, etc.
2. Work areas (reading circle, science table, classroom library, art corner, etc.) are arranged for maximum pupil stimulation and accomplishment.
3. Citizenship training is apparent by the manner in which pupils care for and arrange personal belongings (wraps, books, etc.) and school property (furniture, reference and supplementary books, etc.)
4. Ample, well-adjusted lighting and ventilation contribute to a desirable room atmosphere.
5. Furniture is of appropriate size for individual class members and is arranged so as to contribute to maximum learning opportunities.
6. Audio-visual aids and other instructional materials appropriate to the learning situation are used in a meaningful and purposeful manner.

Page 3

C. *A Goal or Purpose Represents the Most Important Single Factor in the Learning Situation.* Evidences Which Indicate Purposeful, Meaningful Lessons Are:

1. Teachers and pupils are planning and working together to meet those objectives which they have agreed to be important.
2. Goals and purposes are consistent with our understandings of the needs of the learner as determined from our knowledge of child growth and development.
3. Problems of importance to the class as a whole, yet ones which can be differentiated according to the ability, need, and interest of individuals are before the group.
4. A worthwhile problem is being solved and valuable data will be made available for future use.
5. New skills and understandings are acquired or old skills perfected during the period.
6. Proper motivation is present. The lesson is characterized by wide and enthusiastic participation aimed toward achievement of pre-established objectives.
7. Pupils' study habits are fostered by the lesson.
8. Activities are so organized and carried out as to promote integration of learnings.
9. Matters of importance other than subject matter (creative thinking, research, group processes, etc.) received emphasis.

Page 4

D. *The Lesson Is Developed in a Manner Which Gives Meaning to Both the Group and the Individual in Terms of the Established Objectives.*
   1. The lesson shows evidence of careful pre-planning by teacher and/or pupils thus making for clarity and wise use of time.
   2. Necessary materials are ready for immediate use and are distributed and/or collected so as to cause a minimum of confusion.
   3. Children know and understand long-range goals . Short-term objectives are visible in one period of observation.
   4. Vocabulary needs are anticipated by using needed words in meaningful oral and written settings.
   5. Individual abilities, interests, and attitudes are recognized and cared for through grouping techniques and by proper "pacing" of the lesson.
   6. The learning activity builds on what has gone on before and prepared for what is to follow. Continuity is provided by helping pupils understand how the lesson relates to other areas of the curriculum and to daily living.
   7. Fundamental skills are taught in relation to the problem being developed. Necessary practice time for skill development is provided.
   8. Continuing pupil-teacher planning provides for modification and redirecting of individual learning activities.
   9. Democratic procedures are utilized in helping children to learn to work as members of a group.

10. Opportunities are provided for pupils to learn to think critically, to make wise choices and decisions, and to develop self-direction and creativity.
11. Independent activity is provided that is significant to the individual pupil's needs and objectives.
12. Remedial instruction and/or reteaching is offered on the basis of accurate diagnosis of need.

Page 5

E. *The Evaluation of Instruction Should be Concerned with the Total Growth of Each Individual Socially, Emotionally, and Physically—as well as Academically.*
   1. The evaluation of a specific teaching-learning situation is made in terms of the attainment of earlier established goals.
   2. Methods of grading indicate a relation to capacity.
   3. Marks on papers indicate a positive tone; a concern for what is wrong rather than how many are wrong.
   4. Children are grouped and regrouped as growth patterns change.
   5. Efforts are made to develop self-evaluation skills and habits.
   6. Evidence of evaluation of the short-term goals is apparent. The evaluation of long-range objectives may be implied.
   7. Experiences are provided in summarizing and in organizing thoughts and materials.
   8. There will be opportunities, even in a short period, for evaluative experiences.
   9. Evaluation is carried out in a manner so as to stimulate the pupil to improve his level or general performance.
   10. Evaluative techniques encourage the interrelating of subject matter and a proper balance of various activity to develop the "whole" child.
   11. Evaluative procedures may be group and/or individual in approach. In either case the outcome must be significant to *each* individual in order to be effective.

Reporting Teacher Observation

Irving Flinker

At a recent meeting of school principals in our district, my colleagues discussed their plans for observing instruction and reporting their observations. I was struck by the general agreement among supervisors on the criteria of effective teaching, and by the wide diversity of practice in writing the reports. A cursory examination of the professional literature on supervision confirmed my belief that the reporting of classroom visitation has been given inadequate attention. To provoke reaction and thought in this area of supervision, I submit my reflections about the reporting of lessons.

About 40 years ago, when supervision was going through its "scientific period," the school principal emulated the industrial efficiency expert by drawing up an exhaustive checklist of criteria of good teaching. The list was at least two pages long and provided a little space at the end for a summary.

The supervisor generally ticked off each item he observed, or marked it negative if it was lacking. Sometimes these lists were comprised of questions written in the impersonal third person, e.g., "Did the teacher elicit the aim from the children?"

It was impossible for any teacher to have a perfect score. No matter how much the supervisor praised the superior teacher in the subsequent conference the latter was left with a permanent record of not having touched all bases. Moreover, the receipt of a mechanical listing of pedagogic practices left one cold. It was too much like a work-order from a plant superintendent to a shop foreman. If we want our teachers to work like professional people we must treat them as such.

Teacher training is essentially a matter of good teaching on the part of the supervisor. Mastery in all aspects of teaching is achieved after years of experience, and the effective teacher is aware of the importance of gradation in developing concepts and skills. Similarly, the supervisor must plan a sequence of important goals in accordance with the needs of each individual teacher to insure steady and continuous growth. Giving a conscientious first- or second-year teacher a long checklist is enough to drive her into other kinds of employment.

The checklist has a useful function for experienced teachers who wish to become "master teachers" or wish to prepare themselves for supervisory positions. It is an excellent device for self-evaluation. For this purpose, it is best for a teacher to analyze her own teaching and construct her own checklist. She would then find it helpful to compare hers to standard lists and discuss both with her supervisor. Such a job analysis would be very helpful to a conscientious teacher intent on self-improvement, as well as to one interested in supervision.

Fortunately, the checklist as a method of reporting, is losing favor among supervisors today. It is more commonly used as a method of alerting teachers at faculty conferences to good teaching practices. However, the checklist is a training method too extensive for one concentrated program.

A more common form of reporting teaching is the objective description and statement of commendations and recommendations. In many schools such forms are mimeographed thereby limiting the space for each part of the report. The heading generally includes the following data: name of teacher, class, room, subject, date, period. The bottom of the form ends with a brief summary characterizing the lesson and the statement that a conference has been held on a certain date. The teacher is asked to sign the report as evidence of having received it and, of course, the supervisor signs the report. Presented below is an example of this type of report:

Teacher: Miss Alice Brown
Class: 8E1

Date: 11/30/65
Conference: 11/30/65
Length of Observation: 30 minutes

Aim of Lesson: Who was responsible for the Civil War?

Description of Lesson: The teacher began the lesson by setting the ground rules for a panel discussion on the theme of the lesson.

The first speaker denounced the South for its actions in the decade preceding the Civil War as the responsible factor in causing war. The second speaker identified slavery as the crucial issue bringing on conflict. He summarized the historical development of slavery.

The third speaker attacked the North as a repository of industrial slums and crime. She defended slavery as humane compared with child labor and the poverty of the aged, prevailing in the North. The fourth speaker attacked Northern hypocrisy in its attitude toward slavery. The speakers closely questioned each other. Speakers were questioned by the audience.

Commendable Features: The lesson revolved around a central theme and represents an attempt by the teacher to implement a departmental goal, i.e., thematic teaching. The students reviewed tariff policies, land issues, industrial-agrarian rivalries in the course of developing the theme, responsibility for the Civil War.

The research by the students was commendable. It showed familiarity with the material and the content of the unit.

The give-and-take between the speakers was lively and aroused interest and attention. There was a high degree of socialization.

Suggestions: One of the speakers read directly from his notes. This should be avoided.

The youngsters in the audience should have been given more time to question the panel. At the end of each side's presentation, a chairman should be present to summarize views.

Comments: Good emphasis on a "theme," with very good socialization.

CARL DRAKE
Assistant Principal

I have received a copy of this report

The wise supervisor limits the description of the lesson to a succinct account of its development. He commends the teacher for several outstanding procedures and limits his constructive suggestions to a maximum of two. It is better to observe a teacher on three separate days than to overwhelm her with six major recommendations at one time. In the latter instance, the teacher could become so despondent she would give up trying to improve her teaching.

A ratio of five commendations to one or two suggestions provides a fillip to one's ego. The teacher is won over by the supervisor's appreciation of her work. Furthermore, it is reasonable to expect that a teacher can concentrate on self-improvement in one aspect of teaching, and become proficient in that respect within a relatively short time. This means that the supervisor must return in four weeks or so to appraise progress and indicate a new direction for growth. This kind of supervision may be time-consuming, but it is human and effective.

Additional factors and aspects of the lesson may be discussed at the post-observation conference, but the report should not include all the positive and negative characteristics of the lesson, for the same reasons the checklist should not be used (viz., diffusion, confusion, and frustration).

Some supervisors include in this formal report a summary of dialogue and explanation which took place at the conference. Such a statement is superfluous and deleterious. A conference marked by a difference of opinion should be ended in a respectful, amiable manner. To include in a report any innuendoes of conflicts and authoritative pressure is to generate a long-enduring resentment on the part of the teacher.

This brings us to the purpose of the report. All of our work as supervisors is directed toward the improvement of teaching in our schools. We now acknowledge that the authoritarian supervisor failed to inspire and motivate creative teaching because the teacher was undermined by his specific directions. The modern supervisor recognizes the importance of the human relationship in supervision. He seeks to generate enthusiasm, build self-confidence, and release creativity in his teachers. These goals are reached only in an atmosphere of good human relations where each person feels important and trusted.

What is the effect on a teacher's morale when she is required to sign a supervisor's formal report on her lesson? No lesson is perfect and, therefore, almost every report will convey the impression that the teacher needs improvement. She knows that the signed copy is filed and may be used in a final evaluation of her worth as a teacher. She knows, also, that each report bears a different criticism, and she is concerned about the sum total of written criticism. When she signs the report she thinks only of the negative quality of her teaching. Through her mind runs the conclusion that the supervisor is collecting evidence that she has received instructions to improve. She questions the supervisor's need for the evidence. Questioning leads to fear.

I, too, question the need for the teacher's signature. Such a requirement is destructive of mutual trust and a friendly relationship between teacher and supervisor. Teachers should be informed that reports of lessons have functional value for both the supervisor and the teacher. The latter receives a written appraisal of her work and guidance in self-improvement. The supervisor cannot rely on his memory to help each person grow continuously as a teacher and needs a memorandum which refers to the strengths and weaknesses of each one. All teachers are entitled to a written report of their work and to a copy of every statement placed in their personal files. Every teacher should be made aware that she may examine her personal file at any time. Under such conditions the requirement of a teacher's signature becomes needless and should be dropped.

What is the psychological effect of a formal, objective report on the teacher? One way to find out is to question a thousand teachers about it. My educated guess is that the effect is now wholesome.

An objective report lacks personality, warmth, privacy, and feeling. It is an analytical record of behavior revealing competence, disability, growth or deterioration, and authoritative direction. In such a record the teacher is no more human than the dissected frog. This kind of report is not dissimilar to the papers read at a convention of orthodontists. It serves a useful purpose for the supervisor and should be filed for future reference, but it is not a suitable communication to be sent by a thoughtful supervisor to a teacher in whom he wants to infuse hope and determination to work harder. The report is not addressed to her; it is addressed to a folder in a file, and that is where it belongs.

How does the objective, factual report affect creativity in teachers? We are aware that a person's talents are best developed in an atmosphere of freedom to explore and experiment. In the group process of personal dynamic interaction, intelligence is kindled to generate originality. The experienced supervisor knows that each teacher is an individual and must develop her own teaching techniques and devices. While Teacher A may find the developmental method most effective. Teacher B may obtain best results with a socialized pattern of instruction.

The checklist and the formal objective statement restrict the freedom of the teacher to experiment. A lesson consisting of a visiting fireman's talk on safety in the home would draw no plaudits or suggestions in such reports, since the teacher is part of the audience. Similarly, the lecture method, which is advantageously used in large group instruction, provides for a minimum of active group involvement. Such a method would be frowned upon in such reporting.

The objective report leaves little to the imagination of the teacher, for the reader of this report is clearly informed about the kind of teaching the supervisor prefers. The teacher is directed to follow certain procedures, regardless of personal interests or aptitudes, and her personality is not considered in the report. She is not encouraged to create, experiment, or innovate.

A third type of visitation report used by a growing number of supervisors is the personal letter. This may be a formal letter or an informal note conveying praise for commendable practices and questions about other observations. The letter ends with an expression of confidence in the teacher or on some other positive note. A sample of such a letter is presented below:

December 7, 1965

Mrs. Jane Doe Teacher of English
Gershwin J.H.S. 166, Brooklyn

Dear Mrs. Doe:

The fine rapport you have established with your children is an outgrowth of your helpful attitude and constructive lesson planning. Your instruction is focused on the basic needs of the children as evidenced in today's lesson on speaking to an audience. The large cartoons on posture and mannerisms motivated interest in learning propriety in addressing an audience. Your three specific instructions, written on the front board, provided definite guidance in public speaking. Giving children opportunities to speak to the class and evaluate the brief talks will go far to develop good speaking habits in all your children.

At our conference today you showed clear insight into the psychology of the learning process. When you apply to your teaching problems your sound thinking and the criteria of good pedagogy which we discussed, you will achieve more effective results. I refer to the children's identification with the aim and the summation of the lesson.

I am confident that you will continue to evaluate your own lessons so that your professional growth will be maximized.

Sincerely yours,

Irving Flinker
Principal

To summarize, let us review the previously stated questions: Does the objective report place a teacher on the defensive so that she suspects the motives of the supervisor? What is the effect of this report on the receptivity of the teacher to suggested improvement? To what extent does such a report stimulate creativity in teachers? How does a report in letter form affect the human relationship between teacher and supervisor?

The Principal-Teacher Conference: A Case Study

George C. Kyte

The individual conference between principal and teacher is the important supervisory technique for providing professional help to the latter. Recent research findings furnish detailed information regarding the effective conference.[1] They indicate the number of items to include, the relative stress to give each item, the order of occurrence of the points, the use of recurrent discussions of some items, and the methods for making the discussions effective. Applying these findings as criteria of a good conference, the writer analyzed the case study presented below.

This principal-teacher conference is among the best of 30 tape-recorded conferences used in obtaining the research findings. It was selected because it approached the ideal in terms of the criteria. The introductory item, given passing mention, served its purpose of establishing rapport. It included the principal's commendation of the lesson as a whole and his approval of a specific aspect of it. Turning to the second item, he prefaced it with a commendation of the teacher's

[1]Kyte, George C. "The Effective Supervisory Conference." A paper read at the California Educational Research Association meeting, March 3, 1961.

skill. Thus he established the teacher's confidence in herself and her work. Thereafter, he stressed constructive help in which her good work was related to her need for further improvement.

The number of items treated was kept to the amount which the teacher could assimilate. The two major items given marked stress had considerable subsequent effect. One of two other items given lesser stress had moderate effect. The other had slight observable effect because of its specific nature. Among the items were related points which reinforced each other in effecting improvement in the teacher's classwork. The principal supplemented his assistance by lending her a professional textbook with pertinent sections marked for her benefit. The conference was closed commendably. He summarized briefly and definitely the important items discussed. The final conversation indicates mutual friendliness and appreciation. The research study disclosed that this conference had considerable effect on subsequent teaching.

The principal was a well trained and very successful supervisory officer. In his conference with other teachers, the research study had confirmed his supervisory skill. In the selected conference, he supervised the teacher of a second grade regarding her observed spelling lesson. He based his help on his knowledge of her meager professional training and experience. Consequently, he exerted care in giving explicit assistance to her. Throughout the conference is considerable evidence of his careful planning for it. The teacher had completed less than a year of teaching experience, being a beginning teacher in the school. She was inadequately trained and granted a provisional credential because of the teacher shortage. She was enrolled in one extension course and also planned to continue her training during summer sessions. She was employed as a probationary teacher who showed promise of becoming a good one. She was a hard worker, conscientious in her efforts, and willing to learn.

The transcription of the recorded conference discloses the friendly, frank, and professional discussion in which both persons participated freely. In spite of the spontaneity of the oral English, the language errors were not numerous. The detailed research indicated that they had no observable effect on subsequent teaching. Because of this fact, certain superfluous expressions and similar minor speech errors have been eliminated below.

The case study is arranged so that the quoted conference appears in the left-hand column and the writer's annotations appear in the right-hand column. In the latter, the items included in the conference are identified in italics. In both columns, the principal is designated by P and the teacher, by T.

The Conference	The Annotations
P. Now, Mrs. T, I thought that your spelling lesson on the whole was done quite well. However, there are some parts of it that I think you probably could do a little better.	P compliments T on the good lesson. *Passing mention* in establishing rapport.

I liked particularly the way you asked the children to find the small words in the spelling words because I feel that is one way of getting them to be word conscious. Do you do that quite often with your lessons?

P approves a specific teaching technique as an example of the good teaching.

T. I usually do it every week.

P. Every week?

T. Yes.

P. And I also noticed that you developed the meaning of some words quite well. I was wondering why you didn't do it with all the words.

P approves T's skill in developing word meaning and recommends its use with all the words. *Considerable stress.*

T. Well, there was no particular reason except that on Tuesdays we go through the words again–follow-up–and we do have the words used in sentences.

P. Well, I think maybe it could be carried a little further, if you have time. It all depends on how much time you have. For instance, the first word. Maybe you could ask a child to say the word, "came." "Now what does it mean?" and maybe he would say, "Going from one place to another" or something like that. And for instance, there is the word, "fat." Maybe they could explain what "fat" meant by, "When you get heavy" or something like that, you see.

P illustrates a procedure in developing the meaning of words.

T. Yes

P. Well, the psychologists and the experts in the field of spelling do say that if a child does know the meaning of the word he will probably use it more often and that way he'll probably learn how to spell it. Now, your recitation period to me seemed like it was a good learning period. I find sometimes in many classes that the recitation period is not a learning period. It should be. I felt that the boys and girls were learning some of the meanings of the words and they were getting the eye image and the auditory image of the words. I was wondering–now I noticed that you did this a little later–if maybe it shouldn't be done at the beginning of the story or the beginning of the lesson. I noticed that you read the story and discussed the story a little bit after you had gotten into the words. I'm wondering if maybe it wouldn't be a little bit better to do that at the beginning. What do you think about that? Does the book suggest that? Anything like that?

P cites the experts' emphasis on the importance of establishing the meaning of words.

P compliments T on her good learning period.

P suggests developing word meaning at the beginning of the lesson.

P asks T what practice the textbook suggests.

T. Yes, the book suggests that we do it that way.

T replies it recommends the practice.

P. Yes, Well, I noticed that you brought it in. I am not saying that it was the wrong procedure but I'm just wondering. Maybe it should come at the beginning since I notice here that this type of book has the words underlined in the story. And maybe if you could bring that in at the beginning, it would be a little better. I noticed that the boys and girls seemed to have good relations with you. By that I mean they trusted the teacher and the teacher trusted the children and there was good byplay. By that I mean good interaction. They seemed to enjoy the lesson and I think that's good. And I think one way that you can keep it that way is to avoid embarrassing the children. You didn't do that and the interaction between you and the youngsters was very good. I was wondering about that word, "would, w,o,u,l,d." The question came up about what the difference was between "w,o,u,l,d" and "w,o,o,d," which was good. I was wondering if maybe, when words sound alike but are spelled differently, if it wouldn't be a good idea just to put the two words on the board so they can see the difference. Do you think that would be a good idea?

P recommends following this practice.

P compliments T on the teacher-pupil relationship. *Passing mention.*

P reverts to the teaching of meaning of words. In the case of homonyms, suggests the use of the board so pupils can see the two words.

T. Yes.

T approves the suggestion.

P. All right? I imagine you've probably thought of that. Lots of times we know techniques and we just don't happen to use them at that particular time. But I think that when one word sounds like another and is spelled differently, maybe we ought to get what they call a visual image. All right. Now I was wondering there about your vowels. On the word "try, t,r,y," I think sometimes "y" is a vowel. In other words, It's "a,e,i,o,u and sometimes y." And I was wondering about that though usually "y" isn't a vowel. But I think every word has some type of a vowel in it. Let's check and see.

P questions T on her misconception that "y" is never a vowel. *Moderate stress.*

P proposes they check to find out about "y."

T. Maybe my lack of education.

T blames her lack of training.

P. No, it isn't. No, it isn't lack of education at all. There are lots of people that don't remember that. Let's see, Yes, here it is. "Vowels." Let's see here.

P assures T it isn't. . . .

Oh, yes. "Also a letter in English, a,e,i,o,u, and sometimes y representing such a sound." So if you just would—

T. Yes, it would be, wouldn't it?

P. So, if you just keep in mind and I wouldn't be afraid. I mean, the next time it comes up, just tell the youngsters you made a mistake. After all we're all human beings—we do make mistakes. You make them, I make them, everybody does: The thing to remember is that we just don't keep making the same one over and over again.

T. Yes. Well, the "y" in the vowels. We've had an awful lot of trouble with even "a,e,i,o, and u." Most of our books don't use so many vowels. But in our reading books, they don't use the vowel, "u," at all.

P. They don't?

T. In our workbooks or the other books, there is the vowel, "u," but they don't use it in the words at all. The only vowels that we use at all are "a,e,i, and o."

P. Well, that's interesting. I didn't know that.

T. The sentences with the "y," too.

P. Well, it could be. I think what I would try to do, though, when the occasion arises, just correct it.

T. Let them know that there is a "y"?

P. Yes. That's right.

T. And that it's a vowel.

P. Yes. Here are some points that I'm wondering about. Have the children been taught to spell a word? Not how to spell it but I mean how to study a spelling word?

T. Yes.

P. Well, that's fine. And I noticed in our course of study here, there is something to that effect. It's listed under "Second Grade." There's the procedure in learning how to spell the word. In other words, it suggests a method of learning how to spell a word. "Look carefully at the word. Pronounce it by syllables, slowly, distinctly, listening to each syllable as you pronounce it." Of course, you don't have to tell the youngsters about syllables. Just say, "Look at the word carefully and, number two, close your eyes and pronounce the word softly and try to see the

P reads the statement that "y" takes a sound and is then classified as a vowel.

P advises T to correct the concept with the pupils and admit her mistake, which anybody can make.

T digresses from the point.

P utilizes the digression to repeat his advice regarding "y" taught as a vowel when sounded.

P asks T if the pupils have been taught how to study spelling.

T answers affirmatively.

P approves and then reads the procedure suggested in the course of study; initiates a detailed discussion. *Marked stress.*

P suggests a simplified form of directions to pupils.

word as it looked. Open your eyes and look at the word to see whether you had it right. Repeat steps one and two until you are sure you know it. Now write the word without looking at it. If you cannot spell the word, go through and repeat all four steps and, five, write the word again. If correct, cover and write again." Now, I don't think the youngsters have to memorize that or anything like that but it might be a good idea, maybe once in awhile, just to go over that and maybe they could tell you just how we learn to spell a new word. "How do we study when we are studying words by ourselves?" I found that in many classrooms that I visited children do well but as soon as they are left alone, sometimes they get stranded and lost. So if you develop how to study a word when they are by themselves, I think it would help during the week. Don't you think so?

P advises against memorizing a formal procedure.

P illustrates why pupils need to acquire skill in studying spelling.

T. Yes. We often do this. This course of study in particular stresses how to study alone.

T agrees and indicates that the course of study stresses how to study spelling.

P. You've gone over it then?

T. Yes. We've done it quite—well, we usually do it in our—sometimes I like to give them variety. Sometimes we just don't go through it. On Tuesdays we do, however.

T indicates she is trying to get variety in the study but on one day stresses the procedure.

P. Well, that's fine. They have it down very well, don't they?

P compliments T on this point.

T. Oh, yes.

P. As you say, you usually go over it and I would continue doing that. It's good that you are doing that. I was wondering, too, do you usually have the children trace the words? By that I mean, suppose you take the word, "cat." You trace the "c" and then the "a" and then the "t."

P advises T to continue the approved procedure.

P asks T if she uses a certain kinesthetic technique.

T. No, I haven't done that.

T replies in the negative.

P. Sometimes it is good in that it gives the child a kinesthetic sense. There are youngsters who learn how to spell a word kinesthetically. That is, they sort of have to feel how the fingers move. So you might try that, especially if you have youngsters who are poor spellers. Sometimes the kinesthetic might help them to print the word or to spell it.

P advises its use because some children need the technique.

T. I've had them write on the board but not trace them.

T reports that pupils write the words on the board.

P. Yes.

T. But we've spelled them on the board.

P. Yes. Well, sometimes you can do it a little quicker because they're all at their seats. Another thing you can do maybe is have them go over the word with their fingers, right in the book, you see. All right. Now here is a question that I would like to have you help me on. I noticed that you stressed vowels quite a bit. I was wondering why. Is that in relation to some other lesson or something?

P points to the economic efficiency of the suggested technique. Advises another aspect to use.

P asks T why she stressed vowels in the observed lesson.

T. Yes. The first week, in two of the groups, vowels were difficult. The top group seemed to get the idea of vowels very early and they'd had quite a bit of experience with them in their workbooks. But the other groups don't have as much experience with them except in the language class and, of course, in the language class we have other things, too. So I try to bring them into spelling because it certainly won't hurt the top group and it gives the others that much more practice picking vowels out of a word and telling whether they are long or short vowels.

T indicates that many children needed the experience.

P. Well, that's fine. I'm glad to hear that. I was just wondering why you are doing it and I noticed that you were sort of correlating the two things. That's good. I'm glad to hear you are doing that. Do they know what consonants are?

P approves T's procedure, also the correlation involved.

T. Oh, yes.

P. That's fine. I have another notation here. I noticed that when the children spelled the word, they didn't pronounce it before they spelled it. Now, sometimes it's good to do that. The reason I mention it is because the more images that the child has—auditory, kinesthetic, and visual—the more likely he's going to get the word or learn it. For instance, here's an example—take the word, "doing." The child could pronounce the word, "doing," and then spell it, "d,o,i,n,g, doing." I notice that sometimes teachers require the youngsters to pronounce the word at the beginning, then spell it, then pronounce it again. I'm sure the reason is so they'll know what word they're spelling and also give them an auditory image.

P points to the importance of including pronunciation as a phase in the study of spelling.

P illustrates a way to include auditory imagery.

T. Well, I'd like to know how to teach them that. I've tried.

T admits having difficulty using the technique.

P. You have?

T. To have them pronounce the word at least before they spell it. I just felt that if they knew that the word was "doing" and said it, they'd almost feel how to spell it. But it just doesn't seem to register for some reason. I don't know why.

P. Well, maybe they're a little bit anxious. I noticed that there was one boy who was pretty anxious to spell the word. He spelled it so fast you had to ask him again how to spell it. He spelled "wet, w,e,t," just so fast that you could hardly hear it. I'm glad that you have that technique in mind and I would just keep working on it. Of course, they're enthusiastic. That's probably a reason. Maybe if you should explain to them why you'd like them to do that—because it will help them in retaining the words. All right. I'm wondering if a word that you think might be misspelled could be stressed. I would say maybe they would have trouble with the words, "other" and "would," and maybe you could spend more time on those two words. By that I mean, maybe you could put them on the board and just tell the children, "Now these are some words that you might miss so we're going to study them just a little harder or a little bit longer so we won't miss them." In other words, you probably know by now what some of the words are they might miss and, therefore, if you sort of feel that they might miss them, then when you come to them, just stress them a little bit more. Now, I was wondering this. Probably you have some poor spellers in there. Don't you?

P suggests causes of T's difficulty.

P advises T to explain to the pupils the importance of pronouncing words being studied.

P suggests more stress on difficult words by using the board.

P makes the transition to a new item, teaching poor spellers. *Considerable stress.*

T. Oh, yes.

P. You probably know who they are. How do they do now on the words? Do they take the same words as the others?

P asks T if the poor spellers study the same words as the other pupils.

T. Yes. Yes, they do.

T replies affirmatively.

P. How do they do? I mean, I imagine they don't do too well or they wouldn't be poor spellers. I'm wondering if maybe they should have all these words. Do you think maybe it might be too much for them? I don't know. I'm asking you.

P gives T an opportunity to think about the assignment as being too heavy for the poor spellers.

T. Well, it seems to me, I work with my poor spellers more than the others and it seems that they would be able to handle those ten words.

T reports working more with the poor spellers than with the other pupils.

P. You think they can?

T. I don't feel that they would.

P. Are there any children in there that you think cannot? I mean, is there any—

T. No. As far as spelling is concerned, I think it's mostly knowing the word, knowing what the word is. If you see it enough times, you will be able to spell it. And I think that the second-grade children should be able to spell ten words.

T thinks the poor spellers should succeed in the program used.

P. Well, do you find that most of them get them?

T. Yes.

P. Now, is there any youngster that misses them all?

T. Yes.

P. Who is that?

P works on the item from a different approach. Asks T to indicate a poor speller not succeeding to learn.

T. Frances.

T names the poorest speller.

P. Frances? She's the girl that came in late. I'm wondering, maybe in her case, if it wouldn't be better if she would learn five words and learn to spell them rather than try to get ten words and miss them all.

P suggests assigning fewer words in order to get better mastery in spelling.

T. Well, the thing that I have found with Frances is that very often she memorizes the words.

P. She does?

T. Yes. When I give tests, I don't give them in order.

P. You kind of change them around?

T. That is, I don't keep the same order of words.

T digresses to a discussion of why certain poor spellers fail to learn.

P. I think that's good.

T. I don't feel that it's a test unless I do.

P approves one of T's dictation techniques.

P. That's right and I know youngsters do that sometimes. I can remember a case where a youngster had learned the words and when the teacher gave him the words, he said, "Oh, you're not giving them to me the way they are in the book." For some reason or other, they seem to do that and they shouldn't. I was just wondering, why don't you try it with Frances? There's a boy failing too. Why don't you try it and just see what happens to them, too. If they happen to get all five right, then maybe they should just do five. I think that would be better for them because if they get five right and build up their confidence a little bit, later on maybe they could take a little bit more. All right. Just one more thing. At the ending of your lesson, I was wondering about this. I think you made the statement, "Now we'll close our books and put them away," or something like that. I'm wondering if a statement could be made about studying the words. Or do you do that sometimes? I mean, at the end of the lesson, do you tell them, "Now maybe tomorrow, if you have extra time, you can study these words," or something like that?

P reverts to his suggestion that the poorest spellers be assigned fewer words to study. Suggests T try the modified program.

P reverts to teaching procedure, suggesting that T end the lesson telling the pupils to spend other time studying the words.

T. Well, I don't usually. They have studied them and they usually do study them in their spare time and they have other work to do, too. I don't let them use the books during the week except when we have a regular spelling lesson but I do let them work on the board. They are at the board every day of the week.

T reports she usually doesn't, explaining her practice.

P. Oh, I see.

T. So the children can study them. They have scratchpaper and the stuff to write with.

P. Well, I was just kind of wondering. I thought maybe I was in a movie and all of a sudden it ended. And I thought, maybe there ought to be a little bit more. I don't know. Maybe I had the wrong feeling there. I was just wondering if maybe you could say, "Now these words are going to be—these words are a little bit harder than those we usually have. Now when we study tomorrow, we'll want to pay very close attention to them," or something like that. In other words, sort of put a nice little finishing touch to it. It was all right the way you did it but I kind of felt as if there had to be some more coming, for some reason or other. Well, the only other notes I have—maybe you might have some questions you would like to ask me. Oh, here is something you might want to look at. It's one of the professional books I have, *Learning the Three R's* by Gertrude Hildreth. Sometimes I find that I have to go over some of the material that I learned in education courses ten years ago, kind of brush up on it. If you want to take this and just look through it when you have time, you may. Maybe you can look over the sections on learning to spell. There are some pretty good things in there.

P suggests how to give specific direction to pupils regarding their further study of the words.

P calls attention to a helpful professional book including sections on spelling and offers it to T. *Passing mention.*

T. Thanks.

P. Getting back to my question, do you have any questions that you would like to ask?

P gives T an opportunity to ask questions for further help.

T. Oh, none in particular.

P. Well, on the whole I thought your lesson was all right. If you carry on like that every day, I'm sure you're doing all right and, of course, we do vary the lesson from day to day and sometimes we forget to do some things. We're all human about that. Well, let's summarize our particular conference. I think, number one, perhaps we ought to read the story at the beginning and develop the meaning and back-

P repeats his opening compliment about the observed lesson.

P summarizes briefly the important items in the conference, touching on five points.

ground of the words at the beginning. I noticed you did that all right but you did it at a different spot. Then there are the words that sound alike and are spelled differently. Maybe those should be shown on the board so they can see them. And then, number three, I would say to be sure that you give them all types of imagery—auditory, visual, and kinesthetic. And maybe put a little finishing touch on the ending of your lesson. I would say that if you carried that out, you would do quite well. Well, Mrs. T., I've enjoyed this and find you are very cooperative in these things.

P expresses appreciation of T's cooperation.

T. Thank you very much.

T expresses thanks.

P. You're welcome.

Establishing Rapport in the Supervisory Conference

George C. Kyte

In the amount of time devoted to each supervisory technique, the individual conference is second only to the supervisory visit to the classroom. Therefore the supervisory conference must be planned and conducted efficiently. If it is to be effective on the teacher and his subsequent teaching, the establishment of rapport between him and a supervisory officer is an essential aspect of their conference. Both must cooperate in it.

To determine how rapport is established at the beginning of such a conference, the writer conducted the research which yielded the findings reported in this article. The investigation is based on 30 sets of tape recordings of (1) a classroom performance observed by a successful supervisory officer, (2) his planned conference with the teacher, and (3) a subsequent and related classroom performance observed by the supervisor. By means of various analytical, evaluative, and statistical techniques, the writer determined (1) the specific content and nature of the initial item in each conference, (2) the amount of stress given the point, (3) the degree of its subsequent effect on teaching, (4) the amount of stress given the second item, (5) the degree of its subsequent effect, (6) the general effect of the conference on subsequent teaching, and (7) the composite effect of all items included in the conference.

I

In the two research studies cited, both the amount of emphasis on an item in a conference and the subsequent effect on teaching were classified according to two respective sets of values. The amount of stress on a supervisory item was rated as having been given major stress, minor stress, or passing mention. The terms applied to the degree of subsequent effect were: considerable, moderate, slight, and negligible. These seven designations are used throughout the present article.

Below are typical examples of initial items in the conferences and the subsequent effects to which they contributed in establishing rapport between the two professional persons involved. The illustrations are quoted verbatim to show the actual communication which occurred. It should be kept in mind that each conversation is spontaneous, is affected by the personnel relationships it is intended to facilitate, and is characteristic of oral expression as contrasted with written communication.

The following introductory item of a conference consisted of specific commendation by the general supervisor who observed a reading lesson in the third grade. This point was given minor stress. It had considerable effect on the subsequent teaching. The second item was given major stress and also had considerable effect. The general effect of the conference and the composite effect of all supervisory items included in it were considerable. The initial rapport was established as follows:

S. That was a very interesting lesson yesterday. I was amazed at the way the children selected important details in the story and quizzed each other so effectively.

T. Yes, they are good at asking each other questions and answering them. We do that a lot in reading. Of course that was our best group that you heard read.

S. They're reading very well.

Another general supervisor put a teacher at ease by asking for information about her fifth grade class and the arithmetic lessons preceding the observed one and by complimenting her about the latter. This conference item was given passing mention. It had considerable specific effect on the subsequent teaching. The next item, a major point, had considerable effect also. In spite of the inclusion of six items in the conference, both its total effect and the composite effect of all items were more than moderate.

S. Hello, Mrs. J–. Do you have a straight Grade V?

T. Yes.

S. Low?

T. Low and high.

S. Oh. Low and high.

T. The majority of them are in the high V.

S. High V. Well, that was a wonderful lesson, I think. I made so many notes that I thought we should go through, ah, go through them. Tell me first what you did last time, to bring me up to date.

T. Last time, on Thursday, we were working on reducing fractions. We'd been working on that for a day. We were doing some fractions and I found on Thursday that several, quite a few of the children, didn't understand this phrase, lowest terms.

S. Yes?

T. The term that I had been using and suddenly I discovered that that was something which I had not tried to explain to them in great detail, which was the reason I started off the lesson today, thinking that I would try to get across the idea of "lowest terms" by bringing out the fact that the number in the denominator was small when you reduced the fraction to the lowest terms.

S. Don't you think they got it today? Don't you feel that the group got it?

T. As a whole? I could point out the individuals that I know got it, I think.

II

One of the very best conferences occurred between a new fifth grade teacher and a rural school supervisor regarding a social studies lesson. The first item, given passing mention, had a moderate specific effect on the subsequent teaching. The next point, a major one, had considerable effect. Both the general effect of the conference and the composite effect of all items were considerable.

S. Well, Miss J–, that was a remarkable lesson you had this morning. It was the first time I'd been in your room so I was especially interested in how the children reacted to the lesson and to you. They were most responsive and enthusiastic, I thought.

T. Yes, it is a very, very interesting class.

S. How many have you?

T. Twenty-four.

S. Twenty-four! With all the time and the little room you have, you couldn't have many more. (Both laugh.)

T. It's wonderful to have a group that small.

S. Yes, it really is. Since it was the first time I'd been in your room, I'm a little unfamiliar with *what* you've been doing. How long have you been working on South America?

A general supervisor started her conference with a teacher regarding her sixth grade science lesson, by enthusing about the children's experiments and acquired knowledge. The initial item, given minor stress, having dealt with successful teaching, could be expected to have additional slight effect noted. The second point, a major one, had considerable subsequent effect. The general rating and the composite effect indicated considerable effectiveness.

S. That was a wonderful demonstration this morning of how much *children* can learn and know about science just by the experimentation they did. Most of the time I was in the dark as to what they were doing. It was completely beyond me but what a fascinating *thing* it was to learn how easily they spoke and how much information they had about the experiments they were conducting. How long have you been working on this?

T. Well, this was completely spontaneous.

S. It sure was!

T. They actually had no formal work at all on electricity. They were shown a movie more or less as an afterthought and I did assign a little bit of reading. We just came across it in our science study, ah, just the mention of magnetism, and from that some of the boys got to experimenting and before I knew it, why they had everybody working with an experiment.

S. Isn't that wonderful–and some interesting ones, too. Which movies did you see that started this off, this interest in electricity?

In discussing dramatic play with the teacher of a first grade, the general supervisor opened the conference with an introductory treatment of the first major point. Later on further elaboration of the item occurred. The subsequent effect of its entire discussion was considerable. The second point, a related major item, also had considerable effect. The same high degree of effectiveness resulted from the whole conference and the items included in it.

S. Thanks a lot, A–, for coming here to the office. I am sorry that you had to wait and be inconvenienced awhile. I had to settle a matter needing immediate attention to avoid some trouble arising.

T. Well that can happen to anybody.

S. There were lots of interruptions today. Well, I think your dramatic play is coming along very well. The children certainly are getting the concepts of sharing and planning and helping in not only what they are talking about but are beginning to understand and expect it. And the nice thing about it is that they seem to be practicing what they preach instead of just talking about it and then going along ignoring it. I guess you have been doing a lot of work on that.

T. Oh yes. Right from the beginning we emphasized these points and every now and then we have to go over them carefully. If we don't, we certainly see the results.

S. Yeah. I think that's a nice idea, the way you voted for your leaders; and it not only was a democratic principle you were following but also gave a good opportunity to get a number situation in there. I didn't hear the answer to your first question when you said, "How many more votes did Kathy get?" Did they answer?

T. Yes, but it was a child in the back of the room.

S. That was very good. Well, they seem to feel quite free to express themselves. They know what they want to do and how to do it. I guess that field trip to S– helped them a lot.

T. Yes, and the bakery trip, too.

The first item in a principal's conference with a teacher regarding a spelling lesson in the second grade, included both general and specific commendations together with a brief discussion about the conference record blank used in the school system. The passing mention had slight specific effect on subsequent teaching but obviously established rapport. The major item after the initial one had considerable effect. Although the general effect of the conference was also considerable the composite effect of the four items included was nearer moderate than considerable.

P. Miss L–, I thought that your spelling lesson on the whole was done quite well. However, there are some parts of it that I think that you probably could do a little better. Of course you know about the blanks we use here for our conferences. You've seen them before, haven't you? In other words the idea back of this is so that we know what we've talked about in the conference. It's down in black and white and you know it and I know it. I'll give you the original and I'll keep the carbon. Well, as I just said I liked the way you handled the lesson. And particularly the way you asked the children to find the small words in their spelling words because I feel that is one way of getting them to be word conscious. Did you do that quite often in your lessons?

T. I usually do it every week.

III

An assistant principal complimented a teacher of the second grade on a number of conditions he observed in the science lesson. This commendation was given minor stress. Because of its complex content it had the slight effect noted in the subsequent teaching. However, in this case of a weak teacher, the second item, a major point, had moderate effectiveness. Also the total subsequent effect of the conference was moderate and therefore relatively good in this instance.

S. I want to talk to you about your class. The youngsters certainly were interested in the pollywogs and I would like to say especially that I noticed the fine rapport that you had with the children. They don't seem to be a bit afraid of the teacher; that's always a good sign, I think. They work well together; they are most co-operative. I noticed how courteous they were when one was speaking. They gave opportunity to that person to speak and then later on they took turns. Then I think in one part of your discussing with them and asking questions, you noticed that to two or three that would like to have talked all the time, you said, "Let's let someone else have a turn." I think from then on there were others taking part. You would be one to notice that perhaps a little bit more because you didn't come back and ask them again and so I had the feeling of how many were interested and how many were taking part. I would say that you handled that part very well. I feel that a lot of good comes out of this type of program. Another thing I'd like to say is that many times a teacher will stop in the middle of things and correct grammatical errors on the part of children when they made mistakes and I was glad to see that you didn't do that because you kept their interest going by the questions they were asking–and I think that was fine. Sometimes youngsters are afraid to speak up because the teacher said, "What was that?" saying it again and again. Were you surprised at the questions that the children were asking you?

For the opening item of a conference with a teacher regarding a reading lesson in his sixth grade, the superintendent of schools put minor stress on his discussion of the educational environment he observed. Although only slight subsequent effect could and did result from his commendations, his expressed appreciation established the desired rapport. His second item, a major one on an important phase of teaching reading, had considerable subsequent effect. In spite of the inclusion of seven items in the conference, its effectiveness was between moderate and considerable.

S. Hello, J–. I enjoyed my visit very much yesterday. I liked your classroom. You had it well arranged. The environment and setting looked very nice. I liked the way you displayed the various kinds of work that the youngsters are doing, as well as the skills–pointing out the skill subjects and the work you are doing in them. And your youngsters were very attentive. They seemed to enjoy the activity, which is a good sign. I always feel that as a person walks into a room and sees the class right on their toes and following everything the instructor does, they are getting a lot out of it.

When a supervisor confers with a very superior teacher regarding an excellent lesson, the total subsequent effect may be difficult to determine. This condition is to be expected because the conference deals primarily with the improvable good and further small improvement is in reality considerable. The following illustration indicated some discernible results. The supervisor's frank acknowledgement of the teacher's ability and his compliments on her skill constituted the opening item of the conference regarding a reading lesson in the first grade. Although this point was given only passing mention, it had moderate subsequent effect on teaching. The second item, a major point, and the total conference had considerable effect. The composite effect of all items was slight, partly because seven items given minor or less stress were briefly discussed in addition to the two major items.

S. I want you to be sure that I knew that was not a demonstration lesson because it looked so good. It was an excellent lesson, just as if it were. You didn't know I was coming in, did you?

T. No. No I didn't, Miss R–.

S. While I was here, I just knew that I would find a nice lesson in your class. I was here working with Mrs. T–. It was excellent. I wish you could have seen the expressions on the faces of the youngsters and their interest. They are getting great satisfaction out of their first reading.

T. That's because I think they expect to.

S. Yes and they are just all low first graders, aren't they?

T. Yes, low first.

S. Wonderful.

IV

In opening the conference with a teacher regarding her arithmetic lesson in the fourth grade, the superintendent frankly acknowledged the adverse classroom conditions and complimented her on her resourcefulness in meeting them. His evident understanding of her problems and his appreciation of her efforts in solving them served to establish the desired rapport. Consequently the minor item had considerable effect on the teaching. The second point, given somewhat less than major stress, had moderate subsequent effect. The total conference tended to have considerable effect.

S. Mrs. C–, I want to come in and talk about the lesson I observed yesterday. I enjoyed your class very much and I think you've got a nice group of youngsters for a small and very inconvenient room. I think you've done a wonderful job in decorating and making it attractive and your youngsters, I thought, were alert to the situation, which is a fine tribute to you. Do you find the youngsters are of a wide range?

T. Yes the range is wide, particularly in that one group, in arithmetic.

S. I think so too. Still yours is a very pleasant atmosphere.

The above examples illustrate the marked tendency of the supervisory officers to plan their conferences so that the first item serves to establish rapport. As such it tends to set the pattern for the manner in which the discussion then proceeds. Ordinarily the first point is related to some aspect of the observed lesson. Commonly it conveys to the teacher the supervisor's genuine interest in the children and the teacher. Commendation is given from the viewpoint of approving good practices observed. Because the establishment of rapport is the principal purpose of the initial item, it generally receives minor stress or passing mention. Its specific effect on subsequent teaching may even be very slight but if it establishes the professional and cordial relations between the two professional persons, it contributes to the efficacy of the conference and the consequent effectiveness of subsequent teaching. Hence both parties must endeavor to establish the necessary rapport which will result in a constructive conference.

Research on Teacher Evaluation

N. A. Fattu

Studies on teacher effectiveness have been summarized and reviewed periodically since 1926. While empirical study of teacher effectiveness may be said to have begun about 1891, it was not until the period 1913-17 that some momentum was attained. This momentum continued for almost twenty years. The advent of Gestalt psychology and the organismic point of view was reflected by a significant decrease in the number of studies based upon empirical data. Tomlinson has told the story of this movement in detail.[1]

Two major reviews of the literature on teacher effectiveness are those by Domas and Tiedeman[2] and by Morsh and Wilder.[3] These summaries by no means list all of the publications on teacher effectiveness. They exclude the vast majority of the

[1] Tomlinson, L. R. "Pioneer Studies in the Evaluation of Teaching." *Educational Research Bulletin* 34: 63-71; March 1955.

Tomlinson, L. R. "Recent Studies in the Evaluation of Teaching." *Educational Research Bulletin* 34: 172-86; October 1955.

[2] Domas, S. J., and Tiedeman, D. V. "Teacher Competence: An Annotated Bibliography." *Journal of Experimental Education* 19: 101-218; December 1950.

[3] Morsh, J. E., and Wilder, E. W. *Identifying the Effective Instructor: A Review of Quantitative Studies, 1900-52.* Research Bulletin No. AFPTRC-TR-54-44. San Antonio, Texas: USAF Personnel and Training Center, 1954. 151 pp.

publications which were not empirical in some way. These two summaries cover the literature on quantitative studies up to 1952.

Other reviews and summaries that should be read by anyone seriously interested in further exploration of the field are the Mitzel and Gross review of the pupil growth criterion;[4] the series of reviews by Barr over a period of more than thirty years, of which only those in the period 1940-58 are indicated here;[5] the annotated bibliography by Castetter and others;[6] the Leiderman and others summary of teacher behavior studies;[7] the Levin and others comments on the questions asked about, and the reasons for, unproductive studies;[8] the McCall,[9] Mitzel,[10] Remmers and others[11] studies; the American Educational Research Association's *Review of Educational Research* triennial summaries; the Ryans,[12] Tiedeman and Cogan,[13] and Watters[14] studies.

No one seriously interested in teacher evaluation can afford to neglect to read—diligently and frequently—the *Handbook of Research on Teaching.*[15] This book began in 1950 with the appointment of a Committee on the Criteria of Teacher Effectiveness by the American Educational Research Association. In 1956, the Committee, then called the Committee on Teacher Effectiveness, proposed the development of the handbook. In 1957, N. L. Gage, chairman of the Committee,

[4]Mitzel, H. E., and Gross, C. F. *A Critical Review of the Development of Pupil Growth Criteria in Studies of Teacher Effectiveness.* Research Series No. 31. New York: Office of Research and Evaluation, Division of Teacher Education, Board of Higher Education of the City of New York, 1956. 28 pp.

[5]Barr, A. S. and Jones, R. E. "The Measurement and Prediction of Teaching Efficiency." *Review of Educational Research* 28: 256-64; June 1958.

[6]Castetter, D. D.; Standlee, L. S.; and Fattu, N. A.*Teacher Effectiveness: An Annotated Bibliography.* Bulletin of the Institute of Educational Research, Vol. 1, No. 1. Bloomington: Indiana University, 1954.

[7]Leiderman, G. F.; Hilton, T. L.; and Levin, H. "Studies of Teachers' Behavior: A Summary Report." *The Journal of Teacher Education* 8: 433-37; December 1957.

[8]Levin, H.; Hilton, T. L.; and Leiderman, G. F. "Studies of Teacher Behavior." *Journal of Experimental Education* 26: 81-91; September 1957.

[9]McCall, W. A. *Measurement of Teacher Merit.* Publication No. 284. Raleigh, N.C.; State Superintendent of Public Instruction, 1952. 40 pp.

[10]Mitzel, H. E. "Teacher Effectiveness." *Encyclopedia of Educational Research.* Third Edition. (Edited by Chester W. Harris.) New York: Macmillan Co., 1960. pp. 1481-85.

[11]Remmers, H. H., and others. "Report of the Committee on the Criteria of Teacher Effectiveness."*Review of Educational Research 22:* 238-63; June 1952.

Remmers, H. H., and others. "Second Report of the Committee on Criteria of Teacher Effectiveness." *Journal of Educational Research* 46: 641-58; May 1953.

[12]Ryans, D. G. *Characteristics of Teachers.* Washington, D. C.: American Council on Education, 1960. 416 pp.

Ryans, D. G. "Prediction of Teacher Effectiveness." *Encyclopedia of Educational Research.* Third edition. (Edited by Chester W. Harris.) New York: Macmillan Co., 1960. pp. 1486-91.

[13]Tiedeman, D. V., and Cogan, M. "New Horizons in Educational Research." *Phi Delta Kappan* 39:286-91; March 1958.

[14]Watters, W. A. "Annotated Bibliography of Publications Related to Teacher Evaluation." *Journal of Experimental Education* 22: 351-67; June 1954.

[15]Gage, N. L., editor. *Handbook of Research on Teachings.* A project of the American Educational Research Association, NEA.) Chicago: Randy McNally, 1963. 1218 pp.

was named editor. Most relevant to the present discussion are segments of Parts II, III, and IV in the *Handbook.* In Part II on *Methodologies in Research on Teaching,* the following chapters may be most useful to elementary school principals and supervisors: chapter 6, "Measuring Classroom Behavior by Systematic Observation" by Donald Medley and Harold Mitzel; chapter 7, "Rating Methods in Research on Teaching" by H. H. Remmers; chapter 8, "Testing Cognitive Ability and Achievement" by Benjamin S. Bloom; and chapter 9, "Measuring Noncognitive Variables in Research on Teaching" by G. C. Stern. In Part III on *Major Variables and Areas of Research on Teaching,* chapter 11, "The Teacher's Personality and Characteristics" by J. W. Getzels and P. S. Jackson is recommended. Part IV, *Reseach on Teaching Various Grade Levels and Subject Matters,* is addressed largely to high school and college people. Elementary school principals and supervisors would find chapter 15, "Research on Teaching in the Nursery School" by Pauline Sears and Edith Dowley, and chapter 16, "Research on Reading" by David Russell and Henry Fea, most useful.

Obviously, what research says about teacher effectiveness cannot be summarized in a few words. One who wishes to understand the findings should consult the sources indicated, especially the *Handbook of Research on Teaching.*

What is Effectiveness?

A difficult problem in the study of teacher effectiveness has been whether to assume that effectiveness is a statement about an attribute of the teacher in a particular teaching situation or to assume that it is a statement about the results that come out of a teaching situation.

It appears, as indicated by Barr, that most studies of teacher effectiveness are searching for a property of the teacher. As indicated by Remmers, the search has not been successful. But the assumption on which this search is based has not been tested. To do so would require a longitudinal study with repeated measurement of the same teacher on the same criteria under a wide range of teaching conditions. Such a study has not been conducted.

In examining the assumption that effectiveness is an attribute of the teacher, one should recognize that it lies along a continuum of assumptions. At one end is the assumption that effectiveness is determined almost wholly by the teacher, that it is one of his attributes, and that it depends very little on the variables within the situation. As the other end of the continuum is the assumption that effectiveness is almost wholly determined by the particular variables operating in the situation where teaching occurs.

One is free to choose his assumption anywhere along the continuum, but in choosing he implicitly makes a hypothesis about the adaptability of teachers to teaching situations. If he assumes that effectiveness depends on the particular variables operating in a situation in which a teacher teaches, he is saying that teachers simply react without close regard to the appropriateness of that behavior with respect to the variables in the situation. If a teacher happens to react properly for a particular set of conditions, then he is effective.

Or if one proceeds on the assumption that effectiveness is almost wholly attributable to the teacher, he claims that teachers are adaptive in their teaching behavior so that they react with a close regard to its appropriateness. He states that teachers are capable of fine discriminations in their environment and have available the responses appropriate to those discriminations.

Apparently a choice of one assumption or the other is not desirable, because the very act of choosing makes it necessary to exclude one of the assumptions. There is no reason to think that effectiveness depends entirely on variables operating in the situation or that it necessarily depends on the teacher. Perhaps both assumptions are valid, depending on differences among teachers. Some teachers are no doubt capable of producing desirable pupil behaviors in a wide variety of teaching situations. The behavior they display, of course, depends on the situation, but this is not the point. The point is that their behavior is appropriate to that situation and that desirable pupil behaviors result because it is appropriate. These teachers do not have some sort of magical property called "effectiveness," but they are characterized by adaptability to teaching situations, or they have developed a high level of skill in dealing with the problems which arise in the course of their professional work.

There are other teachers who no doubt are capable of producing desirable pupil behaviors under more limited teaching conditions. These teachers are effective within the range of teaching situations for which their responses are appropriate.

Finally, there are no doubt teachers whose patterns of teaching behavior are so poorly developed that they can succeed in only a very few teaching situations or not at all.

In other words, effectiveness has several meanings, and no harm is done in using the term if one is clear as to which meaning is intended.

Teacher Characteristics

The purpose of teacher characteristics studies is to discover which traits or combinations of traits are closely enough associated with teacher competence to permit prediction of such competency. Among these traits are intelligence, knowledge of subject matter, scholarship, educational background, age and experience, professional knowledge, cultural background, socio-economic background, teaching attitude and interest, and voice and speech characteristics.

Intelligence and success. Whether or not intelligence is an important variable in the success of the instructor apparently depends upon the situation. In general, there appears to be only a slight relationship between intelligence and *rated* success of an instructor. Correlation coefficients for high school teachers tend to be somewhat higher and somewhat less variable than those reported for elementary teachers. For all practical purposes, however, this variable appears to be of little value as a *single* predictor of rated instructor competence.

This does not mean that teachers do not need to be intelligent. Rather, those who teach have been selected on the basis of intelligence, and within the range of scores characteristic of teachers, differences in intelligence have not been shown to be crucial. In more refined research where variables are more carefully controlled, intelligence test scores are more closely related to teacher performance.

Knowledge of subject matter and success. A common misconception is that knowledge of subject matter is a major factor in teaching performance. Except for occasional studies in mathematics, chemistry, and physics, research findings report little relationship. Again, whether or not knowledge of subject matter is related to instructor competence seems to be a function of the particular teaching situation and is generally a complex interaction rather than a simple variable.

Professional knowledge and success. It appears that a teacher's rated effectiveness at first increases rather rapidly with experience and then levels off at five years or beyond. The teacher may show little change in rated performance for the next 15 or 20 years, after which, as in most occupations, there tends to be a slow decline.

Cultural background and success. There is no substantial evidence that cultural background is significantly related to teaching effectiveness. Studies reviewed indicate the relation of Cooperative General Culture Test scores to instructor effectiveness is congruent with results reported for other subject-matter areas.

Socio-economic status and success. The relationship of socio-economic status (as measured by such devices as the Sims Socio-Economic Scales) to criteria of instructor effectiveness is low. The research suggests, however, that those from higher groups usually have greater probabilities of success in life than those less fortunate.

Sex and success. No particular differences have been shown when the relative effectiveness of men and women teachers has been compared. (See pp. 22-23 for Ryans' findings on this point.)

Marital status and success. Despite some prejudice to the contrary, there appears to be no evidence that married teachers are in any way inferior to single teachers.

Teaching aptitude and success. Results obtained from measures designed to predict teaching ability show great disparity. Data thus far available either fail to establish the existence of any specified aptitude for teaching with any degree of certainty or indicate the tests used were inappropriate to its measurement.

Teaching attitude and success. Attitude toward teachers and teaching as indicated by the Yeager Scale, which was devised for its measurement, seems to bear a small but positive relationship to teacher success measured in terms of pupil gains.

Job interest and success. In most of the studies reviewed, interest in teaching was measured by interest test scores which indicated similarity between the interests of teachers and the interests of persons undergoing the test. Correlations resulting from the use of several standard interest tests either cluster around zero or are so inconsistent as to render such tests of doubtful value as predictors of teaching success. The common factors that were found through factor analyses to underlie the reasons given for choosing the teaching profession are perhaps provocative of further research, but are based on too few cases to justify any clear-cut interpretation.

Voice-speech and success. On the basis of studies reviewed, it appears that the quality of the teacher's voice is not considered very important by school administrators, teachers, or students. In one study, however, certain speech factors were found to be correlated significantly with student gains and with effectiveness ratings of supervisors. The intercorrelations of the speech factors, however, were so high that general speech ability based on a single factor is probably as useful as a composite of judgments based on several speech factors.

Special abilities and success. Such instructor factors as empathy, professional maturity, general knowledge, mental ability, and social adjustment have been identified through factor analyses by various investigators. The statistical analyses so far reported, however, suffer from inadequacies of criteria, testing instruments, or number of cases.

Teacher failure. In most of the studies of unsuccessful teachers, it has been found that poor maintenance of discipline and lack of cooperation tend to be the chief causes of failure. Health, educational background, preparation, age, and knowledge of subject matter, on the other hand, appear to be relatively unimportant factors in terms of teacher failure.

The attempts made to identify characteristics of successful and unsuccessful instructors by making lists of traits based on opinion appear largely sterile in terms of usability for evaluation or selective purposes.

Ryans' Study of Teacher Characteristics

Perhaps the most extensive study of teacher characteristics ever carried out is that by Ryans.[16] More than a hundred separate research projects were conducted. About 1,700 schools, involving 450 school systems and 6,000 teachers, took part.

Factor analyses of data revealed three patterns of teacher behavior:

Pattern X_0—warm, understanding, friendly vs. aloof, egocentric, restricted teacher behavior. Pattern Y_0—responsible, businesslike, systematic vs. evading, unplanned, slipshod teacher behavior. Pattern Z_0—stimulating, imaginative, surgent vs. dull, routine teacher behavior.

Among elementary school teachers, X_0, Y_0, Z_0 patterns were positively correlated and each seemed to be correlated with pupil behavior in the teachers' classes. X_0, Y_0, Z_0 patterns for married elementary teachers tended to be higher than for single elementary teachers. Patterns did not vary significantly with Minnesota Multiphasic Personality Inventory scores or the Allport-Vernon-Lindzey Study of Values.

Other results were: 1) Educational views of secondary teachers appeared to be more traditional—those of elementary were more permissive; 2) Attitudes of elementary teachers toward pupils, administrators, fellow teachers, and non-administrative personnel were distinctly more favorable than were those of secondary teachers; 3) Male teachers, both at the elementary and secondary school levels, appeared substantially more stable emotionally than female; 4) Observer assessment of pupil behavior in the classroom did not seem to be related to teachers' attitudes; 5) Verbal understanding scores (on vocabulary and verbal analogy problems) of secondary teachers were significantly higher than those of elementary teachers.

[16]Ryans, D. G. *Characteristics of Teachers.* Washington, D. C.: American Council on Education, 1960. 416 pp.

Much of the study was devoted to determination of correlates of teacher classroom behavior. A 300 item multiple-choice and checklist self-report inventory of personal preferences, self-judgments, activities, and biographical data-called the Teacher Characteristics Schedule—was developed. Numerous item analyses were done using observer assessments and direct-response scales as criteria. Scoring keys were developed for a large number of teacher groups.

Comparing characteristics of teachers gave the following results:

- Elementary school married teachers attained more favorable scores on these variables.
- Teachers from large universities achieved higher scores on stimulating classroom behavior and child-centered views.
- Teachers who had been outstanding students scored higher than other groups on most scales. The only exception dealt with emotional stability.
- Teachers who claimed they entered teaching because they liked school and because of its social service usually scored higher on most of the characteristics. Teachers who entered the profession because they were advised to do so or because of favorable prospects for advancement generally scored lower.
- Teachers who reported childhood activities as "reading to children" or "playing school," etc., had higher scores on "friendly, responsible, stimulating" classroom behavior, favorable attitudes toward pupils, and democratic classroom procedures than others.
- Scores of the older teachers (age 55 and over) were not as favorable as those of younger teachers except on warm, understanding, friendly behavior and tradition centered behavior. Trends for experience were like those for age.
- At the elementary school level, men and women teachers differed in only four of the personal-social characteristics studied. Men were less responsible and businesslike in classroom behavior and more favorable toward democratic classroom practices, more inclined toward permissive, child-centered educational viewpoints, and more stable emotionally.
- Teachers from larger schools and larger communities scored substantially higher than others on friendly, stimulating classroom behavior, favorable attitudes toward administrators, verbal understanding, and emotional stability. As a rule, teachers from smaller communities scored lower than those from larger communities, except for teachers from the largest cities (1,000,000 and over) who scored about as low as teachers from very small communities.

Teachers were classified as "high" (at least a standard deviation above the mean) and "low' (at least a standard deviation below the mean) on characteristics. Results are summarized by Ryans as follows:

> There was a general tendency for high teachers to: be extremely generous in appraisals of behavior and motives of other persons; possess strong interest in reading and literary affairs; be interested in music, painting, and the arts in general; participate in social groups; enjoy pupil relationships; prefer non-directive (permissive) classroom procedures; manifest superior verbal intelligence; and be superior with respect to emotional adjustment. On the other hand, low teachers tended generally to: be restrictive and critical in their appraisals of

> other persons; prefer activities which did not involve close personal contacts; express less favorable opinions of pupils; manifest less higher verbal intelligence; show less satisfactory emotional adjustment; and represent older age groups. (pp. 397-98).

The Teacher Characteristics Study was an impressive enterprise, but it is obvious that the author's cautions relative to conclusions are justified.

Personality Patterns

For many years, research on personality characteristics was conducted through opinion studies. On the whole, such studies failed to obtain anything more than agreement on a few general trait designations, such as "interested" and "sympathetic." These provided little insight or help; Guba and Getzels in 1955 commented, "Despite a large number of investigations, relatively little more is known now than in 1900."[17]

Recently, emphasis has shifted to greater use of psychological theory and carefully planned measurement devices. Cook and others developed the Minnesota Teacher Attitude Inventory. Studies by Gage and Cronbach (1955)[18] and Ryans (1960)[19] are recommended for reading. Chapter 11 of the *Handbook of Research on Teaching* summarizes a good deal of the literature.

Results obtained with personality tests of teachers have shown wide variation when correlated with other measures. However, until carefully controlled, well-designed studies employing adequate numbers of instructors have been made, the problem of determining the personality patterns of effective teachers must still remain unsolved.

Assessing Teacher Behavior

Teacher behavior in the classroom obviously would seem to be the most useful source of data on teacher effectiveness, since it would appear to have an authentic on-the-job performance type of validity. Again, the problem is to obtain accurate and comprehensive measures. These measures usually consist of some kind of ranking or rating procedure.

Rating devices. Rating scales are the most frequently used devices for assessing teacher behavior. In practice there is usually no clear delineation regarding what relevant behavior is. Rather, an attempt is made to use rating as a widespread net in the hope of catching some of the unsuspected variables. Rating scales and observation scales exhibit the characteristic features of common sense formulations—vagueness of definition, lack of specificity regarding the range of applicabil-

[17] Guba, E. G., and Getzels, J. W. "Personality and Teacher Effectiveness: A Problem in Theoretical Research." *The Journal of Educational Psychology* 46: 330-44; October 1955.

[18] Gage, N. L., and Cronbach, L. J. "Conceptual and Methodological Problems in Interpersonal Perception." *Psychological Review* 62: 411-22; 1955.

[19] Ryans, D. G. "Prediction of Teacher Effectiveness." *Encyclopedia of Educational Research.* Third edition. (Edited by Chester W. Harris.) New York: Macmillan Co., 1960. pp. 1486-91.

ity, and absence of means of determining the invariant rather than the merely immediate and specific features.

In a sense, the use of rating scales to measure behavioral features tends to emphasize the subjectivity that characterizes broad definitions of behavior, interpretation or inference of goals from actions. Add the "natural" variability among raters, and the residue that is free of experimental error and errors of measurement becomes relatively small.

Surveys of appointment blanks and rating scales in use have failed to provide means for identifying the significant items to be used in setting up rating devices for teacher effectiveness. Frequently mentioned qualities on existing teacher appointment blanks are disciplinary ability, teaching ability, scholarship, and personality. There is no general agreement about what constitute the essential characteristics of a competent teacher. Similarly, items on rating scales tend to be subjective, undefined, and varied; there is little consistency as to what traits a supervisor might be expected to observe and evaluate. Chapter 7 of the *Handbook* contains a comprehensive summary of rating methods.

Administrative ratings. Over-all administrative opinion constitutes the most widely used single measure of teacher competence. Available studies have shown in general that teachers can be reliably rated by administrative and supervisory personnel (usually with correlations of .70 or above). For the most part, administrative ratings do not produce very high correlations with measures of student gain. Intercorrelations of rated traits or categories indicate that traits that are more objectively observable, or are more independent of opinion, tend to be less prone to logical error or halo effect than those traits that are more intangible and more subjectively estimated. Findings suggest that ratings made by a single person are apt to be contaminated by halo effects and that, in many such instances, a single rating of over-all effectiveness is useful only when based on a composite of a number of ratings of separate traits.

Peer ratings. Peer ratings are little used. For administrative purposes they are probably not very useful since teachers tend to have certain misgivings about expressing judgment on fellow teachers. As a rule, ranks probably give better results than ratings. Studies have shown substantial agreement between supervisors and fellow teachers in ratings assigned to teachers. As in the case of administrative ratings, substantial correlation is found among ratings given different traits by the same peer raters. In other words, halo effects influence peer ratings just as they do administrative ratings.

Student ratings. When student ratings are compared with other measures of teacher effectiveness, varying results are found, depending in part upon the criteria employed. Considerable halo effect is usually noted when students rate their instructors on several traits. Results suggest that if the instructor favors the brighter students, he tends to be approved by them and a positive correlation between student ratings and grades results. If he teaches for the weaker students, he is not approved by the brighter students and a negative coefficient tends to be obtained. By and large, such factors as size of class, sex of students, age or maturity of students, and intelligence or mental age of students seem to have little bearing on student ratings. Research has been too sporadic and results too diverse to generalize about the influence of other factors on student ratings.

Self-ratings. Instructors tend to overrate themselves. Self-ratings show negligible relationships with administrative ratings, student ratings, or measures of student gains. On the basis of the few available studies of self-ratings of instructors, the obvious, undisguised self-rating technique appears to offer little encouragement for evaluative or research purposes.

Systematic observation. Systematic observation techniques to determine differences in performance of effective and ineffective teachers were largely neglected until rather recently.[20] Most of the observations seem to depend upon the subjective judgment of the observer. In the case of planned observational recording, the reliability compares favorably with other methods of teacher evaluation. The most general criterion of validity of observation appears to be face validity. No single, specific, observable teacher act has been found whose frequency, or per cent of occurrence, is invariable and significantly correlated with student achievement. There seems to be a suggestion, however, that questions based on student interest and experience rather than on assigned subject matter, the extent to which the instructor challenges students to support ideas, and the amount of spontaneous student discussion are related to student gains. Also, there seem to be no optimal time expenditures for particular class activities; a good teacher could apparently function successfully within a wide range of time distributions.

Critical incident technique. The critical incident technique described by Flanagan (1949) has been used in an attempt to describe teacher behavior. Observers and teachers reported anecdotal incidents in which they thought teachers were particularly effective or ineffective. Incidents were then classified in an attempt to isolate patterns. While many useful incidents were obtained. It has been difficult to put them into significant categories.

Other approaches. Students have been asked to describe their best and poorest teachers; parents and teachers have been asked to recall the behavior of teachers they remembered as being effective; leaders in education have been asked to describe what they regarded as effective and ineffective behavior. These approaches have not been rewarding. The time and effort could better be spent in more precise definition, observation, and analysis of the network of relationships among teacher behaviors, instructional goals, and pupil characteristics.

Pupil Growth and Achievement

Pupil growth and achievement in relation to teacher performance has been

[20]Medley, D. M., and Mitzel, H. E. "Measuring Classroom Behavior by Systematic Observation." *Handbook of Research on Teaching.* (Edited by N. L. Gage.) Chicago: Rand McNally, 1963. pp. 247-328.

reviewed by Ackerman,[21] McCall,[22] Medley and Mitzel,[23] Mitzel and Gross,[24] Morsh and others,[25] Taylor,[26] and Webb and Bowers.[27] If the purpose of teaching is to attain objectives by bringing about desired changes in pupils, the obvious measure of teacher effectiveness is the extent to which the teacher actually produces such changes. Unfortunately, some difficulties intrude upon this happy prospect: 1) It is difficult to measure pupil growth, and 2) it is difficult to determine precisely how much change can be attributed to a particular teacher. It is not surprising that the number of student gain studies is rather low. The great discrepancies in findings of the studies using student gains criteria emphasize the complexity of their relation to instructor performance.

The central difficulty is establishing sufficient experimental controls to show that certain changes in pupil behavior occur if, and only if, these changes are preceded by actions of a teacher.

To attain precise controls is probably impossible, although various statistical controls including matched groups, analysis of covariance, and various randomized and similar designs serve as approximations. A further difficulty in the matter of demonstrating that particular pupil behaviors are associated with actions of a particular teacher lies in the amount of confidence that can be placed in the criterion measure of pupil behavior. For instance: the immediate goal of a teacher may be to get the pupils to perform long division problems of a given level of difficulty. If the pupils learn to do such problems, one has some confidence that the teacher has achieved the goal; but if at a later time the pupils have difficulty in learning to do more difficult problems in division, or have difficulty in learning to use division in algebra, or can't use division to solve elementary science problems, confidence in the criterion is not as firm.

At this point, an interesting paradox appears. As one moves from the more immediate and more convenient criteria for assessing pupil achievement to those that are more distant but more valid, the pupil behavior attributable to a given teacher becomes increasingly confounded with the effect produced by other

[21] Ackerman, W. I. "Teacher Competence and Pupil Change." *Harvard Educational Review* 24: 273-89; Fall 1954.

[22] McCall, W. A. *Measurement of Teacher Merit.* Publication No. 284. Raleigh, N. C.: State Superintendent of Public Instruction, 1952. 40 pp.

[23] Medley, D. M., and Mitzel, H. E. "Pupil Growth in Reading—An Index of Effective Teaching." *The Journal of Educational Psychology* 48: 227-39; April 1957.

[24] Mitzel and Gross, *op. cit.*

[25] Morsh, J. E.; Burgess, G. G.; and Smith, P. N. "Student Achievement as a Measure of Instructor Effectiveness." *The Journal of Educational Psychology.* 47: 79-88; February 1956.

[26] Taylor, H. R. "Teacher Influence on Class Achievement: A Study of the Relationship of Estimated Teaching Ability to Pupil Achievement in Arithmetic." *Genetic Psychology Monographs* 7: 81-175; 1930.

[27] Webb, W. B., and Bowers, N. D. *Student Performance as a Measure of Instructional Proficiency.* Research Project No. NM001077-01-06. Washington, D. C.: U. S. Naval School of Aviation Medicine, 1957. 7 pp. "The Utilization of Student Learning as a Criterion of Instructor Effectiveness." *Journal of Educational Research* 51: 17-23; September 1957.

teachers. Thus, as one's confidence in the criteria of effectiveness increases, the likelihood of being able to attribute it to any one teacher correspondingly decreases. A reason for this is not hard to see. The more distant criteria depend on the transfer of learning. Transfer depends both on initial learning and on what is done later. One of the criteria for how well a fourth-grade teacher teaches arithmetic depends on how well his students learn fifth-grade arithmetic, while one of the criteria of how well a fifth-grade teacher teaches arithmetic is the extent to which he can create situations to which the pupils coming from the fourth grade can transfer their knowledge. The fourth-grade and fifth-grade teachers here become interacting units, and to which of them the arithmetic behavior at the end of the fifth grade is to be attributed is a very interesting problem in logical and statistical analysis.

The problem of inter-teacher influence is further complicated by the other influences that shape pupil growth: home, community, clubs, communication media, books, magazines, and libraries, to name a few. Considering the theoretical importance of pupil gain criteria for the assessment of teacher effectiveness, it is surprising that so few studies have used this measure. Barr's 1948 summary lists only 19 investigations that could possibly be said to use student gain as a criterion. In 1956, Mitzel and Gross found only 20 studies which had used student gain as a criterion. These studies exhibited conflicting results.

The criterion has been used most effectively by Morsh, Burgess, and Smith (1956). However, it should be indicated that the objectives of concern were strictly limited to subject-matter achievement in an Air Force technical specialty school. Mastery involved simply rote learning rather than cultivation of higher mental processes. In this restricted case, clear demonstration of pupil gains in relation to teacher activity was possible.

The Administrator and Teacher Effectiveness Research

So far we have considered only the point of view of researchers. When talking about teacher effectiveness, it is equally important to consider the concerns of teachers and administrators.

Within the arena of practical affairs, concern about teacher effectiveness is frequent. By virtue of local control, it is the responsibility of school officials to obtain an estimate of teacher effectiveness in order that decisions on retention, promotion, salary, or helping teachers to improve may be made.

School officials cannot make a decision as to how well a particular teacher performs without defining, however loosely, the teacher's job. When the job is loosely defined, school officials may base their evaluations on how well they like the teacher; or the number of complaints or commendations received about the teacher from parents; or the extent to which the teacher disrupts or facilitates smooth operation of school machinery.

At a slightly more organized level, administrative officials may work with the school board, the teachers, and the community in attempting to determine what the functions of a teacher in the local schools should be. Decisions of such groups may range from so rigidly specifying the functions and activities that little autonomy is left to the teacher, to stating functions so vaguely that virtually all is left to the judgment of the teacher. Whatever the position of the group, the definitions refer to teacher function only within a limited geographical area.

Under local control, teacher function is free to vary from school system to school system. The job of the teacher thus varies with its location. Given that the functions a teacher should perform are well defined within a particular school system, one must consider the further complication that while first-grade teachers and senior high school teachers perform the same general functions, their specific responsibilities are quite different. Thus the teacher's job also varies with the grade.

Because most administrators are responsible to a local board of education, they can assess teacher performance by reference to locally defined functions. Generally speaking, all evaluations can be categorized as either formal or informal. Within this context, three techniques for local appraisal of teacher performance are typically used—ratings, observations, or student gains measured by standardized tests.

Ratings may consist of an over-all estimate of teacher effectiveness or of separate evaluations of specific teacher behaviors or traits. Self-ratings may be used, or ratings may be determined by the teacher's peers, by students, or by administrative personnel.

Ratings may involve ranking per cent of efficiency, indication of the level of a trait, forced choice, or any of the devices indicated in the *Handbook of Research on Teaching.*

Observation of teachers in the classroom may be used by local school officials; in practice, this technique is seldom the only one used for judgments of teacher effectiveness, and it is rarely used in an objective, scientific fashion.

Student gain, as measured by standardized tests, may be used appropriately to evaluate teacher effectiveness only if extensive controls and adjustments are made to recognize and compensate for factors other than teacher influence.

From the standpoint of the local school administrator, the extent to which any or all of these procedures are used depends on how much and what kind of evidence is desired in making decisions about local school personnel.

If one wants only to make a decision, ratings may be sufficient. If one wants to provide for inservice training and upgrading, ratings are not sufficient. It then becomes necessary to search for more explicit connections between attainment of objectives, teacher behaviors, characteristics and education. The process of joint inquiry, involving both the teachers and administrators, has much to recommend it. Administrators and teachers can help each other clarify their thinking and knowledge, and in the process both gain something in professional fulfillment.

Evaluation of Teaching Competence

Administrative Practice

In a recent survey of teacher evaluation procedures in school systems enrolling 16,000 or more pupils, the Educational Research Service found that only 17 of the 235 responding systems have not established formal procedures for evaluating teachers. Of the 213 systems submitting usable replies, 125 reported that teachers were involved in formulating the evaluation procedures currently in use. Sixty percent of the 213 systems said that their procedures had been revised within the past two years.

Frequency of Evaluations

About 80 percent of the participating systems evaluate probationary teachers more often than continuing teachers. Of the 199 systems which have a probationary period for teachers, 90 conduct evaluations twice a year in the probationary status, and 80 others have annual evaluations for probationers.

Among the 213 systems, 29 do not evaluate teachers once they reach permanent status, and 33 evaluate them only when requested by the teacher or principal or when a change of assignment or performance occurs. More than one-half of the systems with a regular schedule of evaluations for permanent teachers make evaluations an annual occurrence.

Evaluators

In over one-half of the systems the principal is the sole person to evaluate teachers. In other systems he is assisted in his preparation of the form by his assistant principal, supervisor, or department heads; and in a few other systems, the principal and at least one other person each prepare an evaluation form for each teacher.

Unique is the situation in several Michigan school districts. Probationary teachers are evaluated both by their principals and by their peers in the form of a Building Tenure Committee (several tenure teachers appointed by the principal) and a tenure coach (a tenure teacher assigned by the principal to assist the beginning teacher).

Procedures

Table 1 reports the various types of evaluation procedures reported by the responding school systems in the ERS survey. When referring to the figures in the last three columns of the table, it should be remembered that: (a) not all systems have a probationary period for teachers; (b) not all systems evaluate permanent teachers; (c) some systems use different procedures for evaluating permanent and probationary employees, and (d) a few systems reported procedures which could not be placed in one of the eight categories.

Table 1. Teacher Evaluation Procedures, 1968-69

Evaluation procedure	*Number of systems using for:*		
	P–Probationary only	*C–Continuing only*	*Both P and C*
Type A			
1A. Following observation(s) and post-observation conference(s), the evaluator unilaterally rates the evaluatee against prescribed performance standards	2		16
2A. Same as No. 1A above, but also includes post-evaluation conference	29	5	106
3A. Same as No. 2A above, but also includes self-evaluation	3	2	18
4A. Observation(s) and post-observation conference(s) are held during the year. In an evaluation conference, the evaluator and evaluatee discuss the items on the evaluation form as they apply to the evaluatee. The evaluator may or may not complete the evaluation form as each item is discussed			6
5A. Same as No. 4A above, but also includes self-evaluation	1	3	4
6A. Same as No. 5A above, except that the evaluator and the evaluatee discuss their separate evaluations and arrive at an evaluation to which they both agree	1		1
Type B			
1B. Evaluator and evaluatee cooperatively establish specific performance goals which are used by the evaluator to unilaterally judge how well the evaluatee has achieved his performance goals. In addition, the evaluatee may also be rated against prescribed performance standards. At post-evaluation conference evaluator explains his evaluation		1	1
2B. Same as No. 1B above, but also includes self-evaluation.	2		4

The distinction between Type A and Type B (Table 1) procedures is the degree to which the teacher may participate in the evaluation process. Among the Type A procedures, the practice of self-evaluation (Types 3A and 5A) allows the teacher more participation in the actual evaluation, as do the procedures providing for the evaluation "marks" to be determined by the evaluator during a conference with the teacher (Types 4A, 5A, and 6A)

An even greater degree of teacher participation and lessening of the subjective role of the administrator is evident in Type B procedures. At least some of the evaluative criteria are determined by the teacher himself at a conference held before the actual evaluation takes place. During the planning conference, the evaluatee, with the help of his evaluator, establishes realistic job targets or performance goals, tailored to what he believes is lacking in his performance or preparation. In the period between this conference and the post-evaluation conference, the teacher strives to reach these goals, rates himself on how well he has attained them, and is also rated by his evaluator on his achievement of the goals. Thus, much of the responsibility for evaluation rests with the evaluatee himself, and the evaluator becomes more of a coach than an umpire. The real goal of teacher evaluation–the improvement of instruction–becomes the primary result.

Informing Teachers

In all except Type 1A procedures, the evaluatee is naturally aware of his evaluation "score" since it is discussed with him in conference. In most systems at least one additional method is available to inform the teacher of the outcome of his evaluation. Table 2 shows the various apprisal methods reported by the 213 systems.

Table 2. How Teachers Are Apprised of Evaluations, 213 Systems

Procedure	*Frequency*
Signs and receives copy of form	81
Receives copy of form, but does not sign	21
May request copy of form	4
Shown a copy of form, which he signs.	43
May also request a copy	9
Shown copy of form, but does not sign	20
May also request a copy	4
Shown copy of form only on request	3
Informed in post-evaluation conference only	6
May only examine form in personnel file	6[a]
Varies by status or instructional level	4
Not apprised unless unsatisfactory	12

[a]In addition, 43 systems, where teachers are given or shown a copy of the completed evaluation, reported that the forms may also be examined in the personnel files.

Appeal Procedures

Table 3 notes the number of systems in which each procedure is available for teachers wishing to register dissent from the evaluator's assessment of his performance. In many systems several procedures are available. While 93 systems reported that a dissatisfied teacher could invoke formal grievance procedures, respondents from other systems maintained that evaluations are outside the scope of grievance procedures.

Table 3. Appeal Procedures Open to Teachers

Procedure	*Frequency*
Request conference with evaluator's superior	148
Initiate grievance	93
Attach dissenting statement to form	87
Signify dissent on form	33
Request rating by third party	18
File dissenting statement with review board	17
Appeal to personnel office, assistant superintendent, superintendent, or board of education	27
Appeal to professional organization, professional ethics committee, or ombudsman	4
No appeal possible	12
Not applicable	1

Responding administrators in the ERS survey were asked to comment on the impact negotiation is having, or might have, on teacher evaluations. Most respondents were of the opinion that, while there has been little or no impact as yet, it is quite likely that future negotiation will give more attention to objectives and methods in teacher appraisal. In summary, the following opinions were expressed:

Greater care is being taken by evaluators in conducting and recording their evaluations.

There is greater teacher involvement in the evaluation process.

Higher standards have been established for the teaching profession.

There is a tendency to protect the less competent teacher and make it more difficult to dismiss him.

Teacher organizations must start policing their own ranks.

Teachers are demanding the right to evaluate administrators.

Some respondents believed that teacher evaluations are not a negotiable item—there is no need for such a negotiation provision if teachers and administrators view evaluation as a cooperative process wherein the individual being evaluated and the one responsible for making the assessment feel a joint responsibility to focus upon performance areas needing improvement as well as those showing strength, to work together to achieve the best results, and to evaluate the result.

Teacher Opinion

Most teachers think they should be evaluated. Nine in 10 respondents in a nationwide sample survey of public-school classroom teachers, conducted by the NEA Research Division in spring 1969, indicated that they approved of regular evaluation of teachers.

Which Teachers Should Be Evaluated?

Three-fourths of the teachers surveyed responded that both probationary and tenure teachers should receive regular evaluation. In answer to the question, "In your opinion, should teachers be evaluated regularly?" respondents replied thus:

Yes, probationary teachers only	15.4%
Yes, both probationary and tenure teachers	75.1%
I do not believe in evaluation of teachers	9.5%

Analysis of responses revealed slight differences in the distribution of opinion for elementary- and secondary-school teachers, and for teachers in different size school systems. A higher percentage of secondary than of elementary teachers favored evaluation of both probationary and tenure teachers, while the percentage opposed to teacher evaluation was higher among elementary than among secondary teachers.

	Elementary	*Secondary*
Yes, probationary teachers only	16.7%	14.1%
Yes, both probationary and tenure teachers	71.8%	78.4%
I do not believe in evaluation of teachers	11.6%	7.4%

In school systems with 25,000 or more pupils, the proportion of teachers approving evaluation of probationary teachers only, was greater than in smaller systems, and the percentage favoring evaluation of both probationary and tenure teachers was correspondingly smaller.

	25,000 or more pupils	*3,000-24,999 pupils*	*Fewer than 3,000 pupils*
Yes, probationary teachers only	21.2%	14.0%	12.2%
Yes, both probationary and tenure teachers	70.1%	76.8%	77.1%
I do not believe in evaluation of teachers	8.7%	9.2%	10.7%

Who Should Evaluate Teachers

Respondents were almost unanimous in agreeing that the school principal should be responsible for teacher evaluation. About three-fourths of the teachers surveyed offered suggestions in answer to the question: "If teachers are evaluated, by whom should the evaluation be done?" Of those responding, 97 percent said the principal should make the evaluation.

Principal	96.6%
Supervisor	0.6
Principal and supervisor	0.3
Chairman of department	0.5
Teachers	0.7
Other	1.3

All the respondents in school systems with fewer than 25,000 pupils believed the principal should evaluate teachers. In school systems with more than 25,000 pupils, the vast majority of respondents shared the opinion of their colleagues in smaller systems, but several other possible evaluators of teachers were also suggested by small groups of respondents.

	25,000 or more pupils	*3,000-24,999 pupils*	*Fewer than 3,000 pupils*
Principal	87.0%	100.0%	100.0%
Supervisor	2.2		
Principal and supervisor	1.2		
Chairman of department	1.9		
Teachers	2.8		
Other	5.0		

Why Should Teachers Be Evaluated?

A checklist of possible purposes that might be served by teacher evaluation was presented to respondents with this question: "Whether or not you favor teacher evaluation, if teachers are evaluated, for what purpose should this be done? (Check ALL that apply.)" Responses were as follows:

To assist in improving teaching competence	92.8%
To keep the administration aware of what is taking place in the classroom	59.1
To make teachers more responsive to needs of their pupils	56.0
To make it possible to dismiss poor teachers	53.8
To assist in the selection of teachers for promotion to other positions	47.3
To have a statement in the teacher's permanent record for future reference	31.0
To see if the curriculum is being followed	22.9
For advancement on the salary schedule	17.3
For the awarding of merit pay	16.7
Other	2.4

Analysis of responses showed some differences of opinion. More men than women teachers favored evaluation for the purposes of dismissing poor teachers, advancing on the salary schedule, and awarding merit pay. More women than men teachers approved of evaluation to keep the administration aware of classroom activity, to have a statement on the teacher's permanent record, and to see if the curriculum is being followed.

	Men	*Women*
To make it possible to dismiss poor teachers	57.2%	51.9%
For advancement on the salary schedule	22.8	14.3
For the awarding of merit pay	20.9	14.4
To keep the administration aware of what is taking place in the classroom	53.2	62.2
To have a statement in the teacher's permanent record for future reference	27.8	32.7
To see if the curriculum is being followed	20.0	24.5

Opinions of teachers in different size school systems differed on two points. The largest school systems (25,000 or more pupils) had the smallest proportion of teachers (51 percent) approving evaluation for the purpose of keeping the administration aware of classroom activity, as compared with a somewhat larger proportion (60 percent) in medium-size systems (3,000-24,999 pupils), and the largest proportion (65 percent) in the smallest systems (fewer than 3,000 pupils). School systems with 25,000 or more pupils also showed a higher percentage (53 percent) of teachers who approved of evaluation to select teachers for promotion than systems with fewer than 25,000 pupils (3,000-24,999 pupils—44 percent; fewer than 3,000 pupils—47 percent).

Geographic analysis of responses showed a major difference on only one point. A much smaller proportion of teachers in the Southeast (40 percent) than in any other section of the country (Northeast, 58 percent; Middle, 56 percent; and West, 57 percent) thought that teacher evaluation should be used for the purpose of dismissing poor teachers.

As an Item of Negotiation

During the 1967-68 school year, approximately 63 percent of the 603 comprehensive agreements on file with NEA Research Division covering teaching staffs in school systems enrolling 1,000 or more pupils contained clauses on the evaluation of teachers.

Most of the provisions on teacher evaluation include a statement of the procedures to be followed. Some include the actual criteria to be used in evaluating teacher performance. A few merely establish a joint committee of teachers and administrators to study this area and make recommendations.

Evaluation Procedures

The following nine elements are frequently found in negotiated provisions on the procedures to be followed in the evaluation of teaching, although each provision does not include all items:

1. The time schedule for evaluations, including the number, frequency, and length of individual observation sessions.
2. Designation of the evaluator, usually the teacher's immediate supervisor or the school principal.
3. Statement that all observations must be with the knowledge of the teacher, and that monitoring devices may not be used without the teacher's prior consent.
4. Requirement that all evaluations be in writing on a standard form.
5. Provision for the teacher's review of the written evaluation report and opportunity to respond to any adverse comments before the report is placed in his personnel file.
6. Statement that teachers may be accompanied by an organization representative when discussing evaluation reports with supervisors.
7. Grievance procedure indicated as a channel for resolving objections a teacher may have to his evaluation.
8. Provision for special assistance to teachers receiving unsatisfactory evaluations to help them improve their performance. After a specified period of time, such teachers are re-evaluated and improvement, if any, is recorded.

9. Special provisions for the evaluation of new or probationary teachers. Tenure teachers are to be evaluated less frequently than probationary teachers.

The following provision on evaluation procedures was selected to show how the actual negotiated wording may appear in agreements.

ARTICLE XXIII
TEACHER EVALUATION

The following principles shall be applied in the evaluation of teacher performance:

1. a. All monitoring or observation of the work performance of a teacher will be conducted openly and with full knowledge of the teacher. No public address or audio system or other device permitting monitoring or observation of work performance other than by an individual present in the room shall be employed except with the prior knowledge and consent of the teacher.

b. Teacher performance shall be evaluated in light of all evidence pertinent to the discharge of the teacher's professional responsibilities and his exercise of professional judgment and not solely by his work in the classroom. The development of criteria for such evaluation shall be a task of the Professional Conditions Committee under Article VII.

c. A copy of each evaluation report shall be furnished the person evaluated who shall have the right to discuss the same with the maker of the report.

2. a. A teacher will have the right, upon written request, to review the contents of his personnel file and to have a representative of the Association accompany him.

b. No material originating after original hiring which is derogatory to a teacher's conduct, service, character or personality will be placed in his personnel file unless the teacher has had an opportunity to review the material. The teacher shall acknowledge that he has had the opportunity to review such material by affixing his signature to the copy to be filed with the express understanding that such signature in no way indicates agreement with the contents thereof. The teacher will also have the right to submit a written answer to such material and his answer shall be reviewed by the Superintendent and attached to the file copy.

3. Any serious complaints regarding a teacher made to any member of the Committee by, or coming to the Superintendent or the teacher's building principal from, any parent, student or other person will be promptly called to the attention of the teacher.

4. The Association recognizes the authority and responsibility of the Committee to discipline or reprimand, itself or by any administrator, a teacher for delinquency in professional performance. If a teacher is to be disciplined or reprimanded by a member of the administration above the level of the principal, however, he will be entitled to have a representative of the Association present. No teacher will be disciplined or reprimanded or deprived of any professional advantage without good and sufficient reason (Quincy, Mass. (NEA)).

Evaluation Criteria

Provisions on the criteria for teacher evaluation may include only the general categories to be rated, such as "command of subject matter," and "effectiveness of instruction." Others include specific observable traits under each general category; for example, "effectiveness of instruction" may include preparation of lesson plans, use of a variety of instructional materials, attention given to individual pupils, and the like, each of which is rated separately.

A rating scale (i.e., 1-superior, 2-above average, 3-average, 4-needs improvement, 5-unsatisfactory) may be applied to each criterion, or the evaluator may report his observations in a less structured, annotated form. Many agreements include a copy of the actual form to be used for each evaluation report.

Following are sample provisions on evaluation criteria selected from those identified in the NEA Research Division's survey of negotiation agreements.

The following provision includes nine general areas to be evaluated.

> Areas of concern are (a) command of subject matter, (b) effectiveness of instruction, (c) initiative, (d) cooperation, (e) participation, (f) reliability and personal responsibility, (g) leadership, (h) growth potential, (i) and participation in professional activities. (Capac, Mich. (NEA))

The provision below is in the form of a checklist which divides three general categories into more specific traits.

A. EVALUATION SECTION

1. Classroom Effectiveness

Relationship with pupils
Planning
Knowledge of subject (s)
Effectiveness of Communication
Classroom atmosphere and control
Use of new and varied instructional material
Attention to individual needs
Adaptability to changing classroom situations
Attention to study skills and habits
Effectiveness in appraising learning

2. Attitudes and professional responsibilities

Relationship with Parents
Relationship with Colleagues
Willingness to assume responsibility for pupil behavior in all school situations
Takes steps toward self-improvement
Takes part in professional organization
Accepts school staff assignments beyond classroom responsibility
Has respect for channels of authority
Complies with school and school system policies
Responsibility for routines
Attendance and punctuality

3. Personal Characteristics

Mental alertness

Enthusiasm
Dependability
Initiative
Perseverance
Resourcefulness
Tact
Poise and self-confidence
Self-control
Judgment
Dress and Grooming

(Hammond, Ind. (NEA))

The Okemos, Mich. (NEA) agreement specifies that the 10 major areas to be evaluated will be: (a) knowledge of subject matter, (b) techniques of instruction (motivation), (c) pupil-teacher relationships, (d) curriculum development, (e) daily preparation, (f) pupil evaluation, (g) classroom management, (h) character development, (i) school-wide and system effectiveness, and (j) community relationships. Each general area is defined in terms of the responsibility and key duties involved. Following is the description of the second of these 10 categories.

Responsibility: TECHNIQUES OF INSTRUCTION (MOTIVATION)

The standard of performance for this responsibility is met when faculty personnel recognizes and provides for the pupils' interests, needs and abilities and apply instructional techniques which result in the level of learning commensurate with their potential.

KEY DUTIES

1. Stimulates interest in prescribed areas of learning.
2. Challenges, encourages and guides critical thinking through use of stimulating questions and provocative ideas.
3. Uses a variety of methods in presenting subject matter.
4. Encourages a high quality of performance consistent with the individual's ability.
5. Leads pupils in solving problems significant to him.
6. Adapts teaching material and methods to the individual needs of the pupils.
7. Teaches groups and individual pupils in accordance with interests, needs and abilities.
8. Conducts discussions so that pupils learn to express ideas clearly, accurately and completely.
9. Schedules time to meet curriculum requirements through long range planning consistent with philosophy of course.
10. Makes clear assignments and directions with ample time allotment.
11. Develops desirable work and study habits by providing opportunities for the exercise of techniques of reading, organizing materials, etc.
12. Directs pupil who finishes assignments quickly into worthwhile activity.
13. Uses learning aids such as audio-visual material in a profitable manner.
14. Provides for testing and summarization.

Joint Committees

Provisions establishing joint committees to study and recommend teacher evaluation procedures and criteria generally include the following items:

1. Topics to be considered by the committee
2. Manner in which members of the committee will be selected
3. Schedule of meetings and date the final committee report is to be completed
4. Functional guidelines which designate the power and responsibility of the committee
5. Procedures for final disposition of the committee report.

Can Principals Exclude Their Own Personality Characteristics When They Rate Their Teachers?

John H. M. Andrews and Alan F. Brown

The search for an adequate means of measuring teacher effectiveness has attracted considerable attention for many years. It has resulted in the proposal of many different means, some of which appear to be of great promise. But, despite its suspected limitations, the method of rating by the principal persists as probably the most widely used measure for both administrative and research purposes.

Of the suspected limitations inherent in principals' ratings of teacher effectiveness the one investigated in this research is the possibility that the ratings are partly determined by the extent to which the teacher is similar to the principal in certain personality characteristics. If this is so it is clearly a spurious effect and would tend to invalidate the ratings by principals as real measures of teaching effectiveness.

Theoretical considerations seem to point to the existence of such an effect. Guba and Bidwell (*6*) found that the principal's estimate of a teacher's effectiveness is an expression of the degree to which he perceives that the teacher conforms to the principal's expectations for the teacher-rôle. Since the personality of the principal is likely to influence his expectations for teacher behavior and, similarly, the personality of the teacher is, no doubt, a determinant of the teacher's behavior, it would be expected that similarity in personality between the principal and teacher would result in a high rating for the teacher. In support of this argument, Stern, Stein, and Bloom (*8*) suggest that the teacher behavior which a principal rates is a function of transactional relationships between the teacher and his social and non-social environment. In the rating process attention is drawn to the principal as a part of the social environment.

A study by Prince (*7*), however, failed to verify the hypothesis drawn above. The twenty principals and 100 teachers in his investigation showed no significant relationship between degree of teacher-principal congruence of educational values (classified as emergent–traditional) and principal-rated teacher effectiveness. Prince reasoned that, because of the principal's background of experience and training and because of the number of comparisons he makes daily among teachers, it is not necessary that their values coincide with his. It is noted that the term "personality" is used here in a sufficiently broad sense to include such characteristics as structure of educational values.

This study is another attempt, using different measures of personality characteristics, to detect a relationship between teacher-principal similarity and the ratings of effectiveness assigned by the principal to teachers. The personality elements considered are personality needs, dominant values, and educational attitudes. Stated in its positive form, the hypothesis is that effectiveness ratings assigned to teachers by the principal are positively related to the degree to which the teacher's measured needs, values, and educational attitudes are congruent to the principal's measured needs, values, and educational attitudes.

Method

Subjects. The 608 teachers and principals used in this study comprised approximately the total faculties of nine large high schools, were within 150 miles of Chicago–but not inside the Chicago system–and were located in three states: Illinois, Indiana and Wisconsin. The communities represented ranged from residential suburb to industrial suburb and from the semi-rural small town to the city. The data were gathered for a study sponsored by the Midwest Administration Center and reported elsewhere by one of the authors (*1*) (*2*).

Instruments and Scores. Testing the hypothesis necessitated the use of instruments with which to quantify the dependent variable–the principal's estimate of a teacher's effectiveness–and each of the three independent variables–teacher-principal similarities in needs, values and educational attitudes. A six-point Principal-Rated Effectiveness Scale was devised. It was designed to elicit from the principal a subjective judgment of a teacher's global effectiveness in terms of degrees above and below the average effectiveness of teachers in the particular school.

To measure psychological needs, the Edwards Personal Preference Schedule (EPPS) was administered. This is a standardized test purporting to measure fifteen manifest needs found in normals; they are as follows:

(1) *Achievement:* to do one's best, be successful, accomplish tasks requiring great skill and effort, to do things better than others.

(2) *Deference:* to get suggestions from others, find out what others think, praise others, do what is expected, and the like.

(3) *Order:* to have written work neat and organized, make plans before starting a difficult task, and the like.

(4) *Exhibition:* to say witty and clever things, talk about personal adventures and experiences, be the center of attention, and the like.

(5) *Autonomy:* to come and go as desired, say what one thinks, be independent from others when making decisions, and the like.

(6) *Affiliation:* to be loyal to friends, participate in friendly groups, form new friendships, and the like.

(7) *Intraception:* to analyze one's motives and feelings, observe others, understand how others feel, predict how they will act, and the like.

(8) *Succorance:* to have others provide help when in trouble, seek encouragement from others, and the like.

(9) *Dominance:* to argue for one's point of view, to be and to be regarded as a leader, to persuade and influence others, and the like.

(10) *Abasement:* to feel guilt when one does something wrong, to be depressed by inability, give in and avoid a fight, and the like.

(11) *Nurturance:* to help friends when they are in trouble, assist others less fortunate, forgive others, be generous, and the like.

(12) *Change:* to do new and different things, experience change and novelty in daily routine, experiment, and the like.

(13) *Endurance:* to keep at a task until it is finished, avoid being interrupted while working, and the like.

(14) *Heterosexuality:* to go out with members of the opposite sex, engage in social activities with members of the opposite sex, and the like.

(15) *Aggression:* to attack contrary points of view, criticize others publicly, get revenge, become angry, and the like.

The EPPS provides a fifteen-score profile. The degree to which the needs of a teacher and his principal were congruent was determined by the Cronbach-Gleser D^2 method as indicated by the following formula:

$$D^2_{12} = \sum_{j=1}^{k} (x_{j_1} - x_{j_2})^2$$

where j is any of k variables included in the profile. The lower a teacher's D^2 score, the greater is the similarity between his measured needs and those of the principal who has rated his effectiveness.

To determine the similarity of value-orientations between a teacher and his principal, the D^2 method was applied to the six-score profiles obtained from the subjects' responses to the Allport-Vernon-Lindzey "Study of Values" (AVL). These value-orientations, derived from Spranger's *Types of Men*, are as follows:

(1) *Theoretical:* the dominant interest of the theoretical man is the discovery of truth.

(2) *Economic:* the economic man is characteristically interested in what is useful.

(3) *Aesthetic:* the aesthetic man sees his highest value in form and harmony.

(4) *Social:* the highest value for this type is love of people; it is altruistic or philanthropic love that is measured.

(5) *Political:* the political man is interested primarily in power, especially in terms of competition or struggle.

(6) *Religious:* the highest value for the religious man may be called unity; he is directed toward the highest and most satisfying value-experience.

Educational attitudes of the subjects were assessed with the use of the Minnesota Teacher Attitude Inventory (MTAI) which yields a single score. This test is designed to measure the attitudes of teachers toward pupils. A high score indicates those attitudes which are commonly described as progressive. A low score indicates traditional attitudes. The absolute difference between teacher and principal MTAI scores revealed their attitudinal similarity: the lower the absolute difference, the greater the teacher-principal similarity.

Analysis The general hypothesis, that teacher-principal similarity in personality characteristics is related to effectiveness ratings, was broken down for testing purposes into three specific hypotheses. The relationship was sought separately for each of the three personality characteristics under consideration—needs, values, and educational attitudes.

In testing these three hypotheses, the ratings were grouped by school and by sex. Each group was divided into three approximately equal classes (high, medium and low effectiveness ratings) according to the distribution of ratings for that group. Similarly, within each group the congruency scores (absolute difference or D^2) of each variable were divided into three equal classes indicating a high, medium or low degree of similarity with the principal's score or profile. The three hypotheses were then tested by constructing three-by-three chi-square tables.

Results

Attitudes. The specific hypothesis regarding educational attitudes as measured by the teacher-principal MTAI score-differences was not supported. From Table 1 it is observed that of the eight groups tested—males and females in each of nine schools—only two yielded chi-square values significant at the .05 level of confidence. In both instances the teachers were males. The chi-square value for all males is misleading; it appears to indicate that the relationship between congruency scores and effectiveness ratings *of all males* is significant at the .05 level, whereas seven of the nine groups failed to approach significance. When one school is removed from the list, however, it is seen that the relationship of attitudinal similarity to effectiveness rating among males of the remaining eight schools is well below the level of significance (P = .27).

Values. It was not possible to obtain usable AVL data from one of the participating schools. Of the sixteen groups in the remaining eight schools, fourteen of them failed to indicate any significant relationship between effectiveness ratings and teacher-principal congruency score calculated from the AVL. Similarly, the relationship was not significant when considering all the males or all the females whose data were available. From Table 2 it is observed that for School 8 similarity between teacher's and principal's value-orientations was significantly associated with effectiveness ratings among both male and female teachers.

Table 1. The Relationship Between Effectiveness Ratings and Teacher-Principal Similarities in Educational Attitudes

	Males			*Females*		
School	*N*	x^2	p^a	*N*	x^2	p^a
1	56	3.160	–	45	8.474	–
2	63	2.843	–	41	2.756	–
3	28	4.167	–	37	1.692	–
4	28	2.006	–	27	3.983	–
5	22	5.447	–	29	3.394	–
6	39	9.267	.05	35	5.820	–
7	27	6.502	–	21	1.500	–
8	35	18.412	.001	24	1.607	–
9	22	2.972	–	18	8.269	–
Total. . .	320	54.776	.05[b]	277	37.432	–

[a]A dash indicates a probability greater than .05.
[b]When school 8 is subtracted, total remaining x^2 = 36.364 and P = .27.

Table 2. The Relationship Between Effectiveness Ratings and Teacher-Principal Similarities in Value-Orientations

	Males			*Females*		
School	*N*	x^2	p^a	*N*	x^2	*P*
2	62	3.547	–	41	1.321	–
3	26	6.018	–	36	1.752	–
4	28	8.176	–	26	5.207	–
5	21	4.196	–	27	2.284	–
6	40	3.490	–	33	2.488	–
7	27	1.115	–	21	2.500	–
8	36	10.224	.05	22	11.430	.05
9	22	3.781	–	17	4.078	–
Total. . .	262	40.547	–	223	31.060	–

[a]A dash indicates a probability greater than .05.

Clearly, however, the second specific hypothesis of this study failed to obtain general support from the data.

Needs. The subjects used in this part of the study were the male and female teachers of seven schools, or fourteen test groups. Table 3 indicates that among the 379 teachers and their seven principals there was no significant relationship between effectiveness ratings and teacher-principal similarities of manifest needs. Similarly, the chi-square totals, by sex, failed to support the hypothesis.

Table 3. The Relationship Between Effectiveness Ratings and Teacher-Principal Similarities in Manifest Needs

	Males			*Females*		
School	*N*	x^2	*p*,[a]	*N*	x^2	*P*
2	57	2.848	–	30	2.195	–
3	23	6.952	–	30	4.598	–
4	24	2.952	–	24	8.060	–
5	18	2.500	–	23	4.061	–
6	30	7.980	–	28	4.523	–
7	25	8.566	–	17	4.576	–
8	31	3.675	–	19	3.319	–
Total. .	208	35.473	–	171	31.332	–

[a]A dash indicates a probability greater than .05.

Discussion

When it is considered that, of the forty-eight chi-square tests, only four were significant at the .05 level it may reasonably be concluded that this investigation furnishes no support for the general hypothesis. It is interesting to note, however, that three of the four significant relationships refer to the ratings of the same principal (School 8). Quite likely, if the hypothesized effect did exist, it would be demonstrated by some principals to a greater extent than by others. It may be speculated then, that the principal of School 8 is unusually subject to including personal considerations in his ratings of teacher effectiveness.

The lack of support for the general hypothesis may be construed in different ways. It may be, indeed, that the hypothesized effect does not exist. If this were so the principal's rating of teacher effectiveness could be used with a great deal more confidence than it is at present. It would be unwarranted, however, to accept this as a necessary conclusion.

The other possibility is, of course, that the effect does exist but remained undetected. It may have been undetected for any of three reasons: (1) the instruments used may have been grossly inadequate, (2) the statistical definition of "similarity" inherent in the Cronbach-Gleser formula may not have been the appropriate kind of similarity, and (3) the hypothesized effect may exist but in such small quantity as to be negligible as a factor detracting from the usefulness of ratings of teachers.

The instruments used have shown themselves in other studies to be sufficiently useful that they could not be described as grossly inadequate. Their application to this problem, however, should be considered. The personality characteristics of the principal and of the teacher which could influence effectiveness ratings are those which are *perceived* by the principal. Any that are not perceived by him cannot influence his rating. It may be, then, that the hypothesized effect would be found present if measurement of personality characteristics were based upon perceptions by the principal rather than upon instruments completed by both teacher and principal on their own behalf. While this approach has not been used in relation to effectiveness ratings, it was used by one of the authors (*4*) in relation to adolescents' perceptions of parents and peers, and by Bieri (*3*) in relation to learning.

The question of the definition of similarity is raised because the Cronbach-Gleser formula considers, in effect, only the difference between scores of teacher and principal regardless of the direction of difference. A principal who reveals a mild need for orderliness may consider a teacher to be more similar to himself who exhibits a high need for orderliness than a teacher whose score is closer to that of the principal but below it. A formula which accounts for direction in the measurement of similarity (*1*) might well be used in further investigations to account for this possibility.

In conclusion, then, subject to the two qualifying possibilities raised above, it does seem that teacher-principal similarity, in those personality characteristics which were considered, either does not influence the effectiveness rating assigned by a principal to a teacher or else it influences it so little as to be undetectable in a group analysis. It cannot be concluded that all school principals are able to exclude their own personalities from their ratings of teachers as successfully as these large high school principals appear to have done. Indeed, it would likely be more difficult in smaller schools where relationships are more highly personalized. At the same time this study, together with that of Prince, referred to earlier, tends to increase confidence, at least tentatively, that spurious personality considerations are not contaminating effectiveness ratings to any marked degree.

Summary

This study has investigated the extent to which ratings of effectiveness assigned by principals to teachers are contaminated by similarity and difference in personality between principal and teacher. The personality characteristics considered were manifest needs, value-orientations, and educational attitudes. Nine principals and their staff members, ranging in number from forty to 105, comprised the total sample of 608 subjects. Each subject was administered the Edwards Personal Preference Schedule (needs), the Allport-Vernon-Lindzey "Study of Values" (values), and the Minnesota Teacher Attitude Inventory (educational attitudes). Similarity in personality characteristics between teacher and principal was expressed by the absolute score difference and the Cronbach-Gleser D^2 measure of profile similarity. The relationship between effectiveness scores and similarity scores was then tested in contingency tables. Forty-four of the forty-eight tests showed no significant relationship. In result, the study agrees with that of Prince in finding no relationship between teacher-principal similarity in personality elements and principals' ratings of teachers' effectiveness. As such, the study may be interpreted, at least tentatively, as increasing confidence in rating as a measure of effectiveness as far as this spurious personality effect is concerned.

References

(*1*) J. H. M. Andrews, "Administrative Significance of Psychological Differences between Secondary Teachers of Different Subject Matter Fields," *Alberta Journal of Educational Research*, III: 4 (December 1957), pp. 199-208.

(*2*) J. H. M. Andrews, "A Deterrent to Harmony Among Teachers,"Administrator's Notebook, March, 1958.

(*3*) J. Bieri and A. Trieschman, "Learning as a Function of Perceived Similarity to Self," *Journal of Personality*, XXV: 2 (December 1956), pp. 213-223.

(*4*) A. F. Brown, "The Self in Interpersonal Theory: The Relationship between Attitudes Referring to Self and to Significant Others," *Alberta Journal of Educational Research,* III: 3 (September 1957), pp. 138-148.

(*5*) L. J. Cronbach and G. Gleser, "Assessing Similarity between Profiles," *Psychological Bulletin*, L (1953), pp. 456-473.

(*6*) E. G. Guba and C. E. Bidwell, *Administrative Relationships: Teacher Effectiveness, Teacher Satisfaction and Administrative Behavior*, Chicago, Midwest Administration Center, University of Chicago, 1957.

(*7*) R. Prince, "Individual Values and Administrative Effectiveness," *Administrator's Notebook*, VI: 4 (December 1957), pp. 1-4.

(*8*) G. S. Stern, M. I. Stein and B. S. Bloom, *Methods in Personality Assessments*, Glencoe, Illinois, The Free Press, 1956.

In-Service or Continuing Education for Teachers

Jack R. Childress

In-service education and continuing education for teachers are virtually synonymous terms. The in-service program is a natural continuation of the professional pre-service education in which teachers have participated. Such activity is an obligation for teachers and a must for educational programming. Few, if any, deny the fact that one of the imperative needs of American education is continuing education for the professional in the field–teachers, supervisors, specialists and administrators.

Stephen Corey, in the Fifty-sixth Yearbook of the National Society for the Study of Education, *In-Service Education*, has summarized well the problems and issues. He emphasized (planned programs in contrast to independent attempts by teachers to improve themselves,) and stated that wide reading, travel, convention attendance, professional courses or any other means, conducive to professional growth, are not thereby undervalued. Dr. Corey pointed out the necessity for planned programs in in-service education for the improvement of school personnel, expressing the feeling that it is impracticable to depend entirely on pre-service preparation and individual initiative. He called for carefully planned, creative programs, since our rapidly changing culture and its implications, for curriculum change, continually increasing enrollments, the size of the teaching staff, the need for leadership in the schools and the continuing increase in our knowledge of pupils and the learning process make it necessary for school people to strive continuously to keep abreast of what they must know and be prepared to do.[1]

Verbalization runs rampant on the need for such endeavors. Comparable action normally is not in evidence. Definite policies are not adopted by local school districts to implement a vital program which will be of benefit to individual teachers, students, the community and the profession. Many professionals who participate fail to accept the philosophy that this activity is essential regardless of the financial overtones and the salary schedule. Planned programs within the colleges and universities designed for personnel who must be upgraded are limited or unimaginative. Present programs are traditionally designed rather than continuing education oriented.

Four major areas of concern appear to stand out:

1. The creation of a felt obligation on the part of teachers and professionals to undertake a planned and well-designed in-service or continuing education program.
2. The development of a set of guidelines for the "organization" or school district which will implement an appropriate and excellent in-service program.
3. Recognition by community and professional leaders that the rapid expanse of knowledge both in the professional and content fields will require full-time study and that this will necessitate resolution of issues of staffing and finance.
4. The need for schools of education, and other divisions of universities and colleges to plan programs especially for individuals who will be continuing their education on a part-time or a full-time basis—many times on a non-degree basis.

Creation of a Felt Obligation by Teachers

The neophyte in any professional field who is at all dedicated to his or her work will conclude rapidly that the four or five or more years of preservice education has been only modestly adequate. The conscientious and dedicated teacher will normally come to this realization during student teaching and/or the first year of in-the-classroom service.

[1] Corey, Stephen. "Introduction," *In-Service Education,* National Society for the Study of Education, Chicago. University of Chicago Press. 1957. p. 1.

A failure in the educational institutions to instill this fact during the initial preparation program would soon be overcome by the tremendous impact of the "in-the-field" experiences. (The creation of a felt obligation cannot be left, however, only with the individual.) The primary responsibility, will always have to be there if major changes in attitude, methods and knowledge background are to be accomplished.

Preparation programs, regardless of their length, must emphasize that this portion of the work of the professional is only the beginning. It is impossible to incorporate into the academic program of any individual all of the subject matter background and the research and experimental knowledge available in the professional field during any designated or pre-designed period. The completion of a formal educational program is not a climax but is appropriately called a "Commencement" into a new field. Further study and an analysis of the professional area are essential.

A continuing and in-service education program built upon the enthusiasm of the beginning teacher or the dedicated professional will create a need for change in the schools. The potential for altering any given setting must be obvious if the stimulation for continued in-service education is to be maintained. School units, logically organized, will have organized policies and programs to emphasize the need for continued evaluation, alteration and change. This willingness must be expressed through action exemplified by past alterations. A willingness to change when new knowledge is available will create a continued search for new information.

Additional stimulation for the creation of a felt obligation can and will come from outstanding professional organizations. The need to upgrade the profession will be emphasized continuously in the meetings and organizational publications. Definitive steps can be taken, however, to make continued upgrading mandatory for membership. Perhaps in all types of professional organizations, there should be a "college" or group of "fellows" who represent the high achievement levels and continued study necessary for the upgrading of the profession. (The professional organizations will also recognize that conferences and conventions are stimulators for further education and not an end in itself.) The depth study required to gain intimate contact with new knowledge cannot be obtained through short conferences, individual presentations or shot-gun conventions.

A fourth factor in creating a felt-obligation on the part of teachers rests with the institutions for higher learning. Programs and learning experiences which are self-satisfying to the participant must be designed and available in these institutions. Standardized approaches, disregarding the background of the individuals, will produce drones and not enthusiasts.

In every phase of the career activities of a professional, aspects of it must point to the need for continuing education. Any implication that an individual is forever prepared for whatever contingencies must be faced through the pre-service educational program is a forecast of disillusionment. The implementation of a design to aid in the creation of a felt need for further education can be developed even through the obvious means of direct instruction in classrooms and a specific charge at the conclusion of an undergraduate or pre-service educational program. In addition, the professional organizations can point up the need and must give directions. These factors must be combined with followup programs from the university to encourage further study, to exemplify an interest in the graduates and to make evaluations and judgments about the school's program. This latter can be coordinated with the positive attitude of the university faculty toward such programs and to their own need to expand their knowledge and background.

The development of a recognized need is a continuous process shared by the individuals in the profession and by all groups with whom they associate.

The "Organization" Role

The "felt need" can be quickly stifled and retarded in the enthusiastic beginning or experienced teacher by a lack of emphasis on continuing education or inadequate policies and programs to implement change in the local school district. The following proposed set of policies may be overstated in some instances for emphasis. They appear, however, to incorporate premises which must be evaluated carefully by all persons if appropriate "organizational" and individual needs are to be met.

The principles underlying an adequate program of in-service improvement of teachers should be stated as specifically as possible. Every individual employed as a professional staff member in a school system should know the basic philosophy of the school administration and community relative to this area of the teacher's responsibility. The thirteen principles which follow have been designed to point up the essential characteristics which are necessary for the successful in-service program in a given school district.

1. *Participation in an in-service educational program is the professional responsibility of all certified members of the school staff.* Every individual who enters the profession of teachers has the professional and moral responsibility to continue to improve himself and to improve the program in which he is working. Every staff member has the obligation to understand what is expected of him as an individual in a given community and to know the characteristics of the area in which he is to participate as a citizen and teacher. The assumption is made in this principle that every individual can become a better classroom teacher, a better staff member and a better member of the community through having worked to improve himself and the school program.

2. *Individuals in an educational institution can no longer look upon in-service education as only a self-choice, self-selective activity.* Every member of the professional staff must be involved in the program of in-service education. This may be on an assigned basis; at times it may be directed toward a group activity; at other times it may be on a somewhat self-selected program.

In the past it has been considered perfectly satisfactory for the individual to participate or not to participate as he sees fit. This attitude can no longer be countenanced in our schools, regardless of the job held, the educational background which has been developed or the felt outside responsibilities. All members of the school staff must show a willingness to improve themselves and to work for the improvement of the school program and organization.

Most school systems are faced with problems which must be resolved in the formulation of new curricular patterns, in the improvement of classroom instruction in certain subject areas in the utilization of new media of instruction. The assignments of individuals to study such problems should be acceptable to those persons. Definite problems, however, have to be studied. Commitments may have to be secured for faculty to work on them even though these assignments would not normally be the first choice of the teacher.

Complete self-selection of the type of in-service activities will not be possible under such a system. Some self-determination may be possible when there are identifiable areas of needed self-improvement. The individual would be given a choice under such a need of certain acceptable means of carrying through this self-improvement program. Each teacher will have the responsibility to study herself and to work with the administration to determine her own strengths and weaknesses. The results of such a study will then determine the characteristics of the activities in which any given individual may be asked to participate.

3. *A program must be designed for teachers spending their first year and planned with definite activities which enable these individuals to be properly oriented into the school system.* Every individual entering a school district for the first time must become fully aware of the philosophy of the school system and the characteristics of the community in which she is to work. Inexperienced and experienced teachers should share in activity.

The teacher's role will vary from school district to school district. The only logical assumption is that an orientation is necessary to every new position or job. Such an aspect of the program requires that the administration of the schools be willing to explore, in a formalized way, the philosophy of the school system. This statement will encompass such things as expectations from classroom teaching; the areas of learning, which will be emphasized; the responsibility toward the child; the responsibility towards the parent; ways of reporting activities which will be required; obligations which will have to be accepted for group planning and group activity, etc.

Many of the facets of a given school's program will be based upon the characteristics of the community in which the school system is located. Every new teacher should be fully aware of the general characteristics of the neighborhood in which she is to work and the specific characteristics of the attendance unit in which she is to carry on her teaching duties.

The local administrative staff has the responsibility for designing a program for teachers who are in the system for the first time. The sessions of this type of continuing education would take precedence over any other type of meeting.

4. *A definitive program should be planned for all persons on the school staff.* Education is not a static phenomenon. The curriculum is ever changing. Research is available which indicates that new techniques are available which will improve classroom instruction. Community life is undergoing revision. All of these factors must be known by every member of the school staff.

Underlying this general concept of in-service education is the belief that every teacher can improve from year to year. In addition, every teacher must feel a professional responsibility to improve. Within the framework of an in-service education program a definite, well-designed program of in-service education must be included in the activities of every teacher and every school district.

5. *The obvious needs of the school district must be studied.* These needs may be determined by administrative study, by recommendations of the Board of Education, consultation with community groups, decisions by staff members and recommendations of study teams from within and without the school district. The "obvious needs approach" may necessitate that certain priorities be established. The corollary to such determination would be the need for acceptance of an assignment or assignments by various members of the school staff. Once the need is determined, it must be studied and methods determined by resolving any issues. Unless a definite program is established for such study, conclusions may be postponed to the detriment of the school program.

6. *Any in-service education program should be designed specifically for a given school district and the problems which are pertinent to it.* The characteristics of the community, the school program and the teachers working therein will be the prime factors in determining the characteristics, the problems and the issues which may be prevalent in a given school district. The number of inexperienced teachers or the number with longevity in the school system may determine types of action. The social structure of the community will be a determinant of the type of educational program which will be required. The ambitions of the citizens and the Board of Education for the children and the school system will be a major factor which may have to be studied. As the characteristics of any school district are examined, the only conclusion which seems logical is that no generalizations on appropriate specific in-service education program needs can be made for specific school units.

7. *Every in-service education program should be designed to keep the staff members of the individual school district abreast of modern research and study as well as to identify the individual problems facing teachers in that district.* Opportunities to improve classroom teachers are prevalent in all school districts. This improvement can best be done by drawing upon the experience of the individuals who are involved and relating that to the research which has been done in the area under study. Individual problems must be faced, evaluated and resolved. These individual problems may be a part of a larger problem facing the school district and which may require group action.

In addition to the "felt need" of the teachers in a school district, continued emphasis must be given to the need to acquaint the personnel of the staff with new philosophies and research. Those new concepts may be overlooked by persons who are directly involved in solving their individual problems and meeting their individual needs.

8. *In-service education should be designed for both the self-improvement of teachers and the general program improvement of the school.* Every in-service program is designed to provide a learning experience for all involved. These experiences may be limited in nature or extensive in their coverage. The worth of

any person can be evaluated positively only if there has been a change of behavior on the part of those who have been involved. This change of behavior may be directly related to the classroom instruction which the individual carries through, or it may result in a general program improvement in the entire school district. Such results must be looked for and must be observed if the in-service education program is to be deemed a success.

An effort must be made to separate in-service education which is primarily concerned with the personal development of teachers and the curriculum study and administrative consultation which may also be classified as in-service education. This latter phase may also be identified as democratic participation in in-service education. The writer recommends that all in-service education be evaluated on the basis of whether or not it is for individual improvement or for improvement of the total school program. Very little can be justified in carrying through one process if it does not have one of these general goals in mind.

9. *The schedules of teachers should be studied carefully so that time devoted to in-service improvement, curriculum study and participation in democratic administration does not take excessive time from the daily planning of the individual's classes.* Sometime during the school day, a definite block of the time should be set aside for the teacher's daily plans. This period should remain virtually "untouchable" and the teacher should be expected to put this time to good use to plan activities for her classroom day. Such emphasis would place perhaps a proper perspective on the primary responsibility of the teacher—that of classroom instructor. The corollary must be maintained, however, that good classroom instruction cannot occur unless there is continued self-improvement and unless the individual teacher recognizes the place that her instruction and classroom activities play in the total philosophy of the school.

10. *The organization and the direction of the in-service improvement program is an administrative responsibility.* The personnel available in any given school system will determine where the final responsibility is placed. The point of emphasis in this statement is that somewhere in the administrative organization, leadership must develop. The responsibility for an in-service education program cannot be left to the whims and wishes of the individual classroom teachers. A director of research could very logically fill this role.

Recognition by Communities and Professionals of the Need for Continuing Education

Statements in the public press and in virtually every professional meeting include such facts as: 1. Knowledge is doubling every eight to ten years; and, 2. ninety percent of the scientists of history are alive today. These factors emphasize dramatically the need for a continuous upgrading of the background of teachers and a recognition that current practices and content may be out of date in short periods of time. William Patterson has called attention to the fact that the number of scientists in industry, government and universities is doubling the body of knowledge every ten years. Developments that formerly would have required several decades are now occurring in a few years' time. The number of scientists and engineers at work today is greater than the cumulative total since the dawn of recorded history 6000 years ago.[2] According to J. Martin Klotsche, the need to know, which he considers to be the basic foundation of a free society, implies very significant problems, both for the scholar opening up new areas of investigation and the responsible citizen. He directs attention to the tremendous explosion of knowledge, greater in intensity and impact than those of population, metropolitan expansion and even nuclear devices. As more knowledge accumulates, so does the urge to discover more.[3]

Major changes in educational programming will require a clear recognition of the need on the part of community, state and federal government leaders to provide funds for such activity. The professional teacher must have available periods of study expanded dramatically. Practices in vogue today appear to be based upon a belief that individuals from their own time and normally at their own expense must continue to improve themselves for the benefit of the profession and the community. An appropriate in-service or continuing education program for the teaching profession of the future will require periods of concentrated study of six months to a year. Depth analysis of the issues in the teaching field or in professional research will not be possible under other circumstances.

Short-term or part-time study may be appropriate for specific situations and small projects. In addition, the beginning teacher at the outset of her initial assignment should become involved in a formal continuing education program in order to maintain the stimulus and the challenge which they have had in their pre-service program.

Two specific factors will require that time be made available by employing agencies for depth study. The expansion of knowledge has been mentioned already. Truths of the past become the false doctrines of the present. Adherence to previously learned materials and out-of-date publications will produce a false sense of security and inappropriate education for students with whom the individual teacher comes into contact. The development of appropriate skills and knowledges by the individuals registered in our schools, cannot be accomplished through misrepresentation which comes from inappropriate and out-of-date backgrounds.

A second and tangible factor which will enter into the requirement that teachers be given lengthy periods away from the classroom for study is a measureable or objective one. The expansion of summer schools for the elementary and secondary schools and the trend to provide more services for young people during the present off-school-year periods appear to make the conclusion logical that the eleven- or twelve-month schools will become a reality within the next decade. The ramifications of this move are obvious. Teachers will not have scheduled periods of two or three months away from the classroom during which time they can

[2]Patterson, William D. "Six Feet, Six Hours, One World," *Saturday Review*, January 2, 1965. p. 22.

[3]Klotsche, J. Martin. "The Need for Knowing." *The Nature of Knowledge*, The School of Education, The University of Wisconsin, Milwaukee. 1961. p. 2.

undertake professional study. Employment of professionals on a year-round basis will require sabbatical leaves or other arrangements for continued study.

The primary factors are a need for periods of long-term study for six months or a year and for financial policies which will allow for compensation of the individual at their normal salary while undertaking this period of continuing education. This concentration is both for self-improvement and change and for the development of potential for curriculum improvement. Schools may design programs which allow for individuals to be away or for teams to work on new instructional patterns. The latter may be during or after long periods of study for stimulation and relearning.

The felt obligation of teachers to continue their education which has been created by their experiences, their professional attitude, their pre-service education and their professional organizations must be implemented by community recognition of the need to aid in providing time and financial resources for continuing education.

The Obligation of the College and University

The sponsorship of periods of long-term study for teachers and a recognition of this need by the members of the profession will create a demand for improved and expanded formal and informal programs in the colleges and universities. Complacency, which is exemplified by the assumption that existing courses, summer and degree programs in highly-specialized fields will satisfy the need and will create only dissatisfaction and curtailment of the desire for in-service education or continuing educational programs. Basic characteristics for such programs may incorporate the following concepts:

The first premise must be that the programs designed especially for continuing education will be planned individually for the personnel involved. This characteristic does not negate the possibility of having a basic design or philosophy within the school which the professional staff of that unit believes will meet the individual and professional needs of teachers. Clear recognition must be given, however, to two major factors: 1. The background of the individual and his identifiable needs; and 2. The professional program design which represents the best thinking of the staff of the individual college or university. Primacy must be given to the fact that there can be no completely packaged plan for every individual who will enroll in any given field or in any given university. As intimated above, this does not eliminate the professional obligation of the staff of the institution to ascertain if the background elements considered necessary for a good teacher have been incorporated into the experience of the individual. The failure to recognize previous experience or current needs will reduce the benefit to any participant.

In designing the program, specific activities should be developed for persons who are involved in a formal in-service program. For some individuals, practicum experiences in their particular specialization may be appropriate. These practicum experiences would incorporate demonstration teaching, individual counseling, parent relationships and many other programs. In each of the situations, careful evaluation would be made of the activity under scrutiny. Audio and visual taping of the activity, observation of the teaching or counseling situation by pre-service enrollees in a teacher education program, fellow in-service registrants and members of the professional staff can be developed. Criticism for improvement and opportunities for self-analysis are to be available.

The practicum experiences and other activities which will be mentioned will not eliminate the need for regular courses for some individuals. Concepts about the available knowledge in a field can best be obtained in some circumstances through courses and experiences designed to bring about an improvement of the academic background of individuals. Instructional techniques appropriate for a discipline will be used. The opportunity to study in depth in a given field under competent scholars may be an imperative for certain individuals.

As a professional, each in-service teacher has the responsibility to analyze the research information available about teaching in general as well as in the area of specialization. The institution in which the individual is enrolled must accept the obligation of maintaining the best research information available. Through its own initiative or through membership in organizations which provide the service, summaries of available research throughout the nation and world must be provided for students. Judgmental positions on the part of the staff of the institution should be available about the research. Such summaries and positions taken by faculty will be extremely beneficial for the individuals enrolled. Planned programs including research seminars, colloquia and conferences should be available. The evaluation of research and the transmission of information to improve the profession should be a definite part of any planned in-service program.

Institutions of higher learning must accept the obligation for the utilization of the best methods of teaching and the most appropriate resources for knowledge transmission and retrieval. If they are to be approved for in-service education for the teaching profession, the acceptance of programmed testing and teaching, instructional devices such as television and other recorded materials and the potential of the computer must be included in any approved teacher in-service educational program. Human frailties will require that all potential facilities and materials be incorporated into the program. Knowledge about new instructional techniques can be developed through study of the potential and theory of the new devices as well as by utilizing them for learning in the in-service program. Content and skills necessary for the individual to understand new techniques and new knowledge can be incorporated into programmed learning. Those in charge of in-service education should not be averse to utilizing all available techniques for instructional activities.

A sixth major characteristic of in-service education should be individual study. This can be directed study and reading on individually interesting topics or a depth into research projects. The advanced study must incorporate within it an opportunity to create a personal relationship with the in-service teacher which will allow for rapid expansion of interest in depth and for stimulating research in a given field.

Many school districts will need to expand their own program offerings and to make decisions about curriculum projects. Group study and research progams incorporating personnel from a given school district could be carried on under the aegis of an in-service education activity. These projects could be school centered or university centered. Team learning and team teaching could both be incorporated into such an activity as the personnel resources from the school district and from the university are placed in juxtaposition. The needs of the school district and the best professional thinking can be brought to bear on a given problem. The end result can be an excellent design for an educational endeavor within a given community.

In order to ascertain the merits of any program, followup and evaluation must be included. Evaluation should consist of an analysis of the progress of the individuals who have been enrolled and the impact that the programs which have been developed have had on school curricula and programs. Complacency can develop without evaluation. Analysis of results can be a stimulus to improvement, change and better in-service education.

In order to facilitate the entire program for in-service education, any given university must analyze itself carefully in terms of its resources. No implication is intended that every university must be self-contained and able to meet the needs of all individuals. The utilization of the community in which the school is located, the community in which the in-service enrollees are teaching and other educational and community agencies must be examined. The strengths of the entire educational community should be tapped for the experience of a given individual or group. The program of the student should not be handicapped because of the shortcomings of an institution. Through programmed instruction, cross registration, practicum placements, individual study coordinated with correspondence courses, new horizons can be opened for every individual. Emphasis is given again to the fact that these programs must be designed around the needs of individuals rather than around the self-imposed limitation of a given institution or program.

Summary

Continuing education for the teaching profession is crucial. It is crucial for the individuals who are teachers, for the individuals who are students and for the educational upgrading of the entire citizenry. No longer can it be considered an individual choice or a haphazard endeavor.

Every individual who is a teacher must be imbued with the concept that in-service education on a planned basis is a professional necessity. When one accepts the concept that for professional growth a teacher must continue his education, the parallel concept comes into focus that the individual communities and states have a stake in the program. This will require an acceptance of the fact that school community needs and individual needs will have to be coordinated. After the acceptance of this philosophy, implementation of a good continuing education program can only be implemented when adequate resources are available within the University and communities. A new look will have to be taken by universities in terms of their obligation to returning students who are already professionals. Failure to change and modify existing programs can only lead to self-deceit.

The dramatic increase in knowledge and the inability of each individual to keep abreast in his field in any modest way combine to create a situation in which many things are taught which are no longer true. Education for children, youth and adults in the United States can be meaningful only if the teaching staff is knowledgeable and professionally competent in modern technical information and research. Continuing education of the individual and the profession is essential to maintain and to improve educational programs and classroom instruction. Failure to incorporate this concept into the activities of the entire profession will bring chaos and alteration of the prerogatives of the teacher. Control of education will be shifted to other personnel in the society.

A Hard Look at Quality in In-Service Education

Jack D. Roberts

It is hard to imagine a single school system in the United States today that doesn't have a commitment to continuing the professional development of its teachers after they get on the job. It is equally hard to imagine a school system of the future that will not have a much greater commitment to vastly improved professional growth programs.

The need for in-service growth has been part of the professional teaching picture from the time of the earliest schools. But it is only in more recent years that compelling forces have highlighted the necessity for providing teachers with opportunities to increase their knowledge, insight, understanding, and skills in working with young people.

In many communities, the pressure of greatly increased enrollment has resulted in the appointment of many teachers who have been less than fully prepared. These teachers need immediate, on-the-job opportunities to continue their education if a school system is to avoid the serious stresses that can arise when numerous teachers join the staff on an emergency or substitute basis.

Teaching assignments today are becoming more complex. There is not only a greater number of pupils to be served, often with inadequate facilities and less than the needed number of personnel, fully prepared or otherwise, but also a need for teachers to keep apace of rapidly changing areas of knowledge. The demands upon schools to teach more—and to teach it better and faster—are strong and present many instructional problems. Most teachers were prepared well before the explosion of knowledge now under way, and they seek assistance in meeting the instructional problems these demands present. And there is no indication that this need is going to lessen. As programs of research in many fields are expanded, mature and beginning teachers alike will need to continue to extend their knowledge and reshape their practice.

The steady urbanization of our society brings still other pressures. In central city schools, urbanization creates new kinds of educational problems. In the schools of suburbia, the same forces produce a quite different set of problems. Teachers need help in moving ahead, in developing new understandings, in trying out ideas and skills, and in tackling old jobs wsth new insights and new jobs with wisdom and courage.

Importance of Behavioral Change

There are many kinds of programs for the in-service professional growth of teachers. Common to them all is the underlying assumption that teacher's instructional service can be improved. Improvement of instruction eventually requires a change in teachers' classroom behavior. There is much knowledge available in the literature about the processes involved in behavioral change, and this knowledge can be utilized in planning improved programs for professional development.[1] Another article in this issue deals with the process of change and what it takes to bring about significant behavioral modifications. Attention is directed to it.

Within the great range of activities that take place under the general heading of continuing education for teachers, the quality of experience varies widely. Nearly all teachers realize that this is so. An experience of one kind, dealing with just the problems that a teacher faces at the time and treating them in a way which makes the learning most applicable, can rate high in quality. Another, unrelated to a teacher's needs and having no particular application to his teaching situation, can be very poor.

Much of the confusion and frustration associated with some in-service training practices results from a failure to recognize that in-service programs need to seek changes in behavior that lead to more effective teacher-pupil interaction in the classroom in terms of established goals. Further, there is a need for developing ways to determine whether the changes brought about by in-service activities improve the quality of the instructional program.

Certain in-service practices may be classed among the "poorer" professional growth experiences for two principal reasons: 1) They fail to utilize what is known about behavioral change; 2) They appear to be unconcerned with the lack of a positive relationship between the particular activity itself and improvement in the instructional program.

In short, poorer practices seem to have little concern for such questions as: What changes are to be expected in teachers' behavior as an outcome of this in-service experience? Do these changes improve the instructional program?

In thinking through problems of in-service education, it may be helpful to take a

[1] See, for example, Amidon, Edmund J., Flanders, Ned A. *The Role of the Teacher in the Classroom.* Minneapolis: Paul S. Amidon & Associates, 1963. 68 pages.

closer look at some of the most common practices which persist despite the fact that in light of the above, they can be classed as "poorer."

Courses for Point Collectors

The point collectors are those who seek to accumulate credits (in-service or otherwise) to meet what are often rather rigid course requirements for salary advancement or for securing a different license. The collectors simply follow the regulations of their local school systems–regulations which establish a relationship between eligibility for salary or other advancement and certain course work. If the point collectors, as is sometimes alleged, appear to place more stress upon piling up credits than upon the relevance of the courses to their professional growth, they are only utilizing a structure that encourages them to do so.

Whether the courses are given by local school employees or by people outside the school system is beside the point, as is the matter of credit–"in-service" or "university." So long as courses of any kind may be used for license renewal or maintenance, for salary increments, for placement on a higher schedule, or for examination or qualification for another license, there is a real incentive for point collecting quite separate from professional development. Lack of satisfactory ways to determine professional growth is not reason enough to continue practices that too often have only unintended outcomes.

No one really likes this situation–least of all the point collectors who may be looking forward eagerly to the time when course "requirements" will have been met. School administrators and supervisors prefer to stress professional growth, rather than the number of credits collected. Those giving the courses want interested, well-motivated students. Boards of education, knowing of point collectors who appear to be long on credits but short on professional growth, tend to look longingly at a salary schedule that rewards "merit," not credits. No one is really happy about point collecting.

It is high time that we divorce the salary schedule from point collecting and demolish the assumption that courses taken to qualify for advancement of one kind or another somehow promote professional growth. It should be acknowledged that relating salary advancement to the accumulation of course credits hasn't contributed very much to professional growth in many cases. There appears to be little observable relationship between the point collector's salary advancement and improvements in his instructional program. Conant is very outspoken about this when he says, "The mere accumulation of credits without respect to their bearing on the teacher's actual work should not be counted."[2]

Fully adequate salary schedules are of primary importance for all teachers and should be maintained in their own right. That kind of professional growth which fosters individuality, encourages self-fulfillment, stimulates individual professional development, and enhances individual dignity needs to be raised out of the point

[2]Conant, James B. *The Education of American Teachers.* New York: McGraw-Hill Book Company, 1963. p. 196.

collecting category. As more and more attention is directed toward analyses of teaching behavior, perhaps ways will be found to establish first rate salary schedules divorced from point collecting requirements and, at the same time, enable teachers to achieve higher levels of professional development.

"Must" Experiences

A "must" experience is distinguished by two characteristics. First, the content is of relatively high priority for the local school system. Second, it is understood by those in the "know" to be a "must" for certain teachers.

The experience may be any one of a number of different kinds. It may be a course for science background, a workshop on teaching number concepts, a series of lecture-discussion sessions in inter-cultural education, a course in linguistics and its relation to the reading program at a certain level, or intensive work on curriculum change which may involve taking courses, committee work, or other activities. It should be made quite clear that these and similar enterprises can contribute in important ways to professional growth. The nature of the problem is suggested by the question, "Whose growth?"

Who determines the areas around which in-service experiences are planned? Whose problems are dealt with? Are the problems identified for the staff by the administration or someone else, such as a community or parent group? Do teachers have opportunities to define problems and help plan ways to solve them? Who decides what changes should be made? Does the administration encourage teacher participation on the one hand and on the other tend to feel that the staff doesn't identify the "right" problems?

Too often, decisions in such matters are made *for* teachers, as though someone else knows best the problems with which teachers need help. Moffitt puts this point very well when he states, "Only under those circumstances in which teachers find their own problems and want to do something about them can effective in-service education programs exist."[3] It is easy to overlook the importance of involving the learner and to fall back upon the old and discredited idea that lasting change can be effected through mass production methods.

Undoubtedly, there are "priority areas" for a school system or particular school. But professional growth experiences in these areas are of little value unless teachers see a relationship to their own needs. If they do not, chances are there will be little application of the learning that may be reasonably be expected as an outcome.

Occasionally, an experience in a so-called priority area is designed merely to give information. For example, an in-service course on the "new math" may be intended to inform teachers about the changes taking place in elementary school mathematics. Such a course, restricted to information giving, can serve a very limited goal, and it is easy to get into the confusion that exists between "new" programs or content and "better" instruction or learning. Obviously, new content doesn't

[3]Moffitt, John C. *In-Service Education for Teachers.* Washington, D. C.: Center For Applied Research in Education, 1963. p. 59.

necessarily mean better instruction. At this point of information giving, in-service programs and professional growth seem to diverge.

The "must" aspect of these in-service activities makes them of questionable value to genuine professional growth. Every teacher knows what happens when everyone, or everyone worth his salt, is expected to sign up for one of the in-service programs being offered during a particular term. Most teachers probably do one of three things: 1) sign up for the "experience" that seems most closely related to a felt professional need; 2) select whatever experience offers the most credit toward advancement of some kind; or 3) drift into the least offensive enterprise and endure it. One likes to feel that most teachers would be in the first group but has an uneasy feeling that the number in the third group is too large.

The Mutual Admiration Society

Sometimes a mutual admiration society substitutes for in-service education. When this happens, courses given by local system supervisors, administrators, coordinators, or directors stress "the way we do it." Staff members reply in kind, and the sum total of a rather soporific experience is little more or less than a worsening of the inbreeding that is probably already responsible for having local personnel conduct the program in the first place. Too frequently, the problems considered are those of the school or school system as perceived by administrators or supervisors. In addition to being told what the problems are, the participants are often informed just what the solutions should be. If these experiences are expected to bring about change, the change to be wrought is controlled by the "establishment." Any creative ideas teachers may have brought along are smothered. The "establishment" always knows the best answer. As teachers are reminded of this again and again and in many different ways, they come to believe it is so—or at least profess to believe that it is so—and awake to the comforts of mutual admiration.

The mutual admiration society may take other forms—for example, the study group or committee. In such groups, everyone makes a point of cooperating and agreeing. Group members are fairly certain that no real challenges to their commonly held goals and purposes will arise and that they may contentedly discuss the matter at hand without the threat of diversity in thinking. Matters will move along rather smoothly, and nothing of any consequence for the school program or the participating individuals ensues.

Unrelated, Fragmented Experiences

Unrelated, fragmented experiences are of two different kinds. They may be activities which have little if any apparent relationship to professional growth. Aimless travel is an example. Or they may be experiences which presumably have a relationship to professional growth but are independent of an over-all design for professional development. In many ways, the latter represents a grasshopper approach to professional growth. There may be a course now, a workshop later, a study group at another time, travel, intervisitation, or a convention, for example, with no apparent rationale supporting an over-all design for professional growth. It must be said, of course, that each such discrete experience can be important and valuable to a teacher. And teachers should continue to have the opportunities to engage in a variety of these experiences if they wish to do so. But this is not enough. The question "Important and valuable to what end?" needs to be raised.

It seems appropriate at this point to suggest the possibility of differentiating between personal growth and professional growth. The former probably has more to do with the development of the individual as a person, while the latter is concerned more directly with the growth of specialized knowledge and skills. Presumably a teacher's personal growth contributes to his professional growth, and both in turn have a positive relationship to the quality of his instruction. This whole area, however, is badly in need of clarification. If professional growth is separate and distinct from personal growth, then school systems need to define clearly those aspects of growth with which they feel they should be concerned and plan accordingly. If there is no identifiable difference, a much wider range of experiences can be considered in relation to professional growth, and a school system must decide how this is to be managed.

Until these clarifications are made, other salutary measures may be taken. Perhaps more help could be given teachers in planning a series of related and integrative professional growth experiences. This might grow into a kind of "career planning" venture engaged in cooperatively by teachers, local school system supervisors, institutions of higher learning, and professional associations. Too little has been done with this up to now. What career planning there has been has usually taken place in the college or university as part of planning work for graduate study, or it has been attempted in a limited way by local school systems' requiring teachers to obtain advance approval for in-service work. Too often, teachers perceive this latter, rather left-handed attempt at career planning as a coercive administrative device. Counseling a teacher in career development could be carried on over a fairly long period of professional development or as long as it was felt to be needed. How the counseling might take place, what it might include, and who would be engaged and in what manner would need to be explored.

All too frequently, planning for professional growth has overlooked important and valuable resources of the local school system, state departments of education, colleges and universities, professional associations, foundations and the like that with increased cooperative endeavor may be drawn upon. An effective structure for long-range planning of career development can help to provide needed inter-relationships among a number of in-service professional growth experiences.

The grasshopper approach undoubtedly can satisfy certain needs. But it is open to question how much this way of satisfying these needs contributes to professional growth and, further, how much effect it has on the quality of instructional practice. One word of caution seems appropriate here. It is important to avoid the pitfall of planning *for the teacher*, of assuming that someone else knows best a teacher's professional needs or how he may be helped. At this stage, it is crucial to plan cooperatively.

Study Groups

Commonly found in in-service practice is the study group. These formal or informal groups generally seek to increase the participants' understanding of specified professional topics or problem areas. If it is well planned and capably led, the study group can be a good device for promoting in-service growth.[4] It is not, however, as simple to use study groups as it may seem.

A given number of teachers assembled together do not necessarily constitute a group—let alone a study group. It takes a sense of purpose and direction, common interests, and loyalties to have a functioning group. Miles gives a number of examples of group situations involving school people and goes on to say: "These examples suggest the wide range of group situations with which school people are involved. They also underline the complexity of effective work with groups, and the joys, upsets, depressions, and gains which people feel when they work with others."[5]

The practice of bringing a number of teachers together in a "committee" or "study group" on the assumption that the resulting interaction will promote desirable professional growth fails to take into account what is known about groups and how they function. Not only must there be agreement on commonly accepted goals, but also a number of important skills must be drawn upon to produce good results. In addition, what the group members take with them to the group experience is influential. Moffitt points out that "the effectiveness of a group as a means of in-service education of teachers is largely determined by the ability of the group members to free themselves from individual tensions and anxieties. This ability is not possessed by all people."[6]

Depending upon a person's previous experiences, he may look forward eagerly to group work or he may dread it. He may have no particular feeling one way or the other. As an individual who enters a group because he anticipates extended opportunities to talk or because he believes he may dominate or control the situation can make only limited contributions to group progress. And this kind of behavior becomes a real obstacle to the growth of other group members. Interpersonal relationships need to be such that every member of the group can participate freely and effectively and derive a measure of satisfaction from the experience. In a study group where individuals feel anxious or threatened or where the leader or another member manipulates or dominates, the experience may be destructive and produce only frustration and disillusionment. After a few such negative experiences, teachers may quite rightly display unfavorable attitudes toward in-service study groups. These attitudes will be difficult to overcome.

Disintegrative feelings may grow out of group situations characterized by

[4] See Doll, Ronald C. *Curriculum Improvement: Decision-making and Process.* Boston: Allyn and Bacon. 1964, p. 272.

[5] Miles, Matthew B. *Learning to Work in Groups.* New York: Bureau of Publications, Teachers College, Columbia University, 1959. p. 15.

[6] Moffitt, John C. op. cit., p. 68.

aimlessness and failure to come to grips with the basic problems that face the group. When a group member finds in meeting after meeting that he is "enduring" directionless discussion that never gets beneath the surface of the issues involved, he is probably less than enthusiastic about what might have been, under different conditions, a valuable in-service growth experience.

It is quite clear that study groups, to be most effective, need skillful leadership and a willingness on the part of group members to share responsibility for leadership, direction, and progress.

Autocratic Behavior of Leaders

Autocratic behavior on the part of superintendents, principals, supervisors, directors, coordinators, and other responsible leaders can be deadly to the kind of professional growth that schools anticipate for their personnel. It is easy to overlook the fact that for teachers new to the school, its day-to-day functioning is a critical and effective in-service conditioner of growth. The complex system of interrelationships among the members of a school staff and the many daily interactions that express these relationships help the new teacher understand very quickly, for example, that the feelings of the supervisors may be less than warm toward diversity, innovation, or creativity. A supervisor usually doesn't have to frown more than once or twice upon new and divergent approaches to problems for a teacher to get the idea that it's wiser to conform to the established ways.

Autocratic patterns of control can have consequences unintended by school leaders. Teachers who on the one hand are encouraged to become involved in professional growth activities and on the other hand are given little opportunity or responsibility for helping to plan these activities may learn that surface compliance is sufficient, and that no significant changes in behavior are expected or needed.

Limiting Professional Growth Activities To Out-of-School Time

The assumption is often made that the activities of greatest value to professional growth occur largely during out-of-school times–in late afternoon or the evening, on Saturday, or during summers or leaves of absence of one kind or other. When this assumption is made, the professional growth program will not be as strong as it would be if it were recognized that some important experiences can occur only during school time. (The writer excludes from consideration under this heading the usual supervisory activities that take place during the school day.)

For example, the trial use of new ideas in an instructional practice requires a classroom setting. As part of a workshop or other in-service experience in which a teacher may be engaged, the trial and application of new ideas can reinforce new learning. Action research programs conducted by teachers with their own classes can promote professional growth to high levels. The in-service experience that does not promote and encourage adaptations in instructional practice is probably less valuable than one which is not insulated from an immediate application of what is learned to real people in real school settings. Whether it is wisest to limit professional growth experiences to full time study on a campus, for example, where the immediate try-out and revision of an idea in a classroom is not possible, is a question which perhaps has been answered by some too hastily.

The disadvantages of late afternoon and evening classes have been stressed.[7] It needs to be kept in mind, however, that many of these courses have strong reasons to support them, not the least of which may be a close relationship to teacher's current instructional problems.

Perhaps, cooperative plans between school systems and institutions of higher learning could be broadened to include several different kinds of special projects to take place within the school day as well as outside it. Conceivably, a group of teachers from a school could spend a morning a week on the campus, with their professor spending another morning or afternoon with them in school to follow-up and reinforce. A somewhat similar arrangement is commonly found in student teaching programs at both the undergraduate and graduate levels. A variety of such programs to meet different needs could include, for example, intensive work with new teachers cooperatively planned by the teachers, appropriate supervisory staff members, and university personnel. Other such experiences could be planned for groups of teachers involved in special curriculum projects.

There is ample precedent for giving teachers released time for professional work at either local or university centers.[8] For about twenty years, the Metropolitan School Study Council in New York City has had groups of teachers working cooperatively with Study Council personnel on problems of common interest to Council schools. The cost of hiring substitutes to free teachers for a day a month for committee work at Council headquarters is regarded by the local school system as an important investment in professional growth. While the number of teachers who have such opportunities under this kind of arrangement is relatively small, the practice could be developed far more extensively, quite outside a study council framework.

These "in school time" experiences need not be limited to association with an institution of higher learning. Many such projects can be and often are worked out by local school system personnel, with or without the assistance of a consultant. To help solve the problem of "point collecting," a board of education might entirely underwrite certain specified professional growth and development projects without establishing any relationship between the completion of such projects and subsequent salary status.

Unevaluated Programs

It would appear to be less than wise for a school system to provide in-service training programs without making an adequate evaluation of the changes such programs may bring about. Ideally, of course, the plan for evaluation should be built into the activity itself.

[7] See, for example, Conant, James B. op. cit., p. 191.

[8] See, for example, Broadhead, Clare A. "The Reading Center: An In-Service Training Program," *The Elementary School Journal* 52:335-39; February 1952.

The difficulties of identifying teacher growth, measuring it, and relating it to the quality of the instructional program are well known and need not be reviewed here. These difficulties, however, need not hold up all efforts to evaluate in-service programs and their outcomes. Parker, for example, offers some very helpful guidelines for planning, organizing, and conducting in-service education activities and programs in school systems.[9] These guidelines may be helpful in evaluation. Herrick, in considering the evaluation of change in programs of in-service education, states:

> Most programs of in-service education in schools exist for the dual purpose of helping the members of the staff become more competent to deal with their professional roles as teachers and administrators and of improving the quality of the educational program of the school system. It follows, therefore, that the evaluation of change in programs of in-service education should consider the nature and quality for changes in people as individuals and as professional persons and the nature and quality of the changes made in the education program itself.[10]

If the evaluation of an in-service program contents itself with quantitative measures, the goals are indeed limited when contrasted with those of a program which recognizes the importance of teaching behavior and seeks to focus upon where the impact of the activities will rest—the quality of the schools' instructional program.

In-service training programs will merit increasing attention as school systems seek to fulfill their role in an era marked by great scientific and technological complexity and change. The importance of these professional growth programs will be demonstrated again and again as teachers seek practical applications for their conceptualization of the interdependency of technological development, industrialization, and urbanization on the one hand, and the capacity of the educational structure in helping to maintain and promote this development on the other. New insights and skills will be needed, and in-service programs will be called upon to reach levels of effectiveness not expected in a less complex society. The view ahead shows clearly that in the continuing education of teachers, there will be neither room nor time for in-service programs that fail to measure up to high expectations.

[9] Parker, J. Cecil. "Guidelines for In-Service Education." *In-Service Education.* Fifty Sixth Yearbook, Part I. Chicago: National Society for the Study of Education, 1957. pp. 103-128.

[10] *Ibid.* Herrick, Virgil E. "The Evaluation of Change in Programs of In-Service Education," p. 311.

A Study of Orientation and In-Service Education Practices in the Indianapolis Public Schools

Melvin M. Tower

Educators are becoming increasingly aware of the need for helping beginning teachers during their first year of teaching. It is recognized that a certificate gives the teacher the right to start teaching, but much remains to be learned on the job. Public school systems need to assume the responsibility for providing continuous professional growth of those who choose the teaching profession.

It is important for each school system to study the effectiveness of the provisions it makes for caring for the problems of beginning teachers. This study is primarily concerned with an extensive appraisal of the practices and procedures that are used in the Indianapolis public schools.

Statement of the Problem

The purpose of this section of the study was to determine to what degree the orientation and in-service education practices were meeting the needs of beginning experienced and inexperienced teachers. More specifically, this study was concerned with the value which beginning experienced and inexperienced teachers, principals, and consultants placed on certain orientation and in-service education practices. Thus the same list of twenty practices was used to gather data from principals, consultants and teachers.

Although records were not available on the frequency of employment of all orientation and in-service education practices, the comprehensive list in the questionnaire included those services which were described in bulletins by the Indianapolis public school system and by consultants and administrators in their orientation meetings with beginning teachers. Space was provided for the respondents to write additional orientation and in-service education practices that were of value to beginning teachers.

Amount of Help Beginning Teachers Indicated They Gained from Selected Orientation and In-Service Education Practices

Beginning teachers were asked to indicate the amount of help they gained from each practice by checking one of four possibilities: "none," "little," "some," or "much." Values were assigned to their responses as follows: "none" = 0, "little" = 1, "some" = 2, and "much" = 3. After multiplying the percentages of responses to each item by corresponding assigned values, the products were totaled and recorded in the weighted totals column.

As indicated in Table 1, beginning teachers reported they gained the most help

Table 1. Percentage Distribution of Responses, Weighted Totals and Rank Order of the Amount of Help Which Eighty-One Beginning Teachers Indicated They Gained From Various Orientation and In-Service Educational Practices

	Amount of Help Gained						
	Percentages						
Orientation and In-Service Practices	*No response*	*None*	*Little*	*Some*	*Much*	*Weighted totals*	*Rank*
March Conference	1	6	16	25	52	222	1.5
Individual conferences with consultants	2	4	17	26	51	222	1.5
Indianapolis courses of study	9	4	7	31	49	216	3.5
Help from other teachers	2	5	21	21	51	216	3.5
Group meetings: i.e., arithmetic, social studies, science, language arts, chart stories, handwriting	4	9	12	43	32	194	5
Handbook for beginning teachers	1	2	31	37	28	189	6
Regular consultant help	2	12	20	28	37	187	7
General faculty meetings	0	6	28	37	28	186	8
Bulletins from the Instruction Center	1	14	19	49	17	168	9.5
Demonstration teaching by consultants	7	21	14	20	38	168	9.5
Individual conferences with administrators	7	11	25	30	27	166	11
Professional publications	1	7	33	42	16	165	12
Orientation meetings held at Arsenal Technical High School and with the building principal in your school	1	12	33	32	21	160	13
Bulletins from the Central Office	1	31	28	49	9	153	14
Observation of class instruction in your building and/or in other buildings	9	31	14	16	31	139	15
Assistance in making teaching aids or devices	9	27	12	30	22	138	16
The present evaluation system of non-tenure teachers	19	12	19	33	17	136	17
Professional organization	2	27	37	28	5	108	18
Assigned "Big Sister" or "Buddy Teacher"	15	52	4	11	19	83	19
Demonstration teaching by principals	14	53	10	12	11	67	20

from (1) March Conference, (2) individual conferences with consultants, (3) Indianapolis courses of study, and (4) help from other teachers. Approximately fifty per cent of them checked that they gained "much" help from these services.

The March Conference was an annual two-day in-service meeting for all personnel in the Indianapolis public schools. This conference was carefully planned by teachers, consultants and administrators to meet the needs and interests of the entire instructional staff in this school system. All teachers were permitted to choose one area of study for the two-day conference. From an analysis of their registrations, the elementary teachers participated in the following areas: art, music, physical education, kindergarten, science, mathematics, language arts and social studies. Teachers in all areas met in mass meetings and small discussion groups or workshops with twenty-two specialists in the various areas serving as resource leaders.

The elementary consultants sponsored a number of group meetings in arithmetic, social studies, science, language arts, and on the development of primary chart stories throughout the school year. These in-service meetings were open to all elementary teachers in the school system, but the majority of those who attended were non-tenure teachers. Seventy-five per cent of the beginning teachers found these group meetings of "some" or "much" value, and ranked this service fifth in the amount of help gained. Approximately two-thirds of the beginning teachers thought handbooks for beginning teachers and regular consultant services were of "some" or "much" value, ranking them sixth and seventh, respectively. Although no definition of regular consultant help was used in this study, the investigator believed the teachers, consultants and principals interpreted this term to mean the consultant's routine visitations to the classroom. Generally speaking, individual conferences with consultants and group meetings of teachers on common problems are considered as regular consultant services.

Beginning teachers indicated that some of the least valuable services were: (1) the present evaluation system of non-tenure teachers, (2) professional organizations, (3) assigned "Big Sisters" or "Buddy Teachers," and (4) demonstration teaching by principals.

Differences Between Beginning Inexperienced and Experienced Teachers as to the Amount of Help They Indicated They Gained from Selected Services

In an effort to find out whether any significant differences existed between the amount of help that beginning teachers gained from certain orientation and in-service education practices, the investigator organized the data from the respondents according to their teaching experiences. When the criterion of weighted totals was used for appraising the value of each practice, it was evident that the experienced teachers gained more help from orientation and in-service education practices than the inexperienced teachers (Table 2). The experienced teachers reported they gained more help than the inexperienced teachers from the twenty practices with the exception of the following: (1) help from teachers, (2)

Table 2. Percentage Distribution of Responses, Weighted Totals, and Rank Order of the Amount of Help That Beginning Inexperienced and Experienced Teachers Indicated They Gained from Orientation and In-Service Practices

	Amount of Help Gained													
	Amount of help beginning inexperienced teachers gained							*Amount of help beginning experienced teachers gained*						
	Percentages							*Percentages*						
Orientation and In-Service Practices	*No response*	*None*	*Little*	*Some*	*Much*	*Weighted totals*	*Rank*	*No response*	*None*	*Little*	*Some*	*Much*	*Weighted totals*	*Rank*
Help from other teachers	2	5	23	18	53	218	1	4	4	17	29	46	213	4.5
March Conference	2	5	16	30	47	217	2	0	8	17	13	63	232	3
Individual conferences with consultants	4	4	23	21	49	212	3	0	4	4	38	54	242	1
Indianapolis courses of study	12	5	5	26	51	210	4	0	0	13	42	46	235	2
Group meetings: i.e., arithmetic, social studies, science, language arts, chart stories, handwriting	5	9	12	39	35	195	5	0	8	13	54	25	196	9
Handbook for beginning teachers	2	2	33	37	26	185	6	0	4	25	38	33	200	7
Regular consultant help	2	12	23	32	32	183	7	4	13	13	21	50	205	6
General faculty meetings	0	7	32	39	23	179	8	0	4	21	33	42	213	4.5
Demonstration teaching by consultants	7	19	12	23	39	175	9	8	25	17	13	38	157	16
Bulletins from the Instruction Center	2	14	21	49	14	161	10	0	13	13	50	25	188	10.5

Orientation meetings held at Arsenal Technical High School and with the building principal in your school	2	14	32	32	21	159	11	0	8	38	33	21	167	13
Professional publications	2	9	37	39	14	157	12	0	4	25	50	21	188	10.5
Observation of class instruction in your building and/or in other buildings	11	23	18	18	32	150	13	4	50	4	13	29	117	18
Individual conferences with administrators	9	12	33	19	26	149	14	4	8	4	54	29	199	8
Bulletins from the Central Office	0	16	33	42	9	144	15	4	4	17	67	8	175	12
The present evaluation system of non-tenure teachers	21	11	23	32	14	129	16	13	17	8	38	25	159	15
Professional organization	2	30	40	23	5	101	18	4	21	29	42	4	125	17
Assistance in making teaching aids or devices	11	28	14	28	19	127	17	4	25	8	33	29	161	14
Demonstration teaching by principals	18	47	7	14	14	77	20	4	67	17	8	4	45	20
Assigned "Big Sister" or "Buddy Teacher"	14	51	4	12	19	85	19	4	54	4	8	17	71	19
Total	128	323	441	573	542	3,213		57	341	307	677	609	3,488	

demonstration teaching by consultants, (3) observation of class instruction in your building and/or in other buildings, (4) demonstration teaching by principals, and (5) assigned "Big Sister" or "Buddy Teacher."

Although the two groups of teachers were not in complete agreement on the value of all services, they did agree on the services that were of most value by ranking the following practices among the first five: (1) help from other teachers, (2) March Conference, (3) individual conferences with consultants, and (4) Indianapolis courses of study.

Approximately fifty-four per cent of the inexperienced teachers and an even greater per cent of the experienced teachers indicated that demonstration teaching by principals and assigned Big Sister or Buddy Teacher were of little or no value to them.

Amount of Help Principals and Consultants Indicated Beginning Teachers Gained from Orientation and In-Service Education Practices

As mentioned previously, principals and consultants were asked to assess the value to beginning teachers of a selected list of orientation and in-service education practices. An additional column, "I don't know," was provided for principals and consultants to check their choice of responses.

As indicated in Table 3, the seventy-seven administrators and consultants seemed to feel that person-to-person contacts were of most value to beginning teachers. It is significant that all of the principals and consultants indicated that individual conferences with consultants were a valuable service for beginning teachers, and as many as eighty-four per cent of them thought this service was of "much" help to teachers. The practice of individual conferences with administrators was ranked second by principals and consultants as seventy-three per cent of them marked "much" help gained from this service.

Approximately two-thirds of the principals and consultants were of the opinion that beginning teachers gained "much" help from (1) group meetings: i.e., arithmetic, social studies, science, language arts; (2) handbooks for beginning teachers; (3) regular consultant help; and (4) Indianapolis courses of study.

It is interesting to note that three of the first five services were performed by general elementary consultants. These services were: (1) individual conferences with consultants, (2) group meetings, and (3) regular consultant help. The beginning experienced and inexperienced teachers agreed with the principals and consultants on the relative amount of help gained from individual conferences with consultants and from group meetings by ranking them 1.5 and 5, respectively (Table 1).

Principals and consultants thought the following services were of considerable value to beginning teachers: (1) demonstration teaching by consultants, (2) orientation meetings prior to the opening day of school, and (3) teacher visitation.

Although two services, March Conference and help from other teachers, were ranked 1.5 and 3.5 by beginning teachers, the principals and consultants ranked them 12 and 13, respectively.

Principals and consultants were in some agreement with the beginning teachers on

Table 3. Percentage Distribution of Responses, Weighted Totals and Rank Order of the Amount of Help That Principals and Consultants Indicated Beginning Teachers Received from Orientation and In-Service Education Services

	Amount of Help Gained							
	Percentages							
Orientation and In-Service Practices	*No response*	*I don't know*	*None*	*Little*	*Some*	*Much*	*Weighted totals*	*Rank*
Individual conferences with consultants	0	0	0	4	12	84	280	1
Individual conferences with administrators	3	3	0	3	19	73	260	2
Group meetings: i.e., arithmetic, social studies, science, language arts, chart stories, handwriting	4	0	0	3	26	68	259	3.5
Handbook for beginning teachers	3	0	0	3	29	66	259	3.5
Regular consultant help	1	0	0		19	70	257	5
Indianapolis courses of study	3	1	0	4	27	65	253	6
Demonstration teaching by consultants	1	3	1	5	31	58	241	7
Orientation meetings held at Arsenal Technieal High School and with the building principal in their school	3	3	0	6	30	58	240	8.5
Observation of class instruction in their buildings and/or in other buildings	3	0	1	9	30	57	240	8.5
Assistance in making teaching aids or devices	1	0	0	6	45	47	237	10
General faculty meetings	1	3	0	5	47	44	231	11
March Conference	3	0	3	8	40	47	229	12
Help from other teachers	3	0	0	9	48	40	225	13
Bulletins from the Instruction Center	1	1	0	16	44	38	218	14
Bulletins from the Central Office	0	3	0	21	47	30	205	15
Assigned "Big Sister" or "Buddy Teacher"	1	4	6	14	39	35	197	16
Demonstration teaching by principals	0	8	4	16	49	23	183	17
Professional publications	0	4	1	26	57	12	176	18
The present evaluation system of non-tenure teachers	4	3	3	25	53	13	170	19
Professional organizations	4	1	3	38	44	10	156	20

the least valuable services. Table 3 reveals these to be: (1) assigned "Big Sister" or "Buddy Teacher," (2) demonstration teaching by principals, (3) professional publications, (4) evaluation of teaching, and (5) professional organizations.

Amount of Help Beginning Teachers Indicated They Gained from Selected Practices and Amount That Principals and Consultants Indicated the Teachers Gained

A comparison was made of the opinions of beginning inexperienced teachers, beginning teachers, and principals and consultants relative to the amount of help beginning teachers gained from certain orientation and in-service practices. Rank order was used to show the value of these services, because the degree of help gained from each service influenced its weighted total and thereby the rank order of that practice.

Certain services were considered of much value to the beginning experienced and inexperienced teachers, principals and consultants, and thus they were ranked in the upper one-third by the respondents (Table 4). These practices are as follows: (1) individual conferences with consultants, (2) Indianapolis courses of study, (3) handbooks for beginning teachers, and (4) regular consultant help.

The following services were ranked in the middle third of the orientation and in-service practices by the teachers and their superiors: (1) general faculty meetings, (2) bulletins from the Instruction Center, (3) orientation meetings held at Arsenal Technical High School and with the building principal, and (4) individual conferences with the administrators; and the practices they felt were of least value to new teachers were: (1) the present evaluation system of non-tenure teachers, (2) professional organizations, (3) assigned "Big Sister" or "Buddy Teacher." and (4) demonstration teaching by principals.

Summary

Beginning elementary teachers, general elementary consultants and elementary principals were asked to appraise the amount of help beginning elementary teachers gained from a list of orientation and in-service education practices. A summary of these major findings follows:

(1) Beginning teachers indicated they gained the greatest amount of help from (a) personal contacts with consultants and teachers, (b) planned group meetings on common problems, and (c) Indianapolis courses of study.

(2) Beginning experienced teachers gained more help from orientation and in-service education practices than did beginning inexperienced teachers.

(3) According to the beginning elementary teachers, the most helpful services which the elementary consultant performed were the individual conferences and small group meetings of beginning teachers on common problems.

(4) Elementary principals and consultants rated individual conferences with consultants and principals as the most valuable services to beginning teachers. Other practices designed specifically to help beginning teachers that were rated as valuable were: (a) small group meetings on common instructional problems, (b) handbooks for beginning teachers, and (c) regular consultant help. Administrators and consultants did not place as much value on the March Conference and on help from other teachers as did the beginning teachers.

Table 4. Rank Order of the Amount of Help Which Beginning Inexperienced Teachers, Beginning Experienced Teachers, and Principals and Consultants Indicated Beginning Teachers Gained from Certain Orientation and In-Service Practices

	Beginning Teachers			
Orientation and In-Service Practices	*Inexperienced (N = 57)*	*Experienced (N = 24)*	*Total (N = 81)*	*Principals and Consultants (N = 77)*
Help from other teachers	1	4.5	3.5	13
March Conference	2	3	1.5	12
Individual conferences with consultants	3	1	1.5	1
Indianapolis courses of study	4	2	3.5	6
Group meetings: i.e., arithmetic, social studies, science, language arts, chart stories, handwriting	5	9	5	3.5
Handbook for beginning teachers	6	7	6	3.5
Regular consultant help	7	6	7	5
General faculty meetings	8	4.5	8	11
Demonstration teaching by consultants	9	16	9.5	7
Bulletins from the Instruction Center	10	10.5	9.5	14
Orientation meetings held at Arsenal Technical High School and with the building principal	11	13	13	8.5
Professional publications	12	10.5	12	18
Observation of class instruction in your building and/or in other buildings	13	18	15	8.5
Individual conferences with administrators	14	8	11	2
Bulletins from the Central Office	15	12	14	15
Assistance in making teaching aids or devices	16	14	16	10
The present evaluation system of non-tenure teachers	17	15	17	19
Professional organizations	18	17	18	20
Assigned "Big Sister" or "Buddy Teacher"	19	19	19	16
Demonstration teaching by principals	20	20	20	17

Keep Your Meeting on Target

John S. Morgan

"Where did we go off the track?" The meeting should have been productive but it wasn't. Somehow, it never came to grips with the problem it was supposed to solve. A lot was said, but much of it was irrelevant, inconsequential and repetitive.

It's not easy to keep a meeting on target. Assume that you're leading a meeting of ten section supervisors to discuss ways of improving the handling of employee grievances. Each member of the meeting has a slightly different view of the subject. Each one has a different personality. Each one is in a particular kind of mood. It takes skill to keep all these men working together so the meeting can proceed logically and smoothly.

But it's a skill worth learning. Meetings can be tremendously valuable tools for planning, problem-solving, informing and training. Let's take a look at some ways of keeping them on the beam.

Basically, the problem of keeping a meeting on target falls into two areas: setting the goals of the meeting in advance and preventing digression from those goals during the meeting itself.

Robert Young, the late president of the New York Central Railroad, boasted that his weekly staff conferences lasted only five minutes. His meetings obviously had a well-defined goal and a carefully planned agenda. Five minutes, of course, is too short a time for most meetings to accomplish anything. But defining your goals in advance and planning your agenda will help you get the most done in the least time.

Too often, a supervisor starts a meeting with only a vague idea of what he wants to achieve. As a result, the session either doesn't get anywhere or takes twice as long as it should to make progress.

The Purpose

As a first step in goal-setting, decide what the general purpose of the meeting is. Is it primarily to solve a problem, to plan a project, to inform or to train? Once the general purpose is defined, it should be narrowed to more specific terms. Precisely what is the problem to be solved? In how much detail should the project be planned? Exactly what information do you want to convey to the meeting? What points should the training meeting cover?

Always keep in mind that goals for a meeting should be realistic. Often, a manager establishes a goal too broad to be achieved in a single meeting. As a result, the meeting wanders from one aspect of the subject to another, with only superficial coverage of each point. For example, a meeting called to discuss ways of cutting costs might encompass too much. Reducing it to the problem of cutting costs on materials and supplies could result in a far more productive session.

The Agenda

When the meeting's objective is defined, the next task is to develop an agenda that will accomplish it. Let's say the goal of the meeting is to find ways of processing employee grievances with greater speed. You might work out an agenda like this:

1. State the meeting's purpose.
2. Find out the average time needed to process a grievance.
3. Ask for opinions on why grievances take so long to process.
4. Ask for ideas on speeding up the handling of grievances.
5. Make a summation of recommendations.
6. Get agreement on the best suggestions.

Note that the agenda starts off with a statement of goals, goes on to a search for facts, then moves to opinions, and finally summarizes and selects. Take special pains with facts. Not having them can throw a conference off course—especially the problem-solving kind. It's a good idea to make sure in advance that the facts you need will be available, either by digging them up yourself or alerting the meeting participants to come armed with them. This helps avoid wasting time during the meeting while participants leave to get necessary documents.

Other steps also can be taken ahead of time to prevent interruptions from disturbing a meeting. Someone can be stationed outside the meeting room to ward off visitors and to run necessary errands. If the meeting room has a telephone, the operator should be notified to let through only urgent calls.

It also helps to send a copy of the agenda to the participants in advance. This can be a simplified version of the agenda you use in conducting the meeting. Your own agenda should have more detail. It should include a digest of your introduction, notes for the development of the discussion, and notes for the concluding remarks. However, your agenda should be loose enough to allow for unexpected developments during the meeting. For example, it's not practical to plan the summary rigidly because you can't know everything that will turn up. A general outline is the most you need.

Also, in your own agenda, estimate the time you think each topic will need. During the meeting, don't try to keep to this absolutely, but use it to run your meeting approximately on schedule.

Despite the most carefully worked out goals and agendas, meetings can be thrown off target. Here are some problems that can come up:

The hidden agenda. Ocassionally a meeting gets nowhere because the members have certain feelings about the subject that foster resistance to the meeting's goal. For example, the supervisor of an accounting department held a meeting of his key people to decide on an appropriate send-off for a staff member who was retiring. The meeting meandered oddly. Participants went off on tangents and made statements like:

"If anyone, I'm sure, deserves a fine send-off, it's Bill, but I wonder if we want to set too elaborate a precedent."

"Bill would be the first to protest if we went too heavy on a gift for him."

After the meeting had expressed these and similar sentiments, it eventually got to work and decided what to do, how to do it, and when. This took just 15 minutes—but only after 45 minutes of apparently pointless wandering.

Behind this initial resistance lay Bill's unpopularity with the rest of the accounting department. The participants had to get some of their hostility off their chests. The supervisor wisely let them run their course and they eventually took the proper action. If he had tried to cut them short, he might never have achieved his meeting goal.

How do you handle a hidden agenda at a meeting? First, don't pretend that it doesn't exist. Don't ride roughshod over it—the result will be to leave the participants sullen and uncooperative.

CHECK UP ON YOUR CHAIRMANSHIP

If you want to improve your skill in leading meetings, the first step is to pinpoint your weaknesses so you'll know *where* to improve. Immediately after a meeting, when it's still fresh, sit down and ask yourself these questions about your performance:

1. Was my introductory statement too wordy, poorly organized, stilted?
2. Did I neglect to define unfamiliar terms and concepts?
3. Did I talk too much?
4. Did I allow too many side discussions and irrelevant comments?
5. Did I have difficulty making myself understood?
6. Did I fail to involve all the participants in the discussion?
7. Was I patronizing?
8. Did I overlook opportunities to use charts, diagrams, and the blackboard?
9. Did I let the meeting go off schedule, so that there was no time to cover some essential points?
10. Was my summary disorganized and incomplete?

Try this approach:

1. If you sense a hidden agenda, let it express itself and talk about it openly if possible.

2. Help the group overcome its resistance by opening up the problem, collecting as much relevant data as possible, and seeking a solution.

The uneasy silence. Suddenly everybody, including the leader, has talked himself out for a moment. This happens occasionally in every meeting and creates no problem in itself. The problem comes with a panicky reaction to it. Some people can't stand silence. They say the first thing that pops into their heads; it's usually either irrelevant or repetitious. So, off the meeting may go, chasing a hare or replowing old ground.

Don't be upset yourself by silences, and guard against the desperate attempt to break them. Let a silence continue. It rarely lasts longer than a minute or two, and it can actually be useful in giving the participants time to think.

Weariness and boredom. Learn to recognize the symptoms–when sidebar discussions abound, when eyes get that glazed look, when repetitious remarks increase. Sometimes the solution is a five-minute break for coffee. Sometimes the meeting may be snapped out of its lethargy if you *deliberately* go off the subject for a few minutes–by discussing something in a lighter vein, for example.

The rambler. A non-stop talker who gets way off the subject can be a major menace to a meeting because unless he's curbed, the whole meeting may end up discussing his irrelevancies. To cope with him, try a gentle reminder, such as:

"That's interesting, Bill, but how about this sales plan we are supposed to be working on?"

You might also try summarizing what's been done so far–this can get the meeting back on target.

Besides curbing digressions by the meeting members, a leader must watch his own tendencies to get off the subject. One manager in a printing plant had a habit of reminiscing about his early days in the business. He thought he was illustrating the virtues of hard work, but his listeners got bored and felt he was wasting their time.

Many meetings have run off course because the leader didn't follow his own agenda. This doesn't mean you should ignore promising avenues that open up unexpectedly just because they aren't on the agenda. But if you do depart from your agenda, let the members of the meeting know why you're doing it.

Lack of running summaries. Nothing helps keep a meeting on the track as effectively as running summaries. Without such progress reports the meeting wonders where it's going or whether it's going at all. By pointing out the progress that's been made, you will encourage the participants to make even more. The running summaries also serve as a welcome change of pace, and can help stimulate discussion when it lags.

Poor physical facilities. One wonders how politicians ever accomplish much in the legendary "smoke-filled room." Scientific tests indicate that a person's mental efficiency drops sharply when there's not enough oxygen. Make sure there's fresh air, and that the meeting participants are comfortable enough to concentrate on the business at hand.

Lack of orderly procedure. Some meetings fail to generate enough enthusiasm, but there are also meetings where there is too much. In their eagerness to contribute, participants interrupt each other, scarcely allowing anyone to complete a thought. The result can be chaos, unless the leader takes firm steps to create order again. He should rule that only one person may speak at a time, and if necessary he should set a time limit for each speaker.

Every meeting is different, and a meeting leader must be flexible enough to deal with unexpected problems. But if he defines the goal of the meeting, keeps it firmly in mind, and takes quick action when things go off course, he will find that meetings can be genuinely productive.

Part Five

Encouraging Organizational and Personal Improvement

Factors Which Affect Satisfaction and Dissatisfaction of Teachers

Thomas Sergiovanni

Present thought and action relating to satisfaction and motivation of teachers appear to be based on the assumption that job factors which satisfy teachers and job factors which dissatisfy teachers are arranged on a conceptual continuum. This paper tests an alternate assumption which was proposed by Frederick Herzberg and his associates. Herzberg suggests that job factors which satisfy workers and job factors which dissatisfy workers are not arranged on a conceptual continuum but are mutually exclusive. The findings of the study reported here revealed that some factors, reported by teachers as contributing to their job satisfaction and job dissatisfaction, were polar in a positive direction and other factors were polar in a negative direction. Achievement, recognition and responsibility were factors which contributed predominantly to teacher job satisfaction. Interpersonal relations (students), interpersonal relations (peers), "supervision technical", school policy and administration, unfairness, status and personal life were factors which contributed predominantly to teacher dissatisfaction. Further, the satisfaction factors identified for teachers tend to focus on the work itself and the dissatisfaction factors tend to focus on the conditions of work. The results of this study tend to support the universality of Herzberg's findings.

Satisfaction and dissatisfaction of teachers has long been an area of intense interest to researchers in school personnel management. In a recent review of industrial and education job satisfaction research Robinson[1] notes that over 40 per cent of the studies reviewed relate to teachers and their satisfaction or morale. However, the voluminous research in the field to date appears to be lacking in conceptual perspective and may, in fact, be misleading.

An assumption basic to the literature in this area is that factors which account for job satisfaction of teachers and factors which account for job dissatisfaction of teachers are arranged on a conceptual continuum (Fig. 1). Thus, a factor identified as a source of dissatisfaction is also likely to be a potential satisfier. The administrative prescription based on this assumption is that if a factor accounting for dissatisfaction is altered or eliminated, job satisfaction will result. Or, failure to maintain a satisfaction condition will result in teacher dissatisfaction.

[1] Robinson, Alan. Ralph Conners and Ann Robinson. "Job Satisfaction Researches of 1963." *Personnel and Guidance Journal.* XLIII, 1964. p. 361.

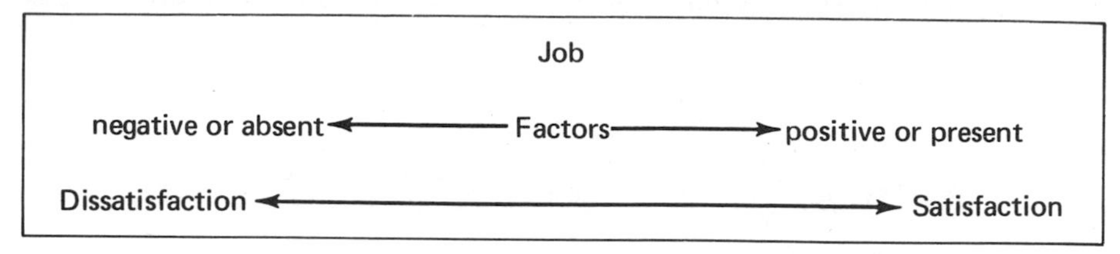

Figure 1. The continuum assumption

The Herzberg Study

The impetus for the research reported here comes from the work of Frederick Herzberg, Bernard Mausner, and Barbara Snyderman.[2] In a review of industrial motivation studies Herzberg observed that a difference in the primacy of work factors appeared depending upon whether the investigator was searching for factors which led to job satisfaction or factors which led to job dissatisfaction.[3] This observation led to the concept that some factors in the work situation were "satisfiers" and other factors were "dissatisfiers." Herzberg hypothesized that some factors were satisfiers when present but not dissatisfiers when absent; other factors were dissatisfiers, but when eliminated as dissatisfiers did not result in positive motivation (Fig. 2).

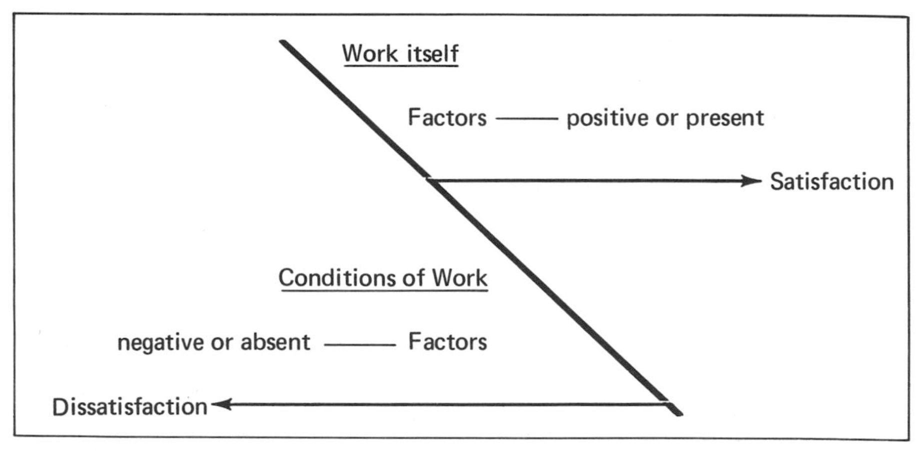

Figure 2. Herzberg hypothesis: Satisfaction factors and dissatisfaction factors are mutually exclusive

Herzberg's research with accountants and engineers[4] tends to confirm the existence of the satisfier and dissatisfier phenomenon. Herzberg found that five

[2]Herzberg, Frederick, Bernard Mausner, and Barbara Snyderman. *The Motivation to Work.* New York. John Wiley and Sons. 1959.

[3]Herzberg, Frederick, Bernard Mausner, Richard Peterson and Dora Capewell. *Job Attitudes: Review of Research and Opinion.* Pittsburg. Psychological Service of Pittsburg. 1957.

[4]Herzberg, *The Motivation to Work.*

factors (achievement, recognition, work itself, responsibility and advancement) tended to affect job attitudes in only a positive direction. The absence of these factors did not necessarily result in job dissatisfaction. The eleven remaining factors, if not present, led to employee dissatisfaction. The absence of these factors tended not to lead to employee satisfaction. Herzberg observed that job factors which resulted in satisfaction were directly related to the work itself. Job factors which resulted in dissatisfaction tended to be related to the environment of work. The factors in their two sub-categories are as follows.

Satisfiers (found in work itself)	*Dissatisfiers (found in the environment of work)*
1. Achievement	1. Salary
2. Recognition	2. Possibility of growth
3. Work itself	3. Interpersonal relations (subordinates)
4. Responsibility	4. Status
5. Advancement	5. Interpersonal relations (superiors)
	6. Interpersonal relations (peers)
	7. Supervision–technical
	8. Company policy and administration
	9. Working conditions
	10. Personal life
	11. Job security

Though arrived at empirically, the Herzberg findings appear to be consistent with the motivational theory proposed by Maslow.[5] Maslow hypothesized a hierarchy into which needs arranged themselves in order of their appearance. The Maslow hierarchy of needs, from lowest order (most prepotent) to highest order (least basic or prepotent), is as follows: physiological needs, security needs, social needs, esteem needs, and the need for self actualization. Needs that are at or near the top of the hierarchy, assuming that lower order needs are met, will tend to be the focus of an individual's attention. As long as lower order needs are satisfied, they cease to motivate the individual; in our society the physiological and security needs are well met for most people, thus they seldom motivate behavior.

Herzberg identified two levels of needs for his subjects; "hygienic" needs (which tend to focus on the dissatisfaction factors identified in his study) and satisfaction needs (which tend to focus on the satisfaction factors identified). According to Herzberg if "hygienic" needs are not met, the individual is unhappy. Provision for "hygienic" needs, however, does not ensure increased motivation. The satisfaction needs have motivational potential but depend upon reasonable satiation of "hygienic" needs before they become operative.[6]

Herzberg's findings have important implications for educational administration

[5] Maslow, A. H. *Motivation and Personality.* New York. Harper & Brothers. 1954.
[6] Herzberg, *The Motivation and Work.* pp. 113-119.

and supervision. They suggest that much of present practice in personnel administration may be directed at controlling the hygienic conditions which have, at best, limited motivating power for professional teachers.

The Problem

The writer undertook a study to determine whether or not the factors reported by teachers would distribute themselves into mutually exclusive satisfaction and dissatisfaction categories. Further, if the satisfaction-dissatisfaction phenomenon existed for teachers, would the factors resulting in satisfaction be concerned with the work itself, and would the factors resulting in dissatisfaction be concerned with the environment of work?

The following questions were raised:

1. Is there one set of factors which tends to satisfy teachers and another set which tends to dissatisfy teachers? Or are these factors better described as being arranged on a continuum with each being a potential satisfier and dissatisfier?

2. Will the distribution of factors vary for subpopulations of teachers? (Subgroups included: (1) male teachers v. female teachers, (2) tenure teachers v. nontenure teachers, (3) elementary school teachers v. secondary school teachers.)

Methodology

The overall design of this study followed, with some additions and modifications, the design developed and used by Herzberg. Respondents were asked to report incidents judged by them to be representative of their job feelings. Each incident or sequence consisted of three phases: (1) the respondent's attitudes expressed in terms of high job feelings and low job feelings, (2) the first-level and second-level factors[7] which accounted for these attitudes, (3) the effects of these attitudes and factors as reported by respondents. Through content analysis the factors which accounted for the expressed attitudes were sorted into the categories developed, defined, and used by Herzberg in the original study. The effects were sorted and categorized in the same manner.

The Population and Sample

The population for this study consisted of teachers in school districts in Monroe County, New York (the City of Rochester was not included in the sample population). The districts ranged from semi-rural to suburban in orientation and in

[7]Herzberg differentiated between the objective events, the actual stories reported by respondents and the subsequent perceptions of respondents of what the objective events meant to them. The actual stories were the basis for the first-level factors and the "interpretation" of the stories by respondents comprised the second-level factors. First-level factors are listed in Table 1 and second-level factors are listed in Table 2.

size from a teaching staff of 36 to a teaching staff of 528. The total sample population consisted of 3,382 teachers.

One hundred and twenty-seven respondents were selected at random from the 3,682 teachers who comprised the study population. The sample was drawn from lists furnished by each of the participating school districts. Administrators, guidance counselors, department chairmen not involved in actual teaching, librarians, supervisors, and other nonteaching personnel were not included in the sample. Seventy-one of the 127 teachers agreed to participate.

The sample included 30 male teachers and 41 female teachers. Elementary school positions were held by 37 respondents and junior high or senior high school positions were held by 34 respondents. Thirty-seven of the 71 respondents held tenure appointments. Respondents ranged in age from 21 years to 64 years with the average age being 37 and the median age being 32. Years of teaching experience ranged from three months to 36 years with the average experience being nine years and the median experience being seven years.

The Interview

The interview outline and interviewing procedure used in this study was a direct adoption of the Herzberg format. Respondents were told that they could start with either a time when they had felt unusually high or good about their job or a time when they had felt unusually low or bad about their job. After the first unusual sequence each respondent was asked to give another. If he had previously given a high story, he was then asked for a low. The same procedure was followed for most recent high feelings and most recent low feelings.

The objective events, the actual stories, which were reported by respondents as being the source of high or low feelings about their jobs were coded as first-level factors. The second-level factors were categories which constituted respondents' feelings as a result of the objective stories they had related and the attitudes they had identified. The analysis of second level factors came primarily from respondents' answers to two questions: "Can you tell me more precisely why you felt the way you did?" and "What did these events mean to you?" One respondent related a story involving a merit salary increase as a source of good feelings about his job. When asked why he felt the way he did, he replied, "It meant that the administration or whoever was responsible for the increase felt that I was doing a good job." The first-level factor in this sequence was coded as salary. This was the objective occurrence. The second-level factor in this sequence, however, was coded as recognition. The respondent perceived the merit increase as a source of recognition.

Respondents were limited to four specific sequences: an unusual high attitude sequence, an unusual low attitude sequence, and a most recent low attitude sequence. Two hundred and eighty-four sequences were collected for the study. The statistical analysis was based on the number of sequences rather than the number of respondents. Focusing on sequences was consistent with the method used by Herzberg.

Analysis of the Interviews

The technique of content analysis was used in coding each sequence. Herzberg suggests two basic approaches to content analysis. The first is an *a priori* approach in which the analysis is based upon a predetermined categorical scheme. The second approach extracts the categories from the raw data itself. Herzberg chose the *a posteriori* approach which produced categories specifically related to the data collected in his study. Herzberg noted, however, that the resulting categorical scheme developed through the *a posteriori* approach was not very different from that which could have been derived from an analysis of the literature.[8]

The scheme used for content analysis in this study was a direct adoption of the categories developed and used by Herzberg, and so represents an *a priori* approach, but one based on empirical evidence.

Coding Procedure

The next step in the analysis of the interviews required that the factors contained in the high and low attitude stories of respondents be identified and coded into the categorical scheme. Further, since several factors could appear in a given story, the factor which contributed most to the expressed feeling was to be isolated for subsequent analysis. Each sequence was coded in terms of expressed attitude (high or low), sequence type (unusual or recent), and level (first and second).

Sequences were coded, independently, by three of five judges. A total of 284 sequences were coded for the study. Coding decisions were classified as unanimous choice, majority choice or consensus choice. First-level coding choices of judges for each of the first 160 sequences included 87 unanimous decisions, 69 majority decisions, and 4 consensus decisions. For the second-level factors there were 96 unanimous decisions and 64 majority decisions. Three-way disagreements did not occur for the second-level factors.

Figure 3 summarizes the basic features of the content analysis.

The Analysis of Results

The results of the study are presented in two sections. The first reports the results relating to the mutual exclusiveness of factors for the total sample. This section includes an analysis of the first-level and second-level factors which appeared in high attitude sequences and an analysis of the first-level and second-level factors which appeared in low attitude sequences.

The second section includes a summary of the difference in responses for male teachers as compared with female teachers, tenure teachers as compared with nontenure teachers, and for elementary as compared with secondary teachers.

High Attitude Sequences Contrasted with Low Attitude Sequences

Table 1 includes the percentages and values of chi-squared for the frequency with

[8] Herzberg, *The Motivation to Work.* p. 38.

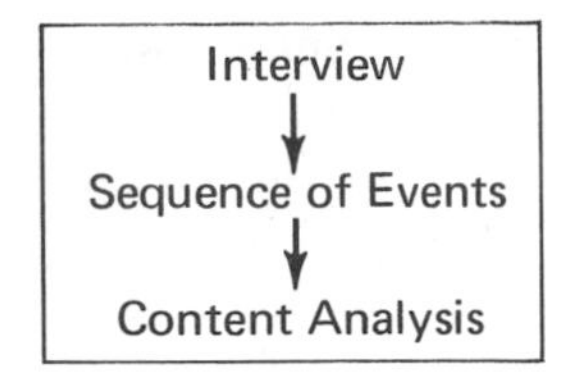

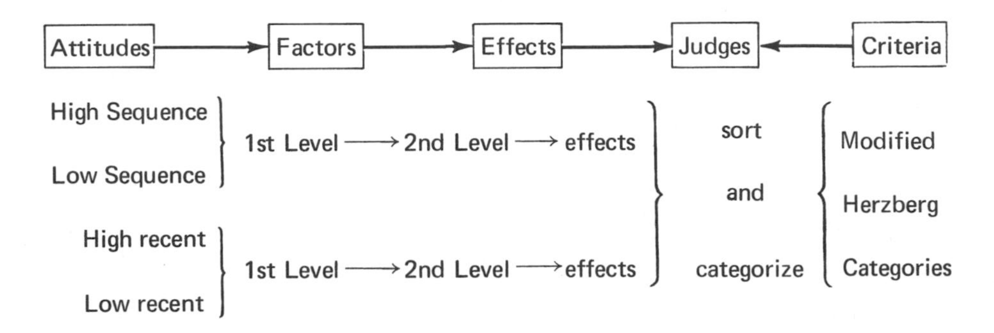

Figure 3. Basic design features of the content analysis

which first-level factors appeared in high attitude sequences as compared with low attitude sequences for the total group.

Sixty-nine percent of the sequences which accounted for high job attitudes included the first-level factors achievement, recognition, and work itself. Responsibility appeared in seven per cent of the high attitude sequences. Advancement did not appear in the 142 high attitude stories.

First-level factors six through 16 (the environment of work factors) appeared in 24 per cent of the high attitude sequences. The major contributors to the 24 per cent were possibility of growth (6%), and interpersonal relations with subordinates (7%). Personal life, status, and security did not appear in the high attitude sequences.

Interpersonal relations (subordinates), interpersonal relations (peers), supervision technical and school policy and administration appeared in 58 per cent of the low attitude sequences. Achievement, recognition, work itself, responsibility and advancement accounted for 21 per cent of the incidence of factors which appeared in the lows. Status did not appear as a first-level factor in low attitude sequences.

The first-level factors which appeared more often in high attitude sequences were achievement*, recognition*, work itself, responsibility*, and possibility of growth. The first level factors which appeared more often in low attitude sequences were advancement, salary, interpersonal relations (subordinates)*, interpersonal relations (superior), interpersonal relations (peers)*, supervision technical*, school policy and administration*, working conditions, personal life*, and security.

The percentages and values of chi-squared for the frequency with which

*Difference between Highs and Lows is significant. Minimum P = .05.

Table 1. Percentages and Values of Chi Squared for the Frequency with Which Each First-Level Factor Appeared in High Attitude Sequences as Contrasted with Low Attitude Sequences for the Total Group

Factor	*High*	*Low*	*Chi Squared*	*P*
	+NS = 142	NS = 142		
1. Achievement–	30*	9	10.500	.01
2. Recognition	28*	2	30.139	.001
3. Work itself	11	8	.346	
4. Responsibility–	7*	1	5.818	.05
5. Advancement	0	1		
6. Salary	2	3		
7. Possibility of growth	6	2	1.454	
8. Interpersonal relations–subordinates)	7	20*	7.605	.01
9. Interpersonal relations (superiors)	3	4	.900	
10. Interpersonal relations–(peers)	1	15*	14.086	.001
11. Supervision–technical–	1	10*	8.470	.01
12. School policy and–administration	2	13*	10.227	.01
13. Working conditions	2	6	2.083	
14. Personal life–	0	5*	5.142	.05
15. Status	0	0		
16. Security	0	1		

+NS in this table and in Table 2 refers to number of sequences.
Percentages in this table and in Table 2 are approximate but do not vary more than .0075.
*Difference between Highs and Lows is significant. Chi Squared value required for significance at the .05 level is 3.841.

second-level factors appeared in high attitude and low attitude sequences are reported in Table 2.

Achievement, which appeared in 50 per cent of the sequences, was the dominant second-level factor for the highs. Recognition appeared in 21 per cent of the sequences involving high job feelings. The remaining factors appeared in 29 per cent of the high attitude sequences.

For second-level low attitude sequences feelings of unfairness, with 32 per cent, was the dominant factor. Feelings of guilt and inadequacy, security, and work itself (6%) and possible growth (6%). The second-level factors advancement, status, salary, and fairness did not appear in high attitude sequences.

For second-level low attitude sequences feelings of unfairness, with 32 per cent, was the dominant factor. Feelings of guilt and inadequacy, security, and work itself appeared in 31 per cent of the low sequences. Recognition with seven per cent and lack of achievement with 13 per cent were other contributors to low job feelings.

The remaining six factors appeared in 15 per cent of the low sequences. The factor advancement did not appear in the lows.

The second-level factors which appeared more often in high attitude sequences were recognition*, achievement*, and possible growth. The second-level factors which appeared more often in low attitude sequences were work itself, status*, security, feelings of unfairness*, feelings of guilt and inadequacy, and salary.

Summary

The results presented in the first section demonstrate that many of the factors which accounted for high job feelings of teachers and many of the factors which accounted for low job feelings of teachers were mutually exclusive.

The first-level factors which appeared significantly as highs (as contrasted with lows) were recognition, achievement, and responsibility. The first-level factors which appeared significantly as lows (as contrasted with highs) were interpersonal relations (subordinates), interpersonal relations (peers), supervision–technical, school policy and administration, and personal life.

Achievement and recognition were the second-level factors which appeared significantly as highs. Feelings of unfairness and low status were the only second-level factors which appeared significantly as lows.

Table 2. Percentages and Values of Chi Squared for the Frequency with Which Each Second-Level Factor Appeared in High Attitude Sequences as Contrasted with Low Attitude Sequences for the Total Group

Factor	*High*	*Low*	*Chi Squared*	*P*
	NS = 142	NS = 142		
1. Recognition	21*	7	9.025	.01
2. Achievement	50*	13	26.677	.001
3. Work itself	6	9	.190	
4. Advancement	0	0		
5. Responsibility	4	4		
6. Group feelings	3	3		
7. Possible growth	6	3	1.230	
8. Status	0	5*	5.1428	.05
9. Security	5	11	1.565	
10. Fairness-unfairness	0	32*	43.022	.001
11. Pride, guilt, inadequacy	5	11	2.782	
12. Salary	0	2		

*Difference between Highs and Lows is significant. Chi squared value required for significance at the .05 level is 3.841.

*Difference between Highs and Lows is significant. Minimum P = .05.

Subgroup Differences

The analysis of results relating to the second question raised in this study strongly suggests that subgroups of teachers tend not to differ in their responses to sources of high and low job feelings. Significant differences were found in only three of 168 possibilities.

Men teachers tended *not* to respond differently from women teachers to sources of high and low job attitudes. No significant exception to this tendency was found.

Tenure teachers and nontenure teachers tended *not* to differ in their responses to sources of high and low job feelings. Three significant exceptions to this tendency were found:

1. The first-level factor interpersonal relations (superior) appeared as a source of low job feelings for tenure teachers in four per cent of the 142 low attitude sequences. This factor did not appear as a source of low job feelings for nontenure teachers.
2. Eleven per cent of the low attitude sequences involved nontenure teachers citing the first-level factor interpersonal relations (peers) as a source of low job attitudes. This was in contrast to four per cent for tenure teachers.
3. Security, a second-level factor, appeared in 11 per cent of the low attitude sequences. Nine of the 11 per cent were cited by nontenure teachers.

Elementary school teachers and secondary school teachers tended *not* to differ in their responses to sources of high job attitudes and low job attitudes. No significant exception to this tendency was found.

Discussion

The Polarity of Factors

The results of this study indicated that achievement, recognition, and responsibility were factors which contributed predominantly to teacher job satisfaction. Interpersonal relations (subordinates), interpersonal relations (peers), supervision–technical, school policy and administration, personal life, and fairness-unfairness were factors which contributed predominantly to teacher job dissatisfaction. The remaining factors appeared to be bi-polar, possessing the potential to contribute to both satisfaction and dissatisfaction (many of the factors did not appear with sufficient frequency to test adequately for polarity).

The Satisfaction Factors

The three dominant factors which appeared in high attitude sequences were achievement, recognition and responsibility. Achievement accounted for nearly one out of three first-level high attitude sequences and for one out of two second-level high attitude sequences. In view of the predominance of the factor achievement, it is interesting to note that most of the teacher achievement-centered stories involved less concrete evidence of actual success and more sensing and feeling by teachers that students had been reached and were presumably affected in some positive way.

This noticeable lack of concrete success reinforces Lortie's notion of psychic gratification as a reward base for teachers. Lortie[9] argues that societal rewards (salary, prestige, and power) are, in general, not perceived by teachers as being in abundance. Thus, teachers tend to focus on psychic gratification as a primary source of reward in their work. One of the major sources of psychic gratification, according to Lortie, is the interaction that the teacher has with individual students and classes where the teacher perceives that something has happened. The teacher senses or believes that, as a result of his activity, a change has taken place in the student or class. Lortie cites the terms "I reached them," "It went today," as being common expressions used by teachers to describe this pheonomenon.

This psychic gratification, which is characterized by a task-oriented interaction with some perceived measurable result, was most typical of many of the success stories related by teachers.

Recognition appeared three times as often in high sequences as in low sequences. Sources of recognition for teachers varied. Teachers talked about feedback from principals, supervisors, parents, students, and fellow teachers. Recognition took the form of letters, oral statements, gifts, incentives, and committee appointments.

The need for recognition, the overt bolstering of self-esteem, appears to be important to teachers. The absence of recognition tends not to affect low job attitudes of teachers.

Responsibility, although significantly found to be a high, appeared in only seven per cent of the high attitude sequences. This percentage is small when one considers that teachers do assume a considerable amount of responsibility. As the classroom door closes behind the teacher, it is implied that she assumes responsibility for her own work. This responsibility is limited, however, and falls within the framework of the rules and regulation of the school, school district, and school board. Further limits are imposed by the state legislature and our society at large. Whatever responsibility a teacher assumes, in terms of what to teach, falls within the framework of the prescribed curriculum.

Perhaps even more interesting than the appearance of achievement, recognition and responsibility as positive polar factors was the absence of advancement and work itself. These factors did appear as satisfiers in Herzberg's study.

The factor advancement was not mentioned by teachers in high attitude stories. Teaching offers little opportunity for concrete advancement (change in status or position) and in fact any particular teaching assignment could be considered as a terminal position. Whatever potential the factor advancement has as a satisfier appears to be lost for teachers under our present system. Capitalizing on this factor,

[9] Lortie, Dan, "The Changing Role of Teachers as a Result of Such Innovations as Television, Programmed Instruction, and Team Teaching." Richard Lonsdale and Carl Steinhoff (eds.). *The Administrative Analysis of Selected Educational Innovations.* Report of the First Inter-university Conference for School Administrators. Syracuse University, 1964.

as a potential source of satisfaction, implies providing overt opportunities for advancement within the ranks of teachers.[10]

Work itself appeared as a bi-polar factor in the study. Although the factor appeared more frequently in teacher high attitude stories, it also appeared as a frequent source of low job feelings. It appears that the job of teacher (although potentially able to provide unlimited opportunity for creative and varied work) requires considerable attention to maintenance type activity. Routine or maintenance tasks range from attendance and scheduling details, daily health checks, study hall assignment, and lunch duty to blowing noses and pouring young scholars into snow suits. The work itself factor, although found to be rich in satisfaction potential, was frequently cited as a source of dissatisfaction for teachers.

The Dissatisfaction Factors

Perhaps of greatest interest among the dissatisfiers was the factor interpersonal relations (subordinates), which appeared in 20 per cent of the low attitude sequences and in seven per cent of the high attitude sequences.

It seems appropriate to assume that since students are the very crux of a teacher's work, they should account for many of the successes and good feelings that teachers have. Indeed, this is so. The students were the raw material for the achievement successes and acts of recognition which teachers perceived as sources of great satisfaction. Establishing an appropriate relationship with students appears to be critical. Once established, the teacher can capitalize on this relationship in pursuit of work-centered or job itself satisfaction. It appears that a happy relationship with students is not in itself potent enough to be a source of job satisfaction. A poor relationship with students, however, can be a source of considerable teacher dissatisfaction.

Responses of Subgroups Tend Not to Differ

A most interesting finding of the study was that subgroups of teachers– tenure and nontenure, male and female, elementary and secondary–tended not to differ in their responses to sources of job satisfaction and dissatisfaction. There were only three exceptions, out of 168 possibilities, to this tendency. All three involved tenure and nontenure teachers.

One interpretation of this finding is that the satisfaction and dissatisfaction factors identified in this study apply to teachers irrespective of their sex, teaching level or tenure status.

[10]Schools frequently contain an informal promotion system for teachers. Advancement within the informal promotion system may include movement to another grade level, being assigned "quality" students, receiving equipment and facility priorities, and moving to a better school within the district. This informal promotion system was not described in teacher high attitude sequences but did appear in low attitude sequences. Judges coded these low attitude sequences into the factor categories working conditions or school policy and administration.

Conclusion

This study provides support for the hypothesis that satisfiers and dissatisfiers tend to be mutually exclusive. Further, it was found that factors which accounted for high attitudes of teachers were related to the work itself and factors which accounted for low attitudes of teachers were related to the conditions or environment of work.

Relative to other activities, teachers derive the most satisfaction from work-centered activity. This finding was reflected in the predominance of achievement, recognition and responsibility as sources of teacher job satisfaction. The low attitude sequences, however, revealed factors which were not in themselves work-centered: rather, they focused on the conditions and people which surround the actual work.

Can we conclude that as long as a teacher experiences personal success, and is recognized for this success, the conditions of work need not be considered? It may be possible (although unlikely) for a teacher, who is immersed in an unsatisfactory work environment, to experience personal success and thus achieve considerable job satisfaction. An environment relatively free from sources of dissatisfaction, however, will tend to increase or enhance the appearance of factors which are direct contributors to job satisfaction.

Herzberg refers to the dissatisfaction factors as "hygienic." In describing these factors, Herzberg states:

> They act in a manner analagous to the principles of medical hygiene. Hygiene operates to remove health hazards from the environment of man. It is not a curative; it is, rather, a preventive.[11]

The "hygienic" factors, according to Herzberg, are essential in preventing dissatisfaction, in making work tolerable. Herzberg describes the satisfaction factors as motivators. These are the job-centred, the task-oriented factors which permit the individual to satisfy his need for self actualization in his work.

The dissatisfaction factors identified for teachers tend to focus on conditions and circumstances which teachers expect to be maintained at acceptable levels. It seems reasonable that teachers should expect fair and adequate supervision, supportive school policies and administrative directives, friendly interpersonal relationships and pleasant working conditions. However, the satisfaction factors focus directly on conditions and circumstances that are not givens, which do not come with the job. These factors constitute rewards that must be earned through performance of the job. The reinforcement potential of the satisfiers is dependent upon a teacher's individual performance.

What then are the implications of the study for administrative behavior? The findings suggest that the present emphasis on "teacher-centered" behavior (supportive supervision, interpersonal relations, effective communications, and

[11] Herzberg, *The Motivation to Work*, p. 113.

group effectiveness) is an important prescription for effective administrative behavior. The "teacher-centered" approach, however, is limited in that it tends to concentrate on the elimination of dissatisfaction factors and thus does not contribute directly to teacher job satisfaction.

"Task-oriented" behavior (organizing and planning work, implementing goal achievement) emerges as an important and direct contributor to teacher job satisfaction. Such behavior, on the part of the administrator, would include increasing the opportunities for teachers to experience personal and professional success. Basic to this undertaking is the proposition that administrators will permit and encourage teachers to (1) exercise more autonomy in making decisions, (intensifying collaborative efforts and consultative management would be a good start), (2) increase individual responsibility in developing and implementing teaching programs, and (3) develop professional skills. These variables will serve to increase individual identification with the task.[12] Task identification appears to be a prerequisite for focusing on achievement as a means to personal and professional success and subsequent job satisfaction.

A corollary to personal success is recognition for such success. Although recognition was not found to be as potent as actual success, it was perceived by teachers as a measure of success. Capitalizing on recognition, as a satisfier for teachers, implies that dispensing of recognition should be as closely associated with successful teacher task-oriented behavior as possible

Finally, effective administrative behavior would not exclude or ignore the sources of job dissatisfaction. Supervisory behavior, interpersonal relationships, and other factors relating to the conditions of work are necessary components in promoting an environment which will enhance job itself satisfaction for teachers. Teachers whose energies are taxed in coping with sources of job dissatisfaction will tend not to be vigorous and dynamic pursuers of work-centered satisfaction.

An inherent assumption, in the discussion above, has been that job satisfiers are reinforcers of behavior and motivators of performance. Considerable evidence has been accumulated which disputes the claim that a satisfied worker is more productive than a dissatisfied one. However, when satisfaction is dependent upon performance in work, satisfaction and productivity are related.[13]

The satisfaction factors identified for teachers cannot be separated from performance and, in fact, are dependent upon performance. It was successful performance which accounted for the high attitudes expressed in achievement-centered stories. Performance was also the basis for recognition-centered sequences. If performance is rewarded in terms of intrinsic personal success and extrinsic recognition for success, it will tend to be repeated.

Summary

The assumption that factors which tend to satisfy teachers and factors which tend to dissatisfy teachers are arranged on a conceptual continuum tends *not* to be

[12] March, John and Herbert Simon. *Organizations.* New York. John Wiley and Sons. 1958. p. 77.

[13] Bass, Bernard. *Organizational Psychology.* Boston. Allyn and Bacon, Inc. 1965. p. 38.

supported by this study. Factors which appeared as sources of high job feelings for teachers, tended to differ from factors which appeared as sources of low job feelings. Further, the satisfaction factors tended to focus on the work itself, and the dissatisfaction factors tended to focus on the conditions of work.

It was concluded that the elimination of the dissatisfiers would tend not to result in job satisfaction. However, it does not appear likely that one can experience work satisfaction *without* the elimination or tempering of the dissatisfiers. Deriving satisfaction from work-centered activity assumes that one's energies and efforts are not taxed or depleted by unsatisfactory conditions of work. The point is not whether satisfiers are more crucial than dissatisfiers, or *vice versa,* but rather the dependence of the satisfiers on the elimination or tempering of the dissatisfiers.

The Supervisor and Staff Morale

Henry A. Crooke

Many considerations of the problems of staff morale which have found their way into print arise directly from the observation of manifestations of low morale and of little else. It has always seemed to me to be obvious that most of these manifestations result from some underlying cause which remains unnoticed or, at least, undiscussed. It is my purpose here to discuss two areas which, when related, provide a valid basis for a consideration of staff morale at a theoretical level. These areas are group dynamics and administrative theory.

It is generally agreed that administration and supervision are not identical. However, it is my firm conviction that in at least one sense there is no difference. I mean in the area of human or personal relations of a superordinate with his subordinates. It is my contention that in terms of human relations, the administrator and the supervisor are in identical positions relative to their subordinates. It is my further contention that what applies to one applies to the other in this area. Finally, it is my firm conviction that good staff morale depends primarily upon good human relations between administrators and supervisors and the teaching staff. With this assumption in mind, let us proceed to the discussion of group processes and administrative theory.

Basic Concepts

Since the problem undertaken, that is the basis for good staff morale, deals with relationships in a personnel–management situation, personnel management seems to provide the logical area in which to begin this discussion. Because the personnel management situation is a group situation, it follows that in a consideration of group structure, roles within the group, and group dynamics is found the matrix in which the teacher–supervisor relationships must be studied if one hopes to gain insight into the nature of personnel problems and staff morale. The first consideration, then, is the group and we begin with a look at group structure.

As a definition we may say that:

> . . . a group, properly speaking, is characterized by the interaction of its members in such a way that each person is changed by his group membership and each would be likely to undergo a change as a result of changes in the group.[1]

This concept of interdependence between individuals and the group as a whole is most important when one is seeking to understand the importance of the actions of individuals within a group. One would be foolhardy to assume that a member of a group could continually order his actions with little or no regard for their effect on the personality of the group as a whole. In fact, there are three aspects of a group which are affected by the actions of its members. The first is the *group structure* which refers to the behavior of individuals toward each other. The second is *group syntality* which is the personality of the group as a whole. The third aspect is *group synergy* which is the sum total of energy which the group can command for self-maintenance and effective action.[2] It is important to the understanding of group behavior to be aware that the structure, syntality, and synergy of a group are influenced by the abilities, motivations, and attitudes of its members, and they in turn are affected by the group. If the behavior of the individuals toward each other and toward the group is pleasant and cooperative, the group structure will be sound. If behavior is strained, unpleasant, and uncooperative, the group structure will certainly be weak.

It has been determined that people belong to groups because they feel they can thus attain satisfactions which are unavailable to them as individuals. This is true of groups regardless of whether they are pressure groups, problem solving groups which make plans for a larger group, or action groups which perform tasks under a supervisor. These findings, the composition of groups and the influence of their members on the group as a whole, have been validated by research that shows that groups, regardless of types, can be apathetic, submissive, active, cooperative, or anarchistic depending upon motivations, attitudes, and behavior of their members.[3]

An obvious question which follows from these findings is whether or not each member of a group exerts the same degree of influence on its syntality and synergy. As difficult and dangerous as it usually is to generalize, it can be said with assurance that different members of a group do have different degrees of influence on its synergy and syntality.

Remembering that individuals join and remain in groups because groups seem to offer corporately what is denied them in isolation, one can expect that within a group there will be problems. These problems have been identified by research as stemming from individual differences in values, temperaments, abilities, and goals.

[1] William Clark Trow, "Group Processes," *Encyclopedia of Educational Research,* p. 602.
[2] *Ibid.,* pp. 602-605.
[3] *Ibid.,* pp. 607-608.

Consequently, we can identify within any group various roles of its members, a prestige hierarchy, and differing degrees of identification by its members with the group. Research shows that each individual member finds or makes a role for himself in every group. This role carries with it more or less status depending upon its position in the hierarchy within the group. A member's status varies directly with his access to such limited resources as money, time, goods, and services. His influence or control over the group varies directly with his status. When his status is high and he exerts control over a group, that member becomes a leader of the group.

However, all roles within a group can not be identified in terms of leadership. Unfortunately, many other roles such as blocker, aggressor, recognition-seeker, dominator, and special-interest pleader have been identified within groups,[4] and when a leader's status declines, for any reason, he finds himself vying for control with one or more of the types of members just mentioned. The resulting conflict can have different outcomes depending upon how the conflict affects the attitudes of the members and, in turn, the structure, syntality, and synergy of the group. Since satisfactions of group members are closely related to the opportunity for full use of their skills, any conflict which tends to deny or impede this opportunity can have a disastrous effect on the group. The point here is that any autocratic actions on the part of the appointed leader which are designed to check the efforts of certain control-seeking members of the group, can have an undesirable effect on all members of the group and, in turn, the syntality, synergy, morale, and efficiency of the group. This is true at least to the extent that the group members perceive the control-seeking actions as being in accord with personal or group goals.

In general terms, then, we find members of groups belonging for personal reasons. There is some common ground, of course, because each member sees in the group an opportunity to gain those satisfactions which he needs but feels he can not gain alone. Because each member of a group retains his own values and goals, there can be great strain and stress among members, and this can result in unsatisfactory group behavior. On the other hand, the degree to which the individual members perceive group goals as identical to their own is directly proportional to the cooperation and accomplishments of the group, or phrased another way, the healthier the syntality and synergy of the group.[5] It is the leader who, through autocratic or democratic processes, exerts the most individual influence over the structure, morale, and efficiency of the group. Through his interpretation of his role, the leader can provide the necessary opportunities for the full use of the other members' skills or deny or minimize such opportunities. If the members have these opportunities, we can expect their satisfaction to be high. Under these circumstances they can be motivated, meaningfully, toward group goals. This we label good morale. If the leader creates the opposite atmosphere, there will be little satisfaction and little real motivation toward group goals. Under the latter circumstances we would find a case of poor morale.

[4]Daniel E. Griffiths, *Human Relations in School Administration,* pp. 178-179.

[5]Roald F. Campbell, "Educational Administration: Is it Unique?," *The School Review,* Vol. 67 (1959), p. 465.

When we identify a group consisting of a supervisor (leader) and a staff of professionally trained teachers (members), we have identified one of the most numerous of the action type groups. In this situation the supervisor's interpretation of his role will have a telling effect on the teachers' group syntality, synergy, efficiency, and morale. When we consider that the attitudes and characteristics exhibited by teachers can be positively correlated with pupil behavior, the morale and efficiency of teacher groups begins to take on a new dimension of importance far beyond the personal happiness of the individual teachers concerned.[6] It becomes imperative that a supervisor identify and understand his role as well as the roles of the staff or group members if he would gain knowledge and understanding of the syntality and synergy of his group, their importance to the total school effort, and ways of maintaining and improving them.

One thing remains to be said before going on to a discussion of administrative theory and practice. It has been established that communication patterns definitely affect the accuracy and satisfactions of an organization as well as the emergence or acceptance of a leader of the organization. Here communication refers not only to the interchange of pertinent information among those concerned in an organization but also the degree to which a speaker makes himself understood. It is through adequate communication in the fullest sense that a leader, be he school supervisor or business executive, exercises his influence on his group. If he fails to establish communication within his group, his leadership will not be accepted by his group for their resulting lack of understanding of group goals and expectations will finally force their efforts toward the fulfillment of their personal goals exclusively. The result is agitation, lack of cooperation, apathy toward group accomplishments, and the emergence of other leaders within the group. It is to be expected that these new leaders, if they are to maintain their acceptability as such, will establish communications with the other members and also establish new group goals more closely aligned with the goals of the members. Under these conditions we see that the stage is set for the rise of the Philadelphia Lawyer, the internal pressure group, and the grapevine.

These few basic concepts of group processes are bases for observable group behavior, and their understanding is necessary to the understanding of the stresses and strains as well as the efforts and accomplishments of groups in general and school staffs in particular.

Morale and the Leader

The previous comments, though relatively general in their review of the commonly accepted principles of behavior in groups, did note that the leader, in his relations with his group, was most important in determining the morale and efficiency of the group. In fact, the W. K. Kellog Foundation of Battle Creek, Michigan, has contributed in excess of $9,000,000 since 1946 to the study of this

[6]David G. Ryans, "Inventory Estimated Teacher Characteristics as Co-variants of Observer Assessed Pupil Behavior," *Journal of Educational Psychology,* Vol. 52 (1961), p. 96.

problem as it applies to education. Although such an expenditure over so short a period of time is quite impressive, one must keep in mind that comparatively little work had been done prior to 1946 in the area of administration and supervision in education. A look at a table taken from a 1943 study of educational supervision as tication in this area only twenty years ago[7] (see Table 1). In terms of sophistication we might identify the year 1954 (less than 10 years ago) as the most significant. It was only then, in their meeting at Denver, that The National Conference of Professors of Educational Administration challenged the whole existing concept of educational administration and supervision. As a result most real efforts to develop a theory of educational administration began after this meeting.

Table 1.[a] Check List of Supervisors Qualities as Presented in Eight Books by Specialists in the Field of Supervision

Qualities	*Barr*	*Burton*	*Kyte*	*Jacobson & Reavis*	*Myers*	*Bolton, Cole, Fessup*	*Cobberly*	*Gist*
Professional co-operation	x	x	x	x	x	x	x	x
Educational leadership	x							
Ability to improve curriculum	x							
Ability properly to organize and conduct conferences	x	x	x	x		x	x	
Knowledge of pupils and teachers	x	x	x	x		x	x	x
Broad scholarship	x							x
Pleasing personality		x						x
Executive ability		x						x
In sympathy with child-centered experiences	x	x	x	x	x		x	x
Ability to evaluate teachers	x	x	x	x			x	x
Respect for personality	x	x	x	x		x	x	x

[a]Daniel E. Griffiths, *Administrative Theory,* p. 24.

Although few people might argue with the statement that "action divorced from theory is the random scurrying of a rat in a new maze,"[8] there has been considerable reluctance in the field of education to put much faith in administrative theory. The major fears seems to have been one of having to accept theory at the

[7]Mary T. Cronin, *Teacher-Supervisor Relationships in the Activity Movements* (unpublished Master's dissertation, St. John's University, 1943), p. 24.
[8]Daniel E. Griffiths, *Administrative Theory,* p. 11.

expense of one's own values. However, theory merely indicates what will probably result if one follows a certain course of action. It does not tell one whether or not one should act. The decision to act or not remains a dictate of one's personal values.

As the rightful place of theory in administration and supervision has come to be understood and generally accepted, many different theories have been put forth. The work of Jacob Getzels, of the Midwest Administration Center at the University of Chicago, is now generally accepted as most accurately describing the nature of administration. He sees administration as a social process in which behavior is conceived as a function of both the *nomothetic* (institutional) and the *idiographic* (individual) dimensions of the social system.

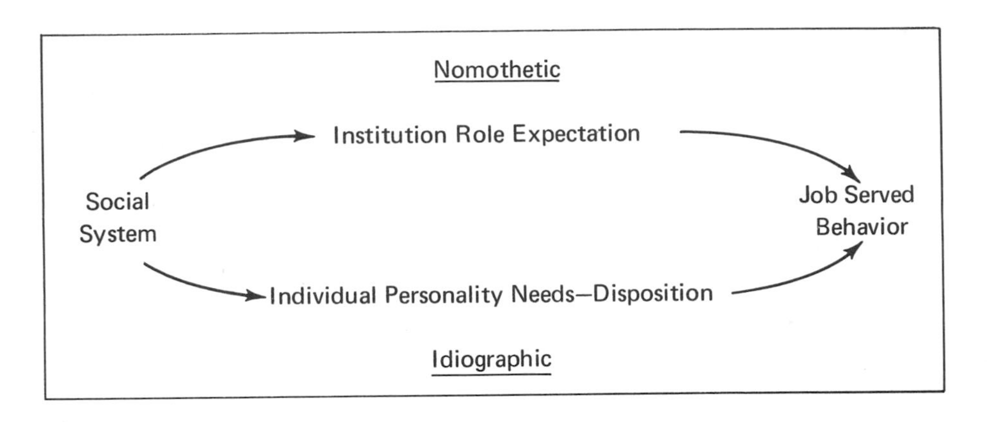

Getzel sees two levels of influence interacting in any society or group. Observable behavior of individuals reflects the degree to which these two opposing influences overlap (see diagram). The degree to which these dimensions or influences are perceived by a member of a group to deviate is indicative of the degree of conflict in the administrative or supervisory setting. The satisfactory functioning of the administrative and supervisory process depends on how much overlap of these two dimensions is perceived to exist by both the superordinate and his subordinates.

This assumption is the basis for a theory of administration which is most compatible with our knowledge of group dynamics. It becomes the function of an administrator or supervisor, then, to establish an atmosphere in which the nomothetic and idiographic dimensions are seen as overlapping if not identical. Using this knowledge and knowing what makes for healthy group syntality and synergy, we can conclude that a supervisor will be performing his function adequately when he creates an atmosphere that enables his subordinates to satisfy their individual needs through identification with, and in pursuit of, the group objectives.

One of the most important outcomes of the work in administrative theory is the effect it has had on administrative and supervisory practices. Many practices which, according to theory, promise success have been adopted and tested by business and education alike. For example, research promoted by the University of Michigan has found that feelings of group belongings and ego needs rather than reward systems set up by management account for superior effort and increased productivity. This approach has been tried successfully in the military as well as in education. It is interesting to note in this regard that Campbell, in his own studies at the Midwest Administration Center, has found a growing conviction that educational administration and supervision has much in common with these areas of business. He finds within any organization three levels of operation. They are the technical (teacher level in education), managerial (administrator and supervisor level in education), and institutional (board level in education) levels. He found that common elements among schools, churches, and profit-making organizations were few at the technical and institutional levels, but many at the managerial level.

Such things as complexity of functions, a need for understanding the intimacy and scope of necessary relationships within an organization, the difficulty of appraising performance, and need for sensitivity to public view are just some of the common areas in management regardless of the field of operation. Our knowledge of groups, a reasonable theory of administration and supervision which is consistent with that knowledge, and a demonstrated ability to identify many common elements of the managerial function regardless of the area of operation, all have combined to foster an interplay of ideas and findings between researchers in industrial management and those in educational management. The result is an ability to synthesize the findings of both areas and label the findings which are applicable to one area rather than the other. There is justification for business managers, therefore, to accept some of the best of the educational supervisors' practices and vice versa. As one expert puts it, the school is an association of people to get something done. This definition can apply to business firms and government agencies alike. In attempting to identify good and bad supervisory practices, then, we can and should look at both fields.

Emphasis on Human Relations

Can we identify any specific principle which research and experimentation have found common to all areas of successful administration and supervision? The answer is yes. The first principle of good administration and supervision has been underlying this entire discussion beginning with the comments on group processes. It can be stated as a keen awareness of group interactions and an understanding of the effects of administrative and supervisory practices on the morale and, as a result, the efficiency and productivity of the entire organization.

What does this mean in practice? It means that building an accepting, understanding pattern of group interaction requires a supervisor to identify with the group physically as well as psychologically; to help participation by encouraging members to speak up; to promote group thinking; and to detect unmet needs of the members of the organization.

It means that the supervisor must be aware that there is clinical evidence that autocratic leadership often leads to apathetic, submissive, or uncooperative organizations.

It means that a supervisor must be aware of the fact that one of the main reasons for low teacher morale is the absence of democratic procedures.

It means that a supervisor must know that a statistically significant negative correlation has been found between his acceptability by the group and the degree of his authoritarianism.

It means that a supervisor should understand that he is perceived fair if it is believed that the interests of all affected by his decision have been considered to the best of his ability, and that under such circumstances, his subordinates will accept the demands of a situation that forces him into an unpopular decision.

It means that a supervisor should realize that consultation with his staff on school policy does not threaten his status or authority.

The statements enumerated above are but a small part of the ramifications and implications of what has been previously stated as the first principle, or underlying principle, of successful administration and supervision. We can conclude that the generally accepted position of experts in the field of administration and supervision is that the first principle of good practice is the awareness of group and individual goals, needs, motivations, and satisfactions. One study of the effects of supervisory practices on teacher efficiency draws this conclusion: the assumption that self-determination in his job is the basis for a great deal of modern practice in personnel management. It is now permissible to speak and act in accordance with the principle that teachers can and should participate in decisions affecting them. Knowledge that certain approaches by a supervisor to staff relations will result in certain reactions of the subordinates involved is the result of sympathetic understanding of human relations. This, in turn, is indispensable to good supervision and health group syntality and synergy.

Does this emphasis on human relations in administration and supervision preclude any need by supervisors for proficiency in other specific techniques? Certainly not. It is assumed in this discussion that some knowledge of his supervisory area and some capacity for coordinating, decision-making, directing, etc., have been sufficiently demonstrated to warrant appointment as a supervisor. However, these proficiencies can more easily be acquired than an effective attitude toward human relations. In addition, it has been demonstrated that a supervisor who is perceived by his subordinates to have considered their interests is permitted to make a larger than average number of reasonable mistakes in technology before being conceived as incompetent by his subordinates. Further, it has been shown in another study that experience need not affect a supervisor's effectiveness if he demonstrates democratic behavior as he works with teachers as individuals or as a group.[9]

One summarizing point remains to be made. Having established the fact that the efficiency, productivity, and morale of a group is primarily dependent upon the degree of understanding and acceptance that exists among all its members, we must ascribe to communication, which is the means of establishing understanding, the same degree of importance. If communication, which we define as information given, received, and understood, is incomplete in an organization, understanding

[9] Vynce Hines, "Searching Through Research," *Overview* (Feb. 1961), p. 31.

will be incomplete, and we can not expect members of the group to make intelligent adjustments to the various situations confronting them. In order to make an intelligent adjustment to a situation, a person must know what it is all about. We can not expect members of a group to identify with group goals if they don't know and understand them. In short, we can't expect a person to act intelligently in a situation if he doesn't understand the situation. We can conclude, then, that communication within an organization is the first step in establishing, maintaining, and improving the morale and effiency of any group. Where communication is missing, incomplete, or ineffective because of misuse, we can expect to find low morale, low productivity, inefficiency, and antagonism against supervision.

Factors That Affect Teacher Morale

Frederick L. Redefer

After buildings are built, after desks have been found for every child, and after the budget has been balanced, it is the educational program that speaks most eloquently as to the superintendent's contribution. In this aspect of his responsibilities, the administrator is dependent on the staff, especially on the teaching staff.

Many superintendents play teacher morale by ear, but even those with developed hearing are surprised by what they do not hear. Principals cannot rely completely on what they think is happening among their staff members.

Why are teachers so important to the successful administration of a superintendent? Teachers are important because they are the professional workers in a school system who determine the quality and quantity of the educational program.

Twenty-Four Cities Studied

In our study of 24 school systems involving 5000 teachers, the following generalizations were established:

1. The morale of teaching faculties is closely related to the *quality of education* in individual schools.

2. The morale score of teachers has a significant correlation with the rating, by administrators, of superiority in teaching.

3. Marital status, sex or age are not the determining factors of morale status.

4. While elementary school faculties seem to have higher morale than junior or senior high school faculties, the level of education is not the determining factor.

5. Salary or salary schedules, while important, do not determine the morale status of the individual teacher or the faculty group.

6. Secondary schools are structured in personnel patterns that differ from the elementary school and this has implications in morale status.

7. The socio-economic status of the school community does not determine the morale status of the faculty.

8. "Problem" schools do not necessarily cause low faculty morale.

Did our study measure the morale status of a faculty or of an individual teacher?

Teachers who scored high on the basic questionnaire say they would do the following:

- would choose teaching as a career again.
- would encourage both sons and daughters to go into the teaching profession.
- would place teachers and teaching higher in community esteem.
- had more positive attitudes toward professional colleagues.
- had fewer personal problems of meaningfulness, loneliness and problems dealing with authority.
- got more satisfaction from teaching.
- carried on more research to improve their teaching.
- took more professional studies in the last five years.
- had joined voluntarily, more professional organizations.
- participated more actively in professional associations.
- felt less fatigued at the end of the school day.
- were less bothered by routines and professional ruts.

Teachers with low morale did not assent to the foregoing. It would seem that, by logic, the opinionnaire used in our study did distinguish morale status among teachers.

How one conceives of teacher morale needs to be understood because some think of it as existing separately.

Teacher morale is a complex and complicated area for investigation. Morale cannot be succinctly defined and minutely measured. Operationally, morale consists of many inter-related factors whose effective weighting may differ with the individual and the situation. Nevertheless, the status for any one factor can be probed and, for a large group of teachers, this status has significance.

At present it is doubtful whether personnel factors that are part of the *gestalt* of teacher morale can be added with mathematical accuracy and scored in exact quantitative terms. Consequently, the phrase Morale Tendency Score (M.T.S.) is used and it indicates *a tendency* rather than an exact amount.

To Discuss Status Study

This article is a discussion of a status study. No report is included of the causes for high or low morale among teachers although many seem self-evident. Causes may have historical roots. Other causes might seem to be related to definite policies, practices or persons. Why do two faculties differ in their reactions so markedly on any factor when such a factor would seem to be effected mainly by system-wide policies and practices? Nor have "comparative norms" with other schools been stressed.

In studies of personnel factors affecting teachers and teaching, it is not so important that a school is higher or lower than others. Each community and school is unique and not comparable factor by factor. What is important is to find out why teachers harbor negative feelings and to take constructive steps to remedy such a situation in terms of that community, that school system, that school personnel, and even with that individual teacher.

Study of One School System

Can the morale status of a staff be determined? Because this is such an important question, our study of teacher morale in one system (to remain nameless) will be described.

This school system was selected because it was sufficiently large to bring out differences within the system, many of which were found between the school systems cooperating in the larger study.

The study was introduced to administrative staff and teachers at a general faculty session. A teacher opinionnaire of 108 items distributed over many fields was presented to the faculty. Voluntary anonymous reponses were received from 781 teachers, 87 per cent of the total faculty.

What personnel factors contributed to the morale of these teachers? To which factors did they respond negatively? To which positively?

Reasonable Standards Used

In reporting positive and negative factors, standards of 80 and 60 per cent have been used. There is no basis, scientifically, for such standards but they seem reasonable. Those personnel factors about which 80 per cent or more of the faculty feel positive are listed as positive factors. This would mean that, in a faculty of 20 teachers, 16 would respond positively. Those personnel factors about which 60 per cent or less of the faculty list as positive are considered negative. This would mean that, in a faculty of 20, only 12 or less respond positively.

In reporting these factors, the percentage figure is the percentage of the faculty who responded *positively* about this factor.

On 32 factors the teachers' responses exceeded a standard of 80 per cent.

On 29 factors a negative response was received in sufficient numbers to warrant a further study of each item and groups of items.

Of these 29 factors, six relate to the board of education, three to administration, seven to personnel practices and policies, seven to school plant and equipment, three to teacher-pupil relations, and three to professional attitudes.

A study of the interrelations between these negative items seems to indicate that action to improve the morale of teachers could well concentrate on four major areas: (1) board of education and central administrative relations with teaching staffs; (2) personnel practices and policies; (3) school equipment and supplies, and (4) educational leadership of the school system as an entity and the leadership of unit schools.

Table 1. Positive Morale Tendencies (Teachers report they agreed with the following statements)

With Respect to Board

84% Board is interested in improving the educational program.

Administration and Its Policies

83% Relationship of headquarters administration and principal does not interfere with educational improvements by faculty.

81% Requests for transfer to another school receive careful study and approval within reasonable administrative considerations.

81% Teaching assignments are well suited to interests and abilities of individual teachers.

80% Professional activities and conferences are encouraged by administrators.

89% Immediate superiors do what they can to make working conditions satisfactory.

80% Differences of opinion within faculty regarding school or classroom practices are so handled by administrators as to achieve solutions satisfying to most everyone.

Curriculum and Practices

87% Field trips are easy to arrange with administration and staff.

84% Teachers share in adapting subject matter content to particular class or grade level.

89% Course of study does not place undue emphasis on content and fundamentals.

87% School is being run sensibly and efficiently.

Teacher-Pupil Relations

88% Teachers are impartial to children regardless of racial, cultural or national backgrounds.

84% Pupils in the school are not headed toward delinquency.

Teacher-Supervisor Relations

86% Superiors are competent in jobs.

85% Teacher committee work operates well.

87% Teachers always cooperate well in arranging activities involving several classes of students.

88% Visits of principals are welcome at any time in classes.

81% Supervisors and principals make reasonable allowances for each teacher's personal limitations and problems.

Teachers, Parents and Community

93% Parents of most of pupils cooperate with teachers.

81% Parents appreciate work teachers are doing.

80% Parents do not interfere with work of teachers.

84% Parent-sponsored school activities receive cooperation and support of teachers.

89% Teachers encourage parents to come to school to discuss children's problems.

80% Teachers' personal standards do not conflict with standards of community and of parents.

85% Relation of teachers with immediate school community is one of mutual respect and trust.

80% Professional association activities are rewarding in many ways.

91% Teachers can be trusted to use information available to them about pupils wisely.

94% Many teachers would prefer to work with children than do anything else.

93% Additional time and effort spent with children are worthwhile.

84% Teachers help one another when it comes to dealing with real problems of children.

Table 2. Negative Morale Tendencies (Factors with less than three-fifths' positive responses. Percentage preceding each statement records negative attitudes and staff agreement)

With Respect to Board

44% Board of education is not vitally interested in welfare of teachers.

42% Headquarters administration is not vitally concerned about teacher welfare.

58% Board of education listens more to community officials than it does to parents or teachers.

67% Superintendent and his assistants are closer to board than they are to teachers.

63% Pressure groups influence board members' decisions.

49% Board is not ready to consider responsible suggestions from individual teachers or groups of staff members.

Administration and Its Policies

47% Personal influence, prejudice and favoritism play parts in selection of principals, licensed supervisors, and teachers.

43% Teachers do not share in determination and evaluation of school policies and practices.

53% There is too much emphasis on mechanics and record keeping rather than on teaching the children.

Personnel Policy and Practice

45% Principals do not know problems of classroom teacher.

48% Teachers are not satisfied with present sick-leave provisions.

77% Teachers are not satisfied with sabbatical leave provisions and decisions.

63% Teachers are not satisfied that their grievances receive prompt and serious consideration.

70% Teachers are not satisfied with retirement benefits.

56% Under present personnel policies poor teachers are not weeded out from schools.

52% Method of selecting administrators or supervisors does not obtain best leadership for teachers.

School Plant, Services, Equipment

47% Classroom furniture is not well designed and sufficiently functional for teaching purposes.

64% Restroom facilities are not pleasant and adequate for the staff.

46% Test materials are inadequate.

52% Books in school library are out of date, insufficient in number.

45% Communication to and from nursing, health personnel, or other special services regarding pupils does not take place in effective manner.

42% Teachers do not feel that mimeographing or other types of duplicating service is adequate and reasonably obtainable.

52% Instructional supplies for classroom teaching are not adequate and not easily obtained.

Teacher-Pupil Relations

53% For many teachers wide difference in ability among students is problem.

Professional Attitudes

47% Extracurricular activity and nonclassroom activity as aspects of professional responsibility are avoided by many teachers.

58% Inservice courses are taken for purpose of salary increment rather than for professional development.

42% Each teacher acts as though his own work is the most important.

Tabulation of teacher and faculty responses reveal differences in attitudes and morale tendencies in the various schools of the school system. A factor-by-factor study of each school's response reveals differences, sometimes widespread. What is the basis for such differences?

Why is it that the board of education seems to be better understood by the faculty of one school in contrast to another? Is it a matter of communication, the channels of communication, or is it some other factor? Why is it that one elementary school faculty has better attitudes toward teacher-supervisor relations than another elementary school?

These questions cannot be answered from the graphs and data alone but answers to them should be sought by principals and teachers.

Elementary Schools

On an average, the elementary schools tend to have higher morale scores than either the junior or senior high school faculties. This, however, is an average. The average MTS for the school system was 71; for the elementary schools, 74. The range for elementary schools was from 58 to 87. Some elementary schools scored as low as either junior or senior high schools. But the high morale tendency scores for some elementary schools were not equaled by any junior or senior high schools.

Personnel factors about which the total elementary school faculty gave positive responses were:

The administration encourages staff members to participate actively in conferences and committee meetings. (The average for all elementary schools was 80%, but one school scored only 17% positive.)

The relationship of the headquarters administration and the principal does not interfere with educational improvements by the school faculty. (The average for all elementary schools was 94%, but one school scored 0%.)

Teaching assignments are well suited to the interests and abilities of the individual teachers. (The average for all elementary schools was 84%, but one school scored only 10%.)

Report deadlines and clerical duties are not given undue significance. (The average for all elementary schools was 76%, but three schools scored 22, 38 and 39%.)

Professional activities and conferences are encouraged by administrators. (The average for all elementary schools was 85%, but one school scored 10%.)

The central administrative staff of the schools is easy to see. (The average for all elementary schools was 61%, but three schools scored 0, 23 and 36%.)

Teachers are satisfied with the present methods of making assignments and establishing equality of load. (The average for all elementary schools was 74%, but three schools scored 23, 25 and 44%.)

These factors, critical in one or a few schools, may indicate the general problems that educational leadership faces.

How does one account for such widespread differences in attitudes among elementary schools? One elementary school had no low ratings except on factors that all elementary schools were low on. In other words, this school would be helped if those factors on which all elementary school faculties were low were raised.

This was not the case with another elementary school, which had 22 factors below the 60% standard, in addition to those factors on which all elementary schools were low. Five of these items fall under "administration." They were:

1. Report deadlines and clerical duties are given undue significance.
2. My immediate superiors do not do what they can to make working conditions as satisfactory as possible.
3. Differences of opinion within the faculty regarding school or classroom practices are not handled by my administrators in such a way as to achieve solutions satisfying to most everyone.
4. Teachers do not have many opportunities to discuss and improve the purposes and objectives of the school.
5. Teachers are not satified with the present methods of making assignments and equalizing load.

These factors indicate the areas in administration in which efforts to improve morale in that school must be considered.

Where Improvement Is Needed

Four of the low factors in this school fell under the heading "School Plant, Services and Equipment." They were: (1) Teachers find it difficult to find and obtain better books. (2) Communication to and from nursing, health personnel, or other special services regarding pupils does not occur in an effective manner.(3) The clerical staff is not adequate and helpful in getting work done. (4) Our building is not kept up as well as other buildings.

Three of these items deal with supply practices and personnel rather than with the equipment or supplies themselves.

A further study of the difference between the elementary schools reveals what are the important personnel relations in low morale schools. Some of them follow:

In the schools with 20 or more negative factors, at least three of the four disagreed that:

1. The teachers often have an opportunity to discuss and improve the purposes and objectives of the school.
2. Teachers share in the determination and evaluation of school policies and practices.
3. The superintendent is vitally concerned about teacher welfare.
4. Superiors handle staff complaints fairly and sympathetically.
5. Supervisors and principals make reasonable allowances for each teacher's personal limitations, problems.
6. New members of the teaching staff receive adequate orientation.
7. Principals know teachers' classroom problems.
8. Board decisions and policies are quickly and accurately transmitted to the teaching staff.

9. In establishing policies, the board relies on the professional advice of the administrative staff.

Understanding Comes First

These factors reveal that administration, in the total sense of the word, is built upon human understanding.

The responses of the teaching staffs of the junior and senior high schools were similar. Yet there are some differences resulting from the differences in structure between elementary and secondary schools.

More important than a school-by-school comparison is a study of the pattern of factors on which a school scores negative attitudes. If this is done with the two secondary schools with the lowest MTS scores, on 11 factors the majority of teachers in these two schools were in common agreement that:

1. Administrators do not give recognition to the contribution of individual classroom teachers.
2. Teachers do not have many opportunities to discuss and improve the purposes and objectives of the school.
3. Teachers do not share in the determination and evaluation of school policies and practices.
4. There is no grade-to-grade coordination and integration in the school program.
5. Organized student records are not used frequently by teachers.
6. Administrators interfere with the expression of teacher opinions in or out of the classroom.
7. Some teachers are left off important school committees.
8. Participation by parents in school policies and practices is not accepted by most teachers.
9. Teachers tend to routinize their teaching.
10. Some teachers act as though their own particular work is the most important.

The same factors were reported negatively in the low scoring elementary schools. Does this indicate that these are factors about which the board of education, the administration, principals and teachers should be more sensitive?

A study of the items on which one high school indicated a sizable percentage of negative responses clearly shows how important human relations factors are in education. A majority of the teachers of this school report that new teachers do not receive adequate orientation, that the superintendent and his assistants are not vitally interested in the welfare of teachers, that they are difficult to see, that grievances do not receive prompt and serious attention, that teachers do not share in the determination of school policies and practices. They record their need for better equipment, more clerical help, more supplies and tests and books. But material things are not more significant for morale than the personal factors.

Study Is Helpful

This report indicates a few of the ways by which a study of teacher morale can be helpful in formulating plans to improve the morale of the teachers and thereby improve the quality of the education of children and youth. It forms guidelines for study and action by the board of education, the superintendent, the administrative staff, and the teachers.

In the report on this school system much more data than this were collected, and these additional data reveal much of importance about teachers and teaching in this school system. This article, however, confines itself to the importance of teacher morale for the superintendent and one way by which it was studied.

A Basis for Viewing Communication

Lawrence Borosage

The ferment in education has raised many questions about our communicative behavior as teachers and administrators: Why do we sense a degree of skepticism among certain segments of the community about some of our practices? How do we account for the antithetical positions sometimes held by different teachers within a school community? What underlies the gulf of misunderstanding that prevails at times between the administrator and teaching staff? While these problems stem from a number of causes, inadequate communication is undeniably a major factor.

If it is of any solace, communication difficulties are common to virtually every segment of society. The perceptive observer recognizes that government, management, labor, professional associations, charitable organizations, religious bodies–the list could be readily augmented–are plagued by persistent communication problems.

Despite bombardment from the literature, platform addresses, and a host of other devices designed to improve communication, the problem continues to rear its ugly head. Like the Hydra, alleviate one misunderstanding and two more appear out of obscurity. This, coupled with our fetish for efficiency and impatience with pedestrian solutions, forces us to try to capture the elusive millennium of "perfect communication" with panaceas of the quickie cookbook how-to-do-it variety.

In any organization such as an elementary school, the assumption that communication difficulties will be nonexistent is false. The central question would seem to be: Given a dynamic organization, is there a basis for minimizing misunderstanding? Certainly, the alert administrator in any forward-looking action program anticipates a certain measure of misunderstanding among those who have an interest in educational matters. He is especially sensitive to the communication problems within his faculty subculture since a school, by its very nature, should represent a holy land of understanding.

An administrator spends a large proportion of his time in communication—for example, talking to professional colleagues, dictating letters, scanning professional journals, reading memoranda, participating in meetings, consulting with parents, preparing reports and schedules. Research evidence reports that the "average American spends seventy per cent of his active hours communicating verbally–listening, speaking, reading and writing in that order. In other words, he spends about 10 to 11 hours a day, everyday, performing communicative behaviors."[1] It is reasonable to assume that the school administrator exceeds this average.

With all this expenditure of time and energy, it is amazing that many individuals do not see their responsibilities in terms of communication. Furthermore, even those who profess a certain degree of sophistication are often unwittingly caught in several traps. The first is viewing communication as if it existed in a vacuum, separate from the contextual environment through which it seeps. The second is the failure to perceive communication as a complex process in which effective or ineffective communication has a residual effect on subsequent communication. The remainder of this discussion will focus on these two points.

Communication in a Social System

Communication affects and is affected by other forces in any social organization such as an elementary school. Jay Jackson has said:

> What we call communication problems are only symptomatic of other difficulties which exist among persons and groups in an organization. I should like to point to four problems which people in organizations must solve in order to overcome barriers to communication.
>
> (1) The problem of trust or lack of trust. Communication flows along friendship channels. When trust exists, content is more freely communicated, and the recipient is more accurate in perceiving the sender's opinion.
>
> (2) The problem of creating interdependence among persons: common goals and agreement about means for achieving them. When persons have different goals and value systems, then it is especially important to create mutual understanding about needs and motives.
>
> (3) The problem of distributing rewards fairly so that people's needs are being met, and so that they are motivated to contribute to the over-all objectives of the organization. Nothing can be so restrictive of the free flow of ideas and information, for example, as the feeling that you may not obtain credit for your contribution.
>
> (4) The exceedingly important problem of understanding and coming to common agreement about the social structure of the organization. I can think of nothing which would facilitate more the free and accurate flow of communication in an organization than consensus about questions of work, authority, prestige, and status relationships.

Despite the continual refinement of media and techniques, communication difficulties will be with us unless we see past the frills and gimmicks to the

[1] Berlo, D. K. *The Process of Communication.* New York: Holt, Rinehart and Winston, 1960. p. 1.

all-pervasive character of communication. A quantitative approach based upon *more* conferences, *more* newsletters, *more* newspaper accounts, *more* brochures will not necessarily bring with it improvement in understanding unless certain attendant prerequisites have been considered.

Using the Bohlen and Beal model of group productivity as a base, we can examine the relationship between communication and the attendant prerequisites. Figure 1 represents a conceptual framework of an elementary school as a social system. We have established the essentiality of communication by giving it central prominence and have indicated by double-headed arrows the reciprocal relationship between communication and eleven other major elements. The model illustrates that effective communication can exist only to the extent that attention is directed to all other elements in the social system. Let us discuss the various elements briefly.

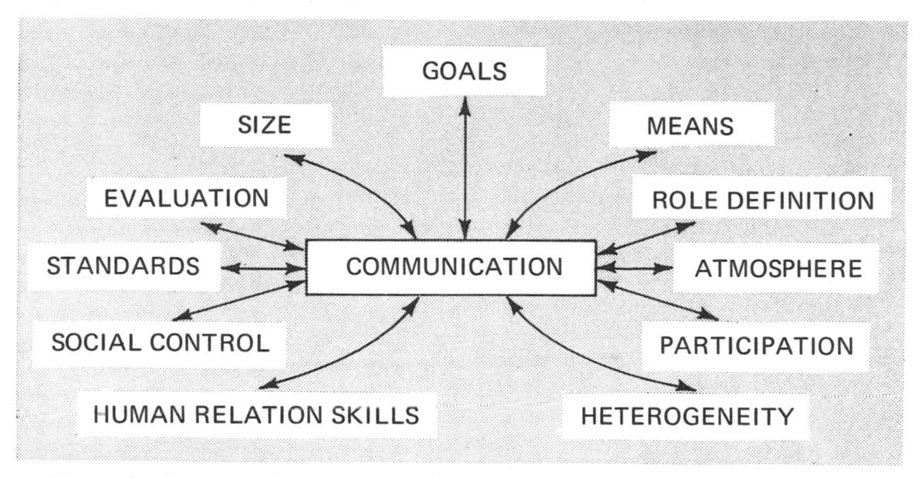

Figure 1. Conceptual Framework of an Elementary School as a Social System

Goals: Effective internal and external communication can exist to the extent that common goals and objectives–the ends of group action–are shared by all individuals within the social system. Without such understanding, Dr. Jackson states, built-in communication barriers will result. Although the research is clear about the importance of goal sharing, behaviorally there may be some glaring lags. To assume that a faculty subscribes to common goals may be the first step toward communication breakdown.

Means: Means are those instrumentalities such as curricula, physical plant, finances, and auxiliary services which enable a faculty community to attain its goals. Once goals have been clarified and formulated, means for attaining them should be considered. Groups which take a systematic approach to identifying means will have a degree of understanding quite different from those employing expediential, disjointed methods.

Definition of roles: In defining roles, two levels should be recognized. First, are general roles which relate to functions expected of individuals in subgroups. 1)

What is the expectation of the teaching staff as contrasted with that of the administrator? 2) Is it the group's expectation that the administrator have major responsibility for initiation, direction, decision, and action, or does the administrator perceive these functions as a diffused responsibility? 3) When a person joins the faculty, is he given any definition of his role, of the responsibilities, obligations, and privileges that go with membership?

The second level of roles deals with individual role definition which helps the individual clarify the group's reactions and expectations in relation to himself. 1) What is the expectation of the administrator regarding the role of a teacher? 2) What expectancies may the teacher have of the administrator who is the official leader? 3) What is the teacher's responsibility to parents and the community at large? 4) What is the responsibility of the teacher to pupils and to other teachers?

Probably no other element in group productivity causes more misunderstanding than the lack of role definition. The author's experience as consultant to many organizations attests to the fact that ill-defined goals and roles are the chief contributors to communication breakdown.

Atmosphere: Atmosphere or climate is the pervading mood, tone, or feeling that surrounds a group. As abrasive as it may seem, Crawford tells us that the major responsibility for creating a proper climate rests with the top administrator.[2] Every faculty reflects the personality and character of the administrator, whether he likes it or not. Crawford pushes in more detail when he says: "Men do things because of pride, greed, fear, vengeance, hate, self-respect, generosity, integrity, justice, love. Every man can be lazy, antagonistic, harsh, scheming, industrious, cooperative, understanding, loyal. Climate helps to determine which emotions shall control. Every man has the potentiality for being something of the hero or something of the villain."[3]

The effect of communication depends on the feelings people have before receiving the communication. The climate may be one of fear and suspicion—fear of being ridiculed or rejected, suspicion in the sense that no one trusts anyone else, his motives or willingness to say what he thinks. Group atmosphere may be aggressive, with people at each other's throats. It may be apathetic, without life or vitality. On the other hand, the feeling may be friendly and warm with people willing to express themselves freely. Again we can see that potentiality for understanding can be reduced or increased depending on the climate.

Participation: Participation means here the mental and emotional involvement of a person in a group situation which encourages him to contribute to group goals and share responsibility for them. There are three ideas in this definition which are significant to those who would practice the art of participation. First, and probably foremost, participation means mental and emotional involvement, rather than mere muscular and physical activity. Some administrators go through the motions of participation, nothing more. They hold meetings and ask opinions, but all the time

[2]Crawford, F. C. *How to Increase Executive Effectiveness:* Cambridge: Harvard University Press, 1953. p. 3.
[3]*Ibid.*, p. 4.

it is perfectly clear to the participants that their leader is an autocrat who wants no ideas. This is busy-work, not participation.

A second important idea is that participation motivates people to contribute to the situation. They are given an opportunity to release their own initiative and creativeness to further the goals of the organization. In this way, participation differs from "consent," which uses only the creativeness and ideas which the administrator brings to the group for consent. The practice of "consent" allows some degree of useful communication (mostly one way), but it does not provide communication in which all members of the group can contribute their ideas.

A third idea in participation is that it encourages people to share responsibility in an activity. Because they are personally involved in an organization, they want to see it work successfully.

Communication through participation is directly related to how well certain prerequisite conditions are met. Some of these conditions occur in participants; some exist in their environment. These conditions are:

1. There must be time to participate before action is required. Participation is hardly appropriate in emergency situations.

2. The financial cost of participation should not exceed the values, economic or otherwise, that come from it.

3. The subject of participation must be relevant to the participants' interest or else they will look upon it as busywork.

4. The participants should have the ability, such as the intelligence and knowledge, with which to participate.

5. The participants must be able to communicate–to talk each other's language–in order to be able to exchange ideas.

6. No one should feel threatened by participation. If a teacher thinks his status or security will be adversely affected, he will not participate. If an administrator feels that his authority is threatened, he will refuse participation or be defensive. Participation, therefore, thrives best in a culture which truly accepts it all the way from top down.

7. Participation in deciding a course of action in an organization can take place only within the group's area of freedom. Some degree of restriction is necessary in order to maintain internal stability. The area of freedom is that which remains after all outside compulsory restrictions have been applied. For example, a group may have freedom to participate in deciding that a change should be made, but may be restricted in making decisions about implementation of the change.

Standards: Group standards may be defined as the level of individual of group operation that is acceptable to the group. Some groups insist on high levels of accomplishment and achievement in teaching performance, curriculum development, decision making, and evaluation. Others are satisfied with mediocrity. In most instances, the difference lies in identifying "what is par for the course." Without group standards against which performance can be measured, the end product may be confusion and misunderstanding.

Social control: Social control is the means by which a group secures conformity to its expectations. Witness the adjustive behavior of the neophyte teacher who brings an image and set of expectations to the new job. The struggle may go on for some time to determine group norms. Usually, this struggle centers on determining the things one can do and cannot do. In the process, the teacher may live up to the group's expectations and be rewarded by group acceptance, or may violate group expectations and be subjected to punitive measures of rejection and ridicule.

It is in this realm of social control that the informal group leader may exercise more power than the official leader in influencing the group to either accept or reject change initiated by the administrator. The astute administrator must recognize the forces of social control which are at work and judiciously temper action accordingly. Resistance may be the residual effect of neglecting this aspect of group productivity.

Heterogeneity: Heterogeneity encompasses the individual differences which exist among teachers as well as pupils. Individuals bring to the teaching situation a variety of motives and expectations that should be identified and reckoned with. One teacher may be highly imaginative and creative and take pride in his innovational ability. Another may find security in following a prescriptive behavior pattern. Still another may revel in leadership responsibilities. Expecting all teachers to reach a single level of interest and performance may result in frustration, insecurity, and, in some cases, apathy.

Human relations skills: This element needs little elaboration. Suffice it to say that it is an imperative to enhance good communication.

Evaluation: Evaluation as here conceived is operative on two levels: first, evaluation that focuses on the extent to which the group has achieved the goals which it has set for itself; second, evaluation of individual performance.

We can readily see in the case of group evaluation that if goals are not clarified, the process of periodic appraisal should enable us to detect this deficiency. However, if we do not engage in any form of group evaluation, we may assume that certain goals are being met when in reality we may be missing the mark substantially. On the other hand, our evaluation may be conducted on a quantitative level with little thought given to the qualitative aspects.

Probably our greatest weakness is our inability to evaluate individual teacher performance. This is due in part to an inability to determine the standards of good teaching, and laxity in identifying the role of the teacher. Because we lack adequate means of individual evaluation or the competence to engage in individual performance review, some teachers may spend their entire careers never really knowing whether they have been successful or not.

We may sharpen up the point by directing our attention to the position in which the administrator may find himself. In Figure 2, let us assume that the larger circle represents the total task responsibility of the administrator and the smaller circle, the ability that he brings to the task. In most instances when an individual becomes an administrator, he does not possess all of the competencies that are required. If after a period of time the administrator feels his competence is increasing and yesterday's insurmountable problems are becoming more manageable, this provides him with positive motivation since success breeds success.

However, if the administrator feels that his competence somehow does not square with his job responsibility and this continues over a period of time, he may find himself enveloped in a climate of fear. The difference between the task responsibility and the competence of the individual may be referred to as the *margin of fear.*

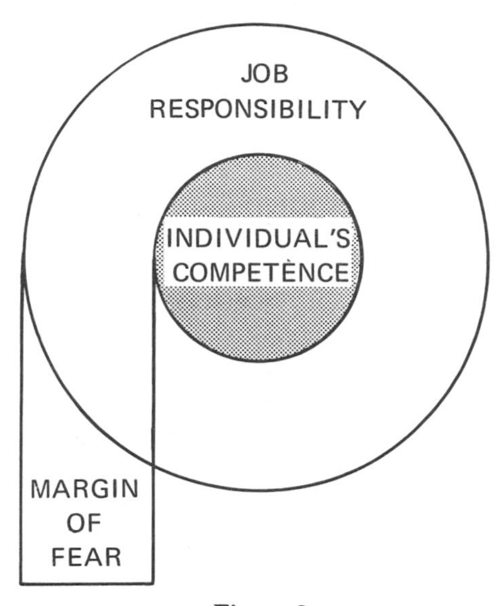

Figure 2

Although a modicum of fear may serve as a motivating factor, an inordinate amount extending over a long period of time may translate itself into lack of confidence. Lack of confidence in turn may be manifested in a variety of behavior patterns. In some individuals, withdrawal will be evidenced and, in extreme cases, may result in the individual's resigning his position. Other individuals may become hostile to faculty, pupils, the community, and, in a sense, themselves. Still others may become apathetic.

Size: The final element in the model is concerned with group size. Blau discusses the effect of size in organization and indicates that four conditions result as an organization undergoes expansion: 1) additional levels of authority are required; 2) more rules and regulations are evidenced; 3) a greater degree of impersonality prevails; and 4) it becomes increasingly difficult to communicate.[4] In considering transmission of information to create understanding, it is important to remember that the greater the organizational distance communication is forced to travel, the greater will be the tendency for it to become diluted in its original intent.

From this discussion, we can see that if an administrator wants to improve internal communication and subsequent external communication, the first step is to attend to the various elements identified in the model. He should not treat communication as if it existed in a vacuum.

[4]Blau, P. N. *Bureaucracy in Modern Society.* New York: Random House, 1956. p. 19-31.

Communication a Complex Process

The second concern of this discussion will deal with perceiving communication as a process. In every communication situation in which we engage, whether we are talking to an individual or group, writing a staff memorandum, reading a novel, or appearing on radio or television, four basic elements are at work. These basic elements are *source, message, channel,* and *receiver.* The relationship of these elements is shown in Figure 3, adapted from Berlo's model.[5] To the extent that we are knowledgeable about these relationships and give them expression, our communication is successful.

The Source in Communication

All communication originates in a source, either in an individual or a group. Certain factors inherent in the source help to enhance or impede communication, and the source must be sensitive to those barriers within itself that are conducive to creating misunderstanding We cannot assume that when a receiver fails to respond or responds incorrectly to our stimulus that the blame rests with the receiver.

Social-cultural context: The first factor affecting our communication, either positively or negatively, is the social-cultural context we bring to the situation. The writer vividly recalls an experience he had in another country. We were trying to teach the people that boiling water prior to drinking would eliminate bacteria. A member of the task force suggested we tell them to boil water for twelve minutes. One of the host country's leaders responded, "This may be a fine solution, but unfortunately our people have no clocks and no concept of time." Thus one can see how mismatched frames of reference interfere with understanding.

An administrator in a large metropolitan center who has reached his station via the teacher-principal-superintendent route must recognize that each change in position changes the social-cultural context in which he moves. A superintendent who has not been in a classroom for twenty years may mistakenly assume that he understands the problems of teachers today because he taught for a few years early in his career.

Knowledge: Another factor we need to reckon with is the quantity and quality of our knowledge–both about the receiver and the subject to be communicated. For example, in an urban renewal project in a large city, the director of adult education distributed reading materials on interior decoration, family finance, and sanitation. He became somewhat anxious because the people were not reading them. When he learned that his intended readership (the audience or receiver) was functionally illiterate, he saw that an entirely different approach was imperative.

We must also consider our knowledge of the subject to be communicated. Does the source possess sufficient credibility to convince the receiver that he should accept the information? If an administrator knows little about various methods of

[5] Berlo, O. K. *Op. cit.*, p. 72.

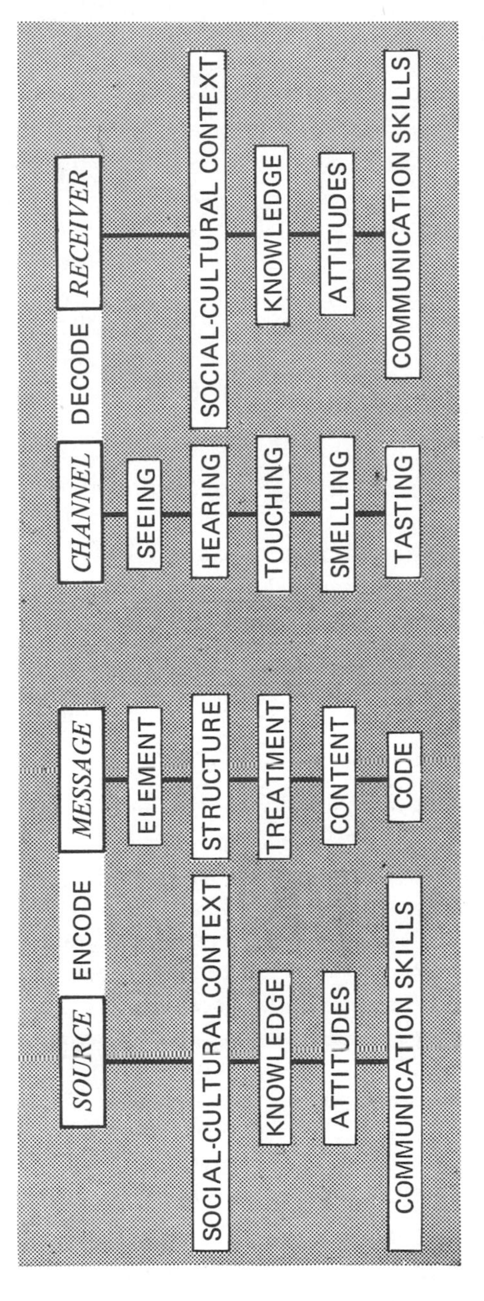

Figure 3. Model of Communication

teaching reading, he should not pretend expertness with a group of teachers who are more knowledgeable than he is in this area.

Attitudes: A third inhibiting mechanism is our attitude toward the receiver, the subject, and ourself. If my attitude as an administrator is that any attempt at curriculum reorganization will be futile because of faculty apathy and disinterest, this attitude will be reflected in my communication. Who has not encountered at least one college instructor who had little interest in the subject he was teaching and would much rather have confined his efforts to sophisticated research? Our self-attitudes as educators can be only too glaring.

Communication skills: The fourth factor pertaining to source centers around our ability to perform communication skills such as writing, speaking, listening, reading, and thinking. Since communication is our stock-in-trade and we have been exposed to courses designed to improve our communication skills, many of us assume that we possess the required competency. However, this is not always the case. Many of us have painful recollections of making a speech when boredom and restiveness were the only response.

The Receiver in the Communication Process

The receiver in the communication process is affected by the same factors that reside in the source. In the transaction, these factors have an influence on the acceptance of the message. Two of the factors, knowledge and communication, have been discussed sufficiently under source.

Social-cultural context: The receiver will respond to messages in terms of his own social-cultural context. This is readily evident in a number of situations. The administrator who engages in educational planning with a board of education comprised of individuals with different occupational orientations and diverse educational backgrounds will sense the tugs and pulls in divergent directions. The teacher who brings a middle-class value system to either a low or high socio-economic audience will experience some frustrating results unless he is aware of the social-cultural context his pupils bring with them.

Attitudes: Earlier, the point was made that communication flows more freely when there is mutual trust between source and receiver. The acceptance of any message depends in large measure on the receiver's attitudes toward the source. In one community, an explosive situation developed between a group of parents and an elementary school staff. Certain parents were informed that their children were making satisfactory progress in reading; however, when they enrolled in junior high school, many of the pupils received unsatisfactory grades. The reason for failure given by the junior high teachers was that the pupils were unable to read. We can readily imagine the parents' skepticism in the future about reporting procedures.

Message in the Communication Process

Any communication transaction between source and receiver must have a message. We may define message as the subject matter or content to be transmitted in order to elicit the desired response. All too frequently, communication fails simply because we focus our attention prematurely on the message rather than on the receiver. In teaching youngsters, we seem to pay some concern to this matter when we say, "Don't teach subject matter, teach the child," or, "Start with the learner where he is." The model indicates that five factors should be attended to in message construction: code, content, treatment, elements, and structure."[6]

Code has been mentioned in discussing knowledge; it refers to the language that we need to use and the level of difficulty that might best suit the receiver. It is obvious that if we were dealing with ethnic groups with low fluency in English, we would use language appropriate to the group in order to facilitate communication. Equally important is the level of difficulty employed within any given language. Differentiation should be made depending upon the language sophistication of the receiver. For example, educational researchers bemoan the fact that practitioners do not read the research literature, much less incorporate the findings into practice; the practitioner, however, says he is unable to understand the outcomes of research that appear in reports. As a result, neither group is really satisfied with the efforts of the other.

Content is the subject matter or substantive material that the source selects in order to achieve his intent. Treatment refers to the way in which content and code are arranged to elicit the most group is really satisfied with the efforts of the other.

Channel in the Communication Process

The final element in the communication process is the channel. Authorities in the field differ in interpreting channel. Some establish a system of ordering based upon sensory receptors for receiving information. Others identify channel as a series of techniques or media used to transmit information.

In the Berlo model, channel is treated in terms of the former classification. Several general principles undergird the use of these channels. First, the more sensory receptors that are put into play for receiving information, the better the chances for more effective communication. The use of audio-visual aids seems to be based upon this principle. Second, the greater the number of sensory receptors involved, the smaller the audience that can be reached. Third, increasing the number of sensory receptors used results in better and immediate feedback. Radio may reach a wider audience, but the source has difficulty in determining the impact of his message and feedback becomes difficult. On the other hand, in small group discussion where source and receiver have an opportunity to interact in a face-to-face situation, a better opportunity is available for feedback and clarification of the message.

In this article, we have discussed two major aspects of communication. First, we have emphasized that communication is inextricably interwoven in the social system in which it is to operate and, therefore, cannot exist in a vacuum. Second, the communication process is composed of four interrelated elements. Disregard

[6] A more exhaustive treatment can be found in Berlo, D. K., *op. cit.*, chapter 3.

any one of the four and the process collapses. Effective communication requires an understanding of both the social system within which the communication occurs and of the basic elements of source, message, channel, and receiver.

Communicating Person to Person

Douglas R. Bunker

The initiated third-grade student, the PTA program chairman, and the young teacher in his second year all "know" what the principal is like and how he is apt to respond to any number of situations. Their perceptions may be distorted and their predictions somewhat inaccurate—or they may sometimes be close to the mark—but each has an image of the principal, an image derived both from his own direct experience and from others' encounters which have been passed about enough to become part of the school legend.

These views of the principal include both perceptions of particular policies or actions and global evaluative impressions. In the processes of seeing and hearing, general impressions and perceptions of specific statements or actions often merge. The message received then consists not alone of the intended verbal content, but also includes and is influenced by the receiver's image of the communication's source, the principal.

This tends to be true for all those whose behavior takes into account the past or anticipated response of the principal: teachers, supporting staff, other administrators, parents, community leaders, students. *The face-to-face encounter is at the core of communication.* Even when the medium is a brief mimeographed statement or a cryptic announcement from an electronically reproduced voice, the receiver's reaction is as much to the person—the source known face-to-face—as to the verbal content of the message.

The importance of the principal's perceived characteristics to his effectiveness as a communicator has several implications:

1) The principal cannot arbitrarily "turn off his transmitter," or confine his impact to official pronouncements. What he says or does casually (and sometimes unintentionally) is communicated as clearly as the carefully worded policy statement.

2) No single message is taken alone. The principal's expressed views are interpreted in the context of continuing relationships and are often "fitted" by the receiver to meet expectations based upon past experience.

3) Because potential hearers walk around with a picture of the principal as well as a sense of history in their mind, messages which fit their image of the principal naturally are likely to be most effectively heard. However elegant our prose, however true to the ideas we are trying to express, it will only evoke confusion or resistance if it is seen to contradict what the receiver "knows" about us.

4) How well a message is going to get across often depends upon the emotional quality of the relationship between the sender and the receiver. If the principal is seen as uncaring, hostile, unduly judgmental, or even as distant and too far removed in the organizational hierarchy, messages from him will come through with difficulty and often be distorted in the process. Economical communication depends upon a minimum of obtruding interpersonal difficulties.

5) Patterns of school leadership which permit the examination and resolution of interpersonal differences facilitate effective communication. Mutual trust and collaborative orientations among the members of a work group are at once a condition for and a consequence of open communication.

These five points underscore the point of view that each communicative act requires on the part of the intended receiver both a response to the content of the message and a complex set of reactions to the source and behavioral context. Thus, the improvement of communication depends as much on the building of relationships as it does on the development of presentation skills.[1]

Getting the Job Done

"But," says a conveniently available straw man, "why this emphasis on the characteristics of the sender and his relationship to the intended receiver? Isn't this an unnecessary psychological detour? If we want to be understood, why shouldn't we concentrate on sharpening the logical structure of our own thinking and polishing our presentation skills? After all, the people we deal with are reasonable, intelligent, and cooperative. As long as people can understand what I am saying, does it make any difference whether I like them or they like me? If you want to get the job done rather than run a social club, the substance of the message is what counts."

"Quite so," say we, "the substance of the message is what counts. But it is the substance of what is heard rather than what is said that is important; and if the two are discrepant, we are obliged to seek an explanation. One kind of hypothesis we can try is that the original message was fuzzy—meaning, of course, that the sender failed. An alternative is that the intended receiver is dense or, more politely, inattentive. But while both of these may often be invoked and may, in fact, be accurate in a particular instance, neither is a satisfactory explanation. The adequate answer must take into account *why* the sender is more or less lucid and compellingly fluent in one situation than in another, and *why* the intended receiver is more or less attentive and comprehending in one set of circumstances than in another. Answers to these questions require consideration of the relationships between people as well as the individual characteristics of each."

While this bit of dialogue is clearly not Socratic, it is unquestionably ancient. It attempts to emphasize that our preocupation with the immediate task and our anxiety to get on with the job may actually interfere with efficient task-centered communication within an organization. This is especially likely to be so if it means

[1] Rogers, Carl R. "The Characteristics of a Helping Relationship." *Personnel and Guidance Journal* 37: 6-16; September 1958.

we are not equally concerned with keeping working relationships in good maintenance.

This impatience with what appear to be inter-personal distractions or human relations byplay is frequently a barrier to effective communication. It is based upon the assumption that we are simple information-processing mechanisms which fail to function only because of limited intellectual capacity or willful contrariness. Closer to the present evidence from cognitive research is the conception that man's communicative efficiency is limited not so much by incapacity or by obstinacy as by motivational factors over which the individual has only partial control.[2, 3]

The interpersonal situation–made up of expectations, influence attempts, unique personalities, status and power differences, and varying perceptions of one another–provides conditions that either arouse or depress particular individual motives. For example, the motive for achievement is operative only when the situation is perceived as one in which success is somewhat probable, and the motive for warm and friendly interpersonal relationships is engaged only by conditions which arouse the expectation of its fulfillment.

The link we are attempting to describe here is that between organizational relationships, individual motivation, and communication. *If a principal's or a teacher's attention and readiness to hear or a student's fluency and clarity in vocal communication are influenced by motivational factors, and if individual motivation is affected by the informal and formal organization, then among the most practical steps we can take toward improving working communication is to examine the quality of the interpersonal relationships within our schools with respect to how well they take into account individual needs and aspirations.*

This examination cannot provide a true picture of the organization, however, unless all within the network of relevant relationships share in it. If it is a participative process, it becomes a means to improve relationships as well as understand them. A vast amount of research is available demonstrating the correlation between participation and personal involvement on the one hand and open communication and organizational effectiveness on the other.[4] A principal conclusion from these sources is that valid communication[5] in a small work group or large organization is only possible when all those involved share responsibility for keeping communication channels open.

[2] Blake, R. R. and Ramsey, G. V., editors. *Perception: An Approach to Personality.* New York: The Ronald Press Company, 1951. 442 p.

[3] Allport, Floyd, A. *Theories of Perception and the Concept of Structure.* New York: John Wiley and Sons, 1955. 709 p.

[4] Likert, R. *New Patterns of Management.* New York: McGraw-Hill, 1961. McGregor, Douglas. *The Human Side of Enterprise.* New York: McGraw-Hill, 1960. Argyris, Chris. *Interpersonal Competence and Organizational Effectiveness.* Homewood, Illinois: Irwin Publishing Company, 1962. Blake, R. R., and Mouton, J. S. *Group Dynamics, Key to Decision Making.* Houston: Gulf Publishing Company, 1961.

[5] Valid communication may be defined as occurring when both the sender and the receiver have functionally identical perceptions both of the message and of the relationship between them.

Handling Conflict

A second block to open communication in an organization is the tendency to suppress conflict to avoid "rocking the boat." To preserve a veneer of cordiality and unity, communication about the important issues in a relationship may be virtually suspended. Potential antagonists may continue to work perfunctorily with one another, but conversation is largely confined by a seeming conspiracy to the trivial, the safe, the conventional.

The paternalistic administrator who operates as a benevolent autocrat and wants to maintain the appearance of congenial staff relations may be especially prone to preserve a contrived peace at the cost of effective working relationships. Unless loyalty and organizational commitment are more than superficial (i.e., based on the recognition and creative use of differences among people rather than their suppression) a communication impasse is created which can be worked through only by confronting the nature of the relationships directly and examining feelings.

Effects of Evaluation

A third important effect of organizational structure on communication derives from the fact that principals, teachers, supervisors, superintendents, and students all occupy positions in an organizational hierarchy. Performance evaluation within such a structure is one of the realities with which all must cope. We acknowledge it as a classroom problem when we consider the effects of grading procedures upon the student-teacher relationship and the learning process,[6] but we do not always directly recognize its importance in influencing the individual effectiveness of professional teachers and administrators and the openness of communication among them. When one person is dependent upon another's approval for salary increases, advancements in rank, or relocation references, he is likely to be quite guarded about revealing anything that might displease the superior. If a supervisor particularly enjoys his role as evaluator and makes the most of it, or if organizational policy emphasizes this function, the communication process may become a game of selective concealment and revelation.

Even in the most favorable situation, evaluation is a barrier to completely open communication and to collaborative relationships. Our cultural norms support "keeping our cards close to our vests" and "not sticking our necks out," but debilitating anxiety about the acceptability of our work is heightened when we are dependent and unsure about how we are doing. This problem of work-interfering individual discomfort becomes a problem for the organization because it creates tension and misunderstanding and makes it difficult to share information that is important to the achievement of organizational goals.

As an illustration, the new teacher who desperately wants to succeed is unlikely to ask for help from a principal whom he considers a severe judge and taskmaster

[6]Cronbach, Lee J. *Educational Psychology.* New York: Harcourt, Brace and Company, 1954. p. 411-517.

lest he risk exposing his weakness. His resulting anxiety about routine class visits and interviews may make his classroom efforts even more difficult. The teacher's effectiveness may then depend upon the creation of relationships between the teacher and the principal which will enable him to seek and receive help from the principal.

Perhaps the only way out of this dilemma is for a work group to find means to develop recognition of the ways in which its members are interdependent. One particularly successful elementary school principal we interviewed reported that he asks his teachers periodically to evaluate him in writing. The fact that these views are written in candor and seriously considered by the principal helps reduce the imbalance of the teachers' subordination and dependence. This procedure and the open relationships it illustrates are a model for the way in which a principal can facilitate open communication by genuine solicitation and acceptance of information.

The Door Is Always Open

In some kinds of relationships, infrequency of contact with the principal is a communication barrier. A principal may be known as accepting and approachable by those who have frequent informal contacts with him, and therefore may have no difficulty in either sending or receiving messages with clarity and effect with this group. To many students, some parents, and one or two new teachers, however, the same principal may seem impersonal and distant. Indeed, in some cases it is not merely a matter of different perceptions but of a realistic difference in the principal's behavior. The uncertainty of a first encounter is always somewhat anxiety evoking, but it tends to be particularly so for those with least social power—the young, the newcomers. When a principal's contacts with a person are so infrequent that each one is essentially a first meeting, the effect is heightened. The probability of both distortion and concealment in the communication process is increased under these conditions.

This problem is further complicated with students who view visits with the principal as punishment. This idea is likely to persist until changed by enough contrasting experience to build relationships based upon trust and understanding of the principal's role.

The remedy would appear to be simply to provide more frequent contact. However, while increased visibility is important, it is not sufficient. There is a difference between being impressed with the grandeur of a snow-capped peak from a distance, and the feeling of relatedness and intimate knowledge that comes from climbing it. Communication is facilitated when the principal is known apart from his position on a public platform. It follows, then, that if the principal is always on the platform—even behind his desk—valid communication is restricted.

Communication may also be restricted by the nature of the concerns the principal expresses in his contacts with others. If, for example, a principal is at the entrance to greet students each morning, but consistently pays more attention to the noise level and muddy shoes than he does to offering a greeting, relationships are not likely to be enhanced. Efforts to feign warmth and acceptance on a sustaining basis are unlikely to succeed. The only recourse, then, is to be somewhat genuinely "people-centered" and accepting, if we want our door to be perceived as open.

All This and People, Too

This discussion of the frequency of contact between the principal and the many others in his daily world leads to consideration of the dimensions of the principal's job. It is undoubtedly a very complex matter, involving administrative, pedagogical, representational, and quasi-parental responsibilities. Most principals we interviewed saw their job ideally to be centered on the direct support of teaching and learning. Some resorted to the traditional role definition—the principal as the principal teacher. A few were frankly resigned to an administrative focus with less idealism about ultimate objectives.

Although they are confronted by a variety of tasks requiring immediate attention, it is probably true that few principals have their time totally preempted by crises. Most exercise some planned initiative in allocating their time and energies. Our observations lead us to believe that those who provide opportunities for brief, informal interviews in which the student, teacher, or parent has the full attention of the principal build relationships which facilitate efficient communication. Often it is the attentiveness and listening skill of the principal which is critical to the success of such sessions.

While it is clearly impossible and usually inappropriate for a principal to spend much time as a counselor to students, teachers, or parents, it is important that the principal's self-defined role requirements include the need to demonstrate his accessibility and express his caring sufficiently to maintain open relationships.

On Staying Awake in Public

A significant portion of our work week and personal energy is committed to communicating with others in scheduled meetings. Principals, like many other harrassed members of large organizations, have long sought deliverance from the length, frequency, and often unsatisfactory consequences of these meetings. "It wouldn't be so bad," we often argue, "if they accomplished their purpose, but they seem to go on interminably without getting the job done." Our meetings very often provide a showcase for symptoms of all the organizational and communications problems and successes we generate, fall into, or have imposed on us.

Meetings can be effective when they are called for the appropriate purposes, when the right people are present, and when both the content and process are motivationally relevant. The "right" purposes are many. Those which are usually appropriate include problem solving or decision making, organizational team building, and the collaborative clarification of information.

Group problem solving is useful when relevant information and skills are distributed among the members of an organization, when the decision will significantly affect the work of the members of an organization, or when the decision's implementation requires the participation of the members. Group problem-solving efficiency is dependent, however, upon the possession of collaborative skills and norms supporting their use in a group. It is important to provide opportunities for their development before a group's problem-solving ability is definitively tested.

With small groups consisting of members with continuing working relationships, it is often important to provide regular opportunities for informal sharing and collective appraisal of work processes. This type of session can be valuable whether there are major problems to be tackled or not, if each member either is committed to the process or feels free to express proposals for alternatives such as adjournment, postponement, optional attendance, or change in format.

The third purpose mentioned above is the collaborative clarification of informational content. A principal may receive a policy communication from the superintendent's office and have to choose between announcing it in a formal memorandum distributed in mail boxes or calling a meeting to read it and distribute copies. If the policy is clear and no strong reactions are expected, the first option may seem appropriate. Not many of our communications, however, are completely lucid and guaranteed to meet agreement. A meeting may facilitate clarification, explore implications, and develop reactions which the principal may represent to the superintendent's office. Participation in this process may ensure that a person accepts the policy because it is understood and seems to make sense, rather than because it comes from a high status source.

In planning invitations to meetings, the distribution of authorized and informal power within the organizational structure should be taken into account. Many wasted hours have been devoted to planning decisions which have been subsequently ignored. In meetings, as in more formal settings, information and opinion exchanges must be seen as purposeful and personally relevant in order for valid communication to occur.

Communication processes may be fully understood and influenced only by taking into account the organic interrelationships of a continuing organization. These relationships are organic because they are characterized by a true interdependency of the several parts. In the school, the principal, because of his central role, may influence the communicative efficiency of his entire organization. Improved understanding between the principal and a teacher may effectively facilitate communication between the teacher and his students by reducing the teacher's anxiety and providing an appropriate relational model. Within organizations, a kind of relational contagion may often be observed. Openness and readiness for collaboration or mistrust and concealment spread quite readily, particularly when they have the sanction of status within the system.

Communicative acts, like all other behavior, are motivationally directed. This is no less true of receiving than of sending behavior. Reception is an active process requiring energy. Receivers respond not only to the substance of the message but also to the source and to what the message connotes with respect to the sender's view of the receiver. One of the critical cues often attended to by potential receivers is the sender's readiness to reverse the process and to listen. We don't hear very well those whom we perceive to be unreceptive. Conversely, one way to engage motives which will increase the probability of being heard is to behave in ways that enable others to communicate to you. Those channels are most useful which have two-way capacity.

Communications in Large Secondary Schools: A Nationwide Study of Practices and Problems

Lloyd E. McCleary

Communication is one of the chief concerns of secondary school principals, and they recognize that effective communication is a key to their success as administrators. These are conclusions to be drawn from the facts and comments provided by about a thousand principals of large high schools who participated in a nationwide study sponsored by the National Association of Secondary School Principals on practices and problems relating to intraschool communication. The present paper contains some of the data developed by the study supplemented by my comments as director of it.

For all that communications have been given attention in professional discussions for many years, actually very little of a factual sort was known about communication procedures and policies as they exist in large high schools. To provide more substance on which to base further discussion of communications problems, NASSP'S Committee on the Larger Secondary School undertook the investigation reported here.

It was decided at the outset to use as the research population those secondary schools that enrolled more than 1,000 students and in which the principals were members of NASSP. More than 5,000 schools were available, as determined by these criteria. (Like most criteria used for selecting a research population, these are somewhat arbitrary; but they appeared to the investigators not to be unreasonable, and no unusual bias seemed inherent in their application.) The questionnaire by which the information was gathered was sent to every fourth name on the list turned out by the computer, a total of 1,240 principals. With usable responses from 80 percent of these men and women—969 individuals—there is every reason to believe that the data as summarized give a reliable picture of conditions as they exist in the schools.

Focus of the Study

The study aimed to obtain information about methods and media of communication, characteristics of communications systems in operation, principals' perceptions of needs and priorities for improvement, and some evaluation of the effectiveness of various practices. These elements of the study are reported in some detail. In addition, the questionnaire was designed so as to test certain hypotheses relating to differences between types of schools and of communities, sizes of schools, and geographic location. Some of these findings are also presented.

An outline of the questionnaire follows to indicate the kind of data that were gathered.

GENERAL INFORMATION: School Enrollment, Grade Pattern, Type; Community Population and Type

Part I. Methods of Communication

A. Means of facilitating communication among staff

Face-to-face	Frequency	Extent of principal's responsibility
Printed	Frequency	Extent of principal's responsibility
Visual-electronic	Frequency	Extent of principal's responsibility

B. Means of communicating: principal and staff

Face-to-face	Frequency	Rating of value
Written	Frequency	Rating of value

Part II. Characteristics of Communications (checklist of conditions that characterize communications as judged by the principal)

Part III. Priorities for Improvement; Greatest Needs; Communications Best Utilized.

In addition to supplying the general information requested about school and community, each principal responded to 101 objective items, 10 items that permitted listing additional media or practices, and three open-ended questions. More than 75 percent of the responding principals made additional entries and more than 65 percent took the time to write one or more full paragraphs for each open-ended question.

Findings of the Study

Basic to the effective functioning of a professional staff are the means available and used to exchange ideas, share understandings, and negotiate differences. The principal is central to all these activities: He not only is largely responsible for planning and supporting the structure by which these kinds of interchange take place; he also sets the tone (and perhaps the unwritten rules) regarding what can be dealt with and how and with whom. One of the concerns of this study, therefore, was to discover the kind and frequency of opportunities for face-to-face communication and the extent of the principal's responsibility for or participation in these opportunities. Table 1 summarizes practices in the 969 schools in the study sample.

The methods most frequently reported by principals for bringing the entire staff or significant parts of it together in face-to-face situations are listed in the table in order of the relative frequency with which they are seemingly used with some regularity; that is, monthly or more often. General faculty meetings, department meetings, principal's cabinet meetings, and meetings of department chairmen lead all other types of gatherings by a significant margin. Of these four, as might be expected, the principal assumes the least direct role in department meetings.

In addition to the procedures specified in Table 1, a scattering of other practices were noted by 18 percent of the schools, but they were so varied that they could not be readily detailed in the table.

Table 1. Frequency of Use of Various Face-to-Face Communications Practices in Large High Schools and Nature of the Principal's Responsibility for Each

	Frequency				*Principal's Responsibility*			
Methods and Media	*Daily or wkly.*	*1 or 2 per month*	*Less than mthly.*	*Not at all*	*Conducts*	*Direct supervision*	*Gen'l supervision*	*No response*
General faculty mtg.	6.6[a]	68.8	23.4	.1	67.0	25.0	5.4	2.5
Department meetings	5.7	66.3	24.6	1.1	4.0	8.1	81.2	6.4
Principal's cabinet	26.1	29.7	12.7	22.9	49.1	12.4	5.1	33.2
Dept. chairmen mtg.	9.6	45.7	28.8	9.8	35.8	19.8	23.8	20.4
Teacher teams mtg.	18.8	8.8	17.6	54.5	1.0	4.5	38.4	56.0
Standing committees	1.3	18.5	49.3	21.2	5.2	12.8	48.7	33.5
Ad hoc committees	2.0	6.2	34.7	28.8	4.2	11.7	26.7	57.3
T-group "self-assessment" groups	1.1	2.5	20.2	55.5	3.2	4.4	16.8	75.8
All other groups	5.7	11.2	1.3	3.4	6.1	6.2	11.6	

[a]All percentages are based on the *total* sample.

Although the responding principals checked only a relatively few methods of communicating with individual staff members in face-to-face settings, all of these few were being used by a large percentage of the principals. Further, these methods were highly valued by the administrators, as is clear from the data in Table 2. Written comments, reported in a later section of this paper, portrayed a strong desire to increase these activities and to make more effective use of them in obtaining staff members' views about problems and conditions and in obtaining a better understanding of their interests and coming to know them better as persons.

Individual, face-to-face communications represent the most perplexing dilemma for the principal of the large school. Repeatedly, respondents reported the frustration of too little time to confer adequately with individual staff members. Several of them listed entries from their appointment books and desk calendars to illustrate the numbers of individuals they were attempting to see during the work day. Some said they set aside Saturday mornings at certain times of the year to confer with individual staff members.

Table 2. Extent of Use by Principal of Various Individual Face-to-Face Communication Practices and Value Placed on These Practices by Administrators Using Them

Communication with Individual Staff Members	*Frequency*			*Principals' Value Ratings*[a]		
	Regularly	*Rarely*	*Never*	*Very helpful*	*Helpful*	*Little help*
Classroom visits	84.1[b]	11.7	3.9	56.2	41.4	2.4
Individual conferences	82.8	9.2	7.9	75.4	23.5	1.1
Small group meetings	74.6	18.1	7.1	51.3	47.0	1.7
Social functions –lunch, coffee, etc.	57.1	35.4	7.2	34.8	47.1	18.1
Systematic interviews	45.9	32.6	21.2	40.2	37.6	22.2
Others	9.5	1.1				

[a]Value ratings are based on responses from principals making some use of practice.
[b]All percentages are based on the total sample.

More than 100 principals wrote that their schools had grown so large that they could no longer maintain an "open door" for staff members. Apparently, by training and disposition principals expect to relate directly with staff members and students; and they feel that school size has definitely limited their opportunities to maintain the kind of individual relationships which they prize highly.

Written Communications

Table 3 lists the written communications most often cited by principals, arranged in descending order of frequency. Although the daily or weekly bulletin to the staff leads the list, it should be noted that in their comments principals expressed dissatisfaction with this means of communication far more frequently than with any other type in any category.

Table 3. Percentages of Schools Using Various Forms of Written Communication and Extent of Principal's Involvement

	Frequency				*Principal's Responsibility*			
Printed Media	*Daily or wkly.*	*1 or 2 per month*	*Less than mthly.*	*Not at all*	*Pre-pares*	*Direct super-vision*	*Gen'l super-vision*	*No re-sponse*
Regular bulletins	68.7[a]	8.4	6.1	16.8	31.4	26.1	24.8	18.7
Special bulletins & announce-ments	45.7	30.1	17.5	11.2	45.8	31.4	9.1	14.4
Staff handbook or manual	8.1	2.3	66.7	22.4	28.3	31.8	18.7	21.2
Staff newsletter	5.1	9.9	11.3	73.4	.5	3.2	19.9	77.4
Reports of work groups	3.9	64.1	25.0	6.7				
Polls of staff opinion	2.9	35.5	48.4	12.5				
Surveys of practices	5.1	32.9	42.4	18.8				
Other printed media	6.0	5.1	6.1					

[a] All percentages are based on the *total* sample.

Writing can be of particular value in communicating information and directions, but it often is of limited value in communicating or in changing attitudes, opinions, and beliefs. Principals cited as most effective the use of written media to reinforce announced decisions, to follow up discussions, and to disseminate results of studies and deliberations. Apparently principals who use written media effectively attempt to link them to other forms of communication and do not rely upon the written word alone to communicate changes in procedures or new ideas that run counter to current practices.

Visual-Electronic Communication

A primary interest in studying communications in the large secondary school was to learn the extent to which visual-electronic media are utilized to overcome the problems caused by size and complexity of operation in such a school. The results of the survey were disappointing in terms of the effectiveness of visual electronic media. Seventy-four percent of the respondents reported that they use public address or intercom systems to communicate with staff on a daily or weekly basis; next most frequently used was the conference telephone. No more than five percent of the respondents reported the use of any other type of visual-electronic media as frequently as weekly. These data are given in Table 4.

Since a total of only 4.4 percent of the schools used any visual-electronic equipment other than the eight kinds specified in Table 4, it appears that newer media of communications are little used. But these newer media do have possibilities worth consideration by schools in which more traditional means of communication are overburdened. These new media can transmit information rapidly and accurately, and some can even facilitate person-to-person contacts.

Table 4. Frequency of Use of Various Visual-Electronic Communications Media and the Nature of the Principal's Involvement with These Media

	Frequency				*Principal's Responsibility*			
Visual Electronic Media	*Daily or wkly.*	*1 or 2 per month*	*Less than mthly.*	*Not at all*	*Conducts*	*Direct supervision*	*Gen'l supervision*	*No response*
Intercom or P.A. system	74.0[a]	2.6	2.6	20.4	18.1	21.9	32.6	27.4
Conference telephone	16.2	2.3	4.5	76.9	6.5	4.9	10.0	78.6
Overhead projector in meetings	4.2	12.7	59.8	23.3	10.8	10.9	43.9	34.4

Table 4. Frequency of Use of Various Visual-Electronic Communications Media and the Nature of the Principal's Involvement with These Media (Continued)

	Frequency				*Principal's Responsibility*			
Visual Electronic Media	*Daily or wkly.*	*1 or 2 per month*	*Less than mthly.*	*Not at all*	*Conducts*	*Direct supervision*	*Gen'l supervision*	*No response*
Slide projector in meetings	3.6	10.2	53.1	44.1	7.9	9.5	40.1	42.5
School-made tapes, voice	5.0	4.9	24.5	65.3	2.1	3.0	25.9	69.0
School-made video tapes, kinescopes	2.7	1.8	6.2	88.9	.5	.5	8.9	90.1
Closed circuit TV	4.9	.7	1.7	91.8	1.1	1.1	6.4	91.4
School radio	4.5	.8	1.1	93.5	1.2	2.6	25.6	90.6
All other	1.8	.6	2.0					

[a]All percentages are based on the *total* sample.

Characteristics of Communication Practices

Each of the participating principals was also asked to respond to a list of questions which asked about the use of some one communications practice or policy. The kinds of responses that were possible are shown in this illustration:

	Yes	Yes, with exceptions	Usually not	No	Cannot answer
Are school policies, rules, and regulations recorded and made readily available to staff, parents, and students?					

Principals typically rated conditions in their schools favorably. The six questions which most frequently received negative responses and the percentages of principals who checked "usually not" or "no" are as follows:

	Usually not or no (percent)
1. Are checks made to see that communications are received and understood?	21.8
2. Are routes of appeal defined in event of disagreement or conflict between staff members and superiors?	19.7
3. Is the staff surveyed in a systematic way for opinions and suggestions relative to problems and issues?	19.4
4. Are communication channels specified in the written materials of the school?	15.2
5. Do staff members complain of the volume of communications?	12.5
6. Do staff members voluntarily report breakdowns in communications?	11.4

When comparisons are made of teachers' responses to similar questions as reported from other studies, and principals' responses as gathered in this investigation, characteristically principals rate conditions more favorably than do teachers. Therefore, indications of inadequate communication such as the foregoing six items point up deserve serious analysis.

Principals ought especially to consider the circumstances indicated by the responses to the first four of the foregoing items. One of the most common observations concerning ineffective administration is that there is a lack of follow-up on directives, announcements, and administrative decisions (Question 1). The next three items—relating to routes of appeal, solicitation of staff opinion, and specified channels of communication—also reflect common dissatisfactions of teachers.

A list of questions like the ones used in this study, asked of a school's teachers by the principal, could initiate a self-study that would lead to significantly improved communication in that school.

Needs, Priorities, and Best Uses

More than 600 of the principals responded to each of three open-ended questions with one or more paragraphs of comment. The principal was asked to identify (1) what he needed most to improve his school, (2) whether time, resources, or help had first priority in improving communications in his school, and (3) what communications were presently best utilized in his school.

Content analysis was employed to provide a substantive listing and frequency count for each of the open-ended questions. As a group, the responses to these three questions reflected a high degree of sensitivity to communications processes in the administration of schools and to the responsibility for facilitating communications.

The greatest needs for improvement indicated by the comments of respondents centered upon the relationship of the principal and the staff. Most frequently reported was the need for time and help to increase personal contacts with staff, to work with new teachers, and to involve staff with planning and decision-making. Next most frequently reported was the desire to consult with staff in order to obtain feedback about the quality of teaching, problems of teacher-pupil and parent relations, and the interests teachers had in professional improvement.

Two other responses followed well behind those but were widely commented upon: (1) use of electronic media to expedite routine messages and information handling and (2) value of expert help to systematize and improve the quality of communications.

Reflecting the needs they saw as greatest, principals gave the highest priority in improving communications to freeing teachers and department chairmen for group work within the school day and to increasing the informal, direct contact of the principal with teachers in order to exchange ideas, discuss problems, and share experiences. Judged next in order of importance were introducing parents and resource people into the school and improving the quality of department and faculty meetings through better planning and concentration upon improved instruction.

Among the communications methods best utilized at present, principals listed in this order: individual conferences, small-group planning meetings, faculty meetings, personal contacts, daily or weekly bulletins, and intercom systems.

Differences Among Types of Schools

Several hypotheses were tested statistically. These related to differences expected among categories of schools. Of the sample, 95.3 percent were public schools, 2.6 percent were parochial schools, and 2.1 percent were independent schools. The statistics which follow concern the kinds of schools and types of communities included in the sample.

A detailed account of the design and statistical treatments will not be undertaken in this article; however, a discussion of certain of the findings are pertinent.

No significant differences were found between categories of schools based upon size of enrollments. An initial error in listing the schools to be used resulted in introducing into the sample about 80 schools smaller than the criterion. Unintentionally, this made possible some unplanned comparisons. The only items in which these smaller schools differed from those schools classified as large was in their having intercom public address systems, and closed circuit TV less often. In all other respects the small schools could not be differentiated from the large ones.

This leads one to wonder whether large schools do indeed have problems quite different from those of smaller schools. Put another way, the question can be raised as to whether principals of large schools are still attempting to administer large schools as though they were small ones.

Schools in metropolitan centers (cities above 200,000) differed from "suburban" schools and from schools "outside of metropolitan areas" in the extent to which

Kind of School

Enrollment	*Percent*	*Grade levels*	*Percent*
Under 999	8.2	6-8, 7-8	1.0
1,000-1,499	43.2	7-9	16.1
1,500-1,999	27.3	9-12	31.8
above 2,000	21.1	10-12, 11-12	34.6
		Other	16.4

Nature of Community

Population	*Percent*		*Percent*
Under 10,000	9.8	City with rural area	30.0
10,000-49,999	42.9	City outside metropolitan area	14.7
50,000-199,999	25.2	Suburban	30.3
Above 200,000	21.9	City, metropolitan center	24.9

they used visual-electronic media but did not differ in use of face-to-face or written methods, as had been hypothesized. Further, no significant differences existed among these categories of schools in the frequency with which principals wrote about the need for direct contacts with staff.

These findings might lead to the conclusions that suburban schools are choosing to move into fuller use of electronic-visual media (and have the means to do so); and that principals of large schools in metropolitan areas value and try to develop direct, face-to-face staff relationships as much as do principals of large schools elsewhere. The myth that secondary schools in large cities are less personal is *not* supported by responses of principals from these schools.

Comments on the Findings

The objective data reported in the tables are open to interpretation by the reader. The nature of the sample and rate of return lend considerable confidence that these data present an accurate picture of the present status of communication conditions and practices in the large secondary school. Then, the question arises as to whether principals of large schools should seek to change this picture in any particular fashion.

Should an effort be made to increase the opportunities for bringing staff together? If so, which methods would be most useful and for what purposes? Should the principal increase his individual contacts with staff? If so, how is he to do this under the conditions of size and complexity of the organization he heads?

Would the increased use of visual-electronic media facilitate communications? Perhaps principals can make use of these data against which to measure practice in measure practice in their own schools.

Suggestions to Principals

Do not fall into the trap of readily blaming problems or the inability to solve problems on a failure in communications. Communications is not a cure-all. The principal might consider communications as (1) a system or network for obtaining and transmitting information and (2) a process for sharing understanding, diagnosing, deciding, and monitoring (or controlling) activity according to decisions made.

Thinking of communications as a network or system for obtaining and transmitting information relative to the operation of the school might mean arranging for such devices as bulletins, a public address system, individual conferences, group meetings, and the like, and training staff to use them. Individuals in the school organization, including the principal, then expect these devices to be available and used when required. The administrator's task is to see that communication devices are sufficient to link together the individuals in the school organization, that the individuals who are to use them understand and anticipate their use, and that the devices are adequate for the purposes they are meant to serve and the "load" of messages they are expected to carry.

The principal also needs to view communications as a process. In this regard, he might think of key administrative functions as a means of examing how he uses communications. Seven axioms which apply are described in the following paragraphs.

Diagnosis

The principal is constantly engaged in diagnostic activity. Whenever he uses questioning or investigating devices such as an interview, questionnaire, and so on to gain information, he is using communications. In the communications system, he is the receiver. For example, he may raise the following kinds of questions: Does the curriculum need revision? Would a self-study lead to improved instruction? Can teachers be involved so they will be motivated to improve?

Any judgments he might reach imply courses of action; and in the process of making judgments the principal uses information-getting devices to reduce uncertainty (omitting the possibility that he may decide *a priori* to make decisions off-the-cuff).

Since time and circumstances never permit getting all the information needed to understand a problem and its conditions, the principal must decide which communications devices to employ.

1. *The principal needs to take into account the nature of his uncertainty as well as the value of the communication devices.* Some communications devices provide little gain in information even though they are valid—if the principal already knows how certain teachers feel, he gains little by interviewing them even though the interview per se is a valuable information-getting device.

2. *The principal must judge the communications devices he wishes to use on the basis of the fidelity required.* He may wish to inquire into many facets of a problem. As he proceeds he might conclude that a particular facet is not important and ignore it; he may remain uncertain about it; or he may decide that it is very important. If he has a range of communications devices at his disposal, he can fix on one facet of a problem and probe for maximum information; *or* he can try to get information about many aspects of a problem and accept less certain information.

Communications devices are either "wide-band" or "narrow-band"—the principal can get fidelity only at the sacrifice of coverage and vice versa. This leads to a third axiom: 3. *The principal should incorporate both wide-band and narrow-band devices into his communications system.* Responses to the study questionnaire lead to the inference that principals tend to base their communications networks on wide-band devices and pay little attention to narrow-band devices that give maximum information on specific questions.

Decision-Making

The band-width and fidelity concepts help to make decisions more rational. One principal may want concrete facts and quick decisions. He decides upon the aspects of a problem he feels to be important; he narrows the field rapidly, obtains accurate information about relatively few things, and reaches a decision. Another principal may wish to consult widely, seek alternatives, delay decisions as long as possible, and attempt to get committees to judge the information obtained. Each, of course, is gambling, which does make administration exciting at times. But in any event, 4. *Principals should be conscious of the approach they are taking and make use of appropriate communications devices for decision making—narrow-band devices for fidelity, wide-band devices for coverage.*

5. *As the principal makes use of communications devices in his decisions, he should make judgments about the accuracy of information they are providing.* Irreversible, terminal decisions should be avoided when the information is incomplete or fallible. This is particularly true when the principal is making decisions about people, and most of his decisions affect people directly and indirectly. The degree of finality of a decision should be proportional to the accuracy of information upon which it is based. Whenever the accuracy of information is in doubt decisions should be cast in as tentative a fashion as possible, monitored, and corrections made as more information becomes available.

Control

Administration, in one sense, is a formalized way of controlling organizational activity to achieve purposes that have been rationally decided. 6. *The principal needs to have a fully functioning communications system that provides continuous, accurate feedback.* Each procedure and process of the school's operation should be monitored so that decisions can be adjusted. Perhaps the greatest shortcoming in school administration occurs in this communications activity.

7. *The principal will need to decide what his communication system is to be sensitive to and how sensitive it shall be.* He can then build in new devices that insure coverage and fidelity, accurate and continuous feedback, and means of determining the accuracy of information he is using.

The foregoing seven principles will be useful to the principal in understanding how he is communicating and may help him to diagnose any communications problems he has. Hopefully, the study reported here and this brief examination of communication concepts will provide insights and useful measures of current practice.

The Relationship of Teacher Communication to Principal Behavior

John A. Peoples

Does a principal's behavior as a leader in the elementary school affect the degree to which teachers communicate their problems to him via the routes he provides? A study[1] conducted by the writer took this question into consideration. The specific concern of this study was the relationship of perceptions of the principal's behavior to the extent to which teachers communicate their problems upwardly (that is, from teacher to principal) through formal routes. Formal routes are those routes of communication set up by the principal. Such communication is referred to in this study as *formal upward communication.*

Formal upward communication is considered as having value to both the principal and the teacher. It helps the principal in many phases of appraisal of the school organization. Moreover, such communication is considered necessary for a determination of the effectiveness of downward communication, that is, communication from the principal to the teacher.[2]

Regarding the value of formal upward communication to the teacher, it satisfies the need of teachers to express their feelings, needs and personal motives.[3] Such communication also provides an opportunity for teachers to contribute to the decision making aspect of administration.

The problem of formal upward communication is seen as relating to barriers which prevent communication. These barriers are looked upon as involving perceptions of the behavior patterns of the principal, such as the tendency to judge,

[1] Peoples, John A. *Formal Upward Communication by Teachers as Affected by Their Perceptions of the Behavior of the Principal,* unpublished Ph.D. dissertation. The University of Chicago, 1961.

[2] Planty, Earl and William Machaver. "Upward Communication: A Project in Management," *Personnel,* XXVIII (January 1952) pp. 306-7.

[3] *Ibid,* p. 308.

evaluate, approve, or disapprove a teacher's effort to communicate her problems. If these barriers to formal upward communication persist, then other communication routes are utilized. These other routes are informal and circumventive with respect to formal upward routes.

The foregoing suggests that the principal would do well to take the necessary steps to provide for optimum formal upward communication. If these steps involve modification of his behavior or perceptions thereof, then he should seek to determine what aspects of his behavior affect formal upward communication.

Hypothesis

This study sets forth the hypothesis that formal upward communication is systematically related to teacher perception of the behavior of the principal. Two dimensions of administrator behavior are posited as significant in this respect. These dimensions are Consideration and Initiating Structure in Interaction as delineated by Halpin.[4] Consideration refers to behavior indicative of friendship, mutual trust, respect, and warmth in the relationship between the principal and members of his staff. Initiating Structure in Interaction refers to the principal's behavior in delineating the relationship between himself and the members of his work-group and in endeavoring to establish well-defined patterns of organization, channels of communication, and methods of procedure.

Thus, the two major variables of the study are formal upward communication, the dependent variable, and teacher perception of the behavior of the principal, the independent variable.

Procedure

Two instruments were used for assessment of data relevant to the variables of the study. The Leader Behavior Description Questionnaire, LBDQ,[5] was used to determine perceptions of the principals' behavior and the Communication Route Indicator, CRI,[6] was used to determine the degree of upward communication perceived in the schools. The instruments were administered to a sample consisting of 120 teachers, five selected randomly from each of 22 participating schools. The setting was the elementary school system of a medium-sized mid-western city.

The LBDQ consists of the 40 descriptive statements indicating ways in which a leader might behave. Responses to the instrument indicate the frequency in which the leader is perceived to behave in a particular manner. A score for each of the behavior dimensions, Consideration and Initiating Structure, can be derived from the responses.

The CRI consists of a checklist of 13 typical teacher problems and eight possible

[4] Halpin, Andrew H. *The Leadership Behavior of School Superintendents* (Chicago: Midwest Administration Center, The University of Chicago, 1959). p. 4.

[5] *Leadership Behavior Description Questionnaire* (Columbus, Ohio: Bureau of Business Research, College of Commerce and Administration, The Ohio State University, 1957).

[6] This instrument was developed by the writer for the present study.

communication routes through which the respondent may indicate the problem would be solved. The number of problems indicated as being solved through formal upward communication routes determines the score on this instrument.

For the design of this study, the Consideration and Initiating Structure scores of the LBDQ were coordinated on a two dimensional graph with the medians of the scores of each dimension used as axes. Figure 1 illustrates this graph.

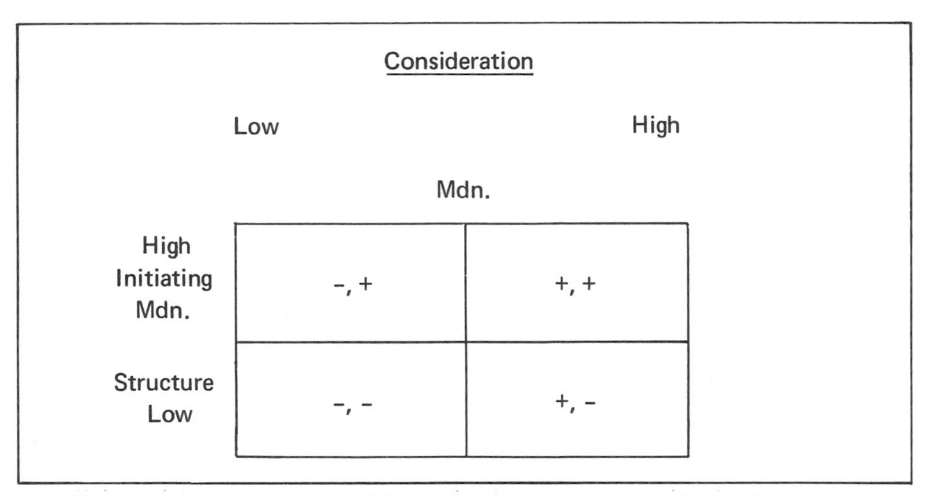

Figure 1. Consideration and Initiating Structure as coordinate dimensions

From this coordination of dimensions, four prototypes of principal behavior were derived. These are as follows:

1. *High Consideration, High Initiating Structure* (+,+) This principal is perceived as one who regards as important the personal feelings, attitudes, and needs of teachers; while at the same time, he maintains a highly structured organization. For example, he does personal favors for group members; he is friendly and approachable, and he finds time to listen to group members. Yet, he maintains definite standards of performance; he criticizes poor work; and he emphasizes the meeting of deadlines.

2. *High Consideration, Low Initiating Structure* (+,–) This principal is seen, on the one hand, as similar to the first type; but on the other hand, he tolerates a very loose organization and has little concern about rules and regulations or uniformity of procedures. For example, he never assigns group members to particular tasks and he never coordinates the work of the group members.

3. *Low Consideration, High Initiating Structure* (–,+) This principal differs from the first type in that he rarely shows warmth in relationships with teachers. He never does personal favors for group members and he never consults with them regarding important decisions.

4. *Low Consideration, Low Initiating Structure* (–,–) This principal is perceived as possessing characteristics of the second and third types. He has little concern about the personal motives of teachers and he is unfriendly and impersonal; on the other

hand, he never coordinates the work of the group and he never makes definite assignments.

Formal upward communication scores of schools are symbolized by "f". The scores of schools with principals of the four prototypes are represented by f(+,+), f(+,–), f(–,+), and f(–,–), respectively. Thus are derived four experimental groups of schools. The general hypothesis can be more specifically expressed in these terms as follows:

$$f(-,-) < f(-,+) < f(+,-) < f(+,+).$$

This expression asserts that formal upward communication, "f", among the experimental groups increases as the behavior of the principal is perceived to range through the prototypes in the order indicated.

The determination of the significance of variation of formal upward communication among the experimental school groups was achieved through analysis of variance and regression.

Ancillary consideration was given to analysis of the relationship of formal upward communication to the factors of sex, race, and age of principals and of sex and teaching experience of the responding teachers.

Findings

The distribution, means, and variances of the formal upward communication scores of the experimental groups are presented in Table 1.

Table 1. Distribution, Means and Variances of "f" Scores of Experimental Groups

	f(–, –)	*f(–, +)*	*f(+, –)*	*f(+, +)*
n	5	6	6	5
Means	8.1	7.4	9.2	10.8
Variances	1.89	2.76	2.47	1.03

Analysis of variance revealed significant difference among the means of the four experimental groups. Regression analysis further revealed that this difference could be accounted for by relatively constant or linear increases in formal upward communication as the perceived principal behavior ranges through the prototypes from low Consideration, low Initiating Structure, (–,–) to high consideration, high Initiating Structure (+,+) in the order indicated in the specific statement of the hypothesis:

$$f(-,-) < f(-,+) < f(+,-) < f(+,+).$$

This analysis, shown in Table 2, confirms the hypothesis of a systematic relationship between formal upward communication among the experimental groups of schools and variation in perceived principal behavior is shown in Figure 2.

Table 2. Analysis of Variance and Regression of Formal Upward Communication Scores of Experimental School Groups

Source of Variation	*df*	*Sum of Squares*	*Square*	*F*	*Prob.*	*Percent of Variation*
Among Means	3	38.208	12.736	5.49	.01	100.0
Linear	1	28.714	28.714	12.38	.005	76.3
Quadratic	1	7.370	7.370	3.18	.05	18.4
Cubic	1	1.900	1.900	.90	.05	5.3
Within Means	18	41.808	2.32			
Total	21	80.036				

This illustration shows an essentially linear increase in "f" as perceived principal behavior ranges through the prototypes in the order indicated.

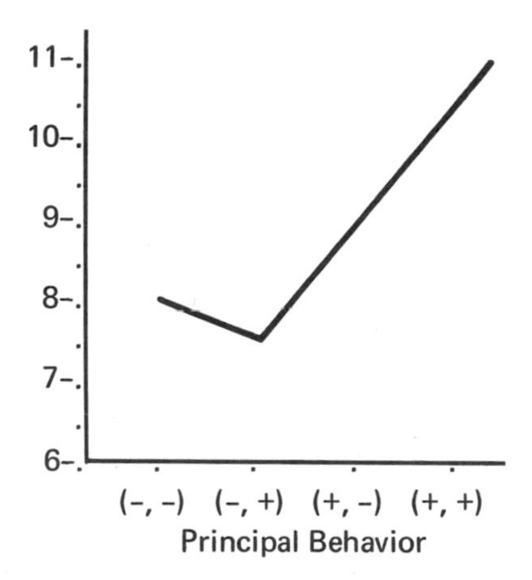

Figure 2. Graphical relationship of means of "f" scores of experimental groups to variation in perceived principal behavior

The race and sex of principals were shown by analysis of covariance to have no significant relationship to formal upward communication by teachers. The age of principals was also shown to have no significant relationship to formal upward communication by teachers. The age of principals was also shown to have no significant relationship to formal upward communication. This was shown by analysis of variance and regression using three age groups of principals, under 40, 40 to 50, and over 50 years of age.

The sex of the teachers was shown by *t*-tests to have a significant bearing on responses to the Communication Route Indicator. Female teachers perceived significantly more formal upward communication than male. The means for male and female were 7.14 and 9.02, respectively. There were no significant sex differences in responses to the LBDQ.

The teaching experience of the respondents was shown by analysis of variance and regression to have a significant relationship to perceived formal upward communication. Formal upward communication was illustrated as following an alternately downward and upward course as teaching experience ranged over four experience levels: 0-5, 6-10, 11-20, and over 20 years of experience. Figure 3 illustrates this trend, the pattern of which may be considered cubic.

Figure 3. Cubic trend of formal upward communication with respect to experience levels of respondents

Discussion of Findings

It would seem that teacher perception of the behavior of the principal has a very definite relationship to formal upward communication by teachers in the elementary school. With reference to the behavior types derived from the LBDQ dimensions, the combination of high Consideration and High Initiating Structure in interaction has a greater positive effect on formal upward communication than any of the three other possible combinations. Formal upward communication tends to increase according to an essentially linear pattern as the principal's behavior is perceived to change from that characterized by having little concern about the personal needs, feelings, and goals of teachers and exhibiting inconsistency as regards lines of authority and procedures for getting the job done to that behavior characterized by high regard for personal feelings, needs, and motives of teachers combined with having definiteness and consistency in delineating lines of authority, channels of communication, and procedures of operation.

Regarding the factors, formal upward communication and perceptions of the behavior of the principal of the elementary school, the findings suggest the following conclusions:

1. Concern about and some degree of control as to how his behavior is perceived is fundamental to the principal's ability to maintain optimum formal upward communication.

2. If the highest degree of formal upward communication is sought, it is not sufficient for the principal's behavior to be perceived as exercising high Consideration or high Initiating Structure alone. A combination of these two behavior

dimensions must be perceived to obtain the highest degree of formal upward communication.

3. Low Consideration in any combination is a greater deterrent to formal upward communication than any combination which includes high Consideration. This indicates that consideration is the main determinant of formal upward communication.

4. High Initiating Structure perceived in the behavior of the principal does not impede formal upward communication. Moreover, this definiteness and consistency seems to have a positive effect when combined with high Consideration.

5. For formal upward communication, the combination of low Consideration and high Initiating structure has no perceptible advantage over that of low Consideration and low Initiating Structure. In fact there was slight indication, although not statistically significant, that the converse might be true.

None of the factors of race, sex, and age of principals seem to have significant relationship to formal upward communication by teachers in elementary schools. It should be noted, however, that in this study, the race of respondents was in almost all instances the same as that of the principal and that only the Negro and white races were included.

As regards the sex of the responding teachers, it seems that male teachers perceive significantly less formal upward communication going on in the school than do female. This suggests either that the male teachers are generally less cognizant of formal upward communication patterns or that they themselves are less communicative upwardly. It might also reflect masculine independence. Female teachers, on the other hand, are more aware of formal upward communication. This might be indicative of their dependence on persons of authority.

Teaching experience of respondents appears to have a definite relationship to the extent of perceived formal upward communication. During the first five years of experience, there is moderate perception of formal upward communication. During the first five years of experience, there is moderate perception of formal upward communication. The least amount seems to occur during the period of from six to ten years of experience. The greatest extent of perceived formal upward communication occurs during the period of from eleven to twenty years of experience. If it can be assumed that the teachers' perceptions of the extent of formal upward communication is indicative of their personal practice, this might suggest an initial period of exploration, during which time the teacher is trying to become acquainted with the communication system. This first period is followed by one that may be characterized by confidence and independence in which there is little inclination to communicate upwardly. The third period might be considered a period of a decrease in self reliance, during which there is a desire to conform and there is continued high formal upward communication.

Suggestions for Further Study

The results of the present study might serve to stimulate further investigation in the fields of educational administration and communication relating to the following questions:

1. Are there perceptions of administrator behavior other than those described by the LBDQ which influence formal upward communication? If so, how may they be ascertained and in what specific ways are they related to formal upward communication?

2. Is there relationship among the factors: perceptions of administrator behavior, actually observed administrator behavior, and formal upward communication? How can actual behavior be determined?

3. Is informal or circumventive communication inversely related to formal upward communication?

4. Does the seeming male independence or female dependence present a problem as regards formal upward communication? How could either or both be dealt with?

5. How can the principal maintain formal upward communication with teachers throughout their tenure?

6. What formal upward communication routes are pertinent to other echelons of the public education system? How does administrator behavior relate to these routes?

It would seem that such investigation would supplement the results of this study as well as throw additional light on administrator behavior.

Diffusion of Innovations

Egon G. Guba

The finest research, the most innovative solutions to practical problems, the best packages of materials, can have no effect on practice if they are not diffused to the level of the practitioner. It is obvious that one cannot hope for any considerable improvement in American education unless one also pays a great deal of attention to the process of diffusion.

Diffusion has been defined in many ways. Rogers' classification of the five stages of diffusion has become classic:

1. *Awareness:* The individual learns of the existence of the innovation.

2. *Interest:* The individual seeks more information and considers the merits of the innovation.

3. *Evaluation:* The individual makes a mental application of the innovation and weighs its merit for his particular situation.

4. *Trial:* The individual applies the innovation on a small scale.
5. *Adoption:* The individual accepts the innovation for continued use on the basis of a previous trial.[1]

Another frequently cited definition is that of Katz *et al.* who define diffusion as " the (1) *acceptance,* (2) over *time,* (3) of some specific *item*—an idea or practice, (4) by individuals, groups, or other adopting *units,* linked (5) to specific *channels* of communication, (6) to a *social structure,* and (7) to a given system of values, or *culture.*"[2]

It is clear that the key element in both these definitions is, to use Katz's term, the *adopting unit.* Both definitions also stress *acceptance.* Thus the end result of diffusion is the *acceptance by an adopting unit,* often as individual, of an "innovation."[3] The purpose of diffusion activities is to gain such acceptance.

Diffusion activity is, of course, carried out by a diffusion agent, whom we shall refer to here simply as a *diffuser.* He may or may not have been involved in the development of the innovation being diffused. He may simply be a huckster who is out to "sell" the innovation wherever he can, for personal gain. We shall limit our discussion, however, to the case in which the diffuser sees himself as engaged in opening viable professional alternatives to practitioners who are confronted with problems. The innovation being diffused is conceivably one alternative way of handling the problem. The diffuser is assumed to operate within the limits of normal professional morality.

Strategy for Diffusion

What the diffuser needs is a *strategy for diffusion,* i.e., some action plan which will result in the innovation involved coming to the attention of those practitioners who ought to know about it. But such a strategy is not easy to devise, because the diffuser, if he is to have a successful strategy, must pay attention to at least five sets of factors:

1. *Diffusion techniques.* There are essentially six modes for the diffuser to use: (a) he can *tell* (newsletters, papers, conference, conversations, etc.); (b) he can *show* (participant observation, demonstration, films, etc.); (c) he can *help* (consultation, service, etc. rendered on the adopter's terms); (d) he can *involve* (include or coopt the adopter); (e) he can *train* (familiarize with the innovation through courses, workshops, T-sessions, etc.); and (f) he can *intervene* (i.e., involve himself in affairs

[1] North Central Rural Sociology Subcommittee on the Diffusion of Farm Practices. *How Farm People Accept New Ideas.* Iowa Agricultural Extension Service Special Report 15. Ames: The Service, 1955.

[2] Elihu Katz, Martin L. Levin, and Herbert Hamilton. "Traditions of Research on the Diffusion of Innovations." *American Sociological Reviews, 27:240; April 1963.*

[3] We shall use the term *innovation* in the sense suggested by Bhola, "An innovation is a concept . . ., an attitude . . ., a tool with accompanying skills . . ., or two or more of these together introduced to an individual, group, institution, or culture that had not functionally incorporated it before." Harbans S. Bhola. "The Configurational Theory of Innovation Diffusion." School of Education, The Ohio State University, 1965. (Mimeographed.)

of the adopter on his [the diffuser's] terms). The diffuser will have to select from among these six that technique or combination of techniques best suited to his purpose.

2. *Assumptions concerning the nature of the adopter.* There are at least seven assumptions which the diffuser can make about the nature of the adopter whom he seeks to cause to consider an innovation: The adopter may be viewed (a) as a *rational* entity who can be *convinced* on the basis of hard data and logical argument of the utility of the proposed innovation; (b) as an *untrained* entity who can be *taught* to perform in relation to the innovation; (c) as a *psychological* entity who can be *persuaded;* (d) as an *economic* entity who can be *compensated* or *deprived;* (e) as a political entity who can be *influenced;* (f) as a member of a *bureaucratic system* who can be *compelled;* or (g) as a *member of a profession* who can be *professionally obligated.*

A *rational* approach might thus, for example, lean heavily on evaluation data: a *didactic* approach on workshops and in-service training experiences (NDEA Institutes); A *psychological* approach on self-actualization devices (COPED); an *economic* approach on financial rewards or punishments (NDEA language laboratory equipment or withdrawal of federal funds from segregated schools); a *political* approach on influence-peddling; an *authority* approach on mandates (elementary language requirement in California); and a *value* approach on moral commitments (what's good for the "kids"). The diffuser will have to decide which of these approaches or combinations of approaches best fits his potential adopter.

3. *Assumptions concerning the end state in which one wishes to leave the adopter.* Very little attention is typically paid to the end state in which the diffuser wishes to leave his subject. This situation may arise, of course, because the diffuser is acting as a mere huckster; hucksterism may "sell" an innovation but it may leave the adopter with very little residual propensity to adopt again. But even with well-intentioned diffusers this difficulty may arise.

What is it that the practitioner should be able to do, to think, or to feel as a result of having been exposed to a diffusion strategy. Is he to be better trained? More skillful? More knowledgeable? More open? It seems particularly ironic that this situation of carelessness about end states should be found in the field of education, which is so generally characterized by concern about behavioral outcomes and objectives. If we applied a little of our usual logic about specifying expected goals, this difficulty might be largely overcome.

4. *Assumptions about the nature of the agency or mechanism carrying out the diffusion activity.* No sensible diffusion strategy can be evolved without careful attention to the matter of who is to carry it out. For not all strategies are within the capabilities of all agents or mechanisms, or congenial to their philosophic or political position. Constraints exist which mandate certain actions for certain agents and which prohibit other actions to them.

So, for example, a regional educational laboratory, acting as a diffusion agent, is hardly in a position to use an intervention technique, since it lacks the necessary than for sensitizing in areas of human relations, etc. Thus we see that the strategy requires department of education may well intervene (and indeed, may be legally mandated to do so in certain instances) but probably would be very suspect if it attempted to use involvement.

An individual teacher can tell and show but probably would be thought ridiculous if he set up a training experience for his fellows. A university could carry out this latter function with impunity, but it must defend itself against a charge of rendering "mere" service when it attempts to use a helping technique. Since the final implementation of a strategy depends upon the agent, the strategy must be one appropriate to the agent's circumstances.

5. *Assumptions concerning the substance of the invention.* Obviously not all inventions are alike; they pose different problems of adoption, and this fact must be taken into account in developing an appropriate diffusion strategy. One way to view this problem is in terms of the *amount of change* mandated by the invention.

Thus Chin[4] characterizes innovations as involving mere *substitution* (e.g., one textbook for another), *alteration* (a minor change such as lengthening the school day by 15 minutes), *perturbation or variation* (e.g., moving a class into a temporary mobile classroom to obviate overcrowding), *restructuring* (e.g., adopting team teaching), and *value orientation change* (e.g., replacing the teacher with a system of computer-assisted instruction). Rogers talks about the characteristics of inventions that make them more or less acceptable, including *relative advantage* (intrinsic superiority), *compatibility* (consistency with existing values and experience), *complexity* (difficulty in use), *divisibility* (degree to which the innovation can be divided into parts and/or tried on a limited basis), and *communicability* (diffusibility).[5]

Whether these or other ways of classifying the substance of innovations are most useful is less important at this moment than to be sure that any diffusion strategy which might be devised takes account of substance in *some* fashion.

We see then that the development of a diffusion strategy is no small chore, involving a number of separate considerations. Some of the involved factors are interrelated so that, for example, when the nature of the diffusion agency is defined, some techniques are more "natural" or "suitable" than are others, as we have already tried to illustrate. On the other hand, some of the dimensions are more or less independent. So, for instance, it is likely that any of the techniques (with few exceptions) could be coupled with any of the assumptions one wished to make about the nature of the adopter.

Consider the differences in use of techniques that might exist between two strategies which made, respectively, a rational or a psychological assumption about the nature of the adopter. The psychological approach, as opposed to the rational, would use "telling" less to inform about hard data than to share experience; "showing" less to illustrate solutions to problems than to demonstrate the enthusiasm of the participants; "training" less for developing skills than for

[4] Robert Chin. "Models and Ideas About Changing." Paper presented at the Symposium on Identifying Techniques and Principles for Gaining Acceptance of Research Results of Use of Newer Media in Education. W. C. Meierhenry, Symposium Director. Lincoln: University of Nebraska, 1963.

[5] Everett M. Rogers. *Diffusion of Innovations.* Glencoe, Illinois: The Free Press, 1962. p. 124.

sensitizing in areas of human relations, etc. Thus we see that the strategy requires an appropriate *blending* of the various factors to produce an effect which is directional, integrated, and effective.

The theory propounded here, if it can properly be called that, is not easy to apply. What is lacking are operational determiners of the four classes of assumptions outlined above. How can one determine which assumption about the nature of the adopter it would be wisest to make? How can one determine appropriate end states? Where are the instruments that will permit the characterization of the nature of the diffusion agent, or of the substance of the invention?

And finally, given that one could determine all of these factors, how is one to tell which techniques are appropriate to the particular configuration of other factors so defined? These questions have no answers. Yet the diffuser who consciously pays attention to these factors, in however "arty" a way he may do it, will derive a better strategy than will the diffuser who fashions his strategy at random.

Bureaucratic Organization and Educational Change

Ralph B. Kimbrough and Eugene A. Todd

Is a bureaucratic structure an efficient organization for bringing about desirable changes in educational programs? Does bureaucracy stimulate or inhibit innovations in education? Are there organizational structures other than bureaucracies that can ensure sequential coordination of student experiences? How can educators design an organization that will bring about the achievement of educational goals?

Today's educational leaders are eagerly searching for the answers to these questions as they attempt to improve their school systems in an era of phenomenal change. Societal forces are exerting much influence on the goals, character, and direction of American education, thus creating pressures on school administrators and supervisors to make educational changes.

In an effort to handle these pressures, numerous educational leaders have concluded that a bureaucratic structure is not designed to accommodate the rapid changes needed. These leaders believe that a bureaucratically organized school system lacks certain desirable characteristics which are evident in a dynamic system, such as the willingness to expand, to probe the unknown, and to even change its very structure. In a bureaucratic school system, the frontiers of today too rarely become the familiar territory of tomorrow.

Dimensions of Bureaucracy

Bureaucracy has been defined in many ways. Bureaucracy is a pattern of ordering and specifying relationships among personnel in an organization. These relationships are based on rationality, with authority being vested in a position rather than in an individual. Ideally, all relationships and activities are directed toward the achievement of organizational goals. Bennis (3) wrote that bureaucracy has the following dimensions:

1. A division of labor based on functional specialization
2. A well-defined hierarchy of authority
3. A system of rules covering the rights and duties of employees
4. Systematic procedures for dealing with work situations
5. Impersonal approach to interpersonal relations and the promotion of rational behavior according to organizational goals
6. Promotion and selection based on technical competence

In the typical bureaucratic organization, importance is placed upon achieving unity of command. Control of programs through attention to gradation of authority is emphasized. The gradations of authority are usually reflected in the differentiation in salaries from top to bottom.

School systems develop specific rules of procedures which are legitimatized by the force of specialized knowledge and weight of hierarchical authority built into the system. These rules are designed to encourage rational behavior—that behavior expected in achieving the goals often predetermined within the hierarchy. Irrational behavior in the form of student or faculty cliques (informal organizations) is neither expected nor condoned in theory. The division of labor along lines of specialization, combined with hierarchical descriptions of authority, produces formidable organizational machinery in school systems.

In addition to the dimensions listed above, four necessary dimensions unique to educational organizations follow:

1. *Sequential coordination of student experiences.* Since students progress through twelve or more grades in different schools and at different levels, school systems have traditionally attempted to ensure a sequential coordination through bureaucratization of content and methodology.

2. *Teacher autonomy.* In attempting to minimize the inherent conflict between hierarchical authority and professional specialization, school systems have attempted to grant autonomy to the teacher as a professional to make discretionary judgments about procedures to be used during the time a student group is in his charge. Studies have shown, however, that bureaucratization tends to result in the lessening of autonomy for teachers as school districts grow in size.

3. *Dual responsibilities.* Unlike some other organizations, the public schools have a responsibility to a student clientele and a responsibility to a public constituencey. In most professional and business organizations, responsibility is centered upon one clientele.

4. *Guaranteed existence.* Legislation at the local, state, and federal levels guarantees the continued existence of public school systems. As a result, innovation may be less likely to be introduced because the need to change has not been a

requirement for organizational survival. The students have to attend and the schools have to serve.

Most students of organizations believe that the dimensions of bureaucracy described above have to be either modified or eliminated if the organizations of the future are to become innovative organizations. One or more of the following criticisms of bureaucracy appear in many recent articles and books written about organizations:

1. The inability to legitimize differences in ideas among personnel depresses creativity.
2. The probability exists that new ideas generated from within will be subjected to vetoes by members of the official hierarchy, especially if these ideas are in conflict with perceived rational teaching behavior.
3. Bureaucracy does not adequately allow for personal growth and the development of mature and healthy personalities.
4. The bureaucratic organization does not have an adequate structure and process for the review of decisions.
5. The bureaucratic structure cannot accommodate the diversity of external inputs needed for a *democratic* school system.
6. The extrinsic reward system stimulates conformity rather than innovation.
7. The prior commitments of organizational resources to subunits within the organization make it difficult to develop innovative solutions for new problems.
8. Bureaucracy does not take into account the "informal organization."
9. The lines of communication are oftentimes closed because of hierarchical divisions.

Needless to say, the bureaucratic organization does not go undefended against criticism. For instance, some writers contend that the faults found in bureaucracy lie in the mismanagement of the organization rather than in the description of qualities inherent in the structure. Instead of being undemocratic, bureaucracy is presented by its advocates as a form of democracy in that it enables schoolmen to organize for goal fulfillment and meet the educational needs of a school district.

According to its advocates, leadership in a bureaucracy is position oriented, thus the irrational behavior of minority cliques is effectively controlled. These authorities also contend that critics of the bureaucratic system have failed to provide the concrete dimensions for a replacement organization. They ask, for example, what alternatives to the division of labor along specialization lines exist. These authorities contend that the bureaucratic structure assures orderly, efficient educational change.

Toward Innovative Organization

The writers believe that the questions posed in the opening paragraph cannot be answered with unqualified "Yeses" or "Nos." We would contend that bureaucracy is not all bad and that some features in an altered form may be retained. Such features as (a) the commitment to the achievement of organizational goals and (b) the system of rules covering the rights and duties of employees have merit and legitimately belong in educational organizations. Nevertheless, we feel that the time has come for educational leaders to make alterations in their bureaucratic structures or to create new systems if their organizations are to become innovative. In initiating organizational changes, educators should give consideration to the propositions reviewed in the following paragraphs.

The organization should have an effective system for planning programs which provide educational opportunities for all students. Educational change is thwarted by a lack of planning. As a consequence of ineffective planning, much organizational energy is wasted in attempts to serve disparate, poorly defined goals. Planning in the traditional bureaucratic organization is an elite process, often resulting in harmful conflict and in apathy toward the suggested goals. The traditional organization is often more concerned with production than with what should be produced. Therefore, identification with educational needs is often lost in organizational management; children have served organizational needs more than their educational needs have been served. We believe that organizational arrangements should be made for effective planning of educational programs and that this planning should be made upon educational needs rather than upon artificial organizational needs.

Organizational machinery should be established to encourage effective communication for continuing development and clarification of a system of educational ideas which has relevance for practice. The educational ideas provide for system unification. Measurement and evaluation of organizational decisions are based upon the educational ideology. An essential factor of any school system operation is the necessity of ensuring sequential coordination of student experiences. Measurement and evaluation of decisions in terms of the relevant system of ideas will help provide the base for the sequential coordination of student experiences. Furthermore, this will help assure the attainment of organizational goals. The authors emphasize, however, that communication concerning "What we are about" is a continuous process. Consequently, the ideas to which the system is committed are undergoing continuous development, clarification, and change.

Pluralism and collegial relations in decision making concerning educational processes should characterize the modern educational organization. Numerous authorities have pointed to the need to establish systematic arrangements for teacher participation in organizational decision making. The bureaucratic organization is inherently in conflict with this objective. As a consequence, teachers are forcing negotiation agreements. In the collegial type organization, specific arrangements are made for cooperative participation in policy making. School systems should achieve maximum utilization of group processes. An analysis of current leadership research indicates that administrators and supervisors are more effective when they help groups to define and achieve their tasks, goals, and purposes.

Administrative activities should be dispersed and decentralized down to the level of the innovative area whenever possible. If school systems are to have the active participation of the professional staff in the change process, the staff must be permitted to introduce innovations at their levels. This right reduces the threat of vetoes now present in bureaucratic organizations. The traditional bureaucratic organization was designed to reduce conflict and focus administrative activity around predetermined goals. We would suggest that the modern organization should be flexible enough to legitimatize conflict which is not destructive. Constructive conflict generates a variety of alternative solutions. Thus, school systems can select from a variety of solutions instead of being forced to accept one solution. This encourages the development of a pluralistic social system.

School systems should establish an environment in which the "search for truth" can flourish from the individual classroom to the meeting room of the Board of Education. School personnel should be encouraged to search for better ways of doing things. Such a search will mean a critical analysis of present practices. An open organizational system will encourage an attitude of inquiry. The "search for truth" also implies the right to experiment and its concomitant result—the right to fail. Experimentation should be legitimatized.

School systems organized for educational change should develop a harmonious balance between the achievement of personal goals and institutional goals. Several writers have observed that the traditional monocratic organization tends to emphasize organizational goals that are in conflict with the personal need dispositions of school personnel. The organization should be sensitive to—and responsive to—the need dispositions of personnel.

The organization should provide for the effective participation of school leaders in the external social systems. The school system does not exist in a political and social vacuum. It is a subsystem of the community power system and of the state and national system. Desirable changes in education often fail because the educational organization did not provide for effective action in politics. Professional personnel at all levels must be knowledgeable about the "politics of education" and at appropriate times function as political activists. Openness to change in school organizations is conditioned by the degree of openness and closedness in the political power systems within which school systems operate.

References

1. Chris Argyris. *Organization and Innovation.* Homewood, Illinois: Richard D. Irwin, Inc., 1965.

2. W. G. Bennis, K. D. Benne, and R. Chin, editors. *The Planning of Change.* New York: Holt, Rinehart and Winston, Inc., 1961.

3. W. G. Bennis. *Changing Organizations.* New York: McGraw-Hill Book Company, Inc., 1966.

4. George Homans. *Social Behavior: Its Elementary Forms.* New York: Harcourt, Brace & World, Inc., 1961.

5. John G. Hutchinson. *Organizations: Theory and Classical Concepts.* New York: Holt, Rinehart and Winston, Inc., 1967.

6. Robert L. Kahn and others. *Organizational Stress: Studies in Role Conflict and Ambiguity.* New York: John Wiley & Sons, Inc., 1964.

7. Ralph B. Kimbrough. *Political Power and Educational Decision- making.* Chicago: Rand McNally & Company, 1964.

8. J. G. March, editor. *Handbook of Organizations.* Chicago: Rand McNally & Company, 1965.

9. Matthew B. Miles, editor. *Innovations in Education.* New York: Bureau of Publications, Teachers College, Columbia University, 1964.

10. E. L. Morphet, R. L. Johns, and T. L. Reller. *Educational Organization and Administration.* (Second edition.) Englewood Cliffs, New Jersey: Prentice-Hall, Inc., 1967.

11. A. H. Rubenstein and C. J. Haverstroh, editors. *Some Theories of Organization.* (Revised edition.) Homewood, Illinois: Richard D. Irwin, Inc., 1966.

12. James D. Thompson, editor. *Approaches to Organizational Design.* Pittsburgh: University of Pittsburgh Press, 1966.

13. Victor B. Thompson. "Bureaucracy and Innovation." *Administrative Science Quarterly* 10 (1): 1-20; June 1965.

14. Eugene A. Todd. *The Administration of Change: A Study of Administrative Tenure.* Houston, Texas: Bureau of Educational Research and Service, University of Houston. 1963.

15. Eugene A. Todd. "Organizing School Districts for Purposeful Change." A paper presented at the annual meeting of The Southern Regional Council on Educational Administration, Atlanta, Georgia, November 14, 1966.

16. Kimball Wiles. *Supervision for Better Schools.* (Third edition.) Englewood Cliffs, New Jersey: Prentice-Hall, Inc., 1967.

Personalities, Teachers, and Curriculum Change

Ronald Urick and Jack R. Frymier

The prospect of the 1960s is one of great significance for American education. Psychological research into the cognitive processes is beginning to bear fruit in broadening and deepening our understanding of the learning process. A resurgence of public awareness of education and insistence on improvement in its quality is bringing about a reexamination of the organization and content of the school curriculum. In recent years national committees of eminent scientists have developed high school science and mathematics programs which have been widely adopted in the schools. More recently, national committees in the social sciences and humanities have begun work of a similar nature.

On the "firing line" in the public schools, teachers and administrators are faced with the problem of conserving the best of the "old" while adopting the best of the "new" within the context of increasing public pressure for "excellence." While it is desirable that outstanding scholars in the various disciplines play an important part in the development of instructional materials for the secondary schools, such programs will not in and of themselves bring improved instruction. An ineffective teacher will not suddenly become effective with the adoption of new curricular materials. If instruction is to be improved, it must be through developments within each school district, in each building, and within each classroom.

Evidence of the crucial nature of local influence on curriculum changes was reported in a recent study by the NEA'.[1] Elementary and secondary principals listed local school officials and faculty members as the two most important groups in bringing changes in instructional practices. There is evidence, however, that it is among these same groups that the major barriers to change are found.[2] Noda indicates that the most important "blocks" to curriculum change arise out of the attitudes of teachers as well as out of the nature of their relationships with administrators, supervisors and students.[3] In another study, Coon found that teachers were more likely to resist significant curriculum change than either administrators, students, or parents.[4]

Resistance to Change

The question immediately arises: How can one account for this apparently widespread resistance to change which is found among teachers in our schools? Several factors should be taken into consideration in any attempt to answer this question.

First, the formal institutional patterns and organizational arrangements of the school may exert a negative influence on teachers' attitudes with regard to change. Administrative failure to initiate opportunity or provide organizational structure for the consideration of change may create a climate in which change itself is actually considered to be inappropriate.

Second, the existence of ill-defined relationships among teachers, administrators and supervisors and of conflicting perceptions of the role each sees himself and others playing may combine to inhibit the consideration of change, and may, therefore, have a negative effect on teachers' attitudes. If teachers see the principal as the leader in bringing about changes while the principal sees the stimulus for change as needing to originate among the faculty, there will likely be a "built-in" resistance to change.

Finally, inasmuch as a teacher's attitudes are a part of his total personality, there

[1] *The Principals Look at the Schools: A Status Study of Selected Instructional Practices.* Washington, D. C.: National Education Association Project on Instruction, 1962. p. 28-29.

[2] Harold B. Alberty and Elsie J. Alberty. *Reorganizing the High School Curriculum.* New York: The Macmillan Company, 1962. p. 18-19.

[3] Daniel S. Noda. "A Study of Successful Practices Used To Remove the Major Blocks to Curriculum Improvement in the Secondary School." Unpublished doctoral dissertation, The Ohio State University, 1952. p. 78.

[4] Herbert Coon. "A Study of the Attitudes of Teachers and Administrators Toward High School Curriculum Reorganization." Unpublished doctoral dissertation, The Ohio State University, 1951. p. 298, 305.

may be certain configurations of personality structures of individual teachers which lead them to be receptive or resistant to a consideration of change. Combs and Snygg describe the "adequate personality" as one who sees himself in essentially positive ways, is capable of acceptance of self and others, and sees himself as closely identified with other persons.[5] The "inadequate personality" is characterized by the reverse of these characteristics. Thus a teacher who sees himself in a basically negative manner and who has difficulty in relating to those around him is likely to react in a highly defensive and resistant way to any suggestions for the consideration of curriculum changes.

Personality Structure

The crucial nature of personality structure in fostering or hindering social change has been discussed by Hagen in another context. In searching for an explanation for the inconsistency of technological progress among different underdeveloped nations, all of which possessed the economic, technological and educational prerequisites, Hagen concluded that the significant element in those countries undergoing rapid change was the existence of a large number of individuals exhibiting what he calls the "innovational personality."[6] On the other hand, in those countries characterized by a remarkable lack of change, the preponderant personality characteristics were those which Hagen classified as "authoritarian." Briefly, among the qualities which characterize the innovational personality are an openness to experience, a confidence in one's own evaluations, a satisfaction in facing and resolving confusion or ambiguity, and a feeling that the world is orderly, and that the phenomenon of life can be understood and explained.[7] Conversely, the authoritarian is characterized by a fear of using his initiative, an uncertainty concerning the quality of his own judgment, a tendency to avoid frustration and anxiety, an uneasiness in facing unresolved situations, and a tendency to see the world as arbitrary and capricious.[8]

Moreover, personality structure or "perceptual organization" is apparently a determining factor in the effectiveness of counselors. According to Combs and Soper, it is possible to distinguish effective counselors from ineffective ones on the basis of how they view themselves, their tasks, their clients, and their clients' purposes.[9] The perceptual organization of effective counselors, as classified by these researchers, follows closely the personality types outlined previously as "innovational" or "adequate."

Finally, Myers and Torrance studied the personality characteristics of teachers

[5] Arthur W. Combs and Donald Snygg. *Individual Behavior: A Perceptual Approach to Behavior.* New York: Harper and Brothers, 1959: p. 248.

[6] Everett E. Hagen. *On the Theory of Social Change.* Homewood, Illinois: The Dorsey Press, Inc., 1962.

[7] *Ibid.,* p. 88-89.

[8] *Ibid.,* p. 97-98.

[9] Arthur W. Combs and Daniel W. Soper. "Perceptual Organization of Effective Counselors." Unpublished report of a study conducted during the 1961-1962 academic year at the University of Florida, p. 1, 8.

who were resistant to change.[10] Among the characteristics which they identified were authoritarianism, defensiveness, insensitivity to pupil needs, preoccupation with information-giving functions, intellectual inertness, disinterest in promoting initiative in pupils, and preoccupation with discipline.

Within the context of this discussion, the following questions might be raised: To what extent can the rigidity of public schools with regard to curriculum change be attributed to teachers with authoritarian or inadequate personalities? Is it possible that persons who possess personality characteristics which lead to resistance to change are attracted to careers in education, or is it possible that such characteristics may arise out of the experiences which the teachers encounter in the profession? Can teachers who *are* willing to consider curriculum changes be distinguished from those who are unwilling to do so in any reliable way prior to actual involvement in curriculum development?

Personality and Change

A study conducted by a graduate class at Ohio State University was concerned with the relationship of teachers' personality structures to their willingness or unwillingness to consider curriculum change. Fifty-four small city and suburban school districts in Ohio which were similar in size, tax valuation, and expenditure per pupil were identified.

The principal of each high school was asked to select the two teachers on his staff whom he considered to be the *most* willing to consider curriculum change and the two teachers whom he considered to be the *least* willing to consider change. He was provided with a series of 11 paired criteria to use as a basis for his selections. For example, included among the criteria for the identification of teachers most willing to consider change were the use of a variety of teaching materials, experimentation in the classroom, the ability for realistic self-evaluation, the viewing of others as capable of making contributions, and the toleration of uncertainty until knowledgeable judgment can be made. On the other hand, criteria for the identification of teachers least willing to consider change included the use of a narrow range of teaching materials, the following of routine procedures in the classroom, defensive self-evaluation, the viewing of others' contributions on the basis of status, and the making of quick judgments to avoid uncertainty.

Each teacher selected was supplied a packet of materials including a personal data sheet and a 100 item questionnaire composed of items from the Dogmatism Scale, the F-Scale, the Junior Index of Motivation, and the GNC Educational Philosophy Scale. An indirect approach was used in that each teacher was asked to respond to each item as he thought an "ideal teacher" would respond.

Of the original group of 216 questionnaires mailed (four to each of the fifty-four selected schools), 137 were returned: 70 from teachers identified as most willing to consider curriculum change and 67 from those identified as least willing. The personal data (sex, marital status, teaching area, educational preparation, etc.) from the returned questionnaires were analyzed and the scores for the Junior Index of

[10] R. E. Myers and E. Paul Torrance. "Can Teachers Encourage Creative Thinking?" *Educational Leadership* 19: 156-59; December 1961.

Motivation and Dogmatism scales were determined. Further, an item analysis was carried out on the questionnaire, in each case comparing those teachers who were classified as most willing to consider curriculum change with those who were classified as least willing to do so.

With respect to the personal data, there were two factors which discriminated significantly between the two groups of teachers beyond the .05 level of confidence. First, 56 percent of the teachers in the group identified as most willing to consider curriculum change held master's degrees as compared with 40 percent of those in the least willing group. Second, among the married teachers, there were more in the group least willing to consider curriculum change with no children (21 percent) than there were in the most willing group (7 percent).

When the motivation scores and the dogmatism scores for the two groups were compared, no significant differences were found.

The item analysis uncovered four items in the questionnaire which discriminated between the two groups beyond the .05 level of confidence. Considering the fact that 100 items were included in the questionnaire, at least five would have been expected to differentiate between the two groups strictly by chance, so no significance can be attributed to these four items.

For all practical purposes, no significant differences were observed in the way these two groups responded to these various items. Indeed, the general pattern of responses for the two groups was in fact quite similar. With minor exceptions, teachers who were identified by their principals as most willing and least willing to consider curriculum change agreed on the way they thought an "ideal" teacher would respond to most of the 100 items included in this study.

This observation raises certain basic questions. Are teachers learning, in their college preparation or in-service education programs, what they "ought to do" or what they "ought to say"? If we can assume that principals were fairly accurate in identifying those teachers whose behaviors were distinctly different, does the fact that these divergent groups say the same thing on pencil and paper tests mean that what teachers say and what they do are entirely different? If this is true, attempting to assess teachers' attitudes or effectiveness or philosophical outlooks by means of conventional instruments may be completely unrealistic. If teachers have learned to "say the right things" to the point that even they are not aware of the discrepancies between their stated sensations and their actual behaviors, the problems involved in helping teachers see where they are in relationship to where they want to go are formidable indeed. This problem should be explored much more deeply and with more elaborate design and procedures in future studies.

In this study the data were collected from teachers in communities which were selected according to certain criteria and which, therefore, were quite similar in some respects. It may be that such communities attract teachers with similar attitudes toward curriculum change. Or, it may be that the communities mold teachers' attitudes to such an extent that significant differences (of the sort examined in this study) cannot be isolated. The relationship between teachers' attitudes toward curriculum change and the type of community in which they are teaching would appear to be a fruitful area for examination.

There may also be a real question whether or not principals can identify teachers criteria employed in this study. On the other hand, it may be that some principals are actually much more accurate than others in classifying teachers according to these criteria.

This study was singularly unsuccessful in its attempt to isolate some differences between teachers who are willing to consider curriculum change and those who are unwilling to do so. It is hoped that this lack of success will not discourage others from studies in what may be a very fruitful area. It may be that the dynamics of curriculum development can only be understood by probing deeply into the personal factors involved in acceptance of or resistance to the notion of change.

Effectiveness of Feedback to Teachers as a Function of Source

Bruce W. Tuckman and Wilmot F. Oliver

286 teachers were separated by years of teaching experience and subjected to 1 of 4 conditions: (*a*) feedback from students only, (*b*) from supervisors, i.e., vice-principals only, (*c*) from both students and supervisors, and (*d*) from neither (no feedback). It was found that student feedback led to a positive change among teachers (as measured by change in students' ratings across a 12 wk. interval). Supervisor feedback added nothing to this effect when combined with student feedback, and when alone, produced change in a direction opposite to the feedback as compared to the no-feedback condition. Less experienced teachers showed greater receptivity to student feedback than their more experienced counterparts while the reverse held true for receptivity to supervisor feedback.

The problem of modifying the behavior of teachers is one that has been submitted to close scrutiny from a variety of vantage points. Techniques such as microteaching and the use of interaction process analysis have been employed, primarily with student teachers, as a means of altering their behavior. Underscoring the entire rationale for this approach, Daw and Gage (1967) recently said:

> It is highly plausible that feedback regarding how others feel about one's behavior will affect one's behavior. Whether this maxim will hold under a given set of practical circumstances must, however, be determined empirically [p. 181].

This study was an attempt to extend this "maxim" to conditions as yet untested.

Bryan (1963) has shown that teachers will alter their behavior as the outcome of receiving feedback from their students. The purpose of this study was to replicate Bryan's basic finding, using his instrument, and then to extend this finding by determining the relative effects of feedback from students and from supervisors (i.e., administrators responsible for instruction) on teachers' behavior. Moreover, Bryan's study did not include control over the variable of amount of teaching experience of teachers whose behavior was to be changed. His experimental and control groups showed an imbalance on this variable at the conclusion of his experiment with the preponderance of less experienced teachers appearing in the experimental group. An additional purpose of the present study was to systematically introduce years of teaching experience as an experimental variable so that its effects, if any, could be determined.

Finally, the present study was carried out with vocational teachers, in order to demonstrate additional generalizability for the basic finding obtained by Bryan using primarily teachers of academic subjects.

The fact that teachers change as the result of student feedback has also been demonstrated by Gage, Runkel, and Chatterjee (1960). Their study also showed that amount of change was related to the interval between pretest and posttest. Daw and Gage (1967) have shown, furthermore, that feedback from teachers can be used to alter the behavior of principals, but that the amount of change is not a function of the pretest-posttest interval.

In this study, as in previous studies in this area, the measurement of change in teacher behavior was inferential. Students were asked to rate their teacher twice, with a 12-week interval separating these ratings (during which time the treatments could take effect). Behavior change by teachers was inferred from a difference between postinterval and preinterval ratings. Remmers (1963) has shown that students, as a measuring instrument, are as reliable as the best mental and educational paper-and-pencil tests and can discriminate between aspects of teacher behavior (see also Tuckman, 1967). Thus, the dependent variable was identified as change in teachers' behavior with the recognition that this was inferential.

The expectation that years of teaching experience would be a significant variable was based on studies such as that of Ryans (1964) and Peterson (1964) who have shown that teachers' behavioral patterns change in a systematic fashion as a function of age. While age and years of teaching experience are not the same variable, they are assuredly related, with the latter being perhaps the more conceptually meaningful in an educational context.

Problem

To determine the relative effects of students and supervisors as feedback sources for teachers, four conditions were run. In the first condition student feedback alone was employed; in the second, supervisor feedback was employed alone (the supervisor being an administrator, usually a principal or vice-principal responsible for the teaching activities of teachers); in the third, both feedback sources were employed concomitantly; and in the fourth, no feedback was given. Teachers were further classified as to teaching experience and systematically assigned to conditions on that basis.

It was hypothesized that: (*a*) teachers receiving feedback would change more than teachers not receiving feedback (essentially a replication of Bryan's results); (*b*) amount of change in teachers' behavior would vary as a function of feedback source; (*c*) years of teaching experience and amount of change would be inversely related.

Method

Sample

The sample consisted of 286 teachers of vocational subjects at the high school or technical institute level. Schools were selected from New Jersey and surrounding out-of-state counties and virtually all the vocational teachers in the schools used took part in the study. Participating teachers had a median class size of 15 students who were either in the tenth, eleventh, or thirteenth grade.

Measurement of Teacher Behavior

Teacher behavior was measured by the Student-Opinion Questionnaire (SOQ) developed by Bryan (1963). This instrument includes 10 rating scales on which teacher is judged as to his (*a*) knowledge of his subject, (*b*) ability to explain, (*c*) fairness, (*d*) ability to maintain discipline, (*e*) degree of sympathetic understanding, (*f*) ability to make you learn, (*g*) ability to be interesting, (*h*) ability to get things done efficiently, (*i*) ability to get students to think for themselves, and (*j*) general all-round teaching ability. Each scale has five points labeled: below average, average, good, very good, and the very best.

Bryan (1963) has reported reliability coefficients for the 10 items on the SOQ of from .75 to .85 for chance-half averages for 50 classes. For whole classes of 28 students on the average, coefficients of from .86 to .92 were obtained.

On the reverse side of the SOQ are four open-ended questions dealing with the course and teacher, reflecting on things that are liked about each and suggestions for the improvement of each.

Feedback Conditions

Students only. Students completed the SOQ, and their ratings on the 10 scales were averaged. The teacher was presented with a graph showing the average student judgment for each item. In addition, a summation of the students' responses on the open-ended questions were provided. Teachers were told that the feedback was from their students.

Supervisor only. The teacher's supervisor (either the principal, vice-principal, or assistant principal) completed the SOQ, and his ratings on each item were given to the teacher in graphical form along with a summary of his answers to the open-ended questions. The teacher was told that this rating was made by the supervisor. (In this condition, student ratings were also obtained although these were not made available to the teacher.)

Students and supervisor. The teacher's supervisor and students completed the

SOQ, and feedback from each was given separately, along with identification of source in the same manner as in the first two conditions.

No feedback. Students completed the SOQ, but no feedback was provided to the teacher.

All initial testing was done in the late fall.

Years of Teaching Experience

Based on information from a personal information form, teachers were categorized as having 1-3 years of teaching experience, 4-10 years of teaching experience, or 11 or more years of teaching experience. Teachers from each group were then randomly assigned to each condition. The overall design of the study and assignment of teachers to conditions is shown in Table 1.

Table 1. Design of the Experiment: Assignment of Teachers to Treatment and Experience Groups

	Years of experience of instructor					
	1-3 years (A_1)		*4-10 years (A_2)*		*11 or more years (A_3)*	
Condition	B_1	B_2	B_1	B_2	B_1	B_2
No student feedback (C_1)	14	18	19	18	18	13
Student feedback (C_2)	39	32	25	31	32	27

Note.–Cell entries are number of observations per cell; N = 286; Abbreviated: B_1 = no supervisory feedback, B_2 = supervisory feedback.

Measurement of Change in Teacher's Behavior

In the late spring, following a 12-week interval after the initial testing, students of each of the teachers in the study completed the SOQ. The measure of change in each condition was the sum of the differences between the preinterval judgments by the students on the 10 items and their postinterval judgments. Ratings on each item were averaged across students and the preinterval average on each item was then subtracted from the postinterval average to yield a change score on each of the 10 items. These 10-item change scores were summed to obtain a total change score. Student judgments were used throughout as a measure of change to maintain a constant measuring instrument across conditions. This was seen as justifiable since preinterval ratings by students did not differ significantly from those of supervisors in conditions where both were obtained and the latter were used as the feedback source.

All test administration was accomplished by the local vocational guidance counselor.

Analysis

For purposes of analysis the four feedback conditions (Conditions 1-4) were treated as two factors: supervisor feedback and student feedback, with two levels on each: present and absent. The four conditions were thus labeled as follows: (b^1c^1) student and supervisor feedback, (b^1c^2) supervisor feedback only, (b^2c^1) student feedback only, and (b^2c^2) no feedback (see Table 1). Years of teaching experience was the first factor and had three levels subsequently, a 3 X 2 X 2 analysis of variance using the unweighted means solution for unequal cell entries (Winer, 1962) was carried out on the total change score for each teacher. (Each teacher was used only once in the design.) In addition, direct mean comparisons were made using the Duncan multiple-range test (Duncan, 1955).[1]

Results

The results of the analysis of variance for the total change score showed that the presence of student feedback (Factor C) had a significant effect on teachers' behavior as compared to its absence ($F = 5.941$; $df = 1/274$, $p < .025$) while the presence of supervisor feedback (Factor B) produced no significant effect ($F = 1.064$; $df = 1/274$). The years-of-experience variable (Factor A) also failed to produce a significant effect ($F = 0.701$; $df = 2/274$) and none of the interactions achieved significance at the .05 level ($F < 1$ in each case).

In an effort to delineate further the feedback effects, means for the four feedback conditions were compared, as shown in Table 2. From the table it can be seen that both conditions involving student feedback showed significantly greater change than both conditions not involving student feedback.[2] Feedback from students alone and from students and supervisors combined were statistically comparable, indicating a failure for feedback from supervisors to generate any change beyond that accounted for by student feedback alone. Finally, feedback from supervisors alone produced a significantly greater negative shift (i.e., a change in the opposite direction of that recommended by the feedback) than no feedback at all.

[1] A fifth condition, called the posttest-only group by Daw and Gage (1967), was also run with an additional 15 teachers. These teachers were rated by their students only at the end of the interval. The purpose of this condition was to determine whether the protest or preinterval measurement had a sensitizing effect on the raters or teachers (cf. Campbell & Stanley, 1963). A comparison of the mean for this posttest-only control group to the mean on the postinterval measurement for the no-feedback group showed them to be comparable. Thus, it was concluded that test sensitization was not a source of invalidity.

[2] Throughout this description, results are referred to as changing "more" or "less." However, in the light of the fact that almost all of the means are negative, changing more means showing a lesser negative shift (i.e., a smaller negative change score) while changing less means showing a greater negative shift (i.e., a larger negative change score). This tendency for ratings to be less positive following the interval as compared to those preceding the interval were not attributable to a testing effect (see the preceding footnote). One must conclude that students as raters are more negatively inclined toward their teachers in the spring (after experiencing them for a year) than in the fall. Thus the positive effect of feedback, when it occurred, was to reduce this tendency toward greater negativity of ratings (i.e., make the negative score smaller or positive).

Table 2. Mean Total Change Scores by Feedback Condition and Their Comparison by Duncan Multiple-Range Test

Students only	*Students and supervisors*	*Supervisors only*	*No feedback*
–.054	–.385	–2.449[a]	–1.234[a]

[a]Significantly different from all other means, $p < .01$ (with exception of difference between second and fourth means, where $p < .05$).

Thus, student feedback "improved" teacher behavior as compared to no feedback would produce greater changes than no feedback, it would have been student feedback, and an adverse effect when used alone.

Discussion

The first hypothesis of this study predicted that feedback (source unspecified) would yield a greater positive change than no feedback, while the second hypothesis predicted different effects for the different feedback sources. The surprising finding of this study was that teachers receiving feedback from supervisors changed more in the opposite direction from the feedback than the spontaneous shift obtained in the no-feedback condition. Thus, the first hypothesis holds true for student feedback (a replication of Bryan's findings) which led to effects in excess of the no-feedback condition. Supervisory feedback added nothing to the student feedback effect when they were combined. (If anything it reduced it, but not significantly so.) Since supervisory feedback had the opposite effect than predicted, the second hypothesis was confirmed—that is, the feedback sources did have different effects. If in the first hypothesis, it was simply predicted that feedback would produce greater changes than no feedback, it would have been confirmed. Certainly this experiment suggests that teachers react to feedback, irrespective of source, with these reactions being positive only in the case of student feedback.

The question of why teachers reacted to feedback from supervisors as they did is immediately raised. It can only be surmised that teachers are defensive toward (or even hostile to) administrators who, in the absence of much basis for judgment, attempt to tell them how to teach. Of interest, though, is the fact that within the educational milieu, the only source of feedback to teachers, typically, are their supervisors. The data collected here indicate that such feedback is doing more harm than good, with the "best" source of feedback, students, overlooked.

The third hypothesis of the present study predicted an inverse relation between years of experience and receptivity to feedback. While the obtained relationship was not sufficiently strong to prove significant, the most experienced teacher group tended to show the least receptivity to feedback from their students, as the hypothesis predicted. However, the least experienced teacher group tended to show the least receptivity (i.e., the least relatively positive shift) to feedback from their supervisor—the reverse of the hypothesis.

Finally, a last question must be raised. Why do all the change scores tend to be negative with positive change being measured in terms of the "smallness" of the negative score? The use of a group of teachers whose students made only the postinterval ratings indicated that the test-retest phenomenon was not responsible for this shift from pre- to postratings. It appeared that students are more critical of their teachers at the end of the term than at the middle. At the time when the teacher is about to evaluate and grade the student, the student perhaps replies in kind. Thus, a positive change appeared as a lessening in the "naturally" occurring negative shift. Researchers interested in using student judgments are cautioned to use the same starting and ending times for all groups to avoid the confusion of this end-of-term effect. September to January will not lead to the same effect as February to June.

References

Bryan, R. C. Reactions to teachers by students, parents, and administrators. United States Office of Education, Cooperative Research Project No. 668. Kalamazoo: Western Michigan University, 1963.

Campbell, D. T., & Stanley, J. C. Experimental and quasi-experimental designs for research on teaching. In N. L. Gage (Ed.), *Handbook of research on teaching.* Chicago: Rand McNally, 1963.

Daw, R. W., & Gage, N. L. Effect of feedback from teachers to principals. *Journal of Educational Psychology,* 1967, **58,** 181-188.

Duncan, D. B. Multiple range and multiple F tests. *Biometrics,* 1955, **11,** 1-42.

Gage, N. L., Runkel, P. J., & Chatterjee, B. B. Equilibrium theory and behavior change: An experiment in feedback from pupils to teachers. Report No. 6 in Studies in the generality and behavioral correlates of social perception. Urbana: Bureau of Educational Research, College of Education, University of Illinois, 1960.

Peterson, W. A. Age, teacher role, and the institutional setting. In B. J. Biddle & W. J. Ellena (Eds.), *Contemporary research on teacher effectiveness.* New York: Holt, Rinehart & Winston, 1964.

Remmers, H. H. Rating methods in research on teaching. In N. L. Gage (Ed.), *Handbook of research on teaching.* Chicago: Rand McNally, 1963.

Ryans, D. G. Characteristics of teachers. In B. J. Biddle & W. J. Ellena (Eds.), *Contemporary research on teacher effectiveness.* New York: Holt, Rinehart & Winston, 1964.

Tuckman, B. W. *A study of the effectivness of directive versus non-directive vocational teachers as a function of student characteristics and course format.* United States Office of Education, Project No. 6-2300, Progress Report No. 1. New Brunswick: Rutgers. The State University, 1967.

Winer, B. J. *Statistical principles in experimental design.* New York: McGraw-Hill, 1962.

Communication Within a Bureaucratic Organizational Framework: Implications for the Educational Administration of Some Recent Investigations

A. R. Crane

The literature has been searched for experiments on communication within organizational frameworks. Some apparently relevant work is cited and discussed in terms of an "anxiety arousal" hypothesis of communication within organizations. The effects upon communication of hierarchical status, organizational mobility, power and ingratiation are discussed. The paper concludes with a series of hypotheses about communication within school systems that could be the subject of empirical investigation by students of educational administration.

There is little doubt that the schools and school systems of the Australian states quite comfortably fit Weber's[1] criteria of bureaucracy, viz,

1. They have a supreme chief with authority defined by regulation.
2. They have a hierarchical structure of positions.
3. Each position has attached to it a defined sphere of control.
4. Positions are filled by selection based upon technical qualifications.
5. Occupants of the positions are remunerated by salary and pursue the occupation as a career.
6. There are established rules for the discipline and control of the occupants of the position.

It has long ago been hypothesized that anxiety is one important factor influencing man's behaviour in such an organizational framework. This was suggested by Merton[2] as long ago as 1940, but it was probably first clearly formulated by Presthus[3] in 1958, although the whole corpus of Argyris's work since 1957[4,5,6] may be looked upon as having anxiety as its central theme.

[1] Weber, M. *The Theory of Social and Economic Organizations.* (ed. T. Parsons). Glencoe, Ill. Free Press. 1947.
[2] Merton, R. K. Bureaucratic Structure and Personality. *Social Forces.* 1940. 17, pp. 560-568.
[3] Presthus, R. V. Towards a Theory of Organizational Behavior. *Admin. Sc. Quart.* 1958. 3, pp. 48-72.
[4] Argyris, C. *Personality and Organization.* New York. Harper. 1957.
[5] Argyris, C. *Understanding Organizational Behavior.* London. Tavistock. 1960.
[6] Argyris, C. *Integrating the Individual and the Organization.* New York. Wiley. 1964. pp. 327.

Presthus went so far as to postulate that "anxiety is probably the most critical variable in organizational behavior."[7] The reason for this is what one might call man's need for status enhancement, or at the very least, for status maintenance. The very fact that an organization is a hierarchy of positions is a threat to each individual occupying a position, no matter what the status of the position happens to be. Any event that occurs in the organization is perceived by personnel through a filter of threatened self-esteem which in turn distorts the perception of those events. One way in which a person occupying a high status position can maintain that status is to act in such a way as to emphasise the inferiority of those beneath him. This can be done in several ways, for example by allocating to himself scarce and valued resources. One such resource is the information which is available to him, but which he can withhold. Mellinger[8] noted this point as worthy of research, but no such investigation has been located. One piece of research which, so far as I know, has never been done would be to ask a school inspector, a school principal and a teacher to give an account of an "inspection" that had just been made of the teacher's work in the principal's school. I have done this informally for my own amusement where all three have been my friends and I have found that, despite mutual goodwill, the three accounts could scarcely be recognised as the same event.

We are here concentrating on one type of event, viz. communication, and it is our aim to see what research evidence there is about the ways in which communication is influenced and distorted by organizational anxiety.

Although there were several investigations of communication within groups before 1950, the key pioneer work was probably the 1950 study of Back and others[9] who planted rumours at various levels in an organization. The nine rumours started produced seventeen recorded acts of communications, eleven of them directed upward, four to the same level and two to a special staff committee. One of the rumours that could be interpreted as critical of persons at the upper level did not spread at all. To this investigation must be added that of Thibaut[10] in the same year, in which he used groups of boys aged ten to twelve who were members of activities clubs and summer camps. He gave to some "High status treatment" and to some "Low status treatment" by giving all the interesting things to do to the Highs and all the uninteresting things to do to the Lows. He also contrived that the Low status teams should sometimes perceive themselves as "successful" and sometimes as "unsuccessful" in group action aimed to improve their under-privileged position. He then examined the communications between the teams and found that after unsuccessful group action the Low status teams initiated more communications with the High status teams, while the teams whose group action was successful greatly reduced their communications. Thus, "the sheer volume of communication tends to be increased as the group's position becomes more negative." His comment

[7] Presthus, R. V. *op. cit.* p. 51.

[8] Mellinger, G. C. "Interpersonal Trust as a Factor in Communication." *Jour. Abn. and Soc. Psych.* 1956. 52, pp. 304-309.

[9] Back, K. *et. al.* "The Methodology of Studying Rumour Transmission." *Human Relations.* 1950. 3, pp. 307-312.

[10] Thibaut, J. "An Experimental Study of the Cohesiveness of Underprivileged Groups." *Human Relations.* 3, pp. 251-178.

on these results was that "upward communication served as a substitute for blocked upward locomotion."

It is clear that in this investigation "status" has no organizational reference; it merely refers to the positive valence of the activities carried on by the group. To extrapolate to an organizational situation is risky but reasonable because positions also carry valence which varies with their status: at least this is so for the "mobile" members of the organization.

I have mentioned these two investigations particularly because they formed the foundation for Kelley's[11] study of communication in experimentally created hierarchies. He accepted Thibaut's equation of communication upward with disappointed upward mobility and interpreted Back's work as pointing "towards the existence of unusual forces to communicate upward, these being thought to indicate the substitute value of communication for upward locomotion. There were also indications of strong restraining forces acting against free communication of specific kinds of content such as, for example, information critical of persons at the upper levels." It is very doubtful indeed if Back and his collaborators would have agreed with this gloss on their work.

Kelley created five experimental groups of college students, a High status mobile group, a High status non-mobile group, a Low status mobile group, a Low status non-mobile group and a control group. He set them at a task of laying bricks and he limited intercommunication to written messages. For his purpose he defined High status as "having the best job" and Low status as "having a poorer job–a more menial and routine one." Mobility was defined as the promise (or threat) "We may move you to the other job". The non-mobiles were told that "We will have to keep you on the better (poorer) job throughout the experiment". He found an inverse relation between "perceived desirability of position (i.e. status) and the amount of task irrelevant communication and that this was initiated more often by the Low status mobile group. He interpreted this as confirming Thibaut's hypothesis and at the same time sharpening that hypothesis in its differentiation of mobile and non-mobile status groups. Some of his other results are also interesting. Low status groups communicated more criticism of the job to fellow High status groups; fewer High status groups than Low status groups criticised their job to the other level. He concluded that, "in criticising other people, restraints introduced by the hierarchy not only operate against criticising other level people 'to their face' but also discourage being critical of them in communication to his own level." When the cohesiveness of the whole group was considered, the High status mobile and Low status non-mobile groups tended to shun other status levels. These were the groups "most destructive of inter-level cohesiveness."

This seminal investigation was based on a contrived situation but much the same results were reported by Zander and others[12] in a study conducted within a real organization. "Tendencies to communicate upward or downward in a hierarchy

[11] Kelley, H. H. "Communication in Experimentally Created Hierarchies." *Human Relations.* 1951. 4, pp. 39-56.

[12] Zander, A., Cohen, A., Hymovitch, B. and Stotland, E. Some Determinants of Role Relations: Reported in Cartwright, D. and Zander, A. *Group Dynamics.* New York. Row, Peterson. 1953. p. 419.

depend greatly upon the specific content of the 'message' and the degree to which this content protects or threatens the (status) relationships between the potential communicators. Thus a study of relationships between professional roles found that persons of Low status are more ready to communicate one type of content upward than are High status persons ready to communicate the same content downward, but the opposite trend is found for other types of content." But they did not specify just what these "types of content" were. One could postulate on the grounds of our anxiety hypothesis that in each case the communication most readily made in either direction would be "status protective" of the person initiating the communication. For example, we would expect persons of Low status to attempt to ensure that the power of the High status persons would be used in a way beneficial to Low status persons. Their communications to High status persons will tend therefore to be deferential and placatory.

In 1958 Cohen[13] used Kelley's 1950 pioneering study as the basis for an investigation in which he added "power" to "status" as a variable. "High power" he defined as "the ability to prevent the need satisfactions of those of Low power. Low power persons are dependent upon Highs for their need satisfactions." He showed that the Low status mobile members' communications to High power persons were in fact deferential and placatory, but that this was less so with the Low status non-mobile members. He also showed that the messages from Low status mobile persons were more task centred. This was to be expected, since this group would wish to impress the High power persons with the fact that the Low status mobile person was "on the job" and therefore promotion-worthy. Since High power persons had it in their hands to satisfy the needs of the Low status mobile person, communication for them was aimed at "maximizing good relations and minimising feelings of unease." Pleasant matters and achievements were more frequently communicated upward than snags and shortcomings. Cohen therefore preferred what he called the "instrumental theory of upward communication" to Kelley's "status–approximation theory."

Bennis[14] studied the "Interaction patterns in formal service-oriented organizations" in the out-patients department of a hospital and showed that the content of nurses' communications differed according to the level of the hierarchy to which they were directed. To their superiors they communicated personal matters and job difficulties. Since most face to face contacts with superiors were initiated by the superiors, they could receive only communications about organizational features of the tasks of the inferiors and showed little understanding of the difficulties and problems faced by the juniors in the execution of these tasks. The investigators pointed out that the "on call" or "open door" policy of a superior was not enough and could lead to serious misunderstandings by the superior, especially an underrating of the problems and complexities of the task as seen by the juniors.

[13] Cohen, A. R. "Upward Communication in Experimentally Created Hierarchies." *Human Relations.* 1958. 9, pp. 41-54.

[14] Berkovitz, N. H. and Bennis, W. G. "Inter-action patterns in Formal Service-oriented Organizations." *Admin. Sc. Quarterly.* 1961. 6, pp. 25-50.

In 1962 Read[15] investigated the accuracy of upward communication in three separate industrial organizations in U.S.A. He conducted interviews on production problems as seen by superiors and by subordinates with the particular purpose of assessing the degree of agreement between the superiors and the subordinates about the relative difficulty of their problems *as seen by the subordinates.* At the same time he administered questionnaires on the strength of mobility motivation of the subordinates and on the trust and perceived influence of the superiors. Read's conclusions were significant:

1. When a supervisor is assessing the problems facing his subordinates his "assessments are not likely to be made with any clear perspective on the problems and obstacles the upward mobile subordinate experiences in his work, unless the supervisor has other sources of information than the subordinate himself. Thus, a judgment about the effectiveness the subordinate has shown in goal achievement cannot be tempered by accurate knowledge of the problems he has encountered in his attempts to achieve the goal."
2. The validity of the decisions made by the superior which concern the subordinate will almost certainly be limited by the superior's lack of awareness of the problems affecting the subordinate.
3. To the extent that the subordinate insulates his superior from clear knowledge of work related problems, he has in effect insulated himself from whatever expert knowledge and judgment the superior might offer or apply in solving these problems.

Up to this point, the investigators mentioned had not taken much notice of developments that had been occurring in the field of social psychology and it was not until 1963 that the relevance of the book by Heider[16]—*The Psychology of Personal Relations* was recognised. Heider built up a communication model using two persons P and O and the content of their communication, X. This model was used as he basis of a significant investigation of "Tactics of ingratiation among leaders and subordinates in a hierarchy" by Jones, Gergen and Jones.[17] Those investigators concentrated on three types of content of P—O communications:

1. Self disclosure about P. (i.e. P talks to O about O)
2. Appraisal of O (i.e. P talks to O about O)
3. About X (i.e. P talks to O about X)

P has therefore, three possible tactics of ingratiation with O.

[15]Read, H. "Upward Communication in Industrial Hierarchies." *Human Relations.* 1962. 15, pp. 3-16.
[16]Heider, F. *The Psychology of Inter-personal Relations.* New York. Wiley. 1959. pp. 322.
[17]Jones, E. E., Gergen, K. J., and Jones, R. G. "Tactics of Ingration Among Leaders and Subordinates in a Status Hierarchy." *Psych. Monog.* 1963. Vol. 77, No. 3.

1. Self presentation
2. Other enhancement
3. Conformity (i.e. "we agree about X")

Where P is subordinate to O, conformity was found to be the most appropriate tactic for P because it bolsters O's view and O is less likely to suspect its tactical origin. He is likely to see P's response not only as "gratifying" but as "correct," and even if he suspects P of being a "yes-man" it is not really easy to distinguish between tactical conformity and genuine agreement. "Other enhancement" was considered not to be a sound tactic for P because it could give the impression that he was comparing O with people of P's own status. In any case flattery is likely to be recognised as a tactic. "Self presentation" is not a sound tactic because it is difficult to find a point between appearing to be "pushing" and seeming to be "deprecatory." The first can annoy and the second might not be seen by O as modesty but as a true statement of P's own inferiority. So far as O, the superordinate, is concerned, his tactics will tend to be directed towards enlisting the liking of P and maintaining P's respect for his task competence. To him therefore, "conformity" is an inappropriate tactic because he must show his ability to form independent judgements. He cannot agree with all his subordinates without losing prestige. For O, "other enhancement" is a useful tactic because it increases P's loyalty to him without reducing the social distance between them. Also P is not likely to see it as a tactic but as O "giving credit where credit is due.""Self presentation" must be used carefully by O: he can be deprecatory on anything except those characteristics central to his status. He can emphasise his weaknesses in non-essential areas (e.g. the poor game of golf he plays) but not in task-essential areas.

These were the bases for the actual investigation carried out into non-task orientated communications in an ROTC group. The general conclusions were:

(a) *Opinion Conformity:* High and Low status persons tended to show approximately the same degree of conformity with each other on issues not especially relevant to the status hierarchy, but on more relevant issues High status persons conformed less with Low Status.

(b) *Self Presentation:* High status persons were more modest when under pressure to be liked; High status persons tended to be modest on "unimportant" issues but less so on important issues.

(c) *Other enhancement:* Low status persons tended to flatter each other more than they flattered High status persons. High status persons tended to flatter Low status persons on unimportant issues.

This investigation will, no doubt, prove as seminal as the earlier Thibaut and Kelley studies although I have not located any similar studies. It is reasonable to assume that task orientated communications carry with them messages of ingratiation in the way they are worded and in the effects they are meant to produce on the receivers.

It was said earlier that each member of an organization will perceive events within the organization (including communication) in terms of status enhancement (if the member can be described as mobile) or in terms of status maintenance (if the member can be described as non-mobile). Here it is relevant to mention Kipnis's[18] 1964 investigation on the relationship between mobility expectations and attitudes towards various aspects of the organization. He put forward four hypotheses:

1. That Low mobile expects will perceive management as less concerned with employee welfare than High mobile expects–confirmed.
2. Low mobile expects will hold less favourable attitudes towards management changes in working procedures than will High mobile expects–confirmed.
3. High mobile expects will maintain a more independent orientation towards co-workers than Low mobile expects–confirmed.
4. Low mobile expects will express less liking for their immediate supervisor than will High mobile expects–confirmed.

Early in 1965 Kelman and Eagly[19] published a paper that is likely to arouse considerable interest amongst administrators. This investigation was also based on Heider's model The basic hypothesis was that a receiver (O) will tend to perceive communication as congruent with his attitude to the communicator (P). This would be so even if the communication is clear, but if it is ambiguous then, if P's attitude to O is negative, the communication will be seen as more discordant with P's position than it actually is. But this mis-perception by P of the communication is not simply a function of the attitude of P to O; it is also a function of the anxiety the communication arouses in P i.e. whether it raises questions of his status which are central to his self concept. It is not merely what O *says* but also what O *is*–a matter of the source as well as the content of the communication. The status anxious person will react primarily to O as *source* of the message and will be more likely to begin ingratiation tactics. The status secure person will react primarily to the *content* of the message and will more likely begin task achievement behaviour.

The foregoing are selected from the published investigations that are perceived as relevant to those interested in communication within organizational frameworks. They are varied in sophistication and some might be considered as only marginally relevant, if not quite irrelevant. But they have one thing in common. They were all carried out in primary groups, with people working together and in such situations where the different levels of the hierarchy–such as it was–were in direct contact with each other. Therefore, if we wish to draw out any implications that might exist for educational administration we must be careful not to extrapolate too glibly outside the primary educational organization i.e. the school, or perhaps in these days of easy travel and of frequent conferences, the schools within an inspectorate. Merely for simplicity and in order to sharpen up the focus a little, I

[18]Kipnis. D. "Mobility Expectations and Attitudes Towards Industrial Structure." *Human Relations.* 1964. 17, pp. 57-72.

[19]Kelman, H. C. and Eagly, A. H. "Attitude to the Communicator: Perception of Communication Content and Attitude Change." *Jour. Pers. and Soc. Psych.* 1965. 1, pp. 63-78.

shall speak in terms of the organizational framework of a school–of Principal and staff particularly.

What hypotheses could we postulate as a guide for investigation by educational administrators? Perhaps the following are some:

1. The Principal will receive proportionally more task irrelevant communications from Low status non-mobile staff members.
2. Few of these communications will contain criticism or disagreement with the Principal.
3. The senior members of staff will criticize their job more often amongst themselves than with the Junior members of staff.
4. Communications from the Principal will be received differently by:
   (a) Mobile and non-mobile staff members.
   (b) Those who agree with the Principal and those who don't.
   (c) Those who like the Principal and those who don't.
5. Communications from the Principal will have overtones of "ingratiation" especially self presentation (status maintenance) and other-enhancement.
6. Communications to the Principal will have overtones of "ingratiation"–especially conformity and self-presentation.
7. Communications to the Principal will not clearly reveal the difficulties being experienced by the staff in achieving the set tasks.
8. The reduction of status anxiety in the sender will be a common feature of both upward and downward communications. It will be the "hidden agenda" of every meeting.
9. Staff unity and cohesiveness is most likely to be endangered by the High status mobile and the low status non-mobile members of staff who will tend to form sub-groups.

It would appear that the Principal who wishes to learn more than he will through formal upward communication should develop what Halpin[20] calls the "informal way of knowing"–a sensitivity to subtle cues and nuances of expression and behaviour, a second sight that detects both in himself and in his staff the tactics of ingratiation and the distortions that they introduce.

Of course, a Principal's knowledge of a school is not confined to what his staff tell him–unless he is a self convicted prisoner in his own office. He can see for himself, but he still has to interpret what he sees and in this he must lean heavily upon what the staff tell him, so he is always working at least at one level removed from daily events. He cannot be everywhere and see everything.

It would be more interesting to speculate what happens to communication as more and more hierarchical levels are added above that of Principal, viz. Inspector, Chief Inspector, Director, Director-General. Do the tactics of ingratiation compound as they go up? Is each level told less and less about the difficulties and problems of classroom teachers?

[20]Campbell, P. O. and Lipham. J. M. *Administration Theory as a Guide to Action.* Chicago. Midwest Administration Centre. 1960. pp. 196.